EDUCATORS' HANDBOOK

EDUCATORS' HANDBOOK
A RESEARCH PERSPECTIVE

Virginia Richardson-Koehler
Senior Editor

Section Editors

David C. Berliner
Ursula Casanova
Christopher M. Clark
Richard H. Hersh
Lee S. Shulman

Longman
New York & London

Educators' Handbook: A Research Perspective

Longman Inc.
95 Church Street
White Plains, N.Y. 10601

Associated companies:
Longman Group Ltd., London
Longman Cheshire Pty., Melbourne
Longman Paul Pty., Auckland
Copp Clark Pitman, Toronto
Pitman Publishing Inc., New York

Executive Editor: Raymond T. O'Connell
Senior Editor: Naomi Silverman
Production Editor: Halley Gatenby
Text Art: J & R Services, Inc.
Production Supervisor: Judith Stern
Compositor: Graphicraft Typesetters Ltd.
Printer and Binder: Interstate Book Manufacturers

Library of Congress Cataloging-in-Publication Data
Main entry under title:

Educators' handbook.

Includes bibliographies and index.
1. Teaching—Addresses, essays, lectures. 2. Teaching—Vocational guidance—United States—Addresses, essays, lectures. I. Richardson-Koehler, Virginia, 1940–   . II. Berliner, David C.
LB1025.2.E39   1986   371.1'02   85-23849
ISBN 0-582-28454-6

87 88 89 90   9 8 7 6 5 4 3 2 1

CONTENTS

INTRODUCTION: TEACHING, SCHOOLING, AND RESEARCH

Virginia Richardson-Koehler

The purpose of this book is to provide teachers, teacher educators, staff developers, and administrators with ways of thinking about instructional practice that have emerged from current research on teaching and schooling. An effort has been made to deemphasize the research methodology aspects of this work to focus on the practical. *Practical,* as used here, however, does not mean telling people what to do. Research cannot provide prescriptions for practice applicable to all settings and all situations. Research can, however, provide alternative ways of thinking and alternative practices that can be considered and tested by practitioners. The term *practical,* then, combines ways of thinking about a particular phenomenon with decriptions of potential approaches to practice that have been, in this case, derived from research.

Note that teaching, in this volume, is portrayed as a profession. Teaching is described as a higher-level decision-making process: The teaching act requires a substantial amount of professional and practical knowledge, teachers make many professional decisions each day, the judgments that teachers make require higher-order thinking processes, and this professional thinking and planning goes on throughout the day, in and out of the classroom. Teaching is also portrayed as a moral activity; that is, the manner in which teachers approach the education of their students strongly affects the ways in which their students approach the subject matter, the world, and other people. The knowledge and ideas extracted from research are placed within this frame of reference.

Further, there are no proposals for "quick fixes." While there is tremendous pressure to come up with *the* answer for improvement—merit pay, longer school days, and so on—experience has taught us that single solutions generally do not work. In fact, they often cause more pain than benefit. Schooling today is an extremely complicated enterprise with numerous goals, clients, personnel roles, and programs. Research has helped us to understand the ways in which community, school district, school, and classroom interact to create environments for learning. Change in one sector can reverberate through all parts of the system. Further, as Elmore (1983) points out, education is a loosely coupled system, and change often happens in a manner quite different from the ways in which its proponents planned it to happen. Change, then, must be a deliberative process; one that assesses the ways in which elements of the system interact and the degree to which change in one element will affect or will be blocked by all others. The kind of knowledge and ways of thinking that are developed in this volume can aid in those deliberative processes.

RESEARCH AND PRACTICE

As editor of a book designed to summarize research on teaching for practitioners and policymakers, I had to confront the often troubled relationship between producers and users of education research. The relationship suffers from communicative and philosophical differences. The thought processes, constructs, methodologies, and understandings involved in conducting research are thought to be so divergent from those involved in teaching that communication becomes impossible. Teachers say that research "isn't relevant," while researchers claim that teachers "don't really want to change." These accusations derive, in part, from the lack of an effective framework for thinking about the lives of teachers and the ways in which they can use professional knowledge gained from research. Recently, we have begun to understand these issues and are thinking more effectively about the relationship between research and practice. It is hoped that the accusations and misunderstandings will diminish and that attention will turn instead to the enterprise of producing and implementing useful professional knowledge. This should improve the quality of education for our students and enhance the status of the teaching profession.

Simplistic arguments that relate research to practice don't work ("Research says that teachers should . . .") not because practitioners are "recalcitrant" and don't want to change but because the relationship between professional knowledge and professional practice is complex and incompletely understood. Don Schön (1983), in a highly influential book that attempts to describe how professionals think in action, presents a rationale for why "professional knowledge" as we have come to define it fails the practitioner. Speaking of all professionals—teachers, doctors, lawyers, architects, and all others—he notes that "professional knowledge is mismatched to the changing characteristics of the situation of practice—the complexity, uncertainty, instability, uniqueness, and value conflicts which are professional practice" (p. 14). Professional practice, he says, has artistic elements that involve finding as well as solving problems and, as Herbert Simon stated, "design," or "changing existing situations into preferred ones" (quoted in Schön, p. 46).

Professional knowledge in occupations other than teaching has been accumulating for many years. In teaching, however, the accumulation of professional knowledge of the teaching act, based on research evidence, is a recent phenomenon. The crisis of confidence in professional knowledge is occurring at a time when such knowledge is growing by leaps and bounds. How, then, can the research be used? Is teaching so much an art, and are classroom situations so unique and complex, that professional knowledge as we know it is useless in setting problems and designing solutions?

There are two extremely useful ways of thinking about how research can inform the practice of teaching. But to understand these, we must first acknowledge that research knowledge is only one of several grounds for action in teaching. Buchman (1984) suggests three other bases that are as valid as research knowledge: common sense, personal commitment, and external policies. She points out that while research knowledge is useful, it is limited because it is "time-bound, theory-dependent, and selective" (p. 422). Therefore, the uses of research knowledge we will describe can only partly guide a teacher's actions.

The first way that research can inform practice concerns the development of a language to describe the wisdom of practitioners. Practical knowledge, based on common sense and experience, is often used by teachers in a manner similar to the conduct of applied research. The teacher develops hypotheses about a situation and ways of acting upon it, experiments, and assesses the results. Often the teacher cannot articulate this knowledge and these processes to others because there is no appropriate language in which to do so. Thus the wisdom accumulated by an individual teacher is often not passed on to others. The role of the researcher, however, is to isolate and explain concepts and to develop language to describe what is going on. The first way in which research can inform practice, then, is to provide teachers with a language that permits them to describe their practical knowledge and the ways they use it.

Practical knowledge is also important in Gary Fenstermacher's (1985) portrayal of the way in which research knowledge can inform practical knowledge, practical arguments, and action. He describes the relationship between practical arguments and action and explains how research can be used in the elaboration of practical arguments. Thus research can be useful to teachers by helping them to elaborate and adjust assumptions in their practical arguments.

These conceptions of the ways in which research can inform practice are important in thinking about the use of the material in this book. The chapters can provide ways of thinking about practice as well as a language for doing so. This material can also be used by practitioners to question and inform their practical arguments.

ORGANIZATION OF THIS VOLUME

This book is organized into five parts, each representing issues that teachers confront daily. Part One, "What Should I Teach?" reviews recent research in subject-matter areas such as mathematics, science, reading, and writing. Part Two, "How Should I Teach It?" looks at issues related to classroom management and organization, instruction, and planning. Part Three, "What Should I Know about My Students?" reviews research on the effects of peer groups on students and research on different categories of students, such as girls and boys, handicapped students, and those of limited English proficiency (LEP); ways in which teachers do and do not treat students differently; and the effects of differential treatment on student learning. Part Four, "The School," places teachers and teaching in the larger context of the school and the community. Effective schools research is reviewed, as is research on teacher collegiality and teacher-administrator relations. Part Five, "Professional Issues," looks at issues related to teaching as a profession and includes discussions of the history and effects of collective bargaining, legal obligations of teachers, stress and burnout, and teachers as collaborators in research.

USING THIS BOOK

This book may be used as a reference text to answer specific questions quickly or to develop an understanding of a complete area such as the teaching of science. Here are some examples of questions that are answered:

- How can I encourage LEP students to use English in class? (Chapter 14)
- How can computers be used in teaching writing? (Chapter 3)
- What is the best way to arrange the room when a classroom has only round worktables (no individual desks allotted for student seating)? (Chapter 10)
- What are some specific techniques for vocabulary development? (Chapter 2)
- What are some student misconceptions in math? (Chapter 1)
- Why do teachers interact more with boys than with girls? (Chapter 13)
- Criterion-referenced tests sound better than norm-referenced tests. Why haven't I seen many of them? (Chapter 11)
- How can parents best help their children with homework? (Chapter 21)
- What are the barriers to good teacher-principal relationships? (Chapter 18)
- What are the nature and roots of student disinterest in social studies? (Chapter 5)
- Should friends be assigned to the same class? (Chapter 12)
- What is the best way to identify gifted students? (Chapter 17)

A number of topics cut across chapters. For example, discussions of the use of *computers* can be found in Chapters 1, 3, 6, and 8. A thorough discussion of how teachers can provide *explanations* is found in Chapter 11, with specific examples of science explanations in Chapter 4. Chapters 9 and 12 discuss *peer teaching,* from different perspectives. *Classroom language* is discussed in Chapters 3, 14, and 15. And how to deal with the *mainstreamed child* is discussed in both Chapters 10 and 16.

This material is meant to help practitioners think about their actions, not to prescribe specific ways of doing things. A teacher, as a professional, is obliged to think about his or her actions and their effects, experiment with new ones, assess the results, and alter the actions accordingly. This book helps in thinking about actions, suggesting alternative actions, and assessing the effects. If we view teaching and the relationship between research and practice in this manner, we will project an image of teaching that emphasizes its professionalism and its need for autonomy.

REFERENCES

Buchman, M. (1984). The use of research knowledge in teacher education and teaching. *American Journal of Education, 92*(4), 421–439.

Elmore, R. F. (1983). Complexity and control: What legislators and administrators can do about implementing public policy. In L. S. Shulman & G. Sykes (Eds.), *Handbook of teaching and policy.* White Plains, N.Y.: Longman.

Fenstermacher, G. (1986). Philosophy of research on teaching: Three aspects. In M. Whitrock (Ed.), *Handbook of research on teaching* (3rd ed.). New York: Macmillan.

Schön, D. (1983). *The reflective practitioner: How professionals think in action.* New York: Basic Books.

CONTRIBUTORS

Charles W. Anderson is assistant professor at Michigan State University and a senior researcher at the Institute for Research on Teaching. He received his doctorate in science education from the University of Texas at Austin. His research interests are in science classroom instruction and student understanding of scientific concepts.

David C. Berliner received his Ph.D. from Stanford University in 1968. Since then he has written extensively on teacher education, teachers' use of time in classrooms, methodology for research on teaching, and the role of the teacher as a decision maker. He has lectured at universities around the world. He is co-author of a widely used text on general educational psychology and is a past president of the American Educational Research Association. He currently is professor of educational psychology at the University of Arizona.

Barbara A. Beyerbach is a lecturer in the Division for the Study of Teaching at Syracuse University. She received her Ph.D. in teaching and curriculum from Syracuse University. She has had five years' experience as an elementary school teacher. Her current research interests focus on assessing changes in teachers' thinking using multiple methodological approaches.

Lovely H. Billups is director of field services for educational issues of the American Federation of Teachers' Educational Issues Department. She calls upon her long experience as a classroom teacher to assist AFT locals in the development of programs and activities focusing on professional issues. The Educational Issues Department effects liaisons between AFT and other educational organizations and provides training programs for teachers in areas such as competency testing, critical thinking, and educational research. The AFT Educational Research and Dissemination Program was the recipient of AERA's 1983 Professional Service Award for relating research to practice.

Robert C. Bogdan is professor of special education, cultural foundations of education, and sociology at Syracuse University. He received his Ph.D. in sociology and his master's degree in education at Syracuse University. Dr. Bogdan has published in such diverse journals as: *The American Psychologist, Educational Technology, Phi Delta Kappan, American Journal of Orthopsychiatry, Social Policy,* and the *National Association of Secondary School Principals Bulletin.* His books *Introduction to Qualitative Research* (with Steve Taylor) and *Qualitative Research for Education* (with Sari Biklen) are widely used in graduate research methods courses.

Hilda Borko is associate professor of educational psychology, Teaching and Curriculum Division, University of Maryland. She received her Ph.D. in educational psychology from UCLA. She is secretary/treasurer of the Division of Educational Psychology (Division 15) of the American Psychological Association. Her current research interests are teacher planning and decision making and the process of learning to teach.

Douglas W. Carnine is associate professor of special education at the University of Oregon. He co-authored *Theory of Instruction, Direct Instruction Reading, Direct Instruction Mathematics,* and *Learning Pascal.* His current research looks at video-disc instruction, computer-assisted instruction, and low-cost networking systems in teaching mathematics, biology, earth science, health promotion, and computer science.

Kathy J. Carter is assistant professor of teacher education at the University of Arizona. She received her Ph.D. in secondary education and educational research from North Texas State University. Her research interests include teacher cognitions, classroom management, and academic work. Her current research is focused on the information processing of expert, novice, and postulant teachers.

Ursula Casanova is assistant professor of education at the University of Arizona. She is a native of Puerto Rico, where she completed secondary education. She has extensive experience as a teacher and school principal. Her major interests are school administration and cross-cultural issues in education. Since 1984 she has published a monthly column, "Putting Research to Work," in *Instructor* magazine.

Christopher M. Clark is professor of educational psychology at Michigan State University. He earned his Ph.D. at Stanford University in 1976 and has been on the MSU faculty since that time, teaching courses on school learning, educational psychology for teachers, and research on teaching. He is also a senior researcher in the MSU Institute for Research on Teaching, directing studies on teacher planning, the teaching of writing, and the relationships between research on teaching and the practice of teaching.

Michael Cohen is director of policy and planning at the National Association of State Boards of Education. He previously served as a senior research associate and team leader at the National Institute of Education, where he directed NIE programs and research on effective schools. Mr. Cohen has graduate training in sociology from Johns Hopkins University. His research interests include effective schools and school improvement, effects of state education policy, and research utilization by state policymakers.

Jere Confrey is assistant professor of mathematics education at Cornell University. She received her Ph.D. from Cornell University in 1980 while working as a senior researcher at the Institute for Research on Teaching at Michigan State University. She founded and directed the SummerMath and SummerMath for Teachers programs at Mount

Holyoke College. Her research interests are conceptual frameworks, and affective variables influencing mathematics learning.

Walter Doyle is professor of teacher education at the University of Arizona. He received his Ph.D. from the University of Notre Dame. He served as editor and associate editor of the *Elementary School Journal* and as associate editor of the *American Educational Research Journal*. His research interests are classroom management, teaching effectiveness, and academic work.

Kenneth Duckworth is professor of educational foundations at the University of Louisville. He received his Ph.D. in the sociology of education from Stanford University. He recently completed two research projects: a study of the management of student absenteeism in high school and a study of high school students' motivational response to teachers' class-testing practices.

Saundra Dunn is a doctoral student in the Department of Counseling, Educational Psychology, and Special Education, and a research intern in the Institute for Research on Teaching, at Michigan State University. Her area of specialization is school psychology, with an emphasis on educational anthropology. Research interests include the role of writing in the identification and remediation of students with learning difficulties, and the use of dialogue journals in teaching these students.

Edmund T. Emmer is professor of educational psychology at the University of Texas at Austin. He received his Ph.D. from the University of Michigan. He has conducted research on classroom management and discipline and has co-authored several books and manuals on these topics. Other related research interests are the development of teacher knowledge and skills, and classroom processes and outcomes.

Elizabeth Fennema is professor of curriculum and instruction at the University of Wisconsin-Madison with a specialty in mathematics education. Her research interests have focused on defining sex-related differences in mathematics and on a search for ways to eliminate them.

Dianne L. Ferguson is assistant professor of education at the University of Oregon. She received her Ph.D. in special education at Syracuse University. Her research interests center around curriculum development for and preparation of educators to work with severely handicapped learners, and relationships between professionals and families of handicapped children.

Philip M. Ferguson is a research associate for the Specialized Training Program, University of Oregon. He received his Ph.D. in special education at Syracuse University. Research interests center on severely handicapped children and their families and the history of public policy toward people with disabilities.

Susan Florio-Ruane is associate professor of teacher education and co-director of the Written Literacy Forum at the Michigan State University Institute for Research on Teaching. She received her doctorate in education from Harvard University. She serves as assistant editor of the *Anthropology and Education Quarterly* and is a member of the board of directors of the Council on Anthropology and Education. She has published extensively on classroom interaction, the teaching of writing, and teachers as researchers of their own practice. Current research interests include the sociolinguistic study of writing in classrooms.

Richard H. Hersh is vice president for academic affairs and professor of education at the University of New Hampshire. He was formerly vice president for research and professor of education at the University of Oregon, director of the Center for Moral Development at Harvard University, and a high school teacher. Among his books are *No G.O.D.'s in the Classroom* (1972), *Promoting Moral Development* (Longman, 1979); *Models of Moral Education* (Longman, 1980), and *The Structure of School Improvement* (Longman, 1984).

Susan Moore Johnson is assistant professor at the Harvard Graduate School of Education, where she earned her doctorate. She has been a public school teacher and administrator and has studied the impact of various educational policies on teachers, teaching, and schools. Her current research interests include incentives for teachers and the character of schools as workplaces. She is the author of *Teacher Unions in Schools* (1984).

Judith Warren Little is senior program director at the Far West Laboratory for Educational Research and Development in San Francisco. She received her Ph.D. in sociology from the University of Colorado. Dr. Little's research has focused on the professional "workplace" environment of schools, support for beginning teachers, and instructional leadership by administrators and teachers.

Jack Lochhead is director of the Cognitive Processes Research Group in the Department of Physics and Astronomy at the University of Massachusetts—Amherst. He received his doctorate from the University of Massachusetts School of Education. His primary interest is in the application of cognitive research findings to the teaching of science and mathematics, and he has written several publications on the topics of problem solving and instruction.

C. June Maker is associate professor of special education at the University of Arizona, Tucson, where she is responsible for the development and coordination of graduate degree concentrations in education of the gifted. She holds national offices in several organizations for the gifted. Her publications are on the subjects of curriculum development for the gifted, teaching models in the education of the gifted, the gifted handicapped, teacher training, the development of talents in exceptional children, and teaching learning-disabled students. She holds a doctorate from the University of Virginia.

Virginia A. Marchman is a doctoral candidate in developmental psychology at the University of California, Berkeley, and a research intern at Far West Laboratory for Educational Research and Development. Her research interests include language acquisition and peer communication.

Carmen I. Mercado is program coordinator for the Instructional Services Component of the New York Bilingual Education Multifunctional Support Center, based at Hunter College of the City University of New York. She is also an adjunct instructor for the Department of Curriculum and Teaching at Hunter. In addition to extensive experience with federally-funded teacher training projects, she was a bilingual teacher for eight years. She is now working toward her doctorate at Fordham University.

John R. Mergendoller is senior program director at the Far West Laboratory for Educational Research and Development in San Francisco. He received his Ph.D. in education and psychology at the University of Michigan. His research and theoretical interests encompass the social-cognitive outcomes of students' classroom experience.

Oliver C. Moles is director of the Education and Society Division in the Office for Educational Research and Improvement of the U.S. Department of Education. He received his Ph.D. in social psychology from the University of Michigan. His research interests are school discipline studies, home-school relations, family structure, and family educational processes.

Greta Morine-Dershimer is a professor in the Division for the Study of Teaching, Syracuse University. She received her Ph.D. in curriculum and teaching from Teachers College, Columbia University. She has taught for 10 years in elementary and secondary schools in New York and California and has worked for 15 years in teacher training in three universities in New York and California. She has published articles, books, and films on child development and teacher education. Her research interests focus on information processing of teachers and pupils during interactive lessons.

Jerome A. Niles is associate professor of elementary education/reading at Virginia Tech. He received his doctorate in reading education at the State University of New York at Albany. He has served as editor for five volumes of the *National Reading Conference Yearbook*. His research interests are teacher thinking related to reading instruction, and learning to teach reading.

George E. Olson is dean of the College of Education of Roosevelt University in Chicago, where prior to his appointment he served for three years as director of the Roosevelt Research and Development Center. A current research interest is the effect of the use of word processors on writing productivity and achievement across a variety of age groups.

Taffy E. Raphael is associate professor in the departments of Teacher Education and Educational Psychology at Michigan State University, and a senior researcher in the Institute for Research on Teaching. She received her doctorate from the University of Illinois, studying at the Center for the Study of Reading. Dr. Raphael's research interests focus on students' comprehension and composition of expository texts, and she edited *Contexts of School-Based Literacy* (1986).

Marilyn Rauth, Executive Director of the American Federation of Teachers' Educational Issues Department, calls upon her extensive experience as a classroom teacher to assist AFT locals in the development of programs and activities focusing on professional issues. The Educational Issues Department effects liaisons between AFT and other educational organizations and provides training programs for teachers in areas such as competency testing, critical thinking, and educational research. The AFT Educational Research and Dissemination Program was the recipient of AERA's 1983 Professional Service Award for relating research to practice.

Virginia Richardson-Koehler is visiting associate professor in the College of Education, University of Arizona. Prior to this she was assistant director of the National Institute of Education, responsible for the research programs on effective teaching, teacher education, and effective schools. She received her Ph.D. in educational foundations from Syracuse University. She is senior editor of the *American Educational Research Journal,* and her research interests focus on teacher education and teachers' thinking in action.

Migdalia Romero is a member of the faculty of the Department of Curriculum and Teaching at Hunter College of the City University of New York. She received her Ph.D. in applied linguistics from New York University. Formerly, Dr. Romero served as director (New York site) of the Significant Bilingual Instructional Features Study. A project associate for the New York Bilingual Education Multifunctional Support Center, which is based at Hunter, she conducts the BEMSC-sponsored language development specialists academies. Her major research interests are the acquisition, learning, retention, and attrition of language.

David Schimmel, a lawyer, is professor of education and co-director of the program in Legal Literacy and Education at the University of Massachusetts—Amherst. He received his J.D. from Yale Law School and is co-author of *The Rights of Students and Teachers, The Rights of Parents,* and *Teachers and the Law.*

Henrietta S. Schwartz is dean of the School of Education and professor of administration and education at San Francisco State University. She received her Ph.D. in administration and education from the University of Chicago. She had done research and published in a variety of disciplines, including multicultural education and equity, ethnography and cultural pluralism, and teacher and administrator stress. She is active on state and national advisory committees. Dr. Schwartz has had extensive teaching and administrative experience at the secondary level. She has taught anthropology and education, curriculum development, and principles and practice of administration, and she has administered a variety of programs.

James P. Shaver is professor and associate dean for research in the College of Education at Utah State University. He received his doctorate from Harvard University. Dr. Shaver was president of the National Council for the Social Studies in 1976 and received the council's Citation for Exemplary Research in Social Studies Education in 1977. Two themes in his extensive publications are the need to develop a sound rationale for social studies education and the need to examine the validity of research and statistical methods in educational research.

Lee S. Shulman is professor of education and affiliated professor of psychology, Stanford University. He did undergraduate and graduate work at the University of Chicago, where he received a Ph.D. in educational psychology. From 1963 to 1982 he was a faculty member at Michigan State University, serving as professor of educational psychology and medical education and as co-director of the Institute for Research on Teaching. His research interests are in the study of teaching, professional education, and the psychology of instruction. His publications include *Medical Problem Solving* (with Elstein and Sprafka) and *Handbook of Teaching and Policy* (with Sykes). He is immediate past president of the American Educational Research Association.

Edward L. Smith is associate professor of teacher education at Michigan State University. He received his Ph.D. in science education from Cornell University and was a member of the professional staff at the Southwest Regional Laboratory before joining the Michigan State University faculty. Dr. Smith has conducted cognitively oriented research on the teaching and learning of science, emphasizing student conceptual development.

Sandra S. Tangri is professor of psychology at Howard University. She received her doctorate in social psychology from the University of Michigan. Her current research areas are women and work, dual-career families, and organizational behavior. She recently completed research on barriers to home-school collaboration on a research grant from the National Institute of Education.

Richard L. Upchurch is assistant professor of computer and information science and director of computer fluency at Southeastern Massachusetts University. His primary interest is the effective and equitable use of information technology to enhance instruction in science and mathematics, particularly in the area of problem solving. He has written numerous papers on problem solving in mathematics and educational computing.

José A. Vázquez-Faría is professor of curriculum and teaching and coordinator of bilingual education programs at Hunter College of the City University of New York. He also directs the New York Bilingual Education Multifunctional Support Center, based at Hunter. Professor Vázquez was educated at Inter-American University in Puerto Rico and Teachers College, Columbia University. Formerly, he served as chief of the Bilingual/Multicultural Division of the National Institute of Education and principal investigator (New York site) for the Significant Bilingual Instructional Features Study. Among his publications is *El Español: Eslabón Cultural*, a text on the Spanish language.

EDUCATORS'
HANDBOOK

PART ONE

What Should I Teach?

Christopher M. Clark, Editor

The academic knowledge exchanged between the participants in a classroom is what most people think of as the major, if not the only, outcome of the schooling process. Although the teacher's skills in classroom management are clearly important, the content of the curriculum defines the limits of what will be learned. Further, we are aware more and more that the teacher's choices of content material to be covered in class strongly affect students' learning and their scores on standardized tests. This book therefore begins with content.

Much of the research on teaching over the past 15 years has focused on *generic* teaching behaviors: effective pedagogical techniques that are appropriate across grade levels and subject matters. The research has been conducted primarily in elementary school in mathematics and reading classrooms, but the concepts that have emerged from this research can be thought of as general teaching models and strategies (see Part Three).

Research on the teaching of a content area, in contrast, combines knowledge and methods of curriculum studies with those of teaching studies. Curriculum studies focus on the individual learner; teaching studies focus on general pedagogical skills appropriate in a classroom of 25 to 30 students. The studies summarized in these chapters describe the teaching of a subject matter not just to an individual learner but to a whole class. Because content-area teaching is an emerging field of research, only limited areas have received such attention.

In reading the chapters in Part One, you will note the powerful influence of cognitive science on our thinking about the teaching of subject matter: writing as a process, science teaching as conceptual change, problem solving on the computer, error and misconception diagnosis in mathematics. All these approaches employ cognitive science as a framework for thinking about how students learn the subject matter and, therefore, how teachers can use these understandings in conducting a lesson, marking homework, diagnosing problems, and so on.

The new research focus on content has great implications for practice. Viewing students' mathematical errors as reasonable, if not correct, or teaching writing as a process rather than a product will fundamentally change the way in which teachers approach these subjects and what students learn.

Virginia Richardson-Koehler
Senior Editor

1 MATHEMATICS LEARNING AND TEACHING

Jere Confrey

Research in mathematics education has been abundant and varied. In early studies, mathematics was frequently selected for examination because of its relative emphasis in the overall curriculum and because researchers expected little variability in how students went about learning the highly structured rules and procedures. However, from the years of disciplined inquiry, a dramatically more complex picture of the instructional setting of mathematics learning and teaching has emerged. Issues involving the learner, the teacher, the organization of groups, and the selection, presentation, and sequencing of curricular topics evolved as significant topics for research studies. Recently, particular attention has been paid to such topics as the implications of the microcomputer, the teaching of problem solving and geometry, and the participation of minorities and women in mathematics-related fields. As a result, the study of mathematics instruction has developed into a discipline that draws from cognitive psychology, sociology, mathematics education, and computer science.

In this chapter I will review a variety of the studies, beginning with a survey of the large existing national data base on mathematics education, moving to more focused examinations of what students learn from instruction and descriptions of different forms of mathematics instruction, including problem solving. Then I will describe some sociological issues arising from mathematics instruction and conclude with a discussion of the research on two current areas of interest: levels of thinking in microcomputers and geometry.

Since research is both a descriptive and an interpretative activity, researchers' commitments are revealed in their selection of the most pressing problems, in their choices of what contexts to examine, and in their methods of examining, analyzing, and interpreting their findings. Because the choice of the problem and method of investigation and analysis has such an impact on the results, I will describe these as well as the results of the studies. By providing this additional information, I hope that teachers will not only gain insight from the results of these studies but will also begin to consider how such methods of examination might be effectively applied in their own classrooms.

STUDENT LEARNING

How Do Our Students Perform?

Concerns for the quality of mathematics and science education have echoed across the country of late. Perhaps most widely reported have been the results of the National Science Board's Commission on Precollege Education in Mathematics, Science, and Technology (1983). This commission was charged with the task of examining, documenting, and proposing possible solutions to the crisis in mathematics, science, and technology education across the nation. As a result of its examination of the research on mathematics education and its consultation with teachers, administrators, teacher educators, business representatives, and textbook publishers, the commission chose this overriding goal:

> By 1995, the nation must provide, for all its youth, a level of mathematics, science, and technology education that is the finest in the world, without sacrificing the American birthright of personal choice, equity, and opportunity. (p. v)

In choosing this goal, the commission commented that although the brightest American students continue to be unsurpassed in their scientific and mathematical knowledge, the majority of the American public is perilously weak in their command of these fields. The commission's proposals for change in mathematics, science, and technology education indicate that our country needs to do the following:

1. Increase leadership at the federal, state, and local levels in both the public and private sectors.
2. Eliminate discrimination due to race, gender, or other irrelevant factors that has resulted in unequal participation.
3. Recruit, attract, and retain excellent teachers through increased compensation and higher certification standards.
4. Develop state resource centers and provide summer opportunities for current teachers.
5. Improve preservice education by requiring computer literacy, more mathematics, knowledge of relevant research, and continued practice teaching.
6. Increase the time devoted to mathematics and science instruction, especially in the elementary grades.
7. Develop and support exemplary programs.
8. Support research on teaching and learning.
9. Integrate technology into our instructional systems.
10. Promote informal educational opportunities through youth organizations, museums, and television and radio broadcasts.

One study that had a major impact on the work of the commission was the Third National Mathematics Assessment by the National Assessment of Educational Progress (1983). The results of the assessment suggest that our students are doing well in computation but that their performance in problem solving remains an area of highest

concern. This study, conducted every four or five years, reported data on the performance of 9-, 13-, and 17-year-olds on a variety of mathematics problems and statements of attitude. The data are presented in relation to the 1973 and 1978 data, so
not only can one compare the performance of various age groups at a single point in
time, but one can monitor their progress over time. The major content areas covered
by the assessment were numbers and numeration, variables and relationships, geometry, measurement, probability and statistics, graphs and tables, and technology. Each
of these content areas was assessed at four levels of cognitive processes based on
Bloom's (1956) taxonomy: (1) knowledge (or the recall of facts and definitions), (2)
skills (or the ability to use algorithms and manipulate symbols), (3) understanding (or
the explanation or illustration of different skills involving a transformation of knowledge), and (4) applications and problem solving.

Through the use of sampling procedures, the items on the assessment test were
administered to 9-, 13-, and 17-year-olds in such a way as to allow the results to be
generalized to the entire population of students in those age groups. Approximately
2,000 students responded to each item. About half of the items were multiple choice,
and the others were open-ended—students supplied the answers. A pool of items used
in the earlier two assessments was repeated in the most recent assessment. Thus the
NAEP represented a large-scale attempt to measure American students' understanding
of mathematics across topics, across cognitive levels, across age groups, and over
time.

Looking at the data for the three age groups over the span of nine years, one can
see that the performance of 9-year-olds has been relatively stable. The 13-year-olds'
scores declined two percentage points between 1973 and 1978 but then improved
four percentage points between 1978 and 1982. The 17-year-olds' scores declined
four percentage points between the first two assessments and remained stable over the
last two assessments.

In the past few years, an increasing amount of emphasis has been given to the
need to improve students' performance in applications and problem solving. Evidence
of this need came from the 1978 NAEP results, which showed dramatic declines in
students' performance at the higher cognitive levels. For example, whereas 75% of
the 17-year-olds are predicted to be able to answer the recall (knowledge) questions
correctly, only an alarming 44% will respond correctly to items on applications and
problem solving.

The NAEP results for 1982 showed no improvement in these skewed performances across cognitive levels for either 9- or 17-year-olds. Although 13-year-olds
performed significantly better in all four areas, they showed the most improvement in
the three lower skill areas of knowledge, skills, and understanding. Their percentages
of success on knowledge, skills, understanding, and applications were, respectively,
73.8% (up 4.5%), 57.6% (up 4.0%), 60.5% (up 3.9%), and 45.6% (up 2.2%).

On particular topics, the NAEP results pointed to improvement in computation
of whole numbers and decimals but not fractions. The students performed well on
items that were presented in standard form, but when that form was varied, adjustments were not made. For instance, when the problem "Subtract 237 from 504" was
presented to 9-year-olds, only a third as many could solve it as when presented in
standard vertical format.

There is also evidence that students performed better on items that could be
learned by rote. As a result, they succeeded in computations that they had done

before and had less success with ones requiring a broader generalization of the concept. For example, at age 13, 86% of the students correctly solved 8.4/4, 50% correctly solved 6.03/.3, and only 39% correctly solved 8.4/.04. When asked to estimate the answer to the problem 3.04 × 5.3, at age 17, 21% responded 1.6, 37% responded correctly 16, 17% responded 160, 11% responded 1,600, and 12% responded "I don't know."

In the areas of noncomputational skills, the pattern was similar. Students performed significantly better on exercises requiring them simply to identify geometric shapes, read simple graphs, or recognize common units of measure. On problems requiring the understanding of the mathematical principles underlying the concepts, such as area or angle measure, their performance dropped dramatically. For example, only about 25% of the 9-year-olds and two-thirds of the 13-year-olds understood that area is defined as the number of units covering a region, although many more of them calculated it correctly as length times width.

In summary, the NAEP findings indicated that students' performance in the basic skill areas has remained stable, with some improvement for 13-year-olds. In all age groups, students' performance remained markedly better in traditional topics and on problems presented in a standard fashion. One interpretation of these results is that students overrely on memorization—thus their performance on nonroutine problems, either presented in a novel format or conceived to test for understanding or application of underlying concepts, was far less satisfactory.

Another source of national data on students' performance in mathematics comes from the Educational Testing Service (1981). ETS provides annual analyses of students' performance on the Scholastic Aptitude Tests. These data are analyzed according to gender, ethnic background, region, school size, and other parameters. From 1967 until 1979, the average score on the mathematics portion of the SAT declined from 492 to 467. Since that time the scores have remained relatively stable, with a slight upturn reported for 1983 and 1984 scores.

The picture that emerges from this review of the research shows a leveling off in the decline in achievement scores, with some improvement in certain age groups. For all students, performance on nonroutine problems or problems requiring deeper conceptualizations, applications, or problem solving is weak.

Why So Poor?

Large survey data can tell how widespread and representative difficulties in learning mathematics are in the entire population, but they provide little information on what causes students' failures on nonroutine problems. To investigate these questions, researchers needed to employ alternative methods. Inspired by the work of Piaget, researchers developed the methods of clinical interviewing in which they posed problems to students and watched and listened as the students attempted to solve the problems. In most cases, the researchers had the students talk aloud as they attempted the problem and asked questions of the students as they proceeded. In other studies, students were asked to describe their method of solution retrospectively. The focus of such research was on the processes and strategies students use to solve problems and on the beliefs and reasons they had for choosing those methods. For these researchers, the paper-and-pencil achievement test was too answer-oriented to be helpful, giving little or no evidence of processes, strategies, or reasons.

Using these alternative methods, researchers opened up to investigation a host of fruitful and intriguing issues. Robust and perplexing responses by students revealed, on the one hand, weak and fragmented conceptual understanding. On the other hand, students were shown to have consistent patterns of errors, to hold intuitive and often conflicting systems of belief that congealed into either misconceptions or alternative conceptions, and to be actively, albeit unsuccessfully, trying to make sense of the instruction. Within single classrooms, the clinical interviews were revealing far more diversity in what students knew, why they believed it, and how they approached and solved problems.

To conduct in-depth investigations of error patterns, the studies involve fewer students, and the data are often presented in the form of case studies. The intent is to come to know the individual case in detail rather than to generalize by the sheer number of cases examined. As Easley (1977) explains:

> Clinical researchers feel that they can generalize from a study of a single case to some other individual cases because they have seen a given phenomenon in one situation in sufficient detail and know its essential workings to be able to recognize it when they encounter it in another situation. (p. 2)

What is Error Analysis?

One of the most fruitful results of the clinical research has been the analysis of student errors. In many instructional settings, errors are treated as stains in performance whose removal should be prompt and complete. This treatment of errors frequently fails. Errors that are eliminated when tested individually resurface when a problem is presented that involves the same knowledge or skill in combination or in another form.

In these studies, most errors in arithmetic were found to be systematic and predictable on further examination. An example of this sort of analysis by Davis, McKnight, Parker, and Elrich (1979) involves column addition. The authors found that the problem

$$
\begin{array}{r}
301 \\
45 \\
+\ 27 \\
\end{array}
$$

is particularly difficult for students because the leftmost column contains only one digit and there is no carry from the tens column. They demonstrated that varying either of these two factors resulted in better student performance and argued that the reason for this is that students have an expectation for addition (they call it an "addition frame") that there will be at least two inputs to the addition operation. Lacking two inputs in the leftmost column, the student is at a loss; he or she may add the 3 to the 2 in 27, getting the erroneous answer 573, or use other strategies to force the problem to fit within his or her expectations.

As is demonstrated in this example, the researchers do more than document errors. Some researchers search for patterns in the errors that may predict a whole series of errors and then test those predictions by constructing tests and analyzing error patterns. Others use the clinical methods of listening to students as they solve the problems to construct their explanations of error patterns.

Radatz (1979) proposed a set of error categories that he believed accounted for many of the errors he had examined. His categorization included errors resulting from the following causes:

1. Clashes between the meanings of words in mathematics and in other contexts.
2. Difficulty in interpreting tables, diagrams, and other visual representations of mathematical tasks.
3. Deficient mastery of prerequisite knowledge.
4. Inflexibility and rigidity in recognizing changes in the fundamental structure of a problem.
5. The application of irrelevant rules or strategies.

Perhaps the most extensive recent work on errors is by J. S. Brown and his colleagues (Brown & Burton, 1977; Brown & Van Lehn, 1980). These researchers have looked at errors as analogous to "bugs" in a computer program, that is, as the result of using the wrong procedure in a systematic way. They constructed "diagnostic models" using computer simulations that replicated the students' patterns of correct and incorrect models. From these "diagnostic models" Brown and his colleagues created a gamelike program, called Buggy, for teaching student teachers to learn to diagnose bugs. The student teacher as diagnostician is presented with a set of problems generated from a single bug or set of bugs. Once a bug has been hypothesized, the diagnostician creates test problems for the computer. Through Buggy, prospective teachers learn that errors are usually not random events, and they learn techniques to probe further to understand the Buggy procedures leading to the observed pattern of errors. An offshoot of this work has been the profound and disconcerting realization that even in an apparently simple arithmetic operation like subtraction, 60 primitive bugs and 270 "buggy" combinations were found. In analyzing the results of a test of over 1,300 fourth, fifth, and sixth graders, 40% of the students exhibited consistently buggy behavior. Ironically, the question of why some students fail to learn mathematics is being transformed into the question of how anyone succeeds in learning mathematics!

The result of this research is an emphasis on the need to attend not only to what students can do successfully but also what students fail to do and to determine the reasons for the failure. It is necessary to determine those reasons before remediation is appropriate. Ginsberg (1977) summed up this attitude toward errors:

> Typically children's errors are based on systematic rules.... Errors are seldom capricious or random. Often children think of mathematics as an isolated game with peculiar sets of rules and no evident relation to reality. At the same time, children's faulty rules have sensible origins. Usually they are a distortion or misrepresentation of sound procedures.... There often exist gaps between children's informal knowledge and their written work.... The gap may originate because instruction does not devote sufficient attention to integrating formal written procedures with children's already existing and relatively powerful informal knowledge. (p. 129)

Students' Misconceptions

In the last sentence, Ginsberg provides a bridge between the research on students' errors and on students' misconceptions. Teachers might infer from the research on errors that the purpose of collecting and categorizing a set of the most prevalent errors would be to design instruction that teaches students explicitly to avoid the errors. This might be possible if all errors were indeed independent sets of incorrect procedures. However, many errors do not fit into this description, especially in more complex mathematics, which is dependent on vast quantities of integrated knowledge. In this case, the errors are captured in a web of factual knowledge, procedures, representations, connected knowledge, justifications for knowledge and procedures, and impressions of mathematics. Errors of this sort are given the name "misconceptions," and they constitute another branch of clinical research.

When students possess misconceptions or alternative conceptions (they are not always erroneous; they may simply differ from the dominant conception), instruction often fails to connect with what they already believe. Most existing instructional models assume minimal variation in students' conceptions in mathematics. Researchers in this tradition have found this assumption to be wrong and stress that the diversity in students' conceptions is far greater than most teachers realize.

Because these misconceptions are so often not examined, students in mathematics develop the kind of survival strategies to which Ginsberg alludes—they learn the formal written procedures by rote and in isolation, as a game to be played by the teacher's rules.

Examples of Misconceptions.   Erlwanger (1977) provided a classic illustration of the development of such misconceptions in his study of Benny, a sixth-grade student studying a curriculum known as Individualized Instruction. From the teacher's point of view, Benny was making better than average progress. However, after interviews, Erlwanger became aware that Benny possessed an idiosyncratic way of solving problems by converting fractions to decimals. Benny would say that 2/10 equals 1.2 and that both 3/5 and 5/3 equal .8. Erlwanger explained Benny's responses by suggesting that Benny interpreted the problem

$$\frac{2}{10} \quad \text{as} \quad \begin{array}{r} 2 \\ +10 \\ \hline \end{array}$$

and that Benny then placed the decimal according to the number of digits in the answer. Benny's success in his class, as measured by his maintenance of a quick pace and consistent mastery at the 80th percentile, resulted from his strategy of attempting the problems, checking the answer sheet, and searching for a pattern that would allow him to predict the correct answer. Thus he modified his answers without concomitant change in his belief system. Erlwanger pointed out that Benny's case illustrated how the mastery of content and skill may not imply understanding when these are packaged under such structured instructional objectives and assessment procedures. The result of Benny's experience was the development of a conception of mathematics in which Benny believed that the answers worked like "magic" and that mathematics consisted of a large variety of different rules invented "by a man or someone who was very smart."

Research on misconceptions has not been limited to arithmetic. Because the misconceptions are described as more complex wholes involving strategies, representations, reasons, and beliefs, they have been used as a basis to describe students' understanding of diverse concepts such as numbers (Gelman & Gallistel, 1978; Confrey, 1980), functions, variables (Rosnick, 1982), volume (Vergnaud, 1983), ratio and proportion (Karplus, Karplus, Formisano, & Paulsen, 1979), and limits (Taback, 1975; Schwarzenberger & Tall, 1975–1978).

For example, Vinner (1983) investigated students' understanding of the concept of function in grades 10 and 11. To do so, he distinguished between a concept definition; a verbal definition accurately explaining a concept in some noncircular way; and a concept-image, which includes the mental picture of a concept and a set of properties associated with the concept. Vinner hypothesized that to understand a concept, a student must be able to integrate the concept definition into the concept-image.

By asking 146 students, several months to a year after studying functions, to answer a five-question, open-ended questionnaire ending with the question "What is a function?" and analyzing those responses, Vinner was able to describe four categories of students' opinions about functions:

1. Approximately 57% of the students responded with the textbook definitions frequently mixed together with elements from their concept-images. In these responses, the requirement for the uniqueness of the $f(x)$ for a given x is often alluded to obscurely or incorrectly. For example, one student wrote, "Every point in the domain has a point in the range" (p. 299).
2. Some 14% of the students thought a function was a well-specified rule of correspondence. An example of this was given by a student who wrote, "It is a relation between two sets of numbers based on a certain law" (p. 299).
3. Another 14% of the students thought a function was an algebraic term, a formula, an equation, or an arithmetic manipulation. For example, one student wrote, "A function is something like an equation. When you put in numbers instead of the unknown you get a solution" (p. 300).
4. Some 7% identified the function with the graph, with the symbols $y = f(x)$, or with the diagram representing the two sets. "A function is a curved line in a coordinate system" (p. 300) is an example of this category of students' beliefs.

(The remaining 8% of the students offered no answer.)

In reporting this research, Vinner emphasized that the concept-images that students hold may or may not be connected with the textbook definitions. Of the 57% of the students who responded with a version of the textbook definition, only 34% acted in accordance with that definition in identifying functions. Their experience of functions and their formal definitions often contained unresolved conflicts of which they were not aware.

Furthermore, included in their concept-images were additional stipulations about functions that exceeded the restrictions in their definition and seemed to have resulted from overgeneralizing their experiences with functions. For example, they had difficulty accepting functions with multiple rules or ones with arbitrary rules and spent much of their efforts in specifying the rules as algebraic statements rather than determining if the example fit the definition.

As this example illustrates, what has united the researchers on misconceptions is the recognition that students are not passive recipients of mathematical knowledge. They actively construct their own meaning and interpretation for what they are learning and use that to guide them in mathematical explorations (Piaget, 1970; Glasersfeld, 1974). At the same time, they will learn the formal mechanics and definitions required of them by rote, and if these conflict with their own constructions, misconceptions are likely to occur. Understanding these misconceptions requires an in-depth examination of what a student believes to be true about a concept, about related concepts, and about what knowledge in mathematics is.

Problem Solving

In examining the research on students' conceptions, it becomes apparent that differences in students' performances are due not only to differences in the facts and procedures that they know but also to differences in how they go about solving problems. As a result, a significant thrust of the research has been devoted to examining problem solving. Early research in mathematics education built heavily on the four phases of good problem solving identified by Polya (1945): understanding the problem, devising a plan, carrying out the plan, and looking back at the solution. From this has come a considerable volume of work on "heuristics." A heuristic is a general technique or strategy for comprehending, solving, or reflecting on a problem. Schoenfeld (1980) provided a list of commonly identified heuristics divided into three stages of solution: analysis, exploration, and verification. These included drawing a diagram, examining special cases, simplifying the number of variables in the problem, looking at equivalent or modified problems, checking solutions for reasonableness, using all relevant data, and considering alternative methods and special cases.

One of the major hurdles in the research on problem solving was how to characterize the problems with which students are faced. Comparisons among findings are difficult and tenuous without such standardization, along with specific information about the context and population of the study (Goldin & McClintock, 1979). Four categories of the structure of tasks were identified by these researchers: the syntax (comprehending the problem), the mathematical and nonmathematical content (devising a plan), the structure, and the heuristic processes required. Such a categorization can be useful to teachers in determining what knowledge students require.

Problem solving in mathematics education has grown at the same time that research on problem solving in cognitive psychology has experienced tremendous growth. Lester and Garofalo (1982) edited a set of writings the intent of which was to build connections between these two bodies of work. The potential gain from doing so is great. From the work in psychology, the mathematics education community has begun to look at such issues as the role and structure of memory in learning mathematics, the importance of metacognitive strategies, or the decisions about which strategies are appropriate, and the importance of "frames" or a "schema," a relatively fixed set of expectations about a mathematical idea that influences one's perception of it, on problem-solving behavior.

Studies of problem solving as it occurs in an instructional setting are just beginning to emerge. Lesh, Landau, and Hamilton (1983) have been studying the processes of problem solving undertaken by groups of three. To study these processes, they have constructed and collected a set of word problems using elementary mathematics concepts involving common practical applications. For example, in the carpentry problem, students are asked to calculate the type and amount of baseboard to purchase for a room of given dimensions. The baseboard comes in preset lengths, and students can choose to attend to such features as the number of doors if they so choose.

In analyzing the group data, Lesh, Surber, and Zawojewski (1983) found that the groups went through cycles in attacking the problem and that these cycles often differed qualitatively. They found that students tended to map over to a potential model for approaching a problem, perform a string of calculations within that model, and then map back to judge the appropriateness of the model. Complete or partial modeling cycles were likely to occur repeatedly for a group during a single problem-solving session.

Research studies such as these have the potential to provide a conceptualization of problem solving that goes well beyond the narrow reassignment of the term *problem solving* to the solution of word problems so prevalent in textbooks. Although such a discussion only barely touches on the wealth of provocative studies emerging in this field, it provides an indication of studies under way.

Mathematical Ability

As researchers have striven to provide an adequate definition of problem-solving ability, interest has been rekindled in the nature of mathematical ability. Many of the processes of solving problems coincide with the characteristics that differentiate more and less able students.

Krutetskii (1976), a Russian psychologist, spent 12 years studying the differences in mathematical problem solving between exceptional students and less successful students. Using interviews and observations of students, questionnaires from teachers and mathematicians, and historical analyses of bibliographies, Krutetskii and his colleagues identified a three-part categorization of abilities that they believed differentiated these groups: the ability to gather information, the ability to process information, and the ability to retain information.

Krutetskii found that the more capable students in mathematics can discern the mathematical structure in a given problem more quickly. He identified three basic quantities in a problem: the relationships that communicate the essential mathematical meaning and structure, quantities not essential for the mathematical structure but essential for solving that particular variant, and superfluous quantities. More capable students would respond to a problem lacking a question with a quick appraisal of the intended question; less capable students would not perceive a hidden question and would focus more characteristically on the particulars of the problem. When a question contained surplus information, the less capable students often used it in their attempts to solve the problem.

Silver (1979) generalized the findings of Krutetskii to groups of nongifted students in a study of how students categorized word problems that varied in their contextual details (subject, location, or action), the mathematical structure, the form of the question, and the pseudostructure (the numeric quantity examined in the problem). He found significant relationships between how frequently students categorized problems by mathematical structure and their performance in solving those problems.

The second category of abilities comes into play as the student is solving a problem. In this category, Krutetskii identified five abilities: generalization, curtailment, flexibility, elegance, and reversibility. Generalization, for Krutetskii, entailed both moving from the particular to the more general or abstract case and recognizing a particular as an instance of a previously known generality. Curtailment was the

appropriate shortening of a reasoning process, combined with the ability to reconstruct that process in its entirety on request. Flexibility and elegance described the
students' ability to diversify their attempts at solution with ease of movement among
methods and to search for the clearest, shortest, and thus most "elegant" path to the
solution. Finally, reversibility was the ability to restructure the direction of a mental
process, such as recognizing the inverse relationships between operations such as
squaring and finding the square root.

In studying information processing, Krutetskii found that the better students in
mathematics were stronger in each of these abilities. They tended to generalize more
quickly and at higher levels of generality. Their curtailment was more rapid and more
often correct, and they could more easily reconstruct the entire process on request.
Multiple methods of solution were attractive to them, and they discerned clear
differences in the elegance of alternative solutions. Finally, they could reverse a
process with ease and independently recognized instances of reversals.

His final category of abilities was that of information retention. Stressing that
how well one retains information is surely a product of how effectively one processes
it, Krutetskii pointed out that poorer mathematics students tend to memorize mechanically and reproduce mathematics unsystematically.

Driscoll (1981, 1982) summarized this work and presented the following charac-
terizations: successful problem solvers do more rereading of the problem, distinguish
between relevant and irrelevant information, plan toward their goals, use a wide
variety of heuristics, discern the mathematical structure in a problem, and generalize
across problems. In contrast, unsuccessful solvers proceed quickly, often on irrelevant
clues, tend to apply a single operation to all the numbers and to rely on memorized
rules or problem types, and have difficulty generalizing.

Using Krutetskii's categories of abilities, Confrey and Lanier (1980) examined
the mathematical abilities of ninth-grade students, half of whom had been placed in
Algebra I and the other half into General Mathematics. Since placement into General
Mathematics often resulted in the termination of a student's mathematics pursuit, the
researchers sought to determine if that placement could be justified on the basis of
ability. Twenty-one students were interviewed for six hours each over a period of six
weeks. Ten students were from an inner-city school, and those students shared the
same teacher, half of them in his algebra class and half in his general mathematics
class. Eleven students from a suburban school also shared one teacher and were in her
algebra or general mathematics class.

No differences were found in the two groups' ability to generalize, to gather
information, or to deal with multiple methods. Slight differences in favor of the
algebra students were found in the students' ability to curtail the reasoning process
and in their recognition of the reversibility of certain mathematical processes. Most
striking to these researchers was not the differences in ability but the weakness
exhibited by all students in these abilities. The students in general were unaccustomed
to focusing on processes, and the conclusion of the researchers was that far more
attention and direct instruction ought to be devoted to the development of these
abilities.

In conducting and analyzing these interviews, the researchers found a set of
themes that characterized how students set about solving mathematical problems.
These were often behaviors that seemed to have resulted from strategies students had
developed from adapting and easing the demands of mathematics instruction. Often

they impeded the investigation of abilities because they masked any real engagement with the problems. Here are four examples of these themes:

1. *Answer frames.* Students believed that the primary aim of mathematics is to get answers; if an answer was incorrect, examining the process was of no use at all to them.
2. *Whole number mentality.* Students believed that if an answer does not come out even, it's wrong; decisions about which operations to choose are based on the likelihood of their producing whole-number answers.
3. *Symbolic manipulations versus representations.* Students lacked any adequate representation for the symbols that were being manipulated. Their ability to explain rules in terms of drawing pictures for fractions and decimals was weak.
4. *Authority and risk.* Students relied heavily on the authority of the teacher or the book to determine the correctness of a response. They expressed little or no commitment to their own answers and were seldom willing to risk being wrong.

These themes indicated that students' conceptions of mathematics and mathematics learning influence how well students can solve problems. They also influence what students come to believe about certain mathematical concepts. And they seem to be the result of patterns of instruction. As such they form a bridge between the research on how students think and the research on teaching in mathematics.

MATHEMATICS TEACHING

How Do Effective Teachers Teach Mathematics?

Fairly recently, researchers have begun to examine instruction as it occurs in classrooms. Known as process-product research, this work has tried systematically to relate the processes teachers use in instruction to their students' performance on one possible product of instruction, the achievement test. One of the most well-regarded investigations in this area was conducted by Good and Grouws (1979) with teachers of fourth-grade mathematics. The study, wherein the researchers hoped to demonstrate that teachers do indeed make a difference in student performance, was designed to identify effective and ineffective teachers as defined by achievement scores and to identify the behaviors that differentiated the two groups.

They found that in both groups, whole-class instruction predominated. Thus the organization of the classroom was not key, but the quality of instruction that took place in that organizational structure was. Factors that contributed to quality instruction included clarity of presentation, an emphasis on questions that demand a single answer (unless difficulty in responding is encountered, in which case a process-oriented explanation is preferred), a willingness to recognize and deal with student failure, an increase in the class time devoted to whole-group instruction, clear definitions of what was to be learned, and carefully monitored daily seatwork. They also found that more effective teachers demand more work, moved at a quicker pace, and provided immediate nonevaluative feedback on tasks.

From this study, Good and Grouws developed a treatment program designed to communicate the results of this study to teachers and to provide a structured program by which they could implement these findings into their own classrooms (Good, Grouws, & Ebmeier, 1983). In the Missouri Mathematics Program, the class period is divided into five parts, with a guideline for the time allocation suggested for each: a daily review (8 minutes), development (20 minutes), seatwork (15 minutes), home-work assignment (15 minutes), and special reviews. Although the divisions are fairly reminiscent of the structure of a secondary class period, the careful and thoughtful implementation of each of the parts makes it an effective method for teaching mathematics.

For example, in the review portion, Good and Grouws recommended that the teacher review and summarize the previous day's concepts, collect and review the homework, and then do several mental computations. In describing the development portion of the program, the authors recommended that the teacher spend 10 minutes or more actively introducing the new concept and then carefully assess students' comprehension; if adequate comprehension is not demonstrated, the teacher should repeat the demonstration. Controlled practice, during which students complete exam-ples of the problems with frequent feedback, is required. The authors stressed the importance of holding students accountable during this portion by continuously alerting them to the performance expected on these problems. Process-oriented ex-planations are emphasized during this time period.

During the seatwork portion of the class, students are given the opportunity to practice the concepts and skills, and this is reinforced by the assignment of homework that provides delayed practice and aids in the recall of the concepts. The authors pointed out the detrimental effects of lengthy homework assignments for which adequate preparation is not provided. If used, they found that students end up practicing errors, and more harm than good results.

The Missouri Mathematics Program represents a significant landmark in the research in mathematics education. First, it is the result of observations and analysis of data on the actual practice of teaching, and hence its relevance and applicability are assured. Second, it represents research that was carried through into a program that has been successfully implemented by a number of school districts. Finally, it introduces the concepts of accountability, clarity, controlled practice, alerting, ex-pectations, and task-orientation, among others, into the mathematics education com-munity.

The primary criticism of the work is that it relies solely on an achievement measure to define effectiveness in teaching mathematics. As demonstrated in the section on misconceptions, it is not universally accepted that students performing well on an achievement measure necessarily understand what they are doing at a deeper level. Good and Grouws are clearly aware of this limitation and have sought more variation in possible outcome measures, such as problem-solving tests.

Are There Viable Alternatives to Whole-Group Instruction?

All of these studies stress the importance of active student participation in the construction of mathematical ideas. The Good-Grouws study does this through "ac-tive teaching," in which the teacher's role in assessing student comprehension and requiring students' accountability is paramount. Other studies have focused on alternative classroom structures for promoting students' participation. Slavin (1981) and Webb (1983) have focused on the use of small groups to promote participation.

Whimbey and Lochhead (1980) have developed a method, known as "paired prob-lem solving," to encourage students' active participation in the processes of mathe-matics. Designed to simulate the clinical interview, the method works as follows:

One student, the problem solver, is required to explain in detail how he or she is approaching the problem. The other student, the questioner, must follow the method of the problem solver, whether it is correct or incorrect, until the questioner understands how the problem solver is approaching the problem. The effectiveness of the method stems from a variety of its characteristics: It teaches students to speak the language of mathematics; it teaches the students to act as resources for each other, freeing time for the teacher to concentrate on deeper instructional challenges; and most important, it focuses reflection by students on the problem-solving process. The role of the teacher using this method becomes one of guidance and encouragement of debate.

Although effectiveness research (Lockhead, 1977) is only emerging now, these methods seem to hold great promise for promoting a more active role on the part of the student.

The Impact of Classroom Activities

A recent study serves as an interesting bridge from the research on student misconceptions to the research on classroom instruction. Recall that some students' misconceptions had to do with students' impressions of mathematics. Frequently those involved what sorts of answers one should get (whole-number mentality), how quickly one should learn a concept (pace), or whom to rely on for correct answers (authority).

One way to organize such student beliefs and behaviors is through a series of constructs first described by Doyle (1980) and more recently by Doyle and Carter (1983). Doyle introduces the concept of a task. A task has three parts: a goal or product, a set of available resources, and a set of operations that can be applied to the resources for reaching the goal. Doyle points out that students spend a considerable amount of time in classrooms figuring out how to accomplish academic tasks. Tasks, as conceptualized by Doyle and Carter, are negotiated between a teacher and the class. If a teacher assigns a set of difficult word problems, students will often pressure the teacher not to grade as stringently, to allow group work, or to give extra time. Doyle suggested that such modifications in the task structure indirectly but significantly affect what the students learn about the subject matter. Thus the notion of a task structure provides a bridge between the subject matter as it is organized and structured within the curriculum and its transformation through the processes of instruction.

Doyle and Carter pointed out that since academic tasks are embedded in an evaluation system, they are accomplished under conditions of ambiguity and risk. Ambiguity refers to the extent to which a precise formula for accomplishing the task can be offered. Risk, tied closely to accountability, refers to the likelihood that the product will be evaluated and the stringency of that evaluation. Students, claim the authors, attempt to minimize ambiguity and risk. For example, a student who asks if an item will be on the test is attempting to reduce risk; a request for the teacher to work through an example step by step on the board is an attempt to decrease ambiguity.

Doyle and his colleagues are currently conducting a study of the task structure of a mathematics class. A study of English classes indicated that when teachers presented students with tasks requiring higher levels of cognitive processes, many opportunities for student judgment and decision making were provided. As the tasks progressed, teachers became more explicit about specifications of the final products, decreased both ambiguity and risk, and had an impact on the difficulty level of the task.

Building on the idea of a task, Confrey (1984) analyzed the responses of young women on a survey designed to elicit their conceptions of mathematics, mathematics learning, and mathematics classrooms. She found that often students do not distinguish between mathematical ideas and nonmathematical classroom activities. Substantial numbers of students said that they relied primarily on memorization and imitation of examples, that they ignored proofs if they were not going to be tested, and that copying examples from the board and handing in homework were examples of mathematics. In journals kept by young women enrolled in a six-week alternative summer program, three dimensions of classroom experience could be postulated to influence dramatically their conceptions of mathematics: the pressure of pace, public exposure of the evaluation system, and the absence of personal identification with the subject.

As a result, Confrey proposed a model of the mathematics classroom in which students must construct a conception of mathematics from their experiences with two filters: the curriculum as it is selected and presented and the task system as it is designed. She warned that to teach problem solving effectively in classrooms, curriculum revision alone is not adequate. Changes in the task system that communicate a different set of expectations for classroom performance are also necessary.

Math and Work Habits

Predating this particular work was one of the first studies to emphasize the multiplicity of roles played by mathematics instruction. In 1978, Stake and Easley conducted a survey of science education for the National Science Foundation. This study compiled a massive amount of data, including a series of case studies, and mathematics instruction was the topic of some of them. In these, mathematics was described as a ritualistic force, in which a work ethic was sometimes stressed over understanding. Stake and Easley described teachers who emphasize that by learning of mathematics, students learn responsibility, diligence, persistence, thoroughness, and neatness. They wrote, "Instilling such disciplinary traits was sometimes a more primary function for the school, it seemed, than disseminating information" (p. 12:35).

THE SOCIAL CONTEXT OF MATHEMATICS INSTRUCTION

In this section, I will review research that describes the underrepresentation of women and minorities in mathematics and examines possible reasons for the imbalance.

On the mathematics portion of the SAT and on the recent NAEP tests, young women and minorities (except Asian-Pacific Americans) continue to score significantly lower than white males. At age 9, no significant differences in the performances of girls and boys on the NAEP are reported; by age 17, however, the males performed three percentage points higher than the females. On the SAT, the gap between young women and young men has widened since 1967 from 42 to 49 points (ETS, 1981).

Consistent with earlier results, the NAEP (1983) showed that black and Hispanic students performed below the national level. At age 9, blacks were performing 11 percentage points below the norm and Hispanics 9 points lower than the norm. At age 17, these gaps had widened to 15 and 11, respectively.

In trying to explain such differences in achievement, researchers have explored a variety of factors. The first factor examined was the differences in participation in mathematics by the different groups. For women, differences in participation in mathematics courses become apparent in higher-level courses such as trigonometry. For minorities, the trend is obvious earlier (NAEP, 1983). By the Algebra I level, significant differences in enrollments were already obvious, with 75% of all whites but only 57% of blacks taking algebra. In geometry, the figures were 55% of the whites and 34% of the blacks. An interesting exception to this pattern was noted in the area of computers, with 11% of the blacks enrolled but only 10% of the whites.

Sells (1976) underscored the importance of overcoming this deficiency of participation of young women and minorities at the secondary level in her study of college freshmen at the University of Maryland. She found that 53% of the white men had at least four years of high-school mathematics, compared to only 20% of the white women. For black men and women, the percentages were 22% and 10%, respectively.

The extent to which the differences in participation are suspected to provide an adequate explanation for differences in achievement tests varies. Reviewing the research on sex differences and taking differences in participation into account, Fennema (1978) concluded that (1) no sex-related differences are evident in elementary school; (2) after elementary school, the differences do not always appear; (3) starting in the seventh grade, differences that do appear favor males, particularly on the higher cognitive skills; and (4) there is some evidence that such differences are decreasing.

Researchers have also sought other factors to explain differences in achievement and participation. Armstrong (1979) reviewed and reexamined these factors, which included attitudes, career and educational aspirations, and encouragement by significant others. She found the strongest predictors of continued participation in mathematics to be enjoyment of, confidence in, and low anxiety about mathematics; a perceived need for mathematics in a career or a belief that mathematics is generally useful; and parental encouragement and high educational expectations and teachers' encouragement.

More recently, researchers have been investigating sex differences in how students experience and interpret their mathematics instruction. Wolleat, Pedro, Becker, and Fennema (1980) studied differences in the attribution patterns of young men and women in mathematics. They found a tendency in young women toward a pattern of "learned helplessness." Young women are more likely to explain their successes by effort rather than ability and their failures by ability and task difficulty. The authors suggested that such a pattern might well be linked to why young women show less confidence in their mathematical ability and less persistence in their participation in mathematics courses.

Becker (1981) examined the treatment of young women and men in geometry classrooms. She found differences in the number of opportunities offered for answering questions, in the level of challenge posed in the questions, in sustenance and persistence after an erroneous response, and in the amount of individual help given. All of the differences favored the male students. "Students were learning," she wrote, that

> mathematics is an environment that sex-typed the subject as male, that provided males more formal and informal reward and support in mathematics, and that

provided males more outlets for classroom academic achievement and recognition.... Females, relatively speaking, were treated with benign neglect. (p. 51)

Minorities lack representation in mathematics-related fields to an even greater degree than do women (National Science Foundation, 1982). Matthews (1983) reviewed the studies of minorities in mathematics and reported three clusters of variables affecting achievement and participation: parent, student, and school. The mothers' educational background, expectations for performance, and attitudes toward mathematics seemed to influence the students' mathematical performance. She found that minority students' attitudes toward mathematics were generally positive, although their awareness of the utility of it for their career choices or for everyday life was low. Finally, a very significant factor for predicting the achievement of minorities in mathematics was the school climate and the racial balance. A school with discipline and attendance difficulties depressed minority achievement in mathematics, as did schools with larger black student populations, possibly due to less available advanced coursework and lower expectations for its pursuit.

Sells's recognition that mathematics acts as a "critical filter" to many lucrative, prestigious, and challenging careers emphasized the importance of considering broader sociological factors involved in the teaching of mathematics. Through the studies of women and minorities in mathematics, it is becoming clear that assumptions teachers hold about mathematics ability, their expectations of students' performance, and their encouragement of students to pursue advanced mathematics coursework exert a profound influence on mathematics-related careers.

INITIATIVES IN MATHEMATICS CURRICULA

Although a comprehensive review of the recent developments in mathematics curricula is beyond the scope of this chapter, two innovations on which a substantial amount of research has been conducted are microcomputers and geometry.

Microcomputers

The impact of microcomputers on the teaching of mathematics is emerging as an important area of research. Designing instructional software for microcomputers has already built on the research on students' errors (Brown & Burton, 1977). The intent of this work was to design systems that predict, diagnose, and remediate common errors. However, another trend has involved the use of the microcomputer to provide students with opportunities to explore fundamental mathematical concepts.

The best-known example of this is the development of Logo by Seymour Papert and his colleagues. Widely publicized through the media and his book *Mindstorms*, Papert (1980) described Logo as creating an environment where students of all ages can actively explore and construct mathematical ideas. By opening the field of programming to access by students at a variety of ages, Papert made it possible to begin to examine some of the intermediate stages of learning programming and provoked the study of the cognitive consequences of computer study.

Interested in determining to what extent programming in Logo could influence higher cognitive processes such as planning, investigators at Bank Street College studied students engaged in learning to program. Their findings offer encouragement and admonitions about the potential of microcomputers to improve thinking.

Pea and Kurland (1984) reviewed the literature on the cognitive demands and consequences of computer learning. The authors point out that the claims for the potential of computer programming to teach critical cognitive processes far exceed current documentation of those claims. This is not surprising, given how recent an innovation the microcomputer is in education; the review, however, also raises significant issues about what is meant by learning to program. Striking an analogy with reading, the authors point out that programming expertise extends beyond knowing the syntax and the definitions of the commands, just as reading is more than decoding. They identify four levels of programming ability and suggest that the demands and consequences of programming will vary with level.

The four levels are (1) program user, who uses prepackaged software; (2) simple programmer, who requires little planning, uses no subroutines or procedures, and inserts no documentation; (3) program generator, who can meet personal objectives but does so without concern for documentation, debugging, or efficiency; and (4) software developer, who has an intimate understanding of how the program works and provides documentation and tests throughout.

The demands of programming depend on which level of programming ability is desired. Pea and Kurland describe the general areas of programming demands that have been researched. These include looking at an individual's memory capacity, mathematical ability, analogical reasoning, conditional reasoning, procedural thinking, and temporal reasoning. In studies of experts, it has been found that expert programmers have in their "repertoire" recurring chunks of programs, a large variety of rules, and mental models of how the computer functions as it encounters a rule or a chunk. Furthermore, experts organize their knowledge differently than novices, attending to deeper features, and when debugging they read programs for the flow of control rather than line by line.

In reviewing the results of research on the consequences of computer learning, Pea and Kurland found the evidence inconclusive for the claims that computer programming improves mathematical understanding by exemplifying and justifying mathematical rigor, by providing opportunities for exploration of mathematical concepts, or by providing a context for problem solving. Again, they pointed out that this may be due to inadequate outcome measures for assessing these effects or the limited number of contexts in which these questions have been explored.

Geometry

After observing the difficulties Dutch students had learning geometry, wife and husband team Dina van Hiele-Geldof and Pierre Marie van Hiele proposed a model describing five levels of thought development in geometry. Although the original work was presented in 1957, American attention to the work (Wirszup, 1976) resulted from its dramatic impact on the Russian curriculum. A vigorous effort to examine and test the model and to derive further implications for the North American curriculum is currently under way.

The levels begin with the recognition of shapes as a whole (level 0), move on to the discovery of properties of figures and informally reasoning about the properties (levels 1 and 2), and end in a rigorous formal study of axioms and proofs (levels 3 and 4) (Fuys, Geddes, & Tischler, 1984). One of the major implications of such work is that the standard axiomatic curriculum of secondary school geometry requires a student to be functioning at level 3 and as a result much effort has been devoted to determining the typical level of the American student.

Usiskin (1982) and Senk (1983) conducted surveys of large numbers of students and found that they were entering geometry at very low levels of geometric thought. Usiskin found that from 40% to 80% of the students entering geometry were at level 0 or below, depending on how rigorous the criteria were. Such weak performance has prompted a renumbering of the levels from 1 to 5, so as to include a level 0 for students who fail to recognize shapes.

In Senk's study, she found that of the students who begin the year without shape recognition, only 10% successfully mastered proofs. Those who could identify shapes, discover properties, and reason informally mastered proofs progressively better, at a level of success of 25%, 50%, and 75%.

One of the compelling qualities of the van Hieles' work is that it discusses a teaching model that seems to promote students' progress through the levels. Described by Senk (1984), in the first phase the teacher introduces vocabulary, raises some questions, and engages students in conversations to ascertain their understanding. In phase 2, activities sequenced to elicit short responses serve to introduce important structures. The third phase has students expressing opinions about the structures. In the fourth and fifth phases, the students engage in open-ended tasks exploring the field and work with the teacher to synthesize the material.

Interestingly, the model integrates a variety of the suggestions from other research areas, such as the work on problem solving and misconceptions. The students are encouraged to be more active and express their own constructions, hands-on materials are frequently used, and the challenging tasks are undertaken by small groups and pairs to promote discussions of mathematical ideas.

CONCLUSIONS

While declines in the mathematics achievement of students seem to have leveled off, national studies of mathematics learning indicate that students continue to be poor in solving nonroutine problems or applications. Clinical studies in which individual students solve problems aloud show prevalent misconceptions about mathematics concepts; yet these studies also show that students are indeed actively attempting to make sense of their mathematical experience. Their errors are systematic, and their misconceptions are often tied to what they believe they ought to be doing in a mathematics classroom.

Studies of classroom instruction prove that individual teachers can make a difference through careful instruction designed to promote more active learning. Variations in instructional models, from whole classes to small groups to pairs, hold promise for increasing this activity. By examining actual teaching practices, it can be discovered that tasks and assignments are not simply given and completed but are mediated and negotiated within a social and temporal task system. Because the task system is social, it can have differential impacts on various subgroups and individuals. In the case of young women and minorities, the evidence points to a systematic lack of encouragement and exclusion in mathematics, which in turn leads to poorer performance by these subgroups on achievement measures.

This picture emerges from a review of the research in mathematics classrooms. New challenges facing teachers, such as problem solving and microcomputers, complicate the picture further. Teachers are in the difficult and challenging position of weighing the components of this picture and working toward creating a satisfying and successful mathematical experience for all students.

FURTHER READING

Driscoll, M. (1981). *Research within Reach: Elementary School Mathematics*. Reston, VA: National Council of Teachers of Mathematics.

Driscoll, M. (1982). *Research within Reach: Secondary School Mathematics*. St Louis, MO: Research and Development Interpretation Service, CEMREL, Inc. A comprehensive survey of recent research.

National Assessment of Educational Progress (1983). *The Third National Mathematics Assessment: Results, Trends and Issues* (Report No. 13-MA-01). Denver: Education Commission of the States. Summarizes the National Assessment of Educational Progress.

Pea, R., & Kurland, M. (1984). "On the Cognitive Effects of Learning Programming." *New Ideas in Psychology, 2*, 137–168. A good review of the relevance of microcomputing.

Reyes, L. H. (1984). "Affective Variables and Mathematics Education." *Elementary School Journal, 84*, 558–581. Excellent summary of research, especially in the areas of mathematics anxiety and learned helplessness.

Senk, S. (1985). "Research and Curriculum Development Based on the van Hiele Model of Geometric Thought." In A. Bell, B. Low, & J. Kilpatrick (Eds.), *Theory, Research and Practice in Mathematical Education: Working Group Reports and Collected Papers.* Knottingham, UK: Shell Center for Mathematical Education.

REFERENCES

Armstrong, J. (1979). *A national assessment of achievement and participation of women in mathematics* (Final report, NIE Grant No. NIE-G-77-0061), pp. 356–366. Washington, DC: National Institute of Education.

Becker, J. (1981). Differential treatment of females and males in mathematics classes. *Journal for Research in Mathematics Education, 12*, 40–53

Bloom, B. (1956). *Taxonomy of educational objectives. Handbook I: The cognitive domain.* New York: McKay.

Brown, J. S., & Burton, R. R. (1977). *Diagnostic models for procedural bugs in basic mathematics skills* (Report No. 3669, ICAI Report No. 8). Cambridge, MA: Bolt, Beranck & Newman, Inc.

Brown, J. S., & Van Lehn, K. (1980). Repair theory: A generative theory of bugs in procedural skills. *Cognitive Science, 4*, 379–426.

Confrey, J. (1980). *Conceptual change, number concepts, and the introduction to calculus.* Unpublished doctoral dissertation, Cornell University, Ithaca, NY.

Confrey, J. (1984, April). *An examination of the conceptions of mathematics of young women in high school.* Paper presented at the Annual Meeting of the American Education Research Association, New Orleans, LA.

Confrey, J., & Lanier, P. (1980). Students' mathematical abilities: A focus for the improvement of teaching general mathematics. *School Science and Mathematics, 80*, 549–556.

Davis, R. B., McKnight, C., Parker, P., & Elrick, D. (1979). Analysis of student answers to signed number arithmetic problems. *Journal of Children's Mathematical Behavior, 2*, 114–130.

Doyle, W. (1980). *Student mediating responses in teaching effectiveness.* (Final report, NIE Grant No. NIE-G-72-00969.) Washington, DC: National Institute of Education.

Doyle, W., & Carter, K. (1983). *Academic tasks in classrooms*. Unpublished manuscript.

Driscoll, M. (1981). *Research within reach: Elementary school mathematics*. Reston, VA: National Council of Teachers of Mathematics.

Driscoll, M. (1982). *Research within reach: Secondary school mathematics*. St. Louis, MO: Research and Development Interpretation Service, CEMREL, Inc.

Easley, J. A. (1977). *On clinical studies in mathematics education*. Columbus: Ohio State University, Reference Center for Science, Mathematics, and Environmental Education.

Educational Testing Service. (1981). Admissions testing program of the College Board. *National report: College-bound seniors, 1979, 1980, 1981, 5*.

Educational Testing Service. (1981). *Profiles: College-bound seniors*. New York: College Entrance Examination Board.

Erlwanger, S. (1977). Case studies of children's conceptions of mathematics (I). *Journal of Children's Mathematical Behavior, 1*, 157–283.

Fennema, E. (1978). Sex-related differences in mathematics achievement: Where and why. In J. Jacobs (Ed.), *Perspectives on Women and Mathematics*. Columbus, OH: Ohio State University, College of Education, ERIC Clearinghouse for Science, Mathematics and Environmental Education.

Fuys, D., Geddes, D., & Tischler, R. (1984). *English translation of selected writings of Dina Van Hiele-Geldof and Pierre M. Van Heile*. Brooklyn, NY: Brooklyn College.

Gelman, R., & Gallistel, C. R. (1978). *The child's understanding of number*. Cambridge, MA: Harvard University Press.

Ginsberg, H. (1977). *Children's arithmetic: How they learn it and how you teach it*. Austin, TX: Pro-Ed.

Glasersfeld, E. von. (1974, March). *Piaget and the radical constructivist epistemology*. Paper presented at the Third Southeastern Conference of the Society for Research on Child Development, Chapel Hill, NC.

Goldin, G., & McClintock, C. E. (1979). *Task variables in mathematical problem solving*. Columbus, OH: Ohio State University, College of Education, ERIC Clearinghouse for Science, Mathematics and Environmental Education. (ERIC Document Reproduction Service No. SE 029 444)

Good, T. L., & Grouws, D. A. (1979). The Missouri mathematics effectiveness project: An experimental study in fourth-grade classrooms. *Journal of Educational Psychology, 71*, 355–362.

Good, T. L., Grouws, D. A., & Ebmeier, H. (1983). *Active mathematics teaching*. White Plains, NY: Longman.

Karplus, R., Karplus, E., Formisano, M., & Paulsen, A. (1979). Proportional reasoning and control of variables in seven countries. In J. Lochhead & J. Clement (Eds.), *Cognitive process instruction*. Philadelphia: Franklin Institute Press.

Krutetskii, V. A. (1976). *The psychology of mathematical abilities in schoolchildren*. Chicago: University of Chicago Press.

Lesh, R., Landau, M., & Hamilton, E. (1983). Conceptual models and applied problem-solving research. In R. Lesh & M. Landau (Eds.), *Applied mathematical problem solving*. Orlando, FL: Academic Press.

Lesh, R., Surber, D., & Zawojewski. (1983). Phases in modelling and phase-related processes. In Bergeron & Herscovics (Eds.), *Proceedings of the 5th Annual Meeting of the North American Chapter of the International Group for the Psychology of Mathematics Education, 2*, 129–136

Lester, F., & Garofalo, J. (Eds.) (1982). *Mathematical problem solving: Issues in research*. Philadelphia: Franklin Institute Press.

Lochhead, J. (1977). *Teaching students how to learn*. Amherst, MA: University of Massachusetts, Cognitive Development Project.

Matthews, W. (1983). *Influences on the learning and participation of minorities in mathematics*. Madison: Wisconsin Center for Education Research.

National Assessment of Educational Progress (1983). *The third national mathematics assessment: Results, trends and issues* (Report No. 13-MA-01). Denver: Education Commission of the States.

National Science Board Commission on Precollege Education in Mathematics, Science, and Technology (1983). *Educating Americans for the 21st century*. Washington, DC: National Science Foundation.

National Science Foundation (1982). *Women and minorities in science and engineering*. Washington, DC: National Science Foundation.

Papert, S. (1980). *Mindstorms: Children, computers and powerful ideas*. New York: Basic Books.

Pea, R., & Kurland, M. (1984). On the cognitive effects of learning programming. *New Ideas in Psychology, 2*, 137–168.

Piaget, J. (1970). *Genetic epistemology*. New York: Norton.

Polya, G. (1945). *How to solve it*. Princeton, NJ: Princeton University Press.

Radatz. H. (1979). Error analysis in mathematics education. *Journal for Research in Mathematics Education, 10*, 163–172.

Rosnick, P. (1982). *Student conceptions of semantically laden letters in algebra: A technical report*. Amherst: University of Massachusetts, Cognitive Development Project.

Schoenfeld, A. (1980). Teaching problem-solving skills. *American Mathematical Monthly, 87*, 794–805.

Schwarzenberger, R.L.E., & Tall, D. O. (1975–1978). *Papers on calculus and catastrophes*. Warwick, England: University of Warwick, Mathematics Institute.

Sells, L. (1976, June). *The mathematics filter and the education of women and minorities*. Paper presented at the meeting of the American Association for the Advancement of Science, Boston.

Senk, S. (1983). *Proof-writing achievement and van Hiele levels among secondary school geometry students*. Unpublished doctoral dissertation, University of Chicago.

Senk, S. (1985). Research and curriculum development based on the van Hiele model of geometric thought. In A. Bell, B. Low, & J. Kilpatrick (Eds.), *Theory, research and practice in mathematical education: Working group reports and collected papers* (pp. 351–357). Knottingham, UK: Shell Center for Mathematical Education.

Silver, E. (1979). Student perceptions of relatedness among mathematical verbal problems. *Journal for Research in Mathematics Education, 10*, 195–210.

Slavin, R. (1981). A case study of psychological research affecting classroom practice: Student team learning. *Elementary School Journal, 82*, 5–17.

Stake, R., & Easley, J. A. (1978). *Case studies in science education* (Booklet 12). Urbana-Champaign: University of Illinois, Center for Instructional Research and Curriculum Education and Committee on Culture and Cognition.

Taback, S. (1975). The child's concept of limit. In M. Rosskopf (Ed.), *Children's mathematical concepts*. New York: Teachers College Press.

Usiskin, Z. (1982). *Van Hiele levels and achievement in secondary school geometry*. Columbus, OH: Ohio State University, College of Education, ERIC Clearinghouse for Science, Mathematics and Environmental Education. (ERIC Document Reproduction Service No. SE 038 813)

Vergnaud, G. (1983, September). Why is an epistemological perspective a necessity for research in mathematics education? In Bergeron & Herscovics (Eds.), *Proceedings of the 5th Annual Meeting of the North American Chapter of the International Group for the Psychology of Mathematics Education, 1*, 2–20.

Vinner, S. (1983). Concept definition, concept image, and the notion of function. *International Journal for Mathematics Education, Science and Technology, 14*, 293–305.

Webb, N. (1983, April). *Sex and race differences in interaction and achievement in low-achieving classes learning in small groups*. Paper presented at the Annual Meeting of the

American Educational Research Association, Montreal, Canada.

Whimbey, A., & Lochhead, J. (1980). *Problem solving and comprehension*. Philadelphia: Franklin Institute Press.

Wirszup, I. (1976). Breakthroughs in the psychology of learning and teaching geometry. In *Space and geometry*. Columbus, OH: ERIC SMEAC.

Wolleat, P., Pedro, J. D., Becker, A. D., & Fennema, E. (1980). Sex differences in high school students' causal attributions of performance in mathematics. *Journal for Research in Mathematics Education, 11*, 356–366.

2 RESEARCH ON READING: BUT WHAT CAN I TEACH ON MONDAY?

Taffy E. Raphael

Concern about reading has been a part of education for centuries, from the Greeks, who thought boys should learn moral standards through reading, to today's concern for a literate nation (Mathews, 1966). Reading research also has a respectable history, though not as long as that of reading instruction. Early in this century, scholars were investigating various processes that underlie the skills involved in reading (e.g., Huey 1908/1968; Thorndike, 1917). More recently, many excellent collections of reviews of research have been published on reading comprehension (e.g., Duffy, Roehler, & Mason, 1984; Guthrie, 1981), on instructional research in reading (e.g., Pearson & Gallagher, 1983), on models of the reading process (e.g., Kamil & Pearson, 1980), and on literacy (Raphael, 1986).

Why do we find such a widespread and continuing attention to reading research and instruction? We as a nation are concerned that a significant portion of our population may not be functionally literate, and even more people may be incapable of learning from text. The National Assessment of Educational Progress (1982) has provided evidence that while reading skills have improved somewhat among 9-year-olds, the performance levels of high school students have actually declined. In colleges, the demand for study skills courses suggests that even for "successful" college-bound students, reading *independently* to learn from text is a process that has not been well developed. While such conditions persist, there is a need to continue to study classroom practices in order to develop and improve effective methods for teaching students to learn independently from text.

The current literature of research on reading is rich with technical terms such as *schema theoretic view of reading* (Anderson, 1979), *metacomprehension* (Raphael & Gavelek, 1984), *inference training* (Hansen & Hubbard, 1984), and *mapping*

(Armbruster & Anderson, 1982). What do such terms have to do with classroom reading instruction? Do they help with the age-old question, "But what should I teach on Monday?" Such research has yet to examine reading in terms of standard classroom structures and the teachers' typical responsibilities, yet the researchers share a common assumption critical to effective instruction in reading: the notions that the learner's role is an active one and that active reading can be taught. The purpose of this chapter is to explore what the research in reading does tell us about reading instruction in today's classrooms, giving particular attention to techniques and methods that stress the need for students' active participation in the reading process and teacher facilitation of this process. Some of the research-derived ideas described here can be found in existing curricula; others could be added to existing curricula. All of these ideas rely on what is perhaps the most critical influence on whether or not children learn how to read, to understand, and to get meaning from what they read—the hard work of the individual practitioner. As Frase (1977) states, "by modifying purpose, by directing reading activities, the teacher influences learning" (p. 42).

My intent is to consider a number of questions, some explicit, some implicit: What makes a skilled reader? What do teachers need to know about learning, reading, and instruction to improve what may already be a reasonable reading program? What can we do to help students become skilled readers? What techniques can be implemented in classrooms today, using available resources?

When discussing research, it is important to distinguish among three types: *descriptive studies* show that a phenomenon exists but do not demonstrate a causal relationship; *training studies* involve the introduction of instructional techniques by a researcher in a classroom or simulated classroom environment; and *instructional studies* involve a test of instructional methods in classrooms taught by teachers. Each type serves a different function. A study can *describe* differences that exist between skilled and less skilled readers, but the description does not necessarily mean that the differences are relevant. For example, skilled readers may read more quickly than less skilled readers, but merely teaching someone to read faster may not result in making him or her a more effective comprehender of text. Training and instructional studies are thus needed. If a teacher teaches less skilled readers a strategy that has been identified in skilled readers and the instruction improves reading ability, we can assume that the strategy was relevant and directly influenced reading ability. Making a distinction between training and instructional studies allows us to indicate whether a relevant strategy was taught under "idealized" conditions, such as a researcher or teacher working with a group of six students in a small room with no distractions, or whether the relevant strategy proved effective when used under normal classroom conditions.

UNDERSTANDING SKILLED READING

If a group of reading researchers, cognitive psychologists, teachers, reading specialists, and teacher educators were sitting in a conference room discussing the cognitive processes involved in reading, implications for teaching, constraints on learning, and other issues vital to reading instruction, there would likely be debate after debate. These debates result from different perceptions of what happens in the reader's mind during reading and have been waged for years—for example, the phonics versus whole-word controversy (Chall, 1967), the top-down versus bottom-up view of the reading process (Kamil & Pearson, 1979), and the direct instruction versus naturalistic learning controversy. But there is one concept about which there is rarely any debate: For successful reading to occur, readers must be *actively involved* in the reading process. Active participation is fundamental to strategic reading. What do we mean by "active"?

Knowing about Knowing

The assumption of the active role of the learner derives from a large body of research in cognitive psychology on metacognition. *Metacognition* is a term used to describe "thinking about thinking." This thinking involves declarative knowledge (knowing *that*), procedural knowledge (knowing *how*), and conditional knowledge (knowing *when* and *why*) (Paris, Lipson, & Wixson, 1983). Skilled reading requires an understanding, at least implicitly, of these three areas of knowledge as they relate to reading.

Declarative knowledge in reading includes both understanding of text and personal characteristics that influence the reading task. For example, declarative knowledge is used when a reader examines a text and recognizes that it can be read, when a reader describes reading as understanding print, or when a reader states that he or she is "good at reading." It does not tell the reader actually how to read a text, but it does address the idea that there are differences in the ways one might read different texts and that different readers may require variation in reading tasks or may experience different degrees of success in completing a reading task. In a descriptive study of children's declarative knowledge of reading, Canney and Winograd (1977) examined good and poor readers, as well as older and younger readers' knowledge of the reading process. They found that the younger and less able readers had an entirely different view than the older and more able readers. The novice readers thought of reading as decoding rather than sense-making and focused on sound-symbol relationships rather than comprehension. Other descriptive research provides further support (e.g., Paris & Myers, 1981, in their interviews with good and poor third- and sixth-grade readers). Implications of this research for instruction include the need to stress the goals of reading (e.g., comprehension) rather than the means (e.g., word attack skills), particularly when working with the less able reader. Descriptive studies by Allington (1980) have demonstrated that, in practice, this rarely occurs.

Procedural knowledge in reading includes all the procedures or strategies that a reader has available to reach a goal successfully in reading. These strategies can take such forms as skimming, study techniques such as outlining, understanding how to use rehearsal to remember specific details in a story, or understanding how to write summaries of text segments. This knowledge is fundamental to strategic behavior: The reader must possess a strategy before he or she can apply it appropriately in a given context. A number of research studies have attempted to teach students about procedural knowledge and will be discussed in detail. Examples of this research are the training and instructional studies conducted at the University of Illinois Center for the Study of Reading and at the University of Utah (Raphael, 1984) in which students were taught how to use different sources of information in answering comprehension questions. This knowledge of question-answer relationships has taken the form of three procedures or strategies for thinking about identifying answers: a "right there" procedure for identifying answers explicitly stated in text, a "think and search" procedure for identifying answers requiring the integration of textual information from more than one sentence, and an "on my own" category for identifying answers from the reader's own knowledge.

Conditional knowledge serves to direct the flexible application of strategies across different contexts and in the service of different goals. Although little research has been conducted to examine conditional knowledge, the importance of orchestrating declarative and procedural knowledge in a variety of contexts has often been discussed (e.g., Rogoff, 1982). Reading is not the same process at all times. Thus successful reading requires differential application of strategies across contexts (Wixson & Lipson, 1986). For example, students may be asked to describe the content of a comic book to one of their friends, to describe the content of a social studies chapter to their teacher, or to describe a newspaper article to a parent. Each of these tasks requires the application of comprehension strategies for recalling text; yet to apply the same strategy in all situations would not be efficient or necessarily effective.

In summary, examining metacognitive knowledge about reading involves studying the readers' knowledge of the reading process, their control over that process, and their underlying motivations in approaching reading tasks. To use declarative, procedural, and conditional knowledge to read successfully requires active cognitive behavior on the part of the reader.

Active Learner, Skilled Reader

As stated earlier, learning to read successfully involves learning a multitude of skills as well as learning to apply strategies that can aid in comprehension of text. Declarative knowledge developed early by skilled readers is concepts of print (Mason, Stewart, & Dunning, 1986). One of the first differences between skilled and less skilled readers is their understanding of such linguistic concepts as word, sentence, and paragraph. Another indication of skilled early readers is their knowledge of reading conventions such as directionality from left to right and what is meant by a book, a page, a story. Baker and Stein (1981) have noted that skilled readers learn that stories have predictable structures. For example, stories have protagonists who have to accomplish certain goals. There are conflicts that are resolved over the course of the story, thus making an interesting plot. Young children may not have these labels available to discuss their knowledge, but skilled young readers show an implicit understanding of such structures.

Second, skilled readers understand that the purpose of reading is to comprehend information, and they have a variety of strategies to achieve that goal. For example, skilled readers have well-developed strategies for coping with unknown words. Descriptive research has detailed skilled readers' strategies for fast word recognition (pronouncing a word) and, perhaps more important, word identification (understanding the meaning underlying the word) (Samuels, Begy, & Chen, 1975–1976). Word knowledge has been shown to be one of the best predictors of skill in reading (for a review of this literature, see Anderson & Freebody, 1981), providing substantial support for instruction for enhancing vocabulary development. In addition to strategies at the word level, skilled readers have strategies for comprehending prose. Comprehension skills have been identified and traced developmentally in a number of research studies, describing the skills that are crucial for developing skilled readers.

Among these skills and strategies are summarization, question answering and asking, and drawing inferences. For a description of the variety of comprehension skills and strategies used by skilled readers, see Ryan (1981) and Johnson and Barrett (1981).

Third, skilled readers are strategic in their application of skills for *comprehension* of text; they perceive a relationship between various means or strategies and ends. This can be contrasted with the reader who is successful at a particular task largely due to luck (see Paris et al., 1983, for a thorough treatment of strategic reading). Paris and colleagues imply that strategic readers can be recognized by the presence of both intent and effort underlying the selection of an action to reach a goal. In a common reading comprehension task, readers are asked to select a correct answer from a number of alternative answers. The strategic reader will integrate information from the text and from background knowledge, will carefully read the question and all possible answers, and will then make a selection. In contrast, the less strategic reader may select one answer because in preceding questions that answer letter had not been used. Though both may end up with the correct answer, only one was strategic in reading behavior. Another aspect of stategic behavior, effectiveness, is also a characteristic of skilled readers. Ryan (1981) suggests that good readers use comprehension strategies more effectively and use more varied strategies than do less skilled readers.

Fourth, skilled readers are adept at the strategic application of *comprehension monitoring* skills (Garner & Reis, 1981). Comprehension monitoring involves not only understanding text but also being aware of failures to understand. Comprehension failures may occur for many reasons, from inconsiderate or poorly written text (Armbruster, 1984) to inconsistencies with background knowledge or of information in text (Markman, 1979). Skilled readers recognize when failures to comprehend occur as well as what "fix-up" strategies to apply (Brown & DeLoache, 1978). Collins and Smith (1980) point out that fix-up strategies can range from least to most disruptive, including (1) ignore the problem and continue reading, (2) suspend judgment, (3) form a tentative hypothesis, using text information, (4) reread the current sentence, (5) reread the previous context, and (6) go to an expert source. Skilled readers are aware not only of their options but also of when to use each one.

Creating Active Learners and Skilled Readers

Understanding the reading process—for instance, that the goal of reading is comprehension—is necessary, but not sufficient, for successsful control over the process. To control the reading process actively, readers must be aware of and use available strategies for comprehending and monitoring their comprehension. That is, their declarative knowledge has to be translated into procedural and conditional knowledge. Some researchers (e.g., Paris et al., 1983) have provided a basis for three general instructional principles in the teaching of strategies. While these principles may not represent a departure from traditional views of learning, they provide a unifying theme for many techniques.

The principles underlying the instructional procedures to be discussed stress the uniqueness of teaching *cognitive*, in contrast to *physical*, strategies and the need for teachers to help create an environment in which these skills can be modeled to help students acquire these strategies. The first instructional principle involves making cognitive activity visible to the novice reader. Unlike the case with learning strategies for a physical activity such as catching a ball, the novice is unlikely to be aided in learning such cognitive activities as reading by watching someone else read. What occurs in the brain must in some way be made visible to the learner, or the chances of developing the requisite cognitive skills are reduced (Vygotsky, 1978). Further, Flavell and Wellman (1977) suggest that the easiest cognitive strategies to learn are external to the learner. For example, in the realm of strategies related to comprehension questions, it would be easier to learn strategies for answering a question asked by an external source (a teacher or a textbook) than it would be for a learner to generate questions to enhance both comprehension and comprehension monitoring as he or she reads a text. A corollary to this first principle is that strategic reading behavior needs to be modeled or demonstrated by skilled readers (e.g., teacher, peer tutor) for those less skilled ones.

A second principle of instruction involves the need to make explicit the application of strategies in the service of higher-order goals (Palincsar & Brown, 1984). Palincsar and Brown suggest that it is not sufficient merely to provide rules for using a strategy. Students must be taught explicitly both the importance of the strategy and how it can be applied *in context*. Duffy, Book, and Roehler (1983) state similarly that teachers' explanations to students should include what the skill or strategy is, how it should be used, and why it is important.

A third principle is the need initially to teach strategies as ends in and of themselves, before applying them in the context of reading independently. Some researchers (e.g., Smirnov & Zinchenko, 1969) have suggested that learners need to learn strategies as ends prior to being able to use them as means to achieve a higher-order goal. One of the most commonly taught lower-order decoding skills concerns the use of phonics rules. These are often taught as part of skill lessons in developmental reading groups and are usually taught as ends in themselves. But much controversy has arisen over the value of such an approach and of the phonics rules themselves, with some researchers suggesting that neither may be of value (Clymer, 1963). One reason the utility of such instruction may be questioned is that students can come to think of reading as "doing phonics worksheets" rather than as comprehending text. This can easily happen if the phonics rules learned as ends are not frequently and visibly modeled by successful readers using them to deal with unknown words in reading. Summarizing texts represents the other side of the problem: the disadvantages of not first teaching a strategy as an end in itself. Students may be asked in content-area subjects to use summary writing as a study skill to help them to remember text. If this skill has not already been learned and practiced so that it can be easily and competently applied, clumsy use of it may actually interfere with the comprehension process.

In summary, the development of skilled readers involves teaching them declarative knowledge of the reading process—what it means to read, what strategies are available for comprehension, and what strengths and weaknesses they bring to the reading task. It also involves teaching them procedural knowledge—how the various strategies can be implemented. Finally, it concerns teaching them conditional knowledge—explicitly stating and modeling for them both when and how the procedural knowledge operates most effectively, to help them understand the final steps in becoming independent strategic readers. Skilled reading has recently been likened to writing (Pearson & Tierney, 1983), suggesting that the reader, much like a writer, is constantly composing messages, planning, and evaluating—cognitively active and demanding skills.

ENCOURAGING ACTIVE READING

Students must be encouraged to process actively information presented in the text, make predictions, draw inferences, and evaluate the quality of written material. The skills needed in successful reading are generally taught in conjunction with a basal reader story in elementary classrooms and in some middle schools. In secondary schools, reading instruction is rarely a separate part of the curriculum and thus must be incorporated as part of content-area courses such as English, science, and social studies. This reading instruction, often known as study skill instruction, is closely related to many of the techniques described here. These techniques have demonstrated their worth in research settings and their potential generalizability across grade levels. In elementary and middle school settings, instruction generally begins with vocabulary instruction, followed by a prereading discussion to set the context and purposes for reading, a guided reading discussion, and independent activities with the story. Included here is a sample of techniques, supported by research, that can be used with existing materials in reading instruction. The organizational framework is intended to mirror the sequence of instruction in a typical series of reading lessons.

General Principles for Vocabulary Instruction

The importance of word knowledge for understanding text has been discussed and documented (Anderson & Freebody, 1981), though it remains unclear exactly how such knowledge assists in reading. One theory is that the relationship is merely correlational, that readers with large vocabularies are either more intelligent or have more general knowledge of the world. In either case, direct instruction in vocabulary would not be warranted. However, another point of view is that the development of word knowledge facilitates comprehension because teaching vocabulary actually increases the reader's conceptual knowledge. Kameenui, Carnine, and Freschi (1982) tested this hypothesis and found evidence that teaching the meanings of words that a reader will encounter in a text facilitates comprehension, thus underscoring both the importance of word knowledge for comprehension and the need specifically to improve readers' word knowledge.

It is apparent that a reader needs many encounters with a new word to learn it. This means that readers must be active in their manipulation of new words before we can expect these words to become a working part of their speaking and reading vocabularies. Activity in learning new vocabulary words has often been interpreted as teaching readers how to use contexts to determine the meaning of unknown words, as well as directing teachers to present words in context. Recently, however, Beck, McKeown, and McCaslin (1983) have suggested that the recommendation of the use of context may have overstated the case, that there are many different types of contexts, and that some may actually mislead readers as to the meanings of words. They classify contexts into two broad categories. Pedagogical contexts are those specifically designed to teach words not in the child's vocabulary. For example, the text might state that

> *Massive* is a word used to describe something that is very large. A mountain is massive, and so is the ocean. Sometimes when you eat an ice cream sundae with three scoops of ice cream, nuts, bananas, and whipped cream, you might say the sundae is "massive"!

The other category of contexts is those that occur naturally in text, and these may or may not give a clue to the meaning of the word. A context may be misdirective in that it leads the reader to conclude that a word has one meaning when in fact it has another. An example quoted by Beck, McKeown, and McCaslin of a misdirective context is from a story about Sandra's successful dance performance: "'Every step she takes is so perfect and graceful,' Ginny said *grudgingly* as she watched Sandra dance" (p. 178). The context leads the reader to assume that *grudgingly* means "with admiration." A nondirective context would give no hint as to the meaning of a word ("Questions are ubiquitous"). A general context would provide some indication of the general meaning, but nothing specific ("The ball was too massive for him to carry by himself"). Finally, a directive context would be similar to the pedagogical context, only it occurs naturally and therefore the author may not have intended to convey the meaning of the word. It is imperative that the teacher select words to be taught, evaluate the quality of the context, and make appropriate adjustments to optimize the chance that the students understand the word to be learned.

Specifically, Beck, McKeown, and McCaslin suggest that the teacher's role in vocabulary development should be to stress the learners' active involvement in using and manipulating the words to be learned. In their general guidelines, they describe that new vocabulary should first be presented in a pedagogical context, followed by discussion of each meaning of the word. Children should have a mechanism for keeping track of newly acquired vocabulary knowledge and should be encouraged to use these words in nonacademic settings.

Techniques for Vocabulary Development

No one method of vocabulary instruction can be used for all words and with students of all levels. Therefore, the teacher needs a number of methods for introducing vocabulary words. Gipe (1978–1979) conducted a training study of four methods of vocabulary instruction, one of which was looking up unknown words in the dictionary. The other three methods all relied on context of one form or another and were found to be superior to the dictionary method. The first method was called free association and introduced a new word by pairing it with a familiar synonym or short definition. This is probably the minimal context one can provide. The second method involved categorizing. Students were given the new word as a heading for a category that contained three familiar words. They were then asked to add more words to the category. The third method involved the extended definition, or pedagogical context as described earlier using the word *massive*. Again, students who were taught by any of these three methods performed at a higher level on a reading comprehension task than those who looked up the same words in a dictionary.

A method used in an instructional study by Hansen and Ahlfors (1982) required somewhat more activity on the part of the learners as they used the words in sentences related to their background knowledge. These researchers adapted a questioning technique developed by Hansen for previewing stories (cf. Hansen & Hubbard, 1984) for use in vocabulary instruction. The principle underlying this technique is that of building from known to new information. In so doing, a word is introduced, defined, and then presented in context: "Recycled means to turn something that is useless into something that is useful. Old pieces of newpapers can be recycled and made into wrapping paper." Then students are asked to relate the vocabulary word to their own experiences: "Can you tell me of something you have recycled?" This activity is conducted orally during the reading group so that students can both have a chance to use the word orally themselves and listen to others give examples, which helps to extend their own conceptual understanding.

McKeown (1985) conducted a training study designed to specify the types of contexts that could be used to provide students with effective repeated experiences to learn new words. Her method could be used by teachers to enhance children's exposure to a word and to increase the probability that the word would become part of the child's vocabulary. In addition, by repeated exposure to the instructional method, students can learn how to use context clues to make decisions about what words mean. McKeown began by presenting an unknown word in context. (For purposes of her study, she actually used artificial words such as *narp*. However, in practice, a teacher would merely select words known to be unfamiliar to the students.) Following the unknown word were six potential synonyms, all familiar words. Students were asked to decide for each choice whether or not it was a plausible meaning for the unknown word. For example, in the sentence "Standing in front of the house, we all agreed that it seemed like a narp house," *brick* and *ordinary* are plausible, but *shy* is not. In the second step, the teacher provided more sentences using the word, and students repeated the decision task of plausible synonyms. For example, presenting the sentence "It was hard finding the right gift because everything in the store was so narp" makes it unlikely that the synonym is *brick* but quite likely that it is *ordinary*. In the third step, the teacher presents three more sentences, based on one of the earlier sentences, further using the target word. In the fourth step, students are asked to define the word. In step five, students are given six sentences using the word. They are asked to tell if the word is used well or if it is used inappropriately. By the end of these activities, the students will have had the opportunity to practice using the word in sentences and talking about the meaning and will thus be more likely to make it part of their permanent vocabulary. However, the time demands are not trivial, so the method should be applied only to words that are important to acquire as part of the students' reading vocabulary.

Beck, McKeown, and McCaslin (1983) note that "many children do not know that they don't know a word" (p. 180). Schwartz and Raphael (1985) suggest that this may be due in part to a lack of a concept of definition. Thus students may have one kind of problem when they come to a word in print that they do not understand and a second, broader problem when they do not have a concept for selecting information from the context that could be useful in determining the meaning of the word. Schwartz and Raphael adapted the technique of semantic mapping to develop a concept of definition that would help readers to understand new words. Semantic maps are based on the notion that concepts are connected to one another in memory through specific relationships such as "example," "property," and "class." Visual "maps" of these semantic relationships can help clarify the meaning of words and longer units of text. Schwartz and Raphael used such visual maps in two training studies designed to teach students how to determine whether they understand a word by explicitly teaching them what constitutes a definition. A sample map is presented in Figure 2.1. The center rectangle shows the word to be defined. The top rectangle gives a synonym or brief descriptor for the defined word ("What is it?"). To the right are explanations or descriptions relating to the new word ("What is it like?"), while the ovals at the bottom present examples of the new word.

Context from which word was mapped: The space shuttle is in space again, this time with five astronauts on board. What an exciting job to have! Astronauts are lucky to be able to travel into outer space. Once there, they have many tasks, from flying the spaceship to conducting experiments. People like John Glenn and Sally Ride must really enjoy their work!

VOCABULARY MAP

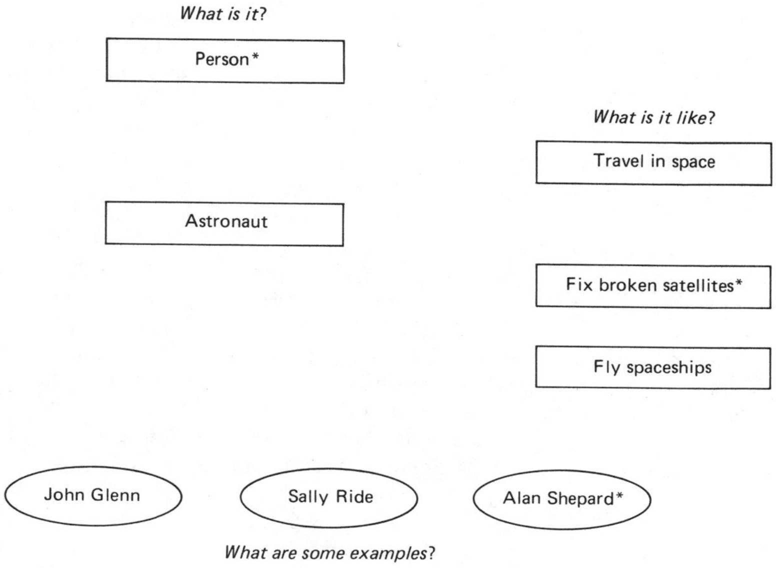

What is it?

Person*

What is it like?

Travel in space

Astronaut

Fix broken satellites*

Fly spaceships

John Glenn   Sally Ride   Alan Shepard*

What are some examples?

*From reader's background knowledge

FIGURE 2.1   Example of vocabulary mapping

The instructional sequence progresses through the four activities shown in Table 2.1. In the first activity, students are introduced to the three components of a definition using the categorization task shown for the word *soup*. The teacher begins by asking students to find a word that answers the very general question "What is it?" for the word to be defined. The general word in the example is *food*. Then the teacher would say that *food* answers the question for many different kinds of foods and directs students to suggest phrases or words that describe a special kind of food, soup. These words answer the question "What is it like?" Finally, examples are identified. In the next phase of instruction, the teacher presents words in complete contexts, *complete* defined as having at least one class, three properties, and three examples. Children map the word and write what it means. The third phase has similar activities but using partial contexts. In this lesson students begin to use their own background knowledge as well as the text. Finally, students use the decision task in which they read a word in context, then a definition of the word, and decide if the definition is a good one. If not, they add the necessary components using their background knowledge, the dictionary, or other source books. With this technique, students are actively engaged in both learning new words from reading and learning to use information from text and background knowledge.

TABLE 2.1   FOUR SEQUENTIAL ACTIVITIES FOR SEMANTIC MAPPING

Categorization Tasks

Soup (carrot)	Clown (policeman)
chicken noodle	wears a lot of makeup
served with sandwiches	Bozo
tastes good	a person
is a liquid	works in a circus
cream of mushroom	does funny things
eat it with a spoon	wears bright colored clothes
vegetable noodle	likes children
made from milk sometimes	rodeo clown
served in a bowl	Oopsy
food	has a large fake red nose

Words in Complete Contexts[1]

Crops

Have you ever been to a farm? Have you ever seen a farmer work with his crops? Crops come from seeds planted by the farmer early in the spring. The farmer takes care of his seeds all spring and summer long. Early in the fall, crops are harvested and taken to market. At the market they are sold to people like you and me. Farmers can plant different kinds of crops. Some plant potatoes. Some plant onions. Some plant corn and tomatoes. Fresh crops sure taste good!

Words in Partial Contexts[2]

Environment

You hear a lot these days about our environment, but what exactly is it? We hear a lot of talk about a clean environment. Many parts of our environment need cleaning. The better our environment, the happier we can be.

Student Decision-Making Task

Astronaut

The space shuttle is in space again, this time with five astronauts on board. What an exciting job to have. I'll bet people like John Glenn and Sally Ride really enjoy their work.

Definition: Astronauts enjoy their work. Examples of astronauts are Sally Ride and John Glenn.

_____ This is a complete definition.

_____ This is not a complete definition.

Things to add are:

---

[1]These examples are considered complete because they refer to one superordinate term, at least three characteristics, and at least three examples.
[2]These are partial contexts because they do not have all the components needed to fill in a map and write what the word means.

In summary, a teacher can use a variety of methods for introducing vocabulary words to students. Thought must be given to the amount of context required for the meaning to be understood, to the method most appropriate to learning a given word, and to the amount of student involvement in manipulating the word. The methods presented here go beyond the less successful means of having students look up words in a dictionary, copy sentences from a workbook or blackboard, or use words in sentences. The underlying theme is to have students use the words in a variety of contexts, selecting words that may indeed become parts of their own vocabularies. Once students become familiar with potentially difficult words, they can begin to focus on the larger meaning units in the story to be read.

Previewing a Story

An outgrowth of the emphasis on the active role of the learner has been a growing realization of how important background knowledge is in understanding stories. Descriptive research (e.g., Bransford & Johnson, 1972; Pearson, Hansen, & Gordon, 1979) has demonstrated conclusively that readers' background knowledge accounts for much of their comprehension of text. This means that for readers to understand a story, it is important that they not only possess the relevant background knowledge but that they also be able to recognize when it is important for them to think about it during the stories they are reading. Beck, McCaslin, and McKeown (1981) examined prereading activities in basal readers designed to set the purpose for reading. They suggest that purpose setting in basals should be designed such that appropriate background knowledge is activated. Instead, they found that the direction-setting activities suggested in the basal manuals are designed to promote information gathering, by having students locate particular story segments. They found three related categories of problems with basal prereading activities. First, some prereading activities may actually misdirect the students, evoking inappropriate expectations of what might be found in the text. Second, the directions may be relevant, but so narrow in scope as to exclude much that is important in the text. Third, some activities give away much of the story, and in such a way that students become less, rather than more, interested in the story after prereading activities. Beck, McCaslin, and McKeown conclude their remarks by stating that "until the developers of reading programs reconsider what should underlie their purpose and begin to formulate it in terms of schematic design, the teachers themselves should do so" (p. 160).

Two prereading programs that can be used with both basal readers and trade books have recently been developed to facilitate children's understanding of text. Au (1979), working with culturally diverse students in Hawaii, and Hansen (Hansen & Hubbard, 1984) have developed prereading questioning procedures designed to build background knowledge when it is not available and to activate the relevant knowledge that can be made available.

Au and her colleagues have worked with Hawaiian students who were not achieving well in reading, sensitizing them through questions to the importance of background knowledge in understanding the stories they read in school. In the first phase of the lesson, students are asked to think about personal experiences relevant to a given topic and then discuss them as a group. After this discussion, the teacher has students make predictions about the content of the text to be read and possible story lines. These predictions are often based on both the discussions and pictures in the stories. After students have read the text, the relationship between their background knowledge and the text information is explicitly drawn. This method is known as ETR—experience, text, relationship.

Hansen and Hubbard (1984) have used a similar method known as inference training to help readers to access the background knowledge relevant to a particular story. Prior to having students read a story, the teacher selects three concepts for which the reader would have to draw inferences to understand the selection. For each concept, two parallel questions are developed—one prior-knowledge question and one prediction question. The procedure begins with asking the students the first prior-knowledge question (e.g., "What things have made you feel embarrassed?"). The students discuss the question, accessing their relevant background knowledge as well as adding to it through their interactions with the other students. Then the students write their own brief answers, ensuring that every child has thought about a relevant experience. The same procedure is then followed for the parallel prediction question (e.g., "In our story today, a young boy is embarrassed in school. What do you think might have made him feel that way?"). The process continues for the two remaining sets of prior-knowledge and prediction questions. Once children have been given a purpose for reading, they read the story silently. However, it is important for their development as readers to reconvene and discuss the story. This discussion leads to a rereading of the story, or what is known as guided reading.

Guided Reading

During the guided reading of text, the effective teacher helps the readers focus on important text elements, identify the central theme of the story, evaluate any predictions made during the prereading activities, and draw inferences necessary for comprehension of the passage. Probably the most commonly used technique during this phase of the reading lesson involves the use of questions, primarily questions generated by others (i.e., by the teacher or the text).

A number of researchers have criticized the comprehension questions asked in basals and by teachers as being too literal (Guszak, 1967), as not having a logical sequence or order (Beck & McKeown, 1981), or as placing too much emphasis on assessment and not enough on instruction (Durkin, 1978–1979). Fortunately, recent instructional studies have examined both question asking by teachers and students' understanding of the sources of information available to them when answering questions asked by teachers or textbooks. The focus of guided reading questions is on the text phase—in Au's terminology of ETR, the activities involved in guiding the students through the passages they are reading.

Pearson (1981) and Beck and McKeown (1981) have suggested teachers' use of story maps to guide them in asking questions relevant to the central theme of a story. A story map is in some ways similar to a vocabulary semantic map. It is a graphic representation of the theme of the story, visually mapped for ease of reference. Pearson suggests three steps, in the form of questions teachers should ask of themselves, for generating a story map and accompanying questions. First, begin with a setting question and ask if it is important information for understanding the story. If it is not important, omit it. Second, ask a question about the protagonist or protagonists, followed by a problem question (e.g., "What is the protagonist's problem?" or

"What is the protagonist's need?"). This second step identifies the goal of the story. Third, identify the steps that the protagonist goes through to attain the goal. From these steps would be developed a cohesive series of questions that help the reader to identify the central elements of the story.

Independent Reading Activities

The teacher must teach students not only the basic strategies for decoding words but also the more complex skills of how to interpret text independently, integrate that information with background knowledge, and monitor comprehension. A number of techniques recently investigated, in addition to those described already, have applied early research in study skills to the need to teach comprehension and comprehension-monitoring abilities. Now the focus shifts from helping children to understand a specific text to helping children understand how to comprehend text as they read independently. The additional techniques to be described can be thought of as organization as well as monitoring aids, divided into graphic aids and text aids.

Graphic aids have been proposed for many years, though more recently the focus has been less on providing students with such aids and more on requiring students to produce graphic representations of text to aid their comprehension. Visual aids known as mapping, networking, and flowcharting have been and continue to be researched with both elementary and secondary school students (Armbruster & Anderson, 1982). These maps are similar to the ones described for definition instruction (cf. p. 16), but rather than developing a single concept, they depict how a number of concepts may be related in texts of different structures.

Armbruster and Anderson describe several text structures and relationships (e.g., cause and effect, definition, comparison and contrast). They have taught students both to recognize such relationships and to display them using a different graphic symbol for each relationship. A definition might be represented by a small box containing a word inside a larger box containing the definition or description. Cause and effect might be represented by two boxes—one containing the cause, one the effect—connected by an arrow showing the direction of the relationship. Although they have not used the mapping technique with large units of texts such as chapters, it has been successfully taught and has improved children's understanding of subsections of science and social studies texts.

Other methods have been used to represent text without the use of visual or graphic aids. Examples include such traditional independent reading skills as SQ3R (survey, question, read, recite, review), summarizing, and outlining. In an instructional study, Adams, Carnine, and Gerston (1982) evaluated the contributions of each of the steps in the SQ3R studying technique. They suggest that the five steps of SQ3R, and an additional step called rehearsal, have a great deal of support in current research. They have observed teachers who taught fifth-grade students to (1) preview a passage by reading all headings and subheadings, (2) recite the subheadings, monitoring the success in recitation by self-checking procedures, (3) generate questions based on the subheadings they had recited, (4) read to find important details related to the questions they had developed, (5) reread the subheading and recite the important details to provide a review of small increments of text, and (6) rehearse by reciting each subheading and important detail. The first five steps are designed to be used with subsections of texts, while step 6 is to be performed after an entire selection has been read. After participating in the instructional program, fifth-grade students improved in their understanding of texts.

Taylor (1982) examined the use of outlining in teaching students to comprehend expository text in content-area subjects such as social studies and science. Outlining is actually one of five steps included in a hierarchical summary procedure children learn, leading to the goal of being able to summarize the important information in a passage. Based on traditional outlining techniques, and modifying them to make explicit the rules of a cognitive skill and to model such skills for students, Taylor has students create outlines in a step-by-step manner, beginning with main headings and subsections; then students reread for detail information; next students write a summary for each section; and finally they retell the story orally to a partner.

Day (1980) and Winograd (1984) have also examined the use of summarizing strategies for comprehension of text. Day worked with junior college students, but the technique is applicable to younger students. She developed a series of six summarization rules that could be taught to poor readers and writers, accompanied by self-checking strategies to assure that the strategy was being used. Two of the rules involved deletion: (1) Delete information that is unnecessary or unimportant, and (2) delete information that is redundant. Two of the rules involved substitution: (1) Substitute a superordinate term for a list of items (e.g., *pets* instead of *dog, cat, canary,* and *goldfish*), and (2) substitute a superordinate term for a list of actions. Two of the rules concern the use of topic sentences: (1) Select the topic sentence, and (2) if there is no topic sentence, invent one. For each set of rules, a different colored pencil could be used. Thus when working independently, students have a built-in self-checking system to assure that all rules have been attempted.

Teaching methods such as inference training, ETR, and mapping all involve teachers asking questions to aid in children's literal and inferential comprehension of text. One common goal of such techniques is that children understand the questioning activities and the strategies that are available to them to answer the questions appropriately. Raphael and her colleagues (Raphael & McKinney, 1983; Raphael & Pearson, 1985; Raphael, Winograd, & Pearson, 1980; Raphael & Wonnacott, 1985) examined students' declarative and procedural knowledge of the question-answering process. They found that even though students tend to spend much of their academic time in answering questions, they actually know very few of the rules that guide the question-answering process. In one training study and two instructional studies, students from fourth through eighth grade were taught to recognize three general categories of question-answer relationships (QARs): "right there," "think and search," and "on my own." A "right there" QAR occurs when the words used to create a comprehension question and the words used to answer the question are "right there" in the same sentence. A "think and search" QAR occurs when an answer can be found in the passage just read but requires the reader to integrate information across sentences or paragraphs. An "on my own" QAR occurs when a question requires readers to access their background knowledge since the answer cannot be found anywhere in the text. Research conducted using the QAR training program consistently demonstrated that making such knowledge available to students improved their ability to answer comprehension questions. Thus, though not something to be used in every story discussion, teaching students about QARs can provide a vocabulary and knowledge set for strategic search of information sources when answering comprehension questions. It also provides a way to help them to use questions themselves when reading independently.

While it is common for students to be guided through their reading by being asked questions as they read, a less common but very effective means of guiding reading has been used in training and instructional studies by Palincsar (1984). She has used a program called reciprocal questioning in which students learn to lead story discussions, first by seeing their teachers model for them appropriate question asking strategies, then by having the teachers gradually transfer the role of question asker to the students. The teacher provides extensive guidance and feedback as to the types and quality of questions asked, gradually turning the control of the discussion over to the students as they develop skills in generating relevant comprehension questions.

In addition to these techniques, several discussed earlier are relevant to this aspect of instruction or can be made relevant by helping readers learn to use effective teacher techniques on their own. For example, Hansen and Hubbard (1984) added a simple component to the instructional program—focusing students' attention on the kinds of questions they were being asked prior to reading (questions about their background knowledge and how this knowledge helps them to make sense of the readings). Then the researchers asked such questions as "If you were going to read a story about children in Alaska, what questions do you think I might ask?" Again, the focus is on the active role of the learner and the need to make explicit the rules and the application of the various study and comprehension-monitoring techniques. In this case, children are being taught directly that before reading a new story, they should think about relevant information from their own experiences. A second example is Schwartz and Raphael's (1985) concept of definition instruction. Students who learn the concept of mapping a word to define it have been taught how to use context clues to understand new words. They have also learned a useful skill for times when defining a word by using the dictionary is necessary.

In summary, many strategies are available to enable students to become successful independent readers, which is our goal as teachers of reading. The important point to note about all of these techniques is that they require the active participation of the learners in developing an understanding of the meaning of texts they are reading. Further, learners can develop this understanding using a variety of techniques, but only if they are explicitly instructed in the rules and the value of the methods (Brown, Campione, & Day, 1981; Duffy, Book, & Roehler, 1983).

SOCIAL FACTORS THAT INFLUENCE READING

Interest in the social context of cognitive processes in general has been on the rise, and reading as a cognitive process is no exception. What do we mean when we consider the social context of reading? One obvious meaning is that we are concerned with the impact of the social environment of the classroom, specifically in terms of the impact of grouping for reading instruction. A second meaning is rooted in research from Soviet psychologists such as Vygotsky and his students. This body of research has examined the role of social mediators in learning—the role of adults such as parents and teachers in explaining, modeling, and directing children's learning experiences. This work is the basis of many of the techniques for developing active readers.

Teachers often group students as one means of coping with the wide range of students' abilities in a single classroom. Grouping can be a valuable step toward providing individual instruction. However, grouping practices can have a negative impact if teachers are not sensitive to the way they may interact with groups differently. Students are quite perceptive of their teachers' opinions and are influenced by these opinions (Weinstein, 1986). Heibert (1983) reviewed the effects of ability grouping on students' reading achievement and suggests that such grouping can affect reading development. Differences in the way teachers interact with groups of low and high ability have been observed (Allington, 1980). For example, students of high ability are given more time to answer questions, and the patterns of question asking and answering tend to be rather analytic compared with teachers' interactions with students of low ability levels. There are also differences in the way teachers interrupt students of differing levels, with students of low ability interrupted more frequently after reading errors, given more cues about letter sounds, and interrupted more by other students in the class seeking the teacher's attention. There was also a difference in the content of reading lessons: high-ability students' lessons focused on silent reading and comprehension, while low-ability students' lessons focused on word attack skills and oral reading. Interestingly, Wonnacott and Raphael (1982) noted that as students get older there is an increasing disparity between high- and low-ability students' metacognitive knowledge—declarative, procedural, and conditional—about comprehension (as measured by their understanding of the process of answering comprehension questions). Perhaps the lower-ability students begin to rely more and more on the adult to monitor their progress, while students of higher ability begin to develop the independence necessary to monitor their own comprehension of text. Developing independent readers within a social context is the focus of the research and practice based on Vygotsky's theoretical work.

The term *social context* takes on a slightly different meaning when considered in Vygotskian terms. From this perspective, reading is a social process in that reading develops in a context in which skills and stategies are "mediated" by an adult or more able peers. Mediation can be used to describe the process of making implicit skills explicit or to describe adult interpretation and modeling of a cognitive process so that the young reader or learner can gradually take over control of his or her own learning process. This transfer of control happens gradually over the course of the students' education. Although Vygotsky presented his theories in terms of individual learning, the transfer of control through mediated learning has been successfully applied to group instruction in reading (Au & Kawakami, 1986).

Underlying Vygotsky's concept of mediated learning is the process of "scaffolding." In building construction, a scaffold is a support that is both flexible and temporary. Similarly, when a new cognitive skill is being introduced, a scaffold is provided in the form of a great deal of teacher support, moving toward little or none. For example, in teaching QARs, the teacher would first give the students a passage followed by a question, an answer, the question-answer relationship, and an explanation. The scaffold provides support at all points in this sequence. When the students seem to understand what has been discussed, the teacher provides the question, answer, and QAR but in this phase removes part of the scaffold, no longer explaining why but asking the students for the explanation. Next the teacher would have students both identify the QAR and tell why, giving them only a passage, question, and answer. Finally, students would provide an answer, the QAR, and their own explanations—the scaffold would be removed entirely. There has been a gradual transfer of control of one cognitive strategy in reading from the teacher to the student.

How can we work toward the transfer of control? What are some techniques for mediating learning? A number of techniques described previously could be adapted to uphold the principles of mediated learning. In Hansen's inference training method, for example, over the course of the year, students could first begin to make up the prediction question after being presented with a prior-knowledge question, then make up both questions when given a concept, and finally be led to select important concepts from stories and think of corresponding questions. The scaffold would take the form of first presenting concepts, prior-knowledge question, and prediction question and gradually removing pieces of the support in a logical order until the reader could stand on his or her own.

The teachers' explanation behavior in mediating learning is critical. The work by Duffy, Book, and Roehler (1983) is relevant to mediating learning in that it is through the teachers' explanations that students come to understand how to implement the various strategies they have been taught. Teachers need to be explicit about why a particular strategy is being taught and how it can help students when they are reading independently. Another way in which mediation can occur is through modeling. Green and Harker (1982) suggest that reading aloud to children takes advantage of a naturally supportive social context and provides ample opportunity for instruction and growth of knowledge of reading. Modeling silent reading has become an integral part of the reading program with the introduction of Sustained Silent Reading (SSR). This procedure is quite simple: The teacher, principal, teacher aides, or any other adult in a classroom setting reads silently along with the students. Student selection of any reading materials of interest is encouraged, and the emphasis is on modeling the satisfaction of reading for pleasure. While there has been little empirical evidence suggesting that SSR by itself can change reading achievement, in conjunction with other forms of mediation it may enhance reading performance (Fielding, Wilson, & Anderson, 1986).

To summarize, research about the social mediation necessary for the development of independent readers has provided us with insight both into the way things are as well as the way things ought to be. A focus on teaching students to control their own reading process can have a large impact on the kinds of changes that would help improve students' chances of becoming successful independent readers.

CONCLUSIONS

As we learn more about the reading process, the notion of teaching such a complex cognitive skill becomes almost overwhelming. Yet it is also clear that we have learned much about what can be done to teach reading effectively. First, it is important to access informally a reader's background knowledge, both at the word level and at the conceptual level. Second, it is important to activate relevant background knowledge prior to reading. Third, strategies for effective independent reading can and should be taught to students as ends in and of themselves, followed by explicit modeling of how learned strategies can be used effectively to comprehend text in a variety of text-learning situations. Finally, reading instructional groups are social settings that have been shown to affect reading progress. In such social settings, teachers and skilled peers can serve as mediating agents, modeling and explaining to novice readers how to master the skills necessary to enjoy reading in a variety of contexts.

FURTHER READING
Research in Reading

Duffy, G. G., Roehler, L. R., & Mason, J. N. (1984). *Comprehension Instruction: Perspectives and Suggestions*. White Plains, NY: Longman. Based on a joint yearlong seminar between staff members of the Institute for Research on Teaching at Michigan State University and of the Center for the Study of Reading at the University of Illinois. Provides a good overview of how information about instruction and information based on cognitive psychology can improve our abilities to teach reading effectively.

Flood, J. (Ed.). (1984). *Understanding Comprehension*. Newark, DE: International Reading Association. A collection of articles by scholars in three areas: cognition, language, and the structure of written language, providing teachers with a basis for reexamining their present teaching practices in light of current research and for evaluating new techniques offered in journals and in graduate and in-service programs.

Guthrie, J. T. (Ed.). (1981). *Comprehension and Teaching: Research Reviews*. Newark, DE: International Reading Association. Provides reviews of research relevant to the classroom. The first half includes overviews of processes in reading, such as making inferences, and how the social context influences these processes. The second half focuses on practices in education, including instructional variables and characteristics of exemplary reading programs.

Pearson, P. D. (Ed.). (1984). *Handbook of Reading Research*. White Plains, NY: Longman. By many of the leading scholars in the field of reading. Each contributor synthesizes an area of research by first providing a brief history of the area, then describing the "state of the art" in terms of what we have learned, finally providing a look toward future issues and questions that professionals in reading must address. This book represents the most current and thorough examination of research in reading today.

Teaching Reading

Flood, J. (Ed.). (1984). *Promoting Reading Comprehension*. Newark, DE: International Reading Association. Companion to Flood's *Understanding Comprehension*. The contributors to this volume describe both specific reading methods and activities and general reading programs consistent with what we have learned from the study of language, cognition, and structure of written language.

Harris, A. J., & Sipay, E. R. (Eds.). (1984). *Readings on Reading Instruction*. White Plains, NY: Longman. A collection of articles from a variety of sources, organized around such topics as contrasting views of reading instruction, language and reading, teaching reading to children with special needs, developing reading vocabulary, and beginning reading instruction. Includes more than 80 articles, some already considered classics. Several viewpoints about both research and instruction are presented.

Johnson, D. D., & Pearson, P. D. (1984). *Teaching Reading Vocabulary*. New York: Holt, Rinehart and Winston. Provides many concrete lessons and activities for the teaching of concepts. The suggested activities focus on the importance of linking new ideas with concepts the children already have. Also covers general principles of instruction to develop children's reading and oral vocabulary.

McNeil, J. (1984). *Reading Comprehension: New Directions for Classroom Practice*. Glenview, IL: Scott, Foresman. Focuses on how to use ideas from research immediately in classroom teaching. Covers such concepts as schema theory, metacognition, and comprehension and provides techniques for applying these concepts in the teaching of reading. For elementary as well as secondary school teachers.

Pearson, P. D., & Johnson, D. D. (1978). *Teaching Reading Comprehension*. New York: Holt, Rinehart and Winston. On its way to becoming a classic, this was one of the first books to describe the processes of how information from print is comprehended, stressing the importance of background knowledge, and the principle of bridging from known to new information. Ideas for drawing these "bridges" are described throughout.

Connecting Reading and Writing

Jensen, J. (Ed.). (1984). *Composing and Comprehending*. Urbana, IL: National Council of Teachers of English. A succinct source for many excellent articles that have been published in the journal *Language Arts*. Articles describe the relationships between reading and writing and the theory underlying these connections; others provide examples of classroom techniques that can lead children to make explicit connections between reading and writing.

Langer, J., & Smith-Burke, T. (1982). *Reader Meets Author: Bridging the Gap*. Newark, DE: International Reading Association. An overview of the position that reading and writing are constructive processes. Points out that authors make certain assumptions about their potential readers and that readers make assumptions about what the authors are trying to convey. Takes the position that reading is as active and as constructive a process as is writing.

Raphael, T. E. (Ed.). 1986. *Contexts of School-based Literacy*. New York: Random House. Based on a conference designed to bring together scholars from areas that are not often directly connected in a single source. Experts in the areas of research on teaching, on reading, on writing, and on cognitive psychology all focused on what their areas can contribute to building a better environment for instruction in literacy.

Assessing Reading Abilities

Gillette, J. W., & Temple, C. W. (1982). *Understanding Reading Problems*. Boston: Little, Brown. Often used as a textbook, this is an excellent source of information about what can lead to reading problems, how teachers can evaulate problems both formally and informally, and potential areas for remediation. It also includes a list of other sources for further information.

Johnston, P. (1983). *Reading Comprehension Assessment: A Cognitive Basis*. Newark, DE: International Reading Association. Provides a sense of future directions in the field of assessment. Johnston describes the comprehension processes, factors that influence the assessment of comprehension, and, perhaps most important, difficulties in measuring problems in comprehension accurately. Future directions are also discussed.

Wixson, K. K., & Lipson, M.Y.L. (1986). "Reading (Dis)ability: An Interactionist Perspective." In T. E. Raphael (Ed.), *Contexts of School-based Literacy*. NY: Random House. A convincing argument that current testing procedures provide little or no information about how to correct a child's reading problems. The authors provide a number of alternatives for assessing children's reading performance in ways that lead immediately to selection of methods for more effective teaching.

History of Reading Research and Practice

Huey, E. B. (1968). *The Psychology and Pedagogy of Reading*. Cambridge, MA: MIT Press. (Originally published in 1908.) A fascinating account of both how much and how little we have learned about how to teach reading. Huey had insight into the major problems in comprehension and intuition about how to study and teach. He was one of the first of the cognitive psychologists to study reading, and this book attests to the traditions begun around the start of this century.

Mathews, M.M. (1966). *Teaching Reading: Historically Considered*. Chicago: University of Chicago Press. Documents the history of reading instruction, from the time of the introduction of the alphabet through the 1960s. Abounds with anecdotes of the people and movements in the expansion of reading instruction. Humorous and always interesting.

Journals

Journal of Reading. Focus on classroom practice, grades 4 through 12; published by the International Reading Association.

Journal of Reading Behavior. Research journal of the National Reading Conference.

Language Arts. Focus on classroom practice, particularly integration of language arts; published by National Council of Teachers of English.

Reading Educator Reports. Dissemination of research and practice from the Center for the Study of Reading, Champaign, IL.

Reading Research Quarterly. Research journal of the International Reading Association.

Reading Teacher. Focus on elementary classroom reading instruction; published by the International Reading Association.

Research in the Teaching of English. Research journal of the National Council of Teachers of English.

REFERENCES

Adams, A., Carnine, D. W., & Gerston, R. (1982). Instructional strategies for studying content area texts in the intermediate grades. *Reading Research Quarterly, 18,* 27–55.

Allington, R. L. (1980). Teacher interruption behaviors during primary-grade oral reading. *Journal of Educational Psychology, 72,* 371–374.

Anderson, R. C. (1979). Schema-directed processes in language comprehension. In A. Lesgold, J. Pelligreno, S. Fokkema, & R. Glaser (Eds.), *Cognitive psychology and instruction.* New York: Plenum.

Anderson, R. C., & Freebody, P. (1981). Vocabulary knowledge. In J. T. Guthrie (Ed.), *Comprehension and teaching: Research reviews.* Newark, DE: International Reading Association.

Armbruster, B. B. (1984). The problem of "inconsiderate text." In G. G. Duffy, L. R. Roehler, & J. N. Mason (Eds.), *Comprehension instruction: Perspectives and suggestions.* White Plains, NY: Longman.

Armbruster, B. B., & Anderson, T. H. (1982). *Idea-mapping: The technique and its use in the classroom* (Reading Education Report No. 36). Urbana: University of Illinois, Center for the Study of Reading.

Au, K. H. (1979). Using the experience-text-relationship method with minority children. *Reading Teacher, 32,* 677–679.

Au, K. H., & Kawakami, A. (1986). The influence of social organization of instruction on children's text comprehension ability: A Vygotskian perspective. In T. E. Raphael (Ed.), *Contexts of school-based literacy.* New York: Random House.

Baker, L., & Stein, N. (1981). The development of prose comprehension skills. In C. M. Santa & B. L. Hayes (Eds.), *Children's prose comprehension: Theory and practice.* Newark, DE: International Reading Association.

Beck, I. L., McCaslin, E. S., & McKeown, M. G. (1981). Basal readers' purpose for story reading: Smoothly paving the road or setting up a detour? *Elementary School Journal, 81,* 156–161.

Beck, I. L., & McKeown, M. G. (1981). Developing questions that promote comprehension: The story map. *Language Arts, 58*, 913–918.

Beck, I. L., McKeown, M. G., & McCaslin, E. S. (1983). Vocabulary development: All contexts are not created equal. *Elementary School Journal, 83*, 177–181.

Bransford, J. D., & Johnson, M. K. (1972). Contextual prerequisites for understanding: Some investigations of comprehension and recall. *Journal of Verbal Learning and Verbal Behavior, 11*, 717–726.

Brown, A. L., Campione, J. C., & Day, J. D. (1981). Learning to learn: On training students to learn from text. *Educational Researcher, 10*, 14–21.

Brown, A. L., & DeLoache, J. S. (1978). Skills, plans, and self-regulation. In R. Siegler (Ed.), *Children's thinking: What develops?* Hillsdale, NJ: Erlbaum.

Canney, G., & Winograd, P. (1977). *Schemata for reading and reading comprehension performance* (Tech. Rep. No. 120). Urbana: University of Illinois, Center for the Study of Reading.

Chall, J. S. (1967). *Learning to read: The great debate.* New York: McGraw-Hill.

Clymer, T. (1963). The utility of phonic generalizations in the primary grades. *Reading Teacher, 16*, 252–258.

Collins, A., & Smith, E. (1980). *Teaching the process of reading comprehension* (Tech. Rep. No. 182). Urbana: University of Illinois, Center for the Study of Reading.

Day, J. D. (1980). *Teaching summarization skills: A comparison of training methods.* Unpublished doctoral dissertation, University of Illinois, Champaign.

Duffy, G. G., Book, C., & Roehler, L. R. (1983). A study of direct teacher explanation during reading instruction. In J. A. Niles & L. A. Harris (Eds.), *Searches for meaning in reading/language processing and instruction.* Rochester, NY: National Reading Conference.

Duffy, G. G., Roehler, L. R., & Mason, J. N. (1984). *Comprehension instruction: Perspectives and suggestions.* White Plains, NY: Longman.

Durkin, D. (1978–1979). What classroom observations reveal about reading comprehension instruction. *Reading Research Quarterly, 14*, 481–533.

Fielding, L. G., Wilson, P. T., & Anderson, R. C. (1986). A new focus on free reading: The role of trade books in reading instruction. In T. E. Raphael (Ed.), *Contexts of school-based literacy.* New York: Random House.

Flavell, J. H., & Wellman, H. M. (1977). Metamemory. In R. V. Kail, Jr., & J. W. Hagen (Eds.), *Perspectives on the development of memory and cognition.* Hillsdale, NJ: Erlbaum.

Frase, L. T. (1977). Purpose in reading. In J. T. Guthrie (Ed.), *Cognition, curriculum, and comprehension.* Newark, DE: International Reading Association.

Garner, R., & Reis, R. (1981). Monitoring and resolving comprehension obstacles: An investigation of spontaneous text lookbacks among upper-grade good and poor comprehenders. *Reading Research Quarterly, 4*, 569–582.

Gipe, J. P. (1978–1979). Investigating techniques for teaching word meanings. *Reading Research Quarterly, 14*, 624–644.

Green, J. L., & Harker, J. O. (1982). Reading to children: A communicative process. In J. A. Langer & M. T. Smith-Burke (Eds.), *Reader meets author/Bridging the gap.* Newark, DE: International Reading Association.

Guszak, F. J. (1967). Teacher questioning and reading. *Reading Teacher, 21*, 227–234.

Guthrie, J. T. (Ed.). (1981). *Comprehension and teaching: Research reviews.* Newark, DE: International Reading Association.

Hansen, J., & Ahlfors, G. (1982). Instruction in inferential comprehension: An extension and summary. In J. A. Niles & L. A. Harris (Eds.), *New inquiries in reading research and instruction.* Rochester, NY: National Reading Conference.

Hansen, J., & Hubbard, R. (1984). Poor readers can draw inferences. *Reading Teacher, 37*, 586–589.

Hiebert, E. F. (1983). An examination of ability grouping for reading instruction. *Reading Research Quarterly, 18*, 231–255.

Huey, E. B. (1968). *Psychology and pedagogy of reading*. Cambridge, MA: MIT Press. (Originally published in 1908.)

Johnson, D. D., & Barrett, T. C. (1981). Prose comprehension: A descriptive analysis of instructional practices. In J. T. Guthrie (Ed.), *Children's prose comprehension: Theory and practice*. Newark, DE: International Reading Association.

Kameenui, E. J., Carnine, D. W., & Freschi, R. (1982). Effects of text construction and instructional procedures for teaching word meanings on comprehension and recall. *Reading Research Quarterly, 17*, 367–388.

Kamil, M. L., & Pearson, P. D. (1979). Toward a theory of reading. *New York University Quarterly, 10*, 10–16.

Markman, E. M. (1979). Realizing that you don't understand: Elementary school children's awareness of inconsistencies. *Child Development, 50*, 643–655.

Mason, J. N., Stewart, J., & Dunning, D. (1986). Measuring early reading: A window into kindergarten children's understanding. In T. E. Raphael (Ed.), *Contexts of school-based literacy*. New York: Random House.

Mathews, M. M. (1966). *Teaching reading: Historically considered*. Chicago: University of Chicago Press.

McKeown, M. G. (1985). The acquisition of word meaning from context by children of high and low ability. *Reading Research Quarterly, 20*, 482–496.

National Assessment of Educational Progress (1982, July). Educational Commission of the States (Report No. 11-R-02). Denver, CO.

Palincsar, A. S. (1984). The quest for meaning from expository text: A teacher-guided journey. In G. Duffy, L. Roehler, & J. Mason (Eds.), *Comprehension instruction: Perspectives and suggestions*. White Plains, NY: Longman.

Palincsar, A. S., & Brown, A. L. (1984). Reciprocal teaching of comprehension-fostering and comprehension-monitoring activities. *Cognition and Instruction, 1*, 117–175.

Paris, S. G., Lipson, M. Y., & Wixson, K. K. (1983). Becoming a strategic reader. *Contemporary Educational Psychology, 8*, 293–316.

Paris, S. G., & Myers, M. (1981). Comprehension monitoring, memory, and study strategies of good and poor readers. *Journal of Reading Behavior, 13*, 5–22.

Pearson, P. D. (1981). *Asking questions about stories*. Occasional Paper Series. Lexington, MA: Ginn.

Pearson, P. D., & Gallagher, M. C. (1983). The instruction of reading comprehension. *Contemporary Educational Psychology, 8*, 317–344.

Pearson, P. D., Hansen, J., & Gordon, C. (1979). The effect of background knowledge on young children's comprehension of explicit and implicit information. *Journal of Reading Behavior, 9*, 201–210.

Pearson, P. D., & Tierney, R. J. (1983). Toward a composing model of reading. *Language Arts, 60*, 568–581.

Raphael, T. E. (1984). Teaching learners about sources of information for answering questions. *Journal of Reading, 27*, 303–311.

Raphael, T. E. (1986). *Contexts of school-based literacy*. New York: Random House.

Raphael, T. E., & Gavelek, J. R. (1984). Successful reading instruction: Orchestrating the learning environment. *Michigan Reading Journal, 17*, 17–21.

Raphael, T. E., & McKinney, J. (1983). An examination of 5th and 8th grade children's question answering behavior: An instructional study in metacognition. *Journal of Reading Behavior, 15*, 67–86.

Raphael, T. E., & Pearson, P. D. (1985). Increasing students' awareness of sources of information for answering questions. *American Educational Research Journal, 22*, 217–235.

Raphael, T. E., Winograd, P., & Pearson, P. D. (1980). Strategies children use when answering questions. In M. L. Kamil & A. J. Moe (Eds.), *Perspectives on reading research and instruction*. Washington, DC: National Reading Conference.

Raphael, T. E., & Wonnacott, C. A. (1985). Heightening fourth-grade students' sensitivity to sources of information for answering questions. *Reading Research Quarterly, 20,* 282–296.

Rogoff, B. (1982). Integrating context and cognitive development. In M. E. Lamb & A. L. Brown (Eds.), *Advances in developmental psychology* (Vol. 2). Hillsdale, NJ: Erlbaum.

Ryan, E. B. (1981). Identifying and remediating failures in reading comprehenders. In T. G. Waller & G. E. McKinnon (Eds.), *Advances in reading research.* Orlando, FL: Academic Press.

Samuels, S. J., Begy, G., & Chen, C. C. (1975–1976). Comparison of word recognition speed and strategies of less skilled and more highly skilled readers. *Reading Research Quarterly, 11,* 72–86.

Schwartz, R. M., & Raphael, T. E. (1985). Concept of definition: A key to improving students' vocabulary. *Reading Teacher, 39,* 198–205.

Smirnov, A. A., & Zinchenko, P. I. (1969). Problems in the psychology of memory. In M. Cole & I. Maltzman (Eds.), *A handbook of contemporary Soviet psychology.* New York: Basic Books.

Taylor, B. M. (1982). A summarizing strategy to improve middle grade students' reading and writing skills. *Reading Teacher, 36,* 202–205.

Thorndike, E. L. (1917). Reading as reasoning: A study of mistakes in paragraph reading. *Journal of Educational Psychology, 8,* 323–332.

Vygotsky, L. S. (1978). *Mind in society: The development of higher psychological processes.* Cambridge, MA: Harvard University Press.

Weinstein, R. S. (1986). The teaching of reading and children's awareness of teacher expectations. In T. E. Raphael (Ed.), *Contexts of school-based literacy.* New York: Random House.

Winograd, P. N. (1984). Strategic difficulties in summarizing texts. *Reading Research Quarterly, 19,* 404–425.

Wixson, K. K., & Lipson, M. Y. (1986). Reading (dis)ability: An interactionist perspective. In T. E. Raphael (Ed.), *Contexts of school-based literacy.* New York: Random House.

Wonnacott, C. A., & Raphael, T. E. (1983). *Children's question-answering ability: A study in metacognition.* Paper presented to the American Educational Research Association, Montreal.

3 TEACHING WRITING: SOME PERENNIAL QUESTIONS AND SOME POSSIBLE ANSWERS

Susan Florio-Ruane and
Saundra Dunn

For the last four years, the authors of this chapter have worked in close collaboration with a group of experienced elementary and secondary school teachers to study the process of writing instruction. Calling ourselves the Written Literacy Forum, we have asked questions, conducted studies, deliberated about our findings, and shared those findings with others (Clark & Florio, 1983). In these efforts, we have learned that often it is in the framing of questions that we gain the most insight into problems of practice.

Over the years, the Written Literacy Forum has encountered a number of perennial questions about writing instruction. These questions, of importance to both the teachers and researchers comprising our group, echo the concerns of teachers around the nation who were surveyed recently by the National Institute of Education. Because of their apparent importance to educators, we have chosen some of these questions as organizers for this chapter on research on writing. Among the questions asked here are the following: What are the current problems and challenges of writing

Preparation of this chapter was supported in part by the Institute for Research on Teaching, College of Education, Michigan State University. The Institute for Research on Teaching is funded primarily by the Program for Teaching and Instruction of the National Institute of Education, United States Department of Education. The opinions expressed do not necessarily reflect the position, policy, or endorsement of the National Institute of Education (Contract No. 400-81-0014).

The authors would like to thank colleagues at the Institute for Research on Teaching, especially Christopher M. Clark, Frederick Erickson, Barbara Diamond, Taffy Raphael, and Laura Roehler, for conversations that helped clarify ideas presented in this chapter. In addition, we thank the past and present members of the Written Literacy Forum for helping us to learn about the teaching of writing. They are, in alphabetical order, James Colando, Jo Ann Dohanich, Janis Elmore, Wayne Hastings, June Martin, Rhoda Maxwell, William Metheny, Marilyn Peterson, Sylvia Stevens, and Daisy Thomas.

instruction in our schools? Why is writing difficult to teach? What roles do teachers play in teaching writing? What is the nature of the classroom as a place to learn to write? What does the future hold for the teaching of writing?

The broad, overlapping questions organizing this chapter do not lend themselves to neat and easy answers. But in asking them, the educator is on the way to interpreting and applying the enormous amount of research that is currently being conducted on writing and its instruction. Approaching research in terms of perennial problems of practice can encourage teachers, administrators, and policymakers to examine more closely and critically the educational process in their own communities.

The research reported here is but a fraction of the work in this growing field. It was selected for its potential to offer new ways of thinking about the writing process, the demands of teaching writing, the environment for writing in school, and the teacher's role in shaping that environment. If research on writing can be useful to educators, it will be to the extent that it offers them conceptual tools to use in framing and solving their own problems. Researchers cannot solve the problems of practitioners, but researchers and practitioners can participate as partners in inquiry into effective teaching and literacy education. It is in the spirit of that inquiry and partnership that this chapter was written.

WHAT IS THE CURRENT STATUS OF WRITING INSTRUCTION?

American education has been much maligned in the research literature and the popular press for its apparent lack of success in teaching students to write. While there is disagreement about the origins of and solutions to these problems, there seems to be consensus among educators and the public that students leave our schools writing less well than we would like and that not all students have equal opportunities to learn and use writing in school (Hillocks, 1982).

Criticisms of writing instruction are many and varied and reflect the shifting and diverse definitions of literacy in our society (Chall, 1983). Some scholars argue that our schools offer learning tasks so narrow in scope that they ultimately limit the writing skills that students can acquire and practice in the classroom (Emig, 1971; Moffett, 1983). Others assert that teachers typically ask students to engage in hollow writing that lacks subject matter richness, purpose, stylistic variety, or meaning (Shuy, 1981; Cook-Gumperz & Gumperz, 1981; Florio, 1979). Still other critics remind us that despite lofty democratic goals of universal literacy, not all students share the same exposure to literacy in school (Hendrix, 1981). Others, criticizing the curriculum for language education, assert that what passes for literacy in school is far from ennobling or emancipating (Friere, 1980; Giroux, 1979).

Many of the criticisms lodged against education for literacy reflect the complex relationship of educational practice, student characteristics, and societal problems and values. These criticisms tend to be borne out in research. One example is a pioneering longitudinal study conducted by Walter Loban among Oakland, California, students from kindergarten to senior year of high school (1976). Loban found that socioeconomic status was a powerful predictor of growth and success in all forms of the language arts. As time went by, school interventions did less and less to remedy the learning problems of children from poorer households. Thus students assessed to be superior in oral language in kindergarten and first grade were the same ones to excel in reading and writing by grade 6 (p. 71). In addition, when high school students were grouped by Loban as "high," "random," and "low" achievers, all showed some growth in writing from grade 9 to grade 10, "but only the High and Random groups showed another velocity surge from grade eleven to twelve. They are the ones who are anticipating a college education" (p. 32).

In Loban's view, the primary predictor of growth and success in all forms of the language arts is not quality of instruction or individual student ability but socioeconomic status. In addition, Loban points out that

> nothing we have ever found supports the idea of any basic ability difference among ethnic groups. What we do find is that those who use the full resources of language usually come from families with reasonably good socioeconomic status. Social injustices, not genetic differences, account most plausibly for the larger number of our minority subjects with lower socioeconomic backgrounds. (p. 87)

It is inappropriate to place sole responsibility for these problems exclusively at the school or classroom door. Teachers know well that problems of literacy and language learning arise from factors both within and outside the classroom. Many historical, social, and political factors limit both our ability to teach writing effectively to all children and our capacity to imagine what such teaching might be like. Still, as professionals with major responsibility for writing instruction, teachers, administrators, and policymakers are confronted with these problems daily and must solve them. Loban challenged educators to respond as follows:

> Pondering the thirteen years of experience with over 200 children in Oakland, the present writer concludes that social conditions we know will continue to exist with gradual modification. Educational preparation for entrance into such a society should include a non-elitist concern with preparation for economic competence: job skills, closer linkage between education and careers, and the option of using informal standard English as part of that non-elitist preparation for the world beyond schooling. Since, obviously, human beings are not merely economic creatures, the schools should also prepare all pupils in a humanistic curriculum which would reveal not only the beauty and power of all language but also the relation between language and society. The study of language itself should be a central feature in all programs, and schools already including such an emphasis have discovered that not only are students fascinated but they are also stimulated "furiously to think." (p. 87)

It is difficult to argue with the wisdom of recommendations such as Loban's, but it is apparently also difficult to follow them. After more than a decade of research on the acquisition and use of language, there continues to be a paucity of broad and rich experiences with written language in our schools. In an extensive survey of high school writing, Applebee (1981) painted a gloomy picture of the writing experience of students both within and beyond the English class. What little writing was done had the teacher/evaluator as an exclusive audience, was largely for demonstration of academic mastery, offered little opportunity for revision, and was initiated almost exclusively by the teacher.

In a similar vein, a review of the data collected for the Third National Assessment of Educational Progress (NAEP, 1980) portrays writing performance and attitudes across grades 4, 7, and 10. One general finding is that while improvement may be subtle and gradual, there appears to be some progress in mastery of writing skills "from age to age and grade to grade" (p. 51). However, this finding is tempered by a strong decline over the school career in students' enjoyment of writing, engagement in extended and meaningful school writing tasks, and opportunities for prewriting activities and revision (p. 7). In addition, what meaningful writing there is in middle and high schools seems largely to be available to the most able writers rather than to those who appear especially to need practice. Thus the National Assessment concludes its summary of survey data on writing experiences and attitudes this way:

> When interpreting these results, one should keep in mind the fact that poor writers are caught in a revolving door of cause and effect; they are poor writers, so they seldom write; and, because they seldom write, they are poor writers. Most of them are likely to be in classes requiring little writing. Good writers are more likely to be engaged in positive writing activities because they are more likely to be writing in the first place. (p. 47)

When we read such reports, we are struck by three things. First, it appears that our efforts at effective writing instruction seem to yield not technically competent and motivated young people ready to use literacy to enrich their lives but variation in technical skills highly correlated with social class and life chances. Second, we are dismayed at the attitudes of students toward writing after they have been taught in our schools. Apparently even the more successful young writers seem to view the process as difficult, dull, and devoid of meaning. Finally, this profile of school writing seems strikingly similar to our own school experiences. We are left wondering whether this is because, when learning to teach, we were offered so little in the way of systematic, theory-based alternatives to the kinds of writing tasks we experienced as children.

Research and evaluation studies can be especially useful when they prompt us to look at our ordinary practices and tacit assumptions about teaching and learning. When such a reflective examination is made of the teaching and learning of writing, the following features seem to emerge:

1. Students generally write in response to teacher initiations.
2. Teachers tend to select the purpose and format of student writing.
3. Teacher response to student writing tends to be limited to product evaluation.
4. Product evaluation tends to focus on surface features of language rather than on meaning.
5. Little or no technical support is offered students during actual writing time.
6. Writing time is limited and considered a private time when peer interaction is discouraged.
7. Little time is spent writing first drafts, and revision is rarely undertaken by student writers.
8. Most school writing never leaves the school or classroom to be read by a wider audience.

WHY IS IT SO HARD TO IMPROVE WRITING INSTRUCTION?

Currently educators have access to a large and diverse body of research on writing. Presumably that research can inform educational planning and curriculum design. But as educators review the many, often competing theories of what writing competence is and how it develops, they are likely to feel that they have received a very mixed blessing. Researchers differ in their formulation of the problems of teaching and learning writing, and the implications of their work are often not clear or do not flow directly from theoretical models (Beach & Bridwell, 1984). In short, research rarely tells practitioners what to teach or how to teach it. This is one reason why the improvement of writing instruction has been slow and difficult.

A second reason why improvement in writing instruction has been difficult is that, of the "three R's," writing has been relatively neglected in the past in educational policy, curriculum development, and teacher training (Graves, 1978). Teachers have generally been left in isolation with respect to writing instruction. They tend to plan and teach with neither the limitations nor the guidance of district policy, published materials, or professional training in theories of the writing process (Clark & Florio, 1982). One consequence is that in many school districts, when writing instruction succeeds, the successes often go unshared and are therefore impossible to incorporate into a working theory of writing instruction that would inform either researchers or practitioners. When this happens, both research and practice suffer.

Often teachers respond to their lack of training and support by choosing simply to teach writing as they were taught. Some teachers find themselves bending to pressures on their time and to other external forces that would define written literacy in an ad hoc way for them. Others manage their difficult situations by "retreating to a basal reading series" as the sole source of their language arts curriculum (Roehler, 1979). Most are forced to compromise their goals for writing in their classrooms with the realities of an already crowded and often interrupted school day. Horace, the fictitious teacher created by Sizer (1984) to illustrate the problems faced by the many high school teachers he studied, experienced the problem this way:

> Horace has high standards. Almost above all, he believes in the importance of writing, having his students learn to use the language well. He believes in "coaching"—in having his students write and be criticized, often. Horace has five classes of fewer than thirty students each, a total of 120. (He is lucky; his colleagues in inner cities like New York, San Diego, Detroit, and St. Louis have a school board–union negotiated "load" base of 175 students.) Horace believes that each student should write something for criticism at least twice a week—but he is realistic. As a rule, his students write once a week.
>
> Most of Horace's students are juniors and seniors, young people who should be beyond the sentence and paragraph exercises and who should be working on short essays, written arguments with moderately complex sequencing and, if not grace exactly, at least clarity. A page or two would be minimum—but Horace is realistic. He assigns but one or two paragraphs.
>
> Being a veteran teacher, Horace takes only fifteen to twenty minutes to check over each student's daily homework, to read the week's theme and to write an analysis of it. (The "good" papers take a shorter time, usually, and the work of inept or demoralized students takes much longer. Horace wonders how his inner-city colleagues, who usually have a far greater percentage of demoralized students, manage.) Horace is realistic: even in his accommodating suburban school, fifteen minutes is too much to spend. He compromises, averaging five minutes for each student's work by cutting all but the most essential corners. (pp. 17–18)

Writing is vulnerable in the school learning environment. It is without the kind of curricular support and limitations present in other school subjects. Moreover, like oral language, writing is not simply a content area in isolation but a medium of communication in the other curricular areas. Thus writing is a complex and powerful aspect of school life that is largely left to the teacher to regulate. However, freed from the "tyranny of the textbook" as they plan and teach about writing, teachers are often left in the difficult position of having to devise their curriculum privately and with insufficient preparation and resources. Researchers have found, for example, that it is unlikely that teachers will integrate their instruction in writing with their goals in the other content areas, not necessarily for lack of knowledge about such integration or its value. Institutional forces including the complexity of the classroom environment, class size, time limitations, and the demands of school-based policies for instruction and evaluation shape the school day and the school curriculum in ways that discourage integration and make extended and meaningful school writing difficult to accomplish (Dunn, Florio-Ruane, & Clark, 1985).

This situation creates a paradox for writing instruction. On the one hand, teachers find themselves acting as autonomous "curriculum builders" in the area of writing far more than is the case when they are guided and limited by textbook series, workbooks, or explicit district mandates. On the other hand, the institutional "invisibility" of writing instruction often means both that teachers have been insufficiently prepared to teach writing and that normative decisions about the organization of the school and classroom unwittingly impede the kind of teaching and learning events needed for genuine written expression to occur (Florio & Clark, 1982; Martin, 1984). Thus writing instruction is a strategic site for research on teaching, learning, and policy since it demands that the teacher answer the essential questions "What should I teach?" and "How should I teach it?" in the context of what is known about the processes of both writing and schooling in our society.

WHAT DOES RESEARCH TELL US ABOUT WRITING INSTRUCTION?

In recent years, research about writing and its instruction has proliferated for at least three reasons. First, due to increased federal funding for research on classroom communication in general (Cazden, 1985) and written literacy in particular, the last decade saw a large number of studies of writing by scholars in many disciplines (Whiteman, 1981; Frederiksen & Dominic, 1981). Second, there has been great public pressure to improve the quality of education in all basic skills areas in the recent past, and writing has benefited from this attention (see, for example, *A Nation at Risk*, National Commission on Excellence in Education, 1983). Third, the current popularity and accessibility of microcomputers at school, at home, and at work has increased interest in the composing process and the ways that new technology may influence how it is learned and undertaken (Lawlor, 1982; Mehan & Souviney, 1984).

Increased research presents educators with both the opportunity and the challenge to review studies of writing and determine ways in which research might lead to more effective instruction. However, while research on writing instruction may be a relatively new enterprise, educators are likely to find that the questions these studies address are perennial ones. Thus, as they attempt to review and apply research, educators are not seeking facile answers to trendy new questions. They seek, instead, enriched ways to think about and solve problems of teaching that have been with us for generations.

Who Studies Writing?

Written literacy has been studied by scholars from many disciplines, among them psychology, education, anthropology, linguistics, English, and rhetoric. In addition, a number of interdisciplinary research teams, some of which include experienced teachers as research collaborators, have investigated the writing process (Mosenthal, Tamor, & Walmsley, 1983).

Researchers from each discipline bring to the investigation of writing different guiding assumptions and ways of viewing the writing process. Frederiksen and Dominic (1981) have proposed a taxonomy of four perspectives on writing that "emphasize different aspects of writing processes and influences on them; yet all are concerned centrally with understanding writing processes" (p. 2). They identify writing as (1) a cognitive activity, (2) a particular form of language and language use, (3) a communicative process, and (4) a contextualized, purposeful activity.

People who focus on writing as a cognitive activity are concerned with the nature and development of the writer's knowledge, strategies, and skills as well as with the general characteristics of the writer's thinking. Cognitive psychologists studying writing attempt to identify the mental processes involved in writing and explain how these processes work and interact (Gregg & Steinberg, 1980; Frase, 1982).

Other researchers choose to focus on particular rhetorical aspects of a writer's knowledge, such as the different language forms an author can use depending on the purpose, audience, and context of the writing. Many of these researchers are concerned not only with the writer's thinking but also with the writing situation and with the characteristics of the texts produced by persons of various levels of literary competence (Britton, 1982; Lloyd-Jones, 1981; Moffett, 1983).

Still another group of researchers focuses on writing as a social process. Like the scholars just mentioned, these researchers are concerned with the writing process and with the author's relation to his or her audience, but they pay special attention to the social norms that govern the forms writing takes in a particular cultural setting (e.g., a community, school, or classroom) and the social purposes served by various written forms (Smith, 1983; Szwed, 1981; Heath, 1983).

WHAT HAVE RESEARCHERS LEARNED?

With so many people working on so many different studies of writing and instruction, it is not easy to summarize or synthesize what they have learned thus far. But several good reviews of research on writing and its implications for practice have been written in the past few years. These reviews cut across the diverse disciplinary approaches to writing research and attempt to distill from them what appear to be the most relevant insights for educators.

Glatthorn (1981), for example, summarizes research on writing for an audience of school administrators, while Kean (1983) does the same for teachers and teacher educators. These two reviews are notable for several reasons. First, they are extremely consistent in what they select to be the most relevant insights from recent research. Second, as we shall see shortly, the educational implications of the research they review seem inconsistent with the ways that most of us were taught to write in school.

Using the work of Glatthorn, Kean, and others, the following list of propositions is presented as food for thought for educators interested in rethinking the approach to writing and its instruction taken in their classrooms, schools, or districts. Though relatively short and general, this list is one about which we think there would be agreement even among the diverse, interdisciplinary collection of researchers currently studying writing and its teaching. In addition, the insights presented here do not readily take the form of prescriptions for practice. Instead, they are statements of what researchers have learned that may stimulate educators to think in new ways about writing instruction in their own particular situations.

Proposition 1: There Is Lack of Consensus about School Writing, Its Purposes, and the Curriculum

A painfully obvious implication of current research on writing instruction is that there exist different definitions of writing and with them different sets of strategies for teaching. While there is general cultural agreement that writing should be taught, when researcher Peter Mosenthal (1983) attempted to frame a taxonomy of the purposes underlying and shaping instruction, he was able to identify at least five. Some of these purposes are recognizable as the sole motivation for writing instruction in some school districts. Other purposes are simultaneously achieved by a variety of integrated writing activities. Several purposes, however, potentially contradict one another and are the source of controversy among language educators and researchers (Hillocks, 1982).

The purposes for teaching writing identified by Mosenthal were the "academic," or writing as a means for conserving and passing on cultural norms; the "utilitarian," or the passing on of traditions and cultural knowledge thought to enable survival in the adult world; the "romantic," or learning to write to develop one's sense of autonomy and worth; the "cognitive-developmental," or writing to promote intellectual growth and lifelong learning; and the "emancipatory," or literacy learning for equality and social justice (Mosenthal, 1983).

In an ethnohistory of literacy education in America, Heath (1981) notes that purposes such as those just mentioned were not always the ones for which writing was taught. Our educational history is marked by shifting definitions of literacy and the values associated with it. However, the purposes identified by Mosenthal seem to capture the contemporary views. They are so much taken for granted in our culture that their validity and utility are rarely questioned. Yet as powerful organizers of our curricula, instruction, and evaluation practices, they merit continual review and examination by educators and other members of the community.

When researchers look at curriculum and instruction they find that different strategies for teaching and evaluating writing tend to reflect the varied, often competing purposes for which writing is taught in school (Katz, 1984). Urging greater awareness and specificity about our definitions and values for writing, Kean (1983) cites James Moffett, who offered five definitions of writing that cover most senses in which the word is used: writing as (1) handwriting—the physical act of drawing letters, making graphic symbols; (2) transcribing and copying—taking dictation, recording one's own words or the words of others; (3) paraphrasing—summarizing the words of others, reporting what others have said or done; (4) crafting—constructing good sentences and paragraphs and overall organization; and (5) authoring—revising inner speech into outer discourse for a specific purpose and a specific audience (Kean 1983, p. 8).

One of the major contributions of research on writing has been descriptive. By reviewing the many forms and functions of writing observed in classrooms or conceived by researchers for study, we begin to appreciate the many purposes writing is thought to serve, the many values connected with literacy by our society, and the many facets of the social and cognitive process we call writing. Thus we know that when students tell us that they "did writing" in school today, they may be referring to any number of activities of differing nature, purpose, and social and intellectual complexity.

Proposition 2: Writing Is a Complex Process

Most mature writers would agree that writing is ultimately all of the operations just mentioned—done simultaneously. Among researchers and practitioners alike, however, there is disagreement about how to attain this mature writing performance. Holding different views both of the writing process and of how it is learned, some researchers argue that people are what Vygotsky called "natural symbolists" (1934/ 1962). Using the metaphor of the acquisition of oral language, these researchers tend to prefer a model of writing development in which children, armed with purpose and occupying a supportive environment, engage in writing as a holistic process of communication. Gradually, with help, encouragement, and models from more experienced writers, their writing takes on the qualities of mature performance in large measure because they have inferred the norms for writing by guided practice, purposeful tasks, and helpful responses from their teachers (Birnbaum & Emig, 1983; Clay, 1975; Martin, 1981).

Also taking research on the acquisition of oral language as their point of departure, other researchers hold a different view of the writing process. Strongly influenced by the operations of the computer as a model or metaphor for human thinking, these researchers consider the writing process to be a many-faceted, complex task of information processing. They assert that the process offers far too many new bits of information for the beginner to hold in consciousness at one time and recommend that the process be divided into constituent parts for teaching and learning. These researchers are often cited in writing curricula that place a high value on practice of isolated parts of the writing process. Among the many kinds of things student writers practice until they have been so routinized as not to demand the writer's conscious attention are spelling, punctuation, and the structuring of sentences. Thus freed from some of the cognitive load of writing, the beginner can work on the more complex aspects of writing that involve meaning and rhetorical purpose (Lawlor, 1983; Daiute, 1984; Bereiter & Scardamalia, 1981).

What is remarkable about these two camps of research on writing is that despite their different views of how it arises and develops, they share consensus on perhaps the essential feature of writing—that it is a process. Most of us learned from dreaded red marks on hastily written tests and themes that writing was the product of our labors. However, significant in current research is the notion that instruction ought to focus on the process rather than the product of writing (Flower, 1981). While this view may contrast sharply with our own school experiences, it flows from more than a decade of research into both the mental processes involved in composing and the social and instructional factors that seem to enhance its development. However, as we shall see when we consider the classroom environment and the roles the teacher plays in the development of writing among students, attention to process does not preclude attention to product. Instead, awareness of the writing process transforms our thinking about that product in important ways.

Proposition 3: The Writing Process Has Phases That Can Guide Instruction

Here some of the oldest myths about and traditions of writing instruction are challenged by the current research on writing. First, research on the composing processes of both beginners and experts shows that writing is undertaken in over-lapping and recursive stages (Flower, 1981). Some researchers state these stages broadly as three: prewriting, writing, and postwriting. Others parse them further into exploration, planning, drafting, revising, and sharing or publication. Regardless of how they are labeled, the important features of the phases are as follows: First, authors appear to engage in an extended period prior to writing in which they generate provisional plans for the text, identify the purpose of their writing, consider the voice they will use as authors, and identify the audience for whom they will write. (One can see in an instant how this fundamental stage of the writing process is truncated when teachers initiate writing tasks, select the topic and format of the writing, leave unexamined the writing's purpose, and serve as the student's sole audience.)

The second phase of the writing process is the one most familiar to us. It occurs when pencil actually touches paper for extended drafting. Here again, however, our tacit assumptions have been challenged by the research. First, writers do not appear relentlessly to follow predetermined formats or plans. In fact, the most mature writers engage in extensive revision of their plans as they write. At this point, thinking and writing appear to shape each other. In addition, this stage requires the writing of a first, rough draft. Attention to spelling, punctuation, and other mechanics related to surface form (and important later when the document is ready for publication) can be suspended at this stage in order to free the author to express thoughts on paper without distraction.

Three things become apparent to the reader of research at this point. First, when writing is construed as a process, teaching it may take more time than is often allocated for writing or language arts in school. Second, the first draft, typically the only one required of students, is in fact just the beginning of the writing process. And third, the teacher, often the critic or even the editor of first drafts in the past, can now be viewed as playing a crucial support role during the early phases of the writing process. All of these have been found to be the case by researchers on writing instruction (Graves, 1983; Shaughnessy, 1977). In particular, the acknowledgment that the teacher's role may turn out to be neither arbiter of a text's form nor editor or evaluator of the first draft implies that the teacher must serve as a coach, an attentive witness to this second stage who can intervene strategically to help authors in their efforts to get their thoughts on paper, to envision their absent audiences, and to clarify the purposes of their writing (Freedman, 1985).

The third phase of the writing process involves much of what we used to teach first. It concerns editing, revising, and otherwise readying the text for sharing with a real audience. Here it is not uncommon for points of grammar and spelling to be taught, but research has found that it is far more effective to do such teaching in the context of the student author's actual text and purposes (Kean, 1983). Even when one wants to drill a particular skill, tying it to the needs of the student seems most effective. Direct teaching of grammar and diagramming sentences have not been found to be useful in helping students write extended and cohesive prose. Though some have found that practice combining sentences into longer, more complex ones can be helpful here (McCutchen & Perfetti, 1983), it appears that the ability to create cohesion between parts of sentences, sentences themselves, or even paragraphs is a competence acquired in general language use rather than in isolated drill and practice (Halliday & Hasan, 1976).

Proposition 4: The Classroom Is a Complex Environment for Writing in Which the Teacher Plays Several Important Roles

Rethinking the writing process in light of the first three propositions, educators reading this chapter might be alarmed at the work that would appear to be involved in coaching each student author to a finished product—particularly when that research also suggests that students who write frequently with coaching and feedback tend to learn to write more effectively. But in fact the research news in this area is potentially very good. Traditional evaluation, where the teacher served as editor, might usefully be replaced by the student as editor of his or her own work. While negative feedback from the teacher does not appear to be helpful, critical feedback from interested readers does (Kean, 1983). Thus writing conferences between teacher and students can replace the armloads of papers that teachers used to have to take home to "correct." In addition, peer conferencing allows this responsibility to be shared, and students learn by reading and responding to others' work. Such responses and even their extension by the publication of student work in the classroom, school, community, and beyond help students see that their writing is of genuine importance and offer practice in writing for diverse audiences (Florio, 1979).

Findings like these highlight the teacher's roles of respondent to the student writer and designer of the learning environment in which writing will occur. Broadening one's conception of the teacher's role in writing instruction and of the school and classroom as places in which to write has implications for teacher education, classroom and school organization, and the allocation of school and community resources.

The current research focus on process and technical support rather than on drill of isolated skills, for example, strongly suggests that students may learn best from teachers who are themselves writers, familiar with all phases of the writing process and role models of its utility and importance. In addition, students appear to learn from reading the writing of others—both the works of their peers and those of published authors.

Writing is evidently not the quiet, solitary, and discrete act we once thought it was. Peer writing and revision are useful; writing one document well takes time—there must be much on-site teacher help and support. Focusing on the process of writing rather than on the product, evaluation needs to be formative rather than summative. We have at our disposal such techniques as holistic scoring and primary-trait scoring, which can be modified by teachers and districts to evaluate their process goals (see Hirsch & Harrington, 1981, for definitions and critiques of these methods). In addition, sensitive record keeping must be undertaken along the way to provide data for teachers about how to help and support the writing of their students rather than how to rank them against some external standard. More will be said about these issues.

WHAT DO WE KNOW ABOUT THE CLASSROOM AS AN ENVIRONMENT FOR WRITING?

In his study of the relation of schooling to thinking, Parker (1983) points out that regardless of the perspective researchers take on the development of the writing process, there appears be to at least tacit agreement that writing—like speaking—is a process with social, historical, and cognitive implications. As children learn to communicate, they learn "to mean" (Halliday, 1975). In so doing, they express and amplify their thinking (Bruner, 1976). This important psychological process takes place not only in the context of social life—that is, in communication with others—but it is also constrained by the communication systems that the culture has developed and passed on over time. Thus in learning to speak or write there are powerful interactions between inner, psychological processes and social and historical forces (Vygotsky, 1978).

Classrooms are the places where the formal business of teaching and learning is accomplished in our society. While many children are educated for literacy informally in the home (Heath, 1983), schools are charged with explicit responsibility to teach our children to read and write. Even a brief visit to an American classroom impresses the observer with the abundance of speaking, listening, reading, and writing being engaged in as part of the daily round of school activities. Because of the sheer volume of language learned and used in school, and in light of the relationship between language as a cultural system and the developing thought of the child, Parker (1983) asserts that researchers and educators must study language learning and use in schools and classrooms. He asks,

> From this viewpoint, what might we hypothesize about important cultural institutions like schools? Schools are "language-saturated" institutions. What are their language policies and practices, what role (or roles) do they play in the growth of mind? (p. 143)

For the past ten years, researchers have been conducting studies of communication in the classroom prompted by just these sorts of questions. Much of this research has been reviewed in recent articles by Cazden (1985) and Green (1983). Among the many things researchers have learned about oral and written language in classrooms, three insights are particularly important to educators. First, classroom language serves a variety of important social and academic functions. Second, language has a number of manifestations across classrooms and across time and activity in even one classroom. Third, classroom life demands of both teacher and student a wide range of social and linguistic competences in order for them appropriately to match language form with social situation and purpose and thus succeed in school.

What Are the Uses of Language in Classrooms?

Before research on classroom communication was initiated, it was well known that the language arts—speaking, listening, reading, and writing—were part of the school's explicit curriculum. Since clear and thoughtful communication seems to mark the educated person in our society and because language learning is fundamental to cultural transmission, it was taken for granted that the school's place was to inculcate both the grammar of English and the understanding of how that grammar worked. This can be thought of as one manifestation of classroom language: *language as a part of the curriculum.*

However, language not only provides us with content for instruction, it is also the medium of instruction in classrooms and the foundation of all social and academic life that occurs there. Viewed in this way, language is part of what Jackson called the school's "hidden curriculum" (1968). Researchers have found, for example, that speech and writing are used by teachers and children not only for the purpose of "skill practice" but also for the creation and maintenance of social relations in the classroom. As in the family, the peer group, or the workplace, we talk, listen, read, and write together in classrooms not exclusively as practice toward some other end but as a practical part of human daily life (Erickson, 1982). Thus a second manifestation of language in the classroom is as *a tool to create and maintain social life.*

Classrooms are special social places. Since they exist within formal institutions accountable for the teaching of the young, it is not surprising to find that evaluation is an important activity in classrooms. Teachers monitor language used in the classroom to assess how well they are teaching and to infer how and what their students are learning. Herein lies a third special manifestation of language in classrooms: *language as a means to assess the learning of students and the effectiveness of teaching.*

How Is Classroom Communication Related to Learning?

Recent research on classroom language has addressed the relationship between the social uses of language and the extent to which children learn (or are assessed as having learned) in school. Particularly among children who for reasons of social class, first language, or culture are less well served by our schools, difficulties in teaching and learning appear to be language-related. These difficulties arise at least in part from conflicting understandings and expectations among the learners, their families, and their teachers about all three of the functions of language in the classroom (Cazden, John, & Hymes, 1972).

Educators know that communication problems can be apparent in all four of the language arts. Research on the writing needs of culturally and linguistically different children, though in its early stages, addresses the relationships among culture, communication, and classroom experience (Cronnell, 1981). Consistent with the findings of research on their oral communication in the classroom, researchers are finding that many of the writing problems experienced by bilingual or culturally different students stem only in part from interference of the structures of their first language with those of the written forms of English. Equally or more important for educators is the insight that teachers often expect less of these students by virtue of their different language experiences or that cultural difference and teacher expectation collaborate to offer students less than optimal classroom experiences (Au & Mason, 1981; McDermott, 1977).

These findings are paralleled in studies of children who are deaf or hearing-impaired. The longstanding assumption that to be without hearing was to be without language has been largely disabused. Yet in many educational settings, hearing-impaired children are isolated from written communication both literally and figuratively when those with whom they might communicate in writing assume that loss of one expressive channel limits communication in another. Here again, important new research on the writing process is beginning to show students as able and eager to learn to write in environments where they are treated as sociolinguistically competent persons with important thoughts to communicate (Whiteman, 1981).

In summary, research has systematically explored and described what experienced teachers have no doubt known for a long time: that when teachers and students engage in daily rounds of classroom communication—be it speaking, listening, reading, or writing—they are doing at least three things. First, they are working on aspects of the school curriculum; second, they are engaged in social exchanges with one another; and third, they are showing each other what they know for purposes of assessment. The simultaneous realization of these three functions of language in the classroom makes that social setting a complicated and unique one in the lives of most children. How a child manages the demands of classroom communication and how a teacher interacts with that child can influence not only the expectations held and opportunities provided for that child but ultimately how and what the child learns about literacy and his or her place in the world.

WHAT IS THE TEACHER'S ROLE IN WRITING INSTRUCTION?

While many social forces external to the classroom influence the communication that occurs there, the teacher has unique authority to influence thought and language in the classroom. It is in this sense that the teacher's role in writing instruction is a central one closely related to issues of the learning environment. These two aspects of literacy education are therefore of considerable interest to educators and researchers alike.

Within the social system of the classroom, teachers and students communicate with each other by means of oral, written, and nonverbal behaviors (Bremme & Erickson, 1977). When writing instruction is viewed as part of this communication system, we find that the interactions of teacher and student matter a great deal to what the student writes and how the student writes it.

In our work with high school writers, for example, we found that adolescents stressed the importance of their personal relationships with their teacher in both the meaningfulness of the writing they did in school and in their willingness to do it. Speaking of their creative writing teacher, for example, students told us, "His interests coincide more with [those of] students than other teachers, so we can relate with him better," and "He treats each poem and writing as a piece of art and personal feelings, not as [something to] grade" (Dunn, 1983).

Now that researchers are examining not only the process of writing but the process of writing instruction, they are finding that the crucial questions may not be those concerned with the teacher's "response to students' writing" but those concerned with the teacher's "response to the student writer." Sondra Perl (1983), a teacher and researcher noted for extensive descriptive studies of writing in class-rooms, explains that when writing was taught, measured, and evaluated exclusively on the basis of a finished *product*, little attention was given to questions such as "What can teachers do to facilitate the writing *process* in the classroom?" The new focus on the understanding of the process of writing highlights the necessity of teachers' talking and listening to students about writing and its purposes. Perl and the teachers with whom she works argue that to do this teachers must be writers themselves. If one thinks of writing as a craft rather than as a product, it is easy to see why it is so important that the teacher be a practicing writer, not just an observer and evaluator.

How Do Teachers Influence the Writing of Their Students?

When we studied writing in elementary and middle school classrooms (Clark & Florio, 1982), we found that we could categorize writing in these classrooms into four broad functions: (1) writing to participate in community, (2) writing to know oneself and others, (3) writing to occupy free time, and (4) writing to demonstrate academic competence (see Table 3.1). Each of these functions took a different form and was marked by particular kinds of teacher-student interactions.

In looking at these categories of writing with the teachers whose classrooms we studied, we found that the teachers were largely unaware of the range of oppor-tunities for writing seized by their students in the course of a day. In addition, viewing their classrooms from the additional vantage point provided by descriptive research, the teachers were dismayed to discover that so much of the day's "official writing" had the teacher as initiator, composer, and audience. In contrast, much of the student writing that went unnoticed by the teachers offered the students nearly complete control of the rights and duties of authorship.

Pondering these findings with the teachers, several questions linking the class-room environment to the teacher's role in school writing emerged: Who initiates writing in the classroom? Who is the primary composer? Who is the intended audience? What is the format of the writing? Is the writing evaluated? If so, how? Finally, what relationship do these contextual factors have to student growth in writing?

When classroom writing is studied in terms of such questions, it becomes apparent that the scope and range of student writing is inevitably shaped by the teacher-student relationship. Often the form of teacher-student interaction during formal writing instruction resembles that identified by sociologist and teacher educator Hugh Mehan (1979) in his study of the oral language of instruction in the classroom. Mehan found that classroom talk during lessons could be described as consisting of three turns—two for the teacher and one for the student. In Mehan's description, the turns took the form of (1) teacher elicitation of information from the students, (2) student response, and (3) teacher evaluation of the response for both academic correctness and social appropriateness.

In writing to demonstrate academic competence, the form of writing most pre-valent in the classrooms we studied and typically the only form of writing used as the basis of formal assessments of learning, we found a communication pattern similar to that described by Mehan. In general, the teacher took responsibility for initiating the writing task, determining such things as its timing, audience, purpose,

TABLE 3.1   THE FUNCTIONS OF WRITING IN AN ELEMENTARY SCHOOL CLASSROOM

Function Type	Sample Activity	Distinctive features						
		Initiator	Composer	Writer/ Speaker	Audience	Format	Fate	Evaluation
Type I: Writing to participate in community	classroom rule setting	teacher	teacher and students	teacher	student	by teacher and students: drafted on chalkboard; printed in colored marker on large white paper	posted; referred to when rules are broken	no
Type II: Writing to know oneself and others	diaries	teacher	student	student	student	by teacher: written or printed on lined paper in student-made booklets	locked in teacher's file cabinet or kept in student desk; occasionally shared with teacher, other students, or family	no
Type III: Writing to occupy free time	letters and cards	student	student	student	other (parents, friends, family)	by student: printed or drawn on lined or construction paper	kept; may be given as gift to parents or friend	no
Type IV: Writing to demonstrate academic competence	science lab booklets	teacher	publisher	publisher and student(s)	teacher	by publisher: printed in commercial booklet	checked by teacher; filed for later use by student; pages sent home to parents by teacher	yes

Source: Florio & Clark, 1982.

and format. Then the students wrote in response to the teacher's initiation. Finally, the teacher read and evaluated the writing of the students—usually serving as its sole audience (Florio & Clark, 1982). Exciting exceptions to this pattern occurred during unexpected "occasions for writing," when teachers found themselves deviating from routine activities to capitalize on unexpected opportunities for their students to write for outside audiences. On these occasions, motivated by real-life purposes for writing and typically addressing audiences beyond the classroom, students tended to engage in extended writing activities in which they exercised more of the author's role, received coaching and support from the teacher, and produced several drafts en route to their final one.

In sharing our insights with the teachers in our study, we found that the routine system of assignment of rights and duties of authorship tended to operate outside the conscious awareness of the teachers. Armed with plans and intentions to motivate students to write, teachers were unaware of the high degree of control they exercised over writing activities or of the ways in which that control served to limit the students' experience of the writing process. It was only when those plans were abandoned by the teacher that students experienced an opening up of the writing process, enabling them to gain some control over purposes, formats, audiences, and evaluation of the writing's effectiveness. This insight suggests that the social organization of the classroom, and the rights and duties of students and teachers, can have powerful effects on the kinds and amounts of experiences students have of written literacy.

The writing that can be observed in classrooms is often not only rhetorically and syntactically limited but is also expressive of the asymmetry of power between student and teacher. Such asymmetry plays itself out in expressive rights and obligations that limit the facets of the author's role the student has an opportunity to practice. If our goals for literacy education extend beyond the classroom walls to the world of adult society and work, these limitations can have profound implications. In many writing activities, the teacher determines the subject matter and form of the writing, the student writes as an academic performance, and the teacher evaluates the written document. Yet this pattern is not typical of most writing that goes on in the world outside the classroom. Rarely in adult writing does the same person play the roles of initiator, audience, and evaluator. Rarely in adult life is the purpose of writing the earning of a grade. Yet this is the type of writing encountered by many students in school.

The consequences of this situation were painfully experienced by the young adults who were taught and studied by Mina Shaughnessy in an open-enrollment program at the City University of New York. Although these students had many other educational and economic disadvantages with which to contend, Shaughnessy's (1977) description of them suggests that one of their disadvantages stemmed directly from their prior schooling. That disadvantage was the absence of opportunities in school for these students to experience the role of author—that is, to take the power and responsibility associated with identifying a purpose and an audience for the writing, drafting a document, revising it, and seeing it through to sharing with others.

Shaughnessy contends that deprived of this role, the students did not think of themselves as having ideas worth writing down. Moreover, their deprivation had implications for their willingness to engage in extended writing and revision. They simply did not know that "good" writers wrote, evaluated, and revised their work many times before it was ultimately published. Writing and revising so little, these students had been deprived of the chance to practice the complex craft of writing. Thus it is not surprising that they experienced many difficulties manipulating both the syntactic and semantic complexities of formal written English. In this regard, Shaughnessy offers the following example:

> Students should be helped to understand, first of all, the need for punctuation, both as a score for intonation, pauses, and other vocal nuances and as a system of marks that help a reader predict grammatical structure. This understanding comes about when the writer is able to view his own work from the reader's perspective. It should not be surprising, however, that BW [basic writing] students, who have generally read very little and who have written only for teachers, have difficulty believing in a real audience. Various strategies can encourage this shift of perspective: exchange reading of student papers, an exposure to unpunctuated passages that students are required to read aloud, [and] audiovisual demonstrations of the way a reader gets derailed by faulty punctuation. (p. 39)

Thus Shaughnessy connects the social context of learning to write with learning how to communicate one's ideas to an absent audience and, ultimately, with the important technical issue of appropriate punctuation.

What Alternative Roles Can Teachers Play in Writing Instruction?

What are the alternatives to this "teacher elicitation–student response–teacher evaluation" structure of classroom interactions? And what are the implications for the teacher's roles? Assuming with researcher Heath (1982) that "there are more literacy events which call for appropriate knowledge of forms and uses of speech events than there are actual occasions for extended reading or writing" (p. 94), many educational theorists are urging the broadening of occasions for writing in school. By redefining the roles of student and teacher in the writing class and by changing the audience and the purpose of school writing, it is possible to open up the range of responses that teachers can make to support student writing, the range of purposes to which writing can be put, and the range of topics and forms that can be used and practiced by students. In short, the manner in which one chooses to perform the role of teacher or student has tremendous influence on the writing that gets done.

In thinking about teacher-student relationships in terms of the social roles enacted by each participant and the ways that they are negotiated in the classroom, we have found the sociological concepts of "role enactment" and "role distance" to be helpful (Goffman, 1961). Goffman defines *role enactment* as "the actual conduct of an individual while on duty in his position" (p. 85). He argues that in role enactment, one has considerable leeway in managing the rights and duties attendant to the position and that enactment is negotiated with others in the context of face-to-face interaction. How one enacts a role has implications for the reciprocal roles of others in the same social situation.

Enactment of a writing teacher's role is negotiated with the students and has implications for the rights and duties that the students will experience in *their* roles as writers. A teacher may at times choose to "embrace" the teacher role, taking the power to initiate student writing, determine its content and format, and be its sole audience and evaluator. Such embracement, Goffman notes, is typical of baseball managers during games and traffic police at rush hour. When the teacher assumes such power and responsibility for student writing, it is clear that he or she can greatly limit the student's role to mere task completion and academic performance for a grade.

In contrast to such role embracement, teachers often distance themselves from the full expression of the putative teacher role. In what Goffman calls *role distance*, the teacher separates self from role, thereby opening up new social options to others in the scene. In doing this, the teacher "apparently withdraws by *actively* manipulating the situation.... The individual is actually denying not the role but the virtual self that is implied in the role for all accepting performers" (pp. 107–108).

By "active manipulation" of the instructional situation and distancing themselves from the role traditionally expected of the writing teacher, teachers are able to support the writing process among students in a variety of ways. Researchers have examined and written about several of the ways that teachers do this.

Three researchers working out of the Center for Applied Linguistics reported extensively on the writing done in the classroom of Leslee Reed, a teacher who has negotiated a special kind of writing with her students (Staton, Shuy, Kreeft, & Reed, 1982). For 17 years Reed kept dialogue journals with her students. Dialogue journal keeping is interactive, functional writing that occurs between two or more people (here, a teacher and each of her students) on a regular basis (here, daily) about topics of interest to the writers. Reed uses dialogue journals both to improve her students' competence with written language and to support their academic and social emotional development.

Much of our own understanding of high school writing has come from the exchanging of dialogue journals with six adolescent writers. Interested in learning more about how they viewed writing, Saundra Dunn corresponded with each student for one semester. She found that unique relationships developed with each of the six student informants.

Much as Kreeft (1982) reported in the analysis of journal writings in Reed's class, the students with whom Dunn exchanged journals approached the purpose and ownership of the journal in very different ways. In several cases, the correspondents had difficulty abandoning the form of adult as questioner and student as respondent. In other journals, Dunn and the student gradually negotiated greater symmetry in their relationship. These journals are marked by the gradual attainment of reciprocity in initiation of new topics and in disclosure of personal information on the parts of both the adult and the student writers (Dunn & Florio-Ruane, 1984).

Although not research on writing instruction per se, the studies just mentioned shed light on issues central to curriculum and instruction in writing. James Moffett, a language arts educator, has argued that a "trinity of discourse" underlies all writing (1983). In this idealized triad, the *author* writes about a *topic* for an *audience* removed in space and time. In many classrooms this triad is distorted such that the student is the author and the teacher is both the determiner of the topic and the audience. This distorted triad limits the range of potential relationships among author and audience, author and subject matter, and audience and subject matter.

Another way to think of this triad is in terms of what might be called "writing for the real world." Teachers can create this triad in their classrooms by refocusing school writing toward purposes and audiences identified by students or otherwise meaningful in their lives. This transformation is more than mere window dressing in the name of relevance. It can actually transform social relations that surround writing. And since writing is an expressive tool, it too is transformed.

To accomplish such a transformation may call upon teachers intentionally to distance themselves from several facets of the roles typically assumed by writing teachers (for example, determiner of subject matter, sole audience, and sole evaluator of the author's written product). This renegotiation also requires that the teacher shift roles in a variety of ways during writing instruction.

We have learned from our dialogue journal exchanges with students, our discussions with teachers, and our extended fieldwork in elementary, middle school, and high school classrooms that the teaching of writing is approached quite differently by each teacher and also by a single teacher at different phases of writing instruction. The primary facets of the teacher's role that we observed in our research and that have been written about by other researchers are those of motivator, resource person, strategist, model, and coach (Shaw, Pettigrew, & Van Nostrand, 1983). At various times in the student's conception, writing, and revision of a document, the teacher may alternately encourage or motivate the writing, offer technical assistance, help the writer to clarify meaning and intentions, and aid in the publication of a student's work. How and when to intervene in the work of the student author becomes the focus of this type of teaching.

The research of Graves (1983) speaks as well of the enterprise of changing the teacher's role and opening up the instructional process. For Graves, the writing conference is one excellent way to engage the student writer. In the conference, typically a face-to-face conversation between student and teacher about the student's work in progress, the norms for classroom speaking and listening are significantly altered. Students maintain ownership of their work, holding it in their own hands and speaking about its purposes and problems. Sitting beside the student rather than across from him or her (see Figure 3.1), the teacher enters the conference to support and extend student thinking and writing.

In this kind of interaction, the written product is important to the teacher and the student, but in new and different ways. It is the basis for a conversation between teacher and student in which both will learn. For the teacher, the document and its discussion can be diagnostic. By listening to the student and reading the work in progress, the teacher can come to understand the young author's intentions, resources, growth, and needs. For the student, talking with a teacher about the work and responding to thoughtful questions is a way to expand and clarify thinking about audience and purpose as well as a moment to receive technical assistance and instruction. One can see at a glance how this kind of attention to the writer and his or her document potentially changes the teacher's role from mere critic or evaluator to what Graves calls an "advocate." One can also see how it transforms the student's role from performer for a grade to author.

Research on the writing process, the learning environment, and the teacher's role encourages us to view the learner in new ways. The learner appears not as an empty vessel to be filled with the formalized rules of English grammar but as a communicator engaged in the acquisition of new knowledge structures from meaningful interactions with people and objects. In looking to the future of writing instruction, there is potential for altering schooling in ways that may dramatically transform the child's experience with writing. It is to that future that we now turn.

THE LANGUAGE OF CONFERENCE SETTINGS

A. *Role of advocate*

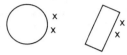

Sits near and next to child.
As close to equal height as possible.
Engages child visually.
Child holds piece, may offer.

B. *Role of adversary*

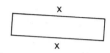

Sits opposite.
Does not want to be next to or near child.
Chair higher.
Ignores eye contact.
Takes child's writing.

FIGURE 3.1   Two ways of interacting with students about their written work. (Graves, 1983)

WHAT'S AHEAD FOR WRITING INSTRUCTION?

It would be naive of us to conclude without giving some attention to an issue that has captured the imagination of researchers, educators, parents, and children: the role that computers will play in literacy education in the coming years. As earlier, our intention is not to give prescriptive solutions but to spark self-examination. We hope that this brief review will encourage teachers to think about whether and how to incorporate computers into the teaching and learning of writing in school.

Such reflection will necessarily call upon educators to examine, and perhaps make more explicit, their curricula for writing and their current classroom organization and teaching strategies. As sociologist Peter Lyman states, "A computer is both a machine and a social relation" (1983, p. 3). We will address issues related to both the technology of educational computers and the social organization of computers in schools.

Computer technology offers a new set of tools to writers and, potentially, new ways of looking at the writing process. Consider, for example, the vision of educator and technologist Seymour Papert:

> Consider an activity which may not occur to most people when they think of computers and children: the use of a computer as a writing instrument. For me, writing means making a rough draft and refining it over a considerable period of time. My image of myself as a writer includes the expectation of an "unacceptable" first draft that will develop with successive editing into presentable form. But I would not be able to afford this image if I were a third grader. The physical act of writing would be slow and laborious. I would have no secretary. For most children rewriting a text is so laborious that the first draft is the final copy, and the skill of rereading with a critical eye is never acquired. This changes dramatically when children have access to computers capable of manipulating text. The first draft is composed at the keyboard. Corrections are made easily. The current copy is always neat and tidy. I have seen a child move from total rejection of writing to an intense involvement (accompanied by rapid improvement of quality) within a few weeks of beginning to write with a computer. Even more dramatic changes are seen when the child has physical handicaps that make writing by hand more than usually difficult or even impossible. (1980, p. 30)

To some this vision may seem exciting and promising. Others are skeptical about the computer's place among other realities of schooling that conspire to make

Papert's child-at-the-terminal vision seem unrealistic indeed. Some educators welcome this technology with open arms, arguing the importance of computer literacy for survival in today's society. Other educators are leery of this new technology, perhaps fearful of buying into another short-lived trend such as educational television or new math.

It remains to be seen whether computers prove to be an educational fad, an educational wonder, or, more likely, something in between. At each end of the continuum, people have voiced strong opinions. Computer scientist J. S. Brown, whose interest is in opening up new areas of human-machine communications, predicts that "by 1990, what's available in the computer marketplace will be constrained not by technology but by what people are capable of understanding" (Gollman, 1984, p. 3). Morris Freedman, professor of English, is more concerned that researchers are failing to address the central questions with respect to writing instruction:

> In the panic to find a panacea (and in the not-so-incidental urgency to corner funds) few pursue such essential questions as what makes good writing in the first place, how it has been attained where it has existed, or who can teach it, and how. (1984, p. 80)

Among those attempting to bridge the gap between an understanding of the capabilities of the technology and an understanding of writing and its instruction is a group of researchers at Harvard (Cazden, Michaels, & Watson-Gegeo, 1983). Their three-year study, begun in the fall of 1983, describes the introduction and use of microcomputers to teach writing in the classroom. A project of this duration allows the researchers to take a long-term look at the relationship between microcomputers and students' literacy. The focus of the first year was to describe the activities and interactions of the students and teacher in two classrooms before and after the introduction of one computer in each room and a program for writing called QUILL (described later). In its second year, the researchers worked with the same teachers and new students. During this second year the researchers focused more on the written texts produced with and without the use of interactive software and on the adjustments that teachers and students had to make in their everyday school lives to accommodate and even exploit the presence of the new technology in their midst. In year 3, applying insights from the first two years for the refinement of the software, the researchers introduced microcomputers into new classrooms and used their research on teaching with computers to help other educators incorporate computers into their programs for writing instruction.

Cazden, Michaels, and Watson-Gegeo, like many other researchers examining the link between microcomputers and literacy, will be able to offer educators rich case studies of teachers and children using computers for writing. Case studies are already being used in preservice teacher education programs as vehicles to help students think more critically about their experiences in the field (Florio & Clark, 1983). Case studies of classrooms with computers can offer teachers an opportunity to examine real-life teaching situations repeatedly and critically and anticipate problems and questions before computers are actually introduced into their classrooms.

How Are Computers Used in Teaching Writing?

Though it is beyond the scope of this chapter to describe the wide range of uses to which computers are being put in educational settings, in reviewing the research on computers and writing, one is struck by the scope and innovativeness of many computer projects. Among the case studies noted were descriptions of a system for teaching children to write before they read (Writing to Read, developed by J. H. Martin, reported in Asbell, 1984), talking computers that have given access to the world of language to children without language (Programs for Early Acquisition of Language, by L. Meyers, in Trachtman, 1984), a program that offers students the opportunity to participate in a pen-pal network that spans the nation (Computer Chronicles Newswire, by J. Levin and R. Scollon, in Riel, 1983), and a community computer site that gives opportunities for computer use to families in a low-income barrio (Computer House, in Adams, 1983).

Researchers and educators have developed various categorization systems for the use of computers in education (for example, Collins, 1982; Cazden et al., 1983). One such categorization (Riel, 1983) draws on Kohlberg and Mayer's (1972) taxonomy of traditions in the development of Western educational thought to describe current uses of educational software. Kohlberg and Mayer identified three traditions —the ideologies of cultural transmission, romanticism, and progressivism—that make somewhat different assumptions regarding the objectives of the educational process.

In the cultural transmission model, the task confronting education is to impart the existing knowledge and moral rules of society to each new generation. The material to be learned and the sequence in which it is learned are fixed by the teacher and the materials. Riel suggests that software known as "computer-assisted instruction," the bulk of all educational software, reflects this philosophy of education. While detailed help and direction are provided by these programs, there is a danger that students will learn a particular task as a series of small steps without ever making sense of the whole activity. With respect to writing instruction, these programs assume that writing can be learned best by isolated drill and practice of various facets of the process.

An example of a program that seems to reflect this cultural transmission philosophy comes from the Southwest Regional Laboratory for Educational Research and Development (Shostak, 1982). This organization's efforts at computer assistance to writing instruction have concentrated on four specific aspects of composing: sentence combining, generating content for a particular discourse type, organizing content, and revising. This work is consistent with the cognitive developmental view of writing described earlier in this chapter. Already tied to computers by the metaphorical relationship between artificial and human intelligence, this view of the writing process and its development seems well suited to the constraints of computer systems.

According to Riel (1983), proponents of the second tradition, the romantic, believe that the school environment should allow each individual's good qualities to unfold. The student is placed in a very rich learning environment in which very little guidance is given with respect to what to learn or how to proceed. Riel proposes that discovery or learning-tool software reflects this philosophy. While this approach exposes the learner to the whole of the activity, the lack of direction may at times be overwhelming to the beginner. LOGO, invented by Seymour Papert (1980), is an example of a discovery-oriented program in which children develop their own programming language.

It is curious that Riel discusses only the cultural transmission and romantic traditions in her categorization of educational software. To extend her analogy, interactive computer programs seem to reflect the tradition of progressivism. Here, the task of education is to stimulate children's development by nourishing their natural interaction with others and with the physical aspects of their environment. The work of Hugh Burns exemplifies an interactive system in which students and computers engage in a prewriting interview. Burns writes:

> I have designed, developed, and programmed three computer programs to encourage thinking, programs I call "artificial intuition." These programs ask writers questions based on particular systems of inquiry, specific heuristics— though at some point I hope students will say to themselves, "Wait a minute, I can ask myself such questions." . . . The strength of these programs is that they imitate a way to investigate a topic, not *the* way by any stretch of the imagination, just one way. (1982, p. 22)

Before choosing a computer program (or before deciding how best to use a preselected program), it is important for educators to examine the assumptions underlying the program in relation to their own views about the teaching of writing. This examination may be difficult on two counts. First, it is not always intuitively obvious what assumptions underlie a particular educational software program for teaching writing. Second, one's own underlying assumptions about writing and how to teach must also be subjects for examination and critical reflection if the computer is to "make sense" in the classroom learning environment.

The critical role that teachers play in shaping the impact of computers on children's literacy has been highlighted by researcher Andee Rubin (1983). Rubin is a coinvestigator of a research project examining the effects of the QUILL program on students' writing (Bruce & Rubin, 1983). QUILL is a software package that offers teachers and children a text editor (Writer's Assistant), an information storage and retrieval system (Library), an electronic mail system (Mailbag), a program to help students plan and organize their thoughts (Planner), and a program that allows children to create stories with alternate branches and endings (Story Maker). Though the project has invested considerable time, energy, and money in the testing and refining of this software, Rubin contends that the teacher's view of the educational importance of computers has much more influence than the features of the software itself. Thus an important facet of their project's work is the development and implementation of a teacher training plan for the use of QUILL software in elementary schools. As computer scientist Tom Moran contends, "It's not enough for the system to provide a powerful functional capability if the user cannot make use of it" (Gollman, 1984, p. 22).

Many of the teachers with whom Bruce and Rubin worked expressed initial and recurring concerns about managing the use of the computer effectively. These concerns are not surprising in light of the newness of computers to teachers and students alike. However, Rubin (1983) has also noted that the interaction of class-room management issues with software features has a greater effect on a program's use than the computer or the software itself. In reporting their work in progress, Bruce and Rubin (1983) offer case studies of the six sites where they are field-testing the QUILL program. Their standard format for the sharing of each of the six descriptions included a section on classroom management of QUILL. In reading the case studies presented by Bruce and Rubin, it seems that some teachers fit QUILL into their normal teaching routine, while others reorganized their writing instruction around the computer.

The issue of classroom organization is strongly tied to the controversial problem of the equity of computer use by students. That there is tremendous diversity among schools and even classrooms within the same school with respect to the use of computers is not a new finding (Miller, 1983). Cohen (1983) has found that this diversity manifests itself along several dimensions: the hardware and software available in schools (in both quantity and quality), the accessibility of computers to students, the activities and content considered appropriate, the arrangement of computers in the classroom, the structure of the lessons, curriculum to be covered, and the attitudes of the teachers toward the use of microcomputers.

The Computer Use Study Group (CUSG) of San Diego notes that while we know something about the number of computers that are in U.S. schools, we know less about the distribution and use of computers in the schools (1983). The CUSG group is interested in "trying to determine whether computers will be tools which facilitate equality among different social groups or whether they will be tools which further stratify groups within society" (p. 51). Looking at 21 schools in five districts in California, they found a very strong relationship among (1) the source of funding for computer acquisition, (2) the type of students who are educated using computers, (3) the type of instruction students are exposed to, and (4) the rationale for computer use in the districts studied.

In the CUSG research, financial support seemed most often to come from sources outside the educational system, as did impetus for the acquisition of computers in the schools studied. The CUSG found that "money available for the education of 'gifted and talented' youngsters, 'economically and culturally disadvantaged' students, school improvement programs and the desegregation effort purchased 93% of the computers in these districts" (p. 52).

The CUSG also found a relationship between the source of funds used for computer acquisition and the students who have access to those computers. Differential access to computers and computer use was reflected in the kinds of instruction students received. Lower-class and ethnic minority students received instruction in basic skills—computer-aided drill and practice in which control of the learning is maintained by the computer. White middle-class and ethnic majority students were more likely to receive instruction in computer literacy—programming and problem solving that encouraged learner initiation. As the CUSG concluded, the tracking of students from different "socioeconomic backgrounds through different computer-based curricula stratifies students' access to information technology. Differential access represents one of the ways in which the microcomputer can be used as a tool to contribute further to stratification of our society" (p. 54).

Neither we nor the CUSG wishes to imply that the introduction of microcomputers into a classroom necessarily results in stratification of students. In fact, Bruce and Rubin (1983) highlight in their case studies of the use of QUILL several ways in which teachers took precautions against differential access to computer use in their classrooms (such as setting up schedules for computer usage time and keeping track of the actual amount of time each student spends with the computer).

Also, the motivational qualities of computers were frequently described in the research (Bruce & Rubin, 1983). Whether due to the novelty of the technology, the privacy of the learning experience, the immediacy of feedback, or any number of other factors, there are "success stories" of lower-socioeconomic and ethnic minority children whose interest in school increased with the introduction of microcomputers in their classrooms. Finally, in many classrooms the students work with partners or in teams. Most of the case studies of these classrooms reported that the students enjoyed working with partners. Bruce and Rubin include student quotes such as "It's fun to share ideas with other people," "You get more help from partners," and "The story can be filled with two people's ideas this way" (p. 17). Not every student appreciates this partnership, however, as was reflected in one child's comment that "partners hog the computer" (p. 10).

How Do Educators Participate in This Innovation?

In a handbook for computers in the classroom, researchers Mehan and Souviney (1984) argue that computers are an educational innovation unlike many of the unsuccessful innovations of the past. Many educational innovations have been imposed from outside the schools or from the top of the hierarchy downward. Often these innovations have been dropped soon after external funding has been withdrawn. Rarely have these innovations made much difference in the organization of education within a school. In contrast, Mehan and Souviney argue that the use of micro-computers to help teach writing in school is far more a "grass roots" movement, with support from teachers, parents, and the business community. From this observation they assert that

> innovative teachers, motivated parents and business interests constitute a coali-tion for change that is unique in educational history. It is important to note that this coalition operates closer to the bottom of the school hierarchy than the top. Knowledgeable and innovative teachers have approached neighborhood com-puter stores and have been successful in receiving free or inexpensive software as well as computer hardware for use in their own classrooms. Teachers have been the driving force behind the introduction and spread of computers within schools. (pp. 15–16)

The research needed to assess both this statement and the roles played by educators in the use of technology in school is in its infancy. Still, from what currently exists, several observations can be made. First, learning to use the computer is a necessary but not a sufficient condition for successful use of computers in teaching writing or any other part of the curriculum. The introduction of the computer brings with it software. Like other published, packaged curricular materials, programs for teaching writing with computers carry with them implicit and explicit assumptions about the nature of the writing process, the role of teacher and student, and the organization of the classroom. Second, integrating the new technology into existing curricula and instructional arrangements requires that educators reexamine their own beliefs, values, assumptions, and techniques. Thus the computer functions not only as an instructional intervention but also as an intervention into the plans and actions of educators.

Educators hold a very special place in this "grass roots" movement to introduce new technologies into the classroom. They are responsible for the curriculum and for the face-to-face learning experiences of their students. Knowledge about the technology, though important, merely scratches the surface of the knowledge required to use that technology effectively. The rest of the knowledge required does not come from outsiders expert in the workings of the computer. It comes from educators who are already thoughtful and knowledgeable about their students and about the things they hope their students will learn.

CONCLUSION

This chapter was organized around some perennial concerns of educators interested in writing instruction. In it we have reviewed a number of studies and attempted to inform and to stimulate readers' thinking about their own situations. Some of the themes in this chapter have been recurring ones. For example, writing has lately been viewed as a social and intellectual process, and this view of writing has implications for how educators interpret research and put it to use. In addition, only recently has the teaching of writing been a focus of research, and this research has raised many new questions about the role of the teacher in the instructional process.

Similarly, recent research on the environments in which writing is taught has underscored writing's sensitivity to social context. Teachers operate within classrooms, where they have considerable leeway to structure learning situations. However, they also operate within the larger institution of the school and the community. The norms, policies, and procedures of the school at large can have powerful impact on the way writing is taught in the classroom. Furthermore, societal norms and values about literacy help to shape school writing. The diversity and inequality present in the wider society can enter the classroom. In the face of these realities, there are many things that educators can do to support and enhance all students' growth as writers.

Finally, the chapter has scratched the surface of the important contemporary issue of the computer's place in classroom writing instruction. Far from leaving the educator in the dust in the scurry toward new and technically complicated ways of teaching, research has already begun to show that this movement requires the educator's guidance if it is to be an effective, equitable, and long-lasting one.

This chapter has not raised all the important questions, nor has it fully answered even the few questions it has raised. However, it has attempted to stimulate conversation, self-examination, inquiry, and criticism among educators concerned with the important and perennial challenge of helping students learn to write.

FURTHER READING

Teaching Writing

Elbow, P. (1973). *Writing without Teachers*. London: Oxford University Press. A critical view of typical methods of teaching writing. Elbow offers his own unique program for learning to write, alone or in a group. A key element is free writing. This activity, intended to get writers beyond "blocks," places the production of text first. Writers put their thoughts on paper without stopping to edit or organize; only later do they return to revise. In this practical and imaginative book, Elbow considers not only thinking processes underlying writing but also the social conditions that seem likely to facilitate or impede the flow of ideas on paper.

Flower, L. (1981). *Problem-solving Strategies for Writing*. San Diego, CA: Harcourt Brace Jovanovich. Drawing on her extensive analysis of the self-reports of writers about their thinking during composing, Flower has applied her cognitive model of the writing process to the very practical problem of teaching young adults to do what she calls "real-world writing." Accompanied by a useful teacher's guide, the book breaks the composing process into a series of steps. For each step, strategies, tactics, and exercises are offered. Flower makes use of examples from her extensive data collection of writing samples and authors' comments on their writing.

Graves, D. (1983). *Writing: Teachers and Children at Work*. Exeter, NH: Heinemann. For teachers who want to improve their teaching of writing. Drawing heavily on his own descriptive research and linking growth in writing to oral exchanges between teachers and students, Graves suggests that the book be read as a "collection of workshops" offering practical guidance and research and theory in such areas as the teacher's role, classroom organization and practices, reporting and record keeping, and child growth in writing.

Moffett, J. (1983). *Teaching the Universe of Discourse*. Boston: Houghton Mifflin. (Originally published in 1968.) Considers curriculum and instruction in writing developmentally and as writing is related to oral language. Moffett offers a way of approaching writing not as an isolated content area but as an expressive process that is taught and learned best as it is used. Ideas for teaching writing in the content areas arise as Moffett traces the various types of written discourse learned by a developing writer.

Shaughnessy, M. P. (1977). *Errors and Expectations: A Guide for the Teaching of Basic Writing*. New York: Oxford University Press. Carefully documents the writing of adult BW (basic writing) students at the City University of New York. Shaughnessy attempts to discover how her students learn from mistakes and how she can learn about beginning writers through analysis of their errors. Her book offers both a window on the writing process that is of considerable research interest in its own right and a way for teachers of beginning writers to think about errors in new and constructive ways. Rules and their application, misapplication, and instruction are treated, as are contextual issues such as the writing situations available in school and the beginning writer's self-concept.

Theory and Research on Writing

Glatthorn, A. A. (1981). *Writing in the Schools: Improvement through Effective Leadership*. Reston, VA: National Association of Secondary School Principals. An overview of the current status of writing research and instruction. Glatthorn's primary audience is administrators. With clear and useful tables and charts and succinct text, the author reviews research on the composing process and moves quickly to such practical problems as evaluation of a school's writing program, staff development in writing, curricular improvement, administrative supervision of writing instruction, assessment, and parental involvement. The book includes inventories and checklists that can be used by educators to initiate inquiry and discussion in their own classrooms, schools, and communities.

Kean, J. M. (1983). *The Teaching of Writing in Our Schools* (Fastback No. 193). Bloomington, IN: Phi Delta Kappa Educational Foundation. A lively, succinct synthesis of current research on the writing process. Kean touches briefly on such important issues as the process approach to writing, the environment for writing, assessment of both student writers and writing programs, special learners and their writing needs, and the integration of writing into the rest of the curriculum. A useful bibliography of related readings is included in this handy booklet.

Newkirk, T., & Atwell, N. (Eds.). (1982). *Understanding Writing: Ways of Observing, Learning, and Teaching (K–8)*. Chelmsford, MA: Northeast Regional Exchange, Inc. Writing research conducted by teachers in their own classrooms and on problems they found important. The potpourri of studies covers topics of practical concern to elementary school teachers and researchers alike. However, as the editors point out, "the articles do more than merely recount teaching procedures....the authors are acting as observers, learners, and teachers." This book can be read both for information about the writing instruction process and as an example of a growing trend for teachers (with or without the collaboration of university-based researchers) to frame research questions, collect and analyze data, and report their findings to colleagues. A well-organized selected bibliography on writing and teaching concludes the book.

Parker, R. P., & Davis, F. A. (Eds.). (1983). *Developing Literacy: Young Children's Use of Language*. Newark, DE: International Reading Association. Many leading researchers and scholars in the areas of oral language and literacy have contributed to this informative and stimulating book. While its theme is broader than writing instruction, the collection tackles difficult theoretical and practical issues such as the models of language acquisition we hold and their relation to decisions we make about formal education, the curriculum for literacy in school and its relation to learning, schools as literate environments, and language as a cognitive, cultural, and political phenomenon. Contributors make many efforts to link theory and research to the problems and realities of educational settings.

Writing and Computers

Lawlor, J. (Ed.). (1982). *Computers in Composition and Instruction*. Los Alamitos, CA: SWRL Educational Research and Development. The proceedings of a conference sponsored by the Southwest Regional Laboratory for Educational Research and Development to consider developments in computer-based learning and their potential applications to teaching composition. This book can be read as an early statement of the state of the art, with chapters dealing with hardware, software, and their selection to chapters laying out theories of the composing process and the ways in which computer programs may enhance and extend the teaching and learning of that process. Since books are being published on these topics rapidly and in large number, this book may be read both for its historical value and as a source for references to other work in the field.

Mehan, H., & Souviney, R. (Eds.). (1984). *The Write Help: A Handbook for Computers in Classrooms*. La Jolla, CA: Center for Human Information Processing, University of California. Produced by researchers and teachers, this handbook reviews the current state of computer use in the California school districts where the authors have worked. In addition, it offers ways to think about how microcomputers can be used to achieve unique educational goals. In a very practical section, ideas on the introduction and use of the computer and the integration of the computer into the classroom social system are offered by a group of teachers and collaborating researchers. An appendix of materials that can be adapted by other teachers for use in their own classrooms is included.

The Writing Curriculum

Hillocks, G., Jr. (Ed.). (1982). *The English Curriculum under Fire: What Are the Real Basics?* Urbana, IL: National Council of Teachers of English. A collection of essays examining the crisis in writing instruction in our country. Both the nature of the attack on English education and the concept of the "basics" to which English teachers have been urged to return are explored. The essays enrich our understanding of the composing process and why it is difficult to teach. They call into question tacit curricular assumptions about what writing is and how and why it should be taught, encouraging reflection and reexamination of the writing curriculum.

Special Needs of Students

Cronnell, B. (Ed.). (1981). *The Writing Needs of Linguistically Different Students*. Los Alamitos, CA: SWRL Educational Research and Development. The proceedings of a conference sponsored by the Southwest Regional Laboratory for Educational Research and Development, this book offers a collection of papers on the writing needs of children who come from a variety of racial, ethnic, linguistic, and geographic backgrounds and who do not speak standard English. Cronnell points out that "although most educators probably agree that such students have special needs, very little research has been done to identify these needs and to establish appropriate instructional strategies that can meet these needs." This book is a good starting point for basic information about cultural differences, their importance in the classroom, and the relation of classroom and culture to the process of learning to write.

Whiteman, M. F. (1981). *Writing: The Nature, Development, and Teaching of Written Communication* (Vol. 1). Hillsdale, NJ: Erlbaum. The final section, "Language Differences and Writing," is one of the few collections of writing on the needs of students who are culturally or linguistically different, including a chapter devoted to the written English of deaf adolescents. The chapters in this section stimulate the reader to rethink not only the difficulties faced by beginning writers who do not speak standard English but also our expectations for these students and the opportunities that schools and classrooms provide for them to communicate in the written mode.

Special Issues of Professional Journals

"Learning to Write and Writing to Learn." (1985). *Volta Review, 87*(5). Special issue on research on writing and its implications for education of the hearing-impaired.

"Learning to Write: An Expression of Language." (1980). *Theory into Practice, 19*(3).

"The Psychology of Writing." (1982). *Educational Psychologist, 17*(3).

Research in the Teaching of English, 16(1–2). (1982). Two-part special issue on research on writing.

"Writing Instruction." (1983). *Elementary School Journal, 84*(1).

REFERENCES

Adams, E. V. (1983). The CEDEN Community Computer Education Program: An experiment in educational equity. *Quarterly Newsletter of the Laboratory of Comparative Human Cognition, 5*(3), 55–59.

Applebee, A. L. (1981). *Writing in the secondary school: English and the content areas* (Research Report No. 21). Urbana, IL: National Council of Teachers of English.

Asbell, B. (1984, February 26). Writers Workshop at age 5. *New York Times Magazine,* pp. 55, 63–65, 69, 72.

Au, K. H., & Mason, J. (1981). Social organizational factors in learning to read: The balance of rights hypothesis. *Reading Research Quarterly, 17*(1), 115–152.

Beach, R., & Bridwell, L. (Eds.). (1984). *New directions in composition research.* New York: Guilford Press.

Bereiter, C., & Scardamalia, M. (1981). From conversation to composition: The role of instruction in a developmental process. In R. Glaser (Ed.), *Advances in instructional psychology* (Vol. 2). Hillsdale, NJ: Erlbaum.

Birnbaum, J., & Emig, J. (1983). Creating minds, created texts: Writing and reading. In R. P. Parker & F. A. Davis (Eds.), *Developing literacy: Young children's use of language.* Newark, DE: International Reading Association.

Bremme, D. W., & Erickson, F. (1977). Relationships among verbal and non-verbal classroom behaviors. *Theory into Practice, 5,* 153–161.

Britton, J. (1982). Spectator role and the beginning of writing. In M. Nystrand (Ed.), *What writers know: The language, process and structure of written discourse.* Orlando, FL: Academic Press.

Bruce, B., & Rubin, A. (1983). Phase II for the QUILL project (BBN & The Network): The utilization of technology in the development of basic skills instruction: Written communications. Unpublished report, Cambridge, MA. (Contract No. 3008100314, Department of Education).

Bruner, J. (1976). Language as an instrument of thought. In A. Davis (Ed.), *Problems in language and learning*. London: Heinemann.

Burns, H. (1982). Computer assisted pre-writing activities: Harmonics for invention. In J. Lawlor (Ed.), *Computers in composition instruction*. Los Alamitos, CA: SWRL Educational Research and Development Center.

Cazden, C. B. (1985). Classroom discourse. In M. C. Wittrock (Ed.), *Handbook of research on teaching* (3rd ed.). New York: Macmillan.

Cazden, C. B., John, V. P., & Hymes, D. (Eds.). (1972). *Functions of language in the classroom*. New York: Teachers College Press.

Cazden, C. B., Michaels, S., & Watson-Gegeo, K. (1983). Microcomputers and literacy: The impact of interactive technology on classroom organization, teacher-student interaction, and student writing. (Funded by an NIE Teaching and Learning Program grant.) Unpublished manuscript.

Chall, J. S. (1983). Literacy: Trends and explanations. *Educational Researcher, 12*(9), 3–8.

Clark, C. M., & Florio, S. (1983). The Written Literacy Forum: Combining research practice. *Teacher Education Quarterly, 10*(3), 58–87.

Clark, C. M., & Florio, S., with Elmore, J. L., Martin, J., Maxwell, R. J., & Methany, W. (1982). *Understanding writing in school: A descriptive case study of writing and its instruction in two classrooms* (Research Series No. 104). East Lansing, MI: Michigan State University, Institute for Research on Teaching.

Clay, M. (1975). *What did I write?* Aukland, NZ: Heinemann.

Cohen, M. (1983). Exemplary computer use in education. *Quarterly Newsletter of the Laboratory of Comparative Human Cognition, 5*(3), 46–51.

Collins, A. (1982). Teaching reading and writing with personal computers. In J. Orasanu (Ed.), *A decade of reading research: Implications for practice*. Hillsdale, NJ: Erlbaum.

Computer Use Study Group. (1983). Computers in schools: Stratifier or equalizer? *Quarterly Newsletter of the Laboratory of Comparative Human Cognition, 5*(3), 51–55.

Cook-Gumperz, J., & Gumperz, J. (1981). From oral to written culture: The transition to literacy. In M. F. Whiteman (Ed.), *Writing: The nature, development, and teaching of written communication* (Vol. 1). Hillsdale, NJ: Erlbaum.

Cronnell, B. (Ed.). (1981). *The writing needs of linguistically different students*. Los Alamitos, CA: SWRL Educational Research and Development.

Daiute, C. (1984). Performance limits on writers. In R. Beach & L. Bridwell (Eds.), *New directions in composition research*. New York: Guilford Press.

Dunn, S. (1983). *Themes and variations in a high school creative writing class*. East Lansing, MI: Unpublished manuscript, Michigan State University, Institute for Research on Teaching.

Dunn, S., & Florio-Ruane, S. (1984, April). *Six high school writers: A dialogue journal study*. Paper presented at the annual meetings of the American Educational Research Association, New Orleans, LA.

Dunn, S., Florio-Ruane, S., & Clark, C. M. (1985). The teacher as respondent to the high school writer. In S. W. Freedman (Ed.), *The acquisition of written language: Response and revision*. Norwood, NJ: Ablex.

Emig, J. (1971). *The composing processes of twelfth graders* (Research Series No. 13). Urbana, IL: National Council of Teachers of English.

Erickson, F. (1982). Classroom discourse as improvisation: Relationships between academic task structure and social participation structure in lessons. In L. C. Wilkinson (Ed.), *Communicating in the classroom*. Orlando, FL: Academic Press.

Florio, S. (1979). The problem of dead letters: Social perspectives on the teaching of writing. *Elementary School Journal, 80,* 1–7.

Florio, S., & Clark, C. M. (1982). The functions of writing in an elementary school classroom. *Research in the Teaching of English, 16,* 115–130.

Florio, S., & Clark, C. M. (1983, February). *A phenomenological approach to the "field" in field-based teacher education.* Paper presented at the annual meeting of the Association of Colleges for Teacher Education, Detroit.

Flower, L. S. (1981). *Problem-solving strategies for writing.* Orlando, FL: Harcourt Brace Jovanovich.

Frase, L. T. (Ed.). (1982). Special issue: The psychology of writing. *Educational Psychologist, 17*(3).

Frederiksen, C. H., & Dominic, J. F. (1981). Introduction: Perspectives on the activity of writing. In C. H. Frederiksen & J. F. Dominic (Eds.), *Writing: The nature, development, and teaching of written communication* (Vol. 2). Hillsdale, NJ: Erlbaum.

Freedman, M. (1984, February 1). Those futile attempts to legislate literacy. *Chronicle of Higher Education,* p. 80.

Freedman, S. W. (Ed.). (1985). *The acquisition of written language: Response and revision.* Norwood, NJ: Ablex.

Friere, P. (1980). The adult literacy process as cultural action for freedom. In M. Wolf, M. K. McQuillan, & E. Radwin (Eds.), *Thought and language/language and reading* (Harvard Educational Review Reprint Series No. 14). Cambridge, MA.

Giroux, H. (1979). Mass culture and the rise of the new illiteracy: Implications for reading. *Interchange, 10*(4), 89–98.

Glatthorn, A. (1981). *Writing in the schools: Improvement through effective leadership.* Reston, VA: National Association of Secondary School Principals.

Goffman, E. (1961). *Encounters: Two studies in the sociology of interaction.* Indianapolis: Bobbs-Merrill.

Gollman, D. (1984, March). The human-computer connection. *Psychology Today,* pp. 20–24.

Graves, D. H. (1978). *Balance the basics: Let them write.* New York: Ford Foundation.

Graves, D. H. (1983). *Writing: Teachers and children at work.* Exeter, NH: Heinemann.

Green, J. (1983). Research on teaching as a linguistic process: A state of the art. In E. W. Gorden (Ed.), *Review of research in education* (Vol. 10). Washington, DC: American Educational Research Association.

Gregg, L. W., & Steinberg, E. R. (Eds.). (1980). *Cognitive processes in writing.* Hillsdale, NJ: Erlbaum.

Halliday, M.A.K. (1975). Learning how to mean. In E. Lenneberg and E. Lenneberg (Eds.), *Foundations of language development: Vol. 2. A multidisciplinary approach.* Orlando, FL: Academic Press.

Halliday, M.A.K., & Hasan, R. (1976). *Cohesion in English.* London: Longman.

Heath, S. B. (1981). Toward an ethnohistory of writing in America. In M. F. Whiteman (Ed.), *Writing: The nature, development, and teaching of written communication* (Vol. 1). Hillsdale, NJ: Erlbaum.

Heath, S. B. (1982). Protean shapes in literacy events: Ever-shifting oral and literate traditions. In D. Tannen (Ed.), *Spoken and written language: Exploring orality and literacy.* Norwood, NJ: Ablex.

Heath, S. B. (1983). *Ways with words: Language, life, and work in communities and class-rooms.* London: Cambridge University Press.

Hendrix, R. (1981). The status and politics of writing instruction. In M. F. Whiteman (Ed.), *Writing: The nature, development, and teaching of written communication* (Vol. 1). Hillsdale, NJ: Erlbaum.

Hillocks, G. (Ed.). (1982). *The English curriculum under fire: What are the real basics?* Urbana, IL: National Council of Teachers of English.

Hirsch, E. D., Jr., & Harrington, D. P. (1981). Measuring the communicative effectiveness of prose. In C. H. Frederiksen & J. F. Dominic (Eds.), *Writing: The nature, development, and teaching of written communication* (Vol. 2). Hillsdale, NJ: Erlbaum.

Jackson, P. W. (1968). *Life in classrooms.* New York: Holt, Rinehart and Winston.

Katz, N. M. (1984). Toward an analysis and comparison of current methods of instruction. *Focus, 29*(4), 9–17.

Kean, J. M. (1983). *The teaching of writing in our schools* (Fastback No. 193). Bloomington, IN: Phi Delta Kappa Educational Foundation.

Kohlberg, L., & Mayer, R. (1972). Development as the aim of education. *Harvard Educational Review, 42,* 449–496.

Kreeft, J. (1982). Mutual conversations: Written dialogue as a basis for student-teacher rapport. In J. Staton, R. W. Shuy, J. Kreeft, & L. Reed, *The analysis of dialogue journal writing as a communicative event.* Final report to the National Institute of Education (NIE-G-80-0122). Washington, DC: Center for Applied Linguistics.

Lawlor, J. (Ed.). (1982). *Computers in composition instruction.* Los Alamitos, CA: SWRL Educational Research and Development Center.

Lawlor, J. (1983). Sentence combining: A sequence for instruction. *Elementary School Journal, 84,* 53–62.

Lloyd-Jones, R. (1981). Rhetorical choices. In C. H. Frederiksen & J. F. Dominic (Eds.), *Writing: The nature, development, and teaching of written communication* (Vol. 2). Hillsdale, NJ: Erlbaum.

Loban, W. (1976). *Language development: Kindergarten through grade twelve* (Research Report No. 18). Urbana, IL: National Council of Teachers of English.

Lyman, P. (1983). *Reading, writing and word processing: Toward a phenomenology of the computer age.* East Lansing, MI: James Madison College, Michigan State University. Unpublished manuscript.

Martin, A. M. (1981). *The words in my pencil: Considering children's writing.* Grand Forks, ND: North Dakota Study Group on Evaluation.

Martin, J. (1984). *Curriculum of middle school: A descriptive study of the teaching of writing.* Unpublished dissertation, Michigan State University, East Lansing.

McCutchen, D., & Perfetti, C. A. (1983). Local coherence: Helping young writers manage a complex task. *Elementary School Journal, 84,* 71–75.

McDermott, R. P. (1977). The ethnography of speaking and reading. In R. Shuy (Ed.), *Linguistic theory: What can it say about reading?* Newark, DE: IRA Publications.

Mehan, H. (1979). *Learning lessons: Social organization in the classroom.* Cambridge, MA: Harvard University Press.

Mehan, H., & Souviney, R. (Eds.). (1984). *The write help: A handbook for computers in classrooms.* La Jolla, CA: University of California, Center for Human Information Processing.

Miller, J. J. (1983). *Microcomputer use in San Diego/Imperial County school districts.* San Diego, CA: San Diego County Department of Education.

Moffett, J. (1983). *Teaching the universe of discourse* (2nd ed.). Boston: Houghton Mifflin.

Mosenthal, P. (1983). Defining classroom writing competence: A paradigmatic perspective. *Review of Educational Research, 53,* 217–251.

Mosenthal, P., Tamor, L., & Walmsley, S. (1983). *Research on writing: Principles and methods.* White Plains, NY: Longman.

National Assessment of Educational Progress. (1980). *Writing achievement, 1969–79: Results from the third writing assessment* (Vols. 1–3). Denver: Education Commission of the States.

National Commission on Excellence in Education. (1983). *A nation at risk: The imperative for educational reform.* Washington, DC: U.S. Department of Education.

Papert, S. (1980). *Mindstorms: Children, computers and powerful ideas.* New York: Basic Books.

Parker, R. P. (1983). Schooling and the growth of mind. In R. P. Parker & F. A. Davis (Eds.), *Developing literacy: Young children's use of language.* Newark, DE: International Reading Association.

Perl, S. (1983). How teachers teach the writing process: Overview of an ethnographic research project. *Elementary School Journal, 84,* 19–24.

Riel, M. (1983). Education and ecstasy: Computer chronicles of students writing together. *Quarterly Newsletter of the Laboratory of Comparative Human Cognition, 5*(3), 59–67.

Roehler, L. (1979). Questions and answers about language arts. In H. Barnes (Ed.), *The integration of language arts, multicultural education, and creative drama in the classroom.* East Lansing, MI: College of Education, Michigan State University.

Rubin, A. (1983, November). *What did I do to deserve this? Teachers' view of writing with computers.* Paper presented at the annual meeting of the National Reading Conference, Austin, TX.

Shaughnessy, M. P. (1977). *Errors and expectations: A guide for the teacher of basic writing.* New York: Oxford University Press.

Shaw, R. A., Pettigrew, J., & Van Nostrand, A. D. (1983). Tactical planning of writing instruction. *Elementary School Journal, 84,* 45–51.

Shostak, R. (1982). Computer-assisted instruction: The state of the art. In J. Lawlor (Ed.), *Computers in composition instruction.* Los Alamitos, CA: SWRL Educational Research Development Center.

Shuy, R. (1981, April). *Relating research on oral language function to research on written discourse.* Paper presented at the annual meeting of the American Educational Research Association, Los Angeles.

Sizer, T. (1984). *Horace's compromise: The dilemma of the American high school.* Boston: Houghton Mifflin.

Smith, D. M. (1983). Reading and writing in the real world: Explorations into the culture of literacy. In R. P. Parker & F. A. Davis (Eds.), *Developing literacy: Young children's use of language.* Newark, DE: International Reading Association.

Staton, J., Shuy, R. W., Kreeft, J., & Reed, L. (1982). *The analysis of dialogue journal writing as a communicative event.* Final report to the National Institute of Education (NIE-G-80-0122). Washington, DC: Center for Applied Linguistics.

Szwed, J. F. (1981). The ethnography of literacy. In M. F. Whiteman (Ed.), *Writing: The nature, development, and teaching of written communication* (Vol. 1). Hillsdale, NJ: Erlbaum.

Trachtman, P. (1984, February). Putting computers into the hands of children without language. *Smithsonian,* pp. 42–51.

Vygotsky, L. S. (1962). *Thought and language.* Cambridge, MA: MIT Press. (Originally published in 1934.)

Vygotsky, L. S. (1978). *Mind in society: The development of higher psychological processes.* M. Cole, S. Scribner, V. John-Steiner, & E. Souberman (Eds.). Cambridge, MA: Harvard University Press.

Whiteman, M. F. (Ed.). (1981). *Writing: The nature, development, and teaching of written communication* (Vol. 1). Hillsdale, NJ: Erlbaum.

4 TEACHING SCIENCE

Charles W. Anderson and
Edward L. Smith

S cience education has received increasing attention over the past few years in both
professional and public forums. This attention has tended to focus on two related
issues. First, we need to know *more* science than we used to, whether the concern is
with coping with an increasing role of technology in our daily lives, protecting our
health, preparing and competing for jobs, or exercising responsible judgment as
citizens. However, it seems that as a nation we actually know *less* science than we
used to. Declines in standardized test scores, lack of preparedness on the part of
individuals or groups of students, and unfavorable comparisons between American
students and those of other nations are all cited as indications that our schools are
failing to prepare students adequately for current or future needs.

In this chapter we will discuss both the evidence that gives rise to these concerns
and possible solutions to our current problems. We will begin by describing three
major areas of concern that are shared by science teachers, science educators, and the
general public: (1) How well are our students learning science? (2) How competent
and well prepared are our science teachers? (3) How can we best improve science
teaching in our schools? We will describe the general nature of each concern and
define specific questions that can be illuminated by available research findings.

Our discussion will draw on two distinct bodies of research. The first looks at
science education on a nationwide scale. This includes a series of studies and reports
from the National Science Foundation's status studies (Helgeson, Blosser, & Howe,
1977; Weiss, 1978; Stake & Easley, 1978) to the report of the National Commission
on Excellence in Education (NCEE, 1983). These studies have been influential
in creating awareness of problems in science education. They identify the extent
of the problems and reflect a variety of proposed directions for solutions. However,

This work is sponsored in part by the Institute for Research on Teaching, College of Education, Michigan
State University. The Institute for Research on Teaching is funded primarily by the Program for Teaching
and Instruction of the National Institute of Education, U.S. Department of Education. The opinions
expressed do not necessarily reflect the position, policy, or endorsement of the National Institute of
Education (Contract No. 400-81-0014).

they don't provide very much new understanding of the underlying nature of the problems.

The best insight into the mechanisms that allow these problems to persist and the best ideas for improvement come from a second body of research, consisting mostly of studies conducted in a few classrooms or with only a few individual students. This is research on the teaching and learning of science. For each of the three concerns defined, we will identify both questions that can be addressed by the status studies and questions that can be addressed by the research on teaching and learning.

HOW WELL ARE OUR STUDENTS LEARNING SCIENCE?

Large-Scale Studies of Student Learning

The status studies and reports are nearly unanimous in answering this question, "Not very well." Studies have cited two types of evidence: achievement test scores and enrollment in science courses. Literature describing a crisis in science education focuses on declines in achievement test scores as a major matter of concern. Declines in Scholastic Aptitude Test (SAT) scores have received considerable attention (National Science Foundation [NSF], 1980, pp. 46–47). Perhaps the best data for looking at the trend in the area of science come from three studies by the National Assessment for Educational Progress (NAEP, 1978) and a follow-up study conducted by the Science Assessment and Research Project (Hueftle, Rakow, & Welch, 1983). Science achievement tests were administered to nationwide samples of 9-, 13-, and 17-year-olds at four different times over the past 15 years. The results of those test administrations are summarized in Table 4.1.

A look at Table 4.1 reveals some clear trends. There are generally small but consistent declines in achievement. These declines are larger for the older students, the ones whose science knowledge comes more from school and less from other sources such as books, television, and personal experience. The current "crisis" thus consists of a long-established trend, which does not seem to be accelerating in recent years. However, the existence of this trend is clearly a reason for concern. A close look at how students perform on individual items shows even more reason for concern. The questions that large numbers of American students are missing just are not very hard. Even in 1969, the American population was not particularly scientifically literate; the NAEP data could best be summarized by saying that our science education system has *never* worked very well for the majority of our students.

Enrollment in Science Courses

A second kind of data cited in support of the judgment that our students are not learning enough science concerns student enrollment in science courses. The proportion of high school students enrolled in science courses declined steadily from 1960 to 1977 (Welch, 1979). As argued by Harnischfeger and Wiley (1977), such declines in curriculum exposure are probably major factors in declining achievement. The NSF report (1980) concludes:

TABLE 4.1   MEAN SCORES (PERCENT CORRECT) ON NAEP SCIENCE TEST

Age of Students	Type of Item	Date of Test			
		1969–1970	1972–1973	1976–1977	1981–1982*
9	Content	—	—	—	—
	Inquiry	—	—	53.6	52.6
	Science, technology, and self	—	—	57.1	59.9[†]
	Attitude	—	—	67.0	66.4
13	Content	55.2	53.5[†]	52.8[†]	52.4
	Inquiry	—	—	58.6	58.0
	Science, technology, and society	—	—	56.8	57.4
	Attitude	—	—	57.7	55.1[†]
17	Content	66.7	63.9[†]	61.7[†]	59.7[†]
	Inquiry	—	—	72.2	69.6[†]
	Science, technology, and society	—	—	67.5	67.0
	Attitude	—	—	57.8	56.3

*Data for 1981–1982 were collected by the Science Assessment and Research Program (Hueftle, Rakow, & Welch, 1983).
[†]Change from previous test administration was statistically significant ($p < .05$)

When combined, the course enrollment patterns and achievement data discussed earlier indicate that the relatively few students who have strong interests in the possibility of science or engineering careers are learning as much science and mathematics as they ever did—perhaps even more. However, many students are ending their studies of these subjects at increasingly early stages and are scoring less and less well on achievement measures. There has always, of course, been a large discrepancy in the amount of science and mathematics training acquired by those who are interested in science and engineering careers and those who are not, but the data show that in recent years that division has been widening. (p. 47)

The argument that declining test scores are related to declining enrollment suggests that the reverse might also hold. Indeed, many proposals for increasing science requirements have been pushed forward, most notably in A Nation at Risk, the report of the National Commission on Excellence in Education (1983). This report recommends that the requirement for high school graduation be increased to include three years of science. In contrast, most school districts currently require one year of high school science (National Research Council, 1979, p. 85).

The approach of raising requirements to increase enrollment and thereby improve achievement undoubtedly has merit. However, we feel that there are some important reasons to be cautious about simply requiring all students to take more science courses. Many students may be avoiding science courses because they have learned little or nothing from the science courses that they have already taken. Thus we need to look not only at the number of science courses that students take but also at what students learn when they enroll in specific courses. To investigate this issue, we will turn to the second body of research: research on classroom teaching and learning of science.

Learning from Specific Courses

A growing body of research indicates that meaningful learning in science courses is usually limited to a small minority of students. The students who are "good in science" understand, while all the rest memorize. We will begin by illustrating this point with four specific examples of learning from different science courses.

Example 1: The Coin Toss Problem and College Physics.   The coin toss problem, which is illustrated in Figure 4.1, is a very simple application of Newton's laws of motion, which are taught in almost all high school and college physics courses. According to Newton, a coin tossed upward in the air is subject to only two forces: a downward force due to gravity and a small additional downward force due to air resistance. (In most instances, respondents are instructed to ignore any air resistance.) These forces eventually slow the coin to a stop, and it begins to fall back toward the earth. However, most students also draw or describe an upward force on the coin, a force in the direction of motion. Furthermore, conventional physics teaching doesn't seem to help a lot of students with this problem. In one study of college engineering majors (most of whom had already taken high school physics), the percentage of students answering the question correctly rose from 12% before the beginning of instruction to 28% after one semester of physics and 30% after two semesters (Clement, 1982). Why weren't the other students able to give the correct answer?

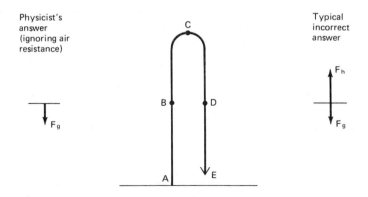

What are the forces on the coin at point B, when it is moving upward through the air?

Physicist's answer (ignoring air resistance)

F_g

Typical incorrect answer

F_h

F_g

Typical incorrect explanation: While the coin is on the way up, the "force from your hand" (F_h) pushes up on the coin. On the way up it must be greater than F_g, otherwise the coin would be moving down.

FIGURE 4.1   The coin toss problem. (Adapted from Clement, 1982)

Example 2: The Rusting Nail and High School Chemistry.   Robert is a student who has completed about four months of instruction in high school chemistry, including instruction on chemical reactions. He is passing the course. When he is asked to explain what happens when a nail rusts, this is his explanation:

> ...the coldness reacts on it [the nail]...plastic doesn't rust because coldness doesn't cause the same reaction...rusting is a breakdown of the iron because it [coldness] brings out the rusting...it [coldness] almost draws it [rust] out, like a magnet...like an attractor it brings it out.

Robert gave similarly unscientific explanations for other chemical changes, including the oxidation of copper and the burning of a match. Yet he consistently indicated that he was satisfied with his explanations, that they made sense to him, and that he thought they were similar to those that would be given by a scientifically trained adult. He believed that the main deficiency in his answers was that he was not using enough scientific terminology (Hesse, 1986). How could Robert (and many students like him) be so unaffected by four months in a chemistry class?

Example 3: Food for Plants and Elementary School Biology.   Table 4.2 displays the answers of four fifth-grade students before and after a six-week unit on "producers" from a widely used and highly respected elementary school science program (Knott, Lawson, Karplus, Thier, & Montgomery, 1978). Students were supposed to learn through a series of experiments and discussions that plants are producers: Rather than consuming food, they produce it themselves through the process of photosynthesis. Renee, Mike, and Andrea are typical of many of the students who experienced this unit. They added sunlight to their previous lists of things that they considered "food for plants." Only 7% of 213 students studied ended the unit learning the intended conception, that plants get food *only* by making it themselves (Roth, Smith, & Anderson, 1983). Why didn't the unit work for the other 93% of the students?

Example 4: Light and Vision and Elementary School Physical Science.   Figure 4.2 shows a question from a test given to 113 fifth-grade students before and after a five-week unit on light and vision (Anderson & Smith, 1983a). Only 5% of the students were able to answer this question correctly before the unit began. The others showed no awareness that the boy sees by detecting light reflected off the tree. At the conclusion of the unit, 24% of the students answered this question correctly. Why didn't the other 76% learn about the role of reflected light in seeing?

TABLE 4.2.   STUDENTS' ANSWERS TO THE QUESTION "DESCRIBE WHAT FOOD IS FOR PLANTS" BEFORE AND AFTER INSTRUCTION ON PHOTOSYNTHESIS

Student	Pretest	Posttest
Renee	Fertilizer, water	Water, fertilizer, light
Mike	Fertile, rich soil	Soil is a food for plants; fertilizer, sun, water
Karin	I don't know	The cotyledon and sunlight and the minerals in the soil
Andrea	Plant food, water, sunshine	Water, dirt, soil, sun (they need it for energy and their making of food)

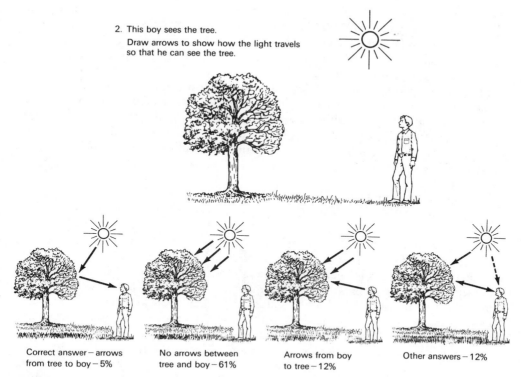

FIGURE 4.2   Percentage of students with various pretest answers to the boy and tree problem. (Anderson & Smith, 1983a)

Implications.   Results like those cited have been documented in dozens of studies covering all scientific disciplines (Driver & Erickson, 1983; Helm & Novak, 1983). Students who successfully memorize formulas and pass courses still fail to apply scientific concepts even to relatively straightforward problems, especially if those problems involve objects or situations that students know from everyday experience. The researchers engaged in these studies have generally been less interested in documenting the extent of failure than in understanding why students fail. It is for their insights into this question that this body of research is most valuable.

Why Is Science So Hard to Learn?

The students just described might have failed to learn because the teaching was bad. However, research on teaching and learning of science has documented many situations where students persist in giving incorrect answers in spite of teaching that is "good" by any reasonable standards. Furthermore, patterns in those incorrect answers suggest another reason that students might stay committed to their incorrect answers. *Those incorrect answers make sense to the students.* Cars, balls, and other objects in our everyday experience come to a stop unless something is done to maintain their motion, so doesn't any motion require a force? We know that nails rust when they are left in cold, damp places, so isn't coldness responsible for the rusting process? We know that *we* get food from a variety of sources; why not plants, too? Can't you buy plant food in the store? Don't we say "I see the tree," rather than "I see the light reflected by the tree"?

In general, there are consistent understandable patterns in the incorrect answers that students give to questions like those in the examples. Researchers in this area attribute these patterns of incorrect answers to knowledge structures that are described by a variety of terms, including misconceptions, naive theories, preconceptions, preconceived notions, and alternative frameworks. Although there are differences among the meanings that researchers attach to these terms, the similarities are more important. An awareness of these alternate theories and their importance has arisen because of parallel revolutions in the philosophies of science and cognitive psychology.

Philosophers and historians of science such as Stephen Toulmin (1972) and Thomas Kuhn (1970) have studied how scientists develop new theories and how those theories come to be accepted by a scientific community. Contrary to most earlier views that theory emerges logically from data, they view theory as creative invention that defines questions, points toward relevant data, and provides the basis for interpreting or giving meaning to data. Prolonged failure of a theory to raise interesting questions or explain data adequately creates conditions favorable to the development of new theories. Rather than simply adding new knowledge, the successful emergence of such alternatives has profound effect on what scientists do, how they do it, and even on what they define as "knowing."

Piaget (Furth, 1969) and many contemporary cognitive psychologists view human thinking as theory-dependent in much the same way. We understand and act on our world in terms of our current theorylike knowledge structures or conceptions. They direct us to seek certain information and provide the basis for interpreting the information we encounter. They provide our immediate options for acting in the world. They are thus the basic mechanisms by which we understand or comprehend. Toulmin (1972) called attention to the parallel between knowledge growth in science and in individuals, referring to "the problem of conceptual change."

Thus students spontaneously construct theories that help them to interpret familiar phenomena before they begin formal science instruction. These naive theories are usually understandable and sensible; they are in accord with common experience and everyday language; and they provide reasonable explanations of what we see around us.

An awareness of these naive theories, however, leads to a very revealing description of what must happen when students learn science. They cannot simply add new knowledge to what they already know. Instead they must abandon habits of thought that they have used successfully for many years in favor of new, more complex, and often counterintuitive ways of thinking. No wonder learning science is so hard!

Conceptual Change and the Science Curriculum

This view of science learning also has important implications for the science curriculum. Rather than treating the science curriculum as a set of facts, concepts, or theories that students must master, a conceptual-change view of learning implies that the curriculum consists of a few major conceptual changes that students must undergo, accompanied by a great deal of "filling in the details." The detailed facts, concepts, and theories of science are meaningful to students only if they can be placed in a meaningful conceptual context.

One of the most valuable contributions of a view of learning as conceptual change is the insight it provides into the nature of learning with *understanding*. This is learning in which students abandon naive conceptions and adopt more scientific alternatives. For students who fail to change their naive conceptions, the only alternatives are to memorize new information without understanding—what Ausubel (1968) calls "rote learning"—or misinterpret that information in terms of their naive misconceptions. Thus teaching that allows students to retain their naive conceptions is doomed to produce only misunderstanding or rote memorization. The available evidence indicates that such teaching is all too common in our schools.

Why does such teaching persist? If science teachers want their students to understand (as most teachers surely do), why do so many students continue to memorize or misunderstand? To answer these questions we turn to research on the background and the behavior of science teachers.

HOW COMPETENT AND WELL PREPARED ARE SCIENCE TEACHERS?

As in the case of student learning, the status studies and the research on science classroom teaching have investigated teacher competence and preparation in quite different ways. As a result, they produce different but complementary types of information. The status studies have looked at teachers' feelings about their own competence and at their professional education and background. The studies of classroom teaching have focused on the actual performance of teachers in science classrooms.

Results from the Status Studies: Teachers' Science Backgrounds and Personal Judgments

Considerable attention has been focused on the science content preparation of teachers who are currently teaching science at the elementary and secondary levels. There is an increasing trend for science to be taught by teachers without a major in the subject that they are teaching. For example, nearly half of those teaching chemistry in Michigan in the early 1980s did not have chemistry majors. Nearly two-thirds of those teaching physics did not have physics majors (Hirsch, 1983). Nationally, more than three-fourths of the states reported shortages of general science, chemistry, and physics teachers during the 1981–1982 school year. Of teachers newly hired to teach high school mathematics or science in 1981, half were unqualified and were teaching with emergency certificates (Hurd, 1982).

At the elementary level, where few teachers have science majors or minors, only 22% of the teachers judge themselves adequately prepared to teach science. In contrast, 67% judge themselves adequately prepared to teach reading (Weiss, 1978; National Research Council, 1979).

These data point toward a need for increased emphasis on both preservice and in-service teacher education in science. However, we feel that they *understate* the extent of the problem. We can accept that teachers who say they have an inadequate background or who lack science content knowledge are not adequately prepared, but is the converse true? Are self-confidence and science content knowledge enough? What other kinds of knowledge do science teachers need?

To answer these questions, we turn from the status studies to investigations of classroom teaching and learning in science. If we can identify and study effective science teachers, then we can understand better what they do that makes them effective and what knowledge they need to perform effectively.

Defining and Describing Effective Science Teaching

Our discussion of classroom research on effective science teaching begins with a question that all researchers on teaching effectiveness must deal with in one way or another: How do you tell good teaching from bad? The performance of teachers can be judged by many different criteria, leading to different conclusions about what effectiveness is. Therefore, we begin by stating and defending our position, admitting that other criteria could lead to other conclusions about effectiveness.

Our definition of effective science teaching focuses on the critical learning problem of conceptual change. At a minimum, science teaching must help students overcome naive conceptions or habits of thought and replace them with scientific concepts and principles. If teachers fail to achieve this minimal goal, misunderstanding or rote memorization is inevitable.

This definition makes it possible to investigate effective science teaching empirically. The techniques developed by researchers into student scientific thinking can be used to identify critical conceptual changes that must take place if students are to understand a scientific topic. Then various teaching techniques can be tried, and the most successful can be described.

A small number of studies describe such empirical investigations. Most of these studies involved development of instructional procedures and materials designed to address specific naive student conceptions and to develop alternative scientific conceptions (Anderson & Smith, 1983b; Minstrell, 1984; Nussbaum & Novick, 1982; Roth, Anderson, & Smith, 1983). These efforts were much more successful than conventional instruction in bringing about conceptual changes in students. In each instance the authors described features of their successful instruction that contrasted with the less successful conventional instruction.

But how can the essential features of teaching for conceptual change be described? One kind of description focuses on teachers' classroom behavior: They asked certain kinds of questions, spent a certain percentage of their time in laboratory activities, and so forth. However, a strictly behavioral approach to describing teaching for conceptual change doesn't work very well. Some of the most important characteristics of conceptual-change teaching concern cognitive issues such as how teachers decide what to do in a classroom or how students think about what is happening. Therefore, our description of effective teaching for conceptual change operates at three different levels:

1. Student thinking. One kind of description of successful teaching focuses on how students think when they are undergoing conceptual change. Successful teaching is then defined as whatever helps students think appropriately.
2. Teaching strategies. Knowing how students should be thinking is not the same as actually making it happen. An adequate description of successful instruction must

therefore also include what happens in classrooms, what teachers *do* to promote appropriate thinking.

3. Teacher knowledge and skills. The study of teachers' performance ultimately leads us back to a question posed earlier: What is the knowledge that underlies effective performance?

Describing Effective Teaching in Terms of Student Thinking

One way of trying to describe what effective teaching consists of is to watch the *students* rather than the teacher. What are they doing and thinking when someone is teaching well? What are they doing and thinking when teaching is ineffective? Our answers to these questions are far from complete, especially at the critical level of student thinking. Even the students themselves are not fully aware of all their thoughts, and those thoughts are inevitably modified by any attempt to verbalize or describe them.

Nevertheless, there are some useful partial answers. Perhaps the best of these is that of Posner, Strike, Hewson, and Gertzog (1982). They suggest that in order for instruction to produce a basic change in students' conceptions, it must meet the following criteria:

1. Students must become dissatisfied with their existing conceptions.
2. Students must achieve a minimal initial understanding of the scientific conception.
3. The scientific conception must appear plausible.
4. Students must see the scientific conception as fruitful or useful in understanding a variety of situations.

These criteria are quite useful in understanding why some teaching strategies seem to work and others don't. The teaching strategies that work include elements that help students achieve all four criteria. The teaching strategies that don't work generally give students little or no help in achieving some of the criteria.

Describing Effective Teaching Strategies

A second way of describing effective teaching for conceptual change is to focus on teachers and what they do in the classroom. What teaching strategies or patterns of behavior contribute most to effectiveness in teaching for conceptual change? In summarizing the results of classroom studies that addressed this question (Roth, Anderson, & Smith, 1983; Minstrell, 1984; Nussbaum & Novick, 1982; Roth, 1984), we focus on how effective teachers for conceptual change accomplish three tasks that confront all science teachers: presenting information, using demonstrations and laboratory activities, and questioning.

Presenting Information.   A first response of many teachers to research findings that students have not learned a particular scientific conception is to ask, "Why not just tell them—explain the scientific conception to the students?" One answer to this question is, "That's what we usually do, and it usually doesn't work." Much instruction, especially at the secondary and postsecondary levels, consists of presenting information. Lecture, lecture-discussion, and having students read textbooks are the primary activities of teaching at those levels. Such presentations almost always include information that students are subsequently found not to have learned or understood. Why don't conventional presentations of information work?

The problems with most presentations to students arise from the teacher's failure to take students' naive conceptions into account. An individual's conceptions serve as the organizing and interpretive framework for new information. Therefore, presentations of detailed information organized according to the scientific conception are not comprehended or are misinterpreted by students who hold naive conceptions. For example, explanations of color vision in terms of the relative absorption and reflection of different colors of light make little sense to students who believe that we see by perceiving objects directly. Understanding this explanation of color vision depends on the underlying conception of vision as the detection of light reflected from objects.

Thus students can understand detailed scientific information only if they understand basic scientific conceptions. However, simply stating the scientific conception is hardly ever sufficient to bring about conceptual change. For example, instruction in Newtonian mechanics almost always includes explanations of Newton's first law: Objects in motion tend to stay in motion unless acted upon by some force. Nonetheless, many students leave such instruction with the contrary notion that motion cannot continue without a force.

Another question often comes from teachers, primarily at the elementary level, who have a strong commitment to a hands-on or discovery approach to teaching. Such teachers tend to ask, "Should we *ever* come right out and tell students the answers?" Briefly, the answer is yes. One of the requirements for conceptual change (from the naive conception to the scientific conception) is that the students develop an initial minimal understanding of the scientific conception (Posner et al., 1982). Students usually cannot come up with these conceptions on their own, so some presentation of such new conceptions is essential (Atkin & Karplus, 1962; Smith & Anderson, 1984). In each of the successful instances of conceptual change that we reviewed, the scientific conception was explained directly to the students.

Thus it seems that presentation of scientific concepts is necessary, but it is usually done in ways that don't work. However, the classroom studies also provide examples of ways of presenting information that *did* work. What did the teachers do right in those situations? Let's look at an example.

In example 4 earlier we showed that most fifth-graders do not understand the role that reflected light plays in seeing. How can we tell students that we see by detecting the light that objects reflect? One approach is incorporated into the textbook (Blecha, Gega, & Green, 1979) that the students were using in classrooms that we observed. For example, this textbook contains the following passage.

Bouncing Light
Have you ever thrown a rubber ball at something?
If you have, you know that when the ball hits
most things, it bounces off them. Like a rubber
ball, light bounces off most things it hits.

When light travels to something opaque, all the
light does not stop. Some of this light bounces off.
When light travels to something translucent or trans-

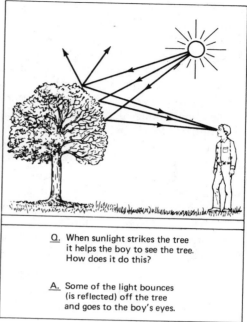

Q. When sunlight strikes the tree
it helps the boy to see the tree.
How does it do this?

Q. When sunlight strikes the tree
it helps the boy to see the tree.
How does it do this?

A. Some of the light bounces
(is reflected) off the tree
and goes to the boy's eyes.

FIGURE 4.3   Overhead transparency presenting a scientific explanation of the role of light in seeing. (Anderson & Smith, 1983a)

parent, all the light does not pass through. Some of
this light bounces off. When light bounces off things
and travels to your eyes, you are able to see.
(p. 154)

However, simply having the students read this passage was not very successful. Only 20% of 113 children in the five classrooms using this text came to understand seeing as detecting reflected light (Anderson & Smith, 1983a).

In contrast, consider another way of presenting similar information. Figure 4.3 illustrates one of a set of 13 overhead projection transparencies made available to the same teachers in the second year of the study. Each transparency first presents a situation and a question calling for an explanation. An overlay presents the scientific conception in the form of an answer to the question.

Using these transparencies and the accompanying information, the teachers were able to help 78% of the students come to understand seeing as the detection of reflected light, a threefold increase over year 1 (Anderson & Smith, 1983a). What accounts for their improvement? One of the major changes between the two years was the nature of the teachers' presentations of the scientific conception.

The question posed in Figure 4.3—How does the light help the boy see the tree?—typically elicits responses reflecting student misconceptions. Thus students see the contrast between their own answers and the scientific alternative presented in the overlay. This kind of contrasting was common to the presentations of scientific conceptions in all the successful teaching instances (Anderson & Smith, 1983b).

Another feature of this example was also common to the successful instances.

The presentation of a scientific conception either involved or was immediately followed by the application of the conception to a specific phenomenon (in this case, seeing a tree): This provided the teachers with an opportunity to diagnose problems in student comprehension and give them corrective feedback.

In the successful instances of teaching for conceptual change, the presentations of the scientific conceptions were also emphasized and distinguished from less important auxiliary information. The key scientific conceptions were not presented as simply single facts among many. These presentations, along with opportunities for application and feedback, were typically repeated several times. The importance of such repetition was expressed by several researchers (Roth, 1985; Minstrell, 1984; Smith & Anderson, 1984).

These three features of presentations of scientific conceptions—direct contrast with student misconceptions, immediate application to explaining a phenomenon, and explicit emphasis with repetition—were common to the successful instances of teaching for conceptual change. These features apparently helped meet the requirements that students achieve a minimal initial understanding of the new conception and find it plausible (criteria 2 and 3, respectively, of Posner et al., 1982).

Laboratory Activities, Demonstrations, and Applications: Relating Concepts to Phenomena

Laboratory and hands-on experiences are widely advocated for the teaching of science. Laboratory activities are a part of many secondary school and college science courses, and most elementary school science programs include recommended hands-on activities. Are hands-on activities essential or important for student learning in science?

To answer this question requires that distinctions be made among the various kinds of things that are learned in science. Skills in performing science processes such as making measurements and manipulating laboratory apparatus can be practiced only with direct experience with appropriate materials and phenomena. For learning science content, however, the answer is less clear-cut. The results of the studies of student learning described earlier show that traditional science laboratory activities are *not* very useful for helping students undergo conceptual change.

However, hands-on activities of some sort played an important role in all the studies of successful teaching for conceptual change. As with presentation of scientific information, teachers who want to teach for conceptual change must ask not *whether* to use laboratory activities but *how* to use them.

In fact, a focus on hands-on or laboratory activities is probably too narrow. In more general terms, successful teaching for conceptual change provides students with many opportunities to relate the scientific concepts they are studying to real-world phenomena through laboratory activities, demonstrations, audiovisual aids, and discussions of familiar phenomena.

One use of phenomena common to the successful instances of conceptual-change teaching was described earlier. Applications of newly presented scientific conceptions to specific phenomena were used to diagnose student misconceptions, provide corrective feedback, and contrast scientific and naive explanations. The phenomena used were often familiar, everyday events. Use of such phenomena helps students realize that science applies to their world, not just to exotic "scientific" phenomena. They help the students to view the scientific conceptions as plausible.

Several researchers (e.g., Nussbaum & Novick, 1982) have proposed challenging students' naive conceptions with "discrepant events," phenomena with results contrary to student expectations. For example, contrary to most novices' predictions, a pad of steel wool gets heavier when it "burns up." Such events do not automatically undermine students' naive conceptions since conceptions, like scientific theories, can be fixed up to account for almost anything (Hewson & Hewson, 1984). But they can be useful in creating dissatisfaction with students' naive conceptions (Posner's criterion 1), especially when the scientific conception is shown to explain such events with relative ease. This contrast can also enhance students' sense of the usefulness of the scientific alternative (criterion 4).

Not only discrepant events but also familiar, everyday events can be used to challenge students' naive conceptions. Students' naive explanations of familiar phenomena often have shortcomings that the students can grasp when pointed out and contrasted with scientific explanations. For example, in another of our overhead transparencies for the unit on light, a girl is shown standing on the opposite side of a wall from a car. The question is posed: "Why can't the girl see around the wall?" A typical answer is "You can see only in straight lines." This is essentially another way of saying "You cannot see around things" and thus constitutes circular reasoning. *Why* can we see only in straight lines? The difficulty students have in answering this question in terms of the naive conception contrasts with the straightforward scientific explanation provided on the overlay to the transparency: "Because light reflecting from objects travels in straight lines, it cannot curve around objects to our eyes." The shortcoming of the naive conception contrasted with the success of the scientific alternative makes this use of an everyday phenomenon effective in both creating student dissatisfaction with their naive conception (criterion 1) and enhancing their sense of the fruitfulness of the scientific alternative (criterion 4).

We have discussed the roles of phenomena in addressing all four of the criteria for conceptual change. In all these instances, the phenomena were chosen because they set up contrasts between naive student conceptions and the scientific conceptions. However, such phenomena do not speak for themselves. For phenomena to be useful in promoting conceptual change, students must not only encounter them but must also become actively involved in trying to *explain* them.

Questions and the Use of Phenomena

The asking of questions is a common occurrence in most classrooms. However, questions differ dramatically in their effects on both students and teachers. Consider the following examples:

1. True or false? Light travels in straight lines.
2. What are some things that help us to see?
3. Why can't the girl see around the wall?

What thinking is each of these questions likely to stimulate in the students?

The true-false question is from the "Test on Understanding" at the end of the unit "Light" in a fifth-grade science textbook (Blecha et al., 1979, p. 190). Even if they understand nothing about light, many students can recognize that this statement is identical to a statement presented earlier in the text and reiterated on the previous page (p. 189) as a "main idea." In fact, Roth (1985) has shown that many students can answer questions like this correctly even if they remember nothing about the text at all! We found that students who had little conceptual understanding of light and vision did quite well on this test (Slinger, Anderson, & Smith, 1983). Some "test on understanding"! Thus the first question, which simply asks students to recall a statement, is of little use in teaching for conceptual change.

The second question is from an introductory page of the same unit (Blecha et al., 1979, p. 145). The "sample answer" included in the teacher's edition is as follows: "Light shines on things and bounces off them to my eyes. My eyes send messages about what I look at to my brain. Then I see things." However, students in the classes we observed seldom mentioned light and never gave any explanation of the role of light in seeing, scientific or naive. Instead they typically talked about eyeglasses and telescopes. The second question, like the first, is of little use in promoting conceptual change. It is too vague and open-ended even to lead to discussion of important issues.

Question 3 is posed on the overhead transparency described earlier. In one classroom this question led to the following discussion:

T: (Puts up transparency #2.) Why can't the girl see around the wall?
ANNIE: The girl can't see around the wall because the wall is opaque.
T: What do you mean when you say the wall is opaque?
ANNIE: You can't see through it. It is solid.
BRIAN: (calling out) The rays are what can't go through the wall.
T: I like that answer better. Why is it better?
BRIAN: The rays of light bounce off the car and go to the wall but they can't go through the wall.
T: Where are the light rays coming from originally?
STUDENT: The sun.
ANNIE: The girl can't see the car because she is not far enough out.
T: So you think her position is what is keeping her from seeing it. (She flips down the overlay with the answer.) Who was better?
CLASS: Brian.
T: (to Annie) Would she be able to see if she moved out beyond the wall?
ANNIE: Yes.
T: Why?
ANNIE: The wall is blocking her view.
T: Is it blocking her view? What is it blocking?
S: Light rays.
T: Light rays that are doing what?
ANNIE: If the girl moves out beyond the wall, then the light rays that bounce off the car are not being blocked.
(Roth, Anderson, & Smith, 1983, p. 12)

This discussion illustrates several important features of teachers' use of questions in the successful instances of conceptual-change teaching. First, the initial question asked for an explanation of a specific phenomenon. Explanation questions tend to drive student thinking beyond recall of specific facts to the application of their conceptions. The resulting responses often provide the teacher with useful evidence about student conceptions. However, the teacher did more than simply pose the question. She followed up in ways that encouraged students to

- clarify and complete their explanations
- compare alternative explanations

- contrast specific aspects of the naive and scientific explanations
- construct a scientific explanation in their own words.

As reflected here, the teacher's use of explanation questions in conjunction with phenomena is an important aspect of teaching for conceptual change. Explanation questions can be usefully posed under several different kinds of circumstances to serve several different functions in teaching for conceptual change:

1. Diagnosing students' conceptions. When the teacher needs to assess the students' naive or current conceptions, explanation questions are especially useful for generating data for such diagnoses. Teachers in the successful instances often encouraged debate among students for this purpose (Anderson & Smith, 1983b; Minstrell, 1984).
2. Challenging students' naive conceptions. To create dissatisfaction with students' naive conceptions, follow-up to explanation questions can be used to drive student thinking to confront discrepancies, contradictions, or gaps in their thinking. Such questions can lead students to recognize the need for or relevance of a new conception (criterion 1).
3. Diagnosing and correcting problems with students' interpretation of a new conception. The posing of an explanation question immediately after the introduction of a new scientific conception drives students' thinking to use their new conception. This provides the teacher with a basis for diagnosing problems in students' interpretations and providing corrective feedback.
4. Applying the scientific conception to new phenomena. This helps students to see that it is useful in a variety of situations (criterion 4). Such applications also help students to understand auxiliary facts and ideas that may be important. They also serve as a basis for continuing to challenge naive conceptions or clarify scientific conceptions, if this is necessary.

Describing the Knowledge Needed for Effective Teaching

Use of the strategies just described leads to superior student learning, especially when conceptual-change learning is considered. These strategies, however, are rarely used in most science classrooms. Why not? We believe that most teachers do not know how to teach this way. What do teachers need to know? We believe that successful teaching for conceptual change depends on two kinds of knowledge. Teachers must have both a proper orientation toward teaching and learning and a good deal of specific information about the subject matter and the students that they are currently teaching.

Teachers' Orientations toward Science Teaching and Learning. In our research we have described four general patterns of thought and behavior related to science teaching and learning. Of the four, only the pattern that we have labeled conceptual-change teaching generally produces conceptual change in students. Let's review all four.

1. ACTIVITY-DRIVEN TEACHING. We have observed this orientation primarily among elementary school teachers who are uncomfortable teaching science. These teachers focus primarily on the activities to be carried out in the classroom: textbook

reading, demonstrations, experiments, answering questions, and the like. These teachers are unsure how specific activities should contribute to student learning. They try to follow the recommendations of the authors of their textbook or teacher's guide as closely as possible, assuming (or hoping) that student learning will result. Unfortunately, this hope is generally not realized. In fact, because they frequently do not understand the rationale for suggested activities, activity-driven teachers often unknowingly modify or delete crucial parts of the program, making learning of the scientific theories almost impossible for their students (Olson, 1983; Smith & Sendelbach, 1982).

2. DIDACTIC TEACHING.   We have encounted this orientation toward teaching far more often than any other among teachers at all levels. Teachers with this orientation treat the teaching of science primarily as a process of organizing and presenting content to students. They expect the students, in turn, to study and to learn the content. Since they focus on presenting content rather than on student thinking, they generally fail to see that their students have misconceptions or that those misconceptions affect students' understanding. Consequently, most students remain committed to their misconceptions (Slinger et al., 1983; Eaton, Anderson, & Smith, 1984).

An important factor in perpetuating didactic teaching is that didactic teachers seldom ask their students the right kinds of questions. Recall questions (e.g., "What is the chemical formula for photosynthesis?") provide teachers with no hint about the existence or the nature of their students' misconceptions. Students can also answer recall questions without ever understanding that the questions are about topics of interest to them. Photosynthesis, for example, is not just "about" chemical formulas, it is also about how plants get their food. Thus didactic teaching and the asking of recall questions tend to be combined in a self-perpetuating cycle.

3. DISCOVERY TEACHING.   Some teachers using activity-based programs try to avoid telling their students answers, encouraging them instead to develop their own ideas from the results of experiments. They ask their students to interpret their observations in open-ended ways, assuming that the performance of the experiments will eventually lead students to develop the appropriate scientific conceptions. In the absence of direct information and feedback from the teachers, however, students generally use their own misconceptions as the basis for interpretation of activities and experiments (Roth, 1984; Smith & Anderson, 1984). Again, the result is that students remain committed to their misconceptions.

Often associated with discovery teaching is an emphasis on the importance of learning science processes: skills such as observing, measuring, and making inferences. The argument goes that students' most important learning from doing experiments is not conceptual but procedural; in doing experiments they are learning and practicing science process skills.

We believe that this argument ignores the interdependence of process and content in science. Scientists developed process skills not because those skills were important for their own sake but because the scientists wanted to understand better how the world works. Thus the pursuit of conceptual understanding is what gives meaning to process skills, and students who practice process skills without gaining conceptual understanding are engaged in another form of rote learning.

4.   CONCEPTUAL-CHANGE TEACHING.   Earlier we described some of the teaching strategies associated with what we call conceptual-change teaching. Teachers can never use those strategies consistently without understanding what their students are thinking. Thus conceptual-change teaching involves both the classroom behavior described and a pattern of thought in which the teacher continually diagnoses student conceptions, considers where they are in the process of conceptual change, and acts accordingly.

Specific Knowledge Needed for Conceptual-Change Teaching.   Although an understanding of the process of conceptual change and an orientation toward conceptual-change teaching are necessary for success in inducing conceptual change, we can testify from our own teaching experience that they are not sufficient. In addition to an appropriate general orientation, conceptual-change teaching must be based on knowledge specific to the topic being taught. When that knowledge is lacking, even teachers who are oriented toward conceptual change must fall back into activity-driven, didactic, or discovery behavior patterns, all of which demand less specific knowledge than conceptual-change teaching.

Our research suggests that effective conceptual-change teaching depends on topic-specific knowledge of at least three different types: knowledge of content, knowledge of students, and knowledge of teaching strategies.

1.   KNOWLEDGE OF CONTENT.   Teaching for conceptual change requires sound knowledge of the topic under study. Rather than viewing the content as a string of facts, as is typical of didactic teachers, conceptual-change teachers must be able to identify the most basic and important principles and organize their knowledge around those, seeing how those principles are related to other ways of understanding the world, including the students' misconceptions. The development of student understanding of these basic conceptions is the primary goal of instruction. Conceptual-change teaching strategies also require that teachers have knowledge of a range of real-world phenomena and how scientific conceptions explain them.

2.   KNOWLEDGE OF STUDENTS.   While all of the approaches to teaching require a certain amount of knowledge about how students typically respond to instruction, the conceptual-change orientation to instruction is unique in requiring knowledge of the misconceptions students bring with them to instruction. Conceptual-change teachers must combine knowledge of content with knowledge of students' misconceptions to construct learning goals for conceptual-change teaching, that is, the changes in students that must be brought about through instruction.

3.   KNOWLEDGE OF TEACHING STRATEGIES.   A teacher's understanding of students and the content to be taught will not ensure that students will learn that content. The teacher must still make learning take place through the use of appropriate teaching strategies and classroom activities. The strategies described earlier in this chapter can be used to help students change their conceptions, but they must be used in a flexible and responsive manner. The teacher must diagnose student misconceptions and monitor student progress, then use that information to select activities that challenge student misconceptions, introduce scientific conceptions, and promote student understanding of the scientific conceptions.

Implications

For us, thinking about the specific knowledge needed for various styles of teaching helps to explain why didactic teaching is so prevalent in our schools, even among the teachers (and there are many) who are sensitive to their students' difficulties with science and concerned about the students they are not reaching. Most textbooks and other teaching materials supply information about content and suggestions about teaching strategies (sometimes sound, sometimes not) but lack specific information about students' misconceptions. Developing an adequate understanding of students' misconceptions is a very long and difficult process, usually requiring months or years of work on a single topic. Thus no teacher can hope to develop such knowledge for all topics in the curriculum without outside help.

But there is no outside help for most teachers. Thus a major cause for the prevalence of didactic science teaching in our schools and the resultant disappointing student learning is that our educational system fails to help teachers acquire the knowledge they need for conceptual-change teaching.

HOW CAN WE IMPROVE SCIENCE TEACHING?

Almost everyone who has examined the available evidence agrees that our present system of science education isn't working very well and that change is needed. But what change is needed, and how can we make it happen? On these issues there is controversy instead of consensus. Here we shall join the fray, proposing our own answers to these questions.

What Change Is Needed?

We have already argued that the ineffectiveness of our science education system can be attributed at least in part to the prevalence of didactic teaching in our schools. This style of teaching is ineffective whenever student understanding depends on conceptual change. It leads to rote memorization or misunderstanding, rather than to conceptual change and true understanding.

However, we also described an alternate style of teaching, one that we call conceptual-change teaching. Using such strategies, it is possible to help students change fundamental conceptions through classroom teaching and thus to learn with understanding rather than simply to memorize.

Thus our suggestions for improvement focus on shifting teachers' orientations and teaching strategies away from didactic teaching toward conceptual-change teaching. As we have suggested, such a change will not take place quickly or easily. Didactic teaching is perpetuated in our schools by many conditions. In particular, most teachers lack either a general orientation toward conceptual change or specific knowledge necessary for conceptual-change teaching.

Improving Teachers' Knowledge

Earlier we identified four kinds of knowledge necessary for conceptual-change teaching: a general orientation toward conceptual change and specific knowledge of science content, of student thinking, and of teaching strategies. How can teachers acquire knowledge in each area?

Changing Orientations toward Science Teaching. Conceptual-change teaching is a new conception of teaching for most teachers, one that is fundamentally different from the conceptions that they now hold. In other words, most teachers must themselves undergo conceptual change in order to engage in conceptual-change teaching.

With this in mind, we have found that the principles and teaching strategies we described are applicable not only to teaching of science content but also to the preservice and in-service education of science teachers. Thus it is possible to apply the criteria of Posner et al. (1982) to the problem of helping teachers understand conceptual-change teaching. Teachers who are accustomed to teaching in another style must (1) become dissatisfied with that other style of teaching, (2) achieve an initial minimal understanding of conceptual-change teaching, (3) see conceptual-change teaching as a plausible alternative to the way they are teaching now, and (4) come to appreciate the usefulness of conceptual-change teaching in a variety of situations.

Similarly, the teaching strategies we described can be adapted to teaching teachers about conceptual change. The phenomena to which the principles of conceptual-change teaching can be applied are classroom episodes and encounters with students. Thus teachers can learn about conceptual-change teaching by dealing with these phenomena, either directly or through indirect methods such as observations of classroom videotapes or reading of case studies. For example, having teachers do interviews to assess the understanding of their own students can be very effective in creating dissatisfaction with the way they are teaching now. Studying case studies of successful and unsuccessful teaching can help teachers see the applicability of conceptual-change teaching to a variety of situations. Lectures or sustained verbal presentations are probably useful but insufficient to meet all four criteria for most teachers.

Improving Teachers' Understanding of Science Content. As we pointed out, most elementary and many secondary school teachers lack adequate academic backgrounds in scientific subjects that they must teach. How can these teachers learn the science content that they need? There are several possible answers to this question, none completely satisfactory.

Taking courses at a local university is undoubtedly helpful but probably not sufficient. Most science content courses ignore some very important issues. What is special about scientific knowledge, for instance? What aspects of scientific thinking are like our "commonsense" thinking? What aspects are different? What are the truly basic conceptions on which knowledge in a scientific discipline is built? These questions are of peripheral interest to career scientists who must learn to work and communicate effectively within a scientific community. They are of central importance, however, to teachers whose careers will be spent communicating about science with nonscientists.

Such issues are typically considered the province not of science courses but of specialized courses in fields such as the history or sociology of science. Science teachers, however, cannot afford to relegate them to such an obscure status. They define an essential aspect of the disciplinary knowledge on which conceptual-change teaching in science must be built. Thus long-term improvement in science teaching depends on reform of the science education that science teachers themselves receive.

Teachers can also gain useful knowledge of science content from sources other than university coursework. Formal in-service programs or informal discussion groups that focus on topics in the school curriculum can be very useful. So can reading. Most textbooks suggest additional reading for teachers or students, and teachers can benefit from both. Trade books written for children are often remarkably informative and helpful to teachers who need to think about science content in ways that their students can understand. Magazines such as *Science '86* or *Scientific American* can also provide a continuing and up-to-date source of information for many teachers.

Improving Teachers' Understanding of Students.   How can information about students be made accessible to practicing teachers? It certainly isn't now. Most investigations of how students understand science are safely locked away in research journals that teachers never read.

We suggest two promising avenues of communication, both of which we have used in our own work. One is teachers' guides and program materials. It is possible to build into program materials both descriptions of important student misconceptions and questions or activities that are diagnostically useful—that is, ones that help teachers to see and diagnose misconceptions in their own students. In our research, we have been successful in developing materials that have these qualities (Anderson & Smith, 1983b; Roth, 1984).

A second way that teachers can learn about students' scientific conceptions is from their own students. We have worked with both preservice teachers and practicing teachers, helping them to design interviews that assess how students understand science. Although designing such interviews is hard, many teachers have been successful; what they have learned about their students has been revealing to them and to us. The benefits of such work can extend beyond the particular topics that the interviews focus on, for teachers can use the skills they gain to investigate students' conceptions of other topics and to grow in their general understanding of student thinking about science.

Improving Teachers' Understanding of Teaching Strategies.   How can teachers learn to use the strategies associated with conceptual-change teaching? Clearly, it will *not* work to treat those strategies as "teaching skills" to be learned and practiced in isolation from a thorough understanding of science content and student conceptions. The strategies we described were the *responses* of intelligent and perceptive teachers to particular learning problems that they had diagnosed in their students.

It is interesting that three of the studies cited in our description of teaching strategies (Anderson & Smith, 1983b; Minstrell, 1984; Roth, 1984) documented cases in which teachers changed from didactic or discovery teaching to the use of conceptual-change teaching strategies. In none of those cases did the teachers receive any explicit instruction in the teaching strategies they were later observed using. Changes in teaching behavior were due to the introduction of new program materials (Anderson & Smith, 1983b; Roth, 1984) or to the teacher's own investigation of students' conceptions and how they could be changed (Minstrell, 1984). In all cases, the teachers were aware that they were teaching differently and attributed their changed behavior primarily to improved understanding of content and of their students' conceptions.

This is not to say that explicit instruction in conceptual-change teaching strategies is never important or necessary. Sometimes it is, especially with preservice or inexperienced teachers. However, these teachers will be able to use the strategies successfully in their classrooms only if they see those strategies as solutions to particular problems in student learning rather than as scripts to be followed while teaching science.

Many experienced teachers are capable of using conceptual-change teaching strategies without special instruction. For these teachers, it is probably more effective to devote available resources to improving their understanding of science content or of their students or to developing program materials that suggest key questions to ask or phenomena to investigate.

Other Improvements

Improving Organization and Administration of Schools.   Many of the proposed improvements in science teaching coming from the status studies and the crisis literature (e.g., NCEE, 1983) focus on school organization and administrative policies at the building, the school district, the state, or the national level. Recommendations include increasing science requirements, more extensive testing of student science achievement, testing of teacher competence, incentives for recruiting or retaining qualified teachers, lengthening the school year, and revising curricula, among many others.

Many of these suggestions focus on the reward systems for teachers and students. They suggest ways in which teachers and students can be encouraged, or compelled, to perform better. Such solutions are clearly of limited usefulness if teachers do not know how to perform better, if they are failing in spite of the fact that they are doing the best they can. We have suggested that this is often the case, and in such cases, administrators must consider their problems to be ones of knowledge dissemination or teacher education. We have already suggested some approaches to this difficult task.

Beyond that, administrators must play a role in encouraging conceptual-change teaching by teachers who do know how. Within our present school systems, changing from didactic to conceptual-change teaching entails considerable personal cost for most teachers. They must work hard to acquire knowledge that they currently lack, they must spend more time in preparation and grading, and they must face the uncertainties that come with aiming for student understanding rather than memorization. In contrast, the benefits of conceptual-change teaching, which include professional growth, personal satisfaction, and improved student understanding, tend to be delayed and not openly valued by most school administrations. Thus changes in reward systems must play an important role in encouraging conceptual-change teaching.

Reform of School Curricula and Curriculum Materials.   We have focused on the instructional effectiveness of science curriculum materials, arguing that reform is clearly necessary because so many students are learning little or nothing from their present science courses. Much of the debate about science curriculum at the national level, however, has focused on the content rather than the effectiveness of science curriculum materials. For instance, many science educators have advocated science courses that are more economically useful or that focus more on relationships among science, technology, and society (NCEE, 1983; Harms & Yager, 1981). While many of these recommended reforms are appropriate, changes in content are likely to be empty without improvements in teaching effectiveness. Students will merely switch from rote memorization of facts about science to rote memorization of facts about science, technology, and society.

Microcomputers and Educational Technology.   The advent of microcomputers promises to have a substantial impact on school science. Because microcomputers and related technology are transforming our society, they affect our perceptions of what is important to teach; thus they will affect the science curriculum. In addition, science teaching will be affected by the use of microcomputers as instructional tools. Like other tools, their impact will depend on how they are used. There are already studies available that demonstrate that microcomputers can be used effectively to promote conceptual-change teaching (Hewson, 1983). A great deal of current educational software, however, promotes the use of microcomputers as tools to aid rote memorization or didactic teaching. Such programs are likely to do more harm than good.

CONCLUSION: WHAT CAN INDIVIDUALS DO?

There is a widespread public perception that science education is in a state of crisis. We suggest that although improvement and reform are clearly needed, the metaphor and language of crisis are potentially counterproductive. We tend to think of crises as arising from sudden changes of circumstance, such as wars or natural disasters, and we respond to crises with intense but relatively short-term efforts. The present "crisis" in science education, however, has not developed suddenly. In the main, it consists of conditions that have prevailed for 20 years. Throughout this period our science education system has functioned relatively well for a few top students and poorly for everyone else. It continues to do so today, in spite of a long period of slow decline.

Just as the present "crisis" was a long time in the making, it will also be a long time in its resolution. We suggest that the problems of science education could better be addressed by modeling our response to the current "crisis" on deeper and slower processes, such as the improvements in agricultural productivity and public health that have occurred over the last century. These improvements have involved the efforts of many different researchers, developers, and practitioners. They have resulted both from theoretical breakthroughs such as the germ theory of disease and from the gradual accumulation of specific knowledge, practical techniques, and technological devices. They have taken place over generations rather than a few years. Ultimately, though, they have transformed our society far more radically than any crisis or its resolution. They have vastly increased our ability to feed and maintain the health of our citizens.

Viewed from this perspective, the present can be seen as a time of opportunity as well as a time of crisis. We have suggested that there are recent developments in science education that could make real, long-term improvements possible. Such improvements, however, can only be the products of efforts by many individuals playing many different roles in the educational system.

Researchers and Theoreticians. In so many areas, our ability to improve is limited by our lack of knowledge. We cannot overcome misconceptions, for example, if we do not know what they are. Deciding what is important to teach may depend on detailed analysis of an expert's knowledge or of the skills that are necessary for functional mastery of a task. Adequate understanding of many of these issues depends on the disciplined pursuit of knowledge by specialists. Research specialists must pursue these and other issues, but always with an eye toward the problems of practice. Significant research problems in science education will always be those that are clearly tied to the practice of science teaching. Researchers must also communicate their knowledge to science teachers as well as develop it.

Curriculum Developers. Most current science curriculum materials simply do not work for most students. Curriculum development in any medium—textbooks, laboratory activities, computer software—must lead to materials that adequately meet the needs of both students and teachers. These materials must provide teachers with adequate descriptions of students' common learning difficulties and of how those difficulties might be overcome. They must also contain instructional strategies that are at least fairly well matched to the needs of students and of their teachers. Finally, materials must communicate to teachers effectively.

Teacher Educators. Teacher educators can also play a critical role in the improvement of science teaching. They can help students to understand the relationships among content knowledge, the processes of student learning, and pedagogical techniques. They can provide students with at least a few successful supervised experiences in classroom situations. Most important, they can provide future teachers with a basis for professional growth by helping them to know what they need to know and by helping them learn where to find information that they lack and how to learn from their own teaching.

School Administrators. School administrators must also play an essential role. They can set policies that encourage students to take more science, and they must support and reward good science teaching. At one level this means being aware of what science teachers are doing and encouraging improved performance. At another level this means helping to select the best available curriculum materials and to develop in-service education opportunities that help teachers acquire essential knowledge that they currently lack.

Teachers. Teachers must help make the support system work better for them than it has in the past. They must demand adequate in-service programs and support materials. (Publishers, for example, are unlikely to improve the quality of their materials unless they see that teachers respond by preferentially selecting those materials.) Teachers must also be aware of how small our systematic knowledge of science education is in comparison with the task that they must do, and they must develop their own personal knowledge bases. This means that teachers must become sensitive observers of their own students, learning to diagnose their students' misconceptions and evaluate how well their instruction is working. The process of development is long and slow, but the rewards in both student understanding and professional growth justify the effort.

FURTHER READING
Conceptual-Change Teaching

Anderson, C. W. (Ed.). (1984). *Observing Science Classrooms: Perspectives from Research and Practice*. 1984 Yearbook of the Association for the Education of Teachers in Science. Columbus, OH: ERIC Centre for Science, Mathematics and Environmental Education. This compilation of classroom studies includes reports of two of the successful instances of teaching for conceptual change cited in this chapter. Roth ("Using Classroom Observations to Improve Science Teaching and Curriculum Materials") describes a three-year study of the teaching of plant growth and photosynthesis at the fifth-grade level. Minstrell ("Teaching for the Understanding of Ideas: Forces on Moving Objects") describes efforts to improve student learning in his own high school physics classroom. Several other chapters also address the issue of classroom teaching for conceptual change.

Driver, R. (1983). *Pupil as Scientist?* Milton Keynes, England: Open University Press. Describes students' efforts to make sense of school science. Rich with examples, the book examines the metaphor of pupil as scientist as a way of thinking about the role of student conceptions in learning.

Roth, K. J. (1986) *Teacher Explanatory Talk during Text-based Content Area Instruction: Case Studies in Science Teaching* (Research Series No. 171). East Lansing; MI: Michigan State University, Institute for Research on Teaching. This analysis contrasts more and less successful cases of science teaching at the fifth-grade level. The cases deal with the topics of light and seeing and plant growth and photosynthesis. The analysis is summarized in terms of a set of "principles" for teacher presentations and class discussions.

Information on Students' Naive Conceptions

Clement, J. (1982). "Students' Preconceptions in Introductory Physics." *American Journal of Physics, 50*, 66–71. A synthesis of the research on one of the best-documented sets of naive conceptions, on the topic of force and motion. Discusses parallels between contemporary naive conceptions and conceptions from the history of science.

Driver, R., & Erickson, G. (1983). "Theories in Action: Some Theoretical and Empirical Issues in the Study of Students' Conceptual Frameworks in Science." *Studies in Science Education, 10*, 37–60. Reviews many studies. Together, this article and the next one provide a relatively complete review of research on student naive conceptions up through early 1983.

Gilbert, J. K., & Watts, D. M. (1983). "Concepts, Misconceptions, and Alternative Conceptions: Changing Perspectives in Science Education." *Studies in Science Education, 10*, 61–98. In addition to reviewing research on naive conceptions of several science topics, this article discusses alternative historical and contemporary definitions of the term *concept*.

Theoretical Underpinnings

Cawthron, E. R., & Rowell, J. A. (1978). "Epistemology and Science Education." *Studies in Science Education, 5*, 31–59. An area in which recent developments have influenced research on student conceptions is the philosophy of science. This article describes these developments in a historical context and discusses the views of science implicit in school science.

Posner, G. J., Strike, K. A., Hewson, P. W., & Gertzog, W. A. (1982). "Accommodation of a Scientific Conception: Toward a Theory of Conceptual Change." *Science Education, 66*, 211–227. Describes a theoretical framework, derived primarily from the philosophy of science, that we have found very useful in interpreting our research findings. Especially useful were the "conditions for conceptual change."

Resnick, L. B. (1983). "Toward a Cognitive Theory of Instruction." In S. G. Parls, G. M. Olson, & H. W. Stevenson (Eds.), *Learning and Motivation in the Classroom*. Hillsdale, NJ: Erlbaum. Describes the "cognitive revolution" that has characterized the last two decades of psychology and then discusses recent progress on three aspects of instructional theory: specification of the capabilities to be acquired; description of the acquisition processes, and principles of intervention.

National Science Foundation Studies

Helgeson, S. L., Blosser, P. E., & Howe, R. W. (1977). *The Status of Precollege Science, Mathematics, and Social Science Education, 1955–1975: Vol. I. Science Education*. Columbus, OH: Ohio State University, Center for Science and Mathematical Education. Documents a review of the literature on the status of science education available in the mid-1970s.

Stake, R. E., & Easley, J. A. (1978). *Case Studies in Science Education* (Vols. 1–2). Urbana, IL: University of Illinois, Center for Instructional Research and Curriculum Evaluation. Case studies of science education in 11 school districts across the United States.

Weiss, I. R. (1978). *Report of the 1977 National Survey of Science, Mathematics, and Social Studies Education*. Research Triangle Park, NC: Research Triangle Institute, Center for Educational Research and Evaluation. Results of a national survey of a stratified random sample of districts, schools, and teachers across the United States.

Responses, Syntheses, and Supplements to the NSF Studies

Harms, N. C., & Yager, R. E. (Eds.). (1981). *Project Synthesis: What Research Says to the Science Teacher* (Vol. 3). Washington, DC: National Science Teachers Association. An attempt to synthesize the findings of the three NSF studies of 1977–1978. The editors adopted a set of broad goals representing a desired state of science education against which they compared the actual state as reflected in the three NSF studies.

National Science Foundation. (1980). *Science and Engineering Education for the 1980s and Beyond*. Washington, DC: U.S. Department of Education. A well-documented review of the NSF studies and related research on the status of science education.

National Science Foundation. (1980). *What Are the Needs in Precollege Science, Mathematics, and Social Science Education? Views from the Field* (Report No. SE80–9). Washington, DC: National Science Foundation. A compilation of responses and recommendations from professional and support organizations following up on the NSF studies.

REFERENCES

Anderson, C. W., & Smith, E. L. (1983a, April). *Children's conceptions of light and color: Developing the concept of unseen rays*. Paper presented at the annual meeting of the American Educational Research Association, Montreal, Canada.

Anderson, C. W., & Smith, E. L. (1983b, April). *Teacher behavior associated with conceptual learning in science*. Paper presented at the annual meeting of the American Educational Research Association, Montreal, Canada.

Atkin, M., & Karplus, R. (1982, September). Discovery or invention? *Science Teacher*, pp. 45–51.

Ausubel, D. P. (1968). *Educational psychology: A cognitive view*. New York: Holt, Rinehart and Winston.

Blecha, M. K., Gega, C., & Green, M. (1979). *Exploring science* (2nd ed.). River Forest, IL: Laidlaw.

Clement, J. (1982). Students' preconceptions in introductory physics. *American Journal of Physics, 50*, 66–71.

Driver, R., & Erickson, G. (1983). Theories in action: Theoretical and empirical issues in the study of students' conceptual frameworks in science. *Studies in Science Education, 10*, 37–60.

Eaton, J. F., Anderson, C. W., & Smith, E. L. (1984). Students' misconceptions interfere with learning: Case studies of fifth-grade students. *Elementary School Journal, 64*, 365–379.

Furth, H. G. (1969). *Piaget and knowledge: Theoretical foundations.* Englewood Cliffs, NJ: Prentice-Hall.

Harms, N. C., & Yager, R. E. (Eds.). (1981). *Project synthesis: What research says to the science teacher* (Vol. 3). Washington, DC: National Science Teachers Association.

Harnischfeger, A., & Wiley, D. (1977). Achievement test scores drop. So what? *Educational Research, 7*, 5–12.

Helgeson, S. L., Blosser, P. E., & Howe, R. W. (1977). *The status of precollege science, mathematics, and social science education, 1955–1975: Vol. 1. Science education.* Columbus, OH: Ohio State University, Center for Science and Mathematics Education.

Helm, H., & Novak, J. D. (1983). *Misconceptions in science and mathematics: Proceedings of the International Seminar.* June 20–22, 1983. Ithaca, NY: Cornell University.

Hesse, J. (1986). *Students' understanding of chemical change.* Unpublished doctoral dissertation, Michigan State University.

Hewson, P. W. (1983, April). *Microcomputers and conceptual change: The use of a microcomputer program to diagnose and remediate an alternative conception of speed.* Paper presented at the annual meeting of the American Educational Research Association, Montreal, Canada.

Hewson, P. W., & Hewson, M.G.A. (1984). The role of conceptual conflict in conceptual change and the design of science instruction. *Instructional Science, 13*, 1–13.

Hirsch, C. R. (1983). A profile of Michigan teachers of high school biology, chemistry, and physics, 1980–83. *Science Education, 68*, 579–587.

Hueftle, S. J., Rakow, S. J., & Welch, W. W. (1983). *Images of science: A summary of results from the 1981–82 National Assessment in Science.* Minneapolis: University of Minnesota, Minnesota Research and Evaluation Center.

Hurd, P. D. (1982). *State of precollege education in mathematics and science.* Report prepared for the National Convocation on Precollege Education in Science and Mathematics, May 12–13, 1982, National Academy of Sciences and National Academy of Engineering, Washington, DC.

Knott, R., Lawson, C., Karplus R., Thier, H., & Montgomery, M. (1978). *SCIIS communities teacher's guide.* Chicago: Rand McNally.

Kuhn, T. (1970). *The structure of scientific revolutions.* Chicago: University of Chicago Press.

Minstrell, J. (1984). Teaching for the understanding of ideas: Forces on moving objects. In C. W. Anderson (Ed.), *Observing science classrooms: Perspectives from research and practice.* 1984 Yearbook of the Association for the Education of Teachers in Science. Columbus, OH: ERIC Center for Science, Mathematics, and Environmental Education.

National Assessment of Educational Progress. (1978). *Three national assessments of science: Changes in achievement, 1967–77* (Report No. 08–S–00). Denver: Education Commission of the States.

National Commission on Excellence in Education. (1983). *A nation at risk: The imperative for educational reform.* Washington, DC: U.S. Department of Education.

National Research Council. (1979). *The state of school science.* Washington, DC: Author.

National Science Foundation. (1980). *Science and engineering education for the 1980s and beyond.* Washington, DC: U.S. Department of Education.

Nussbaum, J., & Novick, S. (1982). Alternative frameworks, conceptual conflict, and accommodation: Toward a principled teaching strategy. *Instructional Science, 11,* 183–200.

Olson, J. K. (1983, April). *Mr. Swift and the clock: Teacher influence in the classroom.* Paper presented at the annual meeting of the American Educational Research Association, Montreal, Canada.

Posner, G. J., Strike, K. A., Hewson, P. W., & Gertzog, W. A. (1982). Accommodation of a scientific conception: Toward a theory of conceptual change. *Science Education, 66,* 211–227.

Roth, K. J. (1984). Using classroom observations to improve science teaching and curriculum materials. In C. W. Anderson (Ed.), *Observing science classrooms: Perspectives from research and practice.* 1984 Yearbook of the Association for the Education of Teachers in Science. Columbus, OH: ERIC Center for Science, Mathematics, and Environmental Education.

Roth, K. J. (1985). *The effect of science text on student misconceptions.* Unpublished doctoral dissertation, Michigan State University.

Roth, K. J., Anderson, C. W., & Smith, E. L. (1983). *Teacher explanatory talk during content area reading: Case studies in science teaching.* Paper presented at the annual meetings of the National Reading Conference, Symposium on Teacher Explanatory Talk, Austin, TX.

Roth, K. J., Smith, E. L., & Anderson, C. W. (1983, April). *Students' conceptions of photosynthesis and food for plants.* Paper presented at the annual meeting of the American Educational Research Association, Montreal, Canada.

Slinger, L., Anderson, C. W., & Smith, E. L. (1983). *Studying light in the fifth grade: A case study of text-based science teaching* (Research Series No. 129). East Lansing: Michigan State University, Institute for Research on Teaching.

Smith, E. L., & Anderson, C. W. (1984). Planning and teaching intermediate science study: Final report (Research Series No. 147). East Lansing: Michigan State University, Institute for Research on Teaching.

Smith, E. L., & Sendelbach, N. B. (1982). The program, the plans, and the activities of the classroom: The demands of activity-based science. In J. K. Olson (Ed.), *Innovation in the science curriculum: Classroom knowledge and curriculum change.* London: Croom-Helm.

Stake, R. E., & Easley, J. (1978). *Case studies in science education* (Vols. 1–2). Urbana: University of Illinois, Center for Instructional Research and Curriculum Evaluation.

Toulmin, S. (1972). *Human understanding.* Princeton, NJ: Princeton University Press.

Weiss, I. R. (1978). *Report of the 1977 national survey of science, mathematics, and social studies education.* Report to the National Science Foundation, Center for Educational Research and Evaluation, Research Triangle Institute (Contract No. C7619848).

Welch, W. W. (1979). Twenty years of science curriculum development: A look backward. In D. Berliner (Ed.), *Review of research in education* (Vol. 2). Washington, DC: American Educational Research Association.

5 IMPLICATIONS FROM RESEARCH: WHAT SHOULD BE TAUGHT IN SOCIAL STUDIES?

James P. Shaver

Questions about what should be taught are difficult to answer in any curricular area. They are particularly perplexing in social studies, for reasons that are both peculiar to the field and general to education. There are three sources of difficulty in formulating such recommendations: (1) the lack of agreement on the meaning of "social studies," (2) the nature of decisions about what "should be" and the relationship of research findings to such decisions, and (3) the state of available research knowledge. The consideration of each is essential to setting an appropriate context for examining the implications of research for what should be taught in social studies.

WHY IS A DEFINITION OF SOCIAL STUDIES IMPORTANT?

"Social studies" has been used to designate an area of curriculum since at least 1916 (Davis, 1981, pp. 26–27), but there have been considerable confusion and disagreement over the years about the meaning of the term (e.g., see Wiley, 1977, pp. 22–24). Most elementary school curricular areas and secondary school courses are referred to by labels, such as science or mathematics, that have clear referents in academic fields. In contrast, *social studies* as a rubric intended to encompass the history, geography, and civics courses that were standard in American schools by the turn of the century is not a term that refers to a commonly recognized academic field of study. As the various social sciences and parts of the humanities became subjects of social studies instruction, the lack of clear identification with an overarching scholarly field became a serious source of ambiguity. While it is not a great oversimplification to say that the commonly accepted task of the elementary or secondary school teacher is to teach the academic content of, for example, mathematics or science (although there are disagreements over what should be taught at different grade levels and over how applied the teaching should be—for example, is business math really mathematics?), that clarity of purpose is not evident in social studies. The situation has been compounded by the longstanding assumption that the courses taught under the social studies label are especially important as foundations for citizenship.

Historically, citizenship education played an implicit role in social studies. That is, it was assumed that studying history, civics, and geography led to good citizenship. In the last 30 years or so, however, teacher educators have tried to make citizenship education an explicit part of the definition of social studies. Some have argued that citizenship is *the* central purpose of social studies, that simply teaching history and the social sciences as academic subjects is not sufficient citizenship education, and that educators should ask what other sources of content, including those of the humanities and of applied fields such as journalism, are relevant (e.g., see Shaver, 1967). Others continue to maintain that teaching the social sciences and history will achieve the essential citizenship goals. This position is often summarized by referring to Wesley's definition of the social studies, in his 1937 textbook, as the social sciences adapted and simplified for instructional purposes. That definition, which is an oversimplification of Wesley's position (Wronski, 1982), is consistent with the content of most elementary and secondary school social studies textbooks (Wiley, 1977, pp. 80–119). In a sophisticated form, with an emphasis on the structure of the disciplines, that definition also fit the orientation of most of the curricular projects of the 1960s, which developed the curricula labeled the "New Social Studies" (Haas, 1977). These two positions—social studies as history and social science and social studies as citizenship education—are at the center of the continuing debate about what social studies is (Wiley, 1977, pp. 22–25, 274–277).

Ambiguities and differences in word usage can confound thought and discussion. Barr, Barth, and Shermis (1977, chap. 1), for example, believe that the lack of a clear definition of *social studies* is a source of much confusion, conflict, and lack of curricular cohesion. Based on a reading of three national studies of the status of social studies sponsored by the National Science Foundation (NSF), Ponder, Brandt, and Ebersole (1980) concluded that lack of agreement "as to what ends social studies education is to serve or the most appropriate subject matter to teach" prevents "internal integrity" in course offerings and provides the basis for "resistance to attempts to unify the social studies program" (p. 171).

The definition of a basic term such as *social studies* is a serious semantic concern as well because our definitions are often persuasive—that is, how we define terms leads us to believe and to act in certain ways. Certainly what a person believes should be taught in social studies will be affected by whether he or she adopts a definition that focuses on history and the social sciences as the source of instructional decisions and content or a definition that focuses on the demands of citizenship as the source.

For these reasons, vagueness in usage of the term *social studies* is a concern not only for an effort, such as this chapter represents, to recommend practice based on research but also for curriculum development generally. Some have argued that clarification of the meaning of social studies is a central need in the field (e.g., Wiley, 1977, pp. 10, 22, 277).

Efforts to define social studies are not, however, viewed as worthwhile by all persons concerned with the field (e.g., Morrissett, 1979). In fact, Mehlinger (1981) has argued that the definition of social studies is a matter of contention to few people other than the college professors who are the so-called leaders in the field. He suggested that for most social studies teachers, the matter of definition is a nonproblem, not even a minor concern, for social studies is, in effect, defined for them by what is contained in the textbooks from which they teach.

Case study research (Stake & Easley, 1978) sponsored by the National Science Foundation, along with a national survey of teachers and school administrators (Weiss, 1978) and reviews of the literature (e.g., Wiley, 1977), to ascertain the status of mathematics, science, and social science/social studies education in this country supports Mehlinger's view. That research indicated not only that teachers and professors have quite different views of what curricular-instructional problems are important but also that the textbook is the central tool of instruction in social studies courses, with the major task for students being the reproduction of information presented in the book (Shaver, Davis, & Helburn, 1979, 1980). (This conclusion was also supported by Goodlad's national study of schooling, 1983a, 1983b.) And a survey of publishers by Schneider and Van Sickle (1979) confirmed that social studies textbooks do and will continue to emphasize the "traditional elements of history, geography, government, civics, and learning skills" (p. 464). In fact, when publishers were asked to indicate the single most important factor in the sale of social studies textbooks, the inclusion of traditional content was the second most commonly mentioned, following only readability (p. 464).

The definition of social studies that teachers accept is a crucial matter. For, as is commonly believed and as the NSF-sponsored case studies of status confirmed, the teacher is the key to what social studies will be for any student (Stake & Easley, 1978, chap. 19).

As important as teachers' beliefs about the meaning of social studies are, little reported research has been aimed at identifying them. One effort has been that of Barr, Barth, and Shermis (1977, 1978). They developed an instrument, the Social Studies Preference Scale, to assess teachers' adherence to three social studies traditions that are viewed as "conceptually different," "not complementary," and "antagonistic, competitive philosophical systems" (1977, pp. 58–59): *social studies as citizenship transmission*, the position that inculcating correct beliefs and values is the major purpose of social studies; *social studies as social science*, which emphasizes social science problems and concepts; and *social studies as reflective inquiry*, which focuses on citizenship decision making and problem solving.

Barr and his associates (1978) have assumed that 60% to 70% of teachers will identify with one of the traditions (p. 152). However, a recent study by White (1982) raised questions about that assumption. White's results must be viewed with some skepticism because of limited sampling (190 secondary school social studies teachers in six Midwest and New England school districts) and a low rate of return (48%). But his finding that 81% of his sample were eclectics—that is, that they selected items indicating an adherence to all three traditions—is provocative. It also is consistent with arguments that all three traditions are essential elements of citizenship (e.g., Shaver, 1977).

What Definition Will Be Used Here?

The view of social studies that underlies this chapter is consistent with the teachers' eclecticism that White's results suggest. Social studies is taken to be that part of the elementary and secondary school curriculum that is specifically concerned with citizenship education—which entails transmitting values, teaching social science and history knowledge, and encouraging the development of competencies in decision making and participation. Citizenship education now seems to be largely accepted as the overarching concern of social studies education (e.g., Barr et al., 1977; Crabtree, 1983), so the definition just given provides a reasonable basis for identifying relevant research. Nevertheless, it is important to remember that stipulating a definition of social studies does not solve the problems created by the persistent lack of agreement about what social studies is.

"SHOULD BE" DECISIONS

As Davis (1981) has pointed out, no history of social studies has been written. However, what is known through scattered reports and anecdotal evidence indicates considerable historical stability in the curriculum. It is possible to delineate a typical kindergarten through twelfth grade course structure (Jarolimek, 1981, p. 4; Morrisett, 1981, pp. 37–38). The elementary courses follow an "expanding environments" pattern that became predominant in the 1930s, and the grade 7 through 12 offerings follow closely recommendations that were published by the U.S. Bureau of Education in 1916. As already noted, course content within that structure tends to be determined by what the textbooks contain, with little variety in that substance (Wiley, 1977). The result, as the NSF studies of status indicated, is stability across the nation, with "a locally accepted nationwide curriculum—so that students face few problems of continuity in moving from district to district, no more so than in moving from one school to another within a district," as well as stability over time, so that "those who graduated from high school twenty years ago or more would, if they visited their local schools, typically find social studies classes to be similar to those they had experienced" (Shaver et al., 1980, p. 17).

When what should be taught is decided by default, by accepting what is, the nature of the decision tends to be obscured. People who are quite aware that a decision to change a curriculum ought to be justified carefully will often assume that to continue past practice does not require justification. Yet both types of decisions affect students, and the grounds for each should be explicated. Unexamined curricula are too likely to be dysfunctional (Shaver, 1977), as the caricature of *The Saber-Tooth Curriculum* (Benjamin, 1939) emphasized so well.

Decisions about what to teach, whether made consciously or not, can be thought of as public policy decisions, for they structure a plan of action to be carried out within a government agency, the school. Even if that seems to be a somewhat grandiose characterization, such decisions should be thought of as political-ethical decisions, because they are decisions about proper or right aims or actions that are subject to negotiation within the political framework of the local, state, and, occasionally, national community (e.g., see Wiley, 1976, pp. 17–25).

What is the relevance of research to such decisions? Charles Beard (1934) commented over 50 years ago:

Since all things known cannot be placed before children in the school room, there must and will be, inevitably, a selection, and the selection will be made with reference to some frame of knowledge and values, more or less consciously established in the mind of the selector.[1] (p. 182)

Educational research is one source of the knowledge that might be used in selecting content. The teacher's own experience, the experiences of his or her colleagues, and non-research-based writings are other sources of knowledge.

As the quote from Beard indicates, along with knowledge, the decision maker's standards or principles of worth—his or her values—play a central role in decisions about what should be taught. Educational research, with its intent to discover what *is*, addresses only indirectly the matter of what *should be*, for research cannot establish values, only determine what values people hold. In fact, when researchers begin to use empirical methods purposely to build support for ideological positions, the usefulness of their findings becomes highly questionable (Bereiter, 1982).

Beard (1934) also addressed the relationship between empiricism and values in the making of ethical decisions: Research cannot tell people what they *ought* to do, although it may provide information about what to do or avoid doing in order to accomplish ends (p. 161). Beard put the matter strongly:

> It is impossible to discover by the fact-finding operation whether this or that change [or lack of change] is desirable. Empiricism may disclose, within limits, whether a proposed change [or goal] is possible, or to what extent it is possible, and the realities which condition its eventuation, but, given possibility or a degree of possibility, empiricism has no way of evaluating value without positing value or setting up a frame of value. (p. 172)

Controversy over MACOS

The important role of values, as compared to research evidence, in making curricular decisions is well illustrated by the MACOS experience. MACOS ("Man: A Course of Study") is an elementary school anthropology curriculum developed with funding from the National Science Foundation. The curriculum was heralded by the American Educational Research Association as "one of the most important efforts of our time to relate research efforts and theory in educational psychology to the development of new and better instructional materials," and it was cited as being "based on unusually sound scholarship" (see National Council for the Social Studies [NCSS] 1975). But MACOS became the center of controversy, nationwide and in Congress (Wiley, 1976).

The frame of reference underlying the development of MACOS was largely a social science view of reality. It was assumed that objectivity in observing cultural matters is desirable and that much can be learned about what it means to be human by a comparative study of lower animals and other cultures, including the moral dilemmas posed by other value systems. These goals are compatible with important American values, such as freedom of opinion and the liberation of intelligence (NCSS,

---

[1]Frame of reference, as used by Beard, is similar to concepts such as "personal perspective," "personal theory," and "implicit theory" that have been used in studies of teachers' thinking (Clark & Yinger, 1979, pp. 251, 259; McCutcheon 1981), except that Beard included values more explicitly as an essential element.

1975, p. 445). But they could also be seen as threatening to children's acceptance of parental and community values.

Other issues were involved, but the conflict between "scientific" and "traditional" values lay at the heart of a storm of criticism of MACOS (Wiley, 1976, pp. 25–33), primarily from persons with fundamentalist religious orientations. Among other things, they saw in the study of different cultures by young children a potential for value relativism, which those with a social science orientation tended to overlook or discount. These value considerations were the major factor in the withdrawal of federal support for MACOS and similar curriculum development and in the general disuse of the program.

Other New Social Studies Projects

The MACOS controversy and the outcome demonstrate the possible effects of values in both national and local educational policymaking. But MACOS was not the only New Social Studies (NSS) curriculum that was not welcomed with open arms in the public schools. Surveys of use of NSS materials (Weiss, 1978; Wiley, 1977) have come up with varying estimates, ranging from 10% to 25%, of social studies teachers who report having used at least one NSS product. However, because of limited samples, small rates of return, and the social desirability of reporting the use of innovative materials,[2] even these small proportions are likely inflated estimates of use.

The MACOS controversy was unusual in that national publicity about a field-tested curriculum had a strong negative impact on adoption. Social studies curricula that are not compatible with traditional instruction are usually quietly ignored, even if effectiveness data are available. The Harvard Social Studies Project (Oliver & Shaver, 1974) is a good example.

Following the same students through the seventh and eighth grades, the Harvard Project produced strong evidence that, with direct instruction and application in the discussion of controversial issues, concepts for use in the analysis of public issues could be taught as part of a two-year junior high school U.S. history sequence. Moreover, that positive result was obtained without a detrimental effect on students' scores on standardized tests that assessed usual social studies objectives, including an American history test selected by the control-group teachers. In addition, on American history items that reflected content covered both as part of the conventional curriculum and as topics in the experimental curriculum, the mean score of experimental students was statistically higher at the end of the two-year period, a result that held up in testing one year later (Oliver & Shaver, 1974, pp. 275–282).

Problem booklets that grew out of the Harvard Project (the AEP Unit Books) were among the most popular of the NSS materials (Wiley, 1977, pp. 317–318), apparently because they were short and could easily be used as the basis for brief units in traditional, textbook courses. Yet acceptance was not high, with reported use ranging from 12% to 20% in studies with limited samples and low rates of return. The positive research evidence for the effectiveness of the projects' jurisprudential approach did not lead to its widespread implementation, either, despite an

---

[2]The effect of social desirability on social studies teachers' reports of books they have read (Baxter, Ferrell, & Wiltz, 1964, pp. 136–138) illustrates the validity of this concern.

enthusiastic reception by professors and social studies supervisors and recognition such as selection by Joyce and Weil (1980) for presentation as a model of teaching.

The Relation of Research Evidence, Practical Knowledge, and Values

The reasons for lack of acceptance of the Harvard Project's approach have not been explored through research, but informal reports indicate that, as with the other NSS curricula, teacher resistance was the major factor. That reluctance was based on perspectives in which research evidence about effectiveness was only one relatively small consideration. Of greater importance were the teachers' values and their practical knowledge about students and about the expectations of their schools and communities.

The New Social Studies curricula were aimed at promoting inquiry among students, whether from the politico-ethical orientation of the Harvard Project or the empirical orientation of the other social science–based projects. They called for experience-centered teaching—students doing things in small groups, in and out of the classroom—and they encouraged students to test the validity of ideas, not reproduce textbook content that was assumed to be valid.

The NSS inquiry orientation ran counter to teachers' previous experiences as students (from kindergarten through college) in which they had played the role of subordinate learner, one who produces assignments and learns content approved by the teacher, rather than the role of independent, speculative thinker and investigator. Consequently, the teachers' own schooling had not provided models of the inquiry, interactive types of teaching called for.[3] Nor had their training provided them with the necessary techniques. In Weiss's (1978) national survey, more than 50% of social studies teachers indicated that they would need help with inquiry teaching (p. 147). Goodlad (1983b) found, too, in his national study that "most teachers do not know how to teach for higher levels of thinking" (p. 15). Equally important, the curricula ran counter to the teachers' beliefs that students did not have the intellectual maturity or self-discipline necessary for inquiry-oriented teaching to work and that the result would be a waste of instructional time (Shaver et al., 1980, p. 8; Goodlad, 1983a, pp. 469–470; 1983b, p. 15).

The new curricula were also seen as creating classroom management problems. And to teachers faced with 30 or more students for a full day in self-contained classrooms at the elementary level or with as many as five classes of up to 40 students each per day at the secondary level, management is a central concern. The inquiry orientation and activities of the NSS curricula not only had potential for creating student control problems but also created resource management difficulties that textbooks do not. Simulation games, for example, often have various parts, such as role cards, to be kept track of. If those elements are lost or misplaced, lessons are disrupted. These are high risks for teachers not convinced that the materials are appropriate for their students anyway.

The view that a "good" teacher keeps students busily working, quiet, and "under control" is reinforced by survival under trying conditions and by the social system of the school. Principals, too, value orderly, quiet schools; they judge teachers and are

---

[3]The lack of models for such teaching has been a serious problem for new science curricula, too (Moore, 1978).

judged themselves by those standards. Moreover, other teachers do not want students "loose in the hallways" or making noise in adjoining classrooms. In addition, a common value of the school is preparation for what lies ahead in the next grade, which is also assumed to be preparation for life. Students are to demonstrate proper demeanor, as well as know prerequisite content, how to study from the textbook, and how to follow instructions. Teachers do not want to be told that their students did not live up to such expectations (Shaver et al., 1980; see also Goodlad, 1983b, p. 10).

Curricula that conflict with teachers' practical knowledge of students and schools and with how to accomplish what is expected of them are not likely to be accepted, despite evidence about effectiveness in achieving goals often espoused for public education. In fact, however, the general NSS aim of teaching students to make better decisions is not always accepted, citizenship goals in curriculum guides notwithstanding. As Goodlad (1983b) noted, in lamenting this discrepancy between goals and practice in the schools, "independent, autonomous individuals can be annoying when young and infuriatingly deviant as adults" (p. 10).

The validity of Goodlad's observation was verified by an incidental Harvard Project experience. A few of our junior high school students attended a town council meeting that had on its agenda a proposal to close the local youth center. The students pointed out value conflicts and discrepancies, asked for definitions of terms, noted relevant factual claims, and requested evidence. The social studies teacher who happened to be present was proud of their performance, but comments indicated that they were viewed by the other adults as young smart alecks who did not know their proper place. Had it been known that at least some of their behavior was due to citizenship-oriented teaching, it would not have led to commendations for the teachers or the school system.

Clearly, the norms of the local community are another important factor in decisions, or nondecisions, about what to teach. As the Harvard Project experience indicated, inquiry- and experience-based curricula are likely to be incompatible not only with the content orientation and the socialization aims common among teachers but with community expectations as well. Boyd (1979) has pointed out that when teaching comes in conflict with community values, opposition and controversy are likely, and educators are inclined to avoid conflict.

That the curriculum is shaped by the desire to avoid conflict is too simple a view, however (Shaver et al., 1980). Teachers see themselves as part of the communities in which they teach and are sensitive to local concerns. In fact, that sensitivity is a common criterion, explicit or implicit, in hiring teachers. When it comes to a choice between conflicting interpretations of American values—for example, between an emphasis on traditional family and religious values or on scientific, intellectual values, as in the case of MACOS (Wiley, 1976, p. 25)—teachers will usually opt for what is valued locally, not because they are cowards but because they tend to share those commitments. In that light, the NSF case studies' finding (Stake & Easley, 1978) that few social studies teachers reported problems in dealing with controversial issues makes sense, despite longstanding concern by the National Council for the Social Studies and university educators that controversial issues "pose a problem of particularly strong significance for social studies teachers, due to the inherently 'hot' nature of the subject matter" (Wiley, 1977, p. 11; see also p. 289). Teachers are tactful about issues because they share local values. Avoiding controversial issues also fits with the view that the subject matter of the textbook is the proper business of the classroom (Shaver et al., 1980).

In short, decisions about what should be taught rest on many elements in a teacher's frame of reference. Research evidence about effectiveness is one element that might have an influence. The teacher's practical knowledge and values are also relevant and are likely to carry greater weight.

Other Types of Research

Research results that address the effectiveness of curricula are not the only findings with potential relevance to the question of what should be taught. Research findings about the state of society are also often cited as considerations. For example, Mehlinger (1978) reported that polls by the University of Michigan Institute for Social Research indicated that the percentage of people distrustful of government had risen from 20% in 1958 to 50% in 1976, and Louis Harris polls showed that the percentage of those expressing confidence in the executive branch of the federal government and in Congress fell from 41% to 23% and from 42% to 17%, respectively, between 1966 and 1977.

What are the implications of these research findings for what should be taught in social studies? Some would say that based on such results, social studies teachers should make renewed efforts to build commitment to the government of our society. Others would say the opposite: that something, perhaps education, is having a good effect in that people are finally recognizing the incompetence and duplicity of those in power. Clearly, again, research evidence can stimulate thought but cannot dictate what should be taught.

What about evidence bearing more directly on the beliefs and attitudes of youth? A survey of 30,000 adolescents from nine countries (Torney, Oppenheim, & Farnen, 1975) indicated that 14-year-olds in this country were the only group less interested in discussing foreign politics than national affairs. The U.S. sample was also less knowledgeable about international political affairs. Torney (1980) used this finding as a partial basis for proposing increased teaching about international human rights in elementary school. But again, such evidence of a "deficit" does not lead directly to a conclusion about what should be taught. Both values and other knowledge are relevant. It would be important to ask if international understanding and interest are as important educational aims as national understanding and interest—a value question. It would also be important to know if efforts to increase international interest and knowledge might lead to decreased domestic interest and knowledge—a factual question of considerable interest in light of the prior value question (Shaver, 1979b).

STATUS OF RESEARCH KNOWLEDGE

An adequate appreciation of the role of educational research in determining what should be taught in social studies also requires that we consider the status of available research knowledge. Two aspects of the status of the available research evidence are germane. First is the matter of relevance: Have researchers addressed questions of interest to social studies practitioners, especially the teachers who ultimately determine what happens in social studies classrooms? Second is the matter of soundness of the research knowledge base: Can research be counted on as a valid source of evidence, when relevant, in making decisions about what should be taught in social studies? Those questions will be dealt with in that order. But first let us consider the use of research findings by teachers.

Are Research Findings Used?

Although a great deal is not known from research about teacher planning (Clark & Yinger, 1979), the available findings are consistent with the research in social studies that indicates that the textbook is the major determinant of what is taught. Generally, teachers do not appear to follow the "rational" model of planning prescribed by teacher trainers, beginning with goals or objectives and then considering alternatives for achieving their aims. Instead, the starting point seems to be the content to be taught, along with consideration of the setting in which the teaching will take place (Clark & Yinger, 1979). Research with social studies teachers portrays a similar picture of daily teaching decisions (McCutcheon, 1981).

In addition, little is known about teachers' decisions to adopt or not adopt new curricula (Hahn, 1977; Kissock & Falk, 1978). But the stages in the adoption of social studies material that Hahn discussed can be taken to include the use of research evidence only by a great stretch of imagination. And Boag and Massey's (1981) case study of two teachers' reactions to new social studies materials notably lacks any reference to research evidence. The NSF studies of status also indicated that elementary and secondary school teachers are not much aware of educational research (Shaver et al., 1980).[4]

Is the Research Relevant?

Why don't teachers use research findings in their decision making? There are several possible reasons. For example, research reports are often not easily accessible to teachers, especially those not near university or large city libraries, and are difficult for teachers to read and interpret when at hand. The proliferation of research reports in education and the social sciences related to teaching and content decisions makes it impossible to keep up to date on all of the potentially relevant findings, and efforts to integrate and synthesize the research literature have not been adequate, methodologically or conceptually (Jackson, 1978). Of particular interest here, reviews of research tend not to address questions of interest to teachers, and even more basic, the original studies themselves tend to address problems that teachers do not see as relevant to their situations (Shaver et al., 1980).

An analogy from the fate of the New Social Studies curriculum materials is appropriate:

> Teachers judged the new materials as likely to work only in exceptional situations, with elite groups of students who had attained the basics and perhaps more important, proper self-discipline. They saw, or sensed, when they were aware of the new materials, the contradictions between the developers' purposes

---

[4]Eisner (1983, pp. 3–4) found in interviews of university faculty what I found in a small, informal survey of colleagues (Shaver, 1982, p. 5): University education faculty members do not use research in their instructional planning either, contrary to what they prescribe for elementary and secondary school teachers.

and their own—the emphasis in the new materials on content, on reasoning and inquiry, and, consequently, the different use of subject matter. Not only was the achievement of goals they thought important threatened by the materials, but their central classroom expectations (e.g., everyone quiet and working on the same assignment) and management techniques were challenged.... The new topics and content organizations and unusual teaching roles not only seemed difficult to carry out but flew in the face of the teacher's view of the needs of students and the school. (Shaver et al., 1980, p. 12)

Just as the NSS curricula did not take into account classroom realities, educational research (and that in social studies education is no exception) tends to be aimed at questions often not viewed by teachers as germane to actual classroom teaching, such as how to teach students to be creative, independent, critical thinkers or how to sequence learning activities to achieve higher-order cognitive and affective outcomes (Shaver et al., 1980). In fact, as Jackson and Kiesler (1977) noted, there is "almost total absorption" on the part of educational researchers "with the goal of improving practice and discovering better techniques...[with little attention to] whether educators might now be doing as well as can be done in many aspects of their endeavor" (p. 15).

Researchers in social studies education rarely treat the difficult problems of classroom management that teachers find pressing, questions of how to use content for management purposes (a use that university professors find difficult to accept as legitimate) or how to achieve the content learning goals, as well as the school socialization goals, that teachers view as important (Shaver et al., 1980).

Given the clear pattern of research findings that teachers rely on the textbook as the basis for the social studies curriculum, it is particularly ironic, especially in light of the 161 analyses of the content of social studies textbooks reported in the two decades before 1976 (Wiley, 1977, p. 83), that little research has been done on the effects on student outcomes of different kinds of content (Wiley, 1977, pp. 167–169, 194–197), including biased content (Ehman, 1977). Ehman and Hahn (1981) noted that not only do we "know little or nothing about what students actually learn from their textbooks" (p. 70), but we "do not yet know what is the best scope and sequence for social studies" (p. 80). The design of social studies curriculum remains largely a "folk art" (p. 70). There have been studies evaluating NSS materials, although the findings have not been synthesized. How textbooks might be used for a greater variety of outcomes has not been addressed by researchers. In short, the questions that interest researchers and social studies teachers are, in large part, so different that it is as if they were dealing with two different worlds of schooling (Shaver et al., 1980; Banks, 1982).

Frames of reference are at the heart of the discrepancy. To some extent, as indicated, the difficulty is that university professors, who are for the most part the educational researchers, view the school from a perspective of the ideal—both in the sense of what might be and in the sense of a focus on the intellectual, nonemotional side of humans—while teachers view the school from a perspective of the real—the constraints imposed by a mass education system in which students often would rather not be in school.

The problem is in part methodological, too. For teachers, the reality is contact with the same students daily for a school year. Researchers, however, want to deal with "manageable" slices of reality. One result, according to Eisner (1983, pp. 17–18), is superficiality. He found, for example, that 10 of the experimental studies published in the 1981 volume of the *American Educational Research Journal* reported the amount of time that students were exposed to the treatment. The median time was 72 minutes. The median treatment time reported in the 1978 volume was even less, 45 minutes.

Moreover, in trying to encapsulate the reality of the classroom, educational researchers have attended to the "physical properties" of human interactions rather than to symbolic meanings. The result has been a disposition toward "equating the underlying meaning and intention of human learning with test scores, rating scales, and preconceived observation categories," and this approach, with its reduction in meaning, has led to limited data that do not speak to "everyday teaching and learning as it occurs in schools" (Bussis, 1980, p. 4).[5] As Eisner (1983) has argued, the language and methods of educational research provide only "gross indicators" of the qualities that make up the realities of the classroom that teachers must address in their work. "They cannot capture nuance—and in teaching as in human relationships [generally,] nuance is everything" (p. 19).[6]

The methodologies and underlying epistemological assumptions of educational research, then, contribute to the lack of relevance to practitioners' concerns, which must be considered in a valid effort to draw implications from research as to what should be taught in social studies. In addition, such an effort depends on the adequacy of the research base upon which it would be mounted.

How Sound Is the Research Base?

The productivity of educational research has often been questioned. For example, Gage (1978) noted that "most reviewers of research on teaching have concluded their reports by saying that past work has been essentially fruitless" (p. 229)—a conclusion, incidentally, with which Gage disagreed.[7] In her extensive review of prior reviews of research in social studies education, Wiley (1977) found that "many reviewers have expressed concern over the lack of a cumulative research base in social studies/social science education" (p. 165).

The reasons given for the lack of productivity are many. Some focus on methodology: the frequently poor design of individual studies, the failure to use randomization, an overreliance on inferential statistics, and a lack of replication. An analysis of the adequacy of research methodology and proposals for improving research are beyond the purview of this chapter. (If interested, see Shaver, 1979a, 1979b; Shaver & Norton, 1980a, 1980b.) It is, however, pertinent to note the need for caution in interpreting research reports and assuming that they provide an adequate base for schooling decisions.

Some critics have proposed that the reasons for the lack of accumulated research

[5]The comments of Bussis and Eisner are directed primarily at the use of traditional quantitative methods. Some researchers try to capture the meaning of the classroom for teachers and students through naturalistic, ethnographic approaches, spending extended periods of time, as long as a school year, in the schools gathering data (e.g., Smith & Geoffrey, 1968).

[6]Ironically, behaviorists argue that traditional educational research has not been productive because researchers are *too* concerned with "mental states"—in a sense, not reductionist enough (e.g., see Greer, 1983).

[7]Gage also provided a summary of research addressed to teachers' classroom management needs (p. 234).

knowledge from educational research, and from social science research as well, lie not with methodological shortcomings (although there frequently are such) but with the unreality of an oft-stated goal: to produce knowledge that will enable us, as theories do in the physical sciences, to know "the necessary and sufficient conditions for a particular result," to forecast outcomes with a reasonable margin of error once parameters are specified, and to state the precise limits of application of principles of behavior (Cronbach, 1975, p. 125).

Gergen (1973), for example, has argued, along lines applicable to educational research, that social psychology "deals with facts that are largely nonrepeatable and which fluctuate over time" (p. 310).[8] Cultural changes over time invalidate findings, in part because the cultural diffusion of research results changes behavior. People become enlightened, more sensitive to the variables, and react accordingly; they may even strive to act contrary to findings with value implications that they view as negative.

Cronbach (1975) concurred with Gergen's analysis. He noted that sociopsychological phenomena do not have a "steady-process property" because they cannot be isolated from other influences, which are themselves changing. Research findings will, therefore, be "partial and distant from real events...and rather short-lived.... [so] that we cannot store up generalizations and constructs" (p. 123). Moreover, Cronbach argued, the complex interactions between variables—the ways in which factors such as teachers' and students' personalities, the climate of the school and/or the community, the age of students, the topic under consideration, and the historical period combine to produce different outcomes—account for many of the inconsistencies in results from one study to another. Such inconsistency makes the building of generalizations about a sociopsychological phenomenon such as schooling extremely difficult, if not impossible.[9]

One reason teachers, and other educators, do not find research helpful, according to Banks (1982), is that it is inconclusive and "can rarely provide specific directions to guide teaching behavior" (p. 2). Gergen and Cronbach agree but suggest that building theories or accumulating generalizations that can be used for precise prescriptions is not a realistic goal for social science or educational research.

What should we hope for from social science and educational research, when it is relevant to our concerns? We might anticipate that it would "sensitize" us—make us more alert to potential influences on behavior and to their relative importance, more perceptive of subtle influences and of assumptions about human behavior that are not useful, more aware of the number of possibilities for bringing about a desired result rather than sure of any one (Gergen, 1973, p. 317). Put somewhat differently, such research might provide "concepts that will help people use their heads" (Cronbach, 1975, p. 126) and suggestions for how to approach our teaching tasks (Martorella, 1977, p. 44). Teachers also ought not overlook the "heuristic" value of research reports; they may stimulate thinking about instructional and curricular alternatives (Shaver, 1979b, p. 41).

---

[8]John Dewey (1929) made the point that "the parent and the educator deal with situations that never repeat one another" (p. 65).

[9]In the context of needed research on teacher decision making, Clark and Yinger (1979) made a parallel observation:

> Each class consists of a unique combination of personalities, constraints, and opportunities. Behavior that is sensible and effective in one setting may be inappropriate in a second setting, and it is the individual teacher who decides what is appropriate and defines the teaching setting. (p. 232)

See also Martorella (1977, pp. 44–47).

This chapter is written from that point of view. It is important that a discussion of research implications for what should be taught in social studies be set in a context of inquiry about the research itself. It is also important to note that the discussion of research vis-à-vis practitioners' decisions about social studies instruction reflects a frame of reference that could underlie the curriculum itself—a recognition that policy ("should be") questions are politicoethical in nature, that values are important influences on such decisions, as is knowledge that is not research-based, and that penetrating questions must be asked about the relevance and soundness of the research evidence that might be brought to bear on such questions (Oliver & Shaver, 1974). Saying that does not discount the potential for research to contribute to consideration of what should be taught in social studies, if that potential is taken realistically to be the sensitization and stimulation of our thinking rather than the provision of precise answers.

RESEARCH ANSWERS TO TEACHERS' QUESTIONS

Social studies is a perplexing field because it draws potentially from so many academic areas—the various fields of history, the humanities, and the social sciences—as well as from the law and applied areas such as journalism. Some people believe that good social studies teachers should be knowledgeable in all of these areas. Whether that was ever possible is questionable; with the explosion in numbers of publications, it is clearly impossible now.

The same frustration of overabundance applies to an attempt to look at research for implications .as to what should be taught in social studies. Clearly, research in history and the social sciences is relevant. It provides the sources of textbook content (albeit much abstracted and overgeneralized, e.g., Metcalf, 1963)[10] and could give us insights into the nature of the society for which students are being prepared for citizenship and into the functioning of individuals in the society. Scholarly activity in the humanities would be relevant as well to efforts in social studies to understand the meaning of humanness and to help students be more reflective about themselves and society. Psychological and educational research is particularly relevant for the hints it might provide about what it is possible to attain in schools, the conditions that affect such attainment, and the relative effectiveness of different ways of seeking outcomes.

Just as social studies teachers cannot be conversant with all of the relevant areas of knowledge, a review of research of that scope is likewise not practicable. What follows is a discussion of educational research that addresses issues of central importance to classroom practice in social studies education. Those issues are not necessarily the ones that receive the most attention in the social studies literature. That distinction parallels the contrast noted earlier between the interests, concerns, and orientations of classroom teachers and those of other social studies professionals, not only professors and researchers but often district supervisors as well.[11] It is the concerns and interests of the latter that tend to get addressed in publications.

---

[10]For example, Patrick (1972) expressed concern that the content of government textbooks did not reflect the most recent research in political science.

[11]The NSF studies of status indicate that teachers rely most heavily on other teachers, persons in touch with the realities of classroom teaching, for information about what and how to teach. Supervisors usually do not teach and, in teachers' eyes, having left the classroom, become insensitive to the real demands of teaching. Graduate work only makes the disconnectedness greater as the supervisor becomes even more attuned to professors' beliefs and attitudes about pedagogy, which are often dissonant with the teachers' frames of reference (Shaver et al., 1980, pp. 11–12).

Student Disinterest

Although there is little research evidence on what students learn from the text-book-oriented teaching prevalent in social studies, the findings on student interest and on students' political knowledge, skills, and attitudes raise provocative questions about the appropriateness of that instruction. There have been consistent findings over the years that students from elementary through high school find social studies to be one of the least interesting school subjects. Recent studies continue to produce similar results. When 46 students randomly selected from grade 6 and grade 12 social studies classes in two schools in a Midwest school district were asked in interviews what was uninteresting about social studies, nearly half replied that it was "boring" (Schug, Todd, & Beery, 1982). In his national study of schooling, Goodlad (1983a) found that students in elementary and high school rated social studies as a low-interest subject. The NSF studies of status produced the same result (Shaver et al., 1980).

The teachers, as persons, do not seem to be the root of the problem. Students do not generally see social studies teachers as lacking in enthusiasm or in concern for them. Students tend to find their social studies classrooms to be comfortable places, and they often like their teachers. In the elementary grades in particular, the teachers tend to be less concerned with covering content than with their students' personal and intellectual development. But secondary school teachers, too, tend to like their students and to be concerned about them personally and scholastically (Shaver et al., 1980; Schug et al., 1982).

It is not surprising, then, that social studies teachers, like mathematics and science teachers, are concerned about student lack of interest. Weiss (1978) reported that 54% of the social studies teachers in her national sample indicated that student lack of interest was either a "serious problem" or "somewhat of a problem" (p. 158). In the NSF case studies of schools (Stake & Easley, 1978), lack of motivation was often mentioned by social studies teachers as a major problem. Hertzberg (1981) put it directly:

> This reader found [in the NSF case studies] a more troubled picture than the one generally conveyed by the [Shaver et al., 1980] report.... For example, the numerous instances of student lack of interest or outright hostility, referred to quietly in the report, emerge vividly in the case studies. (p. 160)

What connection might there be between these findings and the findings, referred to earlier, regarding the *way* social studies is frequently taught? One group of interpreters of the NSF studies of status (Ponder et al., 1980) summarized the mode-of-teaching research as follows:

> At *all* levels, the social studies curriculum is a textbook curriculum. Teachers use the textbook to organize their courses and students encounter the content of these courses largely through textbook pages. Completing worksheets and answering questions at the ends of the chapters are major classroom activities. (p. 171)

And from another summary:

> Knowing for the [social studies] student is largely a matter of having information; and the demonstration of the knowledge frequently involves being able to reproduce the language of the text in class discussions or on tests.... There is

little attention to the development of systematic modes of inquiry and reasoning, including valuing. CSSE [Case Studies in Science Education] observers saw some efforts to get students to think for themselves and develop their own reasoning powers; but more often students were asked to respect understandings that came from others, supposed validated, but by processes that were not explicated, much less brought into the classroom discourse to be applied by students.

As a corollary to [this] mode of teaching. . ., motivation is largely external. One learns for grades, for approval, because it is the thing one does at school, or to get into college. That students will learn through intrinsic motivation —because information or skills are useful for coping with problems of personal importance, or to satisfy curiosity—is not a common assumption among [social studies] teachers. (Shaver et al., 1980, pp. 6–7)[12]

Goodlad noted that there seems to be in social studies classes, nationally, a "preoccupation with the lower intellectual processes" (1983b, p. 15), a "curricular sterility," with the emphasis on recall of textbook information. Topics that seem to be potentially of great human interest are "apparently transformed and homogenized into something of limited appeal." Although teachers list objectives concerned with the development of reasoning, such as "testing in a new situation hypotheses derived from examining other circumstances" and "drawing conclusions from an array of data," few activities implied by such objectives were observed in classrooms, and "tests reflected quite different priorities—mainly the recall of information" (1983a, p. 468).

At the elementary school level, the problem appears to be compounded by the "expanding environment" sequence of elementary social studies, moving in succeeding grades from self to families to neighborhoods to communities, states, nation, and the world (Morrisett, 1981). That pattern persists despite the lack of research evidence to support its effectiveness and in spite of some evidence that at the early grades there is excessive redundancy with what students already know from their out-of-school experiences, especially in a highly mobile society replete with electronic media (McLendon & Penix, 1968; Ehman & Hahn, 1981). That content may also fail to capitalize on the richness of young students' mental lives (Egan, 1980, 1982).

In light of the status-of-instruction findings, it is not surprising to many observers that students refer to social studies as "boring." The questions raised about what should be taught in social studies are serious, undoubtedly the most crucial and most relevant to classroom instruction to be gleaned from research. But if the low-level demands of textbook information recall are one source of student apathy toward social studies, does research indicate any other possible sources with implications for what should be taught?

How Do Students See Social Studies in Their Futures?

Farman, Natriello, and Dornbusch (1978) studied a random sample of the total enrollments of eight San Francisco high schools. They found that only 46% of the

---

[12]Painting an overall picture of teaching is always a hazardous venture, for it is difficult to do justice to the exceptions. For example, Hertzberg (1981) cautioned that her reading of the NSF case studies (Stake & Easley, 1978) indicated a "sufficient number of references to discussions of social issues or problems to raise questions about the. . .assertion that such issues received slight attention" in social studies classes (p. 160).

students thought that learning social studies was more than moderately important, as compared to 75% and 71% for mathematics and English, respectively. The matter of importance is related to the common concern among educators with the "relevance" of content. Although, as Farman and his colleagues have pointed out, the term is ambiguous, relevance is usually taken to refer to the extent to which students can see that their studies will help them to understand and cope with their own lives.

Social studies teachers have often been admonished to make their courses more relevant, but the NSF studies of status indicate that those who try do not necessarily find the task to be an easy one, nor an automatic road to student interest. If an effort is made to select content based on matters of immediate importance in students' lives, it is not easy to anticipate what will be of interest to a variety of students on any one day; on the other hand, a future focus is difficult because students tend to have limited views of the future and its knowledge demands (Shaver, et al., 1980, p. 10).

Farman et al. (1978) approached the problem of relevance by focusing on "articulation," "the extent to which students perceive that course work will be helpful to some future aspect of their life" in the areas of careers, family life, and community work (p. 27). Their analysis of data from their random sample of San Francisco high school students yielded small correlations, indicating that the students saw little articulation between social studies and their future careers or marriages and family life. Students saw social studies as of moderate usefulness to future community work. But only 33% of the students reported involvement in community work to be "very" or "extremely" important to their future happiness (contrasted with 94% for careers and 69% for marriage and family life).

Farman et al. suggested that teachers might attempt to increase the articulation of social studies to careers, marriage, and family life by helping students understand the demands of those adult roles and the ways in which social studies content is pertinent to them.

Of more interest, in the context of the consensus that social studies ought to be centrally concerned with citizenship education, are the implications from the community work data. Earlier analysis of the same San Francisco data by Fernandez, Massey, and Dornbusch (1976) had indicated that students did not perceive social studies courses as emphasizing the social skills and knowledge basic to civic competence. (The students' perceptions are, of course, consistent with the research findings cited earlier with regard to what is taught in social studies.) The analysis by Farman et al. (1978) suggested that even when that emphasis was perceived by students as present, they did not view it as important. This led to the recommendation that social studies teachers stress both the importance of community involvement and the usefulness of social studies content to that involvement.

These findings and recommendations are consistent with those of Schug et al. (1982) based on their interviews of students in the Midwest. While provocative, and perhaps of value to individual teachers who do emphasize sociocivic knowledge and skills, the recommendations fail to take into account a basic reality: The recall of textbook information, which research indicates is the prevalent focus in social studies, is in large part not relevant to or articulated with future citizenship roles. To convince students that it is so articulated hardly seems feasible.

Research suggests other reasons for lack of student interest in social studies, such as the redundancy of content from one year to the next and the teaching methods used (e.g., Schug et al., 1982). But there is no mistaking the strong evidence that the textbook-based curriculum is a major contributor to the dearth of interest. There is also little evidence that teachers are inclined to reckon with the apparent contradiction between their beliefs that they know what is good for students, what students need to know, and how students learn best, as manifested in the textbook-based curriculum, and their own concerns about the lack of student motivation (Shaver et al., 1980).

Political Attitudes and Knowledge

Student interest, as important as it is, would be less of a concern if evidence were available that the citizenship goals so frequently stated in curriculum guides and reflected in teachers' written objectives are being achieved. Such does not seem to be the case, however. The most thorough reviews of literature in this area have been done by Ehman. He has come to conclusions such as these: "The social studies curriculum...does little to alter the political awareness or knowledge of secondary school students" (1980, p. 105); "the number of social studies courses taken by students has little or no relationship to [their] political attitudes" (1977, p. 89); "the civics and government curriculum itself is impotent in the political socialization of attitudes" (1980, p. 107); and "the evidence for [social studies] curriculum effects on [political] participatory orientations is far from suggesting a consistent and robust influence" (1980, p. 108).

The results from the National Assessment of Educational Progress (NAEP, 1978a, 1978b) are no more encouraging. A number of commentators (e.g., Mehlinger, 1978) have expressed concern about the levels of political knowledge and attitudes and the decreases in those levels from the first testing with citizenship exercises in 1969 (NAEP, 1978a) and with social studies exercises[13] in 1972 (NAEP, 1978b) to the second testings in 1976.

Consider the following synopses:[14]

On items assessing recognition and valuing of constitutional rights, there was a slight decline for 13-year-olds and 17-year-olds from the first to the second assessment, with 13-year-olds "succeeding" on the average on 60% to 70% of the items in 1976 and 17-year-olds on 77%. (based on NAEP, 1978a, p. 7)

On items reflecting respect for others, there was a slight decline for both age groups from the first to the second testing, with 65% and 80% success rates for 13-year-olds and 17-year-olds, respectively, in 1976. (p. 15)

Knowledge about the structure of government also declined, with a 58% and approximately 55% success rate for 13- and 17-year-olds, respectively, in 1976. (p. 23)

---

[13]It is interesting that the NAEP chose to have separate citizenship and social studies assessments. To some this choice was perplexing in view of the emerging consensus that citizenship is the central aim of social studies. Others saw the choice as properly reflecting the definitional disagreement in the field and thought that citizenship should be the responsibility of the total school, the family, and the society, not just social studies teachers. Others simply approved the split because it provided two assessments relevant to social studies instead of only one (Fair, 1974, 1975).

[14]The NAEP summaries were largely limited to 13- and 17-year-olds because few items were administered to 9-year-olds. The synopses reflect that limitation. Also, data were not reported for 9-year-olds on the items cited in the paragraph following the synopses.

On items about the political process, decline was also apparent from the first to the second testing, with a 59% average success rate in 1976 for both groups. (p. 31)

Decline was also present for items dealing with international affairs, although the small number of items precluded the calculation of averages. (p. 39)

Although performance on each of the individual items cannot be reviewed here, some examples will indicate that it is often discomforting. For example, in 1976, 40% of the 13-year-olds and 24% of the 17-year-olds did not support the right of a person who believes there is no God to express such views publicly, and 51% and 33% of the 13- and 17-year-olds, respectively, did not support the right of such a person to hold public office (NAEP, 1978a, p. 13). Moreover, 24% and 20% of the two age groups thought, in 1976, that the president could declare an act of Congress unconstitutional (NAEP, 1978b, p. 11).

What to make of such results is not clear. While they seem disappointing in terms of the needs of a democratic society, one group of social studies educators thought that a correct response rate of 61% to 80% would be realistically satisfactory on 34% of the social studies exercises, with at least 80% correct satisfactory on 48% of the exercises (Chapin, 1975). Some reviewers have noted a "heartening...improvement in understanding and acceptance of racial minorities" (Mehlinger, 1978, p. 676). Yet some, as Scriven (1975) did earlier, would express "horror at the plain prejudice" indicated by the results when 42% of the 13-year-olds and 32% of the 17-year-olds in 1976 said they would not be willing to do one or more of the following: have a person of a different race as their barber or beauty operator, come to their church or synagogue, live in their neighborhood, sit beside them on a train or bus, or vote in national elections (NAEP, 1978a, p. 19).

Drawing conclusions from such data is a difficult task. For example, the difficulty level of the exercises could be a factor, although the assessment of "realistically satisfactory performance" by the panel of social studies professionals seems to suggest otherwise, as does my own reading of the exercises. The assessment in 1976 took place after several years of national disruption that might have affected the results (Fair, 1974). It was also a time when test performance on national tests seemed to be falling generally. There is also the riskiness of generalizing from 1976 (the last assessment) to the present: Do the 1976 results validly represent the knowledge and attitudes of same-age young people a decade later? And of course there is the question of social studies and other teachers' accountability for such results, because they are not the only ones who bear responsibility for political attitudes and knowledge (Hunkins, 1975; Mehlinger, 1978).

Even if the declines in scores are ignored, however, it is difficult to escape the provocativeness of the relatively low levels of performance, particularly when one considers that performance on such exercises may not be a strong indicator of applications of knowledge or attitudes in actual life settings. As Scriven (1975) noted with regard to the NAEP data on attitudes toward ethnic groups, there are commonly disparities between what people profess to be morally right and how they actually behave, and the former are usually overestimates of the latter (see Fraenkel, 1981).

All told, there are grave questions as to whether American youth are receiving an education that provides them with essential political attitudes, knowledge, and skills. Such questions have serious implications for what should be taught in social studies.

What Might Be Done?

As Goldenson (1978) has indicated, it is important to distinguish between what *does* occur in schools and what *can* occur when curricula do address political knowledge, skills, and attitudes in nontraditional ways. Experimental research addresses the latter question. For example, Patrick (1972) reported that students in nine schools in various parts of the country who took a high school government course based on the American Political Behavior (APB) curriculum had higher mean political knowledge and critical thinking skills scores than did control students in the same schools. The differences were not only statistically significant, but correlation ratios indicated that a high proportion (.31 to .73) of the variance in political knowledge scores was associated with APB course membership, with moderate to low associations for thinking skills scores. Mean differences on tests of attitudes were slight and not statistically or educationally significant. That finding is interesting in light of the essentially textbook format of the APB materials.

At least two more recent studies have shown that political attitudes are amenable to change. Curtis (1978; Curtis & Shaver, 1980) conducted a study with 225 slow learners, aged 15 to 21, in eight schools throughout British Columbia. As with Patrick's (1972) study, Curtis could not assign students randomly to treatment, but classes were so assigned. The curriculum was based on the common recommendation that the study of contemporary problems is relevant to citizenship education goals and would increase student interest in social studies. Over a four- to five-month period, the students investigated the problems and issues related to housing conditions in their communities, where both rental and purchase costs are high, especially in comparison to the anticipated incomes of the students. The model that the experimental teachers were helped to use called for aiding students to (1) become aware of a problem and the related issues; (2) gather relevant data, including reading government documents and interviewing public officials and private citizens; (3) construct positions on the issues; and (4) propose action.

Curtis (1978; Curtis & Shaver, 1980) found that the experimental students read complex source materials generally thought to be inappropriate for slow learners, had posttest dogmatism mean scores that were statistically significantly lower than those for the control group, and had posttest critical thinking mean scores and self-esteem scores that were statistically higher than those of the control group. There was also a statistically significant difference favoring the experimental group on a test of interest in social issues, with 23% of the variability in scores associated with experimental or control group membership. After completion of the housing study, a questionnaire was distributed to 54 students in three experimental schools (a postal strike precluded getting the questionnaires to the schools in the interior of the province). All of these students indicated, anonymously, that community studies should be part of their regular social studies program.

In a related study, Goldenson (1978) had teachers in two Minnesota high schools teach a three-week unit that exposed students to controversial issues, stressing the implications of constitutional principles for concrete situations. As in Curtis's (1978) study, active participation of the students was sought through group research projects that included interviewing lawyers, law officers, and others in the community. Goldenson found that a larger percentage (about 20%) of the experimental students became more supportive of civil liberties, while about 20% fewer experimental than control students fell into the category of being opposed to civil liberties.

The Curtis and Goldenson studies indicate that what is taught cannot be separated from how it is taught. Both studies emphasized content different from that of the usual textbook along with active student participation, rather than the passive recall of information. The results support Ehman's (1969) conclusion that "if we are to expose students to controversial issues and we desire 'positive' attitude changes, we had better pay close attention to the climate in which these issues are introduced" (p. 578).

The three studies cited have methodological weaknesses common in applied research: None tested for long-range effects; students were not randomly assigned to treatments and teachers were confounded with treatment; and the studies have not been replicated by other researchers. For those reasons, and the other reasons discussed earlier in this chapter, the results do not present an unequivocal mandate for social studies instruction. They do suggest, however, that social studies could be more interesting and more effective in attaining citizenship goals.

Despite the overall portrayal of social studies as dominated by textbook information—oriented teaching, there are exceptions. Each of us knows from personal or anecdotal evidence (perhaps from our own school-attending children) about teachers who select and deal with content in ways that the Patrick (1972), Curtis (1978), and Goldenson (1978) studies indicate are likely to produce knowledge and attitude changes. Research also confirms that such teachers exist but that they are uncommon (Stake & Easley, 1978; Hertzberg, 1981; Jarolimek, 1977: Elliott & Kennedy, 1979).

Student motivation is important to social studies teachers. Moreover, many teachers are interested in teaching political knowledge, and some are interested in skills and attitudes. For those reasons, it is important for teachers to consider the implications of research evidence such as presented in this chapter for their own teaching within the realities of their school setting.

Instruction Time in Elementary Schools

For the most part, the questions raised in this chapter apply to both elementary and secondary school social studies. However, an important question at the elementary school level cannot be ignored. It is whether minimally sufficient time is spent on social studies, especially in nondepartmentalized schools where individual teachers decide how to allocate time among subject areas.

In recent years, there have been frequent expressions of concern that social studies is being neglected in the elementary school because of increased emphasis on the "basics"—reading, writing, and arithmetic (e.g., Gross, 1977; Jarolimek, 1981). There is a lack of baseline data by which to judge whether instructional time for social studies has decreased, but it is clear that the amount of time spent is not great. In Weiss's (1978) national survey, teachers estimated that they spent 21 minutes a day on social studies in grades kindergarten through 3 and 34 minutes a day in grades 4 through 6 (p. 51). Gross (1977) reported that in some school districts less than an hour a week was being spent on social studies by elementary teachers (p. 198). McCutcheon (1981) found that the teachers in her study were spending 60 to 90 minutes a week on social studies and that it was likely to be dropped for assemblies and other special events. And Goodlad (1983b) observed not only that English—language arts and mathematics dominate elementary school instructional time but also that there is a tendency not to test students in social studies, especially in the primary grades.

Whether the concerns about time are justified is not clear. Language arts instruction and reading material often encompass social studies topics. Moreover, because elementary school teachers are concerned with social attitudes and skills often deemed relevant to democratic citizenship, such as working cooperatively, much "non–social studies" instruction and classroom guidance are relevant to social studies goals. Furthermore, Stake and Easley (1978) found that the teachers, elementary and secondary, in their case studies were in accord with the "back to basics" emphasis. Textbook instruction is dependent on students' reading skills; consequently, social studies teachers largely see reading as essential to other learning and believe it a prerequisite, not a skill to be learned through involvement in subject-matter learning. Despite some agreement with efforts by social studies writers (e.g., Jarolimek, 1981) to define citizenship education as "basic," teachers still see the three R's as the "real" basics. The emphasis on the basics in the elementary school and support for that instruction by secondary school social studies teachers are not the result of external coercion (Shaver et al., 1980, pp. 8, 14).

Again, research findings with regard to what is do not indicate what should be. But questions about what should be in social studies may not seem urgent to teachers who devote little explicit instructional time to that curricular area.

CONCLUSION

Rather than the usual general review of research and drawing of implications, this chapter has focused on two matters deemed to be of central importance: (1) the relevance of research to decisions about what should be taught in social studies and the adequacy of that research; and (2) the evidence about what *is* taught in social studies, contrasted with the evidence as to the lack of student interest and the extent to which the political knowledge, skill, and attitude goals of citizenship education are not being achieved. In the face of the paradox implied by the status research, other concerns for social studies practitioners pale in importance.

There is research evidence that what *could be* is significantly different from what *is*; social studies teachers may have options available to alleviate their motivation-learning quandary. How to break from textbook content and from the reading, recitation, information-recall pattern, given the realities of classroom teaching, is the major challenge. Research evidence poses the issue. It suggests that much of what is being taught is inappropriate. What should be taught and how are critical decisions to be made specifically by individual social studies teachers whose separate choices have a collective impact of major importance to the society.

FURTHER READING

Armento, B. J. (1986). "Research on Teaching Social Studies." In M. C. Wittrock (Ed.), *Handbook of Research on Teaching* (3rd ed.). New York: Macmillan. Examines the relation of research to instruction, emphasizing the need for sounder conceptual bases and for research aimed directly at making teaching more effective.

Clifford, J. C. (1973). "A History of the Impact of Research on Teaching." In R.M.W. Travers (Ed.), *Second Handbook of Research on Teaching*. Chicago: Rand McNally. Although this very readable account of the effects of research on teaching does not deal directly with social studies, it will be of interest to all practitioners who wonder about the extent of and reasons for such influence.

Hunkins, F. P., Ehman, L. H., Hahn, C. L., Martorella, P. H., & Tucker, J. L. (1977). *Review of Research in Social Studies Education, 1970–1975.* Washington, DC: National Council for the Social Studies. Reviews of research on social studies curriculum and instruction in the areas of cognitive outcomes and values.

Mehlinger, H. D., & Davis, O. L., Jr. (Eds.). (1981). *The Social Studies.* 80th yearbook of the National Society for the Study of Evaluation, Part 2. Chicago: University of Chicago Press. A comprehensive treatment of social studies education. It has a chapter on research contributions to social studies, and most chapters have references to research.

Metcalf, L. E. (1963). "Research on Teaching the Social Studies." In N. L. Gage (Ed.), *Handbook of Research on Teaching.* Chicago: Rand McNally. This chapter, which laments the lack of research related to a Deweyan theory of reflective teaching and notes conceptual problems with textbooks as a basis for teaching social studies, is still pertinent nearly 25 years after its publication.

Shaver, J. P., & Larkins, A. G. (1973). "Research on Teaching Social Studies." In R.M.W. Travers (Ed.), *Second Handbook of Research on Teaching.* Chicago: Rand McNally. This chapter, like Metcalf's earlier *Handbook* chapter, is not a comprehensive review of the literature; it is a discussion of difficulties in doing research in social studies education. It will be of interest to those concerned with the problems of drawing from research implications for practice.

Stanley, W. B. (Ed.). (1985). *Review of Research in Social Studies Education, 1976–1984.* Washington, DC: National Council for the Social Studies. This volume updates the earlier five-year review by Hunkins and associates. Its currency makes it of special interest to social studies practitioners.

Wiley, K. B. (1977). *The Status of Precollege Science, Mathematics, and Social Science Education, 1955–1975: Vol. 3. Social Science Education.* Washington, DC: Government Printing Office (GPO Stock No. 038–000–00363–1). Wiley has done a monumental job of pulling together studies and summarizing the state of research on social studies education.

REFERENCES

Banks, J. A. (1982, May). Two different worlds: Teachers and researchers. *Social Studies Professional, 64,* 2, 12.

Barr, R. D., Barth, J. L., & Shermis, S. S. (1977). *Defining the social studies.* Washington, DC: National Council for the Social Studies.

Barr, R., Barth, J. L., & Shermis, S. S. (1978). *The nature of the social studies.* Palm Springs, CA: ETC Publications.

Baxter, M. G., Ferrell, R. H., & Wiltz, J. E. (1964). *The teaching of American history in high schools.* Bloomington: Indiana University Press.

Beard, C. A. (1934). *The nature of the social sciences in relation to objectives of instruction.* New York: Scribner.

Benjamin, H. (1939). *The saber-tooth curriculum.* New York: McGraw-Hill.

Bereiter, C. (1982). Structures, doctrines, and polemic ghosts: A response to Feldman. *Educational Researcher, 11*(5), 22–25, 27.

Boag, N., & Massey, D. (1981). Teacher perspectives on program change. *Theory and Research in Social Education, 9*(3), 37–59.

Boyd, W. L. (1979). The politics of curriculum change and stability. *Educational Researcher, 8*(2), 12–18.

Bussis, A. M. (1980, April). Collaboration for what? In P. Hammond (Chair), *Teachers and researchers: Learning from each other.* Symposium presentation at the meeting of the American Educational Research Association, Boston.

Chapin, J. (1975). A rating of social studies exercises by social studies educators. In J. Fair

(Ed.), *National assessment and social studies education: A review of assessments in citizenship and social studies by the National Council for the Social Studies*. Washington, DC: Government Printing Office.

Clark, C. M., & Yinger, R. J. (1979). Teachers' thinking. In P. L. Peterson & H. J. Walberg (Eds.), *Research on teaching*. Berkeley, CA: McCutchan.

Crabtree, C. (1983). A common curriculum in the social studies. In G. D. Fenstermacher & J. I. Goodlad (Eds.), *Individual differences and the common curriculum*. 82nd Yearbook of the National Society for the Study of Education, Part I. Chicago: University of Chicago Press.

Cronbach, L. J. (1975). Beyond the two disciplines of scientific psychology. *American Psychologist, 30*, 116–127.

Curtis, C. K. (1978). *Contemporary community problems in citizenship education for slow-learning secondary students*. Unpublished doctoral dissertation, Utah State University.

Curtis, C. K., & Shaver, J. P. (1980). Slow learners and the study of contemporary problems. *Social Education, 44*, 302–308.

Davis, O. L., Jr. (1981). Understanding the history of the social studies. In H. D. Mehlinger & O. L. Davis, Jr. (Eds.), *The social studies*. 80th Yearbook of the National Society for the Study of Education, Part II. Chicago: University of Chicago Press.

Dewey, J. (1929). *The sources of a science of education*. New York: Liveright.

Egan, K. (1980). John Dewey and the social studies curriculum. *Theory and Research in Social Education, 8*(2), 37–55.

Egan, K. (1982). Teaching history to young children. *Phi Delta Kappan, 63*, 439–441.

Ehman, L. H. (1969). An analysis of the relationships of selected educational variables with the political socialization of high school students. *American Educational Research Journal, 6*, 559–580.

Ehman, L. H. (1977). Research on social studies curriculum and instruction: Values. In F. P. Hunkins et al., *Review of research in social studies education, 1970–1975*. Washington, DC: National Council for the Social Studies.

Ehman, L. H. (1980). The American school in the political socialization process. *Review of Educational Research, 50*, 99–119.

Ehman, L. H., & Hahn, C. L. (1981). Contributions of research to social studies education. In H. D. Mehlinger & O. L. Davis, Jr. (Eds.), *The social studies*. 80th Yearbook of the National Society for the Study of Education, Part II. Chicago: University of Chicago Press.

Eisner, E. (1983, April). *Can educational research inform educational practice?* Division B Vice Presidential Address, presented at the meeting of the American Educational Research Association, Montreal.

Elliott, M. J., & Kennedy, K. J. (1979). Australian impressions of social studies theory and practice in secondary schools in the United States. *Social Education, 43*, 291–296.

Fair, J. (1974). What is national assessment and what does it say to us? *Social Education, 38*, 398–403, 414.

Fair, J. (1975). National assessment and social studies education: The setting. In J. Fair (Ed.), *National assessment and social studies education: A review of assessments in citizenship and social studies by the National Council for the Social Studies*. Washington, DC: Government Printing Office.

Farman, G., Natriello, G., & Dornbusch, S. M. (1978). Social studies and motivation: High school students' perceptions of the articulation of social studies to work, family, and community. *Theory and Research in Social Education, 6*(3), 27–39.

Fernández, C., Massey, G. C., & Dornbusch, S. M. (1976). High school students' perceptions of social studies. *Social Studies, 67*(2), 51–57.

Fraenkel, J. R. (1981). The relationship between moral thought and moral action: Implications for social studies education. *Theory and Research in Social Education, 9*(2), 39–54.

Gage, N. L. (1978). The yield of research on teaching. *Phi Delta Kappan, 60*, 229–235.

Gergen, K. J. (1973). Social psychology as history. *Journal of Personality and Social Psychology, 26*, 309–320.

Goldenson, D. R. (1978). An alternative view about the role of the secondary school in political socialization: A field-experimental study of the development of civil liberties attitudes. *Theory and Research in Social Education, 6*(1), 44–72.

Goodlad, J. I. (1983a). A study of schooling: Some findings and hypotheses. *Phi Delta Kappan, 64*, 465–470.

Goodlad, J. I. (1983b). What some schools and classrooms teach. *Educational Leadership, 40*(7), 8–19.

Greer, R. D. (1983). Contingencies of the science and technology of teaching and pre-behavioristic research practices in education. *Educational Researcher, 12*(1), 3–9.

Gross, R. E. (1977). The status of the social studies in the public schools of the United States: Facts and impressions of a national survey. *Social Education, 41*, 194–200, 205.

Haas, J. D. (1977). *The era of the new social studies*. Boulder, CO: Social Science Education Consortium.

Hahn, C. L. (1977). Attributes and adoption of social studies materials. *Theory and Research in Social Education, 5*(1), 19–40.

Hertzberg, H. W. (1981). *Social studies reform, 1880–1980*. Boulder, CO: Social Science Education Consortium.

Hunkins, F. P. (1975). Validity of social studies and citizenship exercises. In J. Fair (Ed.), *National assessment and social studies education: A review of assessments in citizenship and social studies by the National Council for the Social Studies*. Washington, DC: Government Printing Office.

Jackson, G. B. (1978). *Methods for reviewing and integrating research in the social sciences*. Washington, DC: National Science Foundation. (NTIS No. PB 283–747)

Jackson, P., & Kiesler, S. B. (1977). Fundamental research and education. *Educational Researcher, 6*(8), 13–18.

Jarolimek, J. (1977). The status of social studies education. *Social Education, 41*, 574–579.

Jarolimek, J. (1981). The social studies: An overview. In H. D. Mehlinger & O. L. Davis, Jr. (Eds.), *The social studies*. 80th Yearbook of the National Society for the Study of Education, Part II. Chicago: University of Chicago Press.

Joyce, B., & Weil, M. (1980). *Models of teaching* (2nd ed.). Englewood Cliffs, NJ: Prentice-Hall.

Kissock, C., & Falk, D. R. (1978). A reconsideration of "Attributes and Adoption of New Social Studies Materials." *Theory and Research in Social Education, 6*(3), 56–70.

Martorella, P. H. (1977). Research on social studies learning and instruction: Cognition. In F. P. Hunkins et al., *Review of research on social studies education, 1970–1975*. Washington, DC: National Council for the Social Studies.

McCutcheon, G. (1981). Elementary school teachers' planning for social studies and other subjects. *Theory and Research in Social Education, 9*(1), 45–66.

McLendon, J. C., & Penix, F. C. (1968). *What research says to the teacher: Teaching the social studies*. Washington, DC: National Education Association.

Mehlinger, H. (1978). The NAEP report on changes in political knowledge and attitudes, 1969–76. *Phi Delta Kappan, 59*, 676–678.

Mehlinger, H. D. (1981). Social studies: Some gulfs and priorities. In H. D. Mehlinger & O. L. Davis, Jr. (Eds.), *The social studies*. 80th Yearbook of the National Society for the Study of Education, Part II. Chicago: University of Chicago Press.

Metcalf, L. E. (1963). Research on teaching the social studies. In N. L. Gage (Ed.), *Handbook of research on teaching*. Chicago: Rand McNally.

Moore, J. A. (1978). A new biology: More relevance, less redundancy. *Biological Sciences Curriculum Study Journal, 1*, 10–13.

Morrissett, I. (1979). Citizenship, social studies, and the academician. *Social Education, 43*, 12–17.

Morrissett, I. (1981). The needs of the future and the constraints of the past. In H. D.

Mehlinger & O. L. Davis, Jr. (Eds.), *The social studies*. 80th Yearbook of the National Society for the Study of Education, Part II. Chicago: University of Chicago Press.

National Assessment of Educational Progress. (1978a). *Changes in political knowledge and attitudes, 1969–76*. Denver: Education Commission of the States.

National Assessment of Educational Progress. (1978b). *Changes in social studies performance, 1972–76*. Denver: Education Commission of the States.

National Council for the Social Studies. (1975). The MACOS question. *Social Education, 39,* 445–450.

Oliver, D. W., & Shaver, J. P. (1974). *Teaching public issues in the high school*. Boston: Houghton Mifflin, 1969; reprinted, Logan, UT: Utah State University Press.

Patrick, J. J. (1972). The impact of an experimental course, "American Political Behavior," on the knowledge, skills, and attitudes of secondary school students. *Social Education, 36,* 168–179.

Ponder, G., Brandt, R., & Ebersole, B. (1980). The more things change:...The status of social studies. In *What are the needs in precollege science, mathematics, and social science education? Views from the field*. Washington, DC: Government Printing Office.

Schneider, D. O., & Van Sickle, R. L. (1979). The status of the social studies: The publishers' perspective. *Social Education, 43,* 461–466.

Schug, M. C., Todd, R. J., & Beery, R. (1982, November). *Why kids don't like social studies*. Paper presented at the meeting of the National Council for the Social Studies, Boston.

Scriven, M. (1975). Evaluating social studies and citizenship education: Some alternative approaches. In J. Fair (Ed.), *National assessment and social studies education: A review of assessments in citizenship and social studies by the National Council for the Social Studies*. Washington, DC: Government Printing Office.

Shaver, J. P. (1967). Social studies: The need for redefinition. *Social Education, 31,* 588–593.

Shaver, J. P. (1977). A critical view of the social studies profession. *Social Education, 41,* 300–307.

Shaver, J. P. (1979a). The productivity of educational research and the applied-basic research distinction. *Educational Researcher, 8*(1), 3–9.

Shaver, J. P. (1979b). The usefulness of educational research in curricular/instructional decision-making in social studies. *Theory and Research in Social Education, 7*(3), 21–46.

Shaver, J. P. (1982, November). *Making research useful to teachers*. Invited paper presented at the meeting of the National Council for the Social Studies, Boston.

Shaver, J. P., Davis, O. L., Jr., & Helburn, S. W. (1979). The status of social studies education: Impressions from three NSF studies. *Social Education, 43,* 150–153.

Shaver, J. P., Davis, O. L., Jr., & Helburn, S. W. (1980). An interpretive report on the status of precollege social studies education based on three NSF-funded studies. In *What are the needs in precollege science, mathematics, and social science education? Views from the field*. Washington, DC: Government Printing Office.

Shaver, J. P., & Norton, R. S. (1980a). Populations, samples, randomness, and replication in two social studies journals. *Theory and Research in Social Education, 8*(2), 1–10.

Shaver, J. P., & Norton, R. S. (1980b). Randomness and replication in ten years of the *American Educational Research Journal. Educational Researcher, 9*(1), 9–15.

Smith, L. M., & Geoffrey W. (1968). *The complexities of an urban classroom*. New York: Holt, Rinehart and Winston.

Stake, R. E., & Easley, J. A., Jr. (1978). *Case studies in science education: Vol. II. Design, overview, and findings*. Urbana: University of Illinois, Center for Instructional Research and Curriculum Evaluation.

Torney, J. V. (1980). The elementary school years as an optimal period for learning about international human rights. In L. C. Falkenstein & C. C. Anderson (Eds.), *Daring to dream: Law and the humanities for elementary schools*. Chicago: American Bar Association.

Torney, J. V., Oppenheim, A. N., & Farnen, R. F. (1975). *Civic education in ten countries: An empirical study*. New York: Wiley.

Weiss, I. R. (1978). *National survey of science, mathematics, and social studies education*. Triangle Park, NC: Center for Educational Research and Education.

Wesley, E. B. (1937). *Teaching the social studies: Theory and practice*. Boston: Heath.

White, C. S. (1982). A validation study of the Barth-Shermis Social Studies Preference Scale. *Theory and Research in Social Education, 10*(2), 1–20.

Wiley, K. B. (1976). *The NSF science education controversy: Issues, events, decisions*. Boulder, CO: Social Science Education Consortium.

Wiley, K. B. (1977). *The status of precollege science, mathematics, and social science education, 1955–75: Vol. 3. Social science education*. Washington, DC: Government Printing Office. (GPO Stock No. 038–000–00363–1)

Wronski, S. P. (1982). Edgar Bruce Wesley (1891–1980): His contributions to the past, present, and future of the social studies. *Journal of Thought, 17*(3), 55–67.

6 COMPUTERS AND HIGHER-ORDER THINKING SKILLS

Richard L. Upchurch and Jack Lochhead

Concern for developing higher-level thinking skills has increased in the 1980s; discussion of problem solving, critical thinking, and decision making abounds in conferences and journals. The computer is mentioned numerous times as *the* device to develop these skills. But before focusing on the computer in particular, let us determine what the history of teaching for thinking has to offer.

Until quite recently, Latin was at the core of the curriculum. Latin was taught for two purposes: to preserve a culture and to discipline the mind. The idea of disciplining the mind came from the rigorous logic of Latin grammar. Educators believed that students who had learned that pattern of logic would apply similar patterns when thinking in different domains. Unfortunately, this belief was not supported by the transfer experiments conducted at the beginning of this century (Pressey, 1933). As a result of those findings and the fact that the ancient language had lost much of its cultural relevance, Latin has all but disappeared from our schools. No single subject has emerged to replace it.

For a while mathematics was a candidate to replace Latin as the "builder" of logical or systematic thinking. This began with the required course in geometry for students who wished to continue their studies in higher education, but it was difficult to separate the content of geometry from the desire to produce individuals with unquestionable competence in logical thinking. Now the mathematics curriculum has fallen on hard times. The educational accountability issues of the late 1970s and early 1980s focused primarily on computational ability (South Carolina Department of Education, 1980). The measurability of computational skills combined with the well-defined objectivity of these skills led most states to focus on paper-and-pencil arithmetic, tasks with problem solving sometimes mentioned and other times ignored. The difficulty with portraying mathematics as a developer of higher-level thinking skills, especially in the area of problem solving, faced the same difficulty Latin had in demonstrating the transferability of skills to larger domains.

Today some educational innovators are advocating a role for computer studies and computer programming that is similar to the one Latin and mathematics once enjoyed. They usually do not make the comparison explicit, since both Latin and mathematics have had bad press. Nonetheless, we feel it is useful to view their proposals in that light. First, there is the issue of culture. The impact of computer technology on our current and future culture is at least as great as the Roman impact on eighteenth- and nineteenth-century European thought. It is not difficult to describe why some knowledge of computers and computing is essential. The dynamics of computing and the pervasive nature of computers are well documented, especially since *Time* magazine named a computer 1982's "Man of the Year." The rationale for computing in schools is the need for people to learn to control devices that play such critical functions in their lives (Watt, 1982). The major issue at this point is not that teaching computers is unavoidable but what the nature of that instruction should be and whether it should include a programming language. Consider the case made by Hatfield (1982):

> Contemporary emphases in mathematics instruction typically include rather extensive attention to algorithms, i.e., procedures aimed at "knowing how to." Usually only a single, inflexible, "ready made" procedure is presented. The steps of the procedure are described or exemplified by the textbook, and these are typically "modeled" by the teacher's actions in discussions of specific examples of appropriate algorithmic tasks. Student learning of "the procedure is often expected to be imitative behavior. Little or no attention is given to building up algorithms by each student as possible solutions to a problematically treated algorithmic task. Students are often neither encouraged nor allowed to offer alternative procedures, or to adapt (i.e., personalize) procedures. However, computer programs are often thought of as algorithms. The construction of a computer algorithm can involve many important cognitive processes, as well as emphasize understandings of the mathematical ideas needed to build up, test, "debug," and refine the student's own procedure. Interactive computer programming can allow the student to experience practical heuristic advice as well as concrete notions of algorithms. (p. 33)

The jury may still be out with respect to the need to include programming in the curriculum, but a strong case can be made for it.

We are much more interested in a second argument—that learning to program disciplines the mind. The issue becomes the ways in which programming does this and the types of instructional processes. Some workers in the field simply state that programming teaches problem solving and therefore higher-level thinking skills. The case of Latin does not allow one to let such claims go unchallenged. But reflection on the history of the transfer experiments suggests they may not have given Latin a completely fair evaluation. The experiments did show that skills learned in one area do not transfer rapidly or automatically to another, but they made no attempt to look for fostered transfer or transfer over long periods of time, say, 5 to 10 years. Similar arguments for mathematics, and its lack of transferability in the realm of problem solving, can also be justified. There are reasons for believing that computer programming is an even better method of training the mind. Computer languages are specifically designed for logic processing, and they have a simpler, more coherent structure than Latin. Indeed, the structure and function of computer languages provide a better forum to foster respresentation (Kaput, 1983) and a needed dynamism for encouraging experimentation. When we juxtapose mathematics and programming, we see some of the structures thought to be beneficial in mathematics in a much more malleable form in programming. Furthermore, some languages, such as LOGO (see Papert, 1980), were expressly designed to develop skills in reasoning and logic.

We have mentioned our belief that programming can encourage the development of higher-level thinking skills. Yet the documentation for such occurrences in the light of the number of school-age students subjected to computer-language instruction does not seem to support our supposition (Pea, 1983). In defense, we must distinguish between existing computer-language instruction and what it should be in the educational setting. First, the majority of courses now offered in the schools focus on the teaching of computer language as an end in itself. Too many teachers find the semantics and syntax of a particular language to be the sole reason languages are taught. Second, courses that teach about computers as part of socialization to the technological age often fail to go beyond the most superficial considerations. If computer instruction does not revolve around the theme of problem solving, the educational outcomes are unpredictable. Some students (probably without instruction) will develop into good thinkers and programmers, and others will not; few will view the computer as a problem-solving tool.

But while we believe that learning to program can improve general thinking skills, we also suspect that we educators have not yet learned to take advantage of this environment to achieve maximum benefit. There is evidence that learning to program does not by itself produce dramatic improvements in thinking ability or problem-solving skills (Pea, 1983). It seems sensible to expect, particularly in light of the transfer studies, that if we want skills developed in programming to be used in other contexts, we should specifically teach students how ideas from programming can be used in mathematics, English, and other subjects. Only after we have demonstrated several such examples can we expect students to seek their own. Furthermore, some determination as to the actual goals (explicit and implicit) supposedly built in to learning to program need to be illuminated for teachers whose task it is to teach such subjects.

COMPUTER PROGRAMMING

What Is Programming?

There has been a great deal of discussion of the advantages of teaching programming to students of all ages. To develop a proper perspective of what can happen in programming and the possible relationships of programming, problem solving, and thinking, let's look at the process of programming and program development.

The process begins with the presentation of a situation to the programmer. The usual problem is ill-defined, with a plethora of unanswered conditions and undetermined specifications. At this point in the process the programmer is responsible for constructing an orderly, well-defined problem statement from the givens (not unlike the author of an essay or the composer of a symphony or a painting). The programmer must clarify the goals of the program that is to be written. To reach a point of coherence, the programmer must be capable of asking questions about the situation either of himself or of the provider of the situation. The outcome of the goal clarification process is to determine the program specifications (input and output requirements), possible error conditions, and general processing requirements. The end product of this first stage is a problem definition—a definition of what is to be done with a general sense of how it might be accomplished.

With the problem now in tow, the programmer proceeds to break it into "chunks." This decomposition allows for manageable solution construction because it highlights the intermediate problems that require solution. As an additional benefit of decomposition, the programmer focuses on the intermediate problems, refining the intentions of each subproblem and usually uncovering additional concerns to be dealt with. Design questions that may not have been considered in the original problem definition now must be considered for the program to function successfully. Doing things in this manner, the programmer can impose new design characteristics on the problem that help refine what must actually happen during the execution of the subproblem.

With each subproblem described and the specifications of each determined, the programmer then considers the interaction of the parts, asking, "How do the results of the first action put me in a position to deal with the next process?" From these questions the programmer determines the way in which the pieces of the puzzle fit together and what actions are required to make the pieces fit in a coherent way—again a process of problem decomposition and refinement.

Up to this point, the programmer has not written any program code. It is not until now that the programmer has enough clarity of vision about the problem to attempt a solution by writing the program. But now the coding begins with the programmer describing each situation in terms of the particular language needed to describe the actions and tests required to solve one subproblem at a time. During the coding, the programmer reviews the problem specifications as the code progresses to ensure that what is intended does in fact occur. This coding and problem review process is critical to overall problem solving.

After coding, the programmer reviews the code for a particular process, looking for small syntax and semantic errors. Syntax errors are violations of the grammar rules of the particular language (misplaced punctuation and spelling). Semantic errors, more difficult to locate, are errors in the use of the logic of the language. If not spotted by the programmer, most of these errors are identified by the computer as it tries to make sense of the program. These errors are not difficult to identify or fix since the computer is the assistant and usually ceases work on the program when such errors occur. Most systems have error messages that help the programmer isolate the particular "bug" (error).

Syntax and semantic errors are simple to find because the computer helps us locate them. But another variety of bugs can be more recalcitrant. They appear only when the program is executed. Computer programs, like people, rarely do what they are supposed to the first time. The programmer usually has to go through several cycles of running the program, seeing what the computer does, identifying inappropriate actions, and changing the computer code accordingly. This process is known as debugging. Papert and Solomon (1971) point out that a computer program is, in a sense, a trace of the programmer's thinking. While some program errors are merely grammatical mistakes, others stem from faulty reasoning. Debugging these errors is, in fact, correcting one's own thoughts. If we are optimistic enough to assume that students can learn from their mistakes (that is, from finding and correcting them), we see that debugging can improve the mind. In many ways this is not a new idea. John Dewey saw the development of reflective thinking as the single most important objective in higher education. Binet, creator of the first intelligence tests, believed that self-criticism was the essence of intelligence.

One frequently overlooked task in the programming process is that of verification. If we assume that the code is a specification of a process through which the problem is solved, we should be able to construct data that illuminate particular cases with which the program must deal. Our selection of test data corresponds, to a high degree, with our thoughts about the problem specification and therefore serves as a metric for the goodness of our solution process. The design of the verification-process data is crucial to a properly functioning program, and the skills applied to developing such data are very similar to those used in debugging faulty programs.

Why Should Programming Be Included in the Curriculum?

[If] the essence of problem-solving activity is the representation and processing of information and its structures (this essence may be greatly affected by noncognitive factors, of course), then computers will affect this activity in critical, direct, and fundamental ways because computers deal exclusively with this essence! They provide dramatic new freedom in doing all the things that are at the heart of problem solving: representation of knowledge, manipulation of knowledge, varying the givens of a problem and their relationships, computing potential solutions, and so on. In this way computers are fundamentally different from other technologies, [such as] television, that have bounced off the educational enterprise. These other technologies had to do with transmission of information but not very much to do with varying its representation or transforming its structure. (Kaput, 1983, personal communication)

Computer languages are used for writing precise, detailed instructions. Each statement is a command to the computer ordering it to do something. Adjectives and descriptive statements do not fit into this scheme. While such restrictions have obvious disadvantages, they also help to clarify certain situations. In English we can say, "The green book was on the table." What we really mean is, "Reader, I want you to remember what a table looks like. Place that image in short-term memory. Now remember a book, color it green, and place that book on the table." As computer code it might look like this:

RECALL TABLE

PLACE TABLE IN MEMORY BUFFER

RECALL BOOK

ASSOCIATE COLOR GREEN WITH BOOK

PLACE BOOK ON TABLE IN MEMORY BUFFER

Note that all the underlined words are commands to undertake an action. Consider now the statement "The man was killed by the river." What image did we intend for you to create? Try writing this sentence in computerlike code. Can the ambiguity of the original sentence remain?

One of the best-kept secrets of twentieth-century school mathematics is that algebra is a procedural language. Although millions of students have spent billions of hours studying the subject, few have learned to read equations as instructions for a series of actions, actions that produce results on the left and right sides. This is not the obscure semantic point it may at first appear to be. A failure to read algebra correctly has serious consequences in application to real-world problem solving and in the solving of word problems. It often means that much of the mathematics an individual learned in school is useless in later life.

Imagine that you are looking down on the pasture shown in Figure 6.1. There are other sections of the pasture that you cannot see, but you have reason to believe that the ratio of cows and pigs will remain the same. Write a mathematical equation that describes how the number of cows (C) is related to the number of pigs (P). STOP! Do not read further until you have finished this task.

If you are like most people, you probably wrote $5C = P$ or perhaps $5C + 1P = T$. In any case, you placed the 5 with the C because there are five cows. The C stands for the noun, cows, and the 5 is an adjective modifying cows. But, of course, there are no adjectives in algebra!

Imagine now that someone has told you the number of pigs in the field (perhaps it is 12). Write a procedure with a series of instructions stating what must be done to that number to yield the number of cows you would expect to find. Your result may look like the following:

> *Find* the number of pigs.
> *Multiply* that number by 5.
> *Assign* this new number to the cows.
> The number of cows $\leftarrow$ 5 times the number of pigs,
> > or
> > $$C \leftarrow 5P$$

Note that this equation is the reverse of the first equation. If at this point you feel confused, you are not alone. Even after a course or two in calculus, a majority of students fail to write the correct equation. Most of their mistakes are the writing of $5C = P$ even though the algebraically correct answer is $C = 5P$.

In an international survey of college students, only in Japan did a clear majority favor the correct answer. The reason so few students respond correctly to this question is that natural-language habits are in conflict with algebraic notation. This conflict is so strong that it can persist even after considerable explanation (Rosnick & Clement, 1980). We expect many readers will remain confused, and we will not mention the number of times we have made the reversal even while lecturing on it. In the midst of all this confusion, it is interesting to note that if people are asked to write a computer program for calculating the number of cows from the number of pigs, the error rate is significantly less than it is for the algebraic equation! This is true in spite of the fact that most people have had far fewer hours of computer experience than of algebra. Procedural representations are far easier to learn in the computer context than in regular school mathematics.

Algebra is only one of several areas where the ability to think in procedural terms is a valuable skill. English teachers often use procedural writing assignments—for

A man takes a photograph from an airplane of some of
the animals in a large field of cows and pigs. He is sure
that he has photographed a typical sample of the animals
in the field. Write an equation using the letters C and P
to describe the relationship between C, the number of
cows, and P, the number of pigs, in the field. The
equation should allow you to calculate the number of
cows if given the number of pigs.

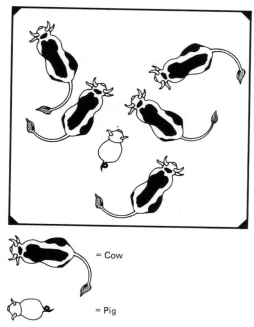

= Cow

= Pig

FIGURE 6.1   The cows and pigs equation problem

example, describe how to tie shoelaces or how to fold a paper airplane—for the
purpose of tightening up vague or sloppy writing habits.

At present there are no research results proving that the computer metaphor
improves student understanding for other types of procedural representation. However, what evidence exists (Soloway, 1982) is consistent with that possibility. We feel
that teachers should exploit this possibility. For example, in the shoelace-tying assignment, ask students to outline the description they will write using a computerlike
language similar to what we used. If even more assistance is needed, the outlining
could be preceded by a class discussion of the operations (commands) required for
tying laces. Here one can stress the need to know what knowledge can be assumed on
the part of the reader—which commands will be understood and which will not. A
similar approach can be used for mathematical word problems; ask students to begin
by writing computer instructions for calculating one of the quantities given or asked
for in the problem.

Is Programming Clearer than Algebra?

There are three distinct sources of complexity in programming: program organization, instruction definition with syntax, and interpretation of variables. Each of these

functions as a part of the process of solving the problem. At the inner level, program variables "hold" the value to be processed in a much more physical sense than algebraic variables, such as x or y. Variables refer to concrete memory locations within the computer, thus avoiding the "what does x mean?" we hear so often in math classrooms. From the variables and the other command words, the student constructs action units called instructions (program statements). The instructions are "bite-sized," in that they are thought of as single actions. The decomposition of a problem-solving task into such small units helps avoid the cognitive overload associated with the algebraic attempt to capture all the given relationships together with their consequences in a single set of statements, often a single equation.

Programming employs four basic structures: declarative, sequential, selective, and iterative (Holoien & Behforooz, 1983). Each of these has an explicit function in the processes that the total program is to perform. A single statement consists of precisely one of these structures and therefore performs exactly one action that can be viewed as distinct from the global problem being solved. This type of representation, then, allows for a line-by-line interpretation of the processes taking place.

The flow of control is well defined, not left to interpretation. Compare the structure of the procedural representation to that of the algebraic equation. The equation is a symbolic representation expressed in a rather compact and perhaps cryptic way. To determine the interactions of the symbols, one must first decode the meaning of each symbol in its context. For example, $3x$ means "3 times x," but 34 does not mean "3 times 4." Once the meaning of each symbol is determined, the individual must refer to a set of rules that govern the interaction of the symbols (order of operation). Thus the equation is a much more complex cognitive structure than the procedural representation. To see this, list the single actions needed in using the quadratic equation to solve the problem $3x = x^2 + 2$.

The major differential between the program as solution and an equation as solution can be based on the goal definition. The programming approach represents a well-defined goal structure with a dynamic flavor. The algebraic problem is not perceived as procedural. What, by the way, is an equation? An equation is a collection of symbols consisting of variables, whose values are undetermined, and operations. But the operations are based on corresponding operations for numbers. Thus by providing programming experience in mathematical problem solving leading to procedural representations, we can (ideally) avoid some of the pitfalls of algebra and at the same time provide a student-centered problem-solving environment. Part of this environment is the computer, whose primary function is to be the student's unemotional referee, considering the precision of the instructions and their organization. The computer signals when it cannot interpret the instructions, providing almost immediate feedback.

There is some evidence that the general technique of procedural representations can provide rich avenues toward deeper understanding and encourage some transfer to other sophisticated tasks. Siegler and Atlas (1976) used procedural representations to teach scientific reasoning. Their representation was in the form of a flowchart. Flowcharts have characteristics similar to those of programming languages in that they have declarative, sequential, selective, and iterative structures. This representation allowed for clearly defined actions at each step of the problem-solving task, and the students were taught to use this device in solving reasoning tasks. Students who understood problem solving in this manner were able to transfer the skill to more complex problems within the same domain in a manner far superior to those who had not had the opportunity to structure problem solving in this way.

Hacker versus Programmer

We have just provided a rationale for including procedural representations in the traditional curriculum, in the form of the computer program, a procedural representation that consists of a series of instructions written in a particular computer language (BASIC, LOGO, PASCAL, etc.). The educationally important benefits of programming do not stem from the details of any particular language but rather from the systematic planning that precedes implementation in computer code. Unfortunately, the popular press and some of the educational establishment have confused mere coding (writing instructions in a specific computer language) with programming. The term *hacker* has become synonymous with a compulsive programmer, and the distinction between serious problem solving and unstructured play has been dangerously blurred.

> How may the compulsive programmer be distinguished from a dedicated, hard-working professional programmer? First, by the fact that the ordinary professional programmer addresses himself to the problem to be solved, whereas the compulsive programmer sees the problem mainly as an opportunity to interact with the computer. The ordinary computer programmer will usually discuss both his substantive and his technical programming problem with others. He will generally do lengthy preparatory work, such as writing and flow diagramming, before beginning work with the computer itself. His sessions with the computer may be comparatively short. He may even let others do the actual console work. He develops his program slowly and systematically. When something doesn't work, he may spend considerable time away from the computer, framing careful hypotheses to account for the malfunction and designing crucial experiments to test them. Again, he may leave the actual running of the computers to others. He is able, while waiting for results from the computer, to attend to other aspects of his work, such as documenting what he has already done. When he has finally composed the program he set out to produce, he is able to complete a sensible description of it and to turn his attention to other things. The professional regards programming as a means to an end, not as an end in itself. (Weizenbaum, 1976, p. 116)

For the programmer, the program is a solution mechanism—a means toward the completion of a problem-solving task, a method for solving a problem with the help of a computer. Note the keywords: *systematic, slow, flow diagramming* (planning), *hypotheses, experiments, test*. All of these terms refer to a method of problem solving, where the problem is given and the program is an attempt at a solution. For the hacker, the purpose is merely to work with the computer; the production of code satisfies that. One would warn against viewing the hacker's cleverness in obtaining solutions, some of which work and some do not, as problem solving. The road to the clever solution may have no rational basis, whereas the well-conceived algorithmic solution (program) does.

The Relationship between Programming and Problem Solving

Let's examine the relationship between true programming and problem solving. Consider the problem diagrammed in Figure 6.2. Here we have a simple industrial task. Material arrives at the parts feeder, is picked up by a robot, and is delivered to the press. Once the press has finished with its process, the robot takes the part and grinds it. When the grinding process is complete, the robot moves the part to quality control for inspection. Finally, the part is put on an outgoing conveyor. The process is simple, but try writing a computer program to control the robot!

Here is a superficial view of the task:

Go over and get the part.
Take it to the press.
Take it to the grinder.
Take it to quality control.
Get rid of the thing by putting it on the conveyor.
Repeat task.

Yet this oversimplification is indeed the correct beginning of the problem-solving approach—decomposing the problem into manageable units, each of which can be dealt with separately. No one should expect an individual to write the full program from scratch as a continuous process. The human brain is not organized to deal with such complexity. Breaking the problem into parts and then dealing with the individual problems separately is proper problem-solving practice, often overridden, unfortunately, by the intricacies of language instruction.

Programming, in its proper perspective, is not a matter of simply writing instructions for the computer. It is a process of structured problem solving:

> Software design is the process of translating a set of task requirements (functional specifications) into a structured description of a computer program that will perform the task. There are three major elements of this description. First, the specifications are decomposed into a collection of modules, each of which satisfies part of the problem requirements. This is often referred to as a modular decomposition. Second, the designer must specify the relationships and interactions among the modules. This includes the control structures, which indicate the order in which modules are activated and the conditions under which they are used.[1] (Jefferies, Turner, Polson & Atwood, 1981, p. 255)

Problem understanding, the first of the set of problem-solving tasks implied by Jefferies et al., is crucial to the proper development of a procedure of any kind. If you do not understand the problem, it is highly unlikely that you will solve it. To redefine the issue, goal definition is a major task in any problem-solving activity. You must query the problem source to obtain the appropriate problem specifications prior to beginning any type of procedural representation. The process of understanding the problem specifications is no simple matter, yet it is neglected in the instructional environment. Problems presented in school mathematics are contained in chapters with well-specified objectives, and the problems reflect precisely those objectives. With such training it is highly unlikely that the student can learn to pose the questions necessary to bring a real-world programming task under control.

---

[1]The final element cited is the data structures involved.

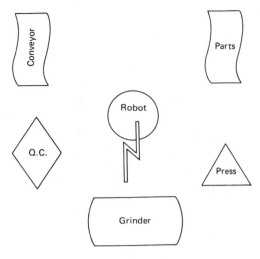

FIGURE 6.2

How can one begin with some vague problem decomposition and develop the intended program from such a description? Today's trend in computer science is to take the initial specification and develop the program as a process of stepwise refinements (sometimes referred to as top-down design). Consider a nonprogramming example:

A sculptor begins with a large piece of stone, from which she must produce a figure. Decisions are made according to what parts are to be described by the resulting piece (problem decomposition). For a full figure, the sculptor might decide on head, torso, trunk, and legs. Within each division, the specification becomes more acute. The head subdivides into ears, eyes, nose, hair, and mouth. Each part is defined in general and then developed into a completed unit. The sculptor also works on the figure in this manner. One would not expect the artist to take hammer and chisel in hand and produce a continuous line from the top of the stone to the bottom. On the contrary, we would expect the artist to complete the details of one specific area before venturing into another.

The process of stepwise refinement relieves the problem solver from action too early in the game. Stepwise refinement allows the problem to be decomposed into smaller and smaller subunits, and at each step the problem solver can submit the design to the scrutiny of the problem statement, reflecting on the conditions specified and those encompassed within the current level of specification.

Let's return to the robot example:

Go to the parts feeder.
   Move to "parts ready" state.
   Check sensor for part.
   Approach part.
   Grasp part.
   Retract.
   Move to "press ready" state.

Take the part to the press.
  Move to press point.
  Check sensor for clearance.
  Approach press.
  Remove finished part.
  Place part in press.
  Release grip.
  Retract.
  Move to "grinder ready" point.

Notice that in the first refinement of the original problem, the number of subtasks has increased dramatically. The number of problems has increased, yet each problem is different from the original; each is smaller and much more manageable. After several trips through the process, we would have the foundations for actually writing the code that would drive the robot to do the task involved. In fact, the actual coding of this problem would be done in pieces and tested in pieces. Such a process is more manageable than attempting to solve the entire problem in a single coding episode.

The process of stepwise refinement allows for one very important feature in a problem-solving environment: interaction of parts. We mentioned the interrelation of the parts when we discussed procedural representations, but now it becomes more critical. Where the outcome of a problem-solving task is a computer program, it is vital that the programmer understand and be able to specify how the pieces fit together. Stepwise refinement encourages exactly that type of thinking. The process of problem solving in this manner allows the programmer to produce modules that perform specific tasks, then write modules that describe the interaction of the parts. Consider the robot again. We have described a brief set of modules that manage the working environment; what is needed now is a way to specify how the modules interact. The languages used by computers allow for structures that provide control of how these modules interact. In most programming languages, the modules can be defined in subprograms (BASIC, FORTRAN) or procedures (LOGO, PASCAL); the programmer then defines within the main body of the global program under what conditions each of the procedures is to be used and when.

```
      MAIN PROGRAM
   REPEAT
      ENTER WAIT STATE;
      CHECK STATUS OF MACHINES;
      SELECT TASK;
   UNTIL JOB FINISHED
      END MAIN PROGRAM
```

The above program calls subprograms that execute specific tasks, then return control to the next instruction of the main program. Though the main program looks simplistic, the subprograms contain the meat of the code and thus can be written and tested initially in isolation from the rest of the program.

The use of subprograms and procedures encourages planning and systematic review of the problem definition. Unfortunately, many programming languages are taught so that the use of this type of language structure is left until the end of the course (this is particularly true of BASIC and FORTRAN). We agree with Mazlack

(1983), who suggests that modularization should be introduced as the first control structure in computer-language instruction.

Debugging

The process of debugging even syntactic and semantic errors can provide an environment where critical thinking is supported, but the location and repair of these other bugs provides a rich domain for developing high-level problem-solving skills. As a programmer you expect to see a certain output and behold a quite unexpected result. How could such a thing happen? What is the cause of this strange behavior? It is this type of occurrence that can be used as the foundation for teaching thinking over brute-force techniques.

Debugging requires several subskills that are worthy of mention in this discussion: hypothesis generation, design of experiments, and testing. When the program is run and produces unexpected results, the programmer should first seek to find the cause of this behavior. (The hacker will skip that search and instead try various patches until the program seems to work properly.) In practice, this pursuit of the underlying bug involves comparison of what was expected and what was actually produced. This differential provides the foundation for determining the bug's "psychology." The programmer generates hypotheses about where the particular bug may be and the cause of the bug. Notice that these are two distinct areas. Due to the interaction of the separate pieces of the program, the programmer must isolate the location within the code prior to determining cause. With hypotheses in hand, the programmer can review the code and inspect the region for possible culprits. Such hypotheses allow the programmer to develop a test case to be run with the program. This test will enable the programmer to establish whether his or her hypotheses are in fact correct. This hypothesis-experiment-test sequence provides the programmer with reliable data about the presence of the bug and its behavior in particular instances. The debugging process is vital to the programming cycle. It forces the programmer to review his or her "logic" and reasoning while coding, thus reflecting on the mental activity that produced the code.

The process of writing down one's ideas has long been recognized as an effective means for clarifying and improving them. It seems likely that it is the rewriting (reading and rephrasing), rather than the original writing, that brings about the improvement. As in the case of programming, written words provide a trace of our thinking. If we bother to read them, we can gain insight into our own reasoning. We identify the assumptions inherent in our work usually by reviewing what we said, not analyzing as we say it.

Unfortunately, reading one's own writing is not as easy as it may sound. Not only students are reluctant to do it, but they also are usually not very good at it. Here programming has a clear advantage. The computer reads the program and does precisely what it is told—it does not do what it assumes or thinks it should have been told. The programmer first sees the result of these instructions and, faced with an undesired outcome, can reread the program with a specific objective in mind. Thus proofreading a program with the aid of a computer is a more focused task than editing an essay.

One of the assumptions of the debugging model is that the program is a good representation of the author's thought process. The validity of this assumption depends in part on the degree to which the language employed reflects basic mental processes. LOGO was specifically designed to incorporate a structure as close to natural human reasoning as possible. For example, in the part of LOGO used to instruct the motion of a "turtle" in space, the commands are FORWARD, BACK, TURN RIGHT, and TURN LEFT. These are, according to Piaget's research, the basic operations a child uses to conceive of his or her own movement. The program that moves the turtle is likely to be an accurate description of how the child first thought about the intended motion.

> Thus, teaching and learning are not a matter of being wrong or right, but rather a process of debugging. Learning and teaching are intertwined and become a process of developing debugging aids as knowledge gaps are discovered and filled in. (Solomon, 1982, p. 208)

But there is still more to this view of how program debugging provides a domain for learning. The form of a given procedural description provides a model through which the programmer conceives of the world he or she is manipulating. Just as LOGO models the child's thinking, programmers learn to model their own reasoning through the structure of the programming languages they have learned. The languages we teach can determine how future generations will think. Thus debugging one's concepts reflects an extraordinarily powerful view of teaching and learning that provides the student with a self-empowering tool to investigate relationships and interactions, while at the same time subtly shaping the style of those investigations. From this perspective, the choice of a computer language to teach should be guided by the effect that thinking in that language has on intellectual development.

USING THE COMPUTER AS A TOOL

Computer Literacy

Suppose we back up for a moment and deal with the issue of basic computer literacy. *Computer literacy* is one of those terms whose existence seems to be one of use without the benefit of definition. Large groups of educators gather and discuss the need for computer literacy without concerning themselves about whether they agree or disagree on the issue. We wish to constrain the confusion by defining computer literacy as the skills and knowledge that will allow a person to function successfully in an information-based society. Such a definition does not exclude programming as a topic but includes it as a part of a much broader conception of computing. With this broader conception we can look at the information processing view of computing to see what the impact on society may be and how that should affect the educational enterprise.

To gain an insight into what computers may become and how they will be used to assist in the development of higher-level thinking skills, let's look at how computers are being used by researchers. The field of artificial intelligence has developed over the past 30 years in an attempt to produce computers that can reason and solve problems. These "knowledge-based" systems provide us with a perspective for viewing computing.

> First is the problem of knowledge representation. How shall knowledge of a domain of work be represented as data structures in the memory of the computer

in a manner in which they can be conveniently accessed for problem solving?

Second is the problem of knowledge utilization. How can this knowledge be used in problem solving? In other words, how should the inference engine be designed?

Third, and most important, is the question of knowledge acquisition. How is it possible to acquire knowledge...automatically, or at least semiautomatically, in a way in which the computer eases the transfer of expertise from humans (practitioners or their texts or their data) to symbolic data structures that constitute the knowledge representation in the machine? (Feigenbaum & McCorduck, 1983, p. 79)

In this view of computers we see several distinctions between what the early computers were used for and what future machines will accomplish. The first issue is that of knowledge representation. The computer has become a knowledge manipulator. Much more than a mere information processor, it is concerned with the structure and access of information. Second, programs have evolved from the sequential, procedural representations to programs that allow inference and decision making based on high-level rules of reasoning. And third, the computer is moving into the sensory realm. Computers are being designed to hear, see, and speak, thus having the capability of "learning" from the environment.

This perspective of the computer, as knowledge manipulator, provides an exciting arena for educational development. Within this arena we can discuss the use of the computer as a tool, not in the programming sense but as a means of solving day-to-day problems, those affecting the quality of life. But alas, there is the issue of the computer as antagonist, one whose attributes are used against us, stealing our jobs, invading our privacy. Values and moral dilemmas slide into the picture, making the literacy issue complex and sensitive.

Today most computers are used in business applications such as word processing, data-base management, electronic spreadsheets, and graphics generation. These applications have prospered because of their impact on productivity and efficiency. They simplify difficult tasks. Each of these applications *can* be used with similar impact in education, reducing the complexity of some learning tasks and freeing students from archaic practices of data manipulation. The hope of these new tools

is that the time and energy devoted to conceptual considerations would indeed be increased. The real problem for the student is setting up the problem—formatting the file in the database, structuring the worksheet, setting the form for the spreadsheet, formatting charts and graphs. (Richards & Wheeler, 1983, p. 209).

To consider the issue further, let's examine some specific applications.

Word Processing in the Classroom

Students' models of the composing process constrast sharply with those of skilled writers. Students strive to make their compositions "right" the first time. Before starting to write, they mentally organize their ideas. Their goal is to tell what they know rather than to refine their understanding or to have a particular effect on the reader. When students write, they start with the first sentence and continue linearly until they are finished. Except for corrections in spelling and punctuation, they rarely modify their texts. Most only do two drafts, the second merely a neater and more legible copy of the first. For student writers, the composing process, with its stages of planning, writing, and revising, is sequential, with revisions primarily limited to corrections in spelling and punctuation and changes in wording and phrasing.

Once a draft is written, changes are mechanically difficult. Erasing makes the paper look sloppy. Adding words, sentences, or paragraphs or reordering the text is impossible without tedious recopying or cutting and pasting. Once a text is written, it may as well be carved in stone. (Kane, 1983, p. 1)

A word processing program for the microcomputer turns the systems memory into an "electronic sheet of paper." The major difference between the electronic sheet and the real paper is the modifiability of the electronic form. Words, sentences, and paragraphs in the computer's memory are alterable with a few keystrokes, thus making corrections easy. Moreover, the software offers the ability to rearrange text, making structural changes in organization quick and easy, as well as less susceptible to the inclusion of additional errors. The use of word processing in the writing activity alleviates the mechanical difficulties of writing and provides the opportunity for both student and teacher to concentrate on the process of writing—the communication of ideas and beliefs.

To speculate for a moment, as we compose the text that you are now reading, we write, modify, and revise as a purposeful activity. The intent is to convey a message to you, the reader. Our choice of language and structure is based on that intention. The use of word processing software allows the discussion of just those issues within the educational environment, and such a discussion is at a higher level than the syntactic issues. As students use word processors in the new focus on writing instruction, the entire composition process changes from simply writing to composing a written document that conveys intent.

In her work with the teaching of writing using word processing software, Kane (1983) points to six ways such technology can support the development of writing skills:

1. Students spend more time composing when they use a word processing system.
2. Students feel free to explore their own ideas in writing because deleting is easy, even from the middle of the text.
3. When using the computer, students consider the overall structure of their text.
4. Using word processing technology may facilitate use of revision strategies students have already learned, eventually resulting in their automatic application.
5. Students will be motivated to learn new strategies for evaluating and revising their texts because changes are easy to execute with a word processor.
6. The computer can influence the extent of collaboration while writing. (pp. 7–8)

Though these are preliminary results from a short educational episode, it appears evident that with appropriate instructional design on the part of the writing instructor, improved levels of writing can be achieved. Writing instruction could begin to focus on more complex forms of expression, such as persuasion, and could eventually produce students whose ability to communicate in written language is fundamentally improved.

Spelling Checker

One aspect of writing that has always invoked the ire of English teachers is the lack of spelling ability in some students. Thus when assessing written assignments, a great deal of time is spent circling misspelled words. The magnitude of the task of identifying and marking these culprits detracts from the task of assessing the written expression of ideas. Furthermore, there is no guarantee that students will correct the circled words properly or that their spelling will improve. More often than not, the graded paper is seen as terminal, and no educational benefits are derived from the assessment.

A spelling checker can solve much of this problem. It is a program that marks all words that do not appear in its file of English words. The writer then determines with a dictionary what the correct spelling should be. Besides checking for misspelled words, the program helps identify typing errors and places where words are run together. Note that the spelling checker *does not* correct the spelling automatically; it only identifies words it does not recognize. Most of these programs also have available an expandable dictionary that lets users add new words.

The use of spelling checkers on word processors seems a significant advance over the old system. Consider the process of correcting spelling errors from the student's perspective. You read the text of an assignment looking for the spelling errors. But how do you find them if you do not know how to spell them in the first place?

Again the use of technology *is not* intended to replace instruction, rather to enhance it by automating some of the more tedious tasks and allowing more instructional time for the higher-level skills. In particular, with the spelling checker, instructional activity can focus on the use of language. Similar to the structural issues discussed earlier, the spelling checker allows experimentation with language without the associated concern for correct spelling. It is even conceivable that students would spend more time selecting words and phrases that communicate precisely.

Data Base

Information organization has become a vital survival skill as the information explosion begins to overwhelm the average citizen. Today's students need to be capable of organizing information for future use and retrieval. By including the fundamental of retrieval in the task, we also incorporate the need for determining what criteria are important in the storage of the information. In storing data electronically, only the salient features can be keyed in for later retrieval, and those salient features must be defined according to the task at hand. Students can best learn about these issues by creating and using their own data bases. Through such experience they can be brought to understand the principles of data-base organization and manipulation. Beginning activities could include a class-interest inventory—likes and dislikes, sports statistics, or series of scientific observations.

Associated with the problem of organizing a local data base is the issue of finding information in the large-scale data bases now available commercially. "Information utilities" such as The Source (Source Telecomputing Corporation) provide access electronically to a wide variety of both current and historical information via computer communications. Instructional uses of such information warehouses are virtually unlimited. Issues that arise from the use of such resources are ones involving the art of asking questions. To make good use of large amounts of data, one must determine what criteria must be contained in the questions asked of it; otherwise, one receives such a volume of data that there is no way to sort through them. Keyword identifiers and sort keys become essential tools in reducing the volume of data to items that are relevant to the issue under investigation.

Another feature of using such computer-based resources is the ability to design real-time problem-solving tasks: An immediate decision must be made based on data, but the data must be found and interpreted first. Such tasks might include stock market analysis, business ventures, and marketing surveys. Embedded in all these tasks are a variety of thinking skills that can be focused on rather than being preoccupied with data gathering. Such skills are basic to real-world problem solving: (1) data acquisition, (2) data storage in a manner amenable to the task presented, (3) data manipulation or feature extraction, (4) data interpretation, and (5) drawing conclusions based on trends and patterns. These activities represent substantial objectives for the educational environment and can be used to enliven student learning.

The data-interpretation task is worthy of special note. Software *is* available for the microcomputer to produce graphs from charted data. This software also allows the user to vary the choice of representation rapidly. Such a capability provides students with rapid, easy options for presenting data persuasively in graphic form. The construction of graphs also provides teachers with a mechanism to discuss trends and patterns by looking at graphs. Activities in business, government, science, and physical education can be envisioned that use such capabilities to make learning "real."

Electronic Spreadsheet

Another useful software tool is the electronic spreadsheet. This software package converts the microcomputer's memory into a scratch pad and calculator for preparing financial reports, cost estimates, and the like. From the broader perspective, the electronic spreadsheet provides the capability to model various quantitative situations easily. This capability allows the user almost effortlessly to view the effects of various variables on the performance of a system, change the values, and update information almost instantaneously.

This is a powerful tool for investigating and developing thinking skills. Identification and manipulation of variables can be the focus of learning activities without the related toil of calculation. Students can rapidly "see" the effect of changes of one variable on the behavior of the system being investigated. Hypotheses can be established and investigated quickly. Students can concentrate on a system's constraints and reactions when its behavior is visible in terms of the quantifiable results.

One important feature of word processing, data bases, graphics, and spreadsheets is that the software for each must be capable of interacting with the others. Information created under the data-base program must be usable with the spreadsheet, and vice versa, for us to realize any time saving from using the computer as a tool for problem solving. Fortunately, such capability exists today and will be increasingly available in the future. In fact, several low-level packages now provide all capabilities on the same program disk, and some high-level packages permit the information from one activity to be used in any of the others.

Perhaps the most interesting area to pursue from the educational perspective is that of feeding the results of spreadsheets or data bases into a graphics-generating program (a program that can produce charts and graphs from data). With such a tool, the instructor can allow the students to manipulate the graphics representation from a given set of data quickly and easily. Such an activity allows the students to investigate the differing "messages" of various pictorial representations and hence investigate the use of differing representations to express a point. Note that this is the quantitative equivalent of the word processor in English.

Computer Tutor

The computer uses we have discussed to this point can be characterized as ones in which the student manipulates the computer. Now we will deal with situations where the computer's program guides and instructs the student. The type of software we are discussing is normally termed CAI, for computer-assisted instruction. The basic design of these programs closely resembles that of the programmed text in that a textual segment is given and then questions regarding the content of the text are presented, with the student's responses guiding the ensuing activities. Of course, the computer version of this approach allows more control over the activities of the student. The programmed text has no way of identifying whether a student actually reviews material when suggested, yet the program version contains some type of decision mechanism that directs the presentation of text, review, and exercises for the student based on the student's answers on portions of the exercises.

> Most programs in this category specify the possible sequences through a program, where different branches are taken depending on the student's responses to questions or problems. The sequence a student follows is usually deterministic, with a branch for each anticipated class of responses by the student (sometimes based on a keyword he might give). Some ingenious programs can be written in this way, such as the Socratic system or the chemistry programs in the Plato system, but there are some inherent limitations to this approach. The student cannot use natural language in his responses, and cannot ask any but specifically anticipated questions. The teacher has a considerable burden in the preparation of questions, answers, keywords, and branching. From a system's point of view, the system has no real initiative or decision power of its own, nor any knowledge that is available other than at fixed points in the sequence. (Collins & Grignetti, 1975, p. 2)

"In many schools today," says Papert (1980), "the phrase 'computer-aided instruction' means making the computer teach the child. One might say the computer is being used to program the child" (p. 2). This use of the computer as tutor may have its place, but we must consider what that place may be and the consequences of such use on higher-level thinking skills. When the program executes its sequence of activities and makes the decision to continue or repeat activities, there is no internal (program) knowledge of the student's needs other than what the student got wrong. Normally, the student can review the material some number of times until the system gives the correct answer and proceeds. It may take a great deal of imagination to see where the "learning" is in this situation. Pursuing this line, consider the task of teaching hypothesis generation, breaking problems into parts, considering similar problems, and developing strategies in this mode. How or when can there be right or wrong answers? These activities require something much more than simple answers; they require the ability to watch and guide development.

An additional complaint with computer-driven lessons is the inability of the program to draw inferences from the student's behavior. Brown and Burton (1977) determined that for some arithmetic tasks, students had developed deep-seated but incorrect procedural methods. The conclusion here is not that students don't know how to work the problems when they get the wrong answer; rather, the method they use is faulty. Using "canned" software, the program would simply assume that the student did not learn the correct method and re-present it. The teaching problem in this case is more difficult, because there must be some method for helping the student recognize fallacies in reasoning and then developing the correct method.

Furthermore, the limitations of the current variety of CAI do not allow students any avenues for exploration. The degree to which the branching and flexibility of this type of software is fixed prevents students from pursuing areas of interest. Thus it is normally beyond the capabilities of the software to meet the needs of the student, either as diagnostician or tutor.

Developments in the area of CAI design may afford us some relief from the frame-based packages of today. Brown and Goldstein (1977) and Burton and Brown (1976) discuss three different roles for the computer in the instructional arena: (1) the computer as consultant, (2) the computer as assistant, and (3) the computer as coach. Each of these portrays the computer program as an intelligent tutor that has information about the knowledge domain being investigated, can build some type of conceptual model of the student using the program, and can discuss the problems at hand with the student in standard English. Consider the power of such a software tool in developing hypotheses about a particular phenomenon. The student could view the data on the behavior of a given system and present a hypothesis rather than select from given alternatives. The computer could then discuss that hypothesis in light of the data presented. During this process, the computer could gain insight into the depth of the student's understanding and choose additional problems or situations to strengthen the given concept or test to see when a given idea fails a crucial test. This conception of an intelligent tutor incorporates the diagnostician, who can view a student's performance and provide a mental model of the processes the student uses. With this information the computer could choose examples and discussions that help the student recognize errant patterns. Such software packages would be a great contribution to existing instructional practices.

COMPUTERS IN CLASSROOMS AND SCHOOLS
Computer Use

Having discussed our view of the use of computers in schools, let us now look at the realities of educational computer use. The Center for Social Organization of Schools performed a survey of 2,209 schools across the country and produced perhaps the most elaborate set of findings concerning school acquisition and use of microcomputers ever (for a summary of the findings, see Rogers, 1984; Schneiderman, 1984).

> By January, 1983, 85% of all high schools, 77% of all junior-senior combinations, and 68% of all middle- and junior high schools had one or more microcomputers. The corresponding figure for elementary schools rose to 42% during the same period. (*School Uses of Microcomputers*, 1983, p. 2)

TABLE 6.1   STUDENT USE OF MICROCOMPUTERS

Activity	Median Use per Week (minutes)		1–15 Minutes per Week		Over 1 Hour per Week	
	Elementary	Secondary	Elementary	Secondary	Elementary	Secondary
Write programs, "computer literacy," etc.	19	55	49%	18%	4%	44%
Do drills, remedial work, unspecified math, language	13	17	60%	48%	.5%	9%
Play learning games, recreational games, etc.	12	11	73%	56%	.5%	9%
Applications: word processing, lab tool, data processing, other use for business class, etc.	—	30	—	28%	—	31%

Source: Rogers, 1984, p. 49.

The rate at which schools are acquiring additional microcomputers is also rising at a high rate.

Computers can be used in classrooms in four ways: (1) as teacher, (2) as object (for programming and computer-literacy training), (3) as facilitator (e.g., word processing), and (4) as a recreational device (for playing games). Table 6.1 gives an indication of the use, by area, for the microcomputers in service as of 1984. In terms of students using computers over an hour each week, at first glance the figure of 44% at the secondary level seems encouraging. But further study of the secondary school data uncovers the frightening inequity of the situation. "Only 13 percent of the students in a typical high school have an opportunity to use a computer in any given week. Most secondary-level computing courses serve a narrow population of above-average students" (Schneiderman, 1984, p. 91). The critical criterion for selection into computer programs is math ability. This excludes a major portion of the high school population. The rush to computerize education is effectively restricting access to computing for ethnic minorities and women.

The computer as object has rushed onto the educational scene over the past five years under the banner of "computer literacy." The collective educational systems of the nation are rushing headlong to guarantee that students can cope with tomorrow's high-tech era. It is estimated that 66% of a high school's computing time is devoted to the teaching of programming or "computer literacy," while only 18% is devoted to computer-assisted instruction or drill. During the same period when systems reverted to "basic skills" as a philosophy, we see the advent of new courses designed to acquaint, teach, or train students in the use of computers. One may ask where the time for such computer instruction is coming from in the light of legislation on basic-skills remediation. We may also ask whether there is a curriculum for introducing students to computers. As an indication, consider the model for computer literacy suggested by the Los Angeles Unified School District (Fischer, 1984). The model provides computer instruction for kindergarten through twelfth grade. The model includes objectives for all students and objectives for every interested and capable student. It may be reasonable to guess that programming appears only in the "interested and capable" category, while "computer awareness and knowledge" appears in the other. Focusing for the moment on the computer-knowledge track of the LA model, we see words such as *identify, use, define,* and *recognize.* In any hierarchy of intellectual skills, these are at the lower levels. Even when we move to the "advanced" track, we do not find any mention of critical thinking, problem solving, or logic. Again, someone is accepting, as fact, that the computer spontaneously and serendipitously generates these abilities in students. We are caught up in the vocational zeal of computer training, lost without purpose or plan.

The Influence of Programming on Intellectual Development

In the beginning of this chapter we placed ourselves clearly on the side of programming as an aid to developing higher-level thinking and problem-solving skills. We have discussed throughout the relationship between programming and the development of thinking skills. Yet we come now to the question, does taking a course in programming per se influence intellectual development? The response we propose is, probably not in most programming courses today. Consider the results of the National Assessment of Education Progress (Anderson, 1980).

1. Very few [students] claimed to be able to program a computer. Only 8% of the 13-year-olds and 13% of the 17-year-olds said they could write a program.
2. Only 11% of the 17-year-olds reported having some coursework in computer programming.
3. Performance on flowchart reading exercises and simple BASIC programs revealed very poor understanding of algorithmic processes involving conditional branching.
4. About half of the students who had taken computer programming classes were still unable to read a simple flowchart.
5. A few students who had taken computer programming classes seemed to have little or no understanding of general computer capabilities, even though students in general, even those lacking computer experience, seem to have such an understanding.
6. Many students both with and without computer programming coursework did not seem to have a sense of the value of computers for themselves personally or for society. (pp. 14–15)

It appears obvious that whatever is happening in the educational setting with regard to "computer literacy," it is not working.

There are four basic models from which one can construct a "programming" version of computer literacy: (1) learning a language, (2) learning programming, (3) programming through problem solving, and (4) problem solving through programming. Each model posits its own unique set of objectives and educational outcomes. Each is very different from the others in the learning activities that would be designed to accomplish the goals of both computer literacy and the development of higher-level thinking skills. In terms of our own view, the fourth, problem solving through programming, is the richest domain to explore, yet the one left untouched by current computer mania. Current events are perhaps best characterized by Martin Schneiderman (1984): "All too often it's a case of old wine in new bottles, a mishmash of old ideas and techniques grafted onto new technology, and the result is largely ineffective teaching and a waste of valuable computing resources" (p. 88). If we wish to make effective, efficient use of new technology as an educational resource, we must rethink the goals to be accomplished. To make programming a viable instructional activity, we must revisit developmental and cognitive psychology, look seriously at learning and instruction theories, and begin to construct the role we wish computers to play in the educational setting.

Teaching Programming to Enhance Intellectual Development

Our initial discussion revolved around the issue of whether programming *could* assist in the development of thinking skills, and our response was yes. Now, however, the question is, *does* programming provide the benefits suggested, and here the answer is "probably not." The distinction is that it can, but not automatically. This distinction forces a discussion of the program elements that must be in place to guarantee intellectual rewards from the teaching of programming.

The first element relates to the issue of programming versus problem solving and concerns intention. The design of the instructional program and the programming environment plays a major role in determining the outcome. If the focus is on programming, with a hope that problem-solving skills may develop, it should not be surprising if some students learn only coding. For problem solving to develop in the arena of programming, the emphasis must be on problem solving, with the program providing either the mechanism or the object. The role of programming must be determined early in the course of this endeavor if the instruction is to attain the intended goal.

Consider the issue of debugging. How does one approach the debugging task to teach problem solving in a programming environment? The answer may seem to be another one of our semantic quibbles, but it does shed some light on the issue. The answer is, debugging is learned, not taught. Debugging is a problem-solving activity, so the instructional activity should support the debugging practice *by the student*. Thus the teacher's role in the debugging activity is one of support and assistance, not problem solver. The attitude we advocate is summed up by Mary Jo Moore (1983):

> Knowing when to intervene and when not to seems to be the secret of artful Logo teaching. Doing it right all the time is an impossible ideal. What helps us do it right at least some of the time is to watch the student, not the screen. And never interfere with intense concentration no matter how repetitious or mindless, no matter what seems to need to come next to make the program at hand more elegant.

The ideal is to let our students know what the Logo language comprises without telling them where to use what. We try not to deprive anyone of his or her "Aha!" We try not to solve problems. We may find ourselves answering questions with further questions. Or the questions the children ask may well show us what to teach next. In lieu of offering a solution, we might offer additional commands in the language. We supply the technology. The child makes the discoveries. We intervene in order to avoid intervening. It is at once a paradox and an ideal. It is how to teach Logo. It is how to avoid teaching Logo. (p. 14)

The second element concerns the choice of language. This is important from the perspective of intent as well as function. It is inconceivable to fit the instruction and the characteristics of the student to the language. It is more appropriate to determine the focus of the instruction and the characteristics of the student, then to determine which language is most suitable for the purpose. Like people, languages have personalities, strengths, weaknesses, functions. One must understand one's instructional intention prior to choosing a language to supplement it. A choice of language should include issues of interactive capability, debugging tools, types of information to be processed (problems used), and interest level of the students. Currently in vogue among languages are BASIC, LOGO, and PASCAL. Each has its strong and weak points. These relative attributes must be considered in relation to the instructional goal. As an example, if one wishes to teach students how programming is correctly used to solve problems in the real world, the choice of BASIC may be appropriate. Yet Pascal would be the choice if the intention was to encourage structured programming techniques and higher-level programming concepts. LOGO can be very effective in focusing students on the computer as a tool for investigating concepts in mathematics (geometry). One must also consider the problems associated with a given language in the instructional environment. There is no evidence indicating direct interference between types of representations (Kaput, 1979; Erlwanger & Belanger, 1983), but this possibility must be on the teacher's mind when faced with a group of eager students. Consider the statement $X = X + 1$ in BASIC. This statement contains an equal sign that has exactly the same form as the one used in mathematics class, yet its meaning is different. If we wrote $x = x + 1$ in mathematics, it would be meaningless, yet in the computing environment it is not. The meaning of the symbols and the interactions of different meanings must be dealt with if we are to gain any benefits from the computing instruction.

Our final element is in some sense a reaffirmation of the earlier statement of Moore. Teachers must as always play a critical role in the learning process. To do this they need to understand the difference between a student's learning and a teacher's dispensing of knowledge. This is no minor task, nor is it ever fully accomplished. In our own struggles, we have found it useful to study aspects of learning theory, educational psychology, and cognitive science. But it is always a challenge to find the proper response, or lack of response, that is crucial to the development of the student's thinking skills.

We have only just begun to explore the ways in which computers can aid education. "For many years we have been trying to get the ship in the water. Now that it's afloat, we've discovered to our horror that we don't know how to steer it" (Arthur Luehrmann, quoted in Kearsley & Hunter, 1983, p. 44).

FURTHER READING

Gundlach, R. (1982). "The Place of Computers in the Teaching of Writing." In *Computers in Education: Realizing the Potential*. Washington, DC: Government Printing Office.

Hansen, V. & Zweng, M. (Eds.). (1984). *Computers in Mathematics Education*. Reston, VA: National Council of Teachers of Mathematics.

Kulik, J. A., Bangert, R. L., & Williams, G. W. (1983). "Effects of Computer-based Teaching on Secondary School Students." *Journal of Educational Psychology, 75.*

Kulik, J. A., Kulik, C. C., & Cohen, P. A. (1980). "Effectiveness of Computer-based College Teaching: A Meta-analysis of Findings." *Review of Educational Research, 50.*

Lesgold, A. (1982). "Paradigms for Computer-based Education." In *Computers in Education: Realizing the Potential*. Washington, DC: Government Printing Office.

Schneiderman, B. (1980). *Software Psychology*. Cambridge, MA: Winthrop.

REFERENCES

Anderson, R. E. (1982). National computer literacy, 1980. In R. J. Seidel, R. E. Anderson, & B. Hunter (Eds.), *Computer literacy: Issues and directions for 1985*. Orlando, FL: Academic Press.

Brown, J. S., & Burton, R. B. (1977). *Diagnostic models for procedural bugs in basic mathematical skills* (Tech. Rep. No. 3669). Cambridge, MA: Bolt, Beranek & Newman.

Brown, J. S., & Goldstein, I. (1977, October). *Computers in a learning society*. Testimony before the House Science and Technology Subcommittee on Domestic and International Planning, Analysis and Cooperation.

Burton, R. B., & Brown, J. S. (1976, February). A tutoring and student modeling paradigm for gaming environments. *Proceedings of the Symposium on Computer Science and Education*, Anaheim, CA.

Collins, A., & Grignetti, M. C. (1975). *Intelligent CAI* (Tech. Rep. No. 3181). Cambridge, MA: Bolt, Beranek & Newman.

Erlwanger, S., & Belanger, M. (1983). Interpretations of the equal sign among elementary school children. In J. C. Bergeron & N. Herscovics (Eds.), *Proceedings of the Fifth Annual Meeting of PME-NA*, Montreal.

Feigenbaum, E. A., & McCorduck, P. (1983). *The fifth generation*. Reading, MA: Addison-Wesley.

Fischer, H. (1984). Computer literacy scope and sequence models: A critical review of two approaches. *SIGCSE Bulletin, 16*(2).

Hatfield, L. L. (1982). Instructional computing in mathematics teacher education. *Journal of Research and Development in Education, 15*(4), 30–44.

Holoien, M. O., & Behforooz, A. (1983). *Problem solving and structured programming with FORTRAN 77*. Monterey, CA: Brooks/Cole.

Jefferies, R., Turner, A. A., Polson, P. G., & Atwood, M. E. (1981). The processes involved in designing software. In J. R. Anderson (Ed.), *Cognitive skills and their acquisition*. Hillsdale, NJ: Erlbaum.

Kane, J. H. (1983). *Computers for composing* (Tech. Rep. No. 21). New York: Bank Street College of Education.

Kaput, J. J. (1979). Learning: Roots of epistemological status. In J. Clement (Ed.), *Cognitive process instruction*. Philadelphia: Franklin Institute Press.

Kaput, J. J. (1983). Representation systems and mathematics. In J. C. Bergeron & N. Herscovics (Eds.), *Proceedings of the Fifth Annual Meeting of PME-NA*, Montreal.

Mazlack, L. J. (1983). Introducing subprograms as the first control structure in an introductory course. *SIGCSE Bulletin, 15*(1), 265–270.

Moore, M. J. (1983). The art of teaching Logo, or when not to bother the learner. *Hands On!* 6(1), 12, 14.

Papert, S. (1980). *Mindstorms: Children, computers and powerful ideas.* New York: Basic Books.

Papert, S., & Solomon, C. (1971). *Twenty things to do with a computer* (Logo Memo 3). Cambridge, MA: MIT Logo Lab.

Pea, R. D., & Kurland, D. M. (1983). *On the cognitive prerequisites of learning computer programming* (Technical Report No. 18). New York: Bank Street College of Education, Center for Children and Technology.

Pressey, S. L. (1933): *Psychology and the new education.* New York: Harper & Row.

Richards, J., & Wheeler, F. (1983). Integrated software for problem solving. In J. C. Bergeron & N. Herscovics, (Eds.), *Proceedings of the Fifth Annual Meeting of PME-NA*, Montreal.

Rogers, J. (1984). Computer use in precollege education. *Computer, 17*(4), 46–52.

Rosnick, P., & Clement, J. (1980). Learning without understanding: The effect of tutoring strategies on algebra misconceptions. *Journal of Mathematical Behavior, 3*(1), 3–27.

Schneiderman, M. (1984). Making the case for innovation. *Popular Computing, 3*(13), 88–95.

School uses of microcomputers: Report from a national survey. (1983, April). Baltimore: Johns Hopkins University.

Siegler, R. J., & Atlas, M. (1976). Acquisition of formal scientific reasoning by 10- and 13-year-olds: Detecting interactive patterns in data. *Journal of Educational Psychology, 68*, 360–370.

Solomon, C. (1982). Introducing Logo to children. *Byte, 6*(8), 90–147.

Soloway, E., Lochhead, J., & Clement, J. (1982). Does computer programming enhance problem solving ability? Some positive evidence on algebra word problems. In R. J. Seidel, R. E. Anderson, & B. Hunter (Eds.), *Computer literacy: Issues and directions for 1985.* Orlando, FL: Academic Press.

South Carolina Department of Education. (1980). *Basic Skills Assessment Program.* Columbia, SC: Author.

Watt, D. H. (1982). Education for citizenship in a computer-based society. In R. J. Seidel, R. E. Anderson, & B. Hunter (Eds.), *Computer literacy: Issues and directions for 1985.* Orlando, FL: Academic Press.

Weizenbaum, J. (1976). *Computer power and human reason: From judgment to calculation.* San Francisco: Freeman.

PART TWO

How Should I Teach It?

David C. Berliner, Editor

This part reviews the very extensive and well-developed literature on pedagogy—from planning through assessment. These chapters represent the bulk of the research on teaching conducted during the 1970s and early 1980s as well as some of the emerging new areas of interest today.

Research on teacher planning has taught us that experienced teachers do not plan in the way that they were taught in preservice teacher education. They focus on activities and content rather than objectives. Does this mean that schools of education should change the way in which they teach planning? The answer is not clear, particularly because, as Chapter 7 points out, beginning teachers have different planning needs than experienced teachers. It could be that novice teachers should begin planning by consideration of objectives; but as they become more experienced and efficient, activities should become paramount.

A relatively new research concern centers on the organization of students to accomplish academic tasks. This work indicates that the way in which students and tasks are organized strongly affects what students learn. The same content can be covered within two different task structures, and the students will learn different things. This work is described in Chapter 8.

During the 1970s, a new line of research on teaching produced information that has entered the consciousness of most teachers across the country. The process-product research, as it was called, equated effective teaching with effective classroom management. Beginning with a criterion of success, in most cases gains on standardized tests, researchers observed teachers of students whose gain scores in reading and math were above and below the average. These observations allowed researchers to differentiate between more and less effective teachers on the basis of their classroom behaviors.

One version of these process-product studies looked at student behavior as well as teacher behavior and learning, and "time on task" emerged. Academic learning time, as described in *Time to Learn* (Denham & Lieberman, 1980), is probably the best known of the time-on-task concepts. Looking at students and how they learn from each other also became an important concern to researchers. This fascinating work is described in Chapter 9, which includes a dialogue around this research among the researchers and several teachers in the Syracuse, NY, area.

Chapter 10 describes the findings about classroom management that resulted from the process-product and other studies of the 1970s and early 1980s. Classroom management has been a topic of great interest but one about which there has been little sense of control. New insights are changing that.

Finally, we turn to the assessment of learning. Chapter 11 combines two important areas: providing explanations and assessing learning. There is no point in assessing what has not been well delivered. Knowledge of assessment should be accompanied by knowledge of the best ways to explain and describe concepts to the students.

Many scholars and practitioners have called for the reform of teacher education through the use of research on teaching (Berliner, 1985; Egbert & Fenstermacher, 1984). By and large, the research referred to is that represented in this section. Its importance has already been felt in preservice and in-service teacher education, teacher evaluation systems, and numerous policies related to the improvement of teacher quality. Its importance to the improvement of practice will continue as the research is refined and different frameworks are explored.

Virginia Richardson-Koehler
Senior Editor

REFERENCES

Berliner, D. (1984). *Contemporary teacher education: Timidity, lack of vision, and ignorance.* Paper presented to the National Academy of Education.

Denham, C., & Lieberman, A. (Eds.). (1980). *Time to learn.* Washington, DC: National Institute of Education.

Egbert, R., & Fenstermacher, G. (Eds.). (1984). How can we use research in teacher education? [Special issue]. *Journal of Teacher Education, 35*(4).

7 DESCRIPTIONS OF TEACHER PLANNING: IDEAS FOR TEACHERS AND RESEARCHERS

Hilda Borko and Jerome A. Niles

To teach successfully, one must plan successfully. Few teachers would disagree with this statement. And, in fact, planning typically is formally structured into many teachers' roles. Teachers are often allocated a planning period on a daily basis. School calendars frequently mark certain days during the contract period as planning days. Many principals require that teachers plan and collect teachers' written plans on a weekly or monthly basis. But what do teachers do when they plan? What resources and information do they consider? Are there notable differences between the planning of more experienced and less experienced teachers? What can teachers do to plan more effectively?

Answering such questions actually proves to be a somewhat difficult task—a state of affairs due at least in part to the nature of planning. Most teachers do produce written plans that are fairly readily accessible as data sources in the study of planning. However, a large part of planning is mental—mental dialogues in which teachers engage, often spontaneously, throughout the day. Teachers may reflect on the past day's experiences and plan for the next as they shower, eat, or drive to and from school. Much of the result of this mental planning never appears on paper. In fact, the aspect of planning represented by written plans, such as daily or weekly plans in a teacher's plan book, represents only a very small portion of what researchers and educators mean by teacher planning. As Clark (1983) recently put it, planning is one of the usually invisible and solitary parts of teaching—characteristics that do not easily lend themselves to investigation.

Despite these difficulties, several recently conducted research studies have made a contribution to our understanding of teacher planning. And what we are learning about planning has the potential to improve instruction. This research, and the insights and recommendations it provides, are the focus of this chapter.

167

THE RESEARCH

Assumptions Underlying Research on Teacher Planning

Most research on teacher planning is based on a conception of teaching as a decision-making process. This conception, in turn, rests on two fundamental assumptions (Shavelson & Stern, 1981). The first assumption is that teachers are professionals who make reasonable judgments and decisions in a complex, uncertain environment (the school and classroom). Given the limited information processing capabilities of the human mind, teachers, like all persons attempting to solve complex problems, construct simplified models of the actual situation and then behave rationally with respect to these simplified models. This view of teachers as operating rationally within the limits of their information processing capabilities leads to the assumption that teachers make *reasonable* (rather than rational) judgments and decisions.

The second assumption is that in teaching there is a relationship between thought and action. More specifically, we assume that teachers' behavior is guided by their thoughts, judgments, and decisions. Thus an understanding of the teaching process depends on both a description of teachers' thoughts, judgments, and decisions and an understanding of how these cognitions are translated into action.

We agree with the argument offered in a report to the National Conference on Studies in Teaching (National Institute of Education, 1975):

> It is obvious that what teachers do is directed in no small measure by what they think.... To the extent that observed or intended teacher behavior is "thought-less," it makes no use of the human teacher's most unique attributes. In doing so, it becomes mechanical and might well be done by a machine. If, however, teaching is done and in all likelihood will continue to be done by human teachers, the question of the relationships between thought and action becomes crucial. (p. 1)

Thus to understand what is uniquely human in the process of teaching, we must study teacher thinking. We intend to further our understanding of teaching by examining one important component of teacher thinking—planning.

Research Questions and Methods

Researchers have examined a number of issues related to planning, issues involving both the thought processes of teachers and the outcomes of these processes. These issues are organized here according to four major questions: (1) Why do teachers plan? (2) How do teachers plan? (3) What factors affect teacher planning? and (4) How does planning affect classroom interactions?

To examine this diverse set of questions, researchers have used a variety of methods. The methods most commonly used are policy capturing, process tracing, stimulated recall, and case study. These methods are often used in combination and are usually supplemented by additional data gathered through questionnaires, interviews, field observations, and examination of written records (e.g., plan books).

In *policy-capturing* experimental studies, teachers are presented with vignettes of classroom life, such as descriptions of hypothetical students who vary in gender, achievement, class participation, ability to work independently, and classroom behavior. They are asked to make one or more instructional decisions for each vignette. Statistical techniques are used to construct equations that are interpreted as models of the teachers' decision policies.

In studies using *process-tracing* procedures, teachers are asked to "think aloud" (verbalize all their thoughts) as they engage in tasks such as organizing the class for instruction, planning a lesson, or making decisions about curricular materials. Teachers' verbalizations are recorded (usually using audiotapes) and later transcribed. These written protocols become the data to be analyzed to produce descriptions of the content sequence of teachers' thought processes.

Stimulated-recall techniques are typically used to study teacher thought processes when process tracing would interfere with the teacher's performance of the task (e.g., while presenting a lesson or otherwise interacting with students). A teaching episode is audiotaped or videotaped and later played back. The viewer (usually the teacher in the episode) is asked to recall the thoughts or decisions that occurred during the taped session.

Case-study approaches are used in educational research to provide detailed descriptions of individual students, teachers, classrooms, school systems, and so on. To construct these detailed accounts, researchers collect data in the actual school setting, using techniques such as participant observation, focused interviewing, and analysis of documents (e.g., plan books, school policies and regulations). In analyzing the data and reporting findings, they are careful to use the language and meanings of the research participants (the teachers, students, and administrators).

Limitations of the Research

Each of these commonly used techniques for the study of teacher planning has its limitations as well as its strengths. For example, policy-capturing studies predict decision outcomes but do not provide information about the cognitive strategies teachers use to make decisions. Also, because the decision models are based on limited information and hypothetical tasks, they may not reflect the full richness and complexity of teachers' decisions in the actual classroom setting. Process-tracing and stimulated-recall techniques use verbal reports as indicators of teachers' thought processes. These methods thus depend on teachers' ability and willingness to articulate their thought processes. Case studies, because they focus on a small number of settings and participants (sometimes only one teacher in one classroom), are open to questions about the generalizability of findings to other situations.

Fortunately the strengths and limitations of the various techniques are complementary. Further, more than one technique has usually been used to study each aspect of planning (sometimes within a single research project). Thus we can be fairly certain that results that are consistent or complementary across studies are generalizable to a broader population of teachers. We will focus in this review on patterns of consistent or complementary findings.

Why Do Teachers Plan?

Not surprisingly, researchers who have asked this question have found that teachers plan for many reasons. To some extent, planning is internally motivated. For example, Clark and Yinger (1979) asked 78 teachers to write responses to the question of why they plan. The researchers categorized the responses into three clusters, each representing a different set of internally motivated reasons. These teachers planned (1) to meet immediate psychological needs (e.g., to reduce anxiety and uncertainty, to find a sense of direction, confidence, and security); (2) to prepare themselves, mentally and physically or instrumentally, for instruction (to learn the material, to collect and organize materials, to organize time and activity flow); and (3) to guide the interactive processes of instruction (to organize students, to get an activity started, to provide a framework for instruction and evaluation). The 12 elementary school teachers who participated in McCutcheon's (1980) study of planning reported similar reasons for planning (reasons that could also be placed into Clark and Yinger's categories): to feel more confident about teaching content, to learn the subject matter better, to help the lesson run more smoothly, to envision and circumvent potential problems.

Planning is also motivated by external sources. For example, McCutcheon (1980) found that a major reason for the written plans developed by teachers in her study was to meet their schools' administrative requirements that they turn in their plans to the school principal or supervisor of instruction on a regular basis.

Several teachers in McCutcheon's study reported another reason for written plans: to provide guidance to substitute teachers. Plans developed for use by substitute teachers are special. These plans tend to include primarily drill and practice activities. They also provide a great deal of background information about how the "system" in a particular classroom and school operates. Some teachers maintain a folder for use by substitute teachers that describes routines to be followed.

Types of Plans.   In addition to these general reasons for planning, some researchers have reported that teachers make different types of plans and that these different types of plans serve different functions. Yinger (1980) studied the planning decisions of a single teacher of first and second grades over a five-month period. Using a case-study approach that included extensive classroom observation, interviews, and process-tracing methods, he identified five types of plans that this teacher made: yearly, term, unit, weekly, and daily.

Clark and Yinger (1979) asked the 78 teachers in their study to select and describe three examples of their own plans representing the three most important types of planning that they did during the school year. Analysis of these descriptions revealed eight distinct types of planning (listed in order of the frequency with which they were mentioned): weekly, daily, unit, long-range, lesson, short-range, yearly, and term. Unit plans were most often identified as the most important type of plan, followed by weekly and daily plans. Only 7% of the teachers listed lesson plans among the types of plans most important to them.

Several studies have examined the roles played by yearly planning and by long-range plans made early in the school year (Clark & Elmore, 1979, 1981; McCutcheon, 1980; Yinger, 1980). In general, these plans are concerned with setting up the physical environment of the classroom, establishing the classroom social system, assessing student ability, fitting the curriculum (framed by the school system curriculum objectives) to the unique teaching situation, developing a general sequence and schedule for instruction, and ordering and reserving materials. They are not often concerned with organizing or sequencing specific sets of learning activities. Teachers in McCutcheon's study gave several reasons for this limitation (and, in fact, for doing little long-range planning of any type): Long-range planning is partly done by textbooks, is counterproductive because it must often be redone, and limits their flexibility to incorporate into the classroom day the children's needs and interests that emerge as the year progresses.

In making sense of these various purposes, Clark (1983) suggests that the major function of early planning is to define a "problem space" within which teachers and students will operate throughout the year. This problem space sets the boundaries within which subsequent planning and decision making will occur. The notion of a problem space, and the powerful influence it exerts on the thought and behavior of teachers and students, is supported by studies demonstrating the importance of establishing an effective management system at the beginning of the school year (e.g., Emmer, Evertson, & Anderson, 1980; Evertson & Emmer, 1982).

Yinger (1980) reported the functions served by other types of planning engaged in by the teacher in his study. Term plans detailed content to be covered during the three-month period and established a weekly schedule of activities and times for that period. In planning units, the teacher developed a sequence of well-organized learning experiences, specified according to content and activities. In her weekly plans, she laid out the week's activities and entered them into her plan book, organized into four daily instructional blocks. Daily planning served the purposes of making any last-minute changes in the day's schedule, setting up and arranging the classroom and materials, and preparing the students by writing the day's schedule on the board. We can understand the various functions served by different types of plans within the framework presented by Clark and Yinger (1979). All types of plans help teachers to meet psychological needs and prepare themselves cognitively for teaching. Daily plans, as opposed to more long-range plans, focus on instrumental preparation for teaching (e.g., organizing materials) and the interactive processes of instruction.

How Do Teachers Plan?

Many teachers can look back to preservice educational programs and recall late-night sessions spent carefully constructing detailed lesson plans to be reviewed by their cooperating teacher and/or university supervisor. Generally, these lesson plans followed some version of the objectives-based, means-end model first proposed by Tyler in 1950. This model describes planning as a four-step process: specifying behavioral objectives, choosing appropriate learning activities, organizing and sequencing the chosen activities, and selecting evaluation procedures. It has been advocated for use by teachers of all levels and all subject-matter areas and has been taught to thousands of preservice teachers over the past 35 years. As users of research, the question we must ask is how well this model fits with research-based descriptions of how teachers plan.

Steps in the Planning Process.   Several studies have examined the components of instruction teachers consider when planning and the order in which they consider these components. These studies explored aspects of planning such as the development of course syllabi (Taylor, 1970), decisions typically made prior to teaching (Zahorik, 1975), and planning for specific experimenter-prescribed lessons (Morine-Dershimer & Vallance, 1976; Peterson, Marx, & Clark, 1978). They used a variety of methods including content analysis of course syllabi and written lesson plans, questionnaires completed by teachers, discussions with small groups of teachers, and think-aloud protocols recorded during planning periods.

Despite the diversity of issues and methods, a consistent pattern is apparent in findings from these studies, namely, that Tyler's model does not fit well with research-based accounts of the planning process. These research-based descriptions differ from Tyler's model in both the relative prominence of the four planning steps and the sequence in which they occur. For example, in terms of frequency of mention, objectives are not a particularly important component of the planning process. They are also seldom the starting point for planning. In fact, some teachers report that they do not actually write down objectives unless they are required to do so by the principal. Objectives are implied in activities and are typically listed in manuals that accompany textbooks. Therefore, to write them down is seen as an unnecessary expenditure of time and energy.

Rather than objectives or evaluation, planning seems to focus primarily on content and activities. The first planning decision made by teachers usually involves subject-matter content. The most frequent planning decisions involve content and activities. The most commonly reported practice for preparing written plans is to begin by identifying the subject matter to be covered and an activity to be used and then to consider other elements such as materials, goals, objectives, and evaluation procedures. In fact, in a stimulated-recall study of lessons taught by kindergarten teachers, McLeod (1981) reported that some intended learning outcomes, particularly those in the social and affective domains, were identified primarily during interactive teaching rather than during planning or preactive teaching. Although some caution must be exercised in interpreting findings from any one of the studies in isolation, the consistency across studies provides some confidence in these descriptions of the planning process.

An Alternate Model of the Planning Process.   Two studies conducted at the Institute for Research on Teaching attempted to describe the processes by which instruction is developed and organized. As one component of his case study of the planning of a teacher of first and second grades, Yinger (1980) developed a three-stage cyclic model to represent this teacher's approach to the planning of instructional activities (the basic structural units of her daily and weekly planning). During the problem-finding stage, the teacher derived an initial conception of the planning problem, based on a consideration of content, goals, and her own knowledge and experience. In the problem formulation and solution stage, she designed instructional activities by repeatedly cycling through a process of elaboration, investigation (mental testing), and adaptation. The third stage consisted of implementation and evaluation of the activities in the actual classroom setting. As a result of these processes, activities were either rejected or modified and (if effective) eventually incorporated into the teacher's repertoire of knowledge and experience to be used in future planning.

Clark and Yinger (1979) found that a similar model could be used to describe unit planning. They asked five teachers to plan a two-week unit on writing, keep journals for three weeks to document their planning, and participate in interviews with the researchers twice during each week. The teachers' unit planning was described by Clark and Yinger as a cyclic process, beginning with a general idea and proceeding through phases of successive elaboration and modification. The teachers differed in the extent to which they developed instructional activities (that is, engaged in problem-finding and problem formulation and solution activities) prior to implementing and evaluating them in the actual classroom situation. However, all participated to some extent in each of the three stages described in Yinger's study.

Both of these studies suggest another way in which research-based descriptions of planning differ from the models typically presented in teacher education programs. These models recommend that teachers identify several alternatives and then select among the alternatives the one best suited to the objectives and learners. In contrast, teachers appear to pursue one idea rather than weighing several alternatives and selecting among them. They report that, given the limited time available for planning, they generally begin with ideas that have worked in the past and spend what time they do have elaborating and embellishing these ideas (see also McCutcheon, 1980).

Mental Planning. The studies described so far all focused on the components of planning that occur during structured planning periods. But what does research tell us about the less formal aspects of planning, the aspects that McCutcheon (1980) refers to as mental planning or mental dialogues? When does mental planning occur? On what does it focus? What are its outcomes?

Many teachers in McCutcheon's study reported that they engaged in mental planning almost continuously throughout the day. For some teachers, the mental dialogue continued through the summer months. Mental planning covered a wide range of concerns, including the teaching of particular skills or concepts to individuals or groups, handling of behavior problems, and tying together of different subject-matter areas. It usually focused on practical problems associated with getting through the day but did not include attempts to relate theory or research findings to these problems. Teachers reported that mental planning helped them to articulate and short-circuit potential problems, elaborate written plans, learn the subject matter to be presented, and feel more confident about teaching.

Morine-Dershimer (1979) also discussed the role of mental plans or images of lessons. She noted that planning is seldom fully reflected in teachers' written plans. Rather, the details recorded on written plans are nested within more comprehensive mental plans or lesson images. The fact that certain planning elements are not part of written plans should not lead to the conclusion that they are not important components of planning. For example, although objectives were not part of her teachers' written plans, they did seem to be part of their lesson images.

In support of Morine-Dershimer's conclusion, Smith and Sendelbach (1979) reported that the principal product of unit planning for sixth-grade science instruction was a mental picture of the unit to be taught, including a sequence of activities and students' probable responses. Notes that accompanied the teachers' mental plans were sketchy, typically consisting of lists of important points to remember. Smith and Sendelbach characterized the process of activating a unit plan as one of reconstructing the plan from memory.

Other than these three investigations, research on teacher planning has not addressed the issue of mental plans. Further, as McCutcheon (1980) pointed out, mental planning is not recognized by theoreticians or teacher educators as an important or legitimate part of planning. Because of this, she suggested, teachers and administrators may not recognize mental planning as an important, legitimate professional activity. Yet "mental planning is probably the part of teaching that has the potential for being the most professional activity of teaching, for it gives teachers the opportunity to relate theoretical knowledge to particular cases" (pp. 8−9). Though we know little about mental planning, we do know enough to suggest that it is an aspect of the planning process that warrants further attention by educational researchers and practitioners.

What Factors Affect Teachers' Plans?

As we have seen, research-based descriptions characterize planning as a process of selecting and elaborating instructional activities, strategies, and techniques. The decision-making conception suggests that teachers have many instructional tools at their disposal and that they select and elaborate these with the intent of helping students to reach some goal (usually academic achievement). The conception further suggests that their decisions are affected by a variety of factors, including information about their students, the nature of the instructional task, their own personal characteristics, and institutional constraints.

Information about Students.   Teachers often report that information about students is the most important factor in determining their planning. This information appears to be particularly salient to teachers early in the school year, as they are getting to know their students and forming instructional groups (Morine-Dershimer, 1979; Mintz, 1979). Based on a review of 32 studies of teacher judgment and decision making, Shavelson and Stern (1981) reported several student characteristics to be important in the majority of studies: general ability or achievement, gender, class participation, self-concept, social competence, independence, classroom behavior, and work habits.

The student characteristic that has the greatest impact on planning decisions is ability. Information about ability is available through standardized achievement test scores and formal (e.g., textbook and teacher-made tests) and informal (e.g., reading aloud in group, seatwork activities) observations of classroom performance. To a lesser extent, teachers take into account nonacademic characteristics such as class participation, classroom behavior, work habits, and patterns of social interaction.

We conducted three studies in which policy-capturing and process-tracing methods were used to examine teachers' planning strategies for grouping students for reading instruction (Borko & Niles, 1982, 1983, 1984). In the first and second studies, experienced teachers and student teachers grouped hypothetical students who varied along five dimensions: standardized reading achievement scores, informal assessments of reading, class participation, classroom behavior, and social competence. In the third, four experienced teachers grouped their own students for the following year's reading program. Results from these studies were complementary and seem to typify findings concerning the roles played by various student characteristics in teachers' planning of instruction. In all three studies, participants formed groups primarily on the basis of reading ability. Nonacademic characteristics, particularly class participation, motivation, work habits, and maturity, were considered when decisions about the best placements for individual students were not easily made solely on the basis of ability.

Nature of the Instructional Task.   Shavelson and Stern (1981) describe the instructional task as the basic unit of planning and action in the classroom. For teachers, the task consists primarily of subject matter (content and structure), activities, and materials. As we have seen in descriptions of the planning process, these three components of the instructional task receive the most consideration during planning. While conceptually distinct, these components are closely linked in actual classroom instruction and planning for instruction.

Often teachers' consideration of subject matter focuses more on the content of the subject matter than on the structure. They accept the textbook as the major, and often only, source of content and frequently do little to modify its orientation to or relative emphasis on various components of the curriculum (e.g., Clark, 1978–1979). Thus once a textbook has been selected (a decision typically not made by the individual teacher or even the individual school), subject-matter concerns in planning translate into concerns about presentation of textbook-prescribed content.

Teachers' planning about presentation of content generally focuses on activities and materials. Here, too, textbooks and associated materials, especially teachers' manuals, play a major role. Several studies have reported that teachers rely on manuals accompanying prescribed textbooks as the primary source of instructional activities and materials (e.g., Clark & Elmore, 1981; McCutcheon, 1980; Smith & Sendelbach, 1979). As an illustration, 85% to 95% of the reading and mathematics activities used by teachers in McCutcheon's study were based on suggestions in teachers' manuals. The figure was somewhat lower in other subject areas, in large part because of time constraints on instruction, which necessitated choosing among topics and limited the kinds of activities that teachers could plan. Also, teachers were more likely to introduce their own interests into areas such as social studies, science, language, and art.

The reliance on textbook series can be explained in part by institutional constraints on teachers' decision making (Borko, Eisenhart, Kello, & Vandett, 1984; McCutcheon, 1980). At one school system in McCutcheon's study, teachers were not permitted to use supplementary materials, even when related to the text, until the end of the year, when the textbook had been completed. Although the teachers in the study of second-grade reading conducted by Borko and colleagues were permitted more flexibility than the extreme cases cited by McCutcheon, students were expected to complete all textbooks, workbooks, and dittos provided by the basal programs. However, while external factors such as institutional constraints clearly provide some limitations, many teachers do not exercise as much decision-making responsibility as they have available with regard to the instructional program (Borko et al., 1984).

Teachers' reliance on textbooks and associated teachers' manuals when selecting and organizing instructional tasks may negatively affect the quality of instruction. For example, McCutcheon (1980) noted a lack of continuity in instruction, which she attributed in part to this reliance on prescribed instructional materials. Teachers assume that textbooks and manuals are structured to provide for continuity across lessons when in fact they may not be. Further, textbooks may be based on assumptions that differ from a teacher's beliefs regarding issues such as the role of the teacher or the nature of the learning process. Such discrepancies between instructional programs and teachers' beliefs or styles may also result in a lack of continuity.

The Context of Instruction.   Teachers' planning for instruction is also affected by the context in which instruction will occur. Consideration of context focuses both on the classroom itself and on the extraclassroom environment (school, school system, community). Ethnographic studies by Janesick (1978) and Florio (1979) help us understand the role played in planning by the sociocultural context of the classroom. The teacher of sixth and seventh grades in Janesick's study was characterized by a concern for creating and maintaining a stable, cohesive group. His planning clearly reflected this concern for "groupness." He designed activities that generated a high level of group cohesiveness and modeled and emphasized cooperation and respect for other group members. During instructional planning, he evaluated classroom activities as to their impact on groupness. The second-grade teacher in Florio's study of writing instruction placed a high priority on creating a sense of community within the classroom. In fact, she actually created a physical community in her classroom, which served as the basis for instruction.

The effects of extraclassroom pressures on teacher planning have been studied both in the laboratory and in actual school settings. One finding, consistent across studies, is that pressures originating outside the classroom significantly affect planning. For example, Floden, Porter, Schmidt, Freeman, and Schwille (1981) used a laboratory policy-capturing approach to study the effects of external constraints (textbooks, media, central division and building administration, other teachers, and parents) on teachers' decisions to incorporate new topics into the mathematics curriculum. The most notable aspect of teachers' responses was their willingness to change content, whatever the pressure for change.

Several naturalistic investigations support this conclusion that external pressures affect planning. In McNeil's (1980) study of high school economics courses, teachers planned instruction in a teacher-directed lecture format, with no reading or writing, little student discussion, and very little use of the school's resources. Their intent was to avoid as many management problems as possible, in order to meet the goals of an administration that expected them to enforce rules of discipline but rarely backed them on that enforcement.

Both McCutcheon (1980) and Borko and colleagues (1984) reported effects of school-level and central administration policy beyond the previously cited restrictions on curriculum and materials. Administratively based influences on planning included policies about class size, scheduling, grouping, and promotion and retention. For example, McCutcheon reported that the policy of grouping across classes for reading and mathematics instruction constrained teachers to adhere more closely to a schedule and resulted in a greater focus on isolated subject matter rather than integrated subjects. With regard to scheduling, Borko and colleagues noted that county and school guidelines specified when reading, language arts, and mathematics would occur during the school day and how much time each subject would occupy. Building administrators further constrained daily and weekly plans by scheduling all extraclassroom activities (e.g., library, physical education). Building administrators in the particular school studied further influenced planning by assigning all students to reading and mathematics groups within classrooms. Despite this clear influence of external forces on the nature of instructional programs, there is room within these constraints for teacher planning and decision making to lead to programs that vary greatly across classrooms (Borko et al., 1984).

Teacher Characteristics. Several researchers have hypothesized that certain characteristics of teachers, such as their conceptions of teaching, beliefs about particular subject areas, and professional experience, affect their instructional planning. In a number of studies, these hypothesized relationships have not been strongly supported. For example, Russo (1978) reported that teachers' progressive and traditional educational beliefs were not related to their grouping of students for reading and mathematics or to their decisions about lesson plans for the groups. She speculated that specific conceptions of reading or mathematics, rather than global views of education, might be associated with differences in planning for these two subject areas. However, Borko and Niles (1982) found that teachers' content-oriented and pupil-oriented conceptions of reading contributed little to their strategies for forming reading groups. Similarly, though Borko (1978) found some relationship between traditional and progressive views of education and teachers' organizing and structuring of educational experiences, the influence of beliefs on planning was small.

In contrast, educational researchers have found significant differences between the planning of "experts" (typically, experienced teachers) and "novices" (typically, student teachers). Teachers in Borko and Niles's (1982) policy-capturing study tended to use more complex decision strategies than did student teachers when forming instructional groups. Specifically, most student teachers placed hypothetical students into reading groups on the basis of information about formal and informal assessments of reading ability. Most experienced teachers used a decision strategy that included one nonacademic characteristic (usually class participation) in addition to the two assessments of reading ability. In a subsequent study that incorporated a process-tracing component, Borko and Niles (1983) found several additional differences between teachers and student teachers. The in-depth analysis of think-aloud protocols for one teacher and one student teacher indicated that the teacher's greater experience in the classroom led to clearer decision rules, applied with much less deliberation. Further, confidence in her ability to manage a reading program enabled the experienced teacher to make decisions based more on student characteristics, with less feeling of being constrained by structural considerations such as number and size of instructional groups.

Sardo (1982) also found a relationship between individual differences in planning style and amount of teaching experience in her study of the planning of four junior high teachers. For the least experienced teacher (with two years of teaching experience), planning consisted primarily of daily and lesson plans. This teacher also followed Tyler's means-ends model more closely than the others. For the more experienced teachers, planning was less systematic, required less time, and focused more on the flow of activities for an entire week rather than the details of individual lessons.

Several possible explanations can be offered for these differences between the planning of experienced teachers and beginning teachers. Experts have more elaborate cognitive schemata (or systems) for understanding and organizing subject matter. When planning instruction, they are more likely to focus on the underlying structure of the subject matter and the task of presenting that subject matter to students. They are also more likely to embellish and transform the information, based on their past teaching experience (Yinger & Clark, 1983; Leinhardt, 1983).

In addition to these differences in understanding of subject matter, novices seem to lack the conceptual structures or have simple, undifferentiated structures with which to make sense of classroom life. They may not, therefore, be aware of the variety of factors that contribute to academic success. For example, experienced teachers may more often consider social and behavioral factors in addition to academic factors when planning instruction because they are more aware of the impact of group dynamics on the learning process (Borko & Niles, 1982).

How Does Planning Affect Classroom Interactions?

Most studies of planning are descriptive in nature and focus on planning in isolation from other components of the teaching process. However, some researchers have begun to examine the role that plans play in teaching and learning. Several studies have shown, for example, that plans made at the beginning of the year are particularly important. The system of schedules, routines, rules, and procedures in operation by the end of the first month of school serves as a framework within which particular units and activities are planned throughout the year. This initial classroom system, which changes very little throughout the year, has a profound influence on instruction and classroom management. Not surprisingly, teachers who fail to plan their classroom systems adequately or to implement their plans effectively are much more likely to experience difficulty in managing their classrooms throughout the year than are teachers who establish initial rules, procedures, and routines (see Clark & Elmore, 1979, 1981; Emmer et al., 1980; Evertson & Emmer, 1982).

A few studies have examined the relationship between plans and the specific instructional units or activities they address. These studies indicate that instructional planning is related to the general structure and focus of interactive teaching. For example, in their study of the teaching of a junior high school social studies unit, Peterson, Marx, and Clark (1978) found that planning directed primarily to content and objectives was associated with "subject-matter focused" teacher behavior and with a somewhat rigid pattern of instruction. In contrast, planning dealing with the learner was positively related to teacher behaviors classified as "group focused." Similarly, in his study of the teaching of a fifth-grade mathematics unit, Carnahan (1980) reported a positive relationship between the emphasis in written plans on individuals or small groups and the extent to which a teacher used small groups in the classroom. He did not find a relationship between plans and the specific details of verbal behavior. Carnahan suggested that the limited relationship of plans to the general organization of teaching is appropriate. Because student responses during interactive teaching are unpredictable, verbal dialogue is not a profitable focus for teacher planning.

Even fewer studies have traced the teaching process from planning through interactive teaching to the effects on student achievement and attitudes. One notable exception is the study by Peterson, Marx, and Clark (1978). These researchers noted that students' achievement and attitudes were lower for teachers who made changes in their plans during interactive teaching than for teachers who did not. However, as is often the case, the teachers who made changes were those whose lessons were not going as planned and whose routines were not maintaining the flow of activity. The skill of planning accurately to maintain the activity flow, rather than any characteristics of interactive decisions, may be the causal factor that best explains the observed link between teacher behavior and student outcomes.

Given the impact of plans on teaching and learning and the importance of planning to maintain the activity flow, is it possible to plan too much? Two investigations suggest that the answer to this question may be yes. As noted, Peterson, Marx, and Clark (1978) found that planning focused solely on objectives and content was associated with rigid patterns of behavior. A similar relationship was found in Zahorik's (1970) study comparing the effects of structured planning with the absence of structured planning on teachers' classroom behavior in a lesson on credit cards. Six teachers were given partial lesson plans two weeks in advance; six were asked to reserve one hour of instructional time and were told just before that hour what they were to teach. Teachers who were given the structured plans were less sensitive to their pupils than were teachers who did not have the opportunity to plan. They did not encourage or develop students' ideas as much and did not foster discussion as well. One possible explanation for this finding is that teachers without the chance to plan had no choice but to explore student ideas and experiences while those who knew the topic in advance were able to focus on the content rather than the students. However, findings from the two studies, considered together, suggest that when planning becomes too structured or too task-oriented, it can lead to instruction that is rigid and unresponsive to students. This interpretation supports Carnahan's (1980) suggestion that the general organization of teaching is the appropriate focus for planning.

IMPLICATIONS FOR PRACTICE

What Can Teachers Learn from Research on Planning?

Both of us have worked with preservice and in-service teachers for a number of years. However, when we began writing this chapter, neither of us had engaged in systematic discussions about planning with either of these groups. To talk in an informed way about what research has to say to teachers, we therefore asked a group of teachers with whom one of us was working to complete a questionnaire and then talk with us about planning. The 30 teachers who shared their perspectives on planning with us were experienced; they had taught for five or more years.

The teachers' responses to several questions clearly identified planning as a significant feature of their professional lives. The overwhelming majority of the teachers agreed that planning was an extremely important factor in determining overall effectiveness as a teacher. Further, planning constituted a significant proportion of their professional work life.

When asked to describe themselves as planners, half of the teachers referred to themselves as overplanners. That is, they reported that they typically plan more activities than they will be able to accomplish during any instructional time period. These teachers seemed to be similar to teachers participating in several of the research studies described earlier in this chapter with respect to their reasons for planning. They reported that they planned to effect good organization, for classroom control, for psychological comfort that comes from being organized and prepared, and to account for any emergency situations that might require a substitute.

Given that planning is an activity that these teachers valued highly, we expected numerous replies to our query "What do teachers want to know about planning?" To our surprise, we were greeted with blank paper and silence. Such a response is even more surprising when one considers that teachers always seem to want to know more about anything that might help them to be better teachers. Not so with planning. In this case, their confident reply was "nothing—we are doing just fine with this important teaching activity."

This contentment with the status quo in planning made us curious and caused us to try a different approach toward discovering what the research on planning has to offer teachers. During our discussions, we recalled that our interactions with preservice teachers are characterized by numerous questions on their part about the what and how of planning. This realization led us to speculate that experience may be a major determining factor in teachers' concerns and questions about planning. It occurred to us that the experienced teachers we talked with may have reached a point at which their planning fulfills their needs for organization, acceptable activity flow, and psychological comfort; in other words, they had reached a "planning plateau." If this is the case, then for these teachers, more planning or different planning will not positively affect their most commonly expressed planning needs.

A Developmental Perspective on Planning.   To account for the role of experience in shaping teachers' expressed planning needs, we decided to attempt to relate findings in the planning literature to a developmental model of teaching (cf. Feiman-Nemser, 1983). As Feiman-Nemser points out, teachers in the different phases of their career—preservice, beginning (years 1 and 2), and experienced—have different needs and priorities with regard to instructional issues. Thus it seems reasonable that they may have different planning needs. If this is the case, the planning literature may be differentially useful to teachers, depending on where they are in their professional development. Sardo (1982) provides some evidence to support this conclusion.

To help us in using a developmental perspective, we returned to our questionnaire and examined the teachers' responses to two questions: "How have you changed as a planner since you began teaching?" and "What are the three most important things you tell your student teachers about planning?" The answers to these questions clearly reflected changing needs and priorities. For example, the teachers' major suggestions to the student teachers were much more lesson-oriented than the planning of experienced teachers, as revealed in the literature (e.g., Clark & Yinger, 1979; Sardo, 1982). With regard to changes in their own planning, the teachers told us that they were able to plan for individual children and groups more effectively. Also, they reported that they knew the material and the individual needs of their students better. Finally, they commented that they were better able to teach to long-range goals.

These reported changes are reasonable, based on what we know about the process of learning to teach. Teachers learn more about their subject matter as they attempt to teach it. Experience helps them to learn what types of prior knowledge their students are likely to bring to a learning event and what content can be particularly troublesome. This acquired knowledge about content and students enables teachers to become better at predicting what types of learning experiences their students will need and thus more able to differentiate instruction. Finally, long-range planning in any area is easier when you have an understanding of the complete picture. For example, those of us who have gone on similar vacations over several years have undoubtedly noticed that planning becomes easier each time. We are more aware of the difficult route changes, sites of interest, and pacing of travel. Teachers' yearlong journeys through content are no different. They are better able to make necessary adjustments in their long-range plans after they have taken the "trip" several times.

According to the teachers we talked with, knowing what you are going to teach, the entering knowledge of those you are going to teach, and where you are headed are three of the most important variables in the planning process. Clearly, there is much less uncertainty about these variables for experienced teachers than for preservice or beginning teachers. Thus we were even more convinced that our decision to evaluate the usefulness of the planning research from a developmental perspective was a sensible one. That is, because beginning teachers and experienced teachers have different teaching needs and different sets of professional knowledge, they may plan differently and therefore may benefit from different information about planning.

Preservice Teachers.   Assuming that preservice teachers have at least a lay sense of the process of planning and its importance, we expect their first question to be "What do typical teachers do when they plan?" The research can be most helpful with this question because it can provide the relevant descriptions. From the research, preservice teachers can learn that typical planning is focused on subject-matter content and the selection of corresponding activities, with relatively little attention to objectives or evaluation.

To use this information about planning effectively, beginning teachers must put it in perspective. They must understand why experienced teachers plan the way they do, why their plans include certain elements and exclude others. The novices will then be able to decide which characteristics of experienced teachers' plans are appropriate for them and which are not. For example, experienced teachers do not specify objectives since they are implied in the materials and in curriculum guides. However, the preservice teacher has not had as many opportunities to abstract these objectives as the experienced teacher has and will most likely need to focus more attention on them. A similar contrast between novice and experienced teachers exists for evaluation. Experienced teachers should be better diagnosticians because they know the material and the youngsters more thoroughly. (This is the claim the teachers we spoke with made). Thus it is natural for an experienced teacher to use more subtle means for evaluation than a novice in deciding who has reached the objectives for a lesson. These differences suggest that Tyler's model, which includes objectives and evaluation, may have more relevance for preservice teachers than for experienced teachers.

The concept of overplanning is an important one for preservice teachers. How much planning should be conducted, and how detailed should plans be? The experienced teachers told us that they urged their student teachers always to overplan. The teachers' definition of overplanning referred to the development of more than enough activities for a given time period, not to the specification of a detailed script. In fact, the teachers discouraged their protégés from using detailed scripts. The planning literature, while initially appearing to contradict this advice, actually supports and clarifies the experienced teachers' view. That is, overplanning may be of value, but not when it entails the construction of detailed scripts that can hinder the fluency of a lesson and create rigidity in a teacher's reactions to students. Thus, just as the research can inform teachers, teachers' understanding of overplanning helps researchers to interpret findings concerning the negative effects of overplanning and to make recommendations based on these interpretations.

Beginning Teachers.   Especially over the first two or three years, teachers are acquiring the knowledge about materials and their students' abilities that will enable them to be effective planners. Upon assuming responsibility for their own classrooms, beginning teachers quickly realize just how important planning is. They soon see the relationship between knowing the subject-matter content, conveying it through appropriate activities, and the concomitant positive effect on the classroom environment. Thus the primary goals of the beginning teacher become mastery of the subject matter and generation of enough varied activities to convey this knowledge. They are successful if they reach a stage where they are in control of the lesson flow. Our feeling is that the descriptions in the literature of experienced teachers' planning are not very helpful to beginning teachers in this difficult endeavor. The beginning teachers' overwhelming need is to survive. To do so, they must rapidly acquire knowledge about their students, the curriculum, and instructional activities. And beginning teachers direct their attention accordingly. They know what has to be done in order to survive from information received in preservice training and from the demands of the teaching task.

However, the literature can be informative to beginning teachers in the sense that it can make them more aware of the relationship between planning and their development as teachers. For example, they can see in studies such as Sardo's (1982) that their planning will initially be detailed and lesson-focused. As they "learn their material" (a comment from the teachers we talked with), they will emphasize lesson flow for the week and will form lesson images rather than detailed lesson plans (Morine-Dershimer, 1979). Finally, descriptions in the literature can provide the prototype of planning for these novice teachers. They can use these descriptions as a developmental benchmark, to ensure continued progress rather than acceptance of the status quo.

Experienced Teachers.   At first glance, it may seem that the planning literature is not very informative to experienced teachers. The teachers we spoke with reflected this view when they commented that there was nothing research could tell them about planning that they didn't already know. We feel this response is a reasonable one, given what teachers see as the primary purposes for planning. These teachers and teachers described in the literature were in agreement that the chief purposes of planning include maintenance of activity flow, classroom control, and self-confidence. Most successful teachers have achieved mastery over activity flow and the associated control that is a precondition for classroom learning (cf. Doyle, 1978). Many feel they have reached their goal and have no need to improve or change.

We would like to suggest, however, that planning can serve an additional purpose. It can act as a tool for experienced teachers to use in improving their teaching. The alternative planning model proposed by Yinger (1980) potentially moves us in such a direction. Yinger's cyclic model portrays planning as a constructive activity represented by continual elaboration, mental testing, and adaptation of ideas. The model views teaching as a problem-solving process and provides a system for carrying out that process. Moreover, the cyclic model of planning has implications for changing teacher practice; that is, if plans are successful, teachers will incorporate the plans in their repertoires for future use. Linear models of planning such as those often presented in preservice teacher education do not convey this constructive aspect of planning. Such models represent planning as a process of selecting strategies from existing repertoires. The result is a maintenance of the status quo.

If the school is to become a setting that encourages teachers to continue to develop their teaching ability throughout their careers, planning can function as an activity to aid this professional growth. Presently, teachers are encouraged to plan, but much of that planning is conducted alone and on their own time. For planning to become a useful developmental vehicle it needs, at least occasionally, to include other teachers. Group planning sessions provide an ideal opportunity for teachers to learn from one another as they talk about the practice of teaching. Planning can be a time during which teachers explore together alternative teaching methods and activities rather than simply calling up routines that have been successful in the past. Cooperative planning can also provide a setting for curriculum review and materials evaluation. Planning used in these ways, as a cyclic process to aid group as well as individual problem solving, can be an exciting opportunity to expand one's repertoire of teaching skills and strategies.

Such a portrayal of teacher planning is admittedly complex. But we believe that given the appropriate resources (e.g., time, availability of colleagues), teachers would welcome the opportunities for instructional problem solving on a regular basis. Such an orientation to planning and teaching would go a long way toward eliminating the routinization and psychological isolation that have characterized the professional environment for experienced teachers (Sarason, 1971). And teachers who approach their own teaching from a problem-solving perspective may find it easier to help their students become problem solvers.

What Can Administrators Learn from Research on Planning?

School administrators can also learn from the research on planning, particularly when they hold as a goal the creation of an environment that facilitates teacher learning as well as student learning. Through the monitoring of plans and the creation of opportunities for planning during the school day, they can encourage the use of planning as a tool for improving teaching. As one example, when determining criteria for plans to be turned in for monitoring or feedback, administrators should keep in mind that planning serves different roles at different phases in teachers' professional development. As a consequence, requirements related to planning should perhaps not be the same for all teachers. Beginning teachers should be encouraged to plan with the goal of creating instructional experiences that will maintain the flow of activity in the classroom. Experienced teachers should be encouraged to use planning as a vehicle for expanding their repertoires of teaching strategies and activities and for optimizing the match between the instructional content and the learners. Clearly, plans oriented toward these two purposes will (and should) look different.

Administrators should also provide time for planning during the school day. And they should structure this time so that teachers have the opportunity to plan together. They should encourage teachers to use their planning time to share ideas about teaching and jointly to design and evaluate instructional activities and materials. In this way, beginning teachers can learn by observing and talking with experienced teachers, and experienced teachers can gain valuable insights and support from colleagues as they attempt to improve their teaching.

CONCLUSIONS

Based on the literature we have reviewed, we can make several statements in response to the research questions posed at the beginning of this chapter.

1. The reasons that teachers give for planning are many and varied. Internally derived reasons include the desire to meet immediate psychological needs, to

prepare themselves for instruction, and to organize the instructional process. The major external impetus for planning is administrative requirement.

2. Teachers typically begin planning by identifying the subject matter to be taught and an activity to be used. Secondarily, they consider elements such as materials, goals, objectives, and evaluation procedures. In developing their plans, they identify and elaborate one idea rather than selecting among alternatives.

3. Teachers consider many factors in planning instruction. They often report that information about students (particularly ability) is the most important factor in determining their planning. Other considerations include the instructional task (subject matter, activities, and materials) and the context in which instruction will occur.

4. Instructional planning is usually related to the general organization and structure of interactive teaching, rather than to the specific details of verbal behavior. In fact, when such details are overplanned, instruction may become rigid and unresponsive to students.

5. Experience appears to be a salient factor in determining the nature of planning. That is, experienced teachers plan differently than do novices.

We believe that these descriptive findings are useful to practitioners. They have documented that teachers behave differently than their preparation would lead us to predict because of the demands of the teaching task. Teachers know what it takes to run a successful classroom, and they direct their planning accordingly. We think the findings are even more informative when they are viewed within a developmental framework for learning to teach. Such a framework can provide guidance in the use of planning as a tool for improving instruction at each phase of a teacher's career.

FURTHER READING

Borko, H., Eisenhart, M., Kello, M., & Vandett, N. (1984). "Teachers as Decision Makers versus Technicians." In J. A. Niles & L. A. Harris (Eds.), *Changing Perspectives in Research in Reading/Language Processing and Instruction.* 33rd Yearbook of the National Reading Conference. New York: National Reading Conference. In a naturalistic investigation of reading instruction, the authors describe four second-grade teachers with similar background characteristics, teaching at the same school. These teachers organized their classrooms and reading programs differently. Moreover, they conceived of their roles in relation to students differently. Based on these findings, the authors suggest that conceptions of the teaching process and the roles and responsibilities of teachers underlie what teachers do in their classrooms. They further suggest that all teachers make some decisions about the nature of their classroom teaching and that these decisions are constrained by their conception of the teaching process.

Clark, C. M. (1983). "Research on Teacher Planning: An Inventory of the Knowledge Base." In D. C. Smith (Ed.), *Essential Knowledge for Beginning Educators.* Washington, DC: American Association of Colleges for Teacher Education. Clark reviews much of the literature on teacher planning, focusing in particular on information and ideas that might be useful to beginning teachers. The article begins with a brief history of research on teacher thinking. The planning literature is then reviewed, organized to address three major questions: (1) What are the types and functions of teacher planning? (2) What models have been used to describe the process of planning? and (3) What is the relationship between teacher planning and subsequent action in the classroom?

Feiman-Nemser, S. (1983). "Learning to Teach." In L. S. Shulman & G. Sykes (Eds.), *Handbook of Teaching and Policy.* White Plains, NY: Longman. Feiman-Nemser describes learning to teach as a process in four phases: pretraining, in which early school and home experiences shape one's ideas about teaching; preservice, or formal preparation; induction, which coincides with the first year of teaching; and in-service, which spans the rest of a teacher's career. Feiman-Nemser pays particular attention to the contributions of formal and informal influences on the teacher's capacity for continued learning.

McCutcheon, G. (1980). "How Do Elementary School Teachers Plan? The Nature of Planning and Influences on It." *Elementary School Journal, 81,* 4–23. This study of the planning of 12 elementary school teachers focuses on three aspects of planning: the planning process, the effects of planning on the curriculum, and the influences on planning. Mental planning and lesson planning are described as two important planning activities. The textbook and such external factors as teachers' isolation, administrative practices and policies, and a lack of education about planning are among the important influences cited. Implications for schools and teacher education are offered.

Peterson, P. L., Marx, R. W., & Clark, C. M. (1978). "Teacher Planning, Teacher Behavior, and Student Achievement." *American Educational Research Journal, 15,* 417–432. In a laboratory situation, the researchers studied the planning of 12 teachers as they prepared to teach a social studies unit to groups of junior high school students whom they had not met previously. The teachers spent the largest amount of their planning time on content and, to a lesser extent, on instructional processes. Behavioral objectives were not a central part of their planning. The authors discuss the relationships of planning focus, teacher behavior patterns, and student outcomes.

Yinger, R. J. (1980). "A Study of Teacher Planning." *Elementary School Journal, 80,* 107–127. Using a case-study approach, Yinger investigated the planning decisions of a single teacher of first and second grades over a five-month period. He describes the five levels of planning engaged in by this teacher: yearly, term, unit, weekly, and daily. He also formulates a process model of teacher planning that characterizes planning as occurring in three stages: problem findings, problem formulation and solution (design), and implementation, evaluation, and routinization.

Zahorik, J. A. (1970). "The Effects of Planning on Teaching." *Elementary School Journal, 71,* 143–151. Zahorik provided six teachers with partial plans for a lesson two weeks in advance. He asked six other teachers to reserve an hour of instructional time and told them just before that hour what they were going to teach. Based on an analysis of the 12 lesson protocols, Zahorik concludes that the teachers who were given partial plans were less sensitive to their pupils than were the teachers who were not given plans.

Zahorik, J. A. (1975). "Teachers' Planning Models." *Educational Leadership, 33,* 134–139. Zahorik asked 194 teachers to list in writing the decisions they made before teaching and to indicate the order in which they made these decisions. He then classified teachers' decisions into eight categories: objectives, content, activities, materials, diagnosis, evaluation, instruction, and organization. The decision made most frequently concerned student activities; the decision most often made first related to content. Based on these findings, Zahorik concludes that the means-end model does not accurately represent these teachers' planning decisions.

REFERENCES

Borko, H. (1978, March). *An examination of some factors contributing to teachers' preinstructional classroom organization and management decisions.* Paper presented at the annual meeting of the American Educational Research Association, Toronto, Canada.

Borko, H., Eisenhart, M., Kello, M., & Vandett, N. (1984). Teachers as decision makers versus technicians. In J. A. Niles & L. A. Harris (Eds.), *Changing perspectives in research in reading/language processing and instruction.* 33rd Yearbook of the National Reading Conference. New York: National Reading Conference.

Borko, H., & Niles, J. A. (1982). Factors contributing to teachers' judgments about students and decisions about grouping students for reading instruction. *Journal of Reading Behavior, 14,* 127–140.

Borko, H., & Niles, J. A. (1983). Teachers' cognitive processes in the formation of reading groups. In J. A. Niles & L. A. Harris (Eds.), *Searches for meaning in reading/language processing and instruction.* 32nd Yearbook of the National Reading Conference. New York: National Reading Conference.

Borko, H., & Niles, J. A. (1984, April). *Teachers' strategies for forming reading groups: Do real students make a difference?* Paper presented at the annual meeting of the American Educational Research Association, New Orleans.

Carnahan, R. S. (1980). The effects of teacher planning on classroom processes (Tech. Rep. No. 541). Madison, WI: University of Wisconsin, Wisconsin Research and Development Center for Individualized Schooling.

Clark, C. M. (1978–1979). A new question for research on teaching. *Educational Research Quarterly, 3,* 53–58.

Clark, C. M. (1983). Research on teacher planning: An inventory of the knowledge base. In D. C. Smith (Ed.), *Essential knowledge for beginning teachers.* Washington, DC: American Association of Colleges for Teacher Education.

Clark, C. M., & Elmore, J. L. (1979). Teacher planning in the first weeks of school (Research Series No. 55). East Lansing: Michigan State University, Institute for Research on Teaching.

Clark, C. M., & Elmore, J. L. (1981). Transforming curriculum in mathematics, science, and writing: A case study of teacher yearly planning (Research Series No. 99). East Lansing: Michigan State University, Institute for Research on Teaching.

Clark, C. M., & Yinger, R. J. (1979). Teachers' thinking. In P. L. Peterson & H. J. Walberg (Eds.), *Research on teaching.* Berkeley, CA: McCutchan.

Doyle, W. (1978). Paradigms for research on teacher effectiveness. In L. S. Shulman (Ed.), *Review of research in education* (Vol. 5). Itasca, IL: F. E. Peacock.

Emmer, E. T., Evertson, C. M., & Anderson, L. M. (1980). Effective classroom management at the beginning of the school year. *Elementary School Journal, 80,* 219–231.

Evertson, C. M., & Emmer, E. T. (1982). Effective management at the beginning of the school year in junior high classes. *Journal of Educational Psychology, 74,* 485–498.

Feiman-Nemser, S. (1983). Learning to teach. In L. S. Shulman & G. Sykes (Eds.), *Handbook of teaching and policy.* White Plains, NY: Longman.

Floden, R. E., Porter, A. C., Schmidt, W. H., Freeman, D. J., & Schwille, J. R. (1981). Responses to curriculum pressures: A policy-capturing study of teacher decisions about content. *Journal of Educational Psychology, 73,* 129–141.

Florio, S. (1979). The problem of dead letters: Social perspectives on the teaching of writing. *Elementary School Journal, 80,* 1–7.

Janesick, V. J. (1978). An ethnographic study of a teacher's classroom perspective: Implications for curriculum (Research Series No. 33). East Lansing: Michigan State University, Institute for Research on Teaching.

Leinhardt, G. (1983). Novice and expert knowledge of individual students' achievement. *Educational Psychologist, 18,* 165–179.

McCutcheon, G. (1980). How do elementary school teachers plan? The nature of planning and influences on it. *Elementary School Journal, 81,* 4–23.

McLeod, M. A. (1981). *The identification of intended learning outcomes by early childhood teachers: An exploratory study.* Unpublished doctoral dissertation, University of Alberta, Edmonton, Canada.

McNeil, L. M. (1980, April). *Knowledge forms and knowledge content.* Paper presented at the annual meeting of the American Educational Research Association, Boston.

Mintz, S. L. (1979, April). *Teacher planning: A simulation study.* Paper presented at the annual meeting of the American Educational Research Association, San Francisco.

Morine-Dershimer, G. (1979). *Teacher plan and classroom reality: The South Bay Study, part*

IV (Research Series No. 60). East Lansing: Michigan State University, Institute for Research on Teaching.

Morine-Dershimer, G., & Vallance, E. (1976). *Teacher planning* (Beginning Teacher Evaluation Study, Special Report C). San Francisco: Far West Laboratory.

National Institute of Education. (1975). *Teaching as clinical information processing* (Report of Panel 6, National Conference on Studies in Teaching). Washington, DC: Author.

Peterson, P. L., Marx, R. W., & Clark, C. M. (1978). Teacher planning, teacher behavior, and student achievement. *American Educational Research Journal, 15*, 417–432.

Russo, N. A. (1978, March). *Capturing teachers' decision policies: An investigation of strategies for teaching reading and mathematics.* Paper presented at the annual meeting of the American Educational Research Association, Toronto, Canada.

Sarason, S. B. (1971). *The culture of the school and the problem of change.* Boston: Allyn & Bacon.

Sardo, D. (1982, October). *Teacher planning styles in the middle school.* Paper presented at the annual meeting of the Eastern Educational Research Association, Ellenville, NY.

Shavelson, R. J., & Stern, P. (1981). Research on teachers' pedagogical thoughts, judgments, decisions and behavior. *Review of Educational Research, 51*, 455–498.

Smith, E. L., & Sendelbach, N. B. (1979, April). *Teacher intentions for science instruction and their antecedents in program materials.* Paper presented at the annual meeting of the American Educational Research Association, San Francisco.

Taylor, P. H. (1970). *How teachers plan their courses.* Slough, England: National Foundation for Educational Research.

Tyler, R. W. (1950). *Basic principles of curriculum and instruction.* Chicago: University of Chicago Press.

Yinger, R. J. (1980). A study of teacher planning. *Elementary School Journal, 80*, 107–127.

Yinger, R. J., & Clark, C. M. (1983). Self-reports of teacher judgment. (Research Series No. 134). East Lansing: Michigan State University, Institute for Research on Teaching.

Zahorik, J. A. (1970). The effects of planning on teaching. *Elementary School Journal, 71*, 143–151.

Zahorik, J. A. (1975). Teachers' planning models. *Educational Leadership, 33*, 134–139.

8 CHOOSING THE MEANS OF INSTRUCTION

Walter Doyle and Kathy Carter

Choosing the means of instruction is one of the most important and perhaps one of the most difficult decisions a teacher makes. In choosing instructional means, a teacher must use his or her knowledge about students, subject matter, resources, purposes, and classroom processes to define a pattern for organizing students to work with academic content. In other words, what a teacher knows is turned into practical procedures for accomplishing educational objectives in the time and space of a specific classroom.

The focus of this chapter is means of instruction as *classroom events* for teachers and students. Such events organize the social dynamics of classrooms, embody the curriculum, and guide student thinking about subject matter.

TEACHING METHODS: A NEW LOOK

Traditionally, choosing the means of instruction has fallen within the province of teaching methods. Teaching methods can take a variety of forms: lecture, recitation, discussion, questioning, small group work, independent study, review, and methods associated with specific technologies such as programmed instruction and computers. Some methods are student-centered and some are teacher-centered; some emphasize problem solving or discovery and some emphasize exposition or rote learning of facts or concepts; some are convergent and some are divergent; some are individualized and some are group-based; and some are "progressive" or "democratic" and some are "traditional" or "authoritarian."

During the writing of this chapter, the first author was supported in part by the National Institute of Education, Contract OB-NIE-G-83-0006, P1, Research on Classroom Learning and Teaching Program. The opinions expressed herein do not necessarily reflect the position or the policy of the NIE and no official endorsement should be inferred.

In the language of teaching methods, decisions about instructional means are based on issues of general curriculum philosophy (e.g., inquiry versus exposition) and broad patterns of teacher behavior (e.g., lecture versus discussion). Issues of curriculum philosophy and instructional effectiveness are certainly important. Teachers must know what they want to accomplish and what conditions promote students' learning. For these reasons, several chapters in this volume are devoted to these topics.

Recent classroom studies have indicated, however, that choosing the means of instruction also requires consideration of the character of the classroom as a context in which methods are enacted (see Doyle, 1983, 1985). This research has called attention to two basic dimensions of classrooms: (1) the social structure by which students are organized to carry out work in classroom settings, and (2) the academic tasks that students accomplish with subject matter. From this perspective, teaching methods or instructional means are viewed as *classroom activities* within which students do *academic work*.

ORGANIZING STUDENTS FOR ACADEMIC WORK

For experienced teachers, thinking about teaching often calls up clear images: students spilling into the room, swapping stories about friends and upcoming social events, complaining about problems they had with homework, commenting on what happened in other classes, asking about grades on papers that were handed in yesterday, wondering about what will happen in class today, and declaring their anger or joy about some crucial event in their lives. Classrooms, in short, are filled with language and motion and people.

The task of choosing the means of instruction for this complex setting requires teachers to combine large amounts of information from several sources into an integrated plan for how work will be done by a particular group of students on a particular occasion. Teachers must, in other words, make executive decisions in the course of shaping classroom events for educational purposes (Berliner, 1983b).

Recent studies of classroom activities have provided useful information for the executive decisions teachers make. In particular, this research has furnished practical ways for thinking about how groups of students can be organized for working in classrooms and how these organizational structures can be managed effectively.

What Kind of Place Is a Classroom?

As settings for instruction, classrooms have special characteristics that affect the behavior of teachers and students. It is important to understand what classrooms are like in order to gain a perspective on more immediate decisions about a particular lesson or class session.

Doyle (1980) has described several dimensions of classroom environments. This list of dimensions is valuable as a framework for thinking about the complexity of these settings and the feasibility of different classroom activities.

Multidimensionality and Simultaneity.   Choices about instructional means would be easier if teachers met each student individually whenever the student wanted to learn something. But teachers meet students in groups at regularly scheduled times to achieve a wide range of purposes with a limited amount of resources. Students differ widely in their abilities, expectations, interests, inclinations to do assigned work, and rates of accomplishing assignments. Some participate actively in classroom events; others passively watch the world go by, intersecting with reality only occasionally. Some demand attention, and others are virtually invisible, ducking the spotlight whenever it is turned toward them. At the same time, teachers are faced with an array of goals, from covering a designated amount of the curriculum and fostering mastery of basic skills to inculcating attitudes of social responsibility and promoting personal development. Finally, classrooms are interactive work settings defined by a fabric of friendships and rivalries, cooperation and disagreement, support and distraction. It is not surprising, then, that teachers have a great deal to think about in planning instructional means.

In addition, many things happen in classrooms at the same time. One student finishes work while another tries to find the correct page and a third waits for permission to sharpen a pencil. The teacher begins to work with a student having difficulty with an assignment, and five other students raise their hands for help. A teacher listens to a student's answer and attempts to understand that student's thoughts about the problem while watching two others in the back of the room who are not paying attention. Because of simultaneity, teachers are often forced to attend to several events at one time, and single actions often have multiple consequences. For example, praising a student's answer can serve to verify correct information and motivate the student. As classroom arrangements become more complex, the number of simultaneous events can increase dramatically.

Immediacy and Unpredictability.   Classrooms are crowded and busy places, and the pace of events is steady and rapid. Teachers frequently answer requests, check comprehension, give feedback, and evaluate behavior. Because classroom order often depends on maintaining momentum and flow in classroom events, teachers often have to react immediately with little time to think before acting (see Kounin, 1970). In addition, abrupt changes can occur in the flow of activity in classrooms, and events can take unexpected turns. Distractions and interruptions are common. Furthermore, because lessons are jointly accomplished with students, it is not always easy for teachers to predict how things will go at a given moment.

Publicness and History.   Classrooms are public places. A teacher's interactions with one student are witnessed by others. Because class groups meet regularly for relatively long periods of time, experiences accumulate and norms develop for acceptable behaviors. Studies suggest that early class meetings shape events for the rest of the term or year (see Emmer, Evertson, & Anderson, 1980). Planning for a single session must therefore take into account the distinctive history and future of a class.

The effect of these dimensions on classroom life varies with lesson type. For example, a class session consisting of several small groups working on science experiments is usually high in simultaneity and perhaps unpredictability, in contrast to a supervised seatwork activity in which students work independently on easy math problems. Nevertheless, these dimensions are present in all classrooms, and they shape in fundamental ways the course of events in these settings.

Organizing Students for Classroom Work

Teachers organize groups of students for work by creating *activities* (Doyle, 1985; Gump, 1969; Ross, 1984). Activities have two major dimensions. First, an activity has *organizational properties,* including (1) a pattern for arranging participants in the room (e.g., small groups versus whole-class presentations), (2) props and resources used (e.g., books versus films), and (3) duration, the time it takes for the activity to run (typically 10 to 20 minutes of class time). Second, an activity has a *program of action* for the teacher and students that guides behavior when an activity is set into motion. The program of action includes (1) roles, responsibilities, and action sequences for carrying out events (e.g., oral answering or writing workbook entries), and (2) "rules of appropriateness" (Erickson & Shultz, 1981, p. 156) that specify the kinds of behaviors that are allowed or disapproved (e.g., talking during snack time or silence during seatwork).

Common activities include seatwork, recitation, discussion, lecture, demon-stration, reports, and group work (see Berliner, 1983a; Stodolsky, Ferguson, & Wimpelberg, 1981). Some activities are named for their focal content, such as reading circle, morning song, spelling, or art, terms that are often associated with particular ways of organizing students for work. On some occasions, more than one activity operates at a time, as in elementary reading when one group works with the teacher and the rest of the class does seatwork.

In principle, students can be organized in a large number of ways in classrooms. In actual practice, students spend approximately 60% to 70% of their time in seatwork and 25% to 35% of their time in whole-class presentation or recitation (see Borg, 1980; Burns, 1984; Gump, 1969; Rosenshine, 1980).

What Factors Need to Be Considered in Selecting Activities?

A teacher's decisions about activities have important consequences for classroom order. Indeed, the program of action in an activity defines what order means for a particular segment of classroom time. In a whole-class recitation, for example, all students are expected to pay attention, one student is allowed to speak at a time, turns are protected from intrusions by other students, and successful bids to speak occur at junctures between turns (see Green & Harker, 1982; McHoul, 1978). During seatwork, students are usually expected to work independently, solicit help from the teacher when necessary, and wait quietly for the teacher's assistance (see Merritt, 1982). Students who behave outside these general guidelines are frequently reprimanded by the teacher, especially if their behavior threatens to divert the course of the primary program or vector of action (see Doyle, 1985).

Researchers have recently identified several features of activities that affect the difficulty of a teacher's task in establishing and maintaining order in classrooms. This information is quite useful in helping teachers anticipate what is likely to happen when selecting activities for a particular class.

Student Engagement.   With a fair amount of consistency, studies have shown that levels of student work involvement or engagement are systematically related to the type of activity in use. In a study of third-grade classes, Gump (1969) found, for example, that average student involvement was higher in teacher-led small groups (approximately 92%) than in whole-class recitations and teacher presentations (approximately 80%). In turn, teachers use more regulatory behaviors (directives, reprimands, etc.) during whole-class recitations than during small group activities. The next highest level of student involvement was in supervised study and independent seatwork (75%), during which teachers either worked with individual students or conducted small group sessions. Engagement was lowest during prolonged pupil presentations, such as sharing, reports, and discussions (about 72%). Silverstein (1979) found a similar pattern in fourth-grade classes: Problematic behaviors from daydreaming and mild distractions to unnecessary movement, disruption, and fighting occurred most during seatwork and silent pleasure reading. During small group and whole-class activities, however, only a few instances of noninvolvement and inappropriate behavior occurred. Comparable figures have been reported by other investigators at other grade levels (see Burns, 1984; Rosenshine, 1980; Ross, 1984).

Engagement is, in part, a student characteristic. Some students, because of ability and motivation, are more likely than others to become involved. In turn, the task of managing activities is very difficult when a class is composed of a large number of students who are unable or unwilling to engage in class work (see Campbell, 1974; Cazden, 1981; Metz, 1978). Under such circumstances, the program of action for an activity lacks durability and is easily pushed aside by interruptions or misbehavior. The composition of a class is therefore an important consideration in selecting activities to organize students for working.

Physical Arrangements.   Given the complexity of the classroom environment, it is understandable that teachers set up the physical arrangements of a classroom carefully. What these teachers seem to know is that the way desks are turned, the distance between desks, the location of supplies, and the patterns for traffic in the room have important consequences for classroom order (see Emmer et al., 1980; Evertson & Emmer, 1982). Although circular tables or U-shaped arrangements of desks may provide an attractive alternative to the traditional pattern of five straight rows, such configurations may lead to special problems of managing student involvement in work.

Studies of physical arrangements in classrooms have focused on the effects of density and noise on student attitudes and attentiveness (see Weinstein, 1979). Noise appears to bother teachers more than students. Greater density, however, increases the likelihood that students will be distracted by the action of others and that many will want to move away from students who interrupt them.

Some studies have found that participation in whole-class discussions is influenced by location in the class (Adams, 1969). In traditional classroom arrangements of rows, students sitting in the front and the center of the room are more attentive and interact more frequently with the teacher. Moreover, the interaction is more likely to be related to the lesson. Although these findings are not universally applicable, they do suggest that a teacher needs to examine whether all students are being given an opportunity to participate in classroom activities.

Bennett and Blundell (1983) reported an interesting field experiment in England in which 10- and 11-year-old students in two classes first spent two weeks working together in their normal classroom groups and then were assigned to work independently in rows. The investigators found that the quantity of work completed increased when students sat in rows and the quality of products remained the same.

In addition, student behavior improved noticeably when students were in rows, although some students complained that they had less work space available.

Complexity of an Activity.   Some attempts have been made to explain differences in engagement rates across activities in terms of the source of pacing for work and the signal systems of a lesson, that is, the instructions available to students for lesson behavior. The work on pacing suggests that student involvement is higher when work is externally paced (recitations, tests) than when it is self-paced (seatwork). When work is externally paced, students are pulled along through the program of action, and momentum can be sustained. During self-pacing, instructions for work are passively available to students, but momentum depends on their motivation and their understanding of the action sequence (see Gump, 1969, 1982).

The research on signal systems suggests that student involvement is highest when there is a continuous source of lesson information (e.g., during teacher presentation), when students are insulated from signals for inappropriate behavior (e.g., during independent construction exercises), and when the behavior of students does not intrude into one another's attention (e.g., during seatwork). Lessons in which information comes from multiple sources or is slow and faltering (e.g., discussions or pupil presentations), in which students share materials (e.g., group construction or laboratory work), or in which actions are intrusive (music or movement lessons) typically have low engagement and high disruption (see Kounin & Gump, 1974).

Complexity would appear to be an underlying theme of these explanations. Very complex activities, such as a science lesson in which several groups of students are required to share instruments and specimens to conduct experiments, are likely to have low engagement and to require a considerable amount of teacher energy to establish and sustain. From this perspective, it is not surprising that whole-class presentations and seatwork are prevalent in classrooms because these activities have relatively simple and familiar programs of action.

Putting Time into Activities.   One of the critical tasks a teacher faces in classrooms is that of scheduling activities to fit the time available. Doyle (1984a) found, for example, that activities in junior high school English classes were often affected by the need to "come out even," that is, to match the externally imposed schedule of 55-minute class sessions. In elementary school classes, the time blocks are longer, but teachers must still plan the duration of activities to allocate sufficient time for different content areas, accommodate different groups of students, and finish before recess or lunch.

One of the special problems of scheduling in classrooms occurs at the end of seatwork segments when students complete their work at different times. Teachers often devise backup systems to keep students who finish early productively engaged in work.

Learning to schedule time for activities requires a considerable amount of classroom experience. Teachers eventually develop a sense of time and use this sense to allocate time to activities and monitor the passing of time during class sessions. Beginning teachers can improve their time allocations by thinking through the sequence of events in an activity and making realistic estimates of the amounts of time needed for each event.

The information reviewed in this section suggests that organizing work to maintain flow or momentum and to guard against competing programs of action promotes order in classrooms. It is important to emphasize, however, that simplicity is not the sole criterion for selecting activities. A teacher should not, in other words, avoid an activity simply because it is complex. Rather, a teacher must anticipate what is likely to affect the success of an activity. Moreover, with careful planning and explicit communication with students, it is possible to enrich classroom experiences through a variety of interesting and challenging activities.

STRUCTURING ACADEMIC WORK FOR STUDENTS

Although organizational factors are central to keeping order in classrooms, instructional means also include academic content. Indeed, most of what students learn in a classroom is organized around the tasks they actually accomplish with subject matter. For example, if students spend their time calculating answers to addition exercises in math, they will learn *how* to add. If, however, they are also asked to solve problems in which they must choose from among several operations the one appropriate for each problem, they will also learn *when* to add. In other words, the quality of the engaged time students spend in a class is shaped by the tasks they work on.

From this perspective, teachers put the curriculum into place in a classroom by constructing tasks for students to accomplish. In choosing the means of instruction, therefore, it is necessary to consider the nature of the academic work students are to accomplish as well as the social organization of the class.

Major Features of Academic Tasks

In a classroom, academic tasks are defined in large measure by the products students are asked to generate, for example, essays, lab reports, or answers to workbook exercises and test items. These products have at least two major components: (1) criteria for judging adequacy, as expressed in such teacher instructions as "Use the correct form of the verb," "Write in complete sentences," "Show your work," or "Write at least five sentences," and (2) value or significance in the grading system of a class, for example, a report that is worth 10% of the term grade versus an exercise that will be averaged with 15 other assignments for 10% of the term grade.

A variety of operations can be used to generate these products. In broad terms, students can be asked to recall information previously encountered, such as spelling words, or to apply a standardized and reliable procedure, such as a math formula. In addition, students can be asked to demonstrate understanding by applying skills to new situations, recognizing transformed versions of principles learned in class, drawing inferences from novel cases, or combining operations learned separately to solve complex problems. These higher-order cognitive skills are involved in solving word problems in math, writing original essays, and conducting science experiments.

How Do Students Approach Tasks?

What students actually do to accomplish academic work is influenced by at least two properties of the tasks themselves (see Doyle, 1984b). First, tasks that are very familiar to the students tend to be done more automatically and with a greater reliance on memory than tasks that are less familiar. Even math word problems that contain a very familiar problem structure can be accomplished fairly easily once the structure is recognized. Second, tasks that require interpretation and assembly of several pieces of information or related skills require higher levels of understanding than tasks that are more unidimensional.

The selection of operations is also affected by the resources available to students, such as instruction from the teachers or text materials, models or examples of acceptable products provided by the teacher or by other students, and the availability of prompts and advice during work time. A task in which students are given short sentences to combine into more complex sentences to produce a paragraph is quite different from a task in which they are required to generate all of their own sentences.

Sometimes students do not follow intended paths in generating products. They copy work from other students, guess at answers rather than carry out appropriate subject-matter operations, invent their own solutions to problems, or avoid the work altogether. Indeed, Tousignant and Siedentop (1982), in a study of students in a gym class, found that some were "competent bystanders" who moved around vigorously during games but avoided key roles (e.g., they always moved from their position before the ball was thrown to them) or fell back in line whenever they got close to having to demonstrate their skills. Such strategies enable students to create products or appear to participate while circumventing the intended demands of assignments. Because academic work is done over long periods of time in group settings, these paths to accomplishment are frequently used.

Academic Work in Classrooms

Academic tasks are a central component of the program of action students carry out in a classroom. For them, academic tasks appear as work to be done under varying conditions of reward and uncertainty. Tasks that are evaluated strictly by the teacher are likely to be taken seriously and to involve greater amounts of risk for students than tasks that are only casually inspected. In addition, tasks involving higher cognitive processes of understanding, reasoning, and problem solving are high in inherent ambiguity; that is, the precise nature of an acceptable product is not completely clear in advance.

Students sometimes respond to academic tasks that are high in ambiguity and risk by direct and indirect attempts to get the teacher to increase the explictness of product specifications or soften the criteria for judging the acceptability of a product. They try, in other words, to push tasks toward familiarity and predictability so that memory or a standard formula can be used to produce answers. At the same time, they try to increase the teacher's generosity in assigning grades. Descriptive studies suggest that the direct negotiation of work demands is successful in many instances (see Davis & McKnight, 1976; Doyle & Carter, 1984). This success happens in part because resistance and negotiation often slow down the flow of classroom activities. This slowing of activity flow in turn creates pressures on the teacher to modify announced tasks.

But even when explicit attempts by students to manage work requirements do not occur, higher-level tasks are often associated with low completion rates and high error rates. These factors also slow the momentum of a class and put pressure on teachers to modify task definitions and accountability (see Doyle, 1984b). In the end, challenging academic work that fosters understanding and the flexible use of subject matter are difficult to establish and sustain in classroom environments.

Managing Academic Work in the Classroom

Some of the factors teachers need to consider in defining and managing the academic work students are to accomplish are (1) the framing of academic tasks, (2) the explicit teaching of task requirements and operations to be used to accomplish work, (3) the monitoring of work conditions, and (4) the management of accountability.

Framing Academic Tasks.   It is helpful to view the curriculum as a kind of lunar landscape for students (see Doyle 1984c). This metaphor suggests that as students progress through the curriculum, they encounter gaps that must be crossed by operations that they perform for themselves. Many gaps are small and can be crossed by remembering a list of words or applying a standardized and predictable formula. Others, such as essay writing or math word problems, are large and require students to interpret the situation, assemble several resources, and make decisions about what should be done.

Teachers create the contours of the curricular landscape by defining the size of the gaps and specifying the operations that are to be used to bridge them. It is here that teachers play a key role in translating curriculum objectives and content into the work that guides students' thinking and learning. Careful thought must be given, therefore, to the framing of academic tasks.

In framing a task, a teacher must consider *what students will need to do in order to complete a task* and whether these operations correspond to the objectives of the curriculum. With this information, a teacher can then design an assignment to give students appropriate practice with the subject matter. This analysis should include not only the intended operations with the content but also any paths students might use to circumvent these operations. For example, a teacher who wants students to learn to recognize when mathematical formulas are applicable must eventually leave the choice of formula for particular problems to the students. In addition, the teacher must plan to remove opportunities for students to have this decision made for them, such as through access to choices made by other students or through prompts from the teacher.

Explicit Instruction.   When a task is introduced in the classroom, a teacher must be prepared to state explicitly the requirements for the final product. Such explicit instructions go a long way toward helping students understand the nature of a task. In addition, a teacher must specify and frequently demonstrate the operations students are to use to accomplish the work (see Brophy, 1982; Duffy & McIntyre, 1982). When the work involves higher-order cognitive operations, it is especially necessary to give students practice with these operations in simplified situations before they are required to accomplish complex tasks. If such practice is not given, students can flounder aimlessly and acquire fundamentally erroneous conceptions of the content. In other words, good teaching means more than simply providing opportunities to accomplish work involving higher-order cognitive operations. Students must also be given instruction in how to do this work.

Some recent work associated with the Kamehameha Early Education Program (see Au & Kawakami, 1984) has suggested that higher-level academic work is best accomplished in a social setting that is structured, familiar, and predictable. Procedural simplicity and familiarity in the organizing of classroom groups appears to provide a context in which students are more willing to tolerate the risk and ambiguity inherent in higher-level tasks. In this framework, the social system of the classroom is put in the service of academic work.

Monitoring Academic Work.   When academic work is being carried out in a classroom, a teacher must be skillful in observing how students are accomplishing assignments, asking questions to indicate whether students understand what they are doing, and watching for paths that circumvent intended operations. This skill in monitoring academic work is especially important when students are accomplishing tasks involving higher-level cognitive operations. When gaps in the curricular landscape are large, tensions are created in a classroom to shrink their size (i.e., reduce ambiguity) or cushion the fall (i.e., reduce risk). These tensions result from the fact that when students cannot or will not do the assigned work, order in the class is threatened. One of the central problems of teaching is to avoid pushing the curriculum aside in an effort to sustain classroom order. Teachers thus need to avoid letting management considerations drive curriculum decisions. When management becomes the primary grounds for a teacher's choices, academic work is reduced to a set of procedures to follow in completing products, and meaningful learning becomes an incidental outcome of schooling.

This tension between management and curriculum is not always easy to resolve. Without order, academic tasks cannot exist. At the same time, when simplified tasks are used to make the work flow smoothly, the quality of the opportunities students have to learn is sharply reduced. Clearly a teacher must master the basic elements of classroom management and learn to anticipate the probable consequences of different forms of academic work on classroom events and processes.

Managing Accountability.   Accountability is one of the key elements in managing academic work. Accountability specifies what "counts" in a class and thus defines the core of academic work for students. Products for which students are held accountable are likely to be taken seriously and receive concentrated student attention. Moreover, the facets a teacher focuses on in grading assignments are crucial in defining students' understanding of an assignment. If, for example, a teacher attends primarily to accuracy of facts and correctness of grammar and spelling in grading writing assignments, students are likely to spend most of their time thinking about these aspects of their written work.

Accountability can take several forms. Most often it involves assigning grades to students' products. At the same time, simply inspecting work implies accountability. Asking students to display products publicly creates peer accountability, a form that can have strong effects.

Some teachers create surplus credit in a class through bonus points used to soften accountability for highly demanding tasks (see Doyle, 1984c). This practice can serve to entice students to try difficult tasks but must be used judiciously so that it does not remove accountability from the task system.

Skillful framing of academic work in a classroom, especially when that work involves higher cognitive operations, requires a solid understanding of the nature of the tasks students are to accomplish, the possible ways in which task demands might be circumvented, and the tensions that are likely to occur in a classroom when the tasks are being carried out. This basic understanding of academic work enables a teacher to communicate expectations clearly to students, track the progress of the work as it is accomplished, and prevent social pressures from pushing the curriculum aside.

A READER'S GUIDE TO CLASSROOM ACTIVITIES

Whole-Class Presentations and Recitations

Teachers select whole-class activities for a variety of purposes, including presenting information about content or procedures, conducting oral exercises, and checking answers to assignments previously completed. Most of the time these activities follow a format that Korth and Cornbleth (1982) have called "QATE," for questions and answers with teacher elaboration. Even during the presentation of new information, teachers often call on students to give short answers or to complete sentences, a practice that appears to sustain student attention and give the teacher feedback concerning understanding.

In orchestrating a whole-class activity, a teacher must divide attention between the development of content and the regulation of behavior. In general, student engagement during whole-class activities is high, probably because the teacher paces the work for the group and provides a continuous information signal. Nevertheless, because of the public nature of these activities, a teacher is usually required to exercise control through nonverbal cues (e.g., looking at or walking toward a student) and reprimands to prevent the spread of misbehavior (see Bossert, 1979). Moreover, a teacher must have sufficient situational awareness and memory to keep track of which students have answered and thus provide opportunities for a wide range of students to participate in the lesson (see Good, 1981). Finally, a teacher must be able to keep the activity moving to sustain attention and prevent a breakdown of order (Kounin, 1970). To be able to attend to the social dynamics of whole-class lessons, a teacher must clearly have a good command of the content.

The use of props, such as worksheets or textbook exercises, appears to reduce complexity, focus student attention, and thus simplify the management of whole-class activities. Oral exercises and checking of completed assignments are typically longer than episodes of content instruction or lecturing. Indeed, lengthy teacher explanations appear to be difficult to sustain in classrooms, and therefore most instruction occurs in close concert with student assignments and often after an assignment has been attempted (Sanford, 1984).

Discussion

Discussion is a special type of whole-class activity in which a teacher relies on questions as the primary means of communicating with a class. This type of activity is widely recommended as a way to stimulate student interest and expression and to push students to think at higher cognitive levels (see Hunkins, 1976).

Discussions occur infrequently in classrooms and appear to be difficult activities to manage. Student involvement is often low and inappropriate behavior high, apparently because of problems associated with prolonged student answers and multiple signal sources. Momentum is also difficult to sustain because the rhythm of discussion is often slow; that is, questions, answers, and the wait time between questions and answers are relatively long (see Rowe, 1974). Moreover, bidding for turns by students can disrupt the continuity of the activity. Finally, the introduction of topics by students can increase the unpredictability of the path through the content in a discussion.

Teachers have been observed to keep discussions moving by calling on higher-ability students, ignoring or excluding lower-ability students, and accepting incorrect answers (Good, 1981; MacLure & French, 1980). As a focus of a discussion becomes more divergent, higher-ability students tend not to participate, and students do not pay attention to one another's answers (Morine-Dershimer, 1983).

All of these factors suggest that the productive use of discussion requires careful planning of questions and preparation of students. In addition, a teacher must have a mastery of academic content and social processes and the ability to maintain awareness of events as they unfold in a classroom.

Seatwork

Seatwork is one of the most common types of activities, accounting for approximately 60% of time in most classrooms. During seatwork, students work independently with their own materials but not necessarily on the same assignments. When the entire class is involved in seatwork, the teacher is free to monitor the group and assist individual students. This form of seatwork is often quite interactive. Seatwork is also commonly used as a means of keeping a class busy when a teacher is working with a small group (e.g., during reading instruction). In this situation, the teacher has less opportunity to monitor work or assist individuals in the seatwork activity.

Student involvement during seatwork is moderately low, in comparison to that typically obtained during teacher-led activities, an effect that appears to be associated with self-pacing of the work (Gump, 1967). DeVoss (1979) has described the rhythm of student engagement during seatwork. Student attention periodically wanes and noise levels increase as students "pass time"—socialize, walk around the room (often carrying a book so that the trip appears to be work-related), daydream, and the like. When such actions become sufficiently visible and the noise sufficiently loud, the teacher typically intervenes to restore attention. Students begin working again, and the cycle is repeated. DeVoss also reported that if a product is required at the end of the seatwork, students typically "spurt," that is, work rapidly to finish when it becomes apparent, often because of a five-minute warning from the teacher, that time is running out. In other words, most of the work during seatwork is actually done during the last few minutes of the activity. In many instances this strategy is reasonable for students because it prevents them from finishing early and risking the possibility of receiving an additional assignment. It is also reasonable from a teacher's perspective because it synchronizes the completion times for most of the students in the group.

The management of seatwork is simplified by the fact that the teacher is not a central public actor in the activity. Nevertheless, orchestrating seatwork is a demanding task for a teacher. During whole-class seatwork, teachers often hover over the activity and usher along the work by inspecting individual progress and helping students who are having difficulty (see Doyle, 1984a). The management of individual contacts with students is especially challenging. When helping a student, a teacher must periodically monitor the rest of the class and acknowledge other attempts to solicit help. In addition, a teacher must decide when to "slot in" contacts, that is, shift attention from one student to another (see Merritt, 1982). At the same time, a teacher must be able to interpret student requests or errors and provide appropriate instructional prompts.

Small Groups

Grouping within classrooms is not a common practice (see Emmer, 1983; Stodolsky, 1984). Teacher-led small groups seldom occur except in reading instruction, in which a technical support system exists in the form of differentiated reading materials and standard procedures to follow. Multiple group arrangements in which students work together on projects and assignments are also rare except for social studies and science labs. When they are used, teacher-led groups are often organized by student ability and are a means for the teacher to "individualize" instruction. Peer work groups, on the other hand, are usually heterogeneous or organized along lines of friendship or interest, and the purpose is to foster creative thinking, interaction, and cooperation.

The relative infrequency of grouping probably reflects the complexity created by simultaneous events in a classroom (see Gump, 1969). Student engagement is normally high in a teacher-led small group but low in the self-paced, unsupervised seatwork that necessarily accompanies this arrangement in a classroom. To use this activity structure, a teacher must be able to divide attention between the program of action in the small group and the tenor of behavior in the rest of the class. In multiple group arrangements, engagement is typically low, peer talk is common, and teachers are required to delegate a considerable amount of authority to students to carry out the work (Wilson, Rosenholtz, & Rosenholtz, 1983). In some situations, the opportunities for such delegation and self-pacing may be limited by student ability and willingness to cooperate in doing academic work (see Metz, 1978).

Recently several attempts have been made to develop a technology to support the use of small cooperative groups in order to improve achievement, group cohesion, friendship patterns, and race relations in classrooms (see Aronson, 1978; Sharan, 1980; Slavin, 1980). One such system developed by Slavin (1980) is called Teams-Games-Tournament (TGT). Students are assigned to heterogeneous teams of four or five members to prepare cooperatively for academic contests with members of other teams. For tournaments, competition is arranged between students of equivalent ability, and each student has a chance to contribute to the team's score. In this system, the teacher structures tasks, and all students are held accountable for their performance. Clearly a great deal of careful planning of content and organizational structures is needed to establish cooperative team arrangements in classrooms.

Individualized Instruction

In classrooms, individualized instruction often appears as an elaborate and complicated form of seatwork in which information and learning tasks are adapted to the abilities, accomplishments, or interests of different students. From the perspective of achievement, research indicates that (1) novices and lower-achieving students often need more structuring by the teacher or instructional system to be successful; (2) individualization works less by adapting to individual characteristics than by arranging time and teacher attention so that all students have access to the main effects of instruction, for example, explanation, practice, accountability, and feedback; (3) adaptation sometimes results in substantial differences in curriculum across ability levels such that lower-achieving students are not given the opportunity to learn what their higher-achieving peers learn; and (4) individualized systems sometimes increase procedural complexity for lower-achieving students, who are likely to have difficulty navigating instructional environments in the first place (see Doyle, 1984c).

An individualized system of instruction is a difficult activity to manage (see Soar & Soar, 1983). In classroom terms, such an activity is very high on multidimensionality, simultaneity, and immediacy. Moreover, time flow is a central problem in individualization. Arlin (1982) found, for example, that mastery learning, a system in which achievement is set at mastery and time needed to learn is allowed to vary, magnified the effect of learning-rate differences among students in a class and created delays as teachers worked with the small number of students who did not achieve mastery. In addition, the problems of lower-achieving students were also idiosyncratic, but teachers lacked the time and resources to do much more than treat these students as a group.

Slavin, Leavey, and Madden (1984) have recently devised a system called team-assisted individualization in which students work together on individualized materials and their performance contributes to team scores. In addition, students correct one another's work so that the teacher is given more time to instruct small groups and work with individuals. This system illustrates the point that individualized instruction requires careful design and preparation. To increase the amount of contact with individual students, a teacher must create a large supply of appropriate instructional materials and put several classroom procedures and routines in place to sustain order.

Instructional Technology

The term *technology* refers to a wide range of devices to supplement conventional classroom teaching or take over the task of instructing students directly. The first category includes broadcast media such as radio and television, sound recorders, and projectors for overhead transparencies, slides, filmstrips, and movies, all of which are designed to enhance the communication of information. These devices are most useful in whole-class presentations or lectures. The second category consists of various forms of programmed instruction, teaching machines, and computer-assisted instruction. These devices are sophisticated types of seatwork materials that are capable of actually providing instruction.

From the perspective of classroom use, communication technologies require careful advance planning to schedule equipment and tie the content of the media to the curriculum of the class. Overhead projectors are perhaps the easiest devices to use because they are readily available in most schools and teachers can quickly prepare their own transparencies. The only management consideration is that the glare from the machine can create blind spots that interfere with the teacher's ability to monitor the class. Other devices using prepared media often elicit high levels of student attention but can be difficult to use because of equipment breakdowns, delays in receiving the media, and a mismatch between the curriculum and the information presented.

Teaching technologies—including programmed texts, audiotutorial and teaching machines, and computers—not only present information but also serve instructional functions of providing practice and feedback. From the perspective of classroom use, these devices allow for differences in the pace at which work is accomplished by individual students. In this sense, they are forms of individualized instruction that take over some of the tasks of instruction from the teacher. Teaching technologies can free the teacher for work with individual students if sufficient equipment is available and programs are keyed to the curriculum. At the same time, differences in pace can increase dramatically the distance between high- and low-achieving students. At some point, the possibility of a whole-class activity is rendered impossible because students are at very different places in the curriculum. Finally, there is some evidence that when teachers turn over instruction to individualized teaching systems, the actual amount of teacher monitoring decreases. Under such circumstances, students can invent their own strategies for getting answers and acquire serious misconceptions of the content (see Erlwanger, 1975).

A special note about computers is in order, given the widespread attention they are receiving. Although very sophisticated programs for decision making, problem solving, and word processing are available, most classroom uses are limited primarily to drill and practice (see Tobias, 1984). In other words, they are being used as fancy workbooks. Part of the problem appears to be the availability of equipment and software and the connection between what the computer can do and what the curriculum specifies as important. From a management perspective, computers share in the promises and problems of all teaching technologies.

Transitions, Rules, and Procedures

Students spend approximately 10% of their classroom time in transitions. Transitions are the activities that occur between major activities, as in the movement from whole-class presentation to seatwork. In contrast to major lesson activities, transitions are often characterized by an increase in disorderly behavior by students and a corresponding rise in the amount of organizing and managing efforts by the teacher (see Bremme & Erickson, 1977). It is important to recognize that transitions are activities in their own right and that a teacher's handling of transitions has important consequences for classroom order. Research indicates that the successful management of transitions has a significant effect on the levels of order and work involvement in a class (Arlin, 1979; Gump, 1969).

In addition to creating activities for accomplishing work, teachers organize students through rules and procedures. Rules specify the appropriate and inappropriate behaviors for students in such areas as arriving on time, bringing textbooks and other materials to class, and not talking during announcements. Procedures specify standard ways of taking care of housekeeping matters, such as sharpening pencils, handing in completed assignments, and leaving the classroom to use the restroom. Teachers often explicitly teach rules and procedures to students and rehearse them until they are virtually automatic routines in a class (see Emmer et al., 1980). In this way, rules and procedures serve as support structures or subroutines that help to prevent disruptions in main lesson activities.[1]

CONCLUSION

Choosing the means of instruction for a class involves selecting activities as contexts for students to accomplish academic work. The choice therefore involves both social-organizational and academic task considerations. Using this framework, we have identified some of the factors a teacher must consider in organizing students for segments of classroom time and in structuring the academic work students are to accomplish. The central premise is that instructional means define a program of action for teachers and students in classrooms. The management task of a teacher is to carry out this program of action in ways that maintain orderliness and provide students with opportunities for high-quality engagement with the curriculum. From this perspective, choosing the means of instruction is at the core of effective teaching.

FURTHER READING
Classroom Activities and Their Management

Berliner, D. C. (1983). "Developing Conceptions of Classroom Environments: Some Light on the T in Classroom Studies of ATI." *Educational Psychologist, 18,* 1–13. Berliner underscores the importance of activities in understanding teaching effects and describes 11 different types of activities found in 75 classrooms from kindergarten to sixth grade. The article is useful in understanding how to identify and describe classroom activities.

Doyle, W. (1980). *Classroom Management.* West Lafayette, IN: Kappa Delta Pi. This 31-page booklet based on the view that activities are the fundamental unit of order in classrooms contains a brief summary of research on characteristics of the classroom environment and on strategies for selecting and arranging activities and monitoring their progress as they are carried out in the classroom.

Doyle, W. (1986). "Classroom Organization and Management." In M. C. Wittrock (Ed.), *Handbook of Research on Teaching* (3rd ed.). New York: Macmillan. This chapter offers a comprehensive review of research on several aspects of classroom activities and their management. A broad interpretative framework for understanding teaching in classroom settings is used to organize a large, diverse collection of studies. Emphasis is placed on the program of action that defines the pace, direction, and contour of classroom events. Attention is also given to the intricate connections between management and curriculum.

Gump, P. V. (1982). "School Settings and Their Keeping." In D. L. Duke (Ed.), *Helping Teachers Manage Classrooms.* Alexandria, VA: Association for Supervision and Curriculum Development. Gump was one of the originators of research on classroom activities. This article is a clear and helpful summary of his main ideas and research projects.

Ross, R. P. (1984). "Classroom Segments: The Structuring of School Time." In L. W. Anderson (Ed.), *Time and School Learning: Theory, Research and Practice.* London: Croom Helm. This chapter is a useful companion to Gump's article. Ross defines the major types of classroom activities and provides an intelligent summary of the research.

Academic Work

Doyle, W. (1983). "Academic Work." *Review of Educational Research, 53,* 159–199. A short version can be found in T. M. Tomlinson & H. J. Walberg (Eds.), *Academic Work and*

---

[1]For more information about transitions, rules, and procedures, see Chapter 10.

Educational Excellence: Raising Student Productivity. Berkeley, CA: McCutchan, 1986. This article provides a somewhat technical introduction to the concept of "academic work" and a review of related research. Academic work is viewed from two perspectives: the inherent demands on students of different academic tasks, and the power of classroom environments to shape the character of academic work.

Doyle, W., & Carter, K. (1983). "Academic Tasks in Classrooms." *Curriculum Inquiry, 14,* 129–149. This article presents a study of academic tasks in junior high school English classes in which emphasis was placed on composition. The report gives examples of classroom tasks and how they can be described.

Grouping and Individualized Instruction

Slavin, R. E., Leavy, M., & Madden, N. A. (1984). "Combining Cooperative Learning and Individualized Instruction: Effects on Student Mathematics Achievement, Attitudes, and Behavior." *Elementary School Journal, 84,* 409–422. Slavin and his colleagues have worked for several years to develop and refine procedures for using cooperative learning groups in classrooms. They have recently combined cooperative learning designs with individualized instruction. This article is a good introduction to these approaches and their consequences.

REFERENCES

Adams, R. S. (1969). Location as a feature of instructional interaction. *Merrill Parker Quarterly, 15,* 309–321.

Arlin, M. (1979). Teacher transitions can disrupt time flow in classrooms. *American Educational Research Journal, 16,* 42–56.

Arlin, M. (1982). Teacher responses to student time differences in mastery learning. *American Journal of Education, 90,* 334–352.

Aronson, E. (1978). *The jigsaw classroom.* Beverly Hills, CA: Sage.

Au, K. H., & Kawakami, A. J. (1984). Vygotskian perspectives on discussion processes in small group reading lessons. In L. C. Wilkinson, P. L. Peterson, & M. Hallinan (Eds.), *The social context of instruction.* Orlando, FL: Academic Press.

Bennett, N., & Blundell, D. (1983). Quantity and quality of work in rows and classroom groups. *Educational Psychology, 3,* 93–105.

Berliner, D. C. (1983a). Developing conceptions of classroom environments: Some light on the T in classroom studies of ATI. *Educational Psychologist, 18,* 1–13.

Berliner, D. C. (1983b). The executive who manages classrooms. In B. J. Fraser (Ed.), *Classroom management.* Bentley, Australia: Western Australian Institute of Technology.

Borg, W. R. (1980). Time and school learning. In C. Denham & A. Lieberman (Eds.), *Time to learn.* Washington, DC: National Institute of Education.

Bossert, S. (1979). *Tasks and social relationships in classrooms.* New York: Cambridge University Press.

Bremme, D., & Erickson, F. (1977). Relationships among verbal and non-verbal classroom behaviors. *Theory into Practice, 5,* 153–161.

Brophy, J. E. (1982). How teachers influence what is taught and learned in classrooms. *Elementary School Journal, 83,* 1–13.

Burns, R. B. (1984). How time is used in elementary schools: The activity structure of classrooms. In L. W. Anderson (Ed.), *Time and school learning: Theory, research and practice.* London: Croom Helm.

Campbell, J. R. (1974). Can a teacher really make the difference? *School Science and Mathematics, 74,* 657–666.

Cazden, C. B. (1981). Social contexts of learning to read. In J. T. Guthrie (Ed.), *Comprehension and teaching: Research reviews*. Newark, DE: International Reading Association.

Davis, R. B., & McKnight, C. (1976). Conceptual, heuristic, and S-algorithmic approaches in mathematics teaching. *Journal of Children's Mathematical Behavior, 1*(Suppl. 1), 271–286.

DeVoss, G. G. (1979). The structure of major lessons and collective student activity. *Elementary School Journal, 80,* 8–18.

Doyle, W. (1980). *Classroom management*. West Lafayette, IN: Kappa Delta Pi.

Doyle, W. (1983). Academic work. *Review of Educational Research, 53,* 159–199.

Doyle, W. (1984a). How order is achieved in classrooms: An interim report. *Journal of Curriculum Studies, 16,* 259–277.

Doyle, W. (1984b). The knowledge base for adaptive instruction: A perspective from classroom research. In M. C. Wang & H. J. Walberg (Eds.), *Adapting instruction to student differences*. Chicago: National Society for Adapting Instruction to Student Differences.

Doyle, W. (1984c, April). *Patterns of academic work in junior high school science, English, and mathematics classes*. Paper presented at the annual meeting of the American Educational Research Association, New Orleans.

Doyle, W. (1985). Classroom organization and management. In M. Wittrock (Ed.), *Handbook of research on teaching* (3rd ed.). New York: Macmillan.

Doyle, W., & Carter, K. (1984). Academic tasks in classrooms. *Curriculum Inquiry, 14,* 129–149.

Duffy, G. C., & McIntyre, L. D. (1982). A naturalistic study of instructional assistance in primary-grade reading. *Elementary School Journal, 83,* 15–23.

Emmer, E. T. (1983, April). *An investigation of heterogeneous elementary school classrooms*. Paper presented at the annual meeting of the American Educational Research Association, Montreal, Canada.

Emmer, E. T., Evertson, C. M., & Anderson, L. M. (1980). Effective classroom management at the beginning of the school year. *Elementary School Journal, 80,* 219–231.

Erickson, F., & Shultz, J. (1981). When is a context? Some issues and methods in the analysis of social competence. In J. L. Green & C. Wallat (Eds.), *Ethnography and language in educational settings*. Norwood, NJ: Ablex.

Erlwanger, S. H. (1975). *Case studies of children's conceptions of mathematics (Part 1)*. Urbana-Champaign: University of Illinois.

Evertson, C. M., & Emmer, E. T. (1982). Effective management at the beginning of the year in junior high classes. *Journal of Educational Psychology, 74,* 485–498.

Good, T. L. (1981). Teacher expectations and student perceptions: A decade of research. *Educational Leadership, 38,* 415–422.

Green, J. L., & Harker, J. O. (1982). Gaining access to learning: Conversational, social, and cognitive demands of group participation. In L. C. Wilkinson (Ed.), *Communicating in classrooms*. Orlando, FL: Academic Press.

Gump, P. V. (1967). *The classroom behavior setting: Its nature and relation to student behavior (final report)*. Washington, DC: Office of Education, Bureau of Research. (ERIC Document No. ED015515)

Gump, P. V. (1969). Intra-setting analysis: The third grade classroom as a special but instructive case. In E. Williams & H. Rausch (Eds.), *Naturalistic viewpoints in psychological research*. New York: Holt, Rinehart and Winston.

Gump, P. V. (1982). School settings and their keeping. In D. L. Duke (Ed.), *Helping teachers manage classrooms*. Alexandria, VA: Association for Supervision and Curriculum Development.

Hunkins, F. P. (1976). *Involving students in questioning*. Boston: Allyn & Bacon.

Korth, W., & Cornbleth, C. (1982, March). *Classroom activities as settings for cognitive learning opportunity and instruction*. Paper presented at the annual meeting of the American Educational Research Association, New York.

Kounin, J. S. (1970). *Discipline and group management in classrooms.* New York: Holt, Rinehart and Winston.

Kounin, J. S., & Gump, P. V. (1974). Signal systems of lesson settings and the task-related behavior of preschool children. *Journal of Educational Psychology, 66,* 554–562.

MacLure, M., & French, P. (1980). Routes to right answers: On pupils' strategies for answering. In P. Woods (Ed.), *Pupil strategies: Explorations in the sociology of the school.* London: Croom Helm.

McHoul, A. (1978). The organization of turns at formal talk in the classroom. *Language in Society, 7,* 183–213.

Merritt, M. (1982). Distributing and directing attention in primary classrooms. In L. C. Wilkinson (Ed.), *Communicating in the classroom.* Orlando, FL: Academic Press.

Metz, M. (1978). *Classrooms and corridors.* Berkeley: University of California Press.

Morine-Dershimer, G. (1983). Instructional strategy and the "creation" of classroom status. *American Educational Research Journal, 20,* 645–661.

Rosenshine, B. V. (1980). How time is spent in elementary classrooms. In C. Denham & A. Lieberman (Eds.), *Time to learn.* Washington, DC: National Institute of Education.

Ross, R. P. (1984). Classroom segments: The structuring of school time. In L. W. Anderson (Ed.), *Time and school learning: Theory, research and practice.* London: Croom Helm.

Rowe, M. B. (1974). Wait-time and rewards as instructional variables, their influence on language, logic, and fate control: I. Wait-time. *Journal of Research in Science Teaching, 11,* 81–94.

Sanford, J. P. (1984). *Classroom management in junior high and middle schools: Findings from two studies* (R&D Rep. 6156). Austin: University of Texas, Research and Development Center for Teacher Education.

Sharan, S. (1980). Cooperative learning in small groups: Recent methods and effects on achievement, attitudes, and ethnic relations. *Review of Educational Research, 50,* 241–272.

Silverstein, J. M. (1979). *Individual and environmental correlates of pupil problematic and nonproblematic classroom behavior.* Unpublished doctoral dissertation, New York University.

Slavin, R. E. (1980). Cooperative learning. *Review of Educational Research, 50,* 315–342.

Slavin, R. E., Leavy, M., & Madden, N. A. (1984). Combining cooperative learning and individualized instruction: Effects on student mathematics achievement, attitudes, and behaviors. *Elementary School Journal, 84,* 409–422.

Soar, R. S., & Soar, R. M. (1983). Context effects in the teaching-learning process. In D. C. Smith (Ed.), *Essential knowledge for beginning educators.* Washington, DC: American Association of Colleges for Teacher Education.

Stodolsky, S. S. (1984). Frameworks for studying instructional processes in peer work-groups. In P. L. Peterson, L. C. Wilkinson, & M. Hallinan (Eds.), *The social context of instruction.* Orlando, FL: Academic Press.

Stodolsky, S. S., Ferguson, T. L., & Wimpelberg, K. (1981). The recitation persists, but what does it look like? *Journal of Curriculum Studies, 13,* 121–130.

Tobias, S. (1984). Macroprocesses, individual differences and instructional methods. In M. C. Wang & H. J. Walberg (Eds.), *Adapting instruction to student differences.* Chicago: National Society for Adapting Instruction to Student Differences.

Tousignant, M., & Siedentop, D. (1982). *A qualitative analysis of task structures in required secondary physical education classes.* Unpublished manuscript, Université Laval, Department of Physical Education, Sainte-Foy, Québec, Canada.

Weinstein, C. S. (1979). The physical environment of the school: A review of the research. *Review of Educational Research, 49,* 557–610.

Wilson, B. L., Rosenholtz, S. J., & Rosenholtz, S. H. (1983, April). *Effect of task and authority structures on student task engagement.* Paper presented at the annual meeting of the American Educational Research Association, Montreal, Canada.

9 MOVING RIGHT ALONG...

Greta Morine-Dershimer and Barbara Beyerbach

There are many images of teaching. Some of the more common include the teacher as doctor (diagnosing and prescribing), the teacher as entertainer (maintaining audience interest), the teacher as computer (taking in, processing, and giving out information), and the teacher as tape recorder (repeating things over and over). Discussions about "moving lessons along" bring to mind the image of the teacher as racer, setting the pace, covering the ground, putting on a burst of speed in the final lap, and crossing the finish line in exhaustion. This highlights both positive and negative aspects of teaching, but the chief problem with the image of the teacher as racer is that it leaves students out of the picture entirely, or else perhaps envisions them as some burden or handicap that the teacher must carry along while racing against time to complete the "course."

Since the point of lessons is student learning, we need an image of teaching that includes students as an integral part. Eisner (1979) and DeVoss (1982) have suggested the image of the class as orchestra and the teacher as conductor, with the appropriate "tempo" for the performance being mutually established. If the tempo is too fast, the musicians cannot play their parts. If the tempo is too slow, they may lose count of the beat and fail to come in at the appropriate time. The conductor must feel out the appropriate tempo by noting how the musicians respond and how harmonious the music sounds as they play their separate parts.

Like a symphony concert, a classroom lesson requires active interpretation of the "score" by both teacher and students. Interpretation transforms, to varying degrees, the original "piece," be it textbook or other prepared material. The vehicle for this interpretive process is communication.

"The teacher's role in orchestrating and managing the many messages, contexts and levels of interaction in the classroom requires considerable skill" (Green & Smith,

The authors were assisted by teachers and staff members of the Edward Smith School and the Dr. Weeks School, Syracuse, NY.

207

1983, p. 361). For example, in any given lesson the teacher must communicate the goals of the academic task, discipline the group, indicate participation "rules," distribute chances to talk, monitor and actively interpret student messages, and clear up misinterpretations. Within the classroom, the teacher must move students from lesson to lesson and place to place, form and monitor groups, and discipline the class without disrupting the flow of instruction. The teacher uses a variety of strategies to orchestrate a variety of goals, and when successful, the classroom is as harmonious as a musical composition (Green & Smith, 1983). As with conductor and musicians in the orchestra, the harmony is the result of a collaborative process.

STUDENTS' ATTEMPTS TO LEARN

There is good evidence that most elementary school students make an effort to collaborate with the teacher in the instructional process. Students attempt to learn from lessons both by listening to the teacher (Winne & Marx, 1982; Peterson & Swing, 1982) and by listening to their peers (Morine-Dershimer, 1982). In addition, most students try to help the teacher to keep an interactive lesson "moving right along" by volunteering to answer the questions the teacher asks. The best-known rule of classroom participation is "If you know the answer, raise your hand" (Morine-Dershimer, 1982).

Of course, not all students volunteer to participate. When a teacher asks a question, there are at least four possible reasons why a student may not respond (Winne & Marx, 1982): (1) The student is not attending, (2) the student is attending but doesn't understand, (3) the student understands what was intended but doesn't have the knowledge and cognitive skills to respond, or (4) the student understands and has the knowledge and cognitive skills to respond but chooses not to (e.g., lacks motivation). Each of these conditions has important implications for pacing of the lesson. What complicates the teacher's task further is that it is possible for all of these conditions to exist in a given classroom group at one time. And all of these conditions can characterize the same student over a period of time.

Listening to Teachers

One thing that research has made clear is that even when students are listening, they are not always hearing what the teacher thinks he or she is saying and that different students are likely to be hearing different things. Teachers and students each bring their own frame of reference (based on past experience) to a situation and interpret what they hear on the basis of this frame of reference (Green & Smith, 1983).

Understanding Teachers' Intentions.   In one study, teachers were asked about their intentions during a lesson, and these were compared to students' reports of their thinking during the same lesson (Winne & Marx, 1982). Teachers had a variety of intentions, which were categorized into three major types:

1. Orienting students: attempting to control goals toward which students worked, to influence their affective states, to identify content to be learned or procedures to be followed
2. Encouraging cognitive processing: getting students to make comparisons, see relationships, or be aware of their own thinking processes

3. Consolidating information: getting students to practice new information in order to promote later recall of content

When these teacher intentions were compared to student reports of their thinking, there was not always a close match. For example, teacher comments intended to create positive affect (e.g., motivation) were misinterpreted; students tended to focus on content rather than feeling. Students were aroused, as teachers intended, when a test was mentioned; however, their understanding of how to learn the material was not improved. This same type of discrepancy between teacher intention and student thinking has been documented elsewhere. Another study (Anderson, 1981) found that first graders felt that the most important aspect of seatwork was simply to get done, not necessarily to learn the content.

In general, teacher intentions were more clearly understood by students when they dealt with smaller units of information (e.g., teacher questions intended to review facts or concepts to be used later in the lesson, teacher rephrasing of pupil responses intended to "model" the appropriate form of response to a task to be practiced later in the lesson). Teacher intentions were less clearly understood by students when larger units of information or more complex thinking skills were involved (e.g., a paragraph read aloud, intended simply to introduce the general topic of the lesson, led students to concentrate on learning the specific content of the paragraph instead). Students were more apt to interpret correctly teacher intentions for processing or consolidating information in a lesson when they understood the content that had been presented in the lesson to that point (Winne & Marx, 1980).

Interestingly, students reported certain teacher intentions even when the teacher made an offhand remark without any particular intention. For example, when a teacher said, "Think hard now," some students interpreted this as a warning that material would be included on a test. Winne and Marx (1980) concluded that students will construct meaning for an activity even though this meaning does not always match the teacher's intentions and that we need procedures for improving teachers' communication of intentions to students. Their work points to the need to address the question of how teachers can make their intentions for student thinking more explicit and how we might teach students to use particular cognitive strategies for learning at appropriate times during lessons. A step in this direction is to look at the cues teachers give students to communicate their intentions.

Strategies for Understanding. Teachers cue students in a variety of direct (i.e., verbal) and indirect ways about instructions for academic tasks and rules for participating in a lesson (Green & Smith, 1983). Not only what is said but also tone of voice, rate of speech, facial expression, intonations, and body movements such as changes in physical distance communicate to students. Sometimes a teacher's direct and indirect messages contradict one another, as when a teacher asks students to raise their hands to respond but then accepts responses that are called out. By far the most frequently used teacher cues are to signal the appropriate place for students to talk in a lesson.

Pupils actively process teacher cues in a variety of ways. In any given classroom, teachers collaborate with students in rule-governed activity. These rules are not static; they evolve in the course of interaction and help maintain the flow of classroom activity. For example, when a student wishes to gain access to a teacher who is working with a small group, the student might signal the teacher nonverbally and wait for the teacher to respond (Green & Smith, 1983). Students have strategies not only for gaining access to the teacher but also for processing information.

Student accomplishment of a given academic task depends on more than spending time on the task or receiving reinforcement for a correct response (Peterson & Swing, 1982). The student must think about the task and may apply appropriate or inappropriate cognitive strategies in attempting to solve it. Asking fifth- and sixth-grade students to recall their thought processes during math instruction led to six findings:

1. Students' attention to the lesson (as reported by students, not observers) was positively related to their achievement.
2. Students' reports of their own understanding were positively related to their achievement.
3. Students who reported specific cognitive strategies scored higher in achievement.
4. Students who reported *general* strategies (e.g., "I was thinking," "I was listening") scored lower in achievement.
5. Students who used two *particular* strategies (relating information being taught to prior knowledge and using multistep problem-solving strategies to try to understand the teacher or problem) scored higher in achievement.
6. Students who reported self-motivational thoughts ("If I do well, I'll treat myself to a cookie") had more positive attitudes toward math after the lessons (initial attitude toward math was controlled for).

This study indicated that students vary in the cognitive strategies they routinely use during instruction and that these variations relate to achievement.

Listening to Peers

Though it is commonly assumed that teacher talk is the primary source of information in a lesson, in one large study of classroom language, when second-, third-, and fourth-grade students in a lower-class, multiethnic urban school were asked to report what they heard being said in lessons, *pupil comments* were reported as heard more than teacher questions or teacher directions, even though teacher talk represented a larger percentage of total classroom talk (Morine-Dershimer, 1982). There were systematic variations in whom and what students listened to.

Students who participated most frequently in discussions were heard more often (proportionately) than those who participated infrequently. Higher achievers were heard more often than lower achievers. Higher achievers also tended to participate more. This pattern related to the student-reported rule "If you know the answer, raise your hand." Students who might be expected to know the answers (high achievers) volunteered more often, were called on more often, and were heard by their classmates more often (even after controlling for their amount of participation). Students appeared to be trying to learn from class discussions by paying particular attention to the comments of pupils who could be expected to know the answers to questions.

Teacher reactions to pupil comments seemed to act as signals that certain answers were important to remember. Pupil comments that were praised by the teacher were reported as heard more often than those that were not praised. It was concluded that teacher praise, beyond providing reinforcement for the pupils who were recipients of the praise, served an instructional function for pupils who were the audience. In addition, pupil comments that were "pursued" by the teacher (i.e., followed by a probing or clarifying question or by asking the same question of another pupil) were reported as heard more often than other comments. This was interpreted as an indication that answers to classroom questions that were extended or expanded by the teacher might be regarded by pupils as more important or informative.

Pupil Listening and Pupil Achievement. Although pupils as a whole reported hearing pupil comments more than teacher questions, higher-achieving pupils reported hearing teacher questions more often than lower-achieving pupils. For higher achievers, then, classroom questions provided important information in addition to the information provided by pupil answers.

Active Listening Is Not Enough

Attending carefully to teacher or peers is not enough to ensure learning. Students can listen to teachers without understanding them or without having the cognitive skills necessary to comply with their requests (Winne & Marx, 1982; Peterson & Swing, 1982). Although pupils in the classroom language study (Morine-Dershimer, 1982) apparently believed that they could learn from class discussions by listening to higher-achieving pupils and frequent participants, this did not prove to be true, for pupils who followed these listening patterns carefully did not achieve any better than those who were more haphazard in their attention patterns. However, pupils who *participated* more in class discussions showed greater achievement gains than those who participated least, and this was true even after entering achievement had been controlled for.

To summarize briefly, research shows that elementary school pupils generally make active efforts to learn through class discussions by listening to the teacher, by trying to understand and accomplish the task presented in the lesson, and by listening to comments of their peers that convey information, especially when the teacher signals somehow that certain comments contain particularly pertinent information. Students' efforts to learn are not always successful because they do not always interpret teachers' intentions in lessons accurately and also because active listening does not seem to be the most important key to achievement.

TEACHER EFFECTS ON PUPIL PARTICIPATION

Participation in class discussions is an important factor in pupil achievement. Through use of direct instruction and other instructional strategies, teachers can affect the ways in which pupils participate, as well as who participates.

Research has indicated that "direct instruction" is very effective for achieving student gains, particularly for teaching basic skills in the primary grades to lower-achieving or minority-group students and particularly with students who participate actively (are "on task") in the lesson. In direct instruction, the teacher attempts to convey content and skills through classroom dialogue in which he or she controls and directs the topic and actively involves students with content-related questioning. Students are asked a series of primarily factual questions related to the development of content. For the lesson to flow smoothly yet still convey new information, the questions must be at a level of difficulty that enables pupils to give correct responses about 85% of the time. The teacher provides corrective feedback for incorrect responses, probing and redirecting questions until correct responses are obtained, and reinforces students for correct responses.

The effectiveness of direct instruction has been documented by a number of studies (e.g., Berliner, 1979; Brophy & Evertson, 1974; Soar, 1973; Stallings & Kaskowitz, 1974), and further studies have demonstrated that when teachers learn these procedures and use them in their classrooms, student achievement can be improved (e.g., Stallings, Needels, & Staybrook, 1979). The term *direct instruction* may carry negative connotations for some educators, who interpret it to mean that the teacher is active and the pupils passive participants in the instructional process. Actually, direct instruction appears to be effective because the majority of pupils are participating very actively.

How does direct instruction facilitate pupil attempts to learn? First, direct instruction may fit in well with teacher intentions to "orient" students (by indicating specific content to be learned) and to "consolidate information" (by getting students to practice new information thoroughly). Second, direct instruction may help to diminish discrepancies between teacher intentions and pupil thinking, because it is clearly focused on the learning of specific content or skills. Third, direct instruction is associated with high attention and task orientation of pupils, and when students report they are attentive in class, they achieve more (Peterson & Swing, 1982). Fourth, direct instruction involves asking factual questions that can be answered correctly by most pupils 85% of the time, which means that more pupils "know the answer" and can participate more frequently in class discussions. Fifth, this high frequency of correct answers means that pupils who are trying to learn by listening to their classmates' answers are hearing correct answers to most teacher questions. Sixth, direct instruction includes reinforcement for correct answers and corrective feedback for incorrect answers (e.g., by use of probing questions), so teachers' reactions to pupil comments may provide signals to students about the answers (information) they should remember.

In all these important ways, direct instruction can operate to assist students in their efforts to learn from class discussion. Thus the collaboration of teacher and pupils in the teaching-learning process is enhanced, and verbal participation of pupils is strongly encouraged.

Verbal Participation Is Not Enough

Although active verbal participation is associated with greater student achievement, simply increasing participation does not guarantee improved learning.

Added insight into how an effective lesson is conducted may be obtained by comparing two lessons covering the same content and objectives. One study compared the lessons of a "more effective" and a "less effective" teacher (in terms of producing student achievement), teaching the same storytelling lessons, each to a group of six students (Green, 1983).

In the more effective lesson, the teacher incorporated discussion of the story more and covered more content with less talk. Participation in her group focused on the text, noting similarities and differences in features of the story and speculating about what might occur. Students were encouraged to explain reasons behind their responses, and a student who disagreed was encouraged to explain his or her reasoning. Students were encouraged to look for recurring patterns in the text and to generate and test hypotheses. They were encouraged to work together to find an answer, and the lesson moved smoothly toward the goal.

Whereas the more effective lesson focused on content, the less effective lesson displayed more management-oriented patterns of demand for student participation. The teacher distributed chances to talk and directed student actions. Students were encouraged to participate for the sake of participating—to tell all they knew regardless of whether it related to the text. Students subsequently focused more on "getting a turn" than on interpreting the text. Thus the two teachers in this comparison constructed different lessons leading to different social and academic demands and performances. Encouragement of cooperative participation, related to developing and expanding on ideas in the text, was related to greater student achievement (Green, 1983).

Another study compared participation patterns in three classrooms and found these to vary with the instructional strategy used (Morine-Dershimer, 1983). In a classroom with textbook-based lessons, where the teacher provided little feedback to signal correct responses, the task became simply to respond, and a wide variety of pupils participated, with those who participated most being heard most. In a classroom where the teacher used "experience-based" teaching, low-achieving pupils could make a contribution by sharing their experiences, while high-achieving pupils related experiences to the textbook content and were heard most or were identified as "pupils you could learn from." In a class with "models-based" lessons (i.e., using instructional models identified by Bruce Joyce and Marsha Weil in *Models of Teaching*, 1972), pupils low in achievement could participate because they were more willing to respond to higher-order divergent questions (questions with more than one right answer) and *they* were identified as "pupils you could learn from." These three classrooms also showed different learning patterns, with pupils in the first classroom, where the task was simply to participate, scoring relatively low in pupil attention and final achievement, while pupils in the other two classrooms, where tasks were clearly cognitive in nature, scored high in pupil attention and final achievement. These results suggest that instructional processes that provide opportunities to involve all students at some point in class discussions related to *cognitive tasks* are most beneficial in ensuring pupil attention and learning.

While the Morine-Dershimer study focused on participation in teacher-led discussions, another study (Webb & Cullian, 1983) found that interaction in small student-led groups in a junior high math program was also a potent predictor of achievement. Participation patterns in these small groups tended to be stable over time, both in average frequency and in individual students' relative level of participation. Type of participation was important here, too. For example, asking a question and receiving no answer was detrimental to achievement, and this type of incomplete interaction occurred more often in uniform-ability groups than in mixed-ability groups.

These studies illustrate two important points relative to pupil participation and achievement. First, participation for the sake of participation alone is not enough. It is important that students of varying abilities participate, but students must be contributing information that is recognized by the teacher and by other pupils as important to the lesson. Second, the content covered in effective discussion lessons need not be limited to factual questions. Both high-achieving and low-achieving pupils can provide useful responses to higher-order questions (interpreting, drawing relationships, explaining, using divergent or creative thinking).

To summarize briefly, pupils who frequently participate verbally in class discussions achieve more than pupils who participate infrequently. The direct-instruction model, which has been demonstrated to be effective in increasing student achievement in basic skills, provides one good means of increasing the verbal participation of pupils in lessons. But simply getting a wide range of students to participate in lessons is not enough. Pupil comments must be contributing useful information in relation to a cognitive task.

POSSIBILITIES FOR IMPROVING PUPIL PARTICIPATION

What can teachers do to help pupils participate in class discussions in ways that may maximize achievement? Several studies suggest productive possibilities.

Teacher Routines

Just as students develop routine ways of seeking teacher attention and of processing information, so do teachers develop classroom routines. These routines are helpful to students who are actively interpreting classroom events in order to determine appropriate and effective means of interacting and learning. Routine ways of dealing with interruptions, distributing chances to talk, or convening and dismissing groups are developed, though these may vary from teacher to teacher. Effective teachers have routines for dealing with inattention before it escalates into disruption—moving near a student, establishing eye contact, or directing a question to the student, for example. Such routines can help to maintain the flow of the lesson, so that maximum time is devoted to instruction.

In addition, teacher routines can assist pupils in their attempts to learn by listening to teachers. In instructional events that students had experienced and practiced repeatedly, teacher signals (intentions) about how to think about lesson content were clearly understood by pupils (Winne & Marx, 1980).

Although teacher routines help make expectations for behavior clear and make life in the classroom more predictable, freeing teachers and students to concentrate on teaching and learning, Shuy (1981) cautions that routines can become too important and that some teachers may focus on teaching students to "do school" to the exclusion of teaching content. Ritualized routines can defeat the purposes for which they were developed—facilitating communication and fostering learning.

"Turn-Taking" Procedures

One interesting study in New York City investigated "turn-taking" procedures and other participation "rules" that commonly operate in classrooms (Brause, Mayher, & Bruno, 1982). Three basic turn-taking procedures were identified: The teacher directs a question to a particular student; the teacher asks a question and students raise their hands and volunteer to respond; the teacher asks a general question to which anyone can respond without waiting to be called on. Each procedure serves a different function in the lesson.

The rules that govern student attempts to get a chance to talk may shift with the context of the lesson. For example, students may sometimes gain a turn by asking a question or calling out, but at certain times, as when the teacher is giving instructions or explaining something, these attempts might be ignored or punished. The teacher may impose turns, say, by calling on nonvolunteers, perhaps to increase involvement of nonvolunteers or to monitor conduct. In general, students are more likely to obtain a turn if they actively solicit it rather than wait to be called on. In discussion lessons, teachers most often seek to involve students who will give correct responses to questions.

Rules for responding and for listening also operate in classroom discussions. For example, individuals who are interacting typically face toward one another. Students are expected to answer promptly or peers begin to bid for the turn. Students are expected to remain seated, to act as if they are listening, to copy "model" students when they are unclear as to what is expected, and in general to follow the teacher's agenda. Students may become adept at imitating others, thereby following the rules without understanding what goes on. Brause et al. (1982) comment that knowing the rules for participation and the contexts in which specific rules operate is a complex task, made even more complex by the fact that teachers do not usually explain these rules to students. Teachers need to become aware of the participation rules that pertain in their classrooms and of how to communicate these to students.

Alternatives for Turn Taking

Asking questions and calling on volunteers may foster competition among students, as in the case mentioned earlier of the less effective lesson, where students tended to volunteer for the sake of "getting a turn" rather than because they knew the answer (Green, 1983). Students whose culture fosters a cooperative, voluntary structure, such as Native Americans, may be at a disadvantage in the typical classroom. Teachers may need to vary turn-taking procedures to ensure the participation of more students (Mehan, 1979).

One interesting study tried this kind of approach with Hawaiian children (Au, 1980). "Talk-story" is a particular pattern of conversation common in the home environment of Hawaiian children, whereby children cooperatively construct a story that is generally a mix of personal experience and folk material. Au explored the possibility of using a talk-story-like structure to improve children's reading achievement. She found that in the traditional classroom where the teacher controlled turn taking, many children would violate traditional turn-taking rules, as by raising hands and not answering when called on or by calling out their answers. The flow of the lessons was thus broken, the teacher lost control of the topic, and the students spent less time on reading and were less successful in practice.

In contrast, in the talk-story lesson, where the teacher controlled the *topic* while allowing children to respond to her questions in turns involving *joint performances* (several children responding together), children spent more time reading and practicing in reading, had a higher rate of success in practice, and processed the text at a higher rate of comprehension. In addition, the lesson flowed more smoothly. Au's work suggests that the teacher needs to be aware of cultural variations in participation patterns typical of home conversations for the children the teacher is working with and of the possibility of varying the turn-taking rules operating in the classroom to make them more similar to home patterns.

"Known Information" versus "Real" Questions

One important difference between conversations at home and lessons in school is in the functions served by questions. At home, we ask a question because we want some information, and we react to the answer by simply acknowledging the information or by thanking the informer ("I can't find the scissors. Do you know where they are?" "Charlie was using them yesterday." "OK, I'll look in his room.") In contrast, the basic pattern of questioning in the classroom consists of a teacher's question, one or more students' responses, and a teacher's reaction (frequently an evaluation). In the classroom, teachers' questions are about "known information" (the teacher knows the answer), and the teacher's reaction to the answer tells the students how well the answer met the teacher's expectations (Mehan, 1979). A positive evaluation of a response terminates the three-part question "cycle," whereas a negative evaluation continues or extends it, for the teacher may repeat or simplify the question or prompt the student to supply a more accurate response.

The discrepancy between use of questions at home and at school is clearly understood by many children (Morine-Dershimer & Tenenberg, 1981) but can cause problems for others. Shuy (1981) suggests that the effective teacher can attempt to reduce the mismatch between school and home talk by eliminating unnecessary characteristics of school talk that are incongruent with home talk. For example, the teacher can ask "real" questions some of the time, questions to which she does *not* know the answer, questions that invite pupils to share their experiences or opinions relative to the content under discussion. This provides more students with opportunities to contribute information to the lesson. This is the procedure used by the teacher mentioned earlier who used the "experience-based" approach. Although pupils in this classroom were generally lower-achieving and came from lower socioeconomic and minority-group backgrounds, they were highly attentive in class discussions and showed strong achievement gains during the school year.

"Recycling" Questions and Repeating Responses

Teachers can *end* a question cycle (question-response-reaction), after a correct response, in a variety of ways (praise, write the answer on the board, build on the answer to provide additional information), and they can *extend* a question cycle, after an incorrect response, in a variety of ways (rephrase the question, give additional information and ask the question again, provide the correct answer). Each of these teacher "moves" conveys information to both the pupil who responded and to other pupils in the classroom.

Two common teacher reaction moves are potentially confusing to pupils because teachers use them to convey a variety of meanings (Tenenberg, 1981). For example, a teacher *repeating a pupil response* may intend to signal any one of the following: (1) "I heard your response"; (2) "That response is correct"; (3) "Is that what you said? I couldn't quite hear you" (with rising inflection); or (4) "You didn't really mean to say that, did you, because it's wrong" (with rising inflection). A teacher who *asks the same question over again* to another child ("recycles" the question) may intend to signal any one of the following: (1) "That answer was wrong; let's see if someone else knows the answer"; (2) "That was partly correct, but I want a little more information"; or (3) "That was a good answer, but there are a lot of possible answers, and I want to know what other students think."

When either of these two reaction moves is used frequently to convey different meanings at different times, both listeners and participants may become confused, and some pupils may refrain from participating. Repeating pupils' responses is a habit that teachers can break by substituting other, less confusing reaction moves. When repeating ("recycling") a question, the teacher can be specific about *why* it is being repeated so that the intention is clear to pupils. Recycling questions for the purpose of getting several different *correct* responses to the same question can serve to include more pupils as active participants in the discussion.

ADDITIONAL INFORMATION TEACHERS HAVE REQUESTED

Kinds of Thinking and Use of Probing Questions

We present five brief segments of interaction in third- and fourth-grade classrooms. In each succeeding segment children are asked to engage in a slightly higher level of thinking. In each segment the teacher moves the lesson along through use of questions, getting the participation of a variety of students and using probing questions and corrective feedback where appropriate.

1. From a fourth-grade lesson on compound words. Children must practice applying the definition they have learned to examples provided for them.

TEACHER: There are pictures at the bottom of the page. Who can find me a compound word? Marcela, do you have one?
MARCELA: Butterfly.
TEACHER: Good. Who can find another one? Steven.
STEVEN: Grasshopper.
TEACHER: Good. Paul.
PAUL: Elephant.
TEACHER: (*corrective feedback*) What does it take to make a compound word, Paul?
PAUL: Two words put together.
TEACHER: And if we take *ele* and *phant*, do we have two words?
PAUL: No.
TEACHER: So that won't be a compound word, will it?

2. From a fourth-grade lesson comparing statements and commands. Children must generate examples of commands to fit a given situation.

TEACHER: This is something that you might actually see happen. A dog is running after a ball out in the street, and there's a car coming. (*Wait time*) What command might you say? Think about it for a minute.... What could you say? John?
JOHN: Get back here!
TEACHER: OK. What were you thinking about, Don?
DON: Get out of the street!

TEACHER: Fine. Another command?

RACHEL: Don't go in the street! There's a car!

TEACHER: Good. Let's try this one. A dog is chasing a cat. What command would you use?...

3. From a third-grade lesson in which children are asked to categorize wooden blocks on the basis of criteria that they themselves choose. They must observe and analyze the features of the blocks in order to do this.

TEACHER: Rachel, would you like to explain how you grouped yours?

RACHEL: I put them in shapes together.

TEACHER: (*probing question*) What do you mean, you put them in shapes together? Would you like to explain a little more?

RACHEL: I put the long ones with the long ones and the red ones with the red ones.

TEACHER: So you kind of grouped them by size and color. Andrew, would you explain what you did?

ANDREW: I put the red, yellow, and blue squares together.

TEACHER: Oh. And then what did you put together?

ANDREW: All the circles.

TEACHER: Very good. So you put them by shapes, not colors.

4. From a third-grade lesson in which children are asked to compare familiar but dissimilar items, as they might in developing analogies. They must imagine possible features of these items.

TEACHER: I'd like you to think for a few seconds about how a balloon is like a tree. Can you think of ways they are alike? Steven?

STEVEN: If you trim a tree, it can be kind of a round shape, and so's a balloon.

TEACHER: (*rephrasing*) Yes. They can be the same shape. Any other ideas? Donald.

DONALD: A balloon can go up in the air, and a tree goes up high in the sky.

TEACHER: OK. So they are both high up. Regina.

REGINA: A tree can have long leaves and a balloon can have a long string.

TEACHER: That's right. They can both have long things hanging from them.

5. From a third-grade lesson in which children are learning to ask questions effectively to find out an idea the teacher has in mind. The teacher can only answer yes or no. Children must synthesize information in order to ask good new questions.

TEACHER: I'm thinking about a particular animal. Melanie, would you like to start the questioning?

MELANIE: Is it brown?

TEACHER: No.

JADE: Is it black?

TEACHER: No. Tina has a quiet hand.

TINA: Is it white?

TEACHER: No. What do we know about this animal so far? What color isn't it?

AMANI: It's not brown, it's not black.

CASSANDRA: It's not white.

TAMMY: Is it gray?

TEACHER: Yes. Tammy.

TAMMY: Is it an elephant?

TEACHER: (*corrective feedback*) Do you think you have enough information to ask that? Can you ask your question a little differently, so you might know whether it's an elephant or not?

TAMMY: Is it big?

TEACHER: Yes. *Good.* That's a much better question. Andy.

ANDY: Does it have a long nose?

TEACHER: No. Not especially....

Wait Time

Several studies have shown that question cycles in many classrooms involve rapid-fire interaction. This rapid pace can make lessons sound like quiz shows, with the contestant (pupil) who presses the buzzer first (raises hand) earning the most points (getting turns to talk). Such lessons may cover more information, but they limit pupil opportunities to participate.

Teachers have been trained to increase the time they waited before and after asking questions, with positive effects on pupil participation (Swift & Gooding, 1983). When teachers increased their wait time to about 1.42 seconds before asking a question and 2.6 seconds after asking a question, students gave longer answers, more relevant responses, and more voluntary contributions, and there was more overall student talk. Training yourself to increase wait time is not difficult (try counting to 3) and can have beneficial outcomes for students.

Classroom lessons "move along" more effectively when teachers and pupils are in tune with each other, in much the same way as a conductor and an orchestra, working cooperatively to interpret and perform a piece of music. Each player needs to be heard from at some point in the performance, and different sections of the orchestra are highlighted in different compositions. The music to be performed should be well within the technical capacity of the musicians, and although the tempo will vary from piece to piece, it should never be so fast that some musicians are unable to keep up, nor so slow that others become inattentive and lose their place in the score. The skillful teacher (conductor) thus leads the class (orchestra) to perform harmoniously, as well as to sharpen their skills with every performance.

WHAT TEACHERS HAVE TO SAY

The following questions and comments come from our conversations with several teachers and staff members at two schools in Syracuse, NY, who volunteered to read and critique the foregoing portion of this chapter. These conversations have been reconstructed from notes and supplemented with additional information from research where appropriate.

Interpreting Research

KATE (sixth-grade teacher): I found myself doing a lot of self-examination as I read this. There are sections in it, like the part on participation not being enough, where I thought, I know from experience that that is true, but I'm not sure that the research convinces me of anything beyond what I already know.

ELEANOR (sixth-grade teacher): Well, I've been teaching a lot longer than you have, Kate. I used to take research as gospel, but I don't take the research results so literally anymore. I rely more on my own experience. Sometimes the research fits my experience, and sometimes it doesn't.

GRETA (researcher): Most of the teachers I've talked to about classroom research feel the same way. Much of the information in the research we're reporting in this chapter comes from teachers and pupils themselves, talking about what they're thinking about and noticing during classroom lessons. For that reason, the findings ring true to other teachers, I suspect.

BILL (second-grade teacher): That's interesting. I noticed that you report on only a few studies here. Is that because there aren't very many studies of this type, or did you just select a few to talk about?

GRETA: A little of both. Research on teacher and pupil thinking and interpretation of classroom language has not been going on for as long as observational studies of verbal interaction in classrooms, so not as many studies have accumulated. But we've also done some selecting here, because most of these studies are what we call "descriptive" studies: A given study looks at only a few teachers or classrooms, but a lot of information has been collected from those few teachers. It seemed more appropriate to us to report on fewer studies and try to give more information from each one. We used our own teaching experiences to help us select.

On Turn Taking

BILL: The part of this chapter that hit home to me was the section on turn taking. I teach second grade, and we work on turn taking every day all year long. It is one of the most critical problems in my classroom. I had one parent who said if her child had the right answer, I should call on her *every time*. She is a "star," and she wants her children to be stars, too. This child needs to be "the best." This is a glaring example, but many children find it difficult to share and take turns. It seems that it's competitive, as suggested in this research report, where you say that children may start to participate just for the sake of participating, not because they know the right answer. Sometimes I think that at the second-grade level it's more egocentric than competitive, but even those kids who get a lot of attention at home compete for attention here.

KATE: It's more than just attention they want; it's positive attention. I have one child who really didn't know the answers to any questions at the beginning of the year. Now she does know, and she really wants to answer every question, to make up for what happened before.

GRETA: It sounds as if students who are too eager to participate can be a real problem for teachers. Obviously, you can't call on everyone at once. The Au study [1980] with Hawaiian children suggests that letting several children answer at once, in cooperating fashion, can be beneficial. Getting choral responses to some questions also lets more children participate.

BILL: I ought to say that this competition to participate is not a problem in DISTAR [Direct Instruction] lessons, because the program is so strict, the children know that everyone will get a chance to answer. So I guess that using that kind of very direct procedure sometimes also helps get around the turn-taking problem.

BARBARA: It may also help to know that some students may use participation rules to *avoid* participation. When Brause and colleagues [1982] identified various rules for getting a turn to talk, they noted that students adept at these rules may use them to avoid participating. For example, they might raise their hand and not turn toward the teacher, or they might appear overeager—flailing their arms and calling out—when such behavior is not allowed. Students may look attentive but not actively solicit turns at talk, so they appear to be involved in a lesson, when really their minds are elsewhere. Some students may present the appearance of being eager to participate, while violating a rule so as to ensure that their participation will not be allowed.

KATE: It seems to me that wait time is related to turn taking. If one child doesn't answer, everyone else wants to jump in. I always say, "Wait, give him a chance." I have one boy who may know the answer, but he just likes to take his time in answering. He's so methodical. And everyone else is trying to jump in. Sometimes they jump in to help their friends out, because they're afraid they don't know the answer. Teachers do have to be trained to wait, but I think maybe kids do, too. They have to learn to respect differences among themselves and give each other time to think and answer.

On Keeping the Lesson Moving

CHARLTON (permanent substitute): Well, kids want to get on with the lesson, too. It's not just teachers. Kids want to get the task done, to keep the lesson "moving right along," as you put it. Covering the content is important to a lot of kids.

DAN (vice principal): I'm not sure that keeping the lesson moving is really important to kids, but I think they know it's important to us as teachers. One problem is that we reinforce them for partial answers. I mean, they may only have part of an answer, but we accept that and go ahead a lot of the time. So kids may learn that they don't have to know the whole answer. They know we'll go on anyway, to keep the lesson moving.

BILL: Part of our wanting to keep the lesson flowing along smoothly is just to avoid stress. Teachers are so pressured. There's always another committee that's meeting or more paperwork to do or another parent to be talked to. I think we accept partial answers or call on kids that we think have the right answer because we don't want to face one more problem. If there's someone who doesn't know the answer, we just don't want to know about it.

ELEANOR: I guess we all have days like that. And calling on kids you can count on to have the right answer does keep the lesson moving. But sometimes I call on someone who I know doesn't have the place, just to get them to realize they have to pay attention.

BILL: We also ought to admit that the teacher can't really know that a particular student *will* have the right answer. Sometimes high achievers think they have the right answer, but they don't.

KATE: We shouldn't talk as if having the right answer is the only important thing. Students can add things to a lesson, even when they don't speak directly to the point of the lesson or give the answer you were looking for.

On Asking Questions

ELEANOR: In my science class, it's not always the gifted children who know the answers. I have a low achiever who doesn't read well, but she talks well. Maybe part of who will know the right answer is tied up in the kind of questions you ask. If you ask factual questions all the time, you get the same kids answering all the time. But science isn't just factual questions. I guess you need a teacher who is a skilled questioner.

GRETA: Asking different kinds of questions is important. Some authors have argued that different instructional strategies require students to play different roles in the classroom, which may require different capabilities. By changing the skills that are needed to participate in a lesson, a teacher can involve a wider variety of students in lessons. For example, the teacher we wrote about who used "experience-based" lessons involved low achievers in reporting their experiences, so they got practice in choosing and describing relevant personal experiences. That's certainly a useful skill. The teacher who used "model-based" lessons involved low achievers in providing divergent, or more creative, ideas, and that's probably a skill that none of us practice enough. We had another teacher in that study [Morine-Dershimer & Tenenberg, 1981] who varied her lessons a lot. In one lesson she had children asking questions of their classmates, getting them to describe characteristics of objects they were holding while they were blindfolded. Some children were getting practice in formulating good questions, and others were getting practice in using different senses to explore and describe objects. In another lesson she had children close their eyes and try to picture something "red that's moving." They had all kinds of ideas: "a red fox running," "a red ball chasing somebody," "a three-headed red snake," "a red horse running around 'cause a cowboy was chasing him," and "this guy carrying a red rectangle and there was blood coming off it." Our sociolinguistic expert, Roger Shuy, said that the skill they were learning in that lesson was "one-upmanship," the kind of skill you need when you're telling stories at a party.

Traditional textbook lessons do seem to involve high achievers as more active participants. They are the kids who know the right answers and get the chance to practice answering factual questions. But much of the research we're reporting on here suggests that teachers need to be versatile in using processes of instruction, not just textbook lessons. This can allow different students to "shine" at different times, and it may contribute to achievement gains. Certainly, in our study, the teachers who used these more varied approaches had classes that achieved well, and these were classes of generally low-achieving, lower-socioeconomic, multiethnic pupils from an urban community.

KATE: That makes sense to me, but it's hard to do. I try to teach lessons with variety, but sometimes I feel guilty when I take time for things like that, that seem to be "extras." For instance, I had my class make picture books, and I know they practiced a lot of useful skills, like group cooperation and writing their own ideas, but I still feel guilty, and I worried about taking the time from the other things we have to cover. Maybe it will help me to think that those kinds of lessons can be contributing to pupil achievement, too.

But, you know, you can have other kinds of problems with lessons that are more varied. For instance, sometimes when I ask an open-ended question, a kid may give a factual answer, and of course it's right, but I want more variety of response. So I have to keep probing to get that.

ELEANOR: I try to probe even with factual questions and correct responses. For instance, in math I'll say, "What was your answer?" Someone will say, "80," and I'll make a sad face. Then I'll ask someone else, "What did you get?" and they'll say, "Gee, I got 80, too." I keep that up until finally they get the idea that 80 is the right answer and that they have to stick by their guns and not be talked out of what they know.

On Peer Teaching

DAN: There's something else that you don't talk about here that provides another way of getting variety in lessons. You mentioned the importance of breaking the habit of repeating pupils' responses. I think that's really a hard habit to break. It helps to train students so that they don't just wait for the teacher to repeat or rephrase but begin to listen to each other because the dialogue is among the students, not just between teacher and student. That business about the students turning to face the teacher in order to get a turn to talk fits here. If you want students to talk to one another, you have to turn them to face one another. I used to set up pairs of students, or groups of four, to talk something over. That provides variety and gives more students a chance to participate in the lesson.

BILL: I'd certainly support that, and I'd go even further. I have a really heterogeneous class this year, and I'm using peer teaching. With such a broad range of students, I have to, and besides, I think peers may be more effective in some ways. They hear other students in different ways than we do. They may understand the problem another student is having even better than the teacher can.

KATE: I'm using peer tutoring, too, and I really support that notion. A student who needs a tutor can learn a lot from a peer who can listen in a different way.

GRETA: The research would definitely support you all on the point of the value of peer interaction in lessons. Peer teaching does provide another type of opportunity for pupils to shift roles, and this can contribute to increased participation in lessons. Besides that, peer-directed interaction gives students a chance to practice different forms of communication skills than they practice in teacher-directed lessons. I think Barbara has some notes on a couple of studies that report interesting findings on peer interaction.

BARBARA: Yes, I do. In one study of peer-directed reading groups [Wilkinson & Calculator, 1982], they looked at 54 first-grade students' requests for information. These children were quite effective in interaction with peers. They initiated turns at talk and addressed requests to specific listeners. Some were effective in complying with requests, that is, providing the information needed. Many did not show skill in revising their original requests for information when these were unsuccessful, suggesting that perhaps these skills had not yet developed. The successful students used a broad repertoire of request forms according to situational demands, persisted in seeking responses to their requests, and attempted to sustain cooperative relationships with listeners, whereas unsuccessful speakers tended to use inexplicit requests and were less likely to revise requests for information if they didn't get a response the first time.

GRETA: Can you give us an example of these requests and responses to requests?

BARBARA: Here's an example. It's a series of interchanges between two boys who were assigned to take turns reading a story to each other.

JAKE: There. There were (pause)
TIM: Were flowers?
JAKE: Flowers. And (pause)
TIM: Remember that story about the tree? "Trees."
JAKE: Trees. There (pause) what does this say. What does this say? What does this say?
TIM: (points to page) With.
JAKE: With.
I can't get that.
TIM: Which one?
JAKE: That one.
TIM: Place.
JAKE: What?
TIM: Place.
JAKE: Place to play and there (pause) what is this word?
TIM: Were, were.
JAKE: Were two
TIM: There were boys.
JAKE: Boys
TIM: And
JAKE: And girls to (pause)
TIM: Play.
JAKE: Play.
TIM: W-w-w (pause) with.
JAKE: With (pause).
TIM: But
JAKE: But Ann
TIM: But Ann was
JAKE: But Ann was
TIM: Lady. Lady. Ann was a lady.
JAKE: Ann was a lady.
TIM: My turn (reads).
Okay, your turn. Read it, read it.
JAKE: I can't get it. Why don't you read this page too, please?
TIM: Okay, I'll tell ya that word. Ann's (Tim and Jake continue reading to end of story.)
TIM: Well, we both did it together.
(Wilkinson & Dollaghan, 1979, pp. 271–272)

In these interchanges, Jake asked Tim for help in a variety of ways, including pausing, asking questions, and making statements. Tim did not always give the information outright, giving Jake clues instead. He declined to read the page for Jake, giving him the first word instead. In the end he provided encouragement, saying, "We both did it together."

ELEANOR: It sounds as if those two students differed a lot in ability.
BARBARA: Children in that study *did* vary in what sociolinguists have called their

"communicative competence." Lower-ability groups were less effective in obtaining appropriate responses to requests and in using direct forms of requests. This study shows the overall effectiveness of peers in working together toward academic goals, but it also indicates that homogeneous grouping of peer-directed study groups may serve to maintain achievement differences in low- versus high-ability groups. The use of peer interaction in heterogeneous groups, which you've been discussing, would be supported by this study.

Another study [Carrasco & Vera, 1977] reported on a cross-age peer-teaching situation with a pair of bilingual students. It was a situation where the teacher taught the child the task, the child rehearsed it back to the teacher, and the child taught one or more students and then reported back to the teacher. The authors document the sophisticated strategies that one peer teacher used in shifting from an "equals" relationship to the role of the teacher. For example, she increased the use of directives and formulated instructions much more fully each time she repeated them. The peer teacher observed in this study demonstrated much more communicative competence in the peer-teaching situation, which was observed on videotape, than she did in the presence of the teacher. This study points to the fact that different contexts may elicit communicative competence in a student. The authors comment that through observation of these peer-teaching sessions, teachers may discover new strengths in their students.

ERNIE (school psychologist): There's something else in that study that I think is important to point out. The teacher was *training* the peer tutor to carry out her role. It seems to me that sometimes when students don't participate in a lesson, it may be because they don't know their role, rather than that they're just not attending. Teachers may need to talk to students and help them examine what their roles are in new learning situations. I know we work very closely with special-ed kids who are being mainstreamed, and that's one of the things we do. We sit down and talk with the child. I'll say, "Now, you're going to be going into Mrs. James's room for reading. What will you do when you're in Mrs. James's room?" We get them to talk about what they think their role will be in that classroom. That works well with special-ed kids. I should think it would work with average children, too.

GRETA: The study of peer-directed reading groups [Wilkinson & Calculator, 1982] is useful in identifying some specific participation skills that are linked to achievement, which might be the focus of explicit instruction or of discussions with children about what their role entails. In peer-directed study groups, students need to be encouraged to take an active part in getting a turn to talk, and they may need to be taught effective strategies for this. For example, effective speakers are clear and direct, and they designate a particular listener when they make a request. They also wait their turn, and they don't interrupt or overlap the conversation of others. These would seem to be skills that could be taught to children, to improve their participation in peer-directed study groups.

On Training Pupils to Think

CHARLTON: It seems to me that we ought to be training students in more than communication skills. We need to train them to think. When I start working with a class, one of the first questions I ask is "What reason do you have for thinking that?" A lot of them can't answer. They're just reporting some fact that they've memorized, but they haven't thought about it.

The other day when my class was working on math problems, I told them that when they finished a problem they should turn the paper over and tell on the back how they got the answer. I said, "Explain in English how you got the answer." They couldn't do it. Now, maybe that's communication skills, but I think it's also not really understanding their own thinking, so I'd like to see us do more work on training them along these lines.

GRETA: The Peterson and Swing study [1982] suggests that you're pointing to an important skill. In that study, students who articulated *specific* cognitive strategies that they engaged in during a math lesson scored higher in achievement on tests of material taught in that lesson. Students who talked only in general terms, like "I was thinking," scored lower in achievement. So being able to explain the thinking that you're doing as you follow a teacher's presentation of a math lesson or as you try to work a math problem seems to be an achievement-related skill. Two specific strategies that the Peterson and Swing study identified were being able to relate information being taught to prior knowledge and trying to understand a math problem by applying a series of problem-solving steps. These would seem to be good candidates for skills that might be taught to students, but it's important to add a word of caution here. This study showed a relationship between students' cognitive strategies and their achievement, but it did not show that students who were *taught* these strategies would improve in achievement, because they didn't try teaching these strategies to students who were not using them. So we don't know yet whether training in these kinds of strategies will improve children's achievement.

On Getting Students to Understand Teachers' Cues

CHARLTON: There's something else that I would like to see happening in classrooms. Teachers need to have ways to cue students as to what kind of language is permissible in response to a question. For example, when a teacher says, "Why...?" students should know that this means to give an explanation. Students probably need to be trained to understand these cues.

GRETA: Winne and Marx [1982] would agree with you there. They found that teacher's instructional signals could communicate different intentions to different pupils, and they suggested that teachers may need to teach some cognitive strategies directly, in order to improve communication of their intentions and thus improve pupils' listening skills and learning outcomes. But a word of caution is in order here, too. Teaching cognitive strategies may actually interfere with the learning of content, at least initially. In one experiment [Winne & Marx, 1980], college students who were trained in particular cognitive strategies for following a lecture scored worse on the final exam than students who were not trained. I think this is analogous to learning a new physical skill. Every time I try to improve my bowling score by throwing the ball a slightly different way, my average drops for several weeks. I seem to get worse at everything, until I begin to integrate the new technique into my whole sequence of moves. Learning a new cognitive strategy may be very similar. We can expect to get less efficient before we get better.

On Combining Skills

DAN: That example reminds me of one of my pet peeves. You've talking about putting skills together in a sequence, and it's the integrated sequence of skills that gets you to throw a strike or a spare in bowling. We emphasize skills, and we have these careful plans for the sequential development of skills, but the skills are taught as *discrete* skills, and the kids never put them together. They never seem to get that integrated set of skills that's so important for applying the skills outside of school. For example, they don't see that reading a newspaper is in any way associated with the reading that they do in their reading groups in school, so they don't apply the skills they've learned in school to that situation.

GRETA: You might be interested in some comments that Roger Shuy has made about that [Morine-Dershimer, Ramirez, Shuy, & Galluzzo, 1981]. He uses what he calls an "iceberg illustration" [Figure 9.1], and he talks about the difference between what's visible, or above the surface, and what's beneath the surface in education. He suggests that teaching is visible, or above the surface, while learning is beneath the surface. Like you, Dan, he's concerned that much of the focus of our instruction in teaching reading, writing, and speaking is at the surface level. We seem to teach "forms," or how to do things, instead of "functions," or why we do things. We say that comprehension is important in reading, but we spend more time on decoding skills. We say that communication of ideas is important in writing, but we focus our teaching on spelling and punctuation. Shuy points out that in their concern to "move along" and cover these skills, teachers might not move beyond the surface level. As a result, children may not get a clear sense of the purpose or function of these skills in terms of their broader use outside of school.

On Understanding Student Thinking

ERNIE: The other side of that coin is that teachers don't have a clear sense of what children are learning, because learning is beneath the surface, or invisible. If we understood more about children's thinking, we might help them make these connections more readily.

BARBARA: Some of these studies seem to demonstrate that we can learn by questioning children about their thought processes. For example, Peterson and Swing [1982] got a lot of interesting information by questioning children about their thinking during math lessons, and the reports of children seemed to be fairly reliable, because children's reports of their attentiveness during lessons was positively related to their achievement. It seems reasonable that students' reports of their thinking during instruction could not only provide teachers with valuable information regarding student understanding but might also provide students with insight into one another's approaches to learning and problem solving.

On Learning from One Another

DAN: It strikes me that you've given us quite a few useful ideas in this chapter, but it's hard for me to keep track of all of them. I think it would be a good idea if you presented a sort of "laundry list" of what the good teacher does, as a summary for us.

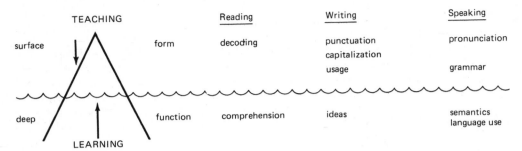

FIGURE 9.1   Iceberg illustration. (From Morine-Dershimer, Ramirez, Shuy, & Galluzzo, 1980)

KATE: Yes, that would be nice. Especially in the section on direct instruction, I found myself reading and rereading, trying to get it all in my head, because you gave so much information in such a small space.

GRETA: All right, we'll put a summary of suggestions at the end of this chapter, but I'd rather not call them a "laundry list." Suppose we label them "ideas to be rehearsed," in keeping with our conductor and orchestra analogy. Also, you have to understand that they are only suggestions of things you might try in your own classrooms. Research of this type can't guarantee that if you do such and such, you will improve children's learning or thinking or communication skills. It can only say, here are some things that have worked in other classrooms, and if you try out some of them that seem to make sense to you, you can find out for yourself whether they work well in your classroom, too. In a sense, you can become researchers yourselves as you test some of these ideas.

BILL: I like that idea. Teachers probably should do some research. They become too close to the problem, and it would help to get out of the classroom. I also think that researchers ought to get into the classroom more, maybe teach once every five years or something.

KATE: We do need to get out of the classroom more, even if it's just to go into one another's classrooms and see what we're doing. I found out some things today about what the rest of you are doing in your classrooms that I never knew.

CONCLUSIONS

Here is a summary of the most important ideas from this chapter, ideas that teachers may want to test out in their own classrooms.

Most pupils are attempting to learn from class discussions. Teachers can help them in these attempts in several ways.

1. By using "direct instruction" techniques to teach basic skills in primary grades or with low achievers, including the following:

- "Orienting" students to the lesson by indicating specific content to be learned
- Getting students to practice new information thoroughly, in order to "consolidate" information
- Asking factual questions that can be answered correctly about 85% of the time, so that most students "know the answer" and can participate in discussions

- Using praise and probing or clarifying questions to signal to pupils that certain information is particularly important to remember
- Establishing routines for dealing with inattention, interruptions, turn taking, and transitions between lessons, so that maximum time is devoted to instruction and lessons flow smoothly

2. By varying instructional procedures, so as to broaden participation and provide opportunities to practice a variety of communication skills and thinking processes, including these:

- Asking questions or presenting tasks that require different levels of thinking
- Asking "real" questions as well as "known information" questions
- "Recycling" questions, in order to get several different correct responses to the same question
- Increasing wait time after asking a question, so that more students can think of better responses
- Varying turn-taking procedures to include "joint" or "choral" responses
- Providing opportunities for pupil-to-pupil interaction in peer-directed study groups or peer-teaching situations
- Encouraging students to discuss their thinking, by providing their interpretation of the question being asked or by describing the cognitive strategies they use in solving problems

3. By being alert to a few potential problems, including these:

- The danger of valuing participation for its own sake; students learn best when they are engaged in content-related discussion
- The danger of varying interaction patterns (level of questions asked, frequency of turns to participate, length of wait time, and types of responses accepted or praised) on the basis of pupil achievement; some teachers ask only factual questions, provide fewer turns at talk and less wait time for responses, and accept or praise partial or incorrect answers in interacting with lower-achieving pupils, and these procedures do not increase pupil learning
- The danger of student misinterpretation of classroom participation rules, particularly when students come from different cultural backgrounds; teachers can be move explicit about the rules governing participation in discussion
- The danger of becoming too routinized in the use of one instructional process; pupils and teachers, like orchestras and conductors, need to keep expanding their "performance repertoire"

FURTHER READING

Fogarty, J. L., & Wang, M. (1982). "An Investigation of the Cross-Age Peer-Tutoring Process: Some Implications for Instructional Design and Motivation." *Elementary School Journal, 82*, 451–470. Reports on a study of interaction in peer-tutoring sessions led by 12 middle school tutors in remedial math and computer literacy. Benefits and limitations of the tutoring process are discussed, and effects on achievement and attitudes of pupils are reported.

Mehan, H. (1979). "'What Time Is It, Denise?': Asking Known Information Questions in Classroom Discourse." *Theory into Practice, 18*, 285–294. Illustrates the ways in which answers are "constructed" cooperatively by pupils and teachers through teacher use of feedback, such as prompts and restated questions. This process is said to be a consequence of teacher use of "known information" questions, where the teacher is testing students' knowledge rather than asking for information.

Morine-Dershimer, G. (1982). "Pupil Perceptions of Teacher Praise." *Elementary School Journal, 82*, 421–434. Describes reports of pupils in six elementary classrooms about teacher praise. Pupils viewed videotapes of lessons they had just had, then reported what they heard being said and why they thought it had been said. Pupils of differing achievement levels gave different reasons for teacher use of praise. Praise seemed to increase pupil attention to certain pupil responses.

Morine-Dershimer, G. (1985). *Talking, Listening, and Learning in Elementary Classrooms.* White Plains, NY: Longman. Compares pupil perceptions of classroom language with their perceptions of language in family conversations and play groups. Rules about who can talk when and ideas about why teachers ask questions are reported. Classroom differences in interaction patterns and pupil perceptions associated with achievement gains are discussed.

Peterson, P. L., & Swing, S. R. (1982). "Beyond Time on Task: Students' Reports of Their Thought Processes during Classroom Instruction." *Elementary School Journal, 82*, 481–492. Describes pupils' reports about their own thinking during math lessons. Fifth and sixth graders were interviewed, and their achievement was tested on seatwork and unit tests. Higher achievers reported being more attentive and indicated specific cognitive strategies they were using to understand content presented in the lessons. Suggestions are made about possible teacher use of such pupil self-reports on their thinking during lessons.

Philips, S. U. (1983). *The Invisible Culture: Communication in Classroom and Community on the Warm Springs Indian Reservation.* White Plains, NY: Longman. Investigates communication patterns into which children on the Warm Springs Indian Reservation are socialized in their family and community life. Problems faced by these children in understanding and participating in the different communication patterns of the classroom are discussed, and suggestions that teachers might use to alleviate such problems are provided.

Wilkinson, L. C., & Dollaghan, C. (1979). "Peer Communication in First-Grade Reading Groups." *Theory into Practice, 18*, 267–274. Describes the communication strategies used by first-grade pupils in peer-directed work groups during reading lessons. Types of successful and unsuccessful requests for information are recounted, as are techniques pupils used to refuse the requests of their peers. The peer-directed group is seen as a setting in which pupils can practice and develop greater communicative competence.

Winne, P. H., & Marx, R. W. (1982). "Students' and Teachers' Views of Thinking Processes for Classroom Learning." *Elementary School Journal, 82*, 493–518. Summarizes five teachers' reports of what they intended pupils to be thinking when they gave certain verbal cues in videotaped lessons. Pupils were interviewed to see what they thought teachers intended by these same cues. The matches and mismatches of teacher intentions and pupil interpretations are explained.

REFERENCES

Anderson, L. (1981). Short-term student responses to classroom instruction. *Elementary School Journal, 82*, 97–108.

Au, K. H. (1980). Participation structures in a reading lesson with Hawaiian children: Analysis of a culturally appropriate instructional event. *Anthropology and Education Quarterly, 11*, 91–115.

Berliner, D. C. (1979). Tempus educare. In P. L. Peterson & H. J. Walberg (Eds.), *Research on teaching.* Berkeley, CA: McCutchan.

Brause, R. S., Mayher, J. S., & Bruno, J. (1982, March). *Turns at talk (and other classroom participation rules*). Paper presented at the annual meeting of the American Educational Research Association, New York.

Brophy, J. E., & Evertson, C. M. (1974). *Process-product correlations in the Texas teacher effectiveness study: Final report*. Austin: University of Texas. (ERIC Document Reproduction Service No. ED 091 394)

Carrasco, R. L., Vera, A., & Cazden, C. B. (1981). Aspects of bilingual students' communicative competence in the classroom: A case study. In R. J. Duran (Ed.), *Latino language and communicative behavior: Advances in discourse processes*, Vol. VI. Norwood, NJ: Ablex.

DeVoss, G. G. (1982). The structure of major lessons and collective student activity. In W. Doyle & T. L. Good (Eds.), *Focus on teaching*. Chicago: University of Chicago Press.

Eisner, E. W. (1979). *The educational imagination*. New York: Macmillan.

Green, J. L. (1983, April). *Lesson construction and student participation*. Paper presented at the annual meeting of the American Educational Research Association, Montreal, Canada.

Green, J. L., & Smith, D. (1983). Teaching and learning: A linguistic perspective. *Elementary School Journal, 83*, 353–391.

Joyce, B., & Weil, M. (1972). *Models of teaching*. Englewood Cliffs, NJ: Prentice-Hall.

Mehan, H. (1979). "What time is it, Denise?": Asking known information questions in classroom discourse. *Theory into Practice, 18*, 285–294.

Morine-Dershimer, G. (1982). Pupil perceptions of teacher praise. *Elementary School Journal, 82*, 421–434.

Morine-Dershimer, G. (1983). Instructional strategy and the "creation" of classroom status. *American Educational Research Journal, 20*, 645–661.

Morine-Dershimer, G., Ramirez, A., Shuy, R., & Galluzzo, G. (1981). *How do we know? (Alternative descriptions of classroom discourse)*. Part 4 of Final Report of Participant Perspectives of Classroom Discourse (NIE-G-78-0161). Syracuse, NY: Syracuse University, Division for the Study of Teaching.

Morine-Dershimer, G., & Tenenberg, M. (1981). *Participant perspectives of classroom discourse: Executive summary*. Hayward: California State University.

Peterson, P. L., & Swing, S. R. (1982). Beyond time on task: Student reports of their thought processes during classroom instruction. *Elementary School Journal, 82*, 481–492.

Shuy, R. (1981, April). *Identifying the dimensions of classroom language*. Paper presented at the annual meeting of the American Educational Research Association, Los Angeles.

Soar, R. S. (1973). *Follow Through classroom process measurement and pupil growth, 1970–71: Final report*. Gainesville: University of Florida, College of Education, Institute for Development of Human Resources.

Stallings, J., & Kaskowitz, D. (1974). *Follow Through classroom observation evaluation, 1972–73*. Menlo Park, CA: Stanford Research Institute.

Stallings, J., Needels, M., & Staybrook, N. (1979). *How to change the process of teaching basic reading skills in secondary schools: Final report*. Washington, DC: U.S. Department of Health, Education and Welfare.

Swift, J. N., & Gooding, C. T. (1983). Interaction of wait time, feedback, and questioning instruction on middle school science teaching. *Journal of Research on Science Teaching, 20*, 721–730.

Tenenberg, M. (1981, April). *Cycling and recycling questions: The "when" of talking in classrooms*. Paper presented at the annual meeting of the American Educational Research Association, Los Angeles.

Webb, N. M., & Culliam, L. K. (1983). Group interaction and achievement in small groups: Stability over time. *American Educational Research Journal, 20*, 411–423.

Wilkinson, L. C., & Calculator, S. (1982). Requests and responses in peer-directed reading groups. *American Educational Research Journal, 19*, 107–120.

Wilkinson, L. C., & Dollaghan, C. (1979). Peer communication in first-grade reading groups. *Theory into Practice, 18,* 267–274.

Winne, P. H., & Marx, R. W. (1980). *Teachers' and students' views of cognitive processes for learning from teaching* (First Year Tech. Rep.). Burnaby, British Columbia, Canada: Simon Fraser University.

Winne, P. H., & Marx, R. W. (1982). Students' and teachers' views of thinking processes for classroom learning. *Elementary School Journal, 82,* 493–518.

10 CLASSROOM MANAGEMENT AND DISCIPLINE

Edmund T. Emmer

Good classroom management and discipline are major components of effective teaching. They are always high on the list of concerns of teachers, students, and the public. Because of their centrality to the teaching role, the topic deserves careful study.

In this chapter the term *discipline* is used to indicate the degree to which students behave appropriately, are involved in activities, are task-oriented, and do not cause disruptions. Classroom management and discipline are related because management is chiefly directed at establishing conditions for good discipline. That is, classroom management is a set of teacher behaviors and activities directed at engaging students in appropriate behavior and minimizing disruptions.

Discipline is sometimes used to indicate the act of administering a punishment, as in "The teacher disciplined the student." However, frequent use of punishment is more indicative of poor discipline than of effective discipline. Furthermore, this sense of the term is misleading, because it focuses attention on the teacher's *reaction* to misbehavior, whereas good discipline is produced mainly by *preventing* problems and by *conducting activities* in ways that keep students actively engaged in them. Of course, punishment is an aspect of discipline, but it is not the teacher's chief tool.

An example will help illustrate this chapter's perspective and demonstrate the relationship of management and discipline.

Mr. Jones uses two groups for instruction in his fourth-grade math class in order to accommodate a wide range of math abilities. While he works with one group, however, students out of the group frequently waste time, wander around the room, and talk loudly among themselves. When he stops his small group lesson to deal with these behaviors, the students in the group become restless and inattentive. Furthermore, his attempts to deal with the disruptions out of the group are generally not successful because in a short while the students resume their misbehavior. Mr. Jones has begun to write names on the chalkboard when students are disruptive and then keep the students after school as punishment. Although this seemed to be effective the first few times he did it, it was difficult to keep track of which students were being excessively noisy, and the noise level and commotion soon exceeded earlier levels. This situation produced the unhappy dilemma of either keeping large numbers of students after school or abandoning the system. In neither case will the original problem be solved.

In this example, the teacher experienced difficulty in obtaining appropriate student behavior, and most observers would probably agree that the students evidenced poor discipline. The causes of the problem, however, are not as obvious as the fact that a problem exists. For one thing, it is likely that the problem developed gradually and was not the result of a single event or student. It can also noted that the teacher's response to the problem of off-task behavior was to punish students, thus reacting to events after they became intrusive. This is a common occurrence—we tend to notice the blemish and try to remove it—and it may be the reason why discussions of discipline often dwell on the exploits of troublesome students and ways of dealing with them. However, suggestions to Mr. Jones about how he should react to the inappropriate behavior would probably not be very helpful to him. Instead Mr. Jones should take action to *prevent* inappropriate behavior and to encourage students to behave appropriately. Identifying how this might be done would require more information than can be presented in a short example, but here are some alternatives:

1. Students out of the group may not know what behaviors are expected of them. Therefore, they need specific directions about what to do when the teacher is working with a group.
2. Students may not be able to complete the assignment without additional help, and they may need more instruction before they begin working.
3. The students may need to be monitored more carefully, and Mr. Jones may need to rearrange seating in order to keep them in clearer view while he is working with the group.
4. Mr. Jones may need to teach students out of the group a signal for correct behavior.
5. Students in the group may need to learn a procedure to follow when Mr. Jones helps another student or leaves the group to deal with a problem.

The example and the suggestions illustrate the likelihood that achieving good discipline depends on much more than just the teacher's response to inappropriate behavior. Good discipline requires managing the classroom so that opportunities for disruption are minimized and so that it is easy for students to engage in learning activities.

Achieving good student discipline is complicated by the necessity of dealing with students in groups. Large numbers of students must be taught a multitude of concepts and skills in one or more subjects in a setting that is filled with distractions, not the least of which are other students of the same age. The pacing of group instruction cannot be optimal for everyone, particularly in heterogeneous classes, and seatwork or other class assignments will vary in their interest or appeal for different students.

The degree to which students exhibit good discipline will be largely determined by the nature of their classroom environment, including the limits it places on students and the opportunities it provides for appropriate or inappropriate behavior. The physical arrangements in the setting, the nature of academic tasks and activities and their demands, the expectations of the teacher, and the reactions of other students will all have an impact on student behavior. Thus the achievement of good discipline is grounded in actions the teacher takes to establish a classroom environment that facilitates appropriate behavior and prevents misbehavior.

The recommendations in this chapter are derived mainly from observational studies of teachers and their classrooms. The approaches presented are not the only ways to build good classroom discipline, nor is every component described here equally important in all settings. Each teacher will need to adapt the suggestions derived from research to fit his or her context. Readers who wish to explore the research literature can examine Duke (1979, 1982), Smith (1983), Brophy (1983), Doyle (1985), Emmer (1984), and Goss and Ingersoll (1981).

PHASES IN CLASSROOM MANAGEMENT AND DISCIPLINE

Three major phases in the process of establishing and maintaining good discipline can be identified. The first phase occurs *before* students arrive at the beginning of the year. It consists of preparing the physical setting, planning beginning-of-year activities, and identifying expectations for student behavior and for work requirements.

The second phase occurs at the beginning of the school year. During this phase the teacher communicates expectations to students, establishes norms for behavior and work, and initiates routines and procedures. Depending on the age and grade level of the students, this phase may take anywhere from a few days to many weeks to complete.

A third phase, which occurs throughout the year, consists of maintaining norms for behavior and involving students in learning activities. During this phase the focus shifts from socializing students into the classroom setting to designing and conducting activities that have high levels of student engagement.

No implication is intended that the planning activities in the first phase and the norm-setting activities in the second phase do not occur at other times than early in the school year. New procedures can be introduced later, and changes in the physical setting or behavior norms can and do occur. Furthermore, students are socialized in the context of classroom activities, so their design and conduct at the *beginning* of the year are also important. Thus the purpose of describing phases is to emphasize their distinctive features and relative importance at different times rather than to imply their complete independence.

Phase 1: Preparing for the Beginning of the Year

Studies of teacher planning for the beginning of school indicate that a major goal for the first few weeks is to make expectations explicit by establishing rules and procedures and by consistent enforcement of them. Thus an important component of the preactive phase is identifying expectations for student behavior and integrating them into an overall system of classroom procedures and rules. Also, studies of planning indicate that teachers concentrate on arranging the classroom, organizing supplies and materials, and planning class activities for the first few days. Because teacher planning influences subsequent teacher behavior and activities, knowledge about critical areas for teacher planning for the beginning of the year can be augmented by research on what teachers actually do when school starts. Several studies have been reported (Anderson, Evertson, & Emmer, 1980; Emmer, 1981; Emmer, Evertson, & Anderson, 1980; Emmer, Sanford, Clements, & Martin, 1982; Evertson & Emmer, 1982; Evertson, Emmer, Sanford, & Clements, 1983; Sanford & Evertson, 1981). These studies were conducted at the Research and Development Center for Teacher Education (R&DCTE) and will henceforth be referred to as the R&DCTE studies. In these studies, observations were made of a total of approximately 200 elementary and junior high school teachers' management practices. Data collected included extensive observations at the beginning of the year as well as at various times later in the year. Some of the data analyses identified teachers as having more effective or less effective discipline, based on their students' levels of disruption and engagement in classroom activities. After matching the classes on the basis of average student ability level, the beginning-of-year classroom management behaviors and activities of more and less effective managers were compared, using both quantitative and qualitative data sources. A number of differentiating characteristics of more effective classroom management that have implications for beginning-of-year planning were identified. These management characteristics are the basis for the suggestions that follow.

Arranging the Classroom.   The relationship between good discipline and physical arrangements may not be apparent at first, but the connection is clear when the negative effects of poor arrangements are considered. For example, the placement of the area for small group instruction can have distracting effects on the remainder of the class or may make it difficult for the teacher to monitor the class when working with the group. Placing students' desks so that they face windows may promote inattention, and the location of the pencil sharpener, supply areas, the wastebasket, or the teacher's desk may also create obstructions or distractions. Consequently, following certain guidelines for good room arrangement can prevent problems and facilitate smoother running classroom activities.

1. Student seating should be arranged to allow easy monitoring by the teacher and to avoid distractions to students.
2. Clear lines of sight are needed from student seating areas to instructional areas.
3. Frequently used areas of the room should be easily accessible, and traffic lanes should not be obstructed.
4. Equipment and materials should be arranged so that they are readily available when needed by the teacher or students.

Once the basic physical arrangements have been set, there is no need to over-dwell on decorating the room. As long as the room is welcoming and appealing, more pressing matters should be considered at the beginning of the year. A blank bulletin board can always be left for a class project.

Identifying Expectations for Behavior.   A major managerial task at the beginning of the year is to establish norms for behavior. Norms are made explicit in classrooms in a variety of ways, including teacher praise of appropriate behavior, corrective feedback, formally presented rules, establishing procedures that regulate behavior during classroom activities, and academic work requirements. The behavior of students and the tasks of accomplishing academic work in a crowded setting are complex, and careful planning is needed to keep activities running smoothly. Selecting and implementing a system of procedures and work requirements, along with some general rules, helps to create a structure for student work and behavior.

Expectations for behavior must be formulated before students arrive. If the teacher is uncertain about what behaviors are or are not acceptable in different types of activities, student behavior that is counterproductive and difficult to change may become established. For example:

> Ms. Andrews provided students with a rule at the beginning of the year—"Listen carefully when others speak"—and she explained that she wanted students to raise their hands during class discussions or presentations. However, no expectation was stated about talking during seatwork or transitions. In fact, Ms. Andrews was not certain whether she would allow talking at other times, and she was not particularly concerned about quiet talk, as long as it did not interfere with or disrupt the class. For the first week or so, students were fairly quiet during seatwork, but gradually the noise built up until Ms. Andrews had to ask for quiet repeatedly.

In this example, Ms. Andrews's rule, while useful for whole-class discussions or presentations, did not generalize to all other types of activities. Because she was not clear about what kind of talk, if any, would be allowed at other times, Ms. Andrews failed to communicate an expectation to students. When students received no feedback for talking during seatwork, the noise level inevitably rose, requiring Ms. Andrews to intervene to try to reduce it. It would have been much simpler if she had formulated an expectation in this area and had communicated it to the students.

The variety of activities and grouping patterns that are used in classrooms makes them complex environments, because different activities require different student behaviors (Berliner, 1983). This complexity makes the formulation of expectations an important task. Studies of classrooms indicate that the following types of activities often require different student behaviors and thus should be "mapped out" prior to their use in the classroom.

1. Whole-class presentations, recitations, and discussions
2. Teacher-led small groups, including expectations for behavior of students not in the group
3. Independent small group or project work
4. Individual seatwork
5. Transitions between activities and into and out of the room
6. Room and equipment use

In addition to expectations in these types of activities, academic work procedures must also be planned. General areas to consider include the following:

1. The communication of assignments and related work requirements
2. Makeup work and other procedures related to student absences
3. Procedures for monitoring student work and the completion of assignments, and assisting students who encounter difficulty with their assignments

4. Feedback to students about their progress and procedures for dealing with students who fail to complete work
5. Grading procedures and related record keeping

   The degree of emphasis placed on particular categories will vary according to the age and grade level of students and the classroom context. Procedures in the area of managing student work are often emphasized somewhat more than behavioral expectations in secondary school classrooms. In the elementary grades, teachers need to give careful attention to procedures associated with various instructional groupings, including how students can obtain assistance when the teacher is occupied with a small group or an individual, and what should be done when students return from out of the room, such as from a resource room or from another teacher's room. At the secondary level, the organization of classes is usually less complex, and by this time students have learned more "going to school" skills, so there are usually fewer procedural concerns. However, careful planning of procedures is still important, and the use of small groups or other non-whole-class instructional formats increases the complexity of a secondary setting.

Planning Consequences.   Another area for preparation at the beginning of the year is the identification of rewards or penalties that will be used as consequences for appropriate and inappropriate student behavior. Having already identified the expectations for student behavior in various procedural and academic work areas makes it easier to identify major classes of behavior that can be rewarded by incentives, such as honor badges, stickers, awards, prizes, or privileges, in addition to the use of grades. It should be noted that student behavior is usually acceptable at the beginning of the year, so extrinsic incentive systems are usually not needed at this time. Student success in academic tasks and teacher feedback, approval, and recognition are generally sufficient to maintain appropriate behavior during the first days or weeks of school. However, if and when extra incentives are introduced, it is important that they be directly associated with the behaviors they are intended to encourage.

   Familiarity with school policies related to punishment and reward at the beginning of the year is essential. When penalty systems or other forms of punishment are used, they should be reserved for behaviors that are easily observable and relatively infrequent. If penalties such as detention, suspension, "fines," or demerit systems are used for frequently occurring behaviors such as social talk among students, or if the behaviors are difficult to monitor, inconsistent teacher use of punishment is much more likely. In addition, frequent use of punishment becomes time-consuming and distracts from the academic work that should be under way in the classroom. Consequences will be discussed later in the chapter, as one aspect of dealing with inappropriate behavior. For the time being, it is sufficient to note that the use of teacher-administered consequences, whether rewards or punishments, is not the major component of an effective system of management and discipline, and the keys to good management and discipline reside in other aspects of the teacher's behavior.

Phase 2: Beginning the School Year

Beginning-of-school activities are needed to establish the teacher's expectations as norms and to create a climate conducive to learning. In addition to the R&DCTE

management studies cited earlier, a number of naturalistic studies at the beginning of the year provide important information about this phase of classroom life (Buckley & Cooper, 1978; Eisenhart, 1977; Moskowitz & Hayman, 1976; Tikunoff, Ward, & Dasho, 1978). Research provides several related principles that can be used to achieve a good start.

Teach Students to Behave.   As noted earlier, classrooms are complex places filled with a variety of activities, such as seatwork, discussions, small groups, and whole-class presentations, all of which may require different behaviors of students, no matter what their age or grade level. The average secondary school student will be in at least six classrooms every day, and procedures and expectations for behavior may vary from one to another, and even elementary school students participate in several types of activities and may receive instruction from other teachers in some subjects. Thus students need to learn what behavior is or is not appropriate in the various settings and activities.

Consider Students' Concerns.   It is not only teachers who are anxious when school begins; many students also approach the beginning of school with trepidation. The sources of anxiety vary, but common ones are a concern about ability to do the required work, fear of peer or teacher rejection, and the change that accompanies entrance into a different school, new subjects, and a higher grade level. Some of the anxiety can be allayed by creating a predictable classroom environment, by designing content activities that students can participate in and complete at a high level of success, and by teacher behavior that is supportive and encouraging.

Lead the Class.   Although the image of the teacher as an authoritarian drill sergeant is overdrawn, its opposite, that of the "laid back, don't sweat the details" type of teacher, is equally inappropriate. At the beginning of the year, it is up to the teacher to define appropriate behavior, provide guidelines for academic work, establish positive expectations about the content to be learned, and to provide students with the information they need to be successful. These tasks require an active role for the teacher. Especially at the beginning of the year, the teacher should be "front and center stage" in the classroom, providing direction, instruction, and guidance. If students have questions or have difficulty in carrying out a procedure or a task, the teacher should be available for assistance and clarification. Teachers need to avoid spending large amounts of time working with individual students or on administrative tasks, because such activities reduce their ability to monitor students and to manage the class as a group.

The following items make these principles operational.

1. A set of three to six general rules should be developed to regulate behavior that is not specific to an individual activity. These rules guide students and create an expectation for appropriate behavior if they are positively stated. A rule or two forbidding particular behaviors may also be used as long as the teacher is prepared to deal with students who test the rule. Also a rule such as "Follow all school policies or rules" is useful because it affirms that the teacher will enforce school regulations. Rules should be discussed with students early on the first day, perhaps immediately after general introductions and basic administrative tasks have been completed. The

discussion should emphasize the rationale for the rules and should clarify the meaning of general terms. Discussions with students sometimes generate negative rationales and examples, so the teacher should be prepared to provide positive reasons that are appropriate for the age and grade level of the students (for example, emphasizing "grown-up" or mature behavior, concern for fellow students, and the desirability of a pleasant class atmosphere conducive to learning). It should be noted that an initial set of rules is only a small portion of the overall expectations for behavior. Teachers also introduce numerous classroom procedures gradually over a period of days or weeks, giving careful explanations of what is expected of students.

2. Other, more specific expectations for behavior—work requirements, classroom procedures, and expected behavior in particular activities—should be introduced as they are needed. No purpose is served by reviewing small group procedures on the first day or two of classes if group instruction will not begin until the second week. However, procedures for student use of the room, storage of materials, bathroom use, movement around the room, and expectations for student talk are all needed on the first day or two. These expectations can be introduced gradually, as they are needed, such as at the beginning of the activities when the procedures are first used.

3. Secondary school teachers should prepare an overview of their courses and highlight their main topics and work requirements. For elementary school teachers, the overview can focus on several topics or skills that will appeal to the students. Because the purpose of the overview of content is to give the students a positive set toward the coming year, the initial presentation should not be too full of details and requirements. Emphasizing the interesting, useful, exciting things that students will be learning keeps the focus on positive reasons for academic work requirements.

4. Procedures and expectations should be *taught* as though they were content. (In some respects, they *are* the content of the beginning of the year.) Good teaching means using clear definitions, examples, and even rehearsal or demonstration of complex behaviors. The latter is usually done at the early grade levels, although even high school students may need demonstration of expected behaviors when safety is a factor, as in industrial arts classes or science laboratories. Once a procedure has been described, careful monitoring to verify compliance is important, and prompt feedback and redirection should be given if a student is observed not following a procedure.

5. Activities for the first several days of classes should be designed to provide high levels of success. Difficult early assignments are problematic because the teacher does not yet know students well enough to predict who will need extra help and because early failure among students whose academic self-concepts are low may further dampen their motivation. From a managerial perspective, difficult early assignments increase the burden on the teacher to provide individual instruction and consequently make monitoring the whole class more difficult. Highly able students in class can be challenged by extra credit or optional assignments.

6. It is important that students be accountable for their work early in the year. Assignments from the first days of classes should be checked, and students should receive feedback promptly. Because early assignments will be easy, this feedback will generally be positive and encouraging. If a student does not complete an early

assignment, reasons should be ascertained immediately in order to prevent a pattern of work avoidance from developing. If ability level is the problem, assignments can be adjusted accordingly. If effort is deficient, early diagnosis and follow-up may improve the situation.

7. Students in the later elementary and secondary levels can be provided with handouts listing class rules, major work requirements, and, at the secondary level, a course outline. To facilitate communication with parents, these descriptions may be sent home to be signed and then retained by students in a folder. Such handouts also make it easier to orient students who are added to the class after the beginning of the year.

8. Whole-class activities, teacher-led instruction, and seatwork predominate for at least the first several days of school. Small groups, individualized instruction, and other complex organizational patterns are usually not introduced until later. From a management perspective, the advantage of these limitations on activities is twofold. Whole-class activities enable the teacher to monitor students readily; also, they do not involve the use of complex procedures that might be difficult to teach students. The use of easier whole-class activities and lessons has the advantage of reducing the likelihood of student failure and also the demands on the teacher's time that might be caused by large numbers of students encountering difficulty with the tasks.

Teachers also establish norms through their handling of inappropriate behavior. Because this aspect of establishing good discipline is also a part of the yearlong maintenance of appropriate behavior, it will be discussed as part of the next section.

Phase 3: Maintaining Good Discipline

Once students have settled into classroom routines, a third phase of classroom management begins. During this phase, teacher skills in maintaining student engagement and preventing disruption of the environment are more prominent than the beginning-of-year tasks of communicating expectations, creating norms, and teaching procedures. Skills for maintaining a well-managed setting can be subdivided into two major areas: (1) monitoring and prompt handling of inappropriate behavior, and (2) organizing and conducting classroom activities.

Teacher Monitoring and Prompt Handling of Inappropriate Behavior. Teacher skills in this area are also important in the norm-setting phase of management at the beginning of the year. Teachers who are good managers and have relatively few discipline problems do *not* ignore large amounts of inappropriate behavior. Instead, they are alert to note students whose behavior is straying from accepted norms and to stop the inappropriate behavior and redirect it to appropriate activities.

Research reported by Kounin (1970) identified "withitness" as an important management variable. Withitness is calculated as the percentage of teacher desists (statements or actions directed at terminating a student behavior) that are both accurate and timely. Whenever a teacher-desist event occurred, Kounin noted whether it was directed at the student who was the cause of the misbehavior and whether the desist occurred before the behavior spread to other students or became intense. Correlations of withitness and management criteria such as on-task behavior or low rates

of deviancy were sufficiently high to conclude that it represents an important component of management capability. Other researchers have examined withitness or
teacher behaviors related to it and corroborated Kounin's results at various grade
levels (Brophy & Evertson, 1976; Copeland, 1983; Emmer, Evertson, & Anderson,
1980; Evertson & Emmer, 1982). Rather than view the concept of withitness as a
single skill, it may be more useful to think of it in terms of two component behaviors,
monitoring and prompt handling of inappropriate behavior. It is apparent that in
order to be "with it," a teacher must be a good monitor—for example, by scanning
the room to see what students are doing, keeping track of individual progress, and in
general being vigilant as to the degree of student involvement in learning activities. If
the teacher does not monitor carefully, there is much greater likelihood that inappropriate student behaviors will escalate into more serious problems or spread to
other students before the teacher is aware of them. Obviously, it is simple to deal with
inappropriate behavior when it is mild and involves only one or a few students. Once
the misbehavior becomes intense or widespread, more time and effort are required to
stop it, and students may have obtained considerable reinforcement from other
students. In addition, widespread misbehavior serves as poor models for other students. Consequently, awareness of what is going on in the room at all times is
essential. Monitoring alone is insufficient, of course; a teacher will not survive for
long as a mere spectator. Thus prompt handling of inappropriate behavior becomes a
complementary component. Research does *not* suggest that it is necessary to respond
to all instances of inappropriate behavior. Instead, it is necessary to deal with those
that are likely to spread or to become more intense. Such student behaviors include
disruption of activities, interference with other students' work, not following
appropriate procedures or work requirements, and aggressive behavior (verbal or
physical, playful or not). Obviously, there are different degrees of intensity of these
types of behavior, and it is important that the teacher avoid overreacting as well as
underreacting. Behaviors that can safely be ignored include those that do not interfere
with other students or an ongoing activity and are of brief duration or those that are
"self-correcting." This latter type includes such things as occasionally failing to raise
one's hand before speaking (if that is a classroom procedure) or inadvertent violation
of some rule. Dealing with such behaviors is seldom necessary because they rarely
persist, nor do they usually serve as a negative model for other students. Furthermore,
a teacher response would attach to them unwarranted significance and might provide
undesirable reinforcing attention.

Research has noted that when effective managers deal with inappropriate behavior, they do so promptly but *relatively unobtrusively*. That is, they handle it in the
context of the activity, without calling undue attention to the behavior, stopping the
lesson, or further disrupting the students. This does not preclude stopping a lesson to
handle a highly disruptive event. However, most inappropriate behavior is less intense, particularly if it is caught in early stages, so frequently, less intrusive measures
can be successful. Consequently, most desists are brief and undramatic and do not
slow down the activity. The following interventions fit this description of unobtru-
sive desists. It should be noted that these would be used with mild or moderate kinds
of inappropriate behavior, not physical aggression, abusive language, or flagrant
violation of rules. These strategies are therefore appropriate for the more "run-of-the-
mill" misbehaviors such as talking too loud, wandering, inattention, or social talk at
inappropriate times.

- Make eye contact with the student and hold it until the student stops the behavior.
- Move closer to the student.
- Give a nonverbal signal (e.g., a finger to the lips to signal quiet).
- State the student's name or briefly request the student to halt the behavior.

These four tactics usually can be executed without seriously interrupting the lesson or distracting other students; thus they are especially useful during teacher-led instruction. Another important class of strategies can be summarized succinctly in one guideline:

- Redirect the students to the appropriate behavior.

This type of strategy has the advantage of indicating what the student is supposed to do, rather than just telling or signaling the student to *stop* doing something. Redirection of student behavior can take many forms, including (1) asking if a student knows what he or she is supposed to be doing; (2) diagnosing whether the student can perform the task and giving corrective feedback; (3) asking the student to state the rule or procedure that is being violated; and (4) simply reminding the student what behavior is appropriate.

Another important type of redirection is group-oriented; the teacher does not react to the student's inappropriate behavior itself but instead focuses students' attention on a desired stimulus or on appropriately behaving students. The principle underlying this type of redirection is to produce behavior that is incompatible with the inappropriate behavior without giving teacher attention to the misbehaving students or allowing them an opportunity to receive peer attention. Examples include verbal signals that direct the students' attention to the teacher or to an aspect of the lesson and that require another overt student response:

"Let me see everyone's eyes, please."

"Everyone look at the chart on page 42."

"Look up at the chalkboard and identify the next step."

"Copy the material on the overhead projector screen into your notebook."

Sometimes a portion of the class will be behaving appropriately while others are inattentive or not following procedures. In such cases, redirection that provides models for appropriate behavior can be used:

"I see two tables whose students have cleaned up really well."

"Most of the class is doing a good job of listening carefully."

"I see ten people who are quiet and have their materials out.... Now I see five more.... Good, three more are ready...."

"I like the way so many of you are working together quietly and sharing the materials without arguing."

In these four examples, the presumption is that a substantial number of students are engaging in the appropriate behavior and that these students receive the teacher's compliment. The other students are thus provided with a model for appropriate behavior. Generally, it is better to avoid singling out one or two students as positive examples unless these students are very popular and cooperative.

Adaptation of the desist and redirection strategies to suit particular grade and age levels will be needed, mainly in the language used by the teacher. The statement used to redirect a few children's behaviors, "I like the way so many of my boys and girls are being good listeners and raising their hands," is appropriate for early and middle elementary grades. With older students, the redirection might become "Is everybody listening?" or "I appreciate how well most of the class is paying attention" or "Let's wait until *everybody* is listening." Also, any of these strategies can be overused. A mixture of responses is more effective than, for example, constantly redirecting students with "I like the way so many are..." Finally, these techniques are not a substitute for basic preventive strategies.

If attention is chronically poor or if students frequently misbehave or do not complete assignments or fail to participate appropriately in class activities, more desists and redirections will not solve the problem. Instead, rules and procedures may need to be revised, and classroom activities and assignments may need to be altered to provide more structure, success, accountability, or appeal.

Organizing and Conducting Activities.   So much of the research on classroom management and discipline focuses on preventing or reacting to inappropriate student behavior that it is easy to lose sight of the fact that most student time is spent in *activities* whose structure determines what students are expected to do. Much of the teacher's planning is aimed at preparing academic activities, and their nature and execution can have a major bearing on the overall quality of student behavior. Research has identified a number of characteristics that contribute to good student discipline because they keep students actively involved in their work at academic tasks. Such characteristics are those that keep the lesson moving, that prevent slow-downs or interruptions, that provide adequate information for the students about what they must do, and that engage and maintain student interest. Because the topic of keeping the lesson moving is treated extensively in Chapter 9, only a few major characteristics will be summarized here.

Clarity of instruction and directions has been consistently identified by research as an attribute of the successful management of activities. Clarity reduces student uncertainty about expectations and provides information that enables students to accomplish their academic work. Vagueness and discontinuity in lessons limit students' ability to complete tasks without assistance and increase distractions caused by students' seeking help or reacting to frustration.

Student success is also another key aspect of activities that maintain student involvement. Several studies have shown that students are better behaved when they are able to perform the tasks required by their classroom activities at a moderate or higher level of success. Highly difficult tasks, especially when they are not accompanied by close teacher supervision and assistance, are likely to produce failure, frustration, and avoidance in all but the most able students. This does not mean that students should not be challenged, but when they are, adequate support should be provided. Pressure exerted by difficult assignments and the consequent fear of criticism and low grades will not enhance motivation.

The continuity and organization of lesson components are also important. Lessons that produce high levels of student involvement have limited intrusions or interruptions and are designed so that students know what they are supposed to be doing. Thus careful planning of lessons to include provisions for adequate directions, examples, needed materials, and other resources is important. Thinking through each task in terms of the demands placed on students and the points at which problems might be encountered also helps the teacher provide greater lesson continuity. Smoothly running activities can be enhanced by being alert during a lesson for interruptions, distractions, or flagging interest and by being ready to redirect student attention and behavior when necessary. Finally, transitions *between* activities can be a source of disruption, but this disruption can be avoided by providing structure to the transitions, for example, by giving students instructions about what they are to do next, by beginning and ending activities as a group, and by providing clear expectations about what is or is not acceptable as students move from one activity or lesson to another.

What makes a lesson flow smoothly and appear well organized is influenced by the type of activity. In particular, success in managing two very common types of activities (teacher-led, large-group instruction and individual student seatwork) depends on somewhat different types of skills. Group instruction formats must be protected from events and behaviors that compete with the teacher's presentation and with the flow of information in the lesson. Thus teachers can themselves cause interruptions through lack of clarity, poor lesson organization, and poor pacing. Students can cause interruptions by prolonged recitation (even if on task) and by noisy or otherwise intrusive behavior. Teacher skills in instructional clarity, lesson organization, and pacing help maintain continuity. Monitoring and prompt handling of inappropriate behavior minimize intrusions by students and help preserve the activity flow. Successful management of individual seatwork activities is more dependent on the teacher's skills in choosing or designing tasks that can be successfully done by the students and in providing prompts and assistance when needed. Material at too difficult a level or lack of clarity about what to do next will detract from students' work involvement.

MANAGEMENT OF CONSEQUENCES

So far my emphasis has been on achieving good discipline by preventing inappropriate behavior or managing such behavior unobtrusively while keeping students focused or involved in lesson activities. Now the use of rewards to encourage appropriate behavior and the use of punishment to discourage inappropriate behavior will be considered.

Before discussing these topics, it should be emphasized that the use of teacher-administered rewards or punishment (or both) cannot be the foundation of a good system of effective discipline and classroom management. Rewards and punishment *can* be used temporarily to increase or to suppress particular behaviors, but they should be supplementary to the primary bases of good discipline just described. It should also be noted that the consequences discussed here refer to "extrinsic" ones, that is, those provided or administered by agents external to the student, and not to "intrinsic" consequences that occur as a result of accomplishment of a task or participation in enjoyable activities. Reviews of research on the use of consequences, and related topics and issues, can be found in Balsam and Bondy (1983), Bates (1979), Brophy (1981, 1983), Deci (1975), and Thoreson (1973).

Rewards

A substantial body of both classroom-based and laboratory research indicates that desirable student behavior and academic achievement can be enhanced by the use of rewards contingent on desired behavior or performance. These desirable changes are often temporary, however, and many studies, though successful in effecting immediate change within the classroom environment created by the research, have experienced problems with establishing generalization or with maintaining effects over longer periods of time (Philips & Ray, 1980). Of course, such a limitation does not necessarily preclude the use of rewards by a teacher simply seeking to enhance the interest of a group of undermotivated students. In fact, a short-term effect (a few weeks or months) may be adequate for many purposes: until students experience enough success to begin enjoying a subject or to finish out the last two or three months of the year. Furthermore, when used as an adjunct to an already smoothly functioning classroom management system, different types of rewards can spark additional interest and excitement without becoming *the* dominant reasons for participation in learning activities.

Major types of rewards include the following:

Social rewards—teacher verbal approval, stickers, stars, written comments on papers, and recognition derived from displays of student work. These are easy to use and common in classrooms. Other types of social rewards are more difficult to use and require careful planning. These types include systems of "honor students," awards, certificates, trophies, and other symbols of accomplishment. Often social rewards function mainly as feedback to students and are useful whether they possess any additional reinforcing properties or not.

Activity rewards—privileges, free time, Friday afternoon popcorn parties, field trips, and any other activity that students find desirable.

Tangible rewards—objects of value such as materials, food, money, prizes, or toys.

Rewards are most likely to have a positive effect on behavior or performance when students perceive them to be contingent on the quality of their performance and not just on participation in an activity. Furthermore, if rewards are to have a desirable effect, it is important that students not attribute manipulative motives to the teacher using the rewards. Thus rewards should be presented as a natural or logical consequence of the students' behavior. When focused on the behavior or performance, teacher praise and other types of social approval are least susceptible to negative attribution effects. Tangible rewards, because they are more external to the setting and not commonly associated with classroom behavior and performance, are most likely to appear externally manipulated. A potential problem is that if extrinsic rewards are emphasized and used extensively, students' intrinsic motivation for engaging in the academic tasks or performing the desired behavior may be reduced. Thus care should be taken to provide students with a clear rationale for the use of extrinsic rewards; other, more intrinsic motives should also be stressed for engaging in the desired behavior (e.g., increased confidence or skill, utility to the student, enjoyment, and interest).

Activity rewards can often be used as group reinforcement. For example, an end-of-the-month field trip or party might be made contingent on all students' satisfactorily completing certain assignments or following class rules. Such rewards can be a strong incentive for many students, but careful planning is needed. For example, the desired behavior or performance must be clearly stated and understood by students. Also, consideration must be given to the possibility that one or a few students will choose not to work for the goal. In such a case, provisions will need to be made for them during the time of the activity. Also, some method for keeping track of progress, such as a chart, chip system, or record of performance, must be maintained.

A combination of several types of rewards can be particularly effective. For example, a school might institute a system of "honor students," meaning those who follow school rules (avoid detention, behave in the cafeteria or hallway, etc.) and who achieve passing grades in all subjects. Such students would receive an honor badge, which they could retain as long as they met the criteria. Honor students would then receive recognition and be eligible for certain privileges (granted because they have demonstrated responsible behavior), such as eating lunch in the courtyard, acting as school representatives for special events, attending a special party, or being granted priority for use of the computer, library, or other facilities.

It is clear that the decision to use systems of rewards other than simpler forms of social approval and recognition involves a consideration of trade-offs. On the negative side are the additional class time and teacher planning that might be needed to begin and maintain a system, along with the possibility that it might distract students from ongoing routines and academic activities. Also, the possible detrimental effects on intrinsic motivation must be considered. Positive features of reward systems include improved student involvement and behavior and stronger motivation for students initially low in this characteristic. In addition, a side benefit may be better student behavior simply as a result of identifying behaviors that are desirable.

Punishment

Negative consequences involve the creation of an unpleasant state for an individual. In classrooms it takes many forms, including detention, withholding privileges or other rewards, the use of penalty systems, teacher disapproval or criticism, and requiring restitution or additional work from students. It is assumed that students usually find such events unpleasant and wish to avoid them. Much research in experimental psychology indicates that negative consequences can suppress undesirable behavior, although they are not sufficient to induce desirable behavior. However, much of the experimental research on the effects of punishment is not necessarily relevant to classrooms because the intensity and types of punishment used are not appropriate in schools or because the research was conducted on animals. Research in classrooms has generally focused on facets of milder punishers such as teacher disapproval or criticism. Reviews of classroom research (e.g., Dunkin & Biddle, 1974; Medley, 1977) have noted that high levels of criticism are often associated with more disruptive or inappropriate student behavior, but it is apparent that such a result could easily be due to the teacher's reaction to student behavior, or vice versa.

I have stressed that the key to good discipline is preventing inappropriate behavior in the first place and, when it occurs, dealing with it promptly and relatively unobtrusively before it escalates or intensifies. However, sometimes punishment is needed because preventive measures are not successful or because a serious infraction occurs before the teacher has a chance to prevent it. Examples include pushing or hitting other students, abusive talk, inappropriate or disruptive behavior that continues in spite of the teacher's initial attempt to stop or redirect it, and damage to property. In addition, punishment is sometimes prescribed as established policy, even when the behavior itself is not grossly inappropriate. For example, some secondary school teachers assess a "fine" or assign detention for tardiness. This is done because it may be simpler and less time-consuming in the long run to deter the behavior by using a penalty rather than using some more positive approach or dealing with each case on an individual basis.

Although it is not possible to prepare for all contingencies, it is helpful to have some general principles in mind for the use of punishment and to plan how to deal with certain types of problems.

1. *Whenever possible, the punishment should relate logically to the misbehavior.* Punishment should not appear capricious or arbitrary to the student. An example of a logical punishment is restitution: If something is broken or damaged, it must be repaired or replaced; if someone makes a mess, that person must clear it up. Other examples include loss of privileges: Excessive social chatter causes students to lose talking privileges during seatwork; a student who bothers others or disrupts the class must sit apart from other students. Even when a punishment is not a direct consequence of some act, a rationale relating it to the punishment can be discussed with the student.

2. *Severe punishment is frequently no more effective than moderate punishment and at times is less so.* Severe punishment means that the unpleasant state created for the student is especially uncomfortable or, more commonly, of long duration. However, 5 or 10 minutes of time out is probably just as effective with an elementary-grade student as an hour; 25 sentences written by a junior high student will make the same point as 100 sentences. Severe punishment may engender feelings of hostility and resentment, and it may provide a convenient excuse for students not to change their ways.

3. *Punishment procedures should be focused on helping the student understand the problem and make a commitment to change to more acceptable behavior.* Schoolwide systems such as the Reality Therapy approach advocated by Glasser (1977) can be helpful to the teacher because they prescribe a sequence of steps for handling repeated offenses by a student. Glasser's idea, which has been used in many schools, is that students need to be aware of the choices they are making and the consequences for themselves and others. Students who misbehave are required to acknowledge their behavior in writing and agree to change. Initial misdemeanors result in only a mild penalty, such as a few minutes of time out. Repeated violations produce stronger punishment, such as in-school suspension or, in extremis, expulsion. At each stage, the student is confronted with the unacceptable behavior and allowed to make a commitment to behave appropriately. Thus the focus is on helping the student to acquire better forms of coping as well as on stopping the disruptive behavior.

When a schoolwide system is not available or its use is not appropriate in a particular instance, the teacher can still use a version of the approach in the classroom. One such procedure is to use a contingency contract with the student. The contract specifies what the student did that was wrong and perhaps why it caused a problem. Desirable alternative behavior is identified, and the student makes a commitment to engage in it. A contract may also specify a reward for a student who lives up to the contract for a period of time. Although contingency contracts can be effective for individual students, their use is time-consuming and requires scheduling a conference with the individual student out of class or conferring with the student during class. In addition, the teacher must monitor compliance carefully. Thus this is not a strategy for everyday use.

4. *When punishment is used, it should not be overused, with respect to either time or frequency.* Less time-consuming types of punishment include the use of "fines" or extra busywork, such as writing sentences, copying a passage from a book, or writing the multiplication tables. Unlike restitution, withholding privileges, or isolation, fines are not logically related to the misbehavior. If they are to be used, therefore, the teacher should supply a clear rationale for their use. Fines have the advantages of being easily altered to suit the circumstances and of requiring very little teacher or class time to administer. They can also be construed as a form of restitution in some cases (e.g., the student who spoke loudly and abusively gets to write repeatedly, "I will speak politely to other students and teachers"). Another type of punishment that is easy to use is a demerit or check system. In such systems, the student's name is recorded on the chalkboard or on a roster when misbehavior occurs. Subsequent violations receive a check or demerit. After accumulating a certain number of checks or demerits, a penalty (such as detention) is assessed. The use of such systems has the advantage of giving students a clear warning and thus allowing the teacher to react promptly to a problem without administering the ultimate punishment (unless the student persists). Problems may be dealt with in early stages at relatively little cost in energy and time.

A problem with fine, demerit, or check systems is that because of their simplicity, they are easy to overuse. Instead of relying on more positive approaches, such as redirecting the student's behavior, the teacher begins to focus more on inappropriate behavior. The classroom climate may degenerate as the teacher tries to catch students misbehaving, and the students develop an oppositional or resentful attitude. Another problem with these systems is that the behavior that is to be punished may not be clearly specified or easily observable, or it may occur very frequently. For example, suppose talking out of turn or to other students is defined as the behavior that results in a fine or check. The teacher in such a circumstance will have difficulty observing each instance of the misbehavior and so will appear to be inconsistent in punishing those that do occur. Furthermore, the behaviors may occur so frequently that the teacher will need to interrupt the lesson constantly and give attention to students when they are caught. Such events will distract students from the lesson and will slow down the activity, producing even more problems.

5. *Consistency is essential.* Inconsistency occurs when behavior that is disapproved or punished by a teacher on one occasion is approved or rewarded on another occasion. For example, a teacher might give detention for excessive talking one day but allow it the next day. Of course, variations in behavior may be necessary, but students should be told that this is the teacher's intention ("Today, because we are working on group projects, you may talk quietly when you need to"). However, unexplained inconsistency in the enforcement of rules and procedures controlling

highly visible behavior will cause some students to produce higher levels of the behavior. This may occur because these students are uncomfortable or anxious about the apparent poor definition of limits. The production of higher rates of inconsistently punished behavior does not occur in all students; some students react to inconsistency by inhibiting the behavior. However, it does not take many students of the first type to disrupt a classroom. Furthermore, when some behavior has been inconsistently punished and higher levels of the misbehavior result, returning the class to more acceptable behavior is extremely difficult.

Thus when punishment must be used, it should be carefully planned, should "fit the crime," and should be logically related to the misbehavior whenever possible or otherwise related to the misbehavior by some rationale. The behavior associated with the punishment should be clearly identified and observable, and it should not be a behavior that is difficult to monitor. When these conditions are met, there is a greater likelihood that the punishment will be used consistently and that it will have the desired effect.

The use of punishment systems such as checks and fines should be reserved for misbehavior that is easily observed and infrequent. Chronic but not seriously disruptive behavior such as excessive talking, out-of-seat wandering, gum chewing, and the like can be dealt with through restitution, withholding of privileges, isolation, or, preferably, less intrusive approaches such as desisting or redirecting student behavior as described earlier.

More serious misbehavior such as physical aggression, intimidation, and verbal abuse directed at other students or at the teacher may be dealt with temporarily by the procedures described here. However, a long-term solution to such behaviors, unless they are the result of a single, specific incident that is very unlikely to recur, will almost surely require consultation with parents and planning with other school personnel such as the administrative staff, special-education resource teacher, counselor, or school psychologist.

QUESTIONS AND ANSWERS

Q. *I like the idea of giving my students input in setting up some of our classroom procedures. Is that appropriate?*

A. Allowing student input into classroom procedures has several advantages, including a potential increase in student acceptance of the procedures and commitment to following them. Also, student input may provide for more discussion of the rationale for the procedures and can promote a greater sense of responsibility in students. Potential disadvantages of student input are that students won't always identify the most appropriate procedures and that too many different procedures are needed in the average classroom to allow discussion of all of them with students in any detail. Consequently, when student input is sought, it is usually limited to general classroom rules and, perhaps, a few procedures in areas identified by the teacher. The nature of the student input can include suggestions for rules, identification of rationales for rules, and suggestions for procedures to govern behavior in specific areas.

Q. *What is the best way to arrange the room when a classroom has only round worktables (no individual desks) allotted for student seating?*

A.   This type of furniture is sometimes chosen for "flexibility" and economy. Unfortunately, at least three types of problems are caused by round worktables and chairs rather than desks: (1) Students do not have adequate storage space for personal supplies, (2) some students may be seated facing away from the teacher when he or she addresses the whole class, and (3) movement about the room may be hampered. Individual plastic tote trays kept under seats or on shelves will help alleviate the storage problem. Because students' belongings will be more visible than if students had interior desk space, it will probably be necessary during discussions of class rules to put a bit more emphasis on respecting others' personal space and belongings, and students should be cautioned not to tempt others by being careless with possessions or by keeping valuables in their storage space. To cope with the seating problem during whole-class activities, arrange the chairs at the tables so that students do not sit with their backs to the area of the room in which you will conduct these activities. A U arrangement may permit satisfactory seating. Students should all be able to see you without needing to turn completely around, and they also should have a surface to write on in front of them. If a satisfactory arrangement isn't possible, you may need to have some students take different seats during whole-class activities. An arrangement of tables and chairs that maximizes visibility, however, may not permit easy movement about the room. Try to leave adequate space around the tables and avoid blocking access to often used areas of the room. Finally, other teachers in your school may be able to offer suggestions that fit your particular classroom constraints.

Q.   *What can I do for students who seem unable to remember our classroom rules?*
A.   Problems with students remembering rules are most common early in the school year or immediately after a long vacation. Try to note which rule students are having difficulty remembering and which students are having problems. Then take a few minutes each day to review and discuss the relevant rules. The following activities may also be useful. Post a copy of the rules so that students can see them easily; be sure to give students positive feedback when they observe the rules; have students copy the rules or give short oral or written quizzes over the rules to see if students have learned them.

Q.   *How can I "salvage" a class whose students consistently ignore my requests to stay in their seats while I conduct my reading groups?*
A.   A first suggestion is to review your procedures for reading groups to be sure they are appropriate and will prevent problems from occurring. Students out of the group should have a sufficient amount of seatwork that is both interesting and varied. They should have necessary materials on hand and adequate directions before they begin their seatwork activities. Some system of providing students with help when they need it is also necessary: Check with students between groups in order to provide help, and have students start another activity if they "get stuck" while you are busy with the group. You should also decide what is a reasonable expectation for student movement during reading groups. It is probably *not* reasonable to prohibit all movement because students may need to return materials, sharpen pencils, and perhaps obtain assistance in completing tasks. It would, of course, be best if they did so without interrupting you or other students. However, out-of-seat behavior for social purposes, to relieve boredom, or to avoid work is clearly not appropriate. Obtaining

help might be a legitimate reason for out-of-seat student behavior, but at this stage you may find it difficult to distinguish this purpose from other, less appropriate reasons. You might consider a "one at a time" rule that allows students with legitimate business to attend to it.

Because your students are already engaged in frequent wandering during reading groups, it may be difficult to obtain initial compliance without an incentive. Therefore, you might tell the class that they can earn 10 points each day that they stay in their seats and follow the "one at a time" rule during reading groups. If they earn 35 or 40 points during the week, they will get a treat on Friday afternoon (e.g., a popcorn party or some free time). If more than one student is out of his or her seat, the class loses one point each time it occurs. If you try this system of incentives and penalties, it will be extremely important for you to monitor students: If you are inconsistent in using this system, it won't work. However, out-of-seat behavior is readily observable, so if you practice reasonable vigilance, you should be successful.

Q. *What can I do about a special-education student who bothers others instead of doing his seatwork? I have simplified and shortened his assignments, but he still won't complete them independently.*

A. First, be sure the modified seatwork assignments are at the student's level. If they are, the following provisions might be helpful. If the student seems very impulsive and distractable, have the student do his seatwork in an area of the room that is away from other students and distractions. You might also try placing the student where you will be able to monitor him most easily during seatwork. You should also be sure that the student understands what behavior is appropriate during seatwork and that he understands the directions for the seatwork assignments. You might appoint another student in the class as a helper for this student if he encounters difficulty.

Another possibility is to use a reward system with this student. Make the focus the satisfactory completion of seatwork as well as "staying seated" because you also want to produce desirable academic behavior. The reward can be a privilege, a treat, a sticker, or some other desirable item. You might use a check or stars on a chart to record satisfactory behavior and then give the reward after the student accumulates a specific number of stars or checks. You might need to start by rewarding 5 or 10 minutes of on-task behavior with a star; however, satisfactory task accomplishment should soon become the criterion. If these strategies are not effective, discuss the situation with the child's special-education teacher. It may be more appropriate or necessary for the student to work on his assignments in the resource room.

Q. *I've been advised to ignore behavior such as shouting out in order to extinguish it, but doesn't "withitness" demand that I respond to it before it escalates? This kind of rule breaking seems to be a constant problem with two or three of my students.*

A. You *can* ignore occasional callouts. If the student gets no response from you or from other students, the behavior is unlikely to continue for very long. Because in your class several students are constantly "shouting out," however, it sounds as though they are getting attention for their behavior, perhaps from each other. It is also possible that you allow callouts at some times but not during other activities.

Begin by reviewing your expectations regarding callouts and handraising. Once you are clear about what procedure you want students to follow, discuss it with them. If your expectations vary with the activity, be sure to make this clear. Continue to ignore occasional callouts, and let students know that you appreciate it when they raise their hands before they answer. If this strategy does not produce a reduction in the frequency of callouts within a week or so, you might try a mild penalty, such as sitting out of class or a short detention period after school. You should make it clear that it is not your intention to punish students each time they call out; rather, you want to stop students who persist in doing it. This will avoid the problem of seeming to be inconsistent when you do not administer a penalty every time someone calls out. You can explain to your class that a few students are making it difficult to conduct lessons because they keep calling out answers or comments without raising their hands. Then if the two or three students begin their "game," give them one clear warning, and assess the penalty if the behavior is repeated.

Q. *I lose a lot of teaching time waiting for my students to get out their materials when we begin a new activity. How can I remedy this?*

A. It may help to give students a specific amount of time to get ready for the new activity: for example, "You should have your notebook, paper, and pens ready in 30 seconds. Let's see how many can do it in that time." You do not have to wait for all of the students. If one or two dawdle, just begin the activity and be sure not to call attention to them. This problem is a specific case of the more general one of handling transitions efficiently and smoothly. Wasted time and inappropriate behavior can be reduced by a number of teacher behaviors, including these:

- Bringing the preceding activity to a halt before beginning the next activity.
- Giving a clear signal when the transition begins.
- Stating what students are expected to do during the transition or developing a routine or procedure for transitions.
- Monitoring student behavior during the transition.

Q. *If I develop a contingency contract with a reward for one student for an expected behavior, how can I address comments of other students who aren't rewarded for that behavior?*

A. One way to deal with the comments is to define the situation to exclude the other students. "This is a private matter between Alfred and me. It does not affect anyone else, so please allow me to do my job as I think it is best to do it."

Another method, appropriate if many students in the class express resentment about a student receiving extra incentives, is to talk to the class about the issue of equal treatment in general. The goal is to help students understand the concept that each person is unique, with different interests, skills, needs, and behaviors. Therefore, sometimes students need to be treated differently in order to help them to learn and to do well in school.

Preventive strategies can also help minimize problems. If possible, discuss the contingency contract in private with the student, and do not give the incentive in front of the class. If this is impossible, consider discussing the matter with the class before you begin to use the system. You don't have to use names, of course; just describe the situation in general terms and encourage students to voice concerns so that you can deal with any potential negative reactions.

Q. *If my discipline policy has failed and needs revision in the middle of the year, what strategies are recommended for introducing the new plan?*

A. First, be sure you know what to change and what to leave alone. Self-diagnosis is an uncertain art, so ask a colleague whose perception and advice you value to observe your class and help you plan changes. It might prove beneficial to write these plans because the process of writing frequently helps clarify problems and it may expose incomplete plans.

Major changes made in midyear are probably best introduced immediately after a vacation or at the beginning of a new grading period. Changes should be treated like the introduction of new procedures or policies at the beginning of the year, with clear explanations of the new policy followed by careful monitoring and prompt handling of inappropriate behavior. It would be particularly important to discuss with students the rationale for changes.

Q. *When I assign projects to students and allow class time for working on them, some students do not manage their time well. How can the project be structured to avoid this problem?*

A. Individual projects require careful planning and monitoring, especially when students are not used to independent work that requires several days or weeks to complete. Try to determine the range of your students' experiences with this type of assignment. Obviously, students with minimal prior experience should be provided with more assistance, and their projects should be more restricted in scope and shorter in duration. Here are some specific things that will help produce more completed projects of good quality:

• Help in selecting the topic or project, including a list of possible topics.
• Handouts describing requirements and a thorough discussion of them.
• Careful monitoring, including checkpoints and intermediate grades.
• Examples of satisfactorily completed projects.
• A checksheet for students to verify that they have met requirements or to use for self-monitoring while they work on the project.
• Early communication with parents regarding the project and due dates. This is critical whenever the project requires the student to procure materials or to complete substantial amounts of the project at home.

Q. *What additional problems are typically encountered in a laboratory class such as in science or home economics? How can these problems be avoided?*

A. Problems can occur in the use of materials and supplies, in assigning students to groups for conducting experiments or other projects, and in organizing laboratory activities. Typically, students are unaccustomed to such activities; therefore, careful description of relevant rules and procedures is necessary, especially those concerned with safe use of equipment. Here are some examples of helpful procedures:

• A handout or posted list of lab rules.
• Specific goals that are described to students along with clear specification of steps to follow during laboratory activities.
• Discussion with students about what behaviors are acceptable during this type of activity.
• Careful planning of each activity so that adequate amounts of needed supplies are available.

- Pacing that allows enough time for getting ready, for teacher demonstrations, cleanup, and so forth.
- Assigning compatible students to workgroups, including at least one student who usually understands directions.

Q. *I teach social studies in a junior high school that does not track students in this subject. Consequently, I have students at all levels of ability. Discipline problems are common, particularly among the lower-achieving students. What are some examples of procedures necessary for instructing different levels in the same class?*

A. Your problems are not unusual because they occur in all subjects with highly heterogeneous student populations. A key to good management in such situations is designing activities so that all students can be successful. This is a tall order indeed when students vary greatly in their ability to read or to comprehend oral instruction. Some procedures that can be used include the following:

- Whenever possible, use instructional materials that are at the reading level of the students. This is of course especially critical for the poorer readers.
- Seat lower-achieving students where they can be more easily monitored during whole-class presentations and during seatwork.
- Check with lower-achieving students at the beginning of seatwork activities to be sure they understand the task and have begun the work. Provide additional directions and instruction to these students, using a small group format if there are several such students.
- Modify assignments (with respect to length and difficulty) so that all students can succeed and higher-achieving students are challenged.
- Arrange peer tutoring, or set up a "buddy system" with mature students assigned to help students who encounter difficulty. A variation of this procedure is to appoint a few students as monitors that anyone can go to for assistance if you are busy. This role can be rotated among students, depending on their interest and ability to work well with other students.
- Use small groups to provide instruction in basic skills. With adequate preassessment, students can be divided into groups based on entering achievement. If a small group format is used, care must be taken to avoid stigmatizing lower groups or communicating negative expectations to them. Nevertheless, if students are at vastly different levels on critical basic skills or if they must use different materials and assignments, the use of small groups may be the most efficient means of giving directions or providing instruction. Because this is a difficult format to plan for and manage in a typical 50- or 55-minute secondary school period, you will find it helpful to do some reading on the topic and to observe another teacher using small group instruction before trying it yourself.

FURTHER READING

Clarizio, H. F. (1980). *Toward Positive Classroom Discipline* (3rd ed.). New York: Wiley. Provides behavior-modification approach to discipline. Although prevention is included, emphasis is on management of consequences to produce behavioral change. Text does a good job of describing classroom applications.

Doyle, W. (1980). *Classroom Management*. West Lafayette, IN: Kappa Delta Phi. A readable, 31-page overview. Doyle argues that teachers encounter classroom management as the task of gaining and maintaining "the cooperation of students in activities that fill classroom time." Using this perspective, he presents major concepts needed to understand how classroom order is achieved.

Doyle, W. (1985). "Classroom Organization and Management." In M. C. Wittrock (Ed.), *Handbook of Research on Teaching* (3rd ed.). New York: Macmillan. Summarizes recent research on classroom management and provides a careful analysis of current knowledge. In addition to its comprehensiveness, the chapter is especially sensitive to the relationship between academic work and student behavior. A key theme is the importance of the teacher's ability to organize and manage student work.

Duke, D. (Ed.). (1979). *Classroom Management.* 78th Yearbook of the National Society for the Study of Education (Part 2). Chicago: University of Chicago Press. Contains chapters written from a variety of theoretical and applied perspectives, providing a scholarly overview of the field.

Duke, D. (Ed.). (1982). *Helping Teachers Manage Classrooms.* Alexandria, VA: Association for Supervision and Curriculum Development. Articles addressed to concerns of practitioners. Both preventive strategies and behavior-change approaches are described, with an emphasis on applications.

Emmer, E. T., Evertson, C. M., Sanford, J. P., Clements, B. S., & Worsham, M. (1984). *Classroom Management for Secondary Teachers.* Englewood Cliffs, NJ: Prentice-Hall. Establishing a good management system at the beginning of the year is emphasized as a cornerstone of effective discipline. Techniques for preventing disruption and for organizing activities are discussed; checklists and case studies are provided to aid in planning.

Evertson, C. M., Emmer, E. T., Clements, B. S., Sanford, J. P., & Worsham, M. E. (1984). *Classroom Management for Elementary Teachers.* Englewood Cliffs, NJ: Prentice-Hall. Similar in format to the preceding reference, this book addresses the needs of the elementary school teacher.

Glasser, W., Bassin, A., Bratter, E., & Rachin, R. (1976). *The Reality Therapy Reader: A Survey of the Work of William Glasser.* New York: Harper & Row. Reality therapy assumes that people will make rational choices if they understand the consequences. Classroom and schoolwide applications stress this key to successful behavior change. Includes a look at a broad spectrum of Glasser's work.

Good, T. L., & Brophy, J. (1983). *Looking in Classrooms* (3rd ed.). New York: Harper & Row. Contains excellent chapters on classroom management and discipline in addition to material on classroom observation, teacher expectations, student motivation, and other classroom topics. The authors provide very readable summaries of recent research and emphasize its classroom applications.

Kounin, J. (1970). *Discipline and Group Management in Classrooms.* New York: Holt, Rinehart and Winston. Kounin conducted a series of research studies investigating how teachers minimize deviant student behavior and maintain on-task behavior. A number of concepts emerged that have strongly influenced subsequent research and conceptualization. Both an interesting account of the progress of research on a useful line of inquiry and a source of descriptions and examples of key concepts.

REFERENCES

Anderson, L., Evertson, C., & Emmer, E. (1980). Dimensions in classroom management derived from recent research. *Journal of Curriculum Studies, 12,* 343–356.

Balsam, P. D., & Bondy, A. S. (1983). The negative side effects of reward. *Journal of Applied Behavior Analysis, 16,* 283–296.

Bates, J. A. (1979). Extrinsic reward and intrinsic motivation: A review with implications for the classroom. *Review of Educational Research, 49,* 557–576.

Berliner, D. C. (1983). Developing conceptions of classroom environments: Some light on the T in classroom studies of ATI. *Educational Psychologist, 18,* 1–13.

Brophy, J. E. (1981). Teacher praise: A functional analysis. *Review of Educational Research*, *51*, 5–32.

Brophy, J. E. (1983). Classroom organization and management. *Elementary School Journal*, *83*, 265–286.

Brophy, J. E., & Evertson, C. M. (1976). *Learning from teaching: A developmental perspective.* Boston: Allyn & Bacon.

Buckley, P. K., & Cooper, J. M. (1978, March). *An ethnographic study of an elementary school teacher's establishment and maintenance of group norms.* Paper presented at the annual meeting of the American Educational Research Association, Toronto, Canada.

Copeland, W. D. (1983, April). *Classroom management and student teachers' cognitive abilities: A relationship.* Paper presented at the annual meeting of the American Educational Research Association, Montreal, Canada.

Deci, E. (1975). *Intrinsic motivation.* New York: Plenum Press.

Doyle, W. (1985). Classroom organization and management. In M. Wittrock (Ed.), *Handbook of research on teaching* (3rd ed.). New York: Macmillan.

Duke, D. (Ed.) (1979). *Classroom management.* 78th Yearbook of the National Society for the Study of Education, Part II. Chicago: University of Chicago Press.

Duke, D. (Ed.) (1982). *Helping teachers manage classrooms.* Alexandria, VA: Association for Supervision and Curriculum Development.

Dunkin, M., & Biddle, B. (1974). *The study of teaching.* New York: Holt, Rinehart and Winston.

Eisenhart, M. (1977, November/December). *Maintaining control: Teacher competence in the classroom.* Paper presented at the annual meeting of the American Anthropological Association, Houston, TX.

Emmer, E. T. (1981). *Effective classroom management in junior high school mathematics classrooms* (R&D Rep. No. 6111). Austin: University of Texas, Research and Development Center for Teacher Education.

Emmer, E. T. (1984). *Classroom management: Research and implications* (R&D Rep. No. 6178). Austin: University of Texas, Research and Development Center for Teacher Education.

Emmer, E. T., Evertson, C. M., & Anderson, L. M. (1980). Effective classroom management at the beginning of the school year. *Elementary School Journal*, *80*, 219–231.

Emmer, E. T., Sanford, J. P., Clements, B. S., & Martin, J. (1982). *Improving classroom management and organization in junior high schools: An experimental investigation* (R&D Rep. No. 6153). Austin: University of Texas, Research and Development Center for Teacher Education.

Evertson, C. M., & Emmer, E. T. (1982). Preventive classroom management. In D. Duke (Ed.), *Helping teachers manage classrooms.* Alexandria, VA: Association for Supervision and Curriculum Development.

Evertson, C. M., Emmer, E. T., Sanford, J. P., & Clements, B. S. (1983). Improving classroom management: An experiment in elementary classrooms. *Elementary School Journal*, *84*, 173–188.

Glasser, W. (1977). Ten steps to good discipline. *Today's Education*, *66*, 61–63.

Goss, S. S., & Ingersoll, G. M. (1981). *Management of disruptive and off-task behaviors: Selected resources.* Washington, DC: ERIC Clearinghouse on Teacher Education.

Kounin, J. (1970). *Discipline and group management in classrooms.* New York: Holt, Rinehart and Winston.

Medley, D. (1977). *Teacher competence and teacher effectiveness: A review of process-product research.* Washington, DC: American Association of Colleges for Teacher Education.

Moskowitz, G., & Hayman, J. (1976). Success strategies of inner-city teachers: A year-long study. *Journal of Educational Research*, *69*, 283–289.

Phillips, J. S., & Ray, R. S. (1980). Behavioral approaches to childhood disorders. *Behavior Modification*, *4*, 3–34.

Sanford, J. P., & Evertson, C. M. (1981). Classroom management in a low SES junior high: Three case studies. *Journal of Teacher Education, 32,* 34–38.

Smith, D. C. (Ed.). (1983). *Essential knowledge for beginning educators.* Washington, DC: American Association of Colleges for Teacher Education.

Thoreson, C. E. (Ed.) (1973). *Behavior modification in education.* 72nd Yearbook of the National Society for the Study of Education (Part 1). Chicago: University of Chicago Press.

Tikunoff, W., Ward, B., & Dasho, S. (1978). *Volume A: Three case studies* (Report A78-7). San Francisco: Far West Laboratory.

11 BUT DO THEY UNDERSTAND?

David C. Berliner

All teachers experience a moment of truth, a moment of great joy or bitter disappointment. It is the moment when teachers check their students' understanding. Did they or didn't they understand what was taught to them? If the students appeared to understand what was taught, teachers feel happy and fulfilled. On the other hand, if the students failed to understand what was taught, teachers usually attribute that failure to the students' lack of preparation, their low ability, poor home conditions, or the difficulty of the test. In other words, teachers take credit for student success but blame student failure on causes other than themselves (Bar-Tal, 1979). This is a very human quality, but it probably is not appropriate professional behavior.

Appropriate professional behavior by teachers requires first the delivery of extremely comprehensible explanations to ensure, as far as is possible, that what is communicated by teachers can be understood by students. After such presentations, teachers need to inquire whether in fact the understanding they wanted to promote actually occurred. These two issues—*explaining for understanding* and *checking for understanding*—are the focus of this chapter. First we will investigate ways to provide "good" explanations so that teachers can justifiably take some credit when students demonstrate that they have understood instruction. Then we will discuss both formal and informal ways in which teachers can check for understanding. Teachers cannot judge their own effectiveness, nor can students evaluate their own progress, unless such checking takes place.

EXPLAINING FOR UNDERSTANDING

Research has examined only a few of the many ways in which a teacher can help ensure that a student understands what the teacher is trying to teach. The research suggests that teachers help students learn more and better if they provide some structure for new information, prompt awareness of the students' own relevant information, and follow a model for organizing explanations. In addition, some helpful tips from the research can make what teachers teach more easily understood by their students.

Providing Structures for New Knowledge

Telling students in advance about what they are going to learn, what the key points to be mastered are, and what they should know at the end of an instructional episode has been positively related to student achievement. This seems to hold for both short instructional episodes and for those lasting over days or weeks. Classroom observations have shown that teachers do not always remember to do this. They often simply plunge into an instructional unit, forgetting to make explicit to students the aims of that instruction.

But over and above such helpful, structuring, prefatory remarks, teachers can help students understand instruction by providing *advance organizers*. An advance organizer provides the learner with some rules for organizing a body of apparently unorganized material, or an organizer can take the form of higher-level propositions about the material to be learned (Ausubel, 1968). Organizers provide concepts under which to subsume other concepts. They are brief statements at a relatively high level of abstraction, generality, and inclusiveness compared to the material to be learned. These high-level rules, propositions, and concepts help students to understand new instructional content by providing them with concepts on which to hang or anchor the new ideas. That is, the advance organizer provides some way to structure the new knowledge that the teacher is trying to impart. These hooks or anchoring concepts have been found to help students identify, store, and retrieve information better. They are intended to provide a kind of "ideational scaffolding" for the content of instruction. An organizer is not just an introduction; it provides verbal structures to aid students in fitting new information into their existing knowledge systems. To "understand" is to have integrated new information into one's personal store of knowledge. Understanding is distinguished from memory by this kind of integration.

Prompting Awareness of Relevant Knowledge

Understanding requires the integration of new information with one's existing knowledge. Teachers can help students to understand by making explicit the relationship of the new instructional content to other knowledge possessed by the students. Whether the content is the addition of negative numbers or the study of the Revolutionary War, new content will be understood better by students if it is explicitly related to what they already know. Teachers either have to create the structure for integrating new material with already known material, or they need to prompt the students deliberately to bring to consciousness the relevant knowledge they have about the topic being taught. In the language of modern cognitive psychology this is called "engaging the relevant schema." Schemata are abstract representations of knowledge that we possess about objects and concepts. The schemata a learner brings to a situation may determine what and how much is understood from that situation.

> Imagine a section from a geography text about an unfamiliar nation. An adult would bring to bear an elaborate nation schema, which would point to subschemata representing generic knowledge about political systems, economics, geography, and climate. Each subschema would have its own infrastructure and interconnect with other subschemata at various points.... The young reader, on the other hand, may not possess a nation schema adequate to assimilate the text. In the worst case, the material will be gibberish...; more likely, the young reader will have partly formed schemata that will allow him or her to make sense of the passage, but will not permit the construction of mental representatives of great depth or breadth. (Anderson, Spiro, & Anderson, 1978, p. 439)

Understanding, as the quote makes clear, depends on engaging appropriate schemata. It is now hypothesized that the reason metaphors are useful in instruction ("electric current is like flowing water"; "programming a computer is like instructing a stupid child") is because new information can be incorporated into already existing schema, with only minor changes. Thus whatever ways a teacher can use to tie new ideas to old ones are likely to help students understand instruction better.

A Model for Explaining

When teachers have to explain why it is warmer in summer than in winter, why time differs in New York and San Francisco, and why multiplying two negative numbers produces a positive number, they must construct a very complex communication. Giving an explanation that results in understanding by most students is not a simple task. In part this is because the content of each explanation is so different and because student questions that often trigger such explanations are so unpredictable. Nevertheless, a simple and learnable model for explaining diverse phenomena in ways that foster understanding has been developed:

Step 1. Make sure you understand the question that a student has asked or that you raise in your presentation. Ask yourself what it is that most students who receive the explanation should be concerned about.

Step 2. Identify the "things" (elements, variables, concepts, events) involved in the relationship needing to be explained.

Step 3. State the relationships between the different "things" you identified in step 2.

Step 4. Show how the relationship identified in step 3 is an instance of a more general relationship or principle.

This model fits the description of what it means to come to "understand" something, as described by J. M. Thyne (1963, pp. 127–129) and illustrated here:

Thyne's Description of Understanding

One stormy Winter evening my neighbor was puzzled by a strange low humming sound which seemed to come out of the walls of his house. After much searching, he traced it to a draught excluder on his front door—a device consisting of a wooden strip to which was attached a long rubber tube. . . . My neighbor understands the eerie noise, not just because he now perceives that it comes from the draught excluder—for that in itself could be puzzling—but because he knows that an air current across the end of a pipe produces this sort of sound. . . . When my noise-haunted neighbor understands, it is not just because he appreciates that air is blowing across this particular tube and making this particular sound. If that were all he knew, he would, of course, know where the noise was coming from, but he would scarely be said to have "understood" it. If that were all he knew, he might as well have discovered that the noise was coming from a piece of cheese in his pantry, for the one thing would make no more sense than the other. He understands the noise in-so-far as he knows that an air current passing over the end of any pipe produces some sort of musical note, and he *sees this particular thing as an instance of that general principle.*

Application of the Model

Step 1. Understand the question (why is there a humming sound coming out of the walls?).

Step 2. Identify the elements (humming sound, coming out of walls, draught excluder, door, wooden strip, rubber tube).

Step 3. State the relationships among elements (air, as in a draught, blowing across the opening of the rubber tube causes the humming sound).

Step 4. Show how the relationship is an instance of a more general principle (air passing over the end of any pipelike object produces some sort of musical note).

So we have a description of understanding and a model for explaining that seems to conform to the description of how one comes to understand something. Can teachers learn this model? If they do, will their explanations be better? The answer to both questions is yes. Thirty preservice teachers explained some instructional material to students, were taught this model, and tried again to explain some similar content to students. Judges who did not know which was the explanation given before or after the short training period rated the posttraining explanations significantly higher on (1) organization of the explanation, (2) clarity of the presentation of the explanation, and (3) overall quality of the explanation itself (Miltz, 1971). Thus providing explanations that are likely to result in understanding is a skill, as learnable as gourmet cooking and just as demanding.

Teaching Tips for Explaining Better

Researchers have examined some commonsense techniques associated with "good" explanations and confirmed their utility. (e.g., Gage & Berliner, 1984; Rosenshine, 1971). They are included here as reminders, because classroom observation has revealed that these techniques are often forgotten during instruction. Teachers can check themselves on the use of these techniques by audiotaping or videotaping their teaching and analyzing their own tapes. Teachers can also team up and rate each other on the use of these well-documented aids to learning.

Avoiding Vague Terms.   There are words that seem to favor approximation rather than precision and ambiguity rather than definitiveness. These do not help students to learn what they are supposed to learn. Here are some examples of such words, grouped by categories:

Ambiguous designations: *somehow, somewhere, thing*

Approximations: *about, a little, just about, somewhat, sort of*

Bluffs and recoveries: *actually, and so forth, and so on, anyway, as you know, in a nutshell, in essence, in fact, in other words, of course, or whatever, to make a long story short, you know, you see*

Error admissions: *excuse me, I'm sorry, I guess*

Indeterminate quantifications: *a bunch, a couple, a few, some, various*

Multiplicities: *kind(s) of, type(s) of*

Possibilities: *chances are, could be, may, maybe, might, perhaps, seems*

Such vague terms were studied by Smith and Cotten (1980). They inserted such terms into mathematical explanations or deleted them completely from the explanations that teachers provided. The following abridged examples illustrate their technique:

High-Vagueness Explanation
The first theory *sort of* involves a *couple of* chords intersecting at *some kind of* point in a circle. *I guess we probably* should look at Figure 1. *You might notice* in that figure....

Low-Vagueness Explanation
The first theory is about two chords that intersect at one point in a circle. Look at Figure 1. Notice in that figure....

Although exposed to the exact same content, students understood much more from the low-vagueness lessons than from the high-vagueness lessons. Moreover, the teachers who presented lessons with low vagueness were rated more favorably by their students.

Explicitness.   Teachers need not only to avoid vague terms when explaining but also to try deliberately to be very explicit. Slower, longer, more expanded explanations have been found to yield better performance by young students. Young students, in particular, profit greatly from explicitness in the directions they receive when a teacher is explaining something. For example, if teachers were explaining some point about geometry, say, something about circles, students were found to understand more from teachers who said, "Pick up your blue pen. First draw a big blue circle and then draw a little blue circle next to it" than from teachers who said, "In blue, after you have drawn a big circle, draw a little one by it."

The importance of explicitness in the teacher's instructions to students about *what* to do is rather obvious. Less obvious is the importance of explicitness in the teacher's instructions to students about *how* to do something. For example, a teacher might introduce an assignment on finding the meaning of words that have prefixes either very simply or by explicitly demonstrating (1) how to divide words into root and prefix, (2) how to determine the meaning of the root, (3) how to determine the meaning of the prefix, and (4) how to put prefix and root together in a meaningful way. Low achievers who did not know how to do this kind of seatwork exercise spent their time copying answers and guessing. They may have understood *what* was expected of them, but they did not understand *how* they were to do it. This is really not surprising, given the fact that when teachers' explanations of seatwork assignments were analyzed, only 1.5% included explicit descriptions of the cognitive processes that the teacher had hoped the students would use. (*Communication Quarterly*, 1984; the specific work referred to in this section is by L. Anderson, G. Duffy, and L. Roehler of the Institute for Research on Teaching, Michigan State University, and by P. Marland, James Cook University, Townsville, Australia.)

Able students apparently seek out and find the cues emitted by their unexplicit teachers. They note the words that seem to be important to their teachers, the concepts used in summaries and introductions, the ideas put on the chalkboard or in a handout, and similar cues. From these they determine what is worth trying to learn. Less able students are "cue-blind." They never learn to identify from the myriad bits of information presented what it is that should be understood.

Explicitness in teaching reading comprehension has also been studied, to try to put an end to the often heard student statement, "I read it, but it sure doesn't make any sense!" Teachers can do a better job of teaching *how* to comprehend written material by doing the following three things:

1. Focusing on the specific mental processes needed to do the task at hand. (The *how* to do, the process, is at least as important to communicate to students as the *what* to do, the product.)
2. Making visible the mental process involved. (For example, the steps toward the solution of a problem can be verbalized, not left silent, allowing a teacher to model the way the relevant mental processes should be employed.)
3. Making instruction cohesive and continuous across lessons. (It is hard to understand what is expected when instruction is disjointed and disconnected.)

When these and some other techniques that were believed to promote understanding were turned into training packages, teachers became more explicit in their instruction. The students of these trained teachers, in comparison to the students of untrained teachers, were more involved in their reading lessons, more concious of their reading skills and strategies, and able to make more sense out of what they read. The researchers noted, however, how hard it was to change people who are not explicit into people who are explicit. Nevertheless, ways to improve explicitness must be worked at. Teachers who give vague directions to students about what to do and who do not make clear to students how they are to think about a problem are not good instructors, and their faults must be corrected.

The Rule-Example-Rule Technique. When compared to less effective communicators, the explanations of very effective communicators were found to contain many more instances of a pattern of phases called rule-example-rule. Here is an excerpt from a teacher who was found to be high in effectiveness. This teacher was explaining aspects of Yugoslavian foreign policy.

> As a communist but not a Soviet-dominated nation, they want to increase peaceful and friendly relations with other nations in Europe. They want to do this by having more trade, through exchanging ideas, and through more personal contact with other nations in Europe. They believe that better relations must be established between countries in Europe.

In this example, the first and last sentences are rules, and the intervening sentence is an example. The sequence of stating a rule, giving examples, and stating the rule again helps students understand explanations.

Using Examples. Even without being part of a rule-example-rule sequence, the liberal use of examples appears to be beneficial. To confirm the positive effect that using examples has on students' understanding is easy. You might try to do your best to provide explanations to a group of students. Then try to redo the presentation to an equivalent group of students, this time inserting two examples to illustrate each concept. Then evaluate your instruction. When this was done as part of a research project, it was found that the students understood more from the revised explanation and rated it more favorably. You will probably get the same result.

Explanatory Links. Rosenshine (1971) has reported that good explainers link their phrases in a special way. They use prepositions and conjunctions that indicate the cause, result, means, or purposes of an event or idea. Examples include *because, in order, of, if...then, therefore, consequently,* and certain uses of *since, by,* and *through.* Explanatory links tie ideas together either within or between sentences. Here are four sentences; the first one does not contain an explanatory link, whereas the last three do.

1. The Chinese dominate Bangkok's economy, and they are a threat.
2. The Chinese dominate Bangkok's economy; *therefore,* they are a threat.
3. The Chinese are a threat *because* they dominate Bangkok's economy.
4. *By* dominating Bangkok's economy, the Chinese became a threat.

Explanatory links probably work *because* (an explanatory link!) they cue the learner that a relationship is being described, and relationships help tie the ideas together, making them more meaningful and easier to learn.

Verbal Markers of Importance. Verbal markers of importance are cues to students that indicate what they should attend to most in an explanation. The cues seem to tell the learners, "This is the key to it!" Examples of such cues are phrases like *Now note this; It is especially important to realize that...; It will help you to understand this better if you remember that...; Now let's discuss the most crucial point of all, namely, that...* From more than a half dozen research studies we have evidence that using such markers in explanations increases students' understanding.

CHECKING FOR UNDERSTANDING

Ultimately, after instruction of a few minutes, hours, or weeks, the time comes to check for understanding. For relatively short instructional episodes, and to help teachers determine the pace and form of instruction in longer episodes, teachers use informal methods of checking. These include interpreting the cues emitted by students in the classroom, framing classroom questions and analyzing their answers, and some other relatively informal, usually unplanned, methods to decide if understanding has taken place. Teachers also use some semiformal methods for assessing student understanding. These include the assignment and monitoring of classroom practice and the assignment and analysis of homework. Formal methods to assess student understanding and to assign marks or grades based on that assessment involve the use of tests.

Informal Methods

The most frequently used methods for checking on understanding are the teachers' interpretation of classroom cues, the use of classroom questions, and conferencing.

Classroom Cues.   Imagine the following situation. A student receives a good explanation about some phenomenon. The student then opens a booklet and answers questions about the phenomenon, one question and answer per page. A hidden camera is focused on the student. This is repeated for many students. The questions are scored; some are found to be answered correctly, and some are clearly incorrect. What this provides, then, are film clips of students who either did or did not understand something. Now imagine that these film clips are shown to teachers, who are asked to make a simple choice: Did the student get a particular item right or wrong? If teachers have learned to read the cues in a classroom, they should do far better than chance when making these kinds of judgments. Teachers who observe students as they respond to questions that check their understanding ought to be able to interpret correctly the dozens of nonverbal cues emitted so as to identify those who do and those who do not understand.

Such a study was actually done by Jecker, Maccoby, Breitrose, & Rose (1964). The results were surprising. Teachers did not do much better than chance. Moreover, even after some training in interpreting nonverbal cues, they were not very proficient at interpreting classroom cues about students' understanding. Confirmation comes from another study of students' states of mind during instruction. In that research it was found "that it is virtually impossible to tell what students are thinking from their [classroom] behavior" (*Communication Quarterly* , 1984, p. 3.)

Unless students are giving very obvious signs of not understanding (lots of puzzled looks and frowns) or very obvious signs of understanding (shaking their heads positively and enthusiastically making notations) teachers should beware of interpreting nonverbal behavior. It appears that the most accurate checking of understanding occurs when teachers ask students to make some sort of verbal response. Questions are the time-honored way to do this. Usually the questions are from the teacher to the student, but students' questions serve also as indicators of students' understanding.

Classroom Questions by Teachers.   Although teachers rely heavily on classroom questions to gauge their students' understanding, those same questions may also serve to *enhance* understanding. The use of classroom questions during instruction may have the effect of providing the following:

Review.   Questions asked during an explanation, lecture or other instructional episode may require learners to review the information recently received by them. The students' covert mental processes after a question may be like a "scan" or a search of all the new information. Thus the use of questions may facilitate learning while providing information to teachers about the efficiency of the instruction.

Attention.   Questions requiring student responses may heighten student attention during the presentation of material to be learned. Lack of attention results in lack of learning.

Self-awareness.   When a question makes students aware that they have not comprehended a point, they may show increased motivation to learn subsequent sections of the presentation. When teachers follow up incorrect responses with correct information, the questions and answers are seen to have direct instructional effects.

Practice.   A response to a question allows students to practice stating their recently acquired understanding. Opportunities to practice usually increase the amount learned. Practice also slows down forgetting.

Emphasis.   Key issues in the presentation of information can be given emphasis by means of the teacher's questions. This provides students with signals about what is important to know.

Apparently, both students and teachers can benefit from the use of classroom questions. Research from many studies supports this belief. In general, there is a positive correlation between the frequency of classroom questions and student achievement in those classrooms (Dunkin & Biddle, 1974). Perhaps that is the reason why the rate of classroom questioning is often very high. From studies reviewed by Gall (1970), we estimate the average frequency of classroom questions to be about 150 per hour in elementary school science and social studies lessons, and presumably, several hundred per day for almost all teachers. A study of teachers' estimates of their own rates of questioning proved interesting. It was found that teachers generally misestimate such rates. The teachers estimated they asked about 15 questions per half-hour lesson, whereas the actual count was 42. They also estimated their students' questions to be about eight per lesson, whereas the actual count was *one!* These rates are equivalent to more than one question per minute by teachers and about one question per month by pupils (Susskind, 1969).

The cognitive level of the questions asked in classrooms (and in workbooks or on tests as well) is a major research issue. To check for understanding, a teacher must frame a question that taps something more than simple memory. Many systems of classifying classroom workbook and test questions have been proposed. The most frequently used system is called Bloom's taxonomy (Bloom, Englehart, Furst, Hill, & Krathwohl, 1956), which is used to classify questions by the kinds of cognitive processes they require of students. The levels of the taxonomy are given here in increasing order of the sophistication and complexity of the cognitive processes that are believed to be involved in answering a question.

> *Knowledge.*   The ability to recall, remember, or recognize ideas or facts. *Example:* "Name the last five presidents of the United States." There is a plethora of useful things to be memorized—poems, dates, mathematical facts and formulas, spelling rules and exceptions, etc. But true understanding involves cognitive processes requiring more than simple memory.
>
> *Comprehension.*   Making use of what is received in instruction, without necessarily relating it to other things or seeing implications. *Examples:* "Explain in your own words the reasons for enmity between the Russian and American governments." "Give some examples of protein-rich foods." Some researchers believe that even success at this level is not yet true understanding.
>
> *Application.*   The ability to use abstractions, rules, principles, ideas, and methods in appropriate situations. *Examples:* "Use the barometer to predict weather." "Determine a healthy diet." All experts agree that this ability demonstrates understanding.
>
> *Analysis.*   The ability to break down communication into its constituent parts or elements. *Examples:* "Determine the different parts of a news story." "Compare and contrast the capitalistic and communistic economic systems."
>
> *Synthesis.*   The ability to take pieces, elements, or parts of things and recombine them into a new pattern or structure. *Examples:* "Prepare a plan for student government." "Determine the lessons learned from the history of the Vietnam War."
>
> *Evaluation.*   The ability to decide if criteria have been satisfied. *Examples:* "Do you like this play?" "Do welfare programs work?" "Is violence ever justified?"

When records of the teacher's classroom questions, workbook questions, and test questions have been catagorized using this taxonomy, it has been found that very large percentages, often over 80%, of all such questions were at the knowledge level (Gall, 1970). Knowledge-level questions do check the contents of students' memories, but that is not the same thing as checking whether students have understood the instructional material. We note also that taxonomic classification depends on the students' previous experience. If students have previously heard or read the answer, a question requires mere recall, no matter how complex the question may seem. Still, getting teachers to frame more complex questions appears to be an enduring educational problem.

How can teachers break the habit of asking so many lower-order (knowledge-level) questions? The answer is practice, practice, practice! Studies of teachers learning to ask other than knowledge-level questions have shown that teachers can learn such skills. In just a few hours of instruction, including detailed analysis of their classroom performance in asking questions, teachers changed their behavior (Borg, Kelly, Langer, & Gall, 1970). The changes in the question-asking behavior of teachers who received this kind of training have proved to be longstanding, with many positive effects still discernible three years after training was completed (Borg, 1972). Thus classroom questioning at a level of the taxonomy high enough to check understanding is a learnable skill. It is not, however, commonly observed in classrooms.

Concern about the level of questions asked by teachers is relevant only if there is some relationship between questions at different levels of the taxonomy and achievement. Lower-order questions certainly have a place. All children, but particularly the young and the low-achieving children of the lower social classes, need a high level of success in their instructional activities (Brophy & Evertson, 1974). Lower-order questions can provide that success. The frequency of such questions was found to correlate positively with achievement for young, lower-achieving students. But higher-order questions, particularly with middle school and older children, seem also to be important. It is estimated, for example, that if an eighth-grade social studies student scored at the 50th percentile on an achievement test with a teacher who asked predominantly lower-order questions, that student would score at the 77th percentile on the achievement test if taught by a teacher who asked predominantly higher-order questions (Redfield & Rousseau, 1981). In addition, Dillon (1982) points out that teachers who ask relatively more higher-cognitive-level questions also tend to elicit student behavior at relatively higher levels. Although the match between the cognitive level of the student's answer and the cognitive level demanded by the form of the teacher's question is not high (the odds are only 50-50 that they will match), higher-order questions still manage to elicit student answers that are more complex than do lower-order questions. Asking higher-order questions "works" in the sense of making students respond to teachers at higher levels.

Teachers who use classroom questions, particularly higher-order questions, to check understanding should keep in mind that analyzing, synthesizing, evaluation, and even just plain remembering take time. Teachers have often been found not to wait long enough after a question to ensure that students have processed their answers. This interval before a student responds to a question is called wait time. (Waiting after a student answers and waiting before a teacher responds to a student's answer are also aspects of wait time.) Teachers generally wait less than one second before requesting a student response. If that wait time is increased to an average of three seconds, through relatively simple training procedures, ten beneficial effects occur (Rowe, 1974):

1. The length of student response increases.
2. The number of unsolicited but appropriate responses increases.
3. Failures to respond by students decrease.
4. Confidence, as reflected in decrease of inflected (questionlike tone of voice) responses, increases.
5. The incidence of speculative responses increases.
6. The incidence of evidence-inference statements increases.
7. The incidence of student-to-student comparisons of data increases.
8. The frequency of student questions increases.
9. The incidence of responses from students rated as slow by teachers shows an increase.
10. The variety in types of actions taken by students increases.

Teachers need specifically to provide enough wait time for the students they regard as less able. Teachers have often been found to give less time to these students than to students whom they believe to be more able (Rowe, 1974; Good, 1983). The data supporting the many beneficial effects reported for increased wait time are very impressive. For example, Fagan, Hassler, and Szabo (1981) worked with 20 elementary school teachers of language arts, who led discussions about literature. The teachers received training in wait time, in higher-order questions, in both, or in neither. Student responses were of greatest length for teachers who were trained in wait time. The students of the teachers who were trained to ask higher-order classroom questions gave more alternative explanations and a greater number of higher-order responses. In the classes of teachers who were trained in both wait time and higher-order questioning, there were a reduction in the number of teacher questions, an increase in the cognitive level of teacher questions, an increase in the cognitive level of student responses, and more alternative student responses. Tobin and Capie (1982) found something similar. Wait time of three seconds together with relevant, clear, higher-cognitive questions was found to improve student attention and achievement in science in grades 6, 7, and 8. They found that wait time correlated substantially with achievement ($r = .69$). Beneficial effects are shown in dozens of studies (Tobin, 1983), and the technique appears to be particularly successful in fostering more complex language from minority groups, such as American Indians (Winterton, 1976).

Now suppose that you waited the requisite three seconds and received an unacceptable response. What should you do? Two alternatives are probing (asking the same student additional questions) and redirecting (asking the same question to a different student). Since both of these teaching techniques are likely to maintain or increase student involvement in the lesson, they are desirable teaching techniques. They also provide the teacher with additional information about the degree to which students have or have not understood instructions. In addition, there is some slight amount of evidence that they also foster learning. In a study by Wright and Nuthall (1970), the frequency of the teacher's redirection of nonanswered questions correlated positively ($r = .54$) with student achievement. The sample was 12 third-grade teachers who taught lessons on nature study. Brophy and Evertson (1974) found redirection to correlate positively with achievement for middle-class students but suggest that probing is a better teaching technique with lower-class students. Probing can then be used to reduce or eliminate the high frequency of "I don't know" responses among such students. This kind of probing can take the form of rephrasing the question, giving clues, and reminding the student of what's already been established, among other techniques. The frequency of such probing procedures correlated positively with achievement (Brophy & Evertson, 1974; Anderson, Evertson, & Brophy, 1979). In addition, probing to improve and clarify answers that have been given (as opposed to probing simply to elicit an answer from a student) was also correlated with achievement (Soar, 1966; Spalding, 1965). This kind of probing helps students to clarify their answers, to develop generalizations, and to hypothesize outcomes and solutions to problems. Such probing needs to be gentle and nonthreatening, as well as precise, to elicit or improve answers to teacher questions. These probes inform the teacher about the depth of a student's understanding as students are led to elaborate on their cognitive processes.

We must remember that questions have instructional effects as well as usefulness for checking understanding. The questions should be answerable questions, because student success is an important factor to consider in instruction. Furthermore, the questions should often be of a higher order; too many questions are not. Teachers need to monitor student answers to their questions because often the answers do not match the cognitive level that the questions were designed to elicit. Student answers can be responded to by redirection and probing, teaching techniques that help determine the breadth and depth of understanding in a class. Finally, we should remember that there are students for whom classroom questions can prove embarrassing. American Indian students, for example, may be socialized not to answer or ask direct questions in order to avoid standing out among their group. For them, the very shy, the speech- or hearing-impaired, and other subpopulations, questioning as a means to infer understanding may have to be more private (more will be said on this point when we discuss conferencing).

Classroom Questions by Students. The reason the rate of student question asking in classrooms is so low is simple. Most teachers discourage real questions from students. It is often costly for a student to ask for another explanation or to express genuine perplexity, yet that is precisely what is needed by teachers who care about checking for understanding. Teachers have to learn to provide a positive climate for student questions to be asked. This means asking for questions and actually waiting long enough for them to be generated, rewarding students who ask questions, appointing student questioners for the day or week, and otherwise encouraging inquiry. When teachers create such environments, students ask interesting questions, and these questions often promote more student-to-student interchanges. Student answers to student questions tend to be more complex and longer than are student answers to teacher questions (Dillon, 1983). Furthermore, just as the level of cognition that is reflected in a teacher's question can be raised by training, so too can the cognitive level of students' questions be raised (Glover & Zimmer, 1982). In one month, using teachers' praise as reinforcement, fifth-grade children showed 20% to 40% increases in asking questions at the application, analysis, and synthesis levels.

Students' questions inform teachers directly about student understanding of what has been taught. Despite the obvious benefits of having instruction take place in a way that allows students to express their misunderstandings genuinely and to ask for clarification and elaboration, classrooms with high rates of student-initiated questions are rarely observed.

Conferencing. One of the best ways for teachers to find out what students do and do not understand is to take them aside and talk to them in private. This technique is not often observed in practice, perhaps because it is so time-consuming. When it is done, however, conferencing becomes more like ordinary conversation than a question-and-answer session. Teachers can use more declarative statements to elicit responses from students. Though not generally recognized, declarative statements ("That's an interesting idea"; "I've often thought that myself") often evoke longer and more complex student responses than questions (Dillon, 1982). In a private conference, teachers can invite some students to elaborate on their thoughts in ways that are not possible in classroom settings. The conference is particularly useful for learning what is known by students who do not participate in classroom activities. Many experts believe that nonparticipants in classroom activities and discussions should not be "forced" by direct questioning into attempting responses. There are five reasons for this (Maier, 1963): (1) Quiet students may have nothing to contribute at that time; (2) the questions may be perceived as threatening in some way, as they might be to minority, bilingual, speech-handicapped, or shy students; (3) other students might wonder why one individual gets special attention; (4) the questioner's actions seem controlling of discussion, not facilitating, and can stifle spontaneous contributions; and (5) if students believe they may be called on at any time, they may spend their time "fishing" for answers rather than reflecting on issues. The private, informal conference is particularly well suited for exploring what nonparticipants or nonresponders know.

Semiformal Methods

Semiformal methods of checking student understanding are not any more or less demanding than informal methods. Both require considerable skill and thoughtfulness. The semiformal methods do, however, require more teacher time for preparing materials and evaluating student products. In the informal methods, the rapid verbal interchanges require immediate analysis of student responses and immediate decisions about how to proceed. In the semiformal methods, the records of students' responses are more durable, allowing the teacher the luxury of more time to analyze the student responses and to decide what to do next. The two semiformal methods we will discuss are the assignment and monitoring of practice in classrooms and the assignment and analysis of homework.

Classroom Practice.   Students spend a good deal of classroom time working individually on workbook exercises, ditto sheets, or practice problems and assignments given out by the teacher. In the elementary school, as much as 60% of the school day may be made up of such seatwork assignments. In secondary schools, the percentage is lower but still significant. However, when questioned, students doing seatwork often do not know what they are doing or why; they do the assignments merely to finish them and get another assignment (Anderson, 1985). As noted earlier, teachers must be explicit about *what* their students are to do and *how* to do it. From Anderson's research on students' cognitions during seatwork, we see that teachers also need to tell students *why* they are doing something. Students who mindlessly do practice problems in workbooks and on dittos have stopped trying to understand anything. Schooling does not make sense to them. Finishing tasks is all they know. To guard against this apparently widespread problem, teachers need to remind students regularly about the relationship between what they are doing and the instruction goals for the class.

The best practice problems offered in workbooks, on dittos, or for boardwork are those that provide the teacher with *diagnostic* information about students' understanding. Carefully constructed diagnostic practice problems can reveal student thinking processes, particularly when students give wrong answers. It is easiest to see how a diagnostic problem works by using an example from mathematics, but the principle is applicable to all subject-matter areas. For example, let us examine the simple problem $248 - 59 =$ _____. You might get the answer 189, which is correct and provides you with no further information. But if you have planned your practice problems with diagnosis in mind, the incorrect answers 211, 299, and 99 can provide you with diagnostic information of very high value. This is because these answers are perfectly correct for people with faulty methods of subtraction. If the method used is always to subtract the smaller number from the larger number in a column, no matter which is on top and which is on bottom, the "right" answer for a student with that fault in understanding subtraction is 211. The student has an algorithm to solve the problem, but it is wrong. Using the language of computer programmers, this is called a "buggy algorithm," as when computer programs have "bugs" in them (Brown & Burton, 1979). An answer of 211 to our sample problem allows the teacher to hypothesize the nature of the bug in the student's subtraction program. With accurate diagnosis, remediation is much easier. Other answers to this simple problem indicate other buggy algorithms a student might be using. For example, the answer 299 indicates that the student is correctly borrowing from the next column over, as needed, but forgets to reduce the numeral in that column by one. Thus 299 is a perfectly correct answer when the student applies a consistent and systematic but completely wrong method of subtraction. The answer 99 indicates another buggy algorithm; it is correct if the algorithm being used is to borrow, when necessary, from the leftmost column of the upper numbers instead of borrowing from the very next column to the left.

The point of this discussion is that student errors are more informative to teachers than correct responses. Errors that are neither random nor careless allow teachers to diagnose problems in students' understanding. Questions to elicit such systematic errors of thinking are difficult to construct, particularly in content areas other than mathematics. Nevertheless, an odd answer to a social studies question might indicate a student's lack of understanding of the differences between communism and socialism. Without such definitional issues clearly in mind, certain kinds of interpretations of social studies problems will necessarily be inadequate. In science, a student's inadequate answer may indicate a failure to understand a principle such as homeostasis or the relationships between velocity and force. In literature, a student may interpret the motives of characters based on current conceptions of the roles of males and females instead of those prevalent in Chaucer's time. In each of these cases, students' incorrect statements or answers indicate bugs in the problem-solving strategies they are using. As often as possible, the teacher's goal should be to use the practice problems in workbooks, on dittos, or on the board to elicit any buggy algorithms that are present. The development of such diagnostic questions is difficult; nevertheless, for hard topics and difficult concepts, a teacher can build up a good set of diagnostic questions over time.

When incorrect answers are due to carelessness, feedback can help students. When students provide no answers or give random answers to practice problems, reteaching is probably required. When students make consistent and systematic but wrong responses, debugging of the students' logic is necessary.

Some other points about classroom practice problems of all types may be helpful. Deep and enduring understanding of subject-matter areas and special topics comes from mastery of basics. It is not easy to progress in physics without thorough understanding of some basic principles, usually learned by extensive practice over a wide range of problems. Math, bridge, chess, historical analysis, curriculum analysis, oil painting, and literary criticism all require practice with the basics in each field. Therefore, practice can be defended as necessary for the development of understanding. Recent research in mathematics instruction (Good, Grouws, & Ebmeier, 1983) identifies practice opportunities as a key element in effective instruction. And Rosenshine (1985) also identifies practice as one of the important instructional functions that every teacher needs in order to create successful instruction.

There is also evidence that overlearning material, through repetitive practice, affects what is learned as well as how much can be retained over long periods of time. For example, when students overlearned unfamiliar scientific information, they were found to transform the material into personally meaningful ideas. They were better able to figure out the main conceptual idea in the material they had learned. The students' repetitive practice was apparently the basis for an increase in problem-solving skill and in transfer (Mayer, 1983). In other studies of reading and mathematics (Samuels, 1985; Resnick & Ford, 1981), when certain levels of automaticity were reached by means of practice, students were found to go on to comprehend more or invent new ways to do the problems they had to master. So practice is not just to provide an opportunity to check understanding or to ensure retention. It is usually a necessary step in the development of deeper forms of understanding.

Homework.   Homework is often another form of practice. Thus what has been said about classroom practice is also applicable to homework. In particular, home assignments of practice should be doable, providing students with opportunities for success. And the homework should also be diagnostic, giving teachers information about the ways in which students are thinking about the content they must learn. In addition, when assigning homework, teachers must be concerned about equity, feedback, and ties between the homework and the curriculum.

Equity issues become important because students' homework completion rates are not always random. They may be associated with racial, ethnic, or socioeconomic factors. It is possible that heavy reliance on homework assignments in classes of mixed social status provides the middle-class students with an advantage on school achievement measures due to differences in family interests and monitoring of school-work. Teachers need to be aware that the monitoring and help with homework that is characteristic of some families is not characteristic of all. In some programs of school improvement, parents have been enlisted to help monitor homework to ensure that it gets done. But not every family has members with the time or knowledge to help a young student with homework. Furthermore, in some families, chores take precedence over homework. Teachers who assign homework to provide students with practice and themselves with a sample of student behavior from which to analyze student thought processes must also consider the variability in family support of homework in their classes.

Feedback is necessary for improved performance in almost all learning situations. If students turn in homework, it deserves to be evaluated. Teachers who assign homework to diagnose problems or provide practice but who do not regularly evaluate student products not only miss the opportunity to help improve student learning but also foster students' belief in the controlling nature of schooling through the assignment of mere busywork.

Homework is a way to control student time at home. Therefore, to take that time away from students, teachers should be sure that the homework assignments have clear instructional purposes. Students are quick to perceive busywork. Their compliance with homework assignments should not be confused with their real attitudes toward schooling, which become negative if they feel too controlled, particularly at the junior and senior high school levels. The easiest forms of homework assignments to defend are those tied closely to the curriculum of the classroom. The classroom curriculum, of course, needs to be aligned with the goals and outcome measures of a district. When there is congruence among all three (goals and outcome measures, classroom activities, and homework), student learning is enhanced.

Homework is not just an opportunity for teachers to evaluate student products. Research indicates that there are direct instructional effects associated with the assignment of homework. Correlational evidence (Wolf, 1979; Keith, 1982) and experimental evidence (Marshall, 1982) suggest a causal relationship between the number of homework hours per week and achievement. The most defensible statement to make about homework is that if assigned in some sensible quantity, if tied to the curriculum, if success is possible or diagnostic information can be derived, and if feedback is regularly provided, homework will be of great utility to teachers and students in fostering learning.

Formal Methods

The most frequently used method of assessing students' understanding of what they have been taught is the test. A heavy reliance on tests—in particular, multiple-choice tests—is a characteristic of the United States of America. Other countries are not nearly so test-oriented, nor are they as enamored of the multiple-choice test. In fact, in many countries a student can go from elementary school to graduate school without ever having encountered a multiple-choice question!

Tests designed to assess students' understanding of what has been taught in schools are usually called achievement tests. A teacher who is informed about achievement testing is aware of at least three things: (1) the purposes and types of achievement tests that exist, (2) the types of items used in achievement testing, and (3) the technical characteristics of acceptable achievement tests.

Purposes and Types of Achievement Tests.   Let us first distinguish between two major types of achievement tests to assess understanding: standardized achievement tests and teacher-made tests of achievement. Standardized achievement tests are usually designed by states or commercial publishers to assess a wide range of school development. The information obtained from such tests is for reporting to parents, local school boards, and state and federal agencies about how well or poorly *schools*, *districts*, and *states* are doing in the preparation of students. The tests often do a poor job of providing teachers with useful information about what *individual students* understand, and they rarely provide diagnostic information to modify instruction. The usual practice is for standardized achievement tests, such as the Metropolitan Achievement Test (MAT), the Stanford Achievement Test (SAT), and the Iowa Tests of Basic Skills (ITBS), to be the cornerstone of a summative evaluation. The tests measure what has been learned after instruction has taken place. Moreover, such tests measure the products of that instruction and provide no information about the processes used by students as they attempt answers to the test items. Finally, standardized achievement tests often measure memory or the comprehension of information and only rarely assess higher and more valued kinds of understandings.

There are, to be sure, standardized tests that claim to diagnose learning disabilities, neurological handicaps, or reading problems or claim that they can identify gifted, retarded, or achievement-oriented students so that instruction can be modified to accommodate their exceptionality. But these standardized tests are not usually *achievement* tests; they are aptitude, ability, intelligence, interest, or personality tests.

Nor do standardized achievement tests provide teachers with information that can guide the course of classroom instruction. Thus we will focus on the purposes and types of teacher-made tests.

A teacher's testing for understanding will be guided by concerns for obtaining information that allows for the *placement* of students, *revision* of instruction, *diagnosis* of student problems, or the *certification* of competency. When information for the placement of students is desired, as when a new student enters the class, a wide-ranging set of questions of different degrees of difficulty and tapping different levels of cognitive functioning is wanted. From such a broad sampling of student cognition, a teacher may decide where in the curriculum or with what instructional groups the new student should be placed. Sometimes, minimal competency testing is called for, as when a teacher must decide if a student has enough algebra to go into the trigonometry class or if a student understands enough about the mechanics of writing to skip the technical writing class and go directly into the creative writing class. Such competency tests for placement are usually short, with relatively easy questions. Their purpose is to determine if certain basic skills are present.

Teachers who want information for revision of instruction create formative tests—tests that give both teachers and students information on how they are doing as instructors and as learners. Such tests take such forms as the 10-item mathematics facts test; a short-answer test requiring definitions of the concepts of ecological niche, adaptation, and natural selection; or a request for a one-page description of how a bill gets through Congress. Formative tests are usually short and are given frequently, perhaps every week or two. They are tied tightly to instructional objectives or to the domains of knowledge that must be mastered. They are often graded in class, or overnight, to provide rapid feedback to teachers and students so that they can modify the process of instruction, if necessary. Such tests are often given back to the students to review or to keep so that they may learn from any errors they might have made. Formative tests permit teachers and students to monitor their progress.

Diagnostic tests are perhaps the most difficult to build. The goal of the diagnostic test is also to provide information that is formative, to revise instruction, but diagnostic tests go beyond measuring progress through the curriculum. They are built to inquire into the cognitive processes used to solve the problems presented to the students. Diagnostic tests must reveal the students' thinking. They concentrate on uncovering the cognitive processes elicited by instruction. Such tests are less oriented to the products of instruction. Diagnostic tests can be quite short, since diagnostic items are so difficult to create.

When it is necessary to attest to the fact that a student has learned something, without any great concerns for placement, formative information, or diagnosis, a summative test is appropriate. Such tests are given at the end of an instructional sequence and are used either to assign grades or to certify some degree of mastery of a body of knowledge. The products, not the processes, of instruction are attended to in scoring such a test. The interpretation of summative tests, however, is a very complex problem.

There are two major ways of interpreting summative tests (and, for that matter, formative, diagnostic, and placement tests as well). The first is with regard to a criterion, and thus such tests are called criterion-referenced tests (CRTs). The second is with regard to norms, and thus such tests are called norm-referenced tests (NRTs). A CRT measures whether a student has or has not reached a criterion or some particular specified level of achievement. A test score depends on the specification of an absolute standard of quality. This standard is independent of a student's actual score. If a student reaches or exceeds the standard, he or she will be judged to be a master, proficient, minimally qualified, able, or whatever. Everyone who passes such a test is proficient, and everyone who fails such a test is not. These tests are constructed in the same way as tests to obtain a driving license. The most desirable situations for using CRTs are for measurement of achievement in individualized programs of instruction, where skills and content areas are often well defined and where students work on different curriculum units. The CRTs do an excellent job of estimating student ability in a well-circumscribed domain, such as two-column addition with regrouping, foreign language verb conjugations, or determining molecular structures. The CRTs serve well for monitoring progress through the curriculum, a formative use, and can be created to diagnose problems as well. Most important, for summative purposes, a CRT measures what a student has actually learned about some domain of knowledge.

On the other hand, with an NRT a student's performance is interpreted in light of the scores achieved by others taking the same test. The NRTs are very useful for classifying students (A knows more than B, and B knows more than C) and for selecting students when quotas exist (placing the top 15% on a science test into an advanced course in science). Unfortunately, with most NRTs the information from scores and grades does not inform us about what a student actually knows. Teachers make judgments about who knows more and who knows less. An NRT may inform us that some students understand physics better than other students, as evidenced by their higher grades or percentile standing on a midterm test of physics achievement. But even when a student is in the 90th percentile or in the A category in the grading system, the *amount* of physics the student actually knows is never clearly revealed! Only the student's relative standing in comparison to other members of the group that took the test is known. With NRTs, there are winners (higher scorers) and losers (lower scorers). With CRTs, it is possible for everyone to win (pass) or everyone to lose (fail) because the criterion for success or failure is chosen by knowledgeable people, and that criterion exists independent of the students' performance.

Which kind of test is better for assessing understanding? That depends on your purposes for testing, the decisions you intend to make from the information you obtain, and the nature of the domain of knowledge in which you are assessing understanding. The domain of knowledge is an important consideration because it is easier to construct CRTs in some content areas than in others. For example, subtraction of up to five columns, with regrouping, is an easy domain from which to create CRTs. Furthermore, it makes no sense to say that Sally is better at subtraction than Don; it makes sense only to say whether Sally and Don can or cannot subtract. When the instructional objective is derived from a well-specified domain of knowledge, such as identifying the writing styles of such American writers as Hemingway or Steinbeck or finding solutions to biochemistry problems or learning geography facts about states and nations, a CRT is not difficult to create. Teachers can set the criterion level where they want it to assure that students meet their standards. Whenever possible, the assessment of students' understanding of school subjects, particularly for summative purposes, should be done with CRTs. Unfortunately, some domains of knowledge do not easily lead to CRT development. Moreover, the creation of enough items at higher levels of cognitive processing to make up a useful CRT is often difficult.

Regardless of the type of test developed and the purposes guiding that development, the key to a good test of students' understanding is having good test questions. We turn now to this issue.

Types of Items Used in Achievement Testing.   One way to classify item types is by means of the taxonomy for classifying objectives and questions presented earlier, whereby the level of cognitive processes that are expected to be used by a student is inferred. Another way to classify questions is by the type of responding called for by students: recalling, recognizing, writing, selecting, and so on.

As shown in Figure 11.1, the major types of test items are essay questions and short-answer questions. Short-answer questions can be subdivided into those that require a student to *supply* the answer and those that require the student to *select* the answer. The select type can be broken down further into true-false, matching, and multiple-choice items. Essay items, as compared to short-answer items, are often heralded because of their potential for calling forth higher levels of cognitive processing, such as analysis and synthesis, which may be required to answer compare-and-contrast-type questions or to answer evaluative questions (see examples in Figure 11.1). While this is generally true, a well-crafted multiple-choice item can also tap these levels of processing. Such an attempt at tapping higher-level processes is seen in the examples of multiple-choice items in Figure 11.1. These are not intended to be simple memory-level items (though, of course, they could be).

Essay questions are also reputed to be easy to prepare in comparison to select-type questions. But good essay questions do not come forth perfect, ready to be answered. The good essay question writer must prepare an answer to the question and design a scoring key for the essay as well. Thus the easy-to-prepare criterion rarely holds for serious essay question writers. The essay question does have two clear advantages over short-answer question: It eliminates the effects of guessing, and it tests writing ability, an important communication skill that is often underemphasized in the schools.

The short-answer formats have some decided advantages, too. They allow a greater sampling of domains of knowledge, thus ensuring that the test covers many curriculum content areas. They are scored more easily and more accurately. Essay tests, with their complex and even creative answers, are more open to interpretation than short-answer questions. Essay answers take longer to score, and errors, misjudgments, and bias in scoring can occur. Nevertheless, essay, even short-essay tests, are the preferred way to get information about a student's knowledge, reasoning, opinions, and creativity.

Of the short-answer questions, the supply type, short-answer recall, and high-grade multiple-choice items allow a teacher to tap into some of the higher levels of cognitive process. True-false, matching, and run-of-the-mill multiple-choice items generally tap memory-level processing only.

What does it take to make a "good" test? Nitko (1983) presents the steps in that process (Figure 11.2). The all too typical classroom test, slapped together in 20 minutes, does not represent the best in the art of achievement test design, as Figure 11.2 makes clear. For more on the art of item writing, see Wesman (1971); for more on testing, see Nitko (1983), Cronbach (1984), and Popham (1981).

Technical Characteristics of Achievement Tests.   Among the most important decisions to be made by a teacher is whether the items of the test for assessing

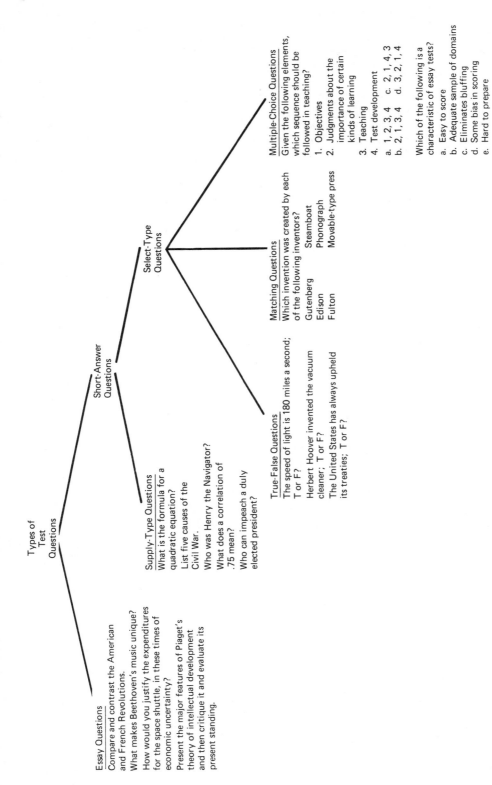

Types of
Test
Questions

Essay Questions
Compare and contrast the American
and French Revolutions.

What makes Beethoven's music unique?

How would you justify the expenditures
for the space shuttle, in these times of
economic uncertainty?

Present the major features of Piaget's
theory of intellectual development
and then critique it and evaluate its
present standing.

Short-Answer
Questions

Supply-Type Questions
What is the formula for a
quadratic equation?

List five causes of the
Civil War.

Who was Henry the Navigator?

What does a correlation of
.75 mean?

Who can impeach a duly
elected president?

Select-Type
Questions

True-False Questions
The speed of light is 180 miles a second;
T or F?

Herbert Hoover invented the vacuum
cleaner; T or F?

The United States has always upheld
its treaties; T or F?

Matching Questions
Which invention was created by each
of the following inventors?

Gutenberg   Steamboat
Edison   Phonograph
Fulton   Movable-type press

Multiple-Choice Questions
Given the following elements,
which sequence should be
followed in teaching?

1. Objectives
2. Judgments about the
   importance of certain
   kinds of learning
3. Teaching
4. Test development

a. 1, 2, 3, 4   c. 2, 1, 4, 3
b. 2, 1, 3, 4   d. 3, 2, 1, 4

Which of the following is a
characteristic of essay tests?

a. Easy to score
b. Adequate sample of domains
c. Eliminates bluffing
d. Some bias in scoring
e. Hard to prepare

FIGURE 11.1   Types and examples of questions for the design of tests by teachers

understanding are derived from the curriculum and match the goals for the course or instructional unit. There is technology to help a teacher do this. It is called the behavior-content matrix, and is the way to accomplish the task specified in box 6 of Figure 11.2. First a teacher must set out columns and rows. The columns are labeled with the types of cognitive behavior that are desired from the students. The Bloom taxonomy provides one way to describe student behavior. An abbreviated version of that taxonomy is provided as an example in Table 11.1, but any designations of student behavior will do as well. The content to be covered is listed in the rows. These can be listings of curriculum units, concepts to be learned, or any other systematic description of the content in an instructional unit. The cells of this matrix are our focus. They can be filled in with questions that tap the important behaviors and contents that should be covered in a test. Table 11.1 shows how this is done. A behavior-content matrix ensures that a teacher-made test covers the important areas of a course or curriculum unit. This is true whether a CRT or an NRT is desired. Either kind of test can be developed to cover the areas in a behavior-content cell or to cover all the desired behavioral competencies across a row of important content.

A test may also cover an entire course, and the matrix helps to delineate all the areas needed to develop a comprehensive test. In fact, to ensure fairness in creating a test, the behavior-content matrix can first be filled out in a way that ensures that a teacher includes the items that match his or her judgment about the most important topics or issues. An example of how this is done is given in Table 11.2.

After the rows and columns of a behavior-content matrix have been created, but before questions are generated, a teacher can weight the matrix. First the teacher can examine the rows and give more weight to content of greater value and emphasis. Then the teacher can weight the columns to emphasize the student behaviors of greater value and emphasis. The row and column percentages in Table 11.2 reflect this kind of weighting for an instructional unit on American novels. In each cell we see the approximate number of questions for a 30-item test that is designed to reflect the teacher's values and instructional emphasis when teaching these American novels. This version of a behavior-content matrix is called a table of specifications—it specifies how to construct an achievement test in a rational manner. Such tables of specifications help avoid generating too many items of one type or too few of another type.

One of the most useful things a teacher can do is generate the behavior-content matrix and tests for assessing instruction *before* instruction begins. The behavior-content matrix and table of specifications can be used to guide the time allocations and content choices that every teacher must make. When this is done, a technical feature of all good tests is automatically taken care of: the content validity of the test. When teachers serve in their role as achievement test developers, the most important of the many kinds of validity they must be concerned about is content validity. Content validity refers to the degree to which a test or test items measure the instructional domains that students have had an opportunity to learn.

Content validity is a logical procedure, dependent on sound judgments about how items relate to the curriculum that was taught. For example, if content is added to a social studies curriculum, say on the People's Republic of China, and students study that content, a teacher's test should include the new material. Even more important, if a unit of instruction is dropped, skipped, or no longer stressed, as when American concern for problems in Southeast Asia waned after the Vietnam War, a

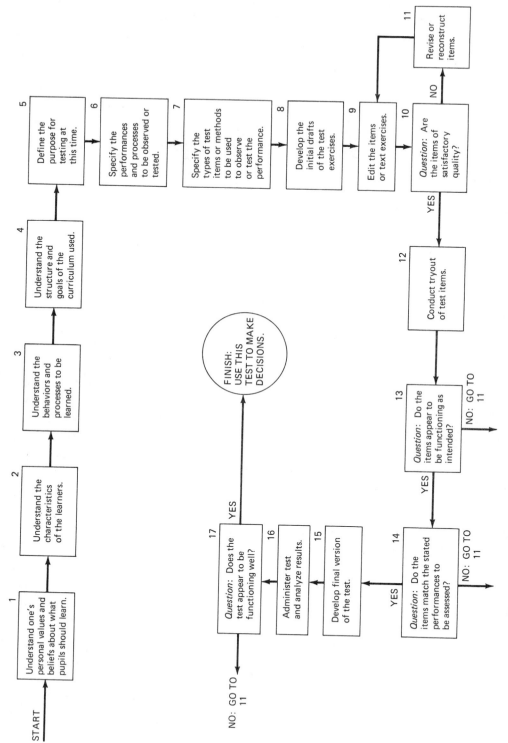

FIGURE 11.2 Steps in making a classroom test of achievement. (Adapted from Nitko, 1983)

TABLE 11.1   BEHAVIOR-CONTENT MATRIX
FOR SOME SECTIONS OF A COURSE IN SAILING

Content Areas	*Desired Behaviors of Students*		
	Knowledge and Comprehension	*Application*	*Analysis/Synthesis and Evaluation*
Knots	Name the 10 most frequently used knots in sailing.	Successfully tie 8 out of 10 of the most frequently used knots in sailing.	Under conditions of rough weather, what kinds of rope and knots do you recommend?
Sailing Positions	Describe the different positions for sailing in front of and into the wind. Name each position.	Describe the sequence of events (or actually perform) a change from a starboard ready to a port tack.	While you are on a port tack, the winds suddenly change from SE at 7 knots to NE at 15 knots. What is the immediate danger in such a situation?
Rules of the Sea and Safety	List the different buoys and markers sanctioned by the U.S. Coast Guard.	Conduct a man-overboard drill.	What should you do when fog prevents you from seeing land or channel markers at 5 P.M. in the Cheasapeake Bay?

test should not still have items about American involvement in Vietnam. Students have a right to demand from teachers and schools the opportunity to learn what is on the achievement tests used to judge their competency. A behavior-content matrix and a table of specifications guide instruction and test-item development to ensure congruence, overlap, or alignment between curriculum and outcome measures. This provides students with the opportunity to learn what is on the test and helps ensure that the test has content validity.

The last important technical consideration for thinking about how teachers can assess understanding by classroom testing is the concept of reliability. For the kind of teacher-made tests of achievement that we have been discussing, reliability refers to whether or not you would make the same decisions about your students if you tested them a second time with no intervening instruction. If you were to measure your students' height with a steel ruler, you usually feel sure that if you measured their height again the next day you would get almost the same results. But notice that even when measuring height, you would not expect to get *exactly* the same results from one measurement occasion to another. The ruler can be expected to expand or contract a little depending on the temperature of the day. Also, the children on different occasions will actually be a bit shorter or taller, depending on whether they had just been sitting, sleeping, or playing athletics. Furthermore, you will read the ruler differently on two occasions according to the angle at which you view the ruler, the amount of wine you drank the night before, the amount of light in the room, and so on. So even when measuring height with a steel instrument, we know to expect some error of measurement. Imagine how much greater the problem of error is when we measure achievement!

TABLE 11.2   TABLE OF SPECIFICATIONS FOR AN ACHIEVEMENT TEST OF UNDERSTANDING OF THREE NOVELS

Analysis of American Novels

| | *Behavioral Competencies Desired* | | | |
Novels Studied	*Knowledge of Facts about Character and Plot*	*Identification of Literary Devices in the Novels*	*Relation to Social History of the Time*	*Weights Desired*
A Farewell to Arms	1 or 2	4 or 5	2 or 3	25%
The Great Gatsby	1 or 2	4 or 5	2 or 3	25%
East of Eden	3 or 4	6 or 7	4 or 5	50%
Weights Desired	20% of test	50% of test	30% of test	100%

The novels and behaviors are not weighted evenly. The approximate number of questions for a 30-item test based on these weights is given in each cell.

When we measure achievement, our instruments, our tests, are not always very good rulers. Our students also vary considerably in what they can retrieve from their memories on different testing occasions. And our scoring of results, particularly with essay tests, is also subject to variation. The problems of achievement testing are therefore very difficult because our measurement is filled with error. The way we estimate the error in tests is by means of a statistic called the reliability coefficient.

If we are going to make important decisions about our students, we should formally determine the reliability coefficient of the tests we are using. This would hold for decisions about whether students should be given or denied entry to certain classes or to programs designed specifically for the gifted or students of low ability. And reliability should be determined when we assign grades that will influence how others will view the student's competency. Determining reliability is not difficult to do, though it is time-consuming. (The methods for computing reliability can be found in Popham, 1981, and Cronbach, 1984.)

Reliability refers to the dependability, consistency, or stability of the scores or decisions about students that you must make. When the reliability of a test is derived, it is often presented as a number between 0 and 1 (it is possible, but rare, for reliability indices to be in the negative range of 0 to -1). The closer the value to $+1$, the more reliable the test. The numerical determination of this figure can be made in many different ways, but conceptually it is done as follows: Develop a large pool of items on the topic of interest, split the items randomly into two parallel forms of a test, administer the two forms of the test to a large and heterogeneous group of students, and determine the correlation coefficient between the two tests. If students score high on both forms of the test, we infer that their scores appear to be dependable.

The same is true if students are at about the middle in scores on one form and also at about the middle in scores on the second form. And you would expect low scorers also to show such consistency over the two test occasions. Such a test would produce a high correlation between the forms, indicating stability, dependability, and a sense of assurance.

Now let us consider the opposite case: Suppose students were found to have very different scores from one test occasion to another. The correlation coefficient would be low, indicating instability, a lack of dependability, and little assurance that the scores on the test are trustworthy. Measurement of height from one occasion to another sometimes may yield correlation coefficients of about .99 or .98. Measuring achievement with the same kind of tests from one occasion to another under the most optimal conditions yields correlation coefficients of about .92 or .90.

So it appears to be possible to build highly reliable tests from which we can make important decisions about our students. With such tests we can feel that our decisions are being made on the basis of dependable data. But in most classrooms the tests built by teachers rarely come close to these levels of reliability. Two forms of a test to assess reliability are not usually created, and thus we must find ways to estimate reliability from a single administration of a test. Also, the typical classroom test is not very long, so we do not get a chance to measure the full range of a student's achievements (it's like estimating height from measuring the length of a person's leg. This technique works, to some extent, but it is not nearly as good as measuring the entire body). Furthermore, the test items are not carefully screened and tried out to get rid of ambiguities, bias, and excessively hard or easy items that provide no useful information. Finally, the size of the student group is small, and in a single class the full range of abilities is usually not represented. All these factors come together so that the typical *teacher-made* test of classroom achievement has a reliability in the range of .50 to .70. This magnitude of reliability is just barely good enough to obtain useful information to guide instruction, but it is not good enough to make important decisions.

There is a direct relationship between the reliability of a test and the magnitude of the error a teacher may be faced with when interpreting a student's score. Whenever we have less than perfect reliability, which is just about all the time, we need to think of scores as bands, not as precise points along some scale. That is, the lower the reliability of a test, the greater the band in which a person's score can be truly located. A person with a score of 68 on a test with perfect reliability ($+1$) is acknowledged to have a true score of 68—there is no error to worry about. In a test with a reliability of .90, that same person may (through statistical techniques) be judged to have an error in measurement of 2, indicating that if we wanted to be reasonably sure of that true score, we would have to think of it as somewhere between 66 and 70 (± 2 points). In fact, to be very certain, we might estimate that the true score was between 64 and 72 (± 4 points). With anything less than perfect reliability, we are not justified to think of a score as a precise point. In the reliability ranges of many teacher-made tests, around .60, the error might easily be about 8 points, indicating that the true score of a person who received a test score of 68 is probably between 60 and 76 (± 8 points) and almost certainly between 52 and 84 (± 16 points). That is a very large range indeed! And that is why you should determine reliability—it tells you how much error there is in your scores. You must have that information in order to judge if you can trust the decisions that will be made on the basis of the test scores.

When dealing with criterion-referenced tests, the computation of reliability is somewhat different. Since only a few items may make up a CRT, we look for the dependability of the decisions that must be made. For example, let us assume that a few short-answer items are developed to assess whether or not students understand the reasons for increased urbanization. We might declare that any student getting three or four right out of the four items presented has mastered the curriculum unit on urbanization. Anyone who answers two, one, or zero items correct has not mastered the curriculum. This short test can be administered a second time, and we can look at the percent of students identified as masters the first time and ask what percent of them were classified the same way the second time. These estimates are usually expressed as percentages or probabilities. A probability of .86 indicates that a test is usually correct in identifying people who do or do not reach criterion standards. A test with a probability of .54 is much less useful—it is accurate only half the time. Whether reliability estimates are computed by correlation or by means of estimates based on percentage or probability does not matter. What we learn to do when we think about reliability is to estimate the degree of dependability of our decisions. When we judge our students' understanding through formal tests (or in any less formal way), we must be sure that the methods we use for making decisions are reliable enough for the purposes at hand. The more important the decisions to be made, the higher the reliability of our methods must be.

We have noted that tests can be designed for many purposes but that teachers really need to be most concerned about their own classroom tests of achievement, both NRTs and CRTs. Teachers should be concerned about developing diagnostic tests and must pick item types to reflect their purposes. Test development, if done well, is a laborious process; it requires much time and many opportunities to administer and redesign the test. The use of behavior-content matrices can help teachers assess understanding more rationally and virtually ensures high content validity—one of the crucial elements of a test. Achievement tests that are reliable and have valid content are useful for decisions about students. Conversely, if a teacher's tests cannot demonstrate content validity and reliability, they cannot be used for decisions of any kind. Testing, the most formal procedure for assessing understanding, is also the procedure with the most highly developed technical methods for evaluating the adequacy of the assessment instruments. Thus with sufficient concern, time, and thought, testing can be done competently and in such a way as to be useful to both instructors and students.

QUESTIONS FROM NEW TEACHERS

Q. *You gave no example of an advance organizer. Can you give us one?*

A. A good example of an advance organizer is hard to come by. Still, in study after study, something that an investigator called an advance organizer worked better than no such thing. Let's try this. Suppose we are to begin teaching a unit on ecology to fifth graders in the northeastern United States. We might start by defining *ecology* and then say, "We are going to study ecosystems, systems of relationships. Keep in mind what you have heard about acid rain, because acid rain is a good example of how some factor far away can influence what goes on close to home. We will look at systems in balance and systems disturbed by factors like acid rain. We will look at cycles like the rain cycle and chains of interrelated events like the food chain. We will talk of change in nature, how slow it is to get things back to balance once they are disturbed, how cycles and chains, once broken, are hard to repair. And in our discussions of balance, harmony, change cycles, chains, and disturbances, we will talk about people—modern, urban; industrial, factory-working, car-driving people—and their contributions to balanced systems and disturbed systems."

That opening to the instructional unit communicates, at an abstract level, some of what will come. It provides "scaffolding" and is different from both an introduction and preview of a lesson. It is designed to help subsume what will come and stresses a number of times the key concepts that will be used.

Q.   *When you emphasize the familiar in teaching children, don't you slow them down too much? You can't help them learn new things if you keep tying them to things they already know.*

A.   What you say sounds logical, and certainly you want to worry about the pace of instruction; but what I am emphasizing need not slow learning or make it trivial. By making the new familiar, we may be able to speed up learning. So I do not agree with you. Nor do a lot of psychological theories and data. The British associationists of the sixteenth and seventeenth centuries discussed how new ideas and new sensory input could only be made comprehensible by means of their relationships to familiar ideas and impressions. The great psychologist of the nineteenth century, Herbart, posited that all new information was understood if it was tied to the "aperceptive mass"—the storage facility for the familiar. The Herbartians, pedogogical theorists around the turn of this century, taught lesson plan designs to reflect these ideas, and their techniques still appear to be sound. They emphasized, as did John Dewey, the role of familiar examples for helping children learn new things. Let me give you an example from a psychological experiment of a few years ago. Listen to this passage and tell me what it is about.

> He begged and pleaded for years, finally getting his way, thanks to her faith and her cleverness in obtaining the money. All the people around him thought he was crazy as he went off with his three sisters. He beat and ran with nature at his back but never reached his goal, stymied by blocks he never imagined, dying a failure in his own eyes, missing his chance for fortune.

Does it make a lot of sense? What if I simply say one word: "Columbus." Instantly the paragraph is perfectly comprehensible. We know that the three sisters are *Niña*, *Pinta*, and *Santa Maria*, that the crew thought him mad, that beating and running are sailors' terms, that the block was a continent, and that the failure was in not finding China. One familiar cue, and suddenly the new is totally comprehensible. The unfamiliar, odd, and divergent is rendered understandable. That is why concern for a learner's schema and an emphasis on examples is important for a teacher. Such concerns need not slow learning down; on the contrary, they can speed it up!

Q.   *OK, but how do you suggest we learn these techniques to explain better?*

A.   Two ways come quickly to mind. One way is to videotape (or audiotape) yourself. The other is to have a colleague observe your teaching. Both provide feedback to you, and it is only on the basis of feedback that we might change what we do. Feedback must, however, be data-based. The videotape or a colleague's observation instrument must be analyzed. The goal is reflection on what was taught and how it could be taught better. The teaching tips, the model of explaining, and the questioning techniques have all been taught to teachers in the past. Therefore, it should be reassuring to know that it has already been demonstrated that such skills of teaching are learnable and not just the conjecture of researchers.

To me, learning these kinds of skills for teaching is not much different from learning to be a gourmet cook instead of a slapdash heater-upper. To be a gourmet cook requires time, practice opportunities, the comments of observers, practice, creativity, and a sense of balnce as well as knowledge of the basic recipe. There are no real substitutes for thinking, practice, and feedback; if you want to explain better or be a different kind of cook, those things cannot be avoided. I believe that teachers get tons of practice and ounces of feedback. If we want teachers to improve, they must have more feedback.

Q. *Student questions really are rare. I keep asking, "Any questions?" but the students simply don't reply. What can I do?*

A. First we have to distinguish between asking for questions as a social convention and as a real invitation. As a social convention, it is often used by instructors the way many people use "How are you?" You tend to be surprised when you get a real answer to that question, like "I've had this pain in my back that began three years ago, so I went to the doctor and..." "How are you?" is really *not* intended to elicit information. Neither are most instructors' requests for questions.

To promote student questions requires training in question asking. You could, for example, learn to use silences—very long silences—after asking for questions. It is so uncomfortable for students to be stared at by an expectant teacher that they *always* break the silence first and will ask a question if you have asked for one. It is not easy to do, but it works, even with generally uncommunicative students.

Once you elicit a question, however, you are obliged to reinforce the student who asked. You not only owe the student a thoughtful answer, but you must also say such things as "Good question!" "That's interesting!" or "Let's really examine that one." Reinforcement, when appropriate and genuine, increases the frequency of student questioning.

Another way to elicit questions is to give stars, awards, tokens, or even raisins for good student questions. The tangible rewards make it fun for the students to get started asking questions. The rewards can be phased out when student question asking becomes more regular.

It is also possible to appoint different students to be official question asker for each lesson, day, or week. When you are through with an explanation, you can turn to the designated student and ask for questions. Ideally, the questions would constitute clues about what to reexplain to the whole class.

Remember that teachers can increase not only the frequency but also the quality of student questions.

Q. *What did you mean when you said practice leads to other things besides achievement of the things that are practiced?*

A. Teachers and parents sometimes forget how practice of one thing lets other desired cognitive events come into play. For example, we may overlook the fact that a child's information processing system may be quite limited. The average child may not be able to concentrate on decoding written verbal material and at the same time comprehend what those words mean. Comprehension for many children occurs only after extensive practice with decoding words, to the point that the decoding is almost automatic. The quicker the word recognition, the more likely that the meaning of the word can be understood. Thus practice in decoding and word recognition is actually the precursor to comprehension for many children. And in mathematics, after much practice with mathematics facts, some children have become quite inventive. When it is very easy for these children to answer a question like $2 + 4 =$ ———, these children often start to invent mental games such as $2 + (2 + 2) =$ ——— or $(2 + 2) + 2 =$ ——— or $(2 - 1) + (4 + 1) =$ ———. That is, after extensive practice with a symbol system, they can invent mathematical rules and mathematical games. These are much more desirable outcomes than simply knowing the mathematics facts themselves. So that is why I said practice has more profound effects than just on the skill areas that are practiced. Practice of simple skills may be a basis for the development of more important outcomes.

Q. *You make it sound as if the only good homework is practice of things done in class. I use homework to "stretch" kids. Do you find that wrong?*

A. Teachers cannot possibly fit into each day all that they might want to teach and all that society wants them to teach. Homework is a perfectly fine way to add to the basic curriculum. Homework might be used in preparation for a future topical event, such as when students are assigned material to interpret an upcoming space mission or to interpret a National Geographic special on television. In the same manner, homework can be used to illuminate a past topical event, such as a worker's strike in the city or a border war between countries. Homework assignments can be enrichment for some children, as when the most able history students in the class get a special project. And homework can be individualized, so that a student who asks a question gets to do research over a few days or weeks in order to answer the question.

But note that unless the achievement-testing program takes into account these kinds of homework assignments, the effects of such homework will never be known. I think such inventive homework assignments are necessary. They have intrinsic merit. I simply remind you that unless the curriculum and the outcome measures are all aligned, there will be no measurable effects of the homework part of the curriculum. Homework is often outside the standard or expected curriculum, and therefore its effects on student achievement are almost always unknown. Homework shows up as a successful mechanism in promoting measured achievement when it is tied directly to the basic curriculum and the basic curriculum is tied to the outcome measures that are used to measure achievement. Do not think I only approve of that kind of homework. I do not. However, that is the kind of homework that is most likely to boost achievement in a direct and demonstrable fashion.

Q. *I don't think that I have seen many criterion-referenced tests. How come? They sound better than norm-referenced tests.*

A. Criterion-referenced tests are not intrinsically better—they are only better for some purposes. When the instructional domain is very discrete, such as with multiplication, a CRT is usually the better test. No one really cares if someone is better than someone else in multiplying. Our society simply wants people to be able to multiply! The reason norm-referenced tests have been developed so extensively is tied into the philosophy and social purposes of schooling. For a long time, schools operated as if one of their jobs was to select and promote the most able students and to drop the least able students along the way. Norm-referenced tests gave information that allowed the least and most able students to be identified. Now that we as a nation have committed ourselves to retain and educate all our youngsters to promote social equality, we find we are still using tests that were designed to promote a different social philosophy. When we need to select the most able people from a pool of people, norm-referenced tests have the edge. But I believe that for most teachers, the measurement of classroom achievement can best be accomplished with a criterion-referenced test.

Q. *You make testing sound so difficult. Have all the tests I have taken and given been so awful?*

A. I hope not! But remember, tests serve so many other functions. They motivate students to do reviews; they provide practice opportunities; they inform students about progress; they inform teachers about who needs further help or whether the class can move on or not. So even when their technical qualities are deficient, tests can still serve very useful purposes. However, if you were ever given a hastily contructed, relatively short achievement test, over a large body of material, I would bet that the technical quality of that test was quite low. And if important decisions about you or your classmates were made on the basis of such a test, they were probably not very accurate.

Q. *Inaccuracy in measurement means that scores kind of float around—they can be as much as 5% or 10% higher or lower. How can I ever assign grades with such uncertainty?*

A. It is true that reliability for any given test may be low, but the reliability of a *set* of tests can give you accurate information. In addition, you can use other indicators of competency, such as essays written at home, other home projects, and classroom participation. Recognize that grading is serious business. You are judging others and affecting their life chances. Such judgments should be made on the basis of as much information as possible and be done as humanely as possible. When you start teaching a new course or a new grade level, the information that you receive from your tests is likely to be filled with error. Nevertheless, each year that you teach the same courses or grade level, you have a chance to improve on the measurement system that you use. Over three or four years, with a similar curriculum, the information you obtain from tests should become more reliable and more valid. In that way, your grades will be based on better information than when you started. It has often been said that a teacher who teaches the same way for 10 years does not have 10 years' experience but one year's experience 10 times. It's only when you use the information you obtain each year to design better courses in subsequent years that you actually profit from your experience as a teacher.

CONCLUSION

The bitter or the sweet of an instructional episode is in the assessment of student understanding. Advance organizers provide cognitive structures for new knowledge to fit within, aiding student understanding. Relating new knowledge to existing knowledge helps too.

The schemata students bring to the instructional situation determine to a large extent what they learn. So does teacher explicitness in explaining. Teachers who are better explainers avoid vague terms, are explicit in stating what is to be learned, and model or communicate how students are to process the information. The plentiful use of examples and the rule-example-rule technique of instruction also further understanding. More effective teachers use explanatory links and verbal markers of importance when speaking. Thus good explanations occur when instructors help students to generate *personal* meaning, carefully communicate what to focus on, are explicit about how students should think about what they are focused on, and emphasize the most salient ideas of the content in their explanations.

Teachers use many methods to elicit information from students. Among the informal methods that teachers use is the interpretation of classroom cues. Research has found this technique to be more misleading than most teachers believe. Classroom questions, both teacher-generated and student-generated, also provide ways to assess student understanding in an informal way. A teacher's questions were shown to have instructional effects as well as utility for assessing instruction. Observation of classroom discourse leads to the conclusion that teachers should require more thought from students than they ordinarily do. Teachers can get lengthier and more complex answers from students if they learn to use wait time and to probe and redirect questions. Students' answers to teacher questions are the most used data from which teachers judge students' comprehension. Students' questions to teachers and classmates are another source of such information, though student-generated questions are surprisingly rare. The private teacher-student conference is a very useful way to assess understanding but may be difficult to arrange.

A little more teacher preparation and analysis are called for when semiformal assessment techniques are used. These include practice in the class and practice in the form of homework. It was noted that diagnostic questions are the best source of data for teachers to modify their instruction. Such questions can be used in both classwork and in homework. The errors students make in answering diagnostic questions provide insight into their problems of understanding. Classroom practice and homework have direct instructional effects as well. When practice in class or at home provides students with success and is directly related to the curriculum and the outcome of instruction, such practice improves student performance.

Finally, we discussed assessing student understanding by tests—a more formal assessment procedure. Teacher-made classroom tests differ in their use. Sometimes tests help in certifying competency, while at other times they aid in placement or in the diagnosis of students' problems. The kinds of information required by a teacher determine whether criterion-referenced or norm-referenced tests should be used and whether one type of test item might be better than another. Tests need to be technically sound for decisions to be made from them. Use of a behavior-content matrix in building a test ensures high content validity. Reliability should be known to judge the technical adequacy of a test and to estimate the width of the band within which a test score might be located.

Explaining and assessing for understanding are not tasks that are easily accomplished. Nevertheless, an increased reliance on research on teaching and the technology of assessment suggests that improvements in classroom instruction are possible.

FURTHER READING

Explaining for Understanding

Gage, N. L., & Berliner, D. C. (1985). *Educational Psychology*. Boston: Houghton Mifflin. One of the best-selling texts over the past 10 years. The first text to have as many chapters about teaching as about learning.

Rosenshine, B. (1971). "Objectively Measured Behavioral Predictors of Effectiveness in Explaining." In I. D. Westbury & A. A. Bellack (Eds.), *Research into Classroom Processes*. New York: Teachers College Press. Puts together the diverse empirical literature in a novel way. The research base underlying "good" explaining in classrooms is described.

Questioning

Dillon, J. T. (1983). *Teaching and the Art of Questioning*. Bloomington, IN: Phi Delta Kappa. A state-of-the-art nontechnical report to teachers about questioning; suggests when and how to question for different purposes.

Orlich, D. C., Harder, R. J., Callahan, R. C., Cravas, C., Kauchak, D. P., Pendergrass, R. A., & Keogh, A. J. (1980). *Teaching Strategies*. Lexington, MA: Heath. A classroom-based view of questioning and other useful instructional strategies.

Achievement Testing

Gronland, N. (1982). *Constructing Achievement Tests* (3rd ed.). Englewood Cliffs, NJ: Prentice-Hall. Practical advice on test construction, administration, and evaluation.

Nitko, A. J. (1983). *Educational Tests and Measurement: An Introduction*. Orlando, FL: Harcourt Brace Jovanovich. A complete reference work on tests and measurement reflecting a very modern viewpoint about the purposes of tests. Ways to put tests together and to judge their adequacy are described. A fine first book for the serious test developer.

REFERENCES

Anderson, L. M. (1985). What are students doing when they are doing all that seatwork? In C. W. Fisher & D. C. Berliner (Eds.), *Perspectives on instructional time*. White Plains, NY: Longman.

Anderson, L. M., Evertson, C. M., & Brophy, J. B. (1979). An experimental study of effective teaching in first-grade reading groups. *Elementary School Journal, 17*, 193–223.

Anderson, R. C., Spiro, R. J., & Anderson, M. C. (1978). Schemata as scaffolding for the representation of information in connected discourse. *American Educational Research Journal, 15*, 433–440.

Ausubel, D. P. (1968). *Educational psychology: A cognitive view*. New York: Holt, Rinehart and Winston.

Bar-Tal, D. (1979). Interactions of teaching and pupils. In I. H. Frieze, D. Bar-Tal, & J. S. Carroll (Eds.), *New approaches to social problems: Applications of attribution theory*. San Francisco: Jossey-Bass.

Bloom, B. S., Englehart, M. B., Furst, E. J., Hill, W. H., & Krathwohl, D. R. (1956). *Taxonomy of educational objectives: The classification of educational goals: Handbook 1. Cognitive domain*. New York: McKay.

Borg, W. R. (1972). The minicourse as a vehicle for changing teacher behavior. *Journal of Educational Psychology, 63*, 572–579.

Borg, W. R., Kelly, M. L., Langer, P., & Gall, M. D. (1970). *The minicourse: A microteaching approach to teacher education*. Beverly Hills, CA: Macmillan Educational Services.

Brophy, J. E., & Evertson, C. M. (1974). *Process-product correlations in the Texas teacher effectiveness study: Final report* (Research Report No. 74-4). Austin: University of Texas, Research and Development Center for Teacher Education.

Brown, J. S., & Burton, R. R. (1979). Diagnostic models for procedural bugs in mathematical skills. In R. W. Tyler & S. H. White (Eds.), *Testing, teaching and learning.* Washington, DC: National Institute of Education.

Communication Quarterly, 6(2). (1984). East Lansing: Michigan State University, Institute for Research on Teaching.

Cronbach, L. J. (1984). *Essentials of psychological testing* (4th ed.). New York: Harper & Row.

Dillon, J. T. (1982). Cognitive correspondence between question/statement and response. *American Educational Research Journal, 19,* 540–551.

Dillon, J. T. (1983). *Teaching and the art of questioning* (Fastback No. 194). Bloomington, IN: Phi Delta Kappa.

Dunkin, M. J., & Biddle, B. J. (1974). *The study of teaching.* New York: Holt, Rinehart and Winston.

Fagan, E. R., Hassler, D. M., & Szabo, M. (1981). Evaluation of questioning strategies in language arts instruction. *Research in Teaching of English, 15,* 267–273.

Gage, N. L., & Berliner, D. C. (1984). *Educational psychology.* Boston: Houghton Mifflin.

Gall, M. D. (1970). The use of questions in teaching. *Review of Educational Research, 40,* 707–721.

Glover, J. A., & Zimmer, J. W. (1982). Procedures to influence levels of questions asked by students. *Journal of General Psychology, 107,* 267–276.

Good, T. L. (1983). Classroom research: A decade of progress. *Educational Psychologist, 18,* 127–144.

Good, T. L., Grouws, D. A., & Ebmeier, H. (1983). *Active mathematics teaching.* White Plains, NY: Longman.

Jecker, J., Maccoby, N., Breitrose, H. S., & Rose, E. (1964). Teacher accuracy in assessing cognitive visual feedback from students. *Journal of Applied Psychology, 48,* 393–397.

Keith, T. Z. (1982). Time spent on homework and high school grades: A large-sample path analysis. *Journal of Educational Psychology, 74,* 248–253.

Maier, N.R.F. (1963). *Problem-solving discussions and conferences: Leadership methods and skills.* New York: McGraw-Hill.

Marshall, P. M. (1982). *Homework and social facilitation theory in teaching elementary school mathematics.* Unpublished doctoral dissertation, Stanford University, Stanford, CA.

Mayer, R. E. (1983). Can you repeat that? Qualitative effects of repetition and advance organizers on learning from prose. *Journal of Educational Psychology, 75,* 40–49.

Miltz, R. J. (1971). *Development and evaluation of a manual for improving teachers' explanations.* Unpublished doctoral dissertation, Stanford University, Stanford, CA.

Nitko, A. (1983). *Educational tests and measurement: An introduction.* Orlando, FL: Harcourt Brace Jovanovich.

Popham, W. J. (1981). *Modern educational measurement.* Englewood Cliffs, NJ: Prentice-Hall.

Redfield, D. L., & Rousseau, E. W. (1981). A meta-analysis of experimental research on teacher questioning behavior. *Review of Educational Research, 51,* 237–245.

Resnick, L. B., & Ford, W. (1981). *The psychology of mathematics for instruction.* Hillsdale, NJ: Erlbaum.

Rosenshine, B. (1971). Objectively measured behavioral predictors of effectiveness in explaining. In O. D. Westbury & A. A. Bellack (Eds.), *Research into classroom processes.* New York: Teachers College Press.

Rosenshine, B. (1985). Teaching functions. In M. C. Wittrock (Ed.), *Handbook of research on teaching* (3rd ed.). New York: Macmillan.

Rowe, M. B. (1974). Wait-time and rewards as instructional variables: Their influence on language, logic, and fate control: Part 1. Wait-time. *Journal of Research in Science Teaching, 11,* 81–94.

Samuels, S. J. (1985). Automaticity and repeated reading. In J. Osborn, P. T. Wilson, & R. C. Anderson (Eds.), *Reading education: Foundations for a literate America.* Lexington, MA: Heath (Lexington Books).

Smith, L. R., & Cotton, M. L. (1980). Effect of lesson vagueness and discontinuity on student achievement and attitudes. *Journal of Educational Psychology, 72,* 670–675.

Soar, R. S. (1966). *An integrative approach to classroom learning.* Philadelphia: Temple University, College of Education.

Spalding, R. L. (1965). *Achievement, creativity, and self-concept correlates of teacher-pupil transactions in elementary schools.* Hempstead, NY: Hofstra University.

Susskind, E. (1969). The role of question-asking in the elementary school classroom. In F. Kaplan & S. B. Sarason (Eds.), *The psychoeducational clinic* (Massachusetts Department of Public Health Monograph Series No. 4). Boston: Department of Public Health.

Thyne, J. M. (1963). *The psychology of learning and techniques of teaching.* London: Hodden & Stoughton.

Tobin, K. G. (1983). Management of time in classrooms. In B. J. Fraser (Ed.), *Classroom management.* Perth, Australia: Western Australian Institute of Technology, Faculty of Education.

Tobin, K. G., & Capie, W. (1982). Relationships between classroom process variables and middle school science achievement. *Journal of Educational Psychology, 14,* 441–454.

Wesman, A. G. (1971). Writing the test item. In R. L. Thorndike (Ed.), *Educational measurement* (2nd ed.). Washington, DC: American Council on Education.

Winterton, W. W. (1976). *The effect of extended wait-time on selected verbal response characteristics of some Pueblo Indian children.* Unpublished doctoral dissertation, University of New Mexico, Albuquerque.

Wolf, R. M. (1979). Achievement in the United States. In H. J. Walberg (Ed.), *Educational environments and effects: Evaluation, policy, and productivity.* Berkeley, CA: McCutchan.

Wright, C. J., & Nuthall, G. (1970). Relationships between teacher behaviors and pupil achievement in three experimental elementary science lessons. *American Educational Research Journal, 7,* 477–491.

PART THREE

What Should I Know about My Students?

Ursula Casanova, Editor

Many observers point to the remarkable continuity of significant features of American schools and classrooms (e.g., Cuban, 1984). Schools are organized much as they were 50 years ago. They are age-graded, and single teachers instruct 25 to 30 students in self-contained classrooms. Classrooms have been remarkably immune to the introduction of new technology: textbooks, blackboard, and teachers remain the primary deliverers of subject matter. Because of this remarkable stability in the surface structures of schooling, many people think that teaching is similar to what it was years ago. But many factors have changed the activities of teachers and what they need to know in order to do an effective job.

Probably the most significant change concerns the student composition in the classroom. Desegregation, mainstreaming, and bilingual education have resulted in much more variety in classes that were traditionally homogeneous. Gifted and talented students must be identified and programs developed for them. Teachers must treat girls and boys equitably in their classrooms. Peer groups, particularly in secondary schools, seem to exert more influence than the school or parents. Further, more students are staying in school longer than in the past. Teachers must develop ways to deal with different needs of very different populations of students all at the same time.

They are also responsible for maintaining the interest of students who, in the past, would have dropped out of the school.

If the various mandates related to special populations of students have created challenges, they have also created opportunities. A classroom with different types of students can be a very important social setting for learning lifelong lessons. Students can begin to understand that there are many different ways of approaching a task and an idea and that different types of skills can contribute to the creation and maintenance of a fascinating, albeit complex, social setting. And the organization and management of a school and classroom can positively affect the formation of and interaction within peer groups. But taking advantage of the opportunities depends on the skills, sensitivity, and understanding of classroom teachers and school administrators.

The chapters in this section address the issues teachers face as they confront the challenges and opportunities of working with special populations of students. Chapter 12 addresses the powerful influences of the peer group on student attitudes and learning at different ages and the ways in which the organization of the school can affect how students choose and use their friends. Chapter 13 explores the literature on sex-related differences in learning and how teachers interact differently with girls and boys, possibly contributing to differences in their interests in subjects such as math and science. Chapter 14 describes very different varieties of students of limited English proficiency and the ways in which teachers can approach their education. For example, students can arrive in the United States highly literate in their first language or as adolescents with little schooling and minimal literacy in their first language. Clearly, these students cannot be instructed in the same way.

Cultural and ethnic differences and their meaning for education are covered in Chapter 15, which reviews such concepts as cognitive style and sociolinguistic variations and describes ways in which teachers can understand their own ethnic and cultural patterns and their effects on the decisions they make in the classroom.

Chapter 16 provides a historical overview of the treatment of handicapped students and explains how this led to the passage of Public Law 94-142. It also discusses the ways in which teachers can approach mainstreamed students. Finally, Chapter 17 provides descriptions of gifted and talented students, the research that has led to the various measures for identifying them, and programs that can be developed for them.

These chapters are exciting because they portray the diversity of American student life and the ways in which teachers can both deal with this diversity and use it to everyone's advantage.

Virginia Richardson-Koehler
Senior Editor

REFERENCE

Cuban, L. (1984). *How teachers taught.* White Plains, NY: Longman.

12 FRIENDS AND ASSOCIATES

John R. Mergendoller and Virginia A. Marchman

Students are naturally social. Much of their time in and out of school is spent with other boys and girls, many of whom are friends. In this chapter we explore the meaning and consequences of these interactions for students and their teachers.

THE SOCIAL CONTEXT

What Is Meant Here by Friend, Associate, Age-mate, and Peer?

Our modern word *friend* traveled through medieval German and English from a word that originally meant "free and loving." This is the general sense of the word in this chapter: Friends (as opposed to age-mates and peers) are freely chosen and are the object of affection and esteem. We use the word *friend* to encompass freely chosen relationships of any degree of intimacy.

One can choose friends but not associates. In classrooms and schools, on Little League teams, in summer camp cabins, children are directed to become members of groups without regard for their social preferences. An *associate* is someone with whom one is required to interact or who is frequently present in the immediate environment. Children may or may not be friends with their associates, but they must spend time with them in any case.

The meaning of *age-mate* is obvious. Because most children are assigned to classes according to their chronological age, the majority of social interactions in

We are indebted to Thomas S. Rounds and Martin J. Packer for their editorial advice and to Jeremy George, Madeline Finch, Betty Hey, and Carol Burkhart for the preparation of the manuscript.

We wish to acknowledge the support of the National Institute of Education, Department of Education, under NIE Contract No. NIE 400-83-0003 to the Far West Laboratory for Educational Research and Development, San Francisco. The opinions expressed herein do not necessarily reflect the position or policy of the NIE, nor should any official endorsement by the NIE be inferred.

school occur among age-mates. Although the intellectual, physical, and social development of individual children in the same classroom can vary considerably, age provides a rough way of categorizing children's development. Most of the research on which this chapter is based has studied children of equivalent ages to reach conclusions regarding the overall trend of children's development.

The word *peer* comes from the Latin word *par*, meaning "equal." In this chapter we use *peer* in its technical sense to refer to "individuals who interact at similar levels of behavior complexity" (Lewis & Rosenblum, 1975). Since children mature at different rates, a fact quite noticeable during the adolescent years, age-mates are not always at similar levels of intellectual or social functioning. In such a case, age-mates may not be developmental peers.

Why Are Children's Relationships with Other Children Important?

If you ask a child why friendship is important, an honest reply might echo the one Hetherington and Morris (1978) received: "It's fun.... Your friends don't tell you to wash your hands all the time, clean up your room, or apologize to your little brother." Beyond the pleasures that friends bring, however, there are important opportunities for learning and development in both the intellectual and social realms that occur only within the context of social relationships.

Children's social competence results in part from the number of social situations in which they have participated; each interaction provides an additional opportunity to practice or refine existing social skills. Popular children tend to interact frequently with their age-mates and as a result have frequent opportunities to develop communication skills, negotiation strategies, or "relationship-enhancing" behaviors that facilitate future social contacts (Wilkinson & Dollaghan, 1979; Oden, 1982). Conversely, poor social relationships may be an early warning of later trouble. Those who become delinquent in adolescence or psychotic as adults frequently did not get along with other children in their early years (Johnson & Johnson, 1980; Roff, 1961).

The notion that social interaction begets social development must, however, be qualified. It is not always the case that children lack social skills because they have not had the opportunity to interact with others. For some children there is no relationship between social acceptance and the amount of time they spend with other children. This suggests that it is the quality of interactions, not merely their quantity, that leads to popularity and social competence (Gottman, 1977). Unpopular children frequently initiate contacts with other children, but they do so aggressively or without regard to others' expectations for appropriate behaviors. Consequently, they fail to establish positive relationships (Hartup, 1983). Increasing the number of opportunities for social interaction among children would thus seem to facilitate the social development of only those children who already have the requisite knowledge and ability to interact successfully with others. For unpopular children, increasing social opportunities is probably not enough; it may also be necessary to improve their social skills.

Interactions with age-mates can contribute to children's understanding of the expectations others hold for them as members of particular social or cultural groups. Through conversation and imitation, young people learn how to act as boys or girls, the latest fad and newest slang, as well as the cultural values and assumptions of the children they play with. During the first half of adolescence, youngsters' use of their friends as standards for personal grooming, behaviors and attitudes appropriate to their sex, and vocational or educational aspirations are most apparent, although children of all ages imitate and influence their friends (Fine, 1981; Hartup, 1983). Boys as young as 3 years old have been observed to reinforce and criticize behavior in accordance with sexual stereotypes during free play (Lamb & Roopnarine, 1979).

Social interaction facilitates children's personal development and self-understanding. Friendships serve as a testing ground for personal interests, beliefs, or values (Fine, 1981). Outside the safe bounds of friendship, children may be reluctant to reveal their inner dreams, try a challenging sport, or take up a new school activity. As adolescents, they may hesitate to discuss their political ideology or sexual desires. It is among friends that one's identity can be most freely questioned, explored, evaluated, and validated.

What Is the Relationship between Children's Social Development and Their Physical and Cognitive Development?

It is impossible to discuss children's social development separately from their physical and cognitive development. While children are gaining social knowledge, they are also growing in stature and changing cognitively. The rate at which children mature physically often plays a part in determining the friends they choose and their activities. Cognitive advances, such as learning to take the perspective of other children and see the world through their eyes, contribute to the acquisition of social skills. At the same time, the ability to relate well to other children affects how efficiently children learn from their companions. The focus of this learning may be on important aspects of children's social worlds (e.g., how to fool a teacher, which rock group is the best), or it may be more directly relevant to academic accomplishment.

Age-related Interactions

Children look to older children for help, advice, and support. Older children offer suggestions to and tend to nurture those who are younger. In these interactions, children gain important skills as they learn to rely on and take care of others. Children are more likely to express aggression toward their age-mates than toward those older or younger than themselves. These patterns of interaction have been observed whether children are acquainted or unacquainted with each other (Hartup, 1983) and are not peculiar to Western cultures (Whiting & Whiting, 1975).

Interpreting the Research

Many psychologists and educators have studied children's social development, and some general conclusions can be drawn. However, the precise ways in which friendships and group relationships occur in specific classrooms or affect specific children vary from classroom to classroom and from child to child. Each student is indeed an *individual* with his or her own level of social and cognitive abilities, personality and temperament, family background, cultural values, and history. The same point can be made for classrooms, which differ according to students, teachers, subject matter, and history. Consequently, general prescriptions are never universally applicable to all students and situations, and the information presented here can only provide a starting place for thinking about the social relationships found in specific classrooms and schools. The final interpretation and judicious use of the research discussed here rest with the reader.

FRIENDS AND FRIENDSHIPS

Very Young Children's Friendships

The first, and some say the most, significant social relationship is between a child and its mother.[1] The intense attachment that develops between child and mother provides a foundation for later social development. Behaviors crucial to the development of social skills, such as looking, reaching, smiling, and making sounds, emerge and allow the child to achieve and maintain contact. A positive child-mother relationship provides a "secure base" from which the infant ventures out to explore the social world (Ainsworth, 1972). Infants 3 to 4 months old are more likely to initiate contact with another infant in the presence of their mother than when they are alone with an age-mate, thus demonstrating the facilitative effect of a secure child-mother bond (Lewis, Young, Brooks, & Michalson, 1975).

By their first birthday, children show interest in playmates and clearly desire to get to know others. Yet they will often "hang back" when confronted with an unfamiliar child their age. Often a parent or other adult plays an important role in facilitating social development by urging the child to play with others (Oden, 1982).

The first move outside the family situation is frequently into a day-care center or preschool, where the child is confronted with opportunities to play with other children. Social relationships with fellow preschoolers generally center around mutual activities or the transfer of toys; if activities cease or toys become unavailable, social interactions cease as well. Peer interaction at this stage is fragile and short-lived (Furman, 1982). Younger preschoolers generally play by themselves or in the vicinity of other children while remaining apparently oblivious to their presence. With age, preschoolers increasingly engage in cooperative activities. Between 3 and 5, social skills such as making eye contact and smiling improve rapidly. Children become more competent at exchanging information, establishing mutual activities, and resolving conflicts. Efficient, smooth interactions begin to replace transient social contacts. These changes reflect the significant cognitive advances that occur during the pre-school years.

Successful social interactions require that children pay attention to the nature of the environment and the corresponding social rules that govern behavior. Play in the block room differs from play outside or in the cooking area. As children learn to discriminate among the behaviors appropriate in different situations, they learn the beginnings of a skill that is fundamental to all successful social relations. (We often call adults who disregard social expectations for behavior "immature.") Children also discover that they can regulate their social interactions according to their personal needs and preferences. They begin to discriminate among potential play partners and practice aggressive or unfriendly behaviors in order to protect shared activities and social relationships from the advances of others. Children also develop the skills that are necessary to form new play groups and to negotiate entry into ongoing groups

---

[1]We recognize that in some cases other adults may take the place of a child's biological mother, and we include other care givers under this generic term.

(Corsaro, 1981). Soon age-mates replace adults as preferred play partners, and children are more likely to seek the attention of a peer than the affection of the teacher (Hartup, 1983).

Preschool children have a limited comprehension of their social relationships and do not make fine distinctions regarding the consequences of liking and disliking others. While they may act toward their peers with affection or animosity, they will tell an interviewer that everyone they play with is a "friend." When asked why they like a playmate, 3- and 4-year-olds cite common activities, material possessions, and physical proximity. Dislike, on the other hand, results from violating the rules or displaying aggressive and aberrant behaviors (Hayes, 1978). This activity-centered conception of friendship reflects children's cognitive inability to conceptualize social relationships as permanent; friendship ends when play ends (Berndt, 1983).

Elementary School-Aged Children's Friendships

If asked "What is a friend?" or "How can you tell if someone is a friend?" children of all ages respond that friends do things together (Berndt, 1983). However, the improved capacity to view another person's perspective and the growing ability to understand abstract social concepts like "group" and "relationship" allow children to expand their rudimentary understanding of friendship. As they become older, children begin to consider the *quality* of their interactions with their peers, not simply the occurrence of these interactions.

During childhood, peer relationships center almost exclusively around same-sex groups, perhaps as a result of adult encouragement, similarity in interests and abilities, and the operation of sex-role stereotypes (Hartup, 1983). Although friendships still center around mutual activity, children learn that friendships take time to build and require getting to know the other person (Smoller & Youniss, 1982). They also learn that others have ideas and points of view different from their own (Hartup, 1983) and begin to appreciate (and scorn) individual differences.

During the elementary school years, friendship begins to assume a moral dimension, and children proclaim that friends should share and help as well as avoid potentially destructive conflicts with each other (Furman, 1982). Some children begin to describe friendships in terms of loyalty or intimacy, although this is more common among girls than boys (Berndt, 1981). Later, children learn that friendships require reciprocity: If a friend does something nice, that favor should be returned. Conceptions of group relationships follow a similar path from self-centered to reciprocal obligations, and by the end of elementary school, most children see groups as arenas for complementary interactions among equals (Oden, 1982).

Adolescents' Friendships

Adolescence is a period of introspection. Youngsters often spend considerable time contemplating what they and their friends are like. As they seek to understand their place in the world, friends provide valued information and standards for comparison. Cognitive advances facilitate increasingly abstract reasoning processes, and teenagers are able to consider their own beliefs and values in social contexts more extensive than their family or friends.

Adolescence is a time when youngsters generally broaden their friendship networks by seeking several friendships that are more intense, enduring, possessive, and demanding than their childhood friendships. At the same time, as they become exposed to and interested in people from a wider variety of backgrounds, adolescents increase their casual acquaintances.

New friends are selected or desired on the basis of their personality, interests, and abilities. Such attention to individual characteristics (including ones that may not be directly apparent to an observer) contrasts with the childhood years when friends are chosen or desired because a friendship brings opportunities for enjoyable activities. Adolescents describe their friendships as reciprocal bonds that offer mutual support, protection from physical and emotional harm, and the occasion for intimate conversation. Although girls are more likely than boys to value friends for their emotional support and intimacy (Smoller & Youniss, 1982), adolescents of both sexes usually reveal inner thoughts and feelings to their close friends. Slight conflicts or arguments do not destroy adolescent friendships. Instead, friendships dissolve as a result of presumed disloyalty or disrespect (Furman, 1982).

As with younger children, friendships among boys and among girls remain a source of support and guidance in adolescence. At the same time, relationships with opposite-sex peers become more frequent and central. Newly meaningful contacts with the opposite sex emerge in the context of structured school activities. The football game or student council meeting brings boys and girls together in situations that establish mutual goals and interests. Cross-sex relationships can also result when several same-sex cliques merge to form a larger heterosexual group. These groups generally contain boys and girls from similar cultural backgrounds or socioeconomic levels. As they explore friends' similarities and differences within this larger group, adolescents have new opportunities to recognize that males and females can have similar values, interests, and attitudes (Fine, 1981). Later, as romantic interests emerge, couple relationships generally arise from within the larger heterosexual group.

Who Are Likely to Be Friends?

Naturally occurring friendships generally form among children from similar socio-economic and ethnic backgrounds who enjoy doing the same things, are of the same sex, and are near the same age. In part it is because friends often share similar backgrounds, interests, values, and lifestyles that they enjoy doing things together. Friendships between boys and girls are more likely to form during adolescence, although the segregation by sex seen in childhood still characterizes the majority of social experience. Friendships between boys and girls at any age are generally less stable than those among boys or among girls (Asher, Oden, & Gottman, 1977).

Popularity

Popularity, or the frequency with which a child is considered by others to be a friend, is influenced by several personal characteristics. Children whom adults and other children find facially and physically attractive are generally more popular than their less comely peers (Hartup, 1983). By the third grade, most children can agree on who is the "best-looking" student in the class (Asher et al., 1977; Cavior & Lombardi, 1973). The relationship between physical beauty and popularity, however, may be most direct and strongest among children who do not know each other very well. As acquaintance progresses, different aspects of an individual's abilities, possessions, or personality may become more important determinants of popularity. It is worth noting that both parents and teachers often expect that attractive youngsters are more intelligent, better students, and better adjusted socially than unattractive youngsters, whether or not they are acquainted with the children in question (Adams, 1978; Clifford & Walster, 1973; Styczynski & Langlois, 1980). These findings with both adults and children document the pervasiveness of the assumption in Western cultures that physical beauty is an outward sign of inner grace. It is not surprising that the perception and behavior of children is not different from that of their parents.

Children who have unusual names are often unpopular. The reason is still a mystery, but people often avoid things that appear strange or unfamiliar. If a teacher suspects that a child's name is impeding popularity, speaking the name in a matter-of-fact way in front of the class will help the other students become familiar with it. This may facilitate friendships with the unusually named child (Asher et al., 1977).

In general, children of high intelligence or who receive high grades are more popular than children of lower intelligence and academic achievement (Austin & Draper, 1981; Roff, Sells, & Golden, 1972). This phenomenon has been shown to be true in middle-class, working-class, and lower-class groups, as well as in American society in general.

Children who have older brothers and sisters are generally more popular than firstborn children (Miller & Maruyama, 1976; Sells & Roff, 1964), perhaps because they are forced to learn how to get along with other children in their own family and can apply this social knowledge to interactions with their age-mates.

Handicapped children usually have fewer friends than the nonhandicapped. This does not seem to depend on the nature of the handicapping condition. Handicaps have significant effects on natural friendship choices; nonhandicapped children actually reject (rather than ignore) their less fortunate peers (Hartup, 1983). In part this seems to result from unusual, negative, aggressive, or antisocial behavior often attributed to the learning-disabled, educable mentally retarded, or behaviorally disordered child (Gottlieb, 1975; Gottlieb, Semmel, & Veldman, 1978; Klein & Young, 1979; Mainville & Friedman, 1976; McMichael, 1980; Pelham & Bender, 1982). Although psychological research contains many contradictory and complex findings, it is striking how frequently and unambiguously the unpopularity of handicapped children has been demonstrated.

Children who are hostile, disruptive, antisocial, who have difficulty expressing themselves and understanding others, or who behave in unusual or nonconforming ways are usually unpopular (Asher & Renshaw, 1981). In contrast, popular children are characterized as helpful, friendly, outgoing, reinforcing, accepting, assured, enthusiastic, and cooperative. Popular children also initiate and maintain more social interactions and participate more frequently in social activities than less popular children (Oden, 1982). In short, popular children have attractive personal characteristics and behaviors that make playing and working with them a rewarding experience.

In adolescence, most friends are of the same age, race, and sex. Boys and girls who possess advanced communicative or social skills are more popular. Physical attractiveness remains a valued characteristic and can have a major influence on popularity, especially as adolescents seek new heterosexual friendships. Social isolates ("loners") generally lack social skills or confidence when interacting with peers. Students rejected by their associates are generally aggressive and insecure (Mussen, Conger, Kagan, & Huston, 1984).

What Are the Differences between Boys' and Girls' Friendships?

We noted that most friendships develop among boys or among girls, but not *between* boys and girls. The quality of friendships among boys and among girls is slightly different. Girls generally limit the number of friendships they form but develop affectionate and emotionally intense bonds within these friendships. In certain situations, girls tend to offer help and share more with friends than with nonfriends, thus cementing friendship through giving. In contrast, boys develop extensive friendship networks or gangs. These chumships are less intimate than those that exist among girls and are often characterized by competitive, rather than cooperative, behaviors. As a result, males sometimes share *less* with friends. This gender difference has been attributed to boys' participation in competitive team sports and societal norms for appropriate behaviors (Berndt, 1982).

Should Friends Be Assigned to the Same Class?

There is no universal answer to this question; it depends on the students and teachers involved, the nature of the classes in question, and the nature of the students' friendships. Teachers or principals faced with parents' requests to place their child in a class with a friend should assess the overall situation. The existing friendship should be only one factor to consider when evaluating what placement is best for the child.

SOCIAL GROUPS

How Is Group Solidarity Established?

Although children's groups vary in size and closeness, being a member of a group carries with it a set of feelings, behaviors, and beliefs to which each member implicitly subscribes (Allen, 1981). An individual's behavior within a group is largely governed by group norms and values; behavior deviant from these norms and values is discouraged. Continued deviancy can lead to expulsion from the group, and since group activities and contacts are enjoyable, group norms can be quite effective in enforcing behavioral conformity.

Groups generally coalesce in the context of joint activity, and group solidarity increases as members work together toward a common goal (Sherif & Sherif, 1953). This effect is amplified when the situation not only requires cooperation among group members but when there is also competition between groups (as in team sports). Here, working against a common opponent fosters cohesiveness within the group while emphasizing the distinction between members of one's own group and members of other groups. Suspicion and hostility among rival groups can be reduced when the pursuit of a common goal brings groups together in mutual, cooperative activity (Sherif, Harvey, White, Hood, & Sherif, 1961).

Why Do Groups Have Leaders?

In general, group members yield power to a leader when this individual is able to attain group goals rewarding to all. At times, however, leaders seem to be chosen because they can gratify group members' desires for friendship and other pleasures rather than as a consequence of their executive skills.

Hierarchies reflecting members' power and status within the groups are an inevitable part of group life and serve to increase the efficiency of group functioning. Once a hierarchy is established, there is no further need to select a leader, unless that leader does not possess the skills necessary for the task at hand. Since organizing a bucket brigade requires different tactics than running a town meeting, within a given group positions of power and status may change as the situation changes.

Who Is Likely to Have Power and Status in a Group?

While those with power usually have high status, this is not always the case, as when a disliked bully controls the activities of a group. An individual's power or status may vary from group to group and is related to the situation in which the group finds itself. The computer whiz who is an outcast on the playground may be a leader during science projects.

In elementary school groups, social structures are generally based on possession of playthings or the social competencies necessary for group activities. Thus as group members meet on the playground, children are usually differentiated by their ability to use toys, play games, or organize activities fairly and efficiently (Hartup, 1983). Often, the characteristics of high-status group members are similar to the characteristics of popular children: They are physically attractive, possess social and practical skills, and are aware of the behavior expected of them within a group. Power and status in a smaller group of friends, however, do not always predict popularity among all the members of a class.

Positions of status and power in adolescent groups are also determined by the possession of skills or abilities that help to guarantee that the group will achieve its objectives. While it is difficult to isolate any one characteristic or attribute that consistently indicates high status or power, research by Savin-Williams (1979) on adolescent groups in a summer camp revealed that adolescents with high group status and power were taller, heavier, tougher, healthier, more athletic, more daring, and more attractive than their peers. In contrast, timid, unsocial, passive, cold, hostile, and nonconforming individuals generally took a position of low status in the group hierarchy. In general, it appears that individuals who interact successfully and confidently are the more liked, as well as the more powerful, group members.

How Much Do Groups Influence Their Members?

The degree to which group membership influences children's behavior varies according to the individual and the situation in question. Different children identify more or less with what a group represents or the members' common characteristics. Like adults, students are members of numerous groups, and different situations provide different opportunities to feel, express, and be influenced by various group memberships. Membership in a specific sixth-grade class may not be very important when cousins gather at Christmas, but its importance and influence increase when it is time to return to school.

Peer groups and their values reflect in part the social and cultural setting in which they exist (Allen, 1981). School achievement, for example, is a more salient basis for peer group formation within communities where academic success is highly valued than it is within communities where athletic success is considered the ultimate accomplishment. Similarly, groups of students espousing certain cultural and racial attitudes generally exist in proportion to the prevalence of these attitudes in their communities. Before denouncing or praising the effect of the peer group on its members' values and behavior, one should question how much these values and behavior reflect the group's unique norms and how much they reflect the larger societal and cultural milieu.

What Role Do Groups Play in Children's Development?

Group experience, in part, can satisfy children's needs for affiliation and facilitate identity formation. In late childhood, children begin to broaden their circle of casual acquaintances, and groups provide increasingly important opportunities for the development of social competence and self-identity (Hartup, 1983). Participation in clubs, after-school sports, or the scouts is increasingly sought by students and provides opportunities to form and solidify relationships with others who share similar interests.

In adolescence, as boys and girls explore the aspects of self that define their identity, they often develop strong affiliations to particular cultural or social groups, such as punkers, jocks, intellectuals, computer hackers, or dopers. While such identifications often revolve around shared activities, they may also take a more ideological, abstract bent. Having achieved the necessary cognitive capacity for identification with larger political, social, or moral ideals, adolescents may feel themselves at one with third world freedom fighters, true Christians, or existentialists. As pride and confidence in personal ideals grow, adolescents gain strength to venture beyond groups based on self-identification and can explore relationships and ideas that are new, dissimilar, or challenging.

GROUPS IN SCHOOL AND CLASSROOM

What Are Classroom Norms and How Can They Influence Students' Interactions?

All groups develop shared expectations about what are considered the "normal" ways of perceiving, evaluating, feeling, and behaving toward others. Group members expect that others in the group will feel the same way about certain styles of music, act roughly the same way in certain situations, and espouse the same standards of dress and deportment. Although group members may vary in the intensity with which they hold a particular norm or the exact definition of the norm, commonalities are more salient than differences. While ninth graders may disagree about the best rock band, few argue the supremacy of classical music. Students striving for admittance to Ivy League universities may differ in how hard they study, but few (if any) do not study at all.

Like any group, a classroom has norms that affect the actions and perceptions of its members—both students and teachers. Some norms are dynamic and emerge, change, or disappear over the course of the year. They may concern the expectations established for a particular assignment or arise as a result of classroom events. Other norms, for example, the noise level permitted and expected during seatwork, are static; once established, they do not change.

We have already mentioned the importance of constructive social interaction in healthy psychological and social development. Peer relationships that "promote feelings of belonging, acceptance, support, and caring, rather than feelings of hostility and rejection," are associated with present and future psychological health (Johnson, 1980, p. 132). If this is considered a worthwhile goal for educators, it is important to consider the norms characterizing individual classrooms and reflect on how norms appropriate for constructive peer interaction can be established. As teachers reprimand students for inappropriate behavior and reward them for proper conduct, they help to establish norms for classroom conduct.

We do not espouse a universal list of norms that teachers should establish in order to facilitate a constructive social climate, as we believe it is best left up to individual instructors to establish expectations appropriate for their subjects, schools, and students. At a minimum, however, we would expect that teachers should model respectful social relationships. Students, like everyone else, are more often influenced by example than by exhortation. In addition, teachers can contribute to the establishment of positive social climates by prohibiting put-downs and other negative forms of interaction. Note that this does not mean that a teacher must accept all answers as correct in class discussion, ignore the distinction between effort and accomplishment, apologize for knowing more than students, or otherwise distort the distinctions that make the relationship between teacher and student different than the relationships students have with their peers. A peer, as noted earlier, is an *equal*, and in classrooms teachers are more than equal. They must maintain positions of legitimate, expert authority if they are to have a constructive influence on students. We advocate that students be given the respect they deserve, mistakes be corrected in a businesslike manner that focuses on the error committed rather than the abilities of the person who made that error, and help be available for all students who seek it.

Classroom norms need to be recognized by both teacher and students. A teacher's expectations will influence student behavior most powerfully when students clearly understand these expectations and observe other students behaving in accordance with them. Such consensual recognition and acceptance can control students' behavior, even in the absence of teachers or other students (Johnson, 1980).

The influence of norms may be more powerful in some classrooms than in others since classrooms contain students who may differ in the extent to which they are affected by norms (Lesser & Abelson, 1959). Students with high self-esteem or who evaluate themselves as competent are generally less influenced by group norms (Hartup, 1983; Landsbaum & Willis, 1971). However, the presence of one or more naysayers who visibly and vocally disregard or violate established norms can diminish the impact of norms on others (Allen & Newtson, 1972). Group norms are generally a significant determinant of behaviors, attitudes, and perceptions when a classroom contains students who like one another, enjoy being and working together, and want to remain members of that class. Such classrooms are termed *cohesive*, and the cohesiveness of a group is related to the power of the group's norms over its members (Cartwright, 1968; Schmuck & Schmuck, 1983).

Effects of Instructional Practices

The way in which teachers organize and conduct instruction can influence students' appraisals of their own and others' abilities as well as the friends they choose. Student friendship patterns have been found to differ in elementary school classrooms where teachers used relatively more recitation or relatively more group work (Bossert, 1979). In the recitation classrooms, students chose friends of the same academic ability: Brighter students were friends with other bright students, and slower students associated with other slow students. This was not the case in classrooms where multiple activities occurred simultaneously in small groups; here, students chose friends of both equal and differing abilities.

When recitation is the predominant mode of instruction, students can observe how well other students answer the teacher's questions. This allows them to judge how smart their classmates are. In multitask classrooms, where student attention is focused on several activities rather than on a single recitation, it is difficult to observe how well other students answer the teacher's questions. Students notice and remember events that provide clues to the ability and accomplishments of their associates. Their summary judgments of other students' competence can influence— consciously or unconsciously—their choice of friends.

Teachers' instructional practices can also affect students' evaluations of their own and other students' abilities (Rosenholtz and Simpson, 1985). In classrooms where teachers' instructional practices made the relative ability of different students obvious (grouping students by ability, for example) classmates agreed about who were the smart and the slow students. Students' perceptions of their own ability also matched their teachers' assessments. When teachers used instructional approaches that allowed different students to shine at different times and in different ways, students more frequently judged themselves and their fellows as being average or above average in ability. In these classrooms students' ratings of their own abilities exceeded the ratings of their teachers.

Researchers have compared how students make friends in open and traditional classrooms (Epstein, 1978; Hallinan, 1973, 1979), and their results complement those just discussed. In the open classrooms, students of different ages worked together and did not receive grades. Teachers typically formed student work groups and changed the membership of those groups from time to time. In the traditional classrooms, students of the same age were generally assigned to work groups on the basis of ability. The membership of these work groups did not change; consequently, students spent much of their time talking to those with whom they were assigned to work. In open classrooms, students had the opportunity for extended conversations with many different students. As would be expected, in traditional classrooms, students made friends with those with whom they worked, and these friends tended to be students of the same ability level. High-ability students also tended to be the most popular. In open classrooms, friendships were sought among a wider variety of students rather than predominantly among the most popular. Fewer students in open classrooms chose friends who did not choose them in return. It appears that providing a range of opportunities for different students to work together and to demonstrate diverse competencies diminishes the number of "psychologically stressful" relationships (Hallinan, 1979) where friendship is sought but not returned.

Educators concerned with fostering friendships among students of differing academic ability and with discouraging a rigid classroom social hierarchy should consider using small group instruction focused on dissimilar tasks and changing the membership of those groups from time to time so that different students may demonstrate different talents.

Effects of Ability Grouping

The impact of ability grouping on students' cognitive and social development has received a great deal of attention. However, there is no consistent evidence that ability grouping results in increased academic achievement and self-esteem and simplifies classroom management (Good & Marshall, 1984; Johnson, 1980; Rosenbaum, 1980). Instead, it appears that ability grouping is detrimental to the social and intellectual development of average and low-ability students (Cowles & Daniel, 1974; Persell, 1977; Rosenbaum, 1980; Schwartz, 1981). These findings have emerged from research in kindergarten (Eminovich, 1981), first grade (Eder, 1982; Rist, 1970), and sixth grade (Cowles & Daniel, 1974), as well as among early adolescents (Mason, 1974; Metz, 1978). We expect the same results from studies conducted in high school classrooms.

Since it has been documented that students in the lower ability groups are less attentive, receive inferior instruction, are less directed toward academic goals, are restricted in the range of friends they establish, and may negatively evaluate their own abilities, we believe there exists a strong case against using ability grouping as an instructional strategy. This argument is strengthened when one considers the inconsistent evidence regarding the supposed advantages of ability grouping. We would urge educators concerned with the social development of their students to experiment with ways to group students heterogeneously with regard to ability.

What Is the Impact of Cooperative Learning on Students' Academic and Social Learning?

While the advantages of various forms of cooperative learning are espoused by their proponents (e.g., Aronson, Blaney, Stephan, Sikes, & Snapp, 1978; Johnson & Johnson, 1975; Sharon & Sharon, 1976; Slavin, 1983a), the adoption of these methods in the classroom generally seems to be lagging. We feel this is unfortunate, for cooperative approaches can have a positive impact on academic achievement in mathematics (Slavin & Karweit, 1982), chemistry (Howe & Durr, 1982), and English composition (Elias, 1982) as well as on general problem solving and the solution of tasks that are complex (Cotton & Cook, 1982; Johnson & Johnson, 1982) or interdependent (Miller & Hamblin, 1983). Students familiar with cooperative learning approaches have been found to use cooperative strategies when confronted with problems that do not explicitly call for cooperation (Bloom & Schuncke, 1979) and to demonstrate higher levels of the ability to understand what others are thinking and feeling when compared to students who received traditional instruction (Bridgeman, 1981; Johnson, 1975). Other studies suggest that cooperative learning facilities the development of self-esteem (Ames, 1981; Ames, Ames, & Felker, 1977;

Johnson, Johnson, & Scott, 1978), mutual concern and liking (De Vries & Mescon, 1975; Slavin, 1981), altruism and helping (Ames, 1981; Bryant, 1977; Johnson et al., 1978; Slavin 1981, 1983b), internal locus of control, and positive attitudes toward achievement (Slavin, 1983b). Cooperative learning approaches are useful in the integration of racially different or handicapped youngsters (Johnson & Johnson, 1980; Slavin, 1980, 1983a; Slavin & Madden, 1979) and may be more effective than traditional instructional approaches with minority pupils (Lucker, Rosenfield, Sikes, & Aronson, 1976).

We do not hold that cooperative learning strategies are always superior to individualistic and competitive learning approaches (e.g., Johnson, Maruyama, Johnson, Nelson, & Skon, 1981), but we do believe that cooperative learning is a viable instructional approach. Because cooperative work is inclusive rather than exclusive, it can contribute to the establishment of a positive social climate for academic work while possibly facilitating students' own social and affective development. There is evidence that friendships in classrooms employing cooperative learning strategies are more inclusive and mutual than those employing traditional teaching methods (De Vries & Slavin, 1978; Hansell, Tackaberry, & Slavin, 1981).

Although positive *social* outcomes appear to accompany almost any cooperative learning approach, certain procedures are necessary to facilitate concurrent *academic* achievement (Slavin, 1983c). Let us consider two commonly used cooperative learning approaches. In the first, students work together to study the same lesson without taking responsibility for learning and teaching others specific parts of the lesson. In the second, a complex lesson is broken down into smaller parts, and each student takes responsibility for mastering and teaching the rest of the group about a specific part. In both cases, the way in which the teacher evaluates students' work and assigns rewards influences how much students learn.

When students work together to learn the same material and are *not* given different parts to master, student achievement increases only when the group is rewarded when all members of the group succeed in learning the material. Making the group's award contingent on individual performance spurs on all members of the group. Approaches that only encourage students working on the same task to "use each other as resources" and then reward the group irrespective of individual accomplishment are no more effective in producing academic achievement than those requiring students to work completely on their own. By contrast, when individual students are assigned *different* parts of a larger task, achievement is encouraged when group rewards are based on the group's overall success rather than the individual successes of its members. If rewards are given according to individual contributions, this will not encourage all group members to contribute.

Not all students (or teachers) are ready to engage in cooperative learning. Cooperative learning is generally a new experience that contradicts much school experience. Students must learn to cooperate in a productive manner, and this may take some time (Schmuck & Schmuck, 1983). Teachers must learn to behave very differently toward students, and this may not come easily. In the Jigsaw cooperative learning approach (Aronson et al., 1978), teachers become "consultant-facilitators" and "information resources" rather than traditional instructors, but findings from a recent study showed that many teachers "substantially modified" the Jigsaw procedure to make it more like traditional instruction (Moskowitz, Malvin, Schaeffer, & Schaps, 1983).

Cooperative learning programs should be more effective if teachers explicitly teach students the skills of cooperation and discuss the roles of all participants. Students should be encouraged to reflect on their actions and become aware of the impact these actions have on the group's progress and their own learning. They may discuss how to ask and answer questions, how to keep the group's attention focused appropriately, and the procedures and steps necessary to complete the assigned task. Training students in the skills necessary for cooperative and productive small group interaction helps them to participate more effectively in the learning group (Swing & Peterson, 1982). If students are faced with a complex or unfamiliar academic task and are unused to working together in small groups, the cognitive and social complexity of the assignment will overload most students' abilities to function and produce chaos rather than learning. Until cooperative learning becomes second nature to students, teachers must take pains to clarify task goals and procedures as well as the social tactics necessary to work together effectively (Blumenfeld, Mergendoller, & Swarthout, in press).

Efficient Management of Small Groups

Clements and Evertson (1982) compared the actions of teachers who were more and less effective managers during small group instruction. They concluded that the better managers excelled in three areas. First, they "set the stage" for small group instruction by making sure students knew what they were supposed to be doing during small group work. They had established classroom rules and procedures and reminded the class at the beginning of group instruction that they were expected to behave accordingly. These teachers monitored the class as students moved in and out of groups and did not begin working with a group until movement was over and the class was settled down. Second, better managers maintained the pace of small group activities while keeping a watchful eye on the entire class. Before leaving a group, better managers often gave members a seatwork assignment to be completed when the group broke up. This helped to maintain the pace of the lesson. Finally, better managers were skilled in responding to inappropriate behavior. They accurately identified misbehaving students and corrected the misbehavior quickly, whether the offender was in or out of the group they were instructing. Better managers reminded their class of appropriate deportment and kept students aware that they were watching for misbehavior.

Though Clements and Evertson were studying effective small group management techniques, the management strategies they isolated have also been found to be characteristic of effective teaching in other instructional formats in both elementary (Doyle, 1979) and secondary school (Mergendoller & Mitman, 1985) classrooms. Consequently, teachers concerned about the effectiveness of their management of small group instruction might better consider the effectiveness of their overall approach to classroom management, a subject considered elsewhere in this handbook.

What Makes Peer-led Instructional Groups Effective?

Recent research has improved our understanding of how students learn from one another in small groups without the teacher. There is consistent evidence from studies in the upper elementary and early secondary grades that students who give academic help to other students in the group learn more than those who do not (Webb, 1984). At the same time, there appears to be no relationship between how much a student talks with other members of a group and how much the student learns (Johnson, 1979), suggesting that it is not talk per se but talk about an academic task that fosters learning. Students who answer others' academic questions are often forced to think carefully about what they are learning, and it is this reflective consideration of the material, during which students clarify their own thinking, that may be the crucial link between academic talk and learning (Bargh & Schul, 1980; Johnson, 1980; Webb & Kenderski, 1984).

The relationship between receiving help and learning is more problematic. Research with above-average students at the secondary level suggests that receiving academic explanations from other students fosters learning, but this has not been demonstrated in research with average elementary or secondary school students. It appears that not all students are capable of answering other students' questions effectively. Students who ask questions and receive either no explanation or who are given the right answer in a truncated fashion do not learn as well as those who receive elaborated answers directed toward resolving their confusion (Webb, 1984; Webb & Kenderski, 1984). Not all students are equally effective in making requests for help. Studies of early elementary school students (Wilkinson & Calculator, 1982; Wilkinson & Spinelli, 1983) have found that sincere, direct, explicit, and task-focused requests directed to a particular peer were most effective in bringing a helpful response.

Earlier we noted that the way in which the teacher rewards students' contributions to a cooperative group effort is related to how much students learn. It is appropriate here to reiterate that rewarding individuals in the group for the performance of all group members has been shown to be an effective way of increasing the amount of help group members provide one another (Webb, 1982).

Organizing Effective Peer-level Instructional Groups

At least three factors should be considered when establishing groups: (1) the number of students necessary to complete the assigned task, (2) the nature and ability of the students in the group, and (3) the time available to complete the project. Although these considerations may lead a teacher to increase or decrease the size of the group, experience suggests that the optimal size for a learning group is four to six members (Johnson, 1980). Groups of this size generally include enough students to ensure the availability of diverse talents without being so large that members feel unimportant, ignored, or redundant. Minimum effort needs to be expended by members of four- to six-person groups to coordinate and monitor their activities.

If students are unfamiliar with group processes and learning activities, are in the early elementary grades, or lack social skills, learning groups should be used carefully. It is generally helpful to allow students at first to work in pairs; once they demonstrate that they can work with partners, a third member can be added. Success with three-member groups points the way to four- or five-member groups. At any time, of course, the teacher can reduce the size of the groups. In general, fewer things go wrong when groups have fewer members (Johnson, 1980).

A final note on the organization of group work concerns the academic ability of the individual students in the group. Research suggests that academic achievement is enhanced when groups are formed among students who do not differ greatly in academic ability. Webb and Kenderski (1984) found that seventh and eighth graders learned more mathematics if they were placed in groups containing both high- and average-ability students or average- and low-ability students rather than groups containing students from all three ability levels. Taken together with the research on ability grouping reviewed by Good and Marshall (1984) and discussed earlier, this would seem to suggest that one must use good judgment when forming heterogeneous work groups to ensure that the range of abilities represented is not so great that it impedes work on common tasks.

What Impact Does Peer Tutoring Have on Students' Learning and Satisfaction?

It is difficult to summarize research on peer tutoring because programs are diverse in the procedures used and the outcomes sought. One survey of peer-tutoring practices, for example, concluded that "successful programs depend on lots of common sense and plain hard work. As long as these two ingredients are present, almost any combination of design alternatives seems capable of producing beneficial outcomes" (Klaus, 1975a). In considering the impact of peer tutoring, it is useful to isolate two possible outcomes of a tutoring program: (1) academic gains for the tutee, and (2) academic gains for the tutor. Research and theory (Hartup, 1983; Rosen & Powell, 1977) as well as practical experience (Klaus, 1975b) suggest that it is unrealistic to expect any one tutoring program to achieve both of these outcomes, and care must be taken to design a program that meets the needs of the teachers and students who will implement it.

A tutoring program divides students into two groups: tutees who receive instruction and tutors who instruct. The first outcome of interest would be to increase the academic performance and motivation of the tutee. A number of studies suggest that tutoring programs can increase the tutee's general achievement as well as performance in reading, mathematics, and computer literacy (Cloward, 1976; Fogarty & Wang, 1982; Willis, Morris & Crowder, 1972). Programs that are long-lasting and well organized and provide one tutor for each tutee are the most effective, although success can also be had with short-term efforts (Hartup, 1983). Given the unsophisticated and restricted teaching behaviors generally used by tutors, as well as many tutors' proclivities for conversation rather than didactic instruction (Fogarty & Wang, 1982), highly structured programs prescribing the "content, sequence, and procedure for each lesson" most consistently facilitate the tutee's learning (Klaus, 1975a). It is thus important to teach tutors how to instruct tutees and to monitor the tutor's progress and problems (Fogarty & Wang, 1982; Hartup, 1983). Teachers should also be aware that student tutors—like any instructor—may misuse their power or ridicule those less fortunate than them. The tutoring relationship must be one in which the basic respect of the teacher for the student is maintained. Tutoring programs should not reward the tutor for the tutee's improvement, as this may encourage tutors to treat tutoring sessions instrumentally as a social means to a personal end rather than an opportunity to help someone else (de Charms, 1983; Garbarino, 1975).

Like tutees, tutors can benefit from participating in tutoring programs, but achievement gains are more inconsistent (Hartup, 1983). Organizing programs to benefit the tutee often precludes the tutor's academic gains (Klaus, 1975a), in part because programs effective for the tutee restrict and define how tutoring should proceed. Tutors learn the most when they are required to "work with and manipulate the instructional content" of the lesson rather than following a preestablished procedure (Klaus, 1975a, p. 2). This does not mean that tutors need no supervision or monitoring to make their own academic gains. In fact, the reverse appears to be true; programs are more likely to benefit tutors if the tutors are carefully trained and supervised, the tutoring sessions extend over time, and the tutors are underachievers who are several years older than the tutees (Hartup, 1983). Although research suggests that both tutors and tutees generally enjoy the tutoring process (Fogarty & Wang, 1982), some studies indicate that tutors learn more rapidly and are more satisfied with the experience of tutoring than are tutees and point to the importance of the tutor's knowing more than the tutee if optimal learning and satisfaction are to result. Such findings lead to the suggestion that students should have experience as both tutors and tutees, although the organizational difficulties inherent in such a suggestion are considerable (Rosen & Powell, 1977).

Students generally prefer to teach younger children and be taught by older students of the same sex, although programs employing tutoring by age-mates or by opposite-sex tutors can also be effective. Tutors generally do not like to participate in the evaluation of the tutee (Hartup, 1983).

When students are given the opportunity, they spontaneously rely on their friends for informal tutoring (Cooper, Marquis, & Ayers-Lopez, 1982; Fogarty & Wang, 1982). Organized peer-tutoring programs mobilize students' abilities as learners and as instructors. Further experimentation by teachers may help to resolve the administrative and organizational barriers to the use of students as active participants in the instructional process.

How Can a Teacher Facilitate the Acceptance of Rejected Students?

Every group, we noted earlier, has its own status hierarchy, and the classroom group is no exception. Children who are handicapped or who lack social skills are often the least admired and least popular students in the classroom (Asher & Renshaw, 1981; Gottlieb, 1975). Several procedures have been shown to be effective in improving the social position and acceptance of low-status students; we will discuss three such procedures: (1) cooperative learning, (2) social skills coaching, and (3) group discussion.

Although we have already discussed and advocated the use of cooperative learning groups, we did not emphasize that by assigning cooperative tasks to groups containing both handicapped and nonhandicapped youngsters, the attitudes of the nonhandicapped toward the handicapped can be improved (Johnson, Johnson, & Maruyama, 1983; Rynders, Johnson, Johnson, & Schmidt, 1980). When the interaction in groups containing both handicapped and nonhandicapped members working on a cooperative task is compared with the interaction occurring in groups working on the same task in a competitive fashion, members of the cooperative groups spend a great deal more of their time together encouraging, praising, and affectionately teasing each other than do members of the competitive groups (Rynders, et al., 1980). This and other research (Gottlieb & Leyser, 1981; Stager & Young, 1981) on the relationships between handicapped and nonhandicapped youngsters suggests that merely providing contact between the two groups is not sufficient to encourage nonhandicapped students to like, appreciate, or act positively toward their less fortunate peers. Organizing cooperative activities where the handicapped can participate equally and can contribute to group achievement is one way to counteract the rejection they might otherwise encounter (Stainback, Stainback, Raschke, & Anderson, 1981).

Sometimes students are unpopular because they lack the skills necessary to establish friendships with others and participate appropriately in group activities. Such students carry their rejection with them. Those who were unpopular in one social group or classroom tend to be unpopular in new groups, even if members of the new groups are unacquainted with them. Once in a new group, previously unpopular students reestablish their unpopularity quite rapidly and generally remain so for the life of the group (Cole & Kupersmidt, 1983). Children often create their own popularity through the way they approach others (Asher, 1983). Consequently, social skills training programs that teach students the skills they need to make and maintain friends can change the way children act toward others and their ability to make friends. Different programs employ somewhat different procedures, but it appears that successful programs are highly structured and focus on both the problems that arise among children and the opportunities that occur for friendly interaction (Asher & Renshaw, 1981; Gottman, Gonso, & Schuler, 1976; Ladd, 1979; Oden, 1982; Schulman, Ford, Busk, & Kaspar, 1973).

Oden (1982) has developed coaching and conflict resolution procedures worthy of description. In the coaching procedure, the teacher talks with students about applying one of four principles of positive interaction (participation, communication, cooperation, and supportiveness) to a concrete social situation. Children are asked, for example, what they would say to classmates who want to play with the same toy. The friendship coach's role is to help students envision positive responses to the hypothetical situation. Studies comparing social skills training with adult versus peer coaches suggest that adult coaches are more effective (Asher & Renshaw, 1981).

Oden uses naturally occurring conflicts as opportunities for teaching students conflict resolution and friendship skills. Her procedure has five steps. The teacher first asks the child to describe the problem or event that has provoked the interpersonal conflict. The student is then encouraged to describe his or her feelings, actions related to the problem, and his or her perspective on the dispute. Next the student is asked to take the perspective of the other party and determine how that person feels. With both perspectives in mind, the student is asked to suggest a strategy for solving the problem. Then the impact of this solution is considered for the student and the other party. If the outcomes are equitable and satisfactory, the solution is accepted. If not, the student is asked to suggest an alternative solution, and the discussion returns to a consideration of the consequences of this solution for both parties.

A final way to facilitate the acceptance of students who might otherwise be rejected is through discussions with the entire class. Oden (1982) suggests that the teacher lead a discussion about what it is like to be a newcomer to the classroom, how to understand the perspective of others, or how different people contribute in different ways. A study by Gottlieb (1980) demonstrates the potential of classroom discussions to affect students' attitudes toward others. He showed students a videotape of a mentally retarded boy playing by himself and working with difficulty in the classroom. After showing the videotape, he asked students to discuss the following questions: (1) Why do you think the boy is retarded? (2) How do you think he feels?

(3) How do the children in his class treat him? (4) Do you think he has many friends? (5) How do you think he would be treated if he were in your class? After participating in the discussion, children's attitudes toward the child improved relative to their attitudes before seeing the videotape and relative to the attitudes of similar groups of students who had viewed and discussed an unrelated videotape.

In closing this discussion, it may be useful to reiterate the behaviors and abilities that children who are well liked demonstrate in their interactions with others. First, they implicitly demonstrate knowledge of what Asher and Renshaw (1981) call "general interaction principles": (1) They participate with others in shared activities; (2) they talk to others about what is happening and how they and their partners are feeling; (3) they cooperate with others and work toward a common goal; and (4) they are friendly and supportive toward others. In addition to these general abilities, they are able to recognize what is required in different situations. Their behavior is flexible and accommodates the needs of others. They are aware of others' goals and act in ways that help others reach those goals. Finally, they are able to recognize and monitor the impact of their actions on others.

How Do School Characteristics Influence Students' Friendships and Social Development?

Researchers have examined the impact of several school characteristics on students' friendships and social development: school size, curriculum grouping (or tracking) at the secondary level, and curriculum structure (e.g., whether a school is open or traditional) at both the elementary and secondary levels. We will consider each characteristic in turn.

Small secondary schools encourage students to participate in more school activities and to make more friends than do larger schools (Barker & Gump, 1964; Karweit, 1976). With fewer students, there is more pressure to become involved in the drama club or go out for the basketball team. As a result of participating in more activities, students have more opportunities to make friends. Since these friendships occur outside the academic classroom, students can recognize and appreciate the nonacademic talents and proclivities of their friends. Consequently, in small schools more friendships form among diverse students such as high and low achievers who would not normally become friends (Karweit, Hansell, & Ricks, 1979).

Curriculum grouping in secondary schools has been a widely researched (and widely debated) topic for several decades. The weight of evidence suggests that track assignment *strongly* influences the friends students make, the kinds of extracurricular activities they participate in and the extent of their participation, the amount of homework they are assigned (and consequently the time remaining for socializing), their self-esteem, their academic self-evaluation, and their attitudes toward other students and school (Alexander & McDill, 1976; Karweit, 1976; Rosenbaum, 1980). By separating large groups of students on the basis of their presumed academic ability, schools can have a major influence on students' friendships, and these friendships can in turn influence students' academic aspirations, social inclinations, and everyday behavior. The importance of these friendships and associations should not be underestimated; one study found clique membership to be a better predictor of grades, social acceptance, attitudes toward school, and self-concept than academic ability (Damico, 1974). Friendship groups formed in college-bound and terminal curriculum tracks in secondary schools can differ widely in their norms for academic achievement and future educational plans. This "polarized socialization" (Shimahara, 1982) encourages high achievers to attend college and expect social and material success while discouraging low achievers.

We mentioned earlier that students seem to make different friends in open and traditional classrooms. The same is true of open and traditional schools. Research comparing students' friendships in grades 6 through 12 suggests that in open schools friendships are less structured, fewer students are isolated, more friendships are reciprocated, and more friends are selected from contacts outside the classroom. Open schools, or schools where "students walk around the room, talk to one another, sit in different places, choose their activities, work with each other, and receive more small than large group attention" produce "looser friendship patterns" apparently as a result of students' fluid engagements with a more diverse range of students and their mutual participation in self-motivated projects (Epstein, 1978).

Minority-Group Students

Minority youngsters sometimes seem united in their disaffection for school. As educators, can we do anything about this? The question does not lend itself to a simple answer. There are tremendous variations in minority youngsters' responses to school—some are high achievers while others drop out. These differences are related to their personalities and abilities, their cultural values and orientations, and the ability of the school to respond to their diverse needs. There is no general prescription to improve minority achievement and motivation, but unless minority students fully believe that they have an opportunity equal to that of majority students to participate and excel in school academic and extracurricular programs, they are likely to give up or rebel rather than try to achieve social and academic success (Ogbu, 1974).

THE INFLUENCE OF FRIENDS AND FAMILY

What Is the Influence of the Family versus Peer Groups in Adolescence?

Traditionally, the transition from childhood to adolescence has been pictured as the time when there is a shift of influence from the family to the peer group. This view maintained that while peer group membership was important during childhood, the family was the primary source of status, nurturance, and information. With the onset of adolescence, however, as children begin striving for independence from the family, it was assumed that they looked exclusively to peer relationships outside the home for the recognition, satisfaction, and information they had formerly found with their parents (Glynn, 1981).

It is now felt that this is probably too simple a description. Several factors suggest that it is inaccurate to assume that either family or peers have an "exclusive" influence at any point in a child's development. First, inevitable differences exist among children in their susceptibility to group pressures to conform. Individuals with high self-esteem and confidence in their social skills, for example, are less likely to accept unthinkingly the dictates of the group and "go along." In contrast, those who respond more strongly to the status of those speaking rather than the content of what is said are more willing to acquiesce to group standards (Hartup, 1983). Adolescents with high educational aspirations are more likely to seek help for a problem from their parents, whereas adolescents with low aspirations generally turn to the peer group (Tillery, Sherman, & Donovan, 1968).

Not only do children differ in their susceptibility to group influence, but parents vary in the influence they exert on their adolescents. Baumrind (1967, 1971) studied the relationship of parental discipline styles to the internalization of parental values and attitudes. She divided parental discipline styles into six categories: (1) *autocratic*—parents dictate how the child should behave without any consideration of the child's point of view; (2) *authoritarian*—parents discuss disciplinary matters with the child, but the child's wishes do not influence parental decisions; (3) *authoritative*—parents discuss disciplinary matters freely and openly with the child and consider the child's point of view while retaining the "final word"; (4) *egalitarian*—parents share decision-making power equally with the child; (5) *permissive*—parents leave decisions to the discretion of the child; and (6) *laissez-faire*—parents do not respond to the child's rejection of or compliance with their wishes.

She found that children with authoritative parents exhibit a relatively low frequency of problem behavior and are high in self-esteem, confidence, and responsible independence. These parents generally establish reasonable rules, legitimate them through clear explanations, and offer unconditional emotional support and affection to their children. In contrast, children of autocratic or authoritarian parents were more likely to reject parental standards or view their rules and principles as unreasonable or wrong. On the other hand, laissez-faire or permissive parents generally encouraged a lack of social responsibility in their children and rarely fostered independent, self-reliant behavior that was oriented toward high standards of achievement (Baumrind, 1971; Burke & Weir, 1977; Glueck & Glueck, 1950; Maccoby, 1980).

Last, peer and parental influences are frequently situation-specific. Peers tend to have more of an immediate influence on an adolescent's behavior by reinforcing, for example, the use of slang or the adherence to the current style of dress. In contrast to these "present-oriented" topics, parents tend to have more influence on "future-oriented" behaviors, such as planning to attend college (Burke & Weir, 1977; Glynn, 1981).

What Accounts for Juvenile Delinquency?

Studies have shown that exposure to delinquent behaviors as well as to attitudes in favor of violating the law predicts an individual's own involvement in delinquent activities. Consequently, both the number of delinquent friends one has and the amount of "trouble" in the neighborhood are associated with the adoption of delinquent attitudes and behaviors (Jensen, 1972). Delinquents often form gangs that engage in and encourage illegal activities. However, Glueck and Glueck (1950) found that nearly half of the delinquents they studied were engaging in criminal behavior before age 8 and before frequent gang participation. This casts doubt that the adolescent gang alone is the cause of juvenile delinquency.

Delinquent behavior can be traced, in part, to family environment and disciplinary approaches. Parents of delinquent children are often, in Baumrind's terms, laissez-faire or autocratic in their discipline techniques and rarely reason with their children about the consequences of misbehavior or the reasons why doing certain things is wrong. The family environment associated with delinquency is marked by hostility, a lack of cohesiveness, or apathy (Glueck & Glueck, 1950).

The overall incidence of delinquency is higher in low socioeconomic groups and urban areas, although delinquency is on the rise among middle-class, suburban youth as well (Mussen et al., 1984). As early as the third grade, future delinquents display less acceptable social behaviors, have more academic difficulties, and suffer from more emotional problems than children who do not go on to break the law. Delinquents generally do not enjoy close personal relationships with peers and are less interested in school parties and organizations (Conger, Miller, & Walsmith, 1970).

No single factor is unambiguously associated with juvenile delinquency. Peers, parents, and the larger social environment are all implicated in its development.

What Roles Do the Family and Peer Groups Play in Encouraging Adolescent Drug Use?

The use of drugs (including alcohol and marijuana) is continually a source of intense and emotional conflicts between adolescents and adults. More adolescents are consuming larger quantities of alcohol at ever younger ages. Today, at least half of all 18- to 21-year-olds have experimented with marijuana. Kandel and her colleagues (Kandel, 1973; Kandel, Kessler, & Margulies, 1978; Davies & Kandel, 1981) have attempted to trace the influence of peers and family on drug use during adolescence. They posit three stages of drug usage: (1) initiation into hard liquor consumption, (2) initiation into marijuana use, and (3) initiation into the use of other illicit drugs. In general, this and other research has found that an adolescent's initiation into any stage of drug usage is not *entirely* influenced by either the family or by peers.

The peer group can increase drug availability, provide opportunities for initiating drug use, and reinforce attitudes favoring drug consumption. The influence of the family, in contrast, flows primarily from the quality of the parent-child relationship and the emotional support children receive at home. Familial influences are thus exerted long before adolescents encounter external pressure from the peer group. Family influence can continue during adolescence—depending, of course, on the family—and results from the general climate and patterns of family interactions as well as the parents' response to drug availability and use (Glynn, 1981).

Do Peer Groups Affect Students' Academic Behavior, Educational Aspirations, and Attitudes toward Schooling?

In general, students who are intelligent, whose parents went to college, and whose friends want to go to college are more likely to continue their education beyond high school (Bain & Anderson, 1974). College-bound youth also tend to have more positive attitudes toward teachers, demonstrate greater desires to master material, and exhibit fewer delinquent behaviors. Relationships, both in the family and in the peer group, have an effect on students' academic performance and the establishment of high educational aspirations (Spenner & Featherman, 1978).

Children and adolescents tend to have friends who are similar to themselves in areas such as need for achievement and self-confidence—personality factors that relate to educational performance and aspirations. Such similarities can strengthen individuals' educational attitudes and expectations. In addition, the extent to which positive attitudes toward school and education are espoused within a peer group is often reflected in an individual's own educational aspirations (Tesser & Campbell, 1982). Peer group attitudes not only affect students' desire to attend college but also influence their assessment of their *ability* to complete college successfully (Bain & Anderson, 1974; Ide, Parkerson, Haertel, & Walberg, 1981). Females seem to be more sensitive to peer pressure than males and thus may be more susceptible to peer influence in the formation of future life plans (Davies & Kandel, 1981; Kandel & Lesser, 1970).

Although the attitudes and college aspirations of a student's friends and associates affect educational plans, parents' educational aspirations for their children seem to play a more significant role. The number of years of schooling to which adolescents aspire relates more closely to parental expectations than the aspirations of their friends (Davies & Kandel, 1981). Parents' occupation and education and the presence of science equipment in the home clearly influence motivation and performance in science and math more than the peers' attitudes toward the subject (Kremer & Walberg, 1981). Rather than declining as the adolescent matures, the importance of parents' expectations for college attendance and achievement, when compared to the importance of peer expectations, seems to increase over time (Davies & Kandel, 1981). Interestingly, parental aspirations for their children's education tend to be based on the number of years the parents spent in college or on their social class rather than on the actual school performance of their child. This may encourage students to hold unrealistic expectations for college acceptance and future academic success.

FURTHER READING

Asher, S. R., & Gottman, J. M. (Eds.). (1981). *The Development of Children's Friendships.* Cambridge, England: Cambridge University Press. This collection brings together current work in psychology, education, and sociology devoted to understanding children's changing relationships to their peers. Questions addressed include, How does children's thinking about friendship develop over time? How does this thinking influence behavior? What social skills underlie peer acceptance? How can acceptance and friendship be fostered between children of different races or intellectual ability? Of particular interest is Asher and Renshaw's article "Children without Friends: Social Knowledge and Social Skill Training," which discusses the identification of social isolates in elementary school classrooms and a coaching technique used to improve the status of children who find it difficult to make friends.

Epstein, J. L., & Karweit, N. (Eds.). (1978). *Friends in School: Patterns of Selection and Influence in Secondary Schools.* Orlando, FL: Academic Press. Examines relationships of the social organization of secondary schools and classrooms, the processes of peer association, friendship selection and social influence, and the social development of students. Of particular interest are discussions of theories of adolescent friendship (Chapter 3), the influence of friends on learning and emotional growth (Chapter 11), the relationship of friendship choice to school and classroom organization (Chapter 5), and participation in extracurricular activities (Chapter 8).

Good, T. L., & Marshall, S. (1984). "Do Students Learn More in Heterogeneous or Homogeneous Groups?" In P. Peterson, L. C. Wilkinson, & M. Hallinan (Eds.), *The Social Context of Instruction: Group Organization and Group Processes.* Orlando, FL: Academic Press. Good and Marshall examine 60 years of studies on ability grouping and consider the complexities inherent in this research. They conclude that the weight of evidence is against ability grouping at both the elementary and high school levels because of its detrimental effect on the learning of low-ability students and the fact that it does not provide convincing learning gains for high-ability students. They point out that it is not necessarily easier (and may be more difficult) to teach students in several small groups rather than in one large group. While not advocating the complete abandonment of classroom ability grouping, the authors urge teachers to "assess carefully their reasons for grouping, and how adequately grouping enables them to meet instructional goals" (p. 32).

Hartup, W. W. (1983). "Peer Relations." In P. Mussen (Ed.), *Handbook of Child Psychology* (4th ed.): *Vol. 4. Socialization, Personality, and Social Development.* New York: Wiley. As part of a comprehensive manual of developmental psychology, Hartup reviews recent research concerning peer relations and friendship and provides a historical and theoretical background to the field. A variety of topics are covered: same-age versus mixed-age interactions, the development of friendships, popularity and isolation, group interactions, the peer group as a factor in the socialization process, and differences among children in social skills and relations.

Klaus, D. J. (1975). *Patterns for Peer Tutoring: Final Report.* Washington, DC: American Institutes for Research in the Behavioral Sciences. (ERIC Document Reproduction Service No. ED 117 695). Teachers wishing to implement peer-tutoring programs in their own classrooms will find this report extremely valuable. It combines descriptions of ongoing tutoring programs with considerations of relevant research and theory and guides teachers in the development of their own tutoring programs. The bibliography is extensive.

Mussen, P. H., Conger, J. J., Kagan, J., & Huston, A. C. (1984). *Child Development and Personality* (6th ed.). New York: Harper & Row. An excellent source of information about theoretical issues as well as the implications and applications of basic research. Traces human development chronologically through infancy, early childhood, childhood, and adolescence while exploring social concerns such as child abuse, adequate day care, drug abuse, and the problems faced by physically and mentally handicapped children.

Schmuck, R. A., & Schmuck, P. A. (1983). *Group Processes in the Classroom.* Dubuque, IA: Brown. The authors apply the results of social psychological research on small groups to the classroom in a readable, jargon-free manner. Their topics include the stages of group development, leadership, friendship and cohesiveness, norms, communication, conflict, and the school as an organization. After discussing research relevant to each topic, they draw specific implications for teachers and provide "action ideas" and exercises for translating research results into classroom practice.

Slavin, R. E. (1983). *Cooperative Learning.* White Plains, NY: Longman. A well-organized and thoughtful review of research on classroom cooperative learning techniques. Although the writing is dense, chapter summaries provide access to the author's conclusions.

REFERENCES

Adams, G. R. (1978). Racial membership and physical attractiveness effects on preschool teachers' expectations. *Child Study Journal, 8,* 29–41.

Ainsworth, M. D. (1972). Attachment and dependency: A comparison. In J. L. Gewirtz (Ed.), *Attachment and dependency.* New York: Wiley

Alexander, K., & McDill, E. L. (1976). Selection and allocation within schools: Some causes and consequences of curriculum placement. *American Sociological Review, 41,* 963–980.

Allen, V. L. (1981). Self, social group, and social structure: Surmises about the study of children's friendships. In S. R. Asher & J. M. Gottman (Eds.), *The development of children's friendships.* Cambridge, England: Cambridge University Press.

Allen, V. L., & Newtson, D. (1972). Development of conformity and independence. *Journal of Personality and Social Psychology, 22,* 18–30.

Ames, C. (1981). Competitive vs. cooperative reward structures: The influence of individual and group performance factors on achievement attributions and affect. *American Educational Research Journal, 18,* 273–287.

Ames, C., Ames, R., & Felker, D. W. (1977). Effects of competitive reward structure and valence of outcome on children's achievement attributions. *Journal of Educational Psychology, 69,* 1–8.

Aronson, E., Blaney, N., Stephan, C., Sikes, J., & Snapp, M. (1978). *The jigsaw classroom.* Beverly Hills, CA: Sage.

Asher, S. R. (1983). Social competence and peer status: Recent advances and future directions. *Child Development, 54,* 1427–1434.

Asher, S. R., Oden, S. L., & Gottman, J. M. (1977). Children's friendships in school settings. In L. G. Katz (Ed.), *Current topics in early childhood education* (Vol. 1). Norwood, NJ: Ablex.

Asher, S. R., & Renshaw, P. D. (1981). Children without friends: Social knowledge and social skill training. In S. R. Asher & J. M. Gottman (Eds.), *The development of children's friendships.* Cambridge, England: Cambridge University Press.

Austin, A. B., & Draper, D. C. (1981). Peer relations of the academically gifted. *Gifted Child Quarterly, 25*(3), 129–133.

Bain, R. K., & Anderson, J. G. (1974). School context and peer influences on educational plans of adolescents. *Review of Educational Research, 44,* 429–445.

Bargh, J. A., & Schul, Y. (1980). On the cognitive benefits of teaching. *Journal of Educational Psychology, 72,* 593–604.

Barker, R. G., & Gump, P. G. (1964). *Big school, small school: High school size and student behavior.* Stanford, CA: Stanford University Press.

Baumrind, D. (1967). Child care practices anteceding three patterns of preschool behavior. *Genetic Psychology Monographs, 75,* 43–88.

Baumrind, D. (1971). Current patterns of parental authority. *Developmental Psychology Monographs, 4*(1, Pt. 2), 1–103.

Berndt, T. J. (1981). Relations between social cognition, nonsocial cognition, and social behavior: The case of friendship. In J. H. Flavell & L. D. Ross (Eds.), *Social cognitive development: Frontiers and possible futures.* Cambridge, England: Cambridge University Press.

Berndt, T. J. (1982). Fairness and friendship. In K. H. Rubin & H. S. Ross (Eds.), *Peer relationships and social skills in childhood.* New York: Springer-Verlag.

Berndt, T. J. (1983). Social cognition, social behavior, and children's friendships. In E. T. Higgins, D. N. Ruble, & W. W. Hartup (Eds.), *Social cognition and social development.* Cambridge, England: Cambridge University Press.

Bloom, J. R., & Schuncke, G. M. (1979). A cooperative curriculum experience and choice of task organization. *Journal of Experimental Education, 48,* 84–90.

Blumenfeld, P. C., Mergendoller, J. R., & Swarthout, D. W. (in press). Tasks as heuristics for understanding student learning and motivation. *Journal of Curriculum Studies.*

Bossert, S. T. (1979). *Tasks and social relationships in classrooms: A study of instructional organization and its consequences.* Cambridge, England: Cambridge University Press.

Bridgeman, D. L. (1981). Enhanced role taking through cooperative independence: A field study. *Child Development, 52,* 1231–1238.

Bryant, B. K. (1977). The effects of the interpersonal context of evaluation on self- and other-enhancement behavior. *Child Development, 48,* 885–892.

Burke, J., & Weir, T. (1977, April). *Helping responses of parents and peers and adolescents' well-being.* Paper presented at the annual meeting of the Western Psychological Association, Seattle.

Cartwright, D. (1968). The nature of group cohesiveness. In D. Cartwright & A. Zander (Eds.), *Group dynamics* (3rd ed.). New York: Harper & Row.

Cavior, N., & Lombardi, D. A. (1973). Developmental aspects of judgment of physical attractiveness in children. *Developmental Psychology, 8*, 67–71.

Clements, B. S., & Evertson, C. M. (1982). *Orchestrating small group instruction in elementary school classrooms.* Austin: University of Texas, Research and Development Center for Teacher Education.

Clifford, M. M., & Walster, E. (1973). The effects of physical attractiveness on teacher expectations. *Sociology of Education, 46*, 248–258.

Cloward, R. (1976). Studies in tutoring. *Journal of Experimental Education, 36*, 14–25.

Coie, J. D., & Kupersmidt, J. B. (1983). A behavioral analysis of emerging social status in boys' groups. *Child Development, 54*, 1400–1416.

Conger, J. J., Miller, W. C., & Walsmith, C. R. (1970). Antecedents of delinquency: Personality, social class, and intelligence. In P. H. Mussen, J. J. Conger, & J. Kagan (Eds.), *Readings in child development and personality* (2nd ed.). New York: Harper & Row.

Cooper, C. R., Marquis, A., & Ayers-Lopez, S. (1982). Peer learning in the classroom: Tracing developmental patterns and consequences of children's spontaneous interactions. In L. C. Wilkinson (Ed.), *Communicating in the classroom.* Orlando, FL: Academic Press.

Corsaro, W. A. (1981). Friendship in the nursery school: Social organization in a peer environment. In S. R. Asher & J. M. Gottman (Eds.), *The development of children's friendships.* Cambridge, England: Cambridge University Press.

Cotton, J. L., & Cook, M. S. (1982). Meta-analyses and the effects of various reward systems: Some different conclusions from Johnson et al. *Psychological Bulletin, 92*, 176–183.

Cowles, J. D., & Daniel, K. B. (1974, August). *Comparative study of certain social and school adjustments of children in two grouping plans.* Paper presented at the annual convention of the American Psychological Association, New Orleans.

Damico, S. (1974). *Education by peers: A clique study.* Gainsville, FL: University of Florida, P. K. Younge Laboratory School. (ERIC Document Reproduction Service No. ED 104 981)

Davies, M., & Kandel, D. B. (1981). Parental and peer influence on adolescents' educational plans: Some further evidence. *American Journal of Sociology, 87*, 363–387.

de Charms, R. (1983). Intrinsic motivation, peer tutoring, and cooperative learning: Practical maxims. In J. M. Levine & M. C. Wang (Eds.), *Teacher and student perceptions: Implications for learning.* Hillsdale, NJ: Erlbaum.

De Vries, D. L., & Mescon, I. T. (1975). *Teams-games-tournaments: An effective task and reward structure in the elementary grades* (Report No. 189). Baltimore: Johns Hopkins University, Center for Social Organization of Schools.

De Vries, D. L., & Slavin, R. E. (1978). Teams-games-tournaments (TGT): Review of ten classroom experiments. *Journal of Research and Development in Education, 12*(1), 28–38.

Doyle, W. (1979). Making managerial decisions in the classroom. In D. L. Duke (Ed.), *Classroom management.* 78th yearbook of the National Society for the Study of Education, Part II. Chicago: University of Chicago Press.

Eder, D. (1982, March). *Peer influence on student attentiveness during classroom lessons.* Paper presented at the annual meeting of the American Educational Research Association, New York.

Elias, K. M. (1982). *Peer interaction: A method of creating voice in writing.* Unpublished manuscript, University of Connecticut, Storrs. (ERIC Document Reproduction Service No. ED 216 356)

Eminovich, C. A. (1981, April). *Shall we cooperate or compete? Social interaction in two integrated kindergartens.* Paper presented at the annual meeting of the American Educational Research Association, Los Angeles.

Epstein, J. L. (1978). *Friends in school: Patterns of selection and influence in secondary schools.* Baltimore: Johns Hopkins University, Center for Social Organization of Schools. (ERIC Document Reproduction Service No. ED 170 198)

Fine, G. A. (1981). Friends, impression management, and preadolescent behavior. In S. R. Asher & J. M. Gottman (Eds.), *The development of children's friendships*. Cambridge, England: Cambridge University Press.

Fogarty, J. L., & Wang, M. C. (1982). An investigation of the cross-age peer tutoring process: Some implications for instructional design and motivation. *Elementary School Journal, 82,* 451–469.

Furman, W. (1982). Children's friendships. In T. M. Field, A. Huston, H. C. Quay, L. Troll, & G. E. Finley (Eds.), *Reviewing human development*. New York: Wiley.

Garbarino, J. (1975). The impact of anticipated reward upon cross-age tutoring. *Journal of Personality and Social Psychology, 32,* 421–428.

Glueck, S., & Glueck, E. (1950). *Unraveling juvenile delinquency*. Cambridge, MA: Harvard University Press.

Glynn, T. J. (1981). From family to peer: A review of transitions of influence among drug-using youth. *Journal of Youth and Adolescence, 10,* 363–383.

Good, T. L., & Marshall, S. (1984). Do students learn more in heterogeneous or homogeneous groups? In P. Peterson, L. C. Wilkinson, & M. Hallinan (Eds.), *The social context of instruction: Group organization and group processes*. Orlando, FL: Academic Press.

Gottlieb, J. (1975). Public, peer and professional attitudes toward mentally retarded persons. In M. J. Begab & S. A. Richardson (Eds.), *The mentally retarded and society: A social science perspective*. Baltimore: University Park Press.

Gottlieb, J. (1980). Improving attitudes toward retarded children by using group discussion. *Exceptional Children, 47,* 106–111.

Gottlieb, J., & Leyser, Y. (1981). Friendship between mentally retarded and non-retarded children. In S. R. Asher & J. M. Gottman (Eds.), *The development of children's friendships*. Cambridge, England: Cambridge University Press.

Gottlieb, J., Semmel, M. I., & Veldman, D. J. (1978). Correlates of social status among mainstreamed mentally retarded children. *Journal of Educational Psychology, 70,* 396–405.

Gottman, J. M. (1977). Toward a definition of social isolation in children. *Child Development, 48,* 513–517.

Gottman, J. M., Gonso, J., & Schuler, P. (1976). Teaching social skills to isolated children. *Journal of Abnormal Child Psychology, 4,* 179–197.

Hallinan, M. T. (1973). *The effect of the structural organization of classroom on the cohesiveness of student peer groups*. Washington, DC: National Institute of Education.

Hallinan, M. T. (1979). Structural effects on children's friendships and cliques. *Social Psychology Quarterly, 42*(1), 43–54.

Hansell, S., Tackaberry, S. N., & Slavin, R. E. (1981). *Cooperation, competition, and the structure of student cliques* (Report No. 309). Baltimore: Johns Hopkins University, Center for Social Organization of Schools.

Hartup, W. W. (1983). Peer relations. In P. Mussen (Ed.), *Handbook of child psychology* (4th ed.): *Vol. 4. Socialization, personality, and social development*. New York: Wiley.

Hayes, D. S. (1978). Cognitive bases for liking and disliking among preschool children. *Child Development, 49,* 906–909.

Hetherington, E. M., & Morris, W. M. (1978). The family and primary groups. In W. H. Holtzman (Ed.), *Introductory psychology in depth: Developmental topics*. New York: Harper & Row.

Howe, A. C., & Durr, B. (1982). Using concrete materials and peer interaction to enhance learning in chemistry. *Journal of Research in Science Teaching, 19,* 225–232.

Ide, J. K., Parkerson, J., Haertel, G. D., & Walberg, H. J. (1981). Peer group influences on educational outcomes: A quantitative synthesis. *Journal of Educational Psychology, 73,* 472–484.

Jensen, G. F. (1972). Parents, peers, and delinquent action: A test of the differential association perspective. *American Journal of Sociology, 78,* 562–575.

Johnson, D. W. (1975). Cooperativeness and social perspective taking. *Journal of Personality and Social Psychology, 31,* 241–244.

Johnson, D. W. (1980). Group processes: Influences of student-student interactions on school outcomes. In J. McMillan (Ed.), *The social psychology of learning.* Orlando, FL: Academic Press.

Johnson, D. W., & Johnson, R. T. (1975). *Learning together and alone: Cooperation, competition, and individualization.* Englewood Cliffs, NJ: Prentice-Hall.

Johnson, D. W., & Johnson, R. T. (1980). Integrating handicapped students into the mainstream. *Exceptional Children, 47,* 90–98.

Johnson, D. W., & Johnson, R. T. (1982, March). *The internal dynamics of cooperative learning groups.* Paper presented at the annual meeting of the American Educational Research Association, New York.

Johnson, D. W., Johnson, R. T., & Maruyama, G. (1983). Interdependence and interpersonal attraction among hetereogeneous and homogeneous individuals: A theoretical formulation and a meta-analysis of the research. *Review of Educational Research, 53,* 5–54.

Johnson, D. W., Johnson, R. T., & Scott, L. (1978). The effects of cooperative vs. individualized instruction on student attitudes and achievement. *Journal of Social Psychology, 104,* 207–216.

Johnson, D. W., Maruyama, G., Johnson, R. T., Nelson, D., & Skon, L. (1981). Effects of cooperative, competitive, and individualistic goal structures on achievement: A meta-analysis. *Psychological Bulletin, 89,* 47–62.

Johnson, J. A. (1979). Learning in peer tutoring interactions: The influence of status, role change, time-on-task, feedback, and verbalization. (Doctoral dissertation, University of California, Los Angeles). Dissertation Abstracts International, 39, 5469A–5470A. (University Microfilms No. 79-06, 175)

Kandel, D. B. (1973). Adolescent marijuana use: Role of parents and peers. *Science, 181,* 1067–1070.

Kandel, D. B., Kessler, R. C., & Margulies, R. S. (1978). Antecedents of adolescent initiation into stages of drug use: A developmental analysis. *Journal of Youth and Adolescence, 7,* 13–40.

Kandel, D. B., & Lesser, G. S. (1970). School, family and peer influences on educational plans of adolescents in the U.S. and Denmark. *Sociology of Education, 43,* 270–287.

Karweit, N. L. (1976). Student friendship networks as a within-school resource. Unpublished doctoral dissertation, Johns Hopkins University, Baltimore.

Karweit, N. L., Hansell, S., & Ricks, M. A. (1979). *The conditions for peer associations in schools.* Baltimore: Johns Hopkins University, Center for Social Organization of Schools. (ERIC Document Reproduction Service No. ED 186 790)

Klaus, D. J. (1975a, March). *Patterns for peer tutoring.* Paper presented at the annual meeting of the American Educational Research Association, Washington, DC. (ERIC Document Reproduction Service No. ED 103 356)

Klaus, D. J. (1975b). *Patterns for peer tutoring: Final report.* Washington, DC: American Institutes for Research in the Behavioral Sciences. (ERIC Document Reproduction Service No. ED 117 695)

Klein, A. R., & Young, R. D. (1979). Hyperactive boys in the classroom: Assessment of teacher and peer perceptions, interactions, and classroom behaviors. *Journal of Abnormal Child Psychology, 7,* 425–442.

Kremer, B. K., & Walberg, H. J. (1981). A synthesis of social and psychological influences on science learning. *Science Education, 65*(1), 1–23.

Ladd, G. W. (1979, March). *Social skills and peer acceptance: Effects of a social learning method for training verbal social skills.* Paper presented at the biennial meeting of the

Society for Research in Child Development, San Francisco. (ERIC Document Reproduction Service No. ED 172 940)

Lamb, E., & Roopnarine, J. L. (1979). Peer influences on sex role development in preschoolers. *Child Development, 50*, 1219–1222.

Landsbaum, J. B., & Willis, R. H. (1971). Conformity in early and late adolescence. *Developmental Psychology, 4*, 334–337.

Lesser, G. S., & Abelson, R. P. (1959). Personality correlates of persuasibility in children. In C. I. Horland & I. L. Janis (Eds.), *Personality and persuasibility*. New Haven, CT: Yale University Press.

Lewis, M., & Rosenblum, L. A. (Eds.). (1975). *Friendship and peer relations*. New York: Wiley.

Lewis, M., Young, G., Brooks, J., & Michalson, L. (1975). The beginning of friendship. In M. Lewis & L. Rosenblum (Eds.), *Friendship and peer relations*. New York: Wiley.

Lucker, W. G., Rosenfield, D., Sikes, J., & Aronson, E. (1976). Performance in the interdependent classroom: A field study. *American Educational Research Journal, 13*, 115–123.

Maccoby, E. E. (1980). *Social development: Psychological growth and the parent-child relationship*. Orlando, FL: Harcourt Brace Jovanovich.

Mainville, F., & Friedman, R. J. (1976). Peer relations of hyperactive children. *Ontario Psychologist, 8*, 17–20.

Mason, G. A. (1974). Ability grouping: An ethnographic study of a structural feature of schools. *Australian and New Zealand Journal of Sociology, 83* 58–77.

McMichael, P. (1980). Reading difficulties, behavior, and social status. *Journal of Educational Psychology, 72*, 76–86.

Mergendoller, J. R., & Mitman, A. L. (1985). The relationship of middle school program features, instructional strategy, instructional performance, and student engagement. *Journal of Early Adolescence, 5*, 183–196.

Metz, M. (1978). *Classrooms and corridors: The crisis of authority in desegregated secondary schools*. Berkeley: University of California Press.

Miller, L. K., & Hamblin, R. L. (1983). Interdependence, differential rewarding, and productivity. *American Sociological Review, 28*, 768–778.

Miller, N., & Maruyama, G. (1976). Ordinal position and peer popularity. *Journal of Personality and Social Psychology, 33*, 123–131.

Moskowitz, J. M., Malvin, J. H., Schaeffer, G. A., & Schaps, E. (1983). Evaluation of a cooperative learning strategy. *American Educational Research Journal, 20*, 687–696.

Mussen, P. H., Conger, J. J., Kagan, J., & Huston, A. C. (1984). *Child development and personality* (6th ed.). New York: Harper & Row.

Oden, S. (1982). Peer relationship development in childhood. In L. Katz (Ed.), *Current topics in early childhood education* (Vol. 4). Norwood, NJ: Ablex.

Ogbu, J. U. (1974). *The next generation: An ethnography of education in an urban neighborhood*. Orlando, FL: Academic Press.

Pelham, W. E., & Bender, M. E. (1982). Peer relationships in hyperactive children: Description and treatment. In K. D. Gordon & I. Bialer (Eds.), *Advances in learning and behavior disabilities*. Greenwich, CT: JAI Press.

Persell, C. (1977). *Education and inequality: The roots and results of stratification in America's schools*. New York: Free Press.

Rist, R. (1970). Student social class and teacher expectations: The self-fulfilling prophecy in ghetto education. *Harvard Educational Review, 40*, 411–451.

Roff, M. (1961). Childhood social interaction and young adult bad conduct. *Journal of Abnormal and Social Psychology, 63*, 333–337.

Roff, M., Sells, S. B., & Golden, M. M. (1972). *Social adjustment and personality development in children*. Minneapolis: University of Minneapolis Press.

Rosen, S., & Powell, R. (1977). *Classroom organizational restructuring to optimize social-

emotional and cognitive growth: Final report. Washington, DC: National Institute of Education. (ERIC Document Reproduction Service No. ED 163 330)

Rosenbaum, J. E. (1980). Social implications of educational grouping. In D. C. Berliner (Ed.), *Review of research in education, 8*, 361–401.

Rosenholtz, S., & Simpson, C. (1985). Elementary classroom structure and the social construction of ability. In J. G. Richardson (Ed.), *Handbook of theory and research in the sociology of education*. Westport, CT: Greenwich Press.

Rynders, J. E., Johnson, R. T., Johnson, D. W., & Schmidt, B. (1980). Producing positive interaction among Down syndrome and nonhandicapped teenagers through cooperative goal structuring. *American Journal of Mental Deficiency, 85*, 268–273.

Savin-Williams, R. C. (1979). Dominance hierarchies in groups of early adolescents. *Child Development, 50*, 923–935.

Schmuck, R. A., & Schmuck, P. A. (1983). *Group processes in the classroom*. Dubuque, IA: Brown.

Schulman, J. L., Ford, R. C., Busk, P., & Kaspar, J. C. (1973). Evaluation of a classroom program to alter friendship practices. *Journal of Education Research, 67*, 99–102.

Schwartz, F. (1981). Supporting or subverting learning: Peer group patterns in four tracked schools. *Anthropology and Education Quarterly, 12*, 99–121.

Sells, S. B., & Roff, M. (1964). Peer acceptance-rejection and birth order. *Psychology in the Schools, 1*, 156–162.

Sharon, S., & Sharon, Y. (1976). *Small group teaching*. Englewood Cliffs, NJ: Educational Technology Publications.

Sherif, M., Harvey, O. J., White, B. J., Hood, W. R., & Sherif, C. W. (1961). *Inter-group conflict and cooperation: The Robbers Cave experiment*. Norman, OK: University of Oklahoma Press.

Sherif, M., & Sherif, C. W. (1953). *Groups in harmony and tension*. New York: Harper & Row.

Shimahara, N. K. (1982, March). *Polarized socialization*. Paper presented at the annual meeting of the American Educational Research Association, New York. (ERIC Document Reproduction Service No. ED 218 552)

Slavin, R. E. (1980). Cooperative learning. *Review of Educational Research, 50*, 315–342.

Slavin, R. E. (1981). Synthesis of research on cooperative learning. *Educational Leadership, 38*, 655–660.

Slavin, R. E. (1983a). *Cooperative learning*. White Plains, NY: Longman.

Slavin, R. E. (1983b). Non-cognitive outcomes of cooperative learning. In J. M. Levine & M. C. Wang (Eds.), *Teacher and student perceptions: Implications for learning*. Hillsdale, NJ: Erlbaum.

Slavin, R. E. (1983c). When does cooperative learning increase student achievement? *Psychological Bulletin, 94*, 429–445.

Slavin, R. E., & Karweit, N. L. (1982). *Student teams and mastery learning: A factorial experiment in nine urban math classes* (Report No. 320). Baltimore: Johns Hopkins University, Center for Social Organization of Schools.

Slavin, R. E., & Madden, N. A. (1979). School practices that improve race relations. *American Educational Research Journal, 16*, 169–180.

Smoller, J., & Youniss, J. (1982). Social development through friendship. In K. H. Rubin & H. S. Ross (Eds.), *Peer relationships and social skills in childhood*. New York: Springer-Verlag.

Spenner, K. I., & Featherman, D. L. (1978). Achievement ambitions. In R. Turner, J. Coleman, & R. Fox (Eds.), *Annual review of sociology* (Vol. 4). Palo Alto, CA: Annual Reviews.

Stager, S. F., & Young, R. D. (1981). Intergroup contact and social outcomes of mainstreamed EMR adolescents. *American Journal of Mental Deficiency, 85*, 497–503.

Stainback, W., Stainback, S., Raschke, D., & Anderson, R. J. (1981). Three methods for encouraging interactions between severely retarded and nonhandicapped students. *Education and Training of the Mentally Retarded, 16,* 188–192.

Styczynski, L. E., & Langlois, J. H. (1980). *Judging the book by its cover: Children's attractiveness and achievement.* Unpublished manuscript, University of Texas, Austin.

Swing, S. R., & Peterson, P. L. (1982). The relationship of student ability and small group interaction to student achievement. *American Educational Research Journal, 19,* 259–274.

Tesser, A., & Campbell, J. (1982). A self-evaluation maintenance approach to school behavior. *Educational Psychologist, 17,* 1–12.

Tillery, D., Sherman, B., & Donovan, D. (1968, August). *Helpfulness of parents, school personnel, and peers to students with different educational aspirations.* Paper presented at the American Psychological Association Convention, San Francisco.

Webb, N. M. (1982, March). *Predicting learning from student interaction: Defining the interaction variables.* Paper presented at the annual meeting of the American Educational Research Association, New York.

Webb, N. M. (1984). Stability of small group interaction and achievement over time. *Journal of Educational Psychology, 76,* 211–224.

Webb, N. M., & Kenderski, C. M. (1984). Student interaction and learning in small-group and whole-class settings. In P. Peterson, L. C. Wilkinson, & M. Hallinan (Eds.), *The social context of instruction: Group organization and group processes.* Orlando, FL: Academic Press.

Whiting, B. B., & Whiting, J. M. (1975). *Children of six cultures.* Cambridge, MA: Harvard University Press.

Wilkinson, L. C., & Calculator, S. (1982). Effective speakers: Students' use of language to request and obtain information in the classroom. In L. C. Wilkinson (Ed.), *Communicating in the classroom.* Orlando, FL: Academic Press.

Wilkinson, L. C., & Dollaghan, C. (1980). Peer communication in first-grade reading groups. *Theory into Practice, 18,* 267–274.

Wilkinson, L. C., & Spinelli, F. (1983). Using requests effectively in peer-directed instructional groups. *American Educational Research Journal, 20,* 479–501.

Willis, J., Morris, B., & Crowder, J. (1972). A remedial reading technique for disabled readers that employs students as behavioral engineers. *Psychology in the Schools, 6,* 67–70.

13 SEX-RELATED DIFFERENCES IN EDUCATION: MYTHS, REALITIES, AND INTERVENTIONS

Elizabeth Fennema

One's gender should not determine what one learns in school. However, schools have not yet met that challenge. Certainly schools alone do not determine what girls and boys learn; society exerts a large influence. The media, church, and family must accept a major portion of the responsibility for the inequities that exist in education. Recognition of that fact does not help a great deal. But even though schools and their personnel cannot change the media, the church, and the family, they can change themselves.

Though it is commonly believed that females and males are treated in a more egalitarian way in schools than in other institutions, in reality schools are training girls and boys to believe that males and females should play specific, well-defined roles in society. Females, it is taught, are better suited for subordinate roles, and males are more suited for leadership roles. This is not a new situation. Since the beginning of the country, the unstated goals of education have included training males and females for the separate and not equal spheres of men's and women's lives. Women's sphere comprises dependent, helpful, nurturant, and domestic behaviors. The hidden purpose of schools is to educate females "for dutiful and dependent lives for subordination and powerlessness" (Greene, 1984, p. 21).

While some women, and even a few men, have recognized the inherent inequity of forcing females and males to function in their own well-defined spheres, most females and males have accepted this idea, and many women continue to believe in the rightness of their own oppression. When women have stepped outside their own sphere of spirituality, domesticity, and dependency, they have been considered aberrant and perceived as less feminine. The same is true of men: When they take over a homemaker's role, become a nurse, or work in some other "typically female" occupation, they are considered by many as emasculated.

Before the twentieth century, goals of education for females and males were explicit. Rousseau stated that "the whole of education of women ought to be relative to men" (Boyd, 1960, pp. 134–135). Catherine Beecher, an early advocate of education for females, suggested that in order to do their "proper work," females should be trained to be good housewives. It was more important that women be "virtuous, useful, and pious than that they become learned and accomplished" (quoted in Greene, 1984, p. 26). Females were to be educated, if at all, to become the helpmates of males and parents of future generations. As an extension of this latter role, women were also educated to be teachers, particularly for the elementary school. However, they were accorded little respect and less money, ensuring that their role would remain separate, subordinate, and unequal to that of men.

To most people in the field of education today, such overt, explicit notions about the education of females seem humorous and archaic. Public schools in the United States have been coeducational since about 1850. The stated goals of education are the same for both sexes. Boys and girls are taught in the same classes, apparently have the right to elect the same courses in high school, and are attending postsecondary education at about the same rate. Civil rights legislation, originally designed to protect ethnic groups, has been broadened to prohibit discrimination by sex. Affirmative action plans, in place in most school systems and universities, are designed to ensure equality of opportunity in administrative and academic positions.

If the overt goals of education are the same for boys and girls and educational opportunity is equal, the outcomes of schooling should be the same for females and males. This is one of the biggest myths in education today.

THE PROBLEM

Educational outcomes for females and males are not equal. Differences exist in specific cognitive and affective areas, and major differences exist in more general outcomes.

Cognitive Outcomes

Cognitive variables have to do with intellectual factors. It has long been assumed that there are certain cognitive areas in which females achieve at higher levels than do males and other areas where the reverse is true. It is so commonly accepted that girls are better at verbal skills such as reading (Leinhardt, Seewald, & Engel, 1979; Dwyer, 1973) that authors don't even bother to document the differences anymore. By the third or fourth grade, girls are one-third to one-half a grade level ahead of boys, and girls' superiority in a variety of verbal skills persists into high school and beyond (Bank, Biddle, & Good, 1980). Results from the second and third National Writing Assessments, conducted in 1974 and 1979, report female superiority in writing skills. These assessments, done with a large, national random sample, measured various narrative writing skills including those called humorous, persuasive, explanatory, and cohesive. The interpreters of the results state that "females wrote significantly more successful papers than males in each assessment with the exception of the humorous task. On that one, the males had an advantage in 1974, but lost it by 1979" (National Assessment of Educational Progress [NAEP], 1980, p. 1). "The male/female difference did not change appreciably for any age group" from 1974 to 1979 (p. 51).

The situation in mathematics and science achievement is reversed, with males achieving at higher levels than females. The onset of sex-related differences in mathematics occurs somewhat later than sex-related differences in verbal skills. Females and males perform at about the same level in early elementary school, but starting in the upper elementary years and lasting until adulthood, male superiority in mathematical tasks of high cognitive complexity, such as true problem solving, is found. Male superiority increases as the difficulty level of mathematics increases and is clearly evident even when the number of mathematics courses taken by girls and boys is held constant (Fennema, 1984).

There have been strong sex-related differences in the percentage of females and males who are enrolled in mathematics classes in secondary schools. In 1967, Husén reported that in the 12 countries studied in the International Study of Achievement, the ratio of males to females enrolled in mathematics at the end of secondary education ranged from 1.73 to 7.13, with an average ratio of 3.70 (p. 234). Basically, these data are similar to those reported by Fennema and Sherman (1977) in the United States in the 1974–1975 school year. The third National Mathematics Assessment reports results from a national sample on enrollment in high school mathematics courses by sex (Table 13.1) for two years. It should be noted that the

TABLE 13.1   CHANGES IN PERCENTAGES OF MALES AND FEMALES TAKING
MATHEMATICS COURSES, AGE 17

Course	Percentages of 17-Year-Olds Who Have Taken at Least ½ Year	
	Males	Females
Algebra 1		
1978	70.7	73.6
1982	69.4	72.2
Geometry		
1978	52.1	50.5
1982	51.8	51.8
Algebra 2		
1978	37.8	36.1
1982	38.9	38.0
Trigonometry		
1978	14.7	11.1
1982	15.0	12.7
Precalculus/Calculus		
1978	4.7	3.1
1982	4.7	3.6
Computer		
1978	5.9	4.1
1982	11.1	8.6

Source: National Assessment of Educational Progress. (1983). *Third National Mathematics Assessment: Results, Trends, and Issues* (Report No. 13-MA-01). Denver: Education Commission of the States.

male-female differential is not large at any time, but is largest in the most advanced classes. It is also known that enrollment patterns differ widely by school, with some schools reporting more females than males enrolled in advanced courses but many more schools reporting just the opposite. Although there continue to be differences in enrollment patterns between girls and boys, adult differences in mathematics-related careers cannot be totally traced to differences in course taking.

Science learning has also been measured by NAEP. While it is difficult to understand the magnitude and thus the importance of the differences, the data interpreters state that "the achievement level of males at each age was higher than that of females in all three assessments of science" (1969, 1972, 1976; NAEP, 1978, p. xiii).

Although results seem clear-cut, caution must be taken in drawing broad, general conclusions about sex-related differences in school achievement. Large data sets (such as NAEP) tend to disguise differences within smaller subgroups. Sex-related differences in mathematics achievement vary widely by school and even by state (see Fennema, 1984, for a more in-depth discussion). Results from certain schools show few sex-related differences in any area, while results from other schools show larger differences than have been reported here. For example, Fulkerson, Furr, and Brown (1983) found no sex-related differences in mathematics achievement in one large school system in grades 3, 6, or 9. The Profile of American Youth Study (Administration of the Armed Services Vocational Aptitude Battery [AASVAB], 1982), which used a large national sample, reported that the "mean estimated reading grade level for the total sample of males ($n = 5,944$, ages 14–20) was three months higher than the same score for females ($n = 5,934$)," while National Assessment results showed that males do read better than females (NAEP, 1981). Other discrepant results could be cited.

Are sex-related differences in verbal skills, science, or mathematics large enough so that educational change needs to be made to ensure equality of outcomes? The most quoted authorities to report cognitive differences between the sexes are Maccoby and Jacklin (1974), who concur that there are well-established sex-related differences in cognitive functioning, with boys excelling in mathematical abilities and girls excelling in verbal skills. They came to the conclusions they did because of the number of studies found that reported statistically significant differences in one direction. However, after performing a metanalysis of these studies, Hyde (1981) discovered that "the main conclusion that can be reached from the analysis is that the gender differences in verbal ability [and] quantitative ability...are all small" (pp. 895–896).

In other words, all cognitive differences between the sexes reported by Maccoby and Jacklin were, in reality, quite small. Figures 13.1 and 13.2 show two normal distribution curves that represent the magnitude of the sex differences in verbal ability (Figure 13.1) and mathematical abilities (Figure 13.2). As one can readily see, intrasex differences are much larger than intersex differences, and the overlap in performance is quite large.

Some cautions ought to be made concerning both the Maccoby-Jacklin and Hyde conclusions. Both sets of conclusions were drawn from approximately the same studies, done before 1972. The tests used to assess the various abilities varied greatly, and one must question the across-test construct validity. Verbal skills assessed varied from reading comprehension to vocabulary to spelling. The components of quanti-

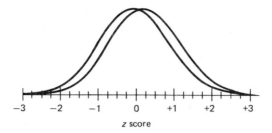

FIGURE 13.1   Two normal distributions with means .25 *SD* apart, that is, with a *d* of .25. This is approximately the magnitude of the gender difference in verbal ability. (Hyde, 1981)

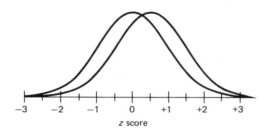

FIGURE 13.2   Two normal distributions with means .50 *SD* apart, that is, with a *d* of .50. This is approximately the magnitude of the gender differences in quantitative ability, visual-spatial ability, and field articulation. (Hyde, 1981)

tative or mathematical ability assessed varied from digit processing (how fast one can repeat digits) to mathematical synthesis. Perhaps the purpose of trying to assess general sex differences in a large, amorphous area such as verbal or quantitative skills is impossible.

The cognitive differences that exist between males and females do not appear overall to be large, and if the entire case for inequity of educational outcomes were to rest with cognitive outcomes, it would be quite weak. However, there are other than cognitive goals for education, and it is in affective outcomes where many differences are found.

Affective Outcomes

Affective variables have to do with internal beliefs systems, including factors such as interests, attitudes, and values. A major goal of education is to develop an internal belief system that enables one to function well in society. There are several areas in this affective dimension where sex-related differences exist. Perhaps the most important area is in the development of independence in learning. Females, more than males, do not emerge from public schools as learners who are able, confident, and motivated to continue as self-reliant learners and participants in society. Boys and girls enter school differing in independent or dependent behavior. It appears that schools reinforce and enlarge these differences.

Dependence is usually defined as need for reward, help, or attention from another person. The actual behaviors that constitute dependency include seeking physical contact, seeking proximity and attention, seeking praise and approval, resisting separation, and seeking help in performing tasks. An independent person is self-reliant, whereas a dependent person relies on others. Although some conflicting evidence exists, most authors conclude that females exhibit more dependent behaviors than do males, and this difference appears at a very young age. A global definition of dependency and overgeneralization of results from limited studies should be questioned. It does appear, however, that females, more than males, exhibit behaviors that suggest a greater need for interaction, attention, reinforcement, and help.

Such dependence in school is often demonstrated by continually asking for teacher approval or help, particularly when high-level thinking is required. Many teachers report that during problem-solving activities, many more girls than boys request directions or passively wait for help. Young girls tend to stay closer to the teacher than do young boys. Many girls appear helpless when faced with challenges.

It is believed that dependent or independent behaviors are developed by the socialization process, mainly within social interactions. Young girls, more so than boys, are encouraged to be dependent. Girls receive more protection and less pressure for establishing themselves as individuals separate from parents. Because of this, girls are less likely to engage in independent exploration of their worlds. Because of the sex-typed social reinforcement of dependent or independent behaviors, children enter school with girls tending to be more dependent on others and boys tending to be more self-reliant.

Little research, or even theorizing, in educational literature relates directly to how independence in learning is achieved. But it is assumed, almost without question, that a major goal of education is to develop individuals who are independent thinkers and problem solvers. However, what appears to happen is that schools merely reinforce and further develop in girls and boys the dependent or independent behaviors they bring to school.

It is evident from the achievement motivation literature that to have strong achievement strivings and thus achievement success, one must be an independent individual. To become increasingly independent, one must develop confidence in one's ability to do difficult learning tasks and also believe that one is in control of the outcomes of achievement striving.

While it has long been believed that females are lower in general self-esteem than are males, this sex-related difference in general self-esteem has been shown to be largely myth. However, when one looks at specific content areas, a different picture emerges. In mathematics, starting at least by grade 6 and persisting through high school, even when females achieve at the same level as males, females report significantly less confidence in their ability to perform mathematical tasks or to learn new mathematics (Fennema, 1984). How confident one feels about succeeding at a task appears to be related to the stereotyped appropriateness of that task to one's sex.

There are sex-related differences in perceptions of control of achievement outcomes. The model of causations of success-failure experiences proposed by Weiner (1974) is helpful in understanding causal attributions. In this model, attributions of success and failure are categorized into a 2 × 2 matrix with locus of control (internal-external) being one dimension and stability-instability the other. In a somewhat simplistic summary, if one attributes success to an internal, stable dimension (ability), one expects success in the future and will continue to strive in that area. If one attributes success to an external cause (e.g., the teacher) or an unstable one (e.g., effort), one will not be as confident of success in the future and will cease to strive. A somewhat different situation is true of failure attributions. If one attributes failure to unstable causes, such as effort, failure can be avoided in the future, so the tendency to approach or persist at tasks will be encouraged. Attribution of failure to a stable cause, on the other hand, will lead one to believe that one can't avoid failure.

Although one should be extremely careful of overgeneralizing data and concluding that all males behave one way and all females behave another way, many studies have reported that females and males tend to exhibit different attributional patterns (Bar-Tal & Frieze, 1977). Males tend to attribute successes to internal causes and failures to external or unstable causes. Females tend to attribute successes to external or unstable causes and failures to internal causes. This particular combination of attributions has become hypothesized to affect strongly academic achievement and, in particular, females' achievement. Bar-Tal (1978) states that "females and individuals with certain causal perceptions may perform in a classroom below their abilities because of their maladaptive patterns of attributions" (p. 267).

General Outcomes

General variables have to do with broad factors not easily identified as cognitive or affective. Two such variables indicate major inequities in education: the dropout rate of high school boys and girls and the development of leadership skills.

Girls have limited opportunities to develop leadership skills. Lockheed (1984) has documented that more boys than girls report that they have had leadership opportunities and that boys are more influential than girls in mixed-sex groups. Boys are selected more often than girls by teachers and peers to assume leadership roles in small group activities and whole-class activities. Boys are also more assertive in claiming leadership roles. Not only do boys have more opportunities to serve as leaders and thus learn to be leaders, but both boys and girls perceive boys to be leaders more often than girls. In one study, children in four-person groups were asked to identify the leader of their group. Even though no sex differences were found for either the amount or type of contribution made to the task or for actual influence of the group members, boys received 94% of the children's votes as leaders (Lockheed, 1984).

Documentation of gender-related differences in high school dropout rates is almost as difficult as documentation of gender-related cognitive differences. One study (AASVAB, 1982) with a very large data base of youths aged 16 to 23 in 1980 (n = ca. 12,000) found that only 72% of males but 77% of females graduate from high school. In this large nationwide sample, only 4% of male dropouts and 3% of female dropouts complete the Graduate Equivalency Diploma (GED) high school degree.

Another large sample of youths aged 14 to 21 in 1979 (n = ca. 6,000) reports large ethnic differences in dropout rate but few sex differences (Pallas & Alexander, 1983). It appears reasonable to believe that if a sex difference in dropout rate occurs, more males than females drop out of school before high school graduation.

In summary, what inequities in educational outcomes exist? Males do not develop their verbal skills to the same level as females, and females achieve at lower levels than males in mathematics and science. Perhaps more important, fewer females than males develop leadership skills, but more demonstrate lowered self-esteem in their ability to learn, negative attributional styles, and habits of dependency. Such inequities in educational outcomes hinder many females from participating fully and contributing significantly in adulthood.

THE CAUSES

Why do sex-related differences in educational outcomes exist? For many years researchers have been unconcerned with answering this question, but with the recent increase in concern over educational equity, causes have been sought. Reasons advanced range from biologically based differences to overt sexism. Let us examine several of these hypotheses.

Biological Differences

Are there biological differences that would explain the educational discrepancies? Crockett and Peterson (1984) divide biological influences into two categories: direct effects (X-linked gene transmission of traits, brain organization, hormonal influences) and indirect effects. After thoroughly examining the literature, they conclude that the evidence supporting any of the direct effects as an explanation of sex-related differences in cognition is largely inconclusive. However, other biological factors, such as size and height, indirectly influence the educational experience of girls and boys. Higher expectancies are reported for tall children, and size is likely to help determine who is dominant in a peer group.

The most important indirect effect is how society responds to a person's gender. Starting at birth, being a boy or a girl directly influences the educational experiences one participates in. Whether a newborn is a boy or a girl is of primary importance to parents. By 2 or 3 years of age, children know whether they are boys or girls and whether their peers are girls or boys. One of the first facts adults learn about children is their sex. It is not difficult to believe that much of children's experience is colored by their sex. What parents, peers, and all of society expect of a child is directly related to the child's gender.

By the time children enter school, they have many traits that have been developed by the interactions they have had with society, and these interactions have been different for girls and boys. Schools continue selecting experiences for children on the basis of gender. This selection of experiences is not done overtly, or even consciously, in most cases. It is subtle, unrecognized but extremely pervasive. It is done by administrators, custodians, secretaries, teachers, peers, as well as the children themselves.

Differences in Verbal Skills

There has been much thinking and writing on why boys do not learn to read as well as do girls. Bank, Biddle, and Good (1980) explore six hypotheses as to why boys learn to read more slowly than girls:

1. *Boys mature physically more slowly than girls, and this affects boys' readiness to decipher symbols.* This hypothesis is rejected because of studies that show male superiority in learning to read in other cultures.

2. *Female elementary teachers are biased against boys.* This hypothesis is supported by weak and contradictory evidence. It may be worthy of further investigation, but it is based on the dubious assumption that all female teachers behave in one way that is different from the way all male teachers behave.

3. *Elementary school teachers discriminate against boys with more negative treatment.* Boys do receive more discipline contacts from teachers but also more positive contacts. It also has been argued (Dweck, Davidson, Nelson, & Enna, 1978) that discipline contacts are beneficial to boys, not negative. Little evidence supports this hypothesis.

4. *Reading is perceived to be a feminine subject.* According to this hypothesis, both teachers and learners believe that reading is more appropriate for females than for males, so males won't strive to achieve in reading, and teachers have lower expectations for boys than for girls. Bank, Biddle, and Good feel that this hypothesis offers a "promising approach to the understanding of differential reading achievement" (p. 123). However, they also raise the question that stereotyping of reading as feminine may be a result, rather than a cause, of differential achievement.

5. *Teachers respond differentially to boys and girls, and this results in differential achievement.* Boys and girls bring many differences to the classroom, including those associated with sex. Teachers respond to these differences. If boys are treated differently than girls, it is because boys behave differently than girls. It is the "teachers' *expectations about* and *responses to what different students do and say*" that affect relative achievement levels" (p. 124).

6. *Teachers use sex-related teaching styles.* Teachers stereotype reading as a feminine domain and subconsciously use a teaching style favorable for female learning. Components of this teaching style, such as pace of instruction or an emphasis on cooperation, might be more suitable to females than to males. Such a hypothesis has some support.

Hypotheses 3 through 6, all supported by some data, appear to be interrelated. All six suggest that reading is stereotyped as feminine by society as a whole, which includes both teachers and learners. Learners, both boys and girls, do not expect boys to learn to read as well as do girls. Teachers also hold lower expectations for boys. Reading materials and the classroom reading environment are more appropriate for girls. As a result of all of these interrelated factors, boys do not learn to read as well as do girls.

What Causes the Differences in Mathematics and Science?

Whereas sex-related differences in achievement in elementary and secondary school mathematics are not large, major differences exist between participation in post—secondary school mathematics study and mathematics- or science-related careers. Both income and status are directly related to the amount of mathematics used in an occupation. Females' lack of participation in mathematics-related careers often results in lower status for them in society as well as lower-paying occupations. Therefore, in looking at causation, both mathematics achievement and participation in mathematics-related careers must be considered. One hypothesis linking the two problems that has received a great deal of attention is the differential course-taking hypothesis.

First proposed by Fennema and Sherman in 1977, it simply states that *differential mathematics course taking in high school is the cause of sex-related differences in mathematics achievement.* It has led to a number of studies (Perl, 1979; Steele & Wise, 1979; Benbow & Stanley, 1980; Pallas & Alexander, 1983).

Most studies specifically designed to investigate the hypothesis and done with representative samples of the general population have concluded that differential course taking partly accounts for sex differences in learning. Benbow and Stanley conclude just the opposite. However, their study was not designed specifically to investigate the hypothesis and was conducted primarily with highly precocious learners. As a result, it is difficult to generalize from their work. The NAEP data appear to provide the best information. Even when amount of course taking was controlled, girls did not perform at the same level on problem-solving tasks (see Fennema & Carpenter, 1981, and Fennema, 1984, for a complete discussion). Undoubtedly, differential course taking is a partial explanation of the differences found, but in some ways it is an irrelevant explanation. The important question is why. Why do girls take fewer courses, and why do they achieve less well? These two questions are highly interrelated. Knowing the answer to one helps in knowing the answer to the other.

Another hypothesis is that *females and males differ on the important cognitive trait of spatial visualization, and this explains differential learning.* Spatial visualization is a particular subset of spatial skills. It involves visual imagery of objects, movement of the objects, or changes in their properties that must be manipulated in the "mind's eye."

Male superiority in spatial visualization is often reported. However, statements about sex differences in spatial visualization made over a period of years by one author indicates that "truth" is not constant. In 1966, Maccoby said that "by the early school years, boys consistently do better on spatial tasks and this difference continues through the high school and college years" (p. 26). In 1972, Maccoby and Jacklin said that sex differences in spatial ability "remain minimal and inconsistent until approximately the age of 10 or 11, when the superiority of boys becomes consistent on a wide range of populations and tests" (p. 41). In 1974, Maccoby and Jacklin state that "male superiority on spatial-visual tasks is fairly consistently found in adolescence and adulthood, but not in childhood" (p. 351).

The first statement said that spatial differences begin during early school years and last until adolescence. The last statement said that the differences are found in adolescence. The specification of the trait narrowed from general spatial tasks to a very specific skill called visual-spatial ability. Commenting about this trend, Jacklin said in 1979 that if the trend continues, "we can predict that the actual demographics for a sex-related difference in visuospatial ability will lessen and perhaps disappear" (p. 359).

The impact of spatial visualization skills on learning is also not very clear. It has been hypothesized to be an important influence on the learning of mathematics. The relationship between mathematics and spatial visualization is logically evident. In mathematical terms, spatial visualization requires rotation, reflection, or translation of rigid figures, all of which are important ideas in geometry. Many mathematicians believe that all mathematical thought involves geometric ideas. Therefore, if spatial visualization items are geometric in character and if mathematical thought involves geometric ideas, spatial visualization and mathematics are inseparably intertwined.

Not only are spatial visualization skills related to ideas within the structure of mathematics, but spatial representations are being increasingly included in the teaching of mathematics. For example, the Piagetian conservation tasks, which are becoming part of many school programs, involve focusing on correct spatial attributes before quantity, length, and volume are conserved. Most concrete and pictorial representations of arithmetic, geometric, and algebraic ideas are heavily reliant on spatial attributes. The number line, which is used extensively to represent whole numbers and operations on them, is a spatial representation. Illustrating the commutativity of multiplication by turning an array 90 degrees involves a direct spatial visualization skill.

Although the relation of the content of mathematics, instruction in mathematics, and spatial visualization skills appears logical, results from empirical studies that have explored the relationship are not consistent. Some investigators have concluded definitely that spatial skills and learning of mathematics are not related, while others feel that the data indicate a positive relationship (Fennema, 1975). While it appears that tasks that measure spatial visualization skills have components that can be mathematically analyzed or described, one could hypothesize a direct relationship between mathematics and spatial visualization. However, this direct relationship has been difficult to document, and some theorists question whether it exists at all.

The relationship between sex-related differences in mathematics and spatial visualization has been the subject of much speculation and some research. One indication of its importance is the concurrent development of sex-related differences in favor of males in both. The two are related with correlations found to be about .45. The sex-related differences found in a recent three-year longitudinal study (Fennema & Tartre, 1983) give credibility to the belief that sex-related differences in problem solving may be due to how girls and boys use their spatial visualization skills. Girls and boys with equivalent spatial visualization skills did not solve the same number of problems, nor did they use the same processes in solving problems. It also appears that a low level of spatial visualization skills was more debilitating for girls than for boys.

It is increasingly believed that there is no direct causal relationship between spatial visualization skills and the learning of mathematics in a broad, general sense. In American schools, teachers do not appear to use mathematical representations that either encourage or require the use of spatial visualization skills. While some primary mathematics programs encourage the use of concrete and pictorial representations of mathematical ideas, by the time children are 10 or 11 years old, symbolic representations are used almost exclusively. Perhaps boys more than girls use concrete representations during primary years and thus develop higher skills in using spatial visualization.

Whatever influence spatial visualization skills have on learning is subtle, to say the least. It is proving an interesting area of investigation and discussion, but it is not expected that an emphasis on the development of spatial visualization skills will do very much to eliminate sex-related differences in various types of achievement.

A third hypothesis is that *females perceive mathematics as less useful to them than males do*. As a result, girls neither exert as much effort to learn nor elect to take the advanced math courses at the same level as boys. There is a great deal of evidence to support this hypothesis as a partial explanation. Females' career interests expressed in high school and college often do not include math-related occupations. Mathematics is a difficult subject and not particularly enjoyable for many learners. Why should one study if it is of no future use? Females in secondary schools, as a group, indicate that they do not feel they will use mathematics in the future. Females, more often than males, respond negatively to such items as "I'll need mathematics for my future work" and "Mathematics is a worthwhile and useful subject." Males, as a group, are much more apt to report that mathematics is essential for whatever career they plan. These sex differences appear as early as sixth grade. If females do not see mathematics-related careers as possibilities, they will also not see mathematics as useful.

Females lack confidence in their ability to learn mathematics, and this affects achievement and election of courses. The literature strongly supports the fact that there are sex-related differences in confidence in learning mathematics. In the Fennema and Sherman study (1978), at each grade level from 6 to 12, boys were significantly more confident than girls in their abilities to deal with mathematics, even, in most instances, when there were no significant sex-related differences in mathematics achievement. In addition, confidence in learning mathematics and achievement were more highly correlated than any other affective variable and achievement ($r = .40$). Confidence was almost as highly related to achievement as were verbal ability and spatial visualization.

While evidence exists in abundance that there are sex-related differences in confidence in the learning of mathematics, much is unknown about its true effect or how such feelings are developed. The relationship between spatial-visual processes and the confidence-anxiety dimension has not been explored. What effect do feelings of confidence have on cognitive processes involved in learning mathematics and in solving mathematical problems, and vice versa? Are feelings of confidence stable across time and across a variety of mathematics activities? Does lessening anxiety increase either learning or the willingness to elect to study mathematics? Do low levels of confidence affect females differently than males? Are there really sex differences in confidence toward mathematics, or, as many have hypothesized, are females more willing than males to admit their feelings?

Many studies are currently under way that will help in answering these questions. Until the results are available, though, one must accept the evidence that females, across a wide age range, do report more anxiety and less confidence about mathematics than males.

Females, more than males, exhibit a causal attributional style that is detrimental to their learning and election of mathematics. Some data do support this hypothesis. Girls are more apt than boys to attribute success in mathematics to effort and environment and failure to ability (Wolleat, Pedro, Becker, & Fennema, 1980).

Teachers have lower expectations of girls in mathematics than they have of boys. This hypothesis is not totally supported by data. Parsons, Kaczala, and Meece (1982) found that fifth- through ninth-grade math teachers had expectations for their female students equal to or higher than those they had for their male students. However, Fennema and Koehler (1983) report a decline in perceived expectations of females by both boys and girls from grade 6 to grade 8. Becker (1979) contends that the sex-related differences she found in teacher-student interactions in geometry classes were strongly related to differential teacher expectancies.

Teachers interact differently with boys and girls in mathematics classes and thus affect their learning. Teachers interact more with boys than they do with girls. Boys generally receive more criticism for their behavior but also more praise and positive feedback. In short, boys get more of the teacher's attention.

Boys who are high in confidence interact more with mathematics teachers than any other groups of students (Fennema, Wolleat, Pedro, & Becker, 1980). Interestingly, girls who are high in confidence interact with teachers *less* than any other group. In sixth-grade classrooms, large numbers of girls have no mathematics interaction with the teacher at all on many days. Why this differential interaction pattern occurs is unclear.

As with all generalizations, one must be very cautious about believing that all teachers interact with girls and boys in the same way. For example, Reyes (1981) found tremendous variation in the behavior of 12 seventh-grade teachers. Some teachers asked many more high-level questions of boys than they did of girls; others asked approximately equivalent numbers.

The problem of teachers' differential treatment of male and female students is well documented, and probably influences learning. However, the longer the problem is studied, the more complex it becomes. Most overt behavior by teachers appears to be nonsexist and fair to most students. In many cases, teachers interact more with boys because they feel that they must in order to maintain control. Many negative interactions occur between boys and teachers. On the surface, teachers' interactions with girls are more positive and appear to be what has been considered good educational practice. However, the end result appears to be negative.

Mathematics is stereotyped as a male domain and thus has a detrimental effect on females' learning. This simplistically worded hypothesis, which encompasses all the other hypotheses, offers the best explanation of why sex differences in mathematics exists. Sex role acts as a mediator of learning.

DIFFERENCES IN EDUCATIONAL EXPERIENCE

Boys and girls have different educational experiences. Teachers interact differently with girls and with boys, and girls and boys choose to participate in different learning and social behavior. These differences develop because perceived sex role acts as a mediator influencing what boys and girls do and, as a consequence, what they learn. Teachers, students, and the entire educational community hold beliefs about appropriate roles for females and males. Part of that belief includes stereotyping learning in specific areas as masculine or feminine. When a content area such as reading is stereotyped as being feminine (reading) or masculine (mathematics), it is more difficult for boys and girls to achieve equally.

Sex-role identity is important to everyone. A portion of that identity is achievement in domains seen as appropriate for one's sex—usually a reflection of traditional achievement areas for the sexes. Achievement in an "inappropriate" domain is perceived as a failure to fulfill one's sex-role identity. Such achievers are aware that others see them as somewhat less feminine or masculine, and they may become increasingly uncomfortable with achievement in that area. They also realize that teachers and peers have lowered expectations of success because of their "inappropriate" gender and may come to value success less highly as a result.

Nash (1979) has reviewed the literature dealing with sex role as a mediator of intellectual functioning. She concludes that "beginning in second grade and persisting through the 12th grade, children perceive social, verbal, and artistic skills as feminine whereas spatial, mechanical, and athletic skills are viewed as masculine" (p. 265). Starting at the onset of puberty, mathematics and science are viewed as masculine. This stereotyping of subjects by learners can affect performance in a variety of ways. Children choose tasks they identify as sex-appropiate. Persistence is longer on tasks labeled as suitable for one's own sex. Attitude toward the tasks is improved and success is both valued more and expected more when the task is sex-appropriate.

Teachers also convey subtle messages to boys and girls about the importance of achievement. One major set of studies explored the notion of equality of treatment of girls and boys. Boys interact much more with teachers than girls do, and on many days teachers do not interact at all with their female students (Fennema et al., 1980). Boys initiate more contacts with teachers than girls do, and teachers initiate more contacts with boys (Brophy & Good, 1974; Fennema et al., 1980). Boys receive more discipline contacts (Serbin, O'Leary, Kent, & Tonick, 1973) as well as more praise. Teachers accept wrong or poor answers more often from boys (Good, Sikes, & Brophy, 1973). Teachers tend to criticize boys for their lack of effort and criticize girls for the academic quality of their work (Dweck et al., 1978). Teachers respond more frequently to requests for help from boys than from girls (Serbin et al., 1973).

When one looks at specific subgroups of boys and girls, some other interesting differences emerge. Teachers interact more with high-achieving boys than with high-achieving girls (Good et al., 1973). Teachers interact less with girls who have high confidence in learning mathematics than with high-confidence boys. High-confidence boys interact at higher cognitive levels with their teachers more often than high-confidence girls (Fennema et al., 1980).

Not many studies relate teacher behavior directly to dependency. One study does indicate that teachers differ in their interactions with children whom teachers perceive to be different in dependency. In particular, according to this study, teacher praise, criticism, and feedback differed for boys and girls, and there appeared to be a sex-dependency interaction (Hollinger, 1978). The series of studies by Dweck and colleagues (1978) concerned with sex differences in learned helplessness provides some additional clues to important teacher behaviors. Learned helplessness exists when failure is seen as insurmountable and is attributed to uncontrollable factors such as lack of ability. Dweck's results emphasize the importance of teachers, particularly in their feedback for failure. In a study of teacher-student interactions at the fifth-grade level, 54.4% of work-related criticism to boys referred to intellectual inadequacy, while 88.9% of work-related criticism to girls concerned things other than intellectual performance. In conclusion, the researchers state "that the pattern of evaluative feedback given to boys and girls in the classroom can result directly in girls' greater tendency to view failure feedback as indicative of their level of ability" (p. 274).

Why do teachers interact more with boys than with girls? Perhaps teachers are responding to the more insistent demands by boys. The demands could be quite direct if boys volunteer (raise their hands) more to answer questions posed by teachers. Perhaps boys also just initiate more interactions than girls. Brophy and Evertson (1981) report that boys have more total contacts with teachers partly because the teacher initiated such contacts and partly because the behavior of the boys demanded more contacts. In this study, girls showed their dependency by seeking teacher approval in private contacts. No doubt teacher actions result partially from pupil actions. However, both teacher action and student action directly reflect the stereotyping of the activity as appropriate for females or males.

A Model of Classroom Influences

Learning is dependent on what each child actually does in the classroom. What a child does is determined by teachers and by that child. Figure 13.3 is a model representing the classroom components of a sequence that results in the sex-related differences in educational outcomes that have been found. The model illustrates that what students actually do in classrooms directly affects their learning and the development of sex-related differences in learning. Boys and girls participate at different levels in certain activities. This differential participation includes things like the zeal with which a learner approaches and works on a task, persistence at a task, type and amount of interactions with a teacher, and role in small group activities. Differential participation by girls and boys in learning activities is probably not very great. However, this differential participation over a number of years could easily account for the differential educational outcomes of boys and girls.

Why students participate differentially is also explained by the model. Both teachers and individual learners hold a view of appropriate behaviors for females and males. A portion of these appropriate behaviors is achievement in specified content areas and the development of certain traits such as leadership and independence. The view of appropriate sex role is pervasive and influences expectations, interactions, and participation in classroom activities.

An individual develops an internal belief system (confidence, attributional style)

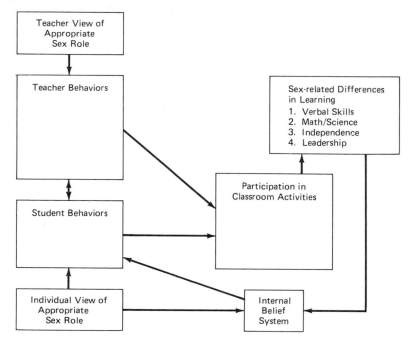

FIGURE 13.3   Classroom influences on development of sex-related differences in learning.

partly as a result of three things: (1) personal view of appropriate sex role, (2) interactions with teachers, and (3) personal achievement. This internal belief system influences how a child initiates interactions with a teacher as well as responses to the teacher's initiations of interactions. The development of this internal belief system also depends on what the child has learned in the past.

Teacher-pupil interactions are a result of a teacher's view of appropriate sex roles as well as responses to individuals' behavior (which has partly been caused by the teacher's behavior). Thus what happens is a result of both learner and teacher behaviors, which are in turn partly a result of the view of sex role held by each.

INTERVENTION

Can anything be done to eliminate sex-related differences in outcomes? The answer is yes. Concerned parents, teachers, and school personnel can ensure that sex is an irrelevant variable and that all children learn as much as they can, regardless of gender. The details of how this should be done are beyond the scope of this chapter, but must involve modifying views about appropriate behavior for females and males. Educational decision makers must become truly blind to gender. The specifics are determined by the situation in each school and by the abilities, interest, and motivation of individual teachers. Programs need to be developed to address each situation. Many resources are available to help schools or teachers to develop intervention plans (see "Further Reading"). Here are a few criteria that may be helpful in making decisions about what to use:

1. To be most effective, a program designed to eliminate sex-related differences in educational outcomes needs to be carried out over a period of years. Since the problem of stereotyping behavior as appropriate for females or males permeates society, only long-term interventions can alleviate the problem.
2. Short-term, sharply focused programs can sometimes attack a symptom of sex-role stereotyping and as such are valuable. For example, the Multiplying Options and Subtracting Bias intervention program (Fennema et al., 1980) is designed to change females' perception of a very narrow belief: the usefulness of mathematics for them. Because it is so narrow, it has been quite effective at changing this narrow belief and has resulted in more girls' enrolling in mathematics courses.
3. Changing perception of sex role must be done with all significant groups, not just the group targeted to benefit. For example, many people have decided that females' achievement in mathematics should be improved, and many programs have been developed to change girls' attitudes toward mathematics. However, a heavy burden is being placed on the girls when they are the only ones asked to change. If all others continue to believe that to learn mathematics, a girl has to become less feminine, girls will still receive that message. It would take a very strong girl indeed to change when all others around her are suggesting, however subtly, that she shouldn't change.

Keeping these criteria in mind, can individual teachers do anything? Here are some specific things teachers can do:

1. Be very aware of who is assuming leadership roles in the classroom. If girls are not, structure small groups so that girls must assume the leader's position.

2. Talk about sex-role stereotyping in society so that both girls and boys become aware of it.
3. Be sure all learners recognize the importance of all content areas to their future life.
4. Be sure your expectations of learning are high for all students.
5. Ensure that both girls and boys learn to be self-reliant and to value independence.
6. Be sure that instructional materials are nonbiased.

FURTHER READING

Sadker, M. P., & Sadker, D. M. (1982). *Sex Equity Handbook for Schools*. White Plains, NY: Longman. Discusses many issues concerned with achieving equity for girls and boys in schools. Included is an extensive Research Directory for Sex Equity in Education.

Fennema, E., Becker, A. D., Wolleat, P. L., & Pedro, J. D. (1981). *Multiplying Options and Subtracting Bias*. Reston, VA: National Council of Teachers of Mathematics. The title is that of an intervention program, but the Facilitators' Guide includes information about many additional programs designed to increase equity in mathematics education.

Women's Educational Equity Act Program. (Published yearly). *216 Resources for Educational Equity*. Newton, MA: Educational Development Corporation/Women's Educational Equity Act Publishing Center. The WEEA has sponsored the development of many intervention programs in all areas.

REFERENCES

Administration of the Armed Services Vocational Aptitude Battery. (1982). *Profile of American youth: 1980 nationwide*. Washington, DC: Office of the Assistant Secretary of Defense.

Bank, B. J., Biddle, B. J., & Good, T. L. (1980). Sex roles, classroom instruction, and reading achievement. *Journal of Educational Psychology, 72*, 119–132.

Bar-Tal, D. (1978). Attributional analysis of achievement-related behavior. *Review of Educational Research, 48*, 259–271.

Bar-Tal, D., & Frieze, J. H. (1977). Achievement motivation for males and females as a determinant of attribution for success and failure. *Sex Roles, 3*, 301–313.

Becker, J. (1979). *A study of differential treatment of females and males in mathematics classes*. Unpublished doctoral dissertation, University of Maryland, College Park.

Benbow, C. P., & Stanley, J. C. (1980). Sex differences in mathematical ability: Fact or artifact? *Science, 210*, 1262–1264.

Boyd, W. (1960). *The Emile of Jean-Jacques Rousseau*. New York: Teachers College Press.

Borphy, J. E., & Evertson, C. M. (1981). *Student characteristics and teaching*. White Plains, NY: Longman.

Brophy, J. E., & Good, T. L. (1974). *Teacher-student relationships: Causes and consequences*. New York: Holt, Rinehart and Winston.

Crockett, L. J., & Petersen, A. C. (1984). Biology: Its role in gender-related educational experiences. In E. Fennema & M. J. Ayer (Eds.), *Women and education: Equity or equality?* Berkeley, CA: McCutchan.

Dweck, C., Davidson, W., Nelson, S., & Enna, B. (1978). Sex differences in learned helplessness: II. The contingencies of evaluative feedback in the classroom; III. An experimental analysis. *Developmental Psychology, 14*, 268–276.

Dwyer, C. A. (1973). Sex differences in reading: An evaluation and a critique of current theories. *Review of Educational Research, 43*, 455–468.

Fennema, E. (1975). Spatial ability, mathematics, and the sexes. In E. Fennema (Ed.), *Mathe-

matics learning: What research says about sex differences. Columbus, OH: ERIC Center for Science, Mathematics, and Environmental Education.

Fennema, E. (1984). Girls, women, and mathematics. In E. Fennema & M. J. Ayer (Eds.) *Women and education: Equity or equality?* Berkeley, CA: McCutchan.

Fennema, E., & Carpenter, T. P. (1981). Sex-related differences in mathematics: Results from National Assessment. *Mathematics Teacher, 74,* 554–560.

Fennema, E., & Koehler, M. S. (1983). Expectations and feelings about females' and males' achievement in mathematics. In E. Fennema (Ed.), *Research on relationship of spatial visualization and confidence to male/female mathematics achievement in grades 6–8.* Final Report, National Science Foundation Project SED78-17330.

Fennema, E., & Sherman, J. A. (1977). Sex-related differences in mathematics achievement, spatial visualization, and affective factors. *American Educational Research Journal, 14,* 51–72.

Fennema, E., & Sherman, J. A. (1978). Sex-related differences in mathematics achievement and related factors: A further study. *Journal for Research in Mathematics Education, 9,* 189–203.

Fennema, E., & Tartre, L. A. (1983). The use of spatial skills in mathematics by girls and boys: A longitudinal study. In E. Fennema (Ed.), *Research on relationship of spatial visualization and confidence to male/female achievement in grades 6–8.* Final Report, National Science Foundation Project SED78-17330.

Fennema, E., Wolleat, P., Pedro, J. D., & Becker, A. (1980). Increasing women's participation in mathematics: An intervention program. *Journal for Research in Mathematics Education, 12,* 3–14.

Fulkerson, K. F., Furr, S., & Brown, D. (1983). Expectations and achievement among third, sixth, and ninth grade black and white males and females. *Developmental Psychology, 19,* 231–236.

Good, T. L., Sikes, N., & Brophy, J. E. (1973). Effects of teacher sex and student sex on classroom interaction. *Journal of Educational Psychology, 65,* 74–87.

Greene, M. (1984). The impacts of irrelevance: Women in the history of American education. In E. Fennema and M. J. Ayer (Eds.), *Women and education: Equity or equality?* Berkeley, CA: McCutchan.

Hollinger, C. (1978). *The effects of student dependency, sex, birth order, and teacher control ideology on teacher-student interaction.* Unpublished doctoral dissertation, Case Western Reserve University, Cleveland, OH.

Husén T. (Ed.) (1967) *International study of achievement in mathematics: A comparison of 12 countries* (2 vols.). New York: Wiley.

Hyde, J. S. (1981). How large are cognitive gender differences? *American Psychologist, 36,* 892–901.

Jacklin, C. N. (1979). Epilogue. In M. A. Wittig & A. C. Petersen (Eds.), *Sex-related differences in cognitive functioning.* Orlando, FL: Academic Press.

Leinhardt, G., Seewald, A. M., & Engel, M. (1979). Learning what's taught: Sex differences in instruction. *Journal of Educational Psychology, 79,* 432–439.

Lockheed, M. E. (1984). Sex segregation and male preeminence in elementary classrooms. In E. Fennema & M. J. Ayer (Eds.), *Women and education: Equity or equality?* Berkeley, CA: McCutchan.

Maccoby, E. E. (1966). Sex differences in intellectual functioning. In E. E. Maccoby (Ed.), *The development of sex differences.* Stanford, CA: Stanford University Press.

Maccoby, E. E., & Jacklin, C. N. (1972). Sex differences in intellectual functioning. In A. Anastasi (Ed.), *Assessment in a pluralistic society.* Proceedings of the 1972 Invitational Conference on Testing Problems, Educational Testing Service, Princeton, NJ.

Maccoby, E. E., & Jacklin, C. N. (1974). *The psychology of sex differences.* Stanford, CA: Stanford University Press.

Nash, S. C. (1979). Sex role as a mediator of intellectual functioning. In M. A. Wittig & A. C. Petersen (Eds.), *Sex-related differences in cognitive functioning.* Orlando, FL: Academic Press.

National Assessment of Educational Progress. (1978). *Reading change, 1970–75: Summary volume* (Reading Report No. 06–R–21). Denver: Author.

National Assessment of Educational Progress. (1980). *Writing Achievement, 1969–79: Results from the Third National Writing Assessment: Vol. 1. 17-year-olds* (Report No. 10-W-01). Denver: Education Commission of the States.

National Assessment of Educational Progress. (1981). *Three National Assessments of reading: Changes in performance, 1970–1980.* Denver: Education Commission of the States.

Pallas, A. M., & Alexander, K. L. (1983). Sex differences in quantitative SAT performance: New evidence on the differential coursework hypothesis. *American Educational Research Journal, 20,* 165–182.

Parsons, J. E., Kaczala, C. M., & Meece, J. L. (1982). Socialization of achievement attitudes and beliefs: Classroom influences. *Child Development, 53,* 322–339.

Perl, T. H. (1979). Discriminating factors and sex differences in electing mathematics. Unpublished doctoral dissertation, Stanford University, Stanford, CA.

Reyes, L. H. (1981). *Classroom processes, sex of student, and confidence in learning mathematics.* Unpublished doctoral dissertation, University of Wisconsin, Madison.

Serbin, L., O'Leary, K., Kent, R., & Tonick, I. (1973). A comparison of teacher responses to the preacademic and problem behavior of boys and girls. *Child Development, 44,* 796–804.

Steele, L., & Wise, L. K. (1979, April). Origins of sex differences in high school mathematics achievement and participation. Paper presented at the annual meeting of the American Educational Research Association, San Francisco.

Weiner, B. (1974). *Achievement motivation and attribution theory.* Morristown, NJ: General Learning Press.

Wolleat, P. L., Pedro, J. D., Becker, A. D., & Fennema, E. (1980). Sex differences in high school students' causal attributions of performance in mathematics. *Journal for Research in Mathematics Education, 11,* 356–366.

14 STUDENTS OF LIMITED ENGLISH PROFICIENCY

Migdalia Romero, Carmen Mercado, and José A. Vázquez-Faría

Eddie was born in Mexico and has been in this country for two years. Though more proficient in Spanish than in English, he nonetheless speaks English fairly well. He tends to stutter when speaking either language. He arrived in this country in April and two months later was held over in grade 2. The following September he was placed in a bilingual second-grade class for children who had been held over. In this class Eddie quickly picked up English; he excelled in mathematics and was frequently observed serving as a peer tutor. His teacher described him as being a risk taker and highly motivated, frequently asking questions and volunteering responses. As a result of his performance and progress in the second grade, Eddie was assigned to a bilingual third-grade class, but this time for gifted bilingual students.

THE PROBLEM

Scope

Eddie is only one of many children entering school in the United States unable to speak English. Over the past two decades, increased attention has been focused on the educational needs of children who come to school speaking little or no English. Many of these children experience academic failure and drop out of school prematurely. They are often from lower-income families and represent a variety of ethnolinguistic minority groups. In some ways Eddie is a typical language minority student (LMS).[1]

---

[1]The authors realize that the terms *language minority student* (LMS) and *limited English proficient* (LEP) *student* are not synonymous. LEP refers to a subclassification of LMS, since not every LMS is limited in English proficiency. Therefore, the use of each term in context represents a deliberate choice on the part of the authors.

348

However, he is not a prototype, nor does he represent the prototype of any language minority group. Instead, he is an individual member of a larger group that is all too often stereotyped.

The problem that Eddie typifies is national in scope, involving a wide variety of language minority groups. It is projected that in the United States the non-English-language-background (NELB) population, of which Eddie is a member, will have grown from 30 million in 1980 to 39.5 million in the year 2000 (Oxford-Carpenter, 1980). Projections do not take into account large unexpected migrations resulting from political and economic factors abroad. Although the two largest non-English-language groups in the United States, speakers of Spanish and the various Chinese languages, are most heavily concentrated in California, Texas, and New York, all 50 states have and will continue to have NELB populations. The diversity among the Hispanics and East Asians is as great as the states in which these groups have settled. Central Americans, Cubans, Mexicans, Puerto Ricans, South Americans, and Spaniards are numbered among the Hispanics. Chinese, Filipinos, Japanese, Koreans, and Vietnamese are numbered among the East Asians. Languages represented by other linguistic minority groups in this country include Arabic, Armenian, French, Greek, Haitian Creole, Italian, Russian, and a variety of American Indian languages. Among school-age children it is estimated that 2.5 million speak a language other than English or live in households in which a language other than English is spoken. Current statistics do not take into account undocumented immigrants who are not counted by the census.

The need to design effective instructional programs for the student population just described continues to be one of the most pressing problems confronting educators and policymakers at all levels of government. Traditionally, the presence of language minority students was either ignored or, if they received any special assistance in learning English, it was usually in the form of special English-language classes, requiring that they be taken out of regular classes for periods of the day. Thus, while they indeed learned English, they lost time in the content areas, and consequently many fell behind academically.

The plight of children who come to school speaking a language other than English has always posed a multifaceted challenge for American educators. Because English is the medium of instruction in U.S. schools, students of limited English proficiency (LEP) are denied access to instruction until they can understand the language in which it is delivered. Thus the educators' first challenge is to develop their students' proficiency in the English language. At the same time, however, it is expected that LEP students will progress academically at a normal rate for children of their age. If this is a problem for educators and policymakers, it is even more of a challenge for the student.

The fact that the education of the LMS is both a language-related issue and an educational issue is best evinced by the questions most frequently raised in its discussion. While some see the problem as one of English language development, others see it more globally as one of assuring educational achievement for the LEP student while developing English language proficiency. The goal from either perspective is learning both English and other academic content. Given the diversity of students and of class compositions, it is naive to presume that there is a single solution or only one viable approach to the problem.

Responses

Since the late 1960s, a major federal response to the perceived needs of these students has been bilingual education. It was defined by the Bilingual Education Act—added as Title VII to the Elementary and Secondary Act of 1965—as the use of a student's native language as a medium of instruction for teaching a part of the curriculum. The act provided financial assistance to state and local educational agencies to develop and carry on "new and innovative elementary and secondary programs . . . to meet the needs of the large numbers of children of limited English ability." It stipulated as its goal the development of children's English language proficiency, but not at the expense of their continuing to progress in the acquisition of academic and basic skills as well. This implied that while learning English the student was to receive native language instruction in all content areas prescribed in the curriculum for students proficient in English, who were of a similar age and educational experience in a given classroom. Although the use of two languages for instruction was not new to this country (its antecedents date back to the 1700s), it was perceived as a new approach to preventing the academic failure and alarming dropout rates of LEP students.

However, whether the use of two languages for instruction is the best means by which to accomplish these educational goals remains a subject of debate. Although the effectiveness of a bilingual approach has been verified by such research as the Significant Bilingual Instructional Features Study (1980–1983), it is also clear that bilingual education is not necessarily the most appropriate approach for all students of limited English proficiency in all situations. For example, if there are too few LEP students in a particular school or district, or if such students come from diverse ethnolinguistic groups, other approaches that are more intensive in the use of English might be more practical. In fact, Part A of the Education Amendments of 1984 (U.S. Congress, 1984) delineates the programs for which federal assistance is available. The criteria for funding bilingual education programs have been expanded to accommodate a variety of approaches, including

> programs of transitional bilingual education; programs of developmental bilingual education; special alternative instructional programs for students of limited English proficiency; programs of academic excellence; family English literacy programs; bilingual preschool, special education, and gifted and talented programs preparatory or supplementary to programs such as those assisted under this Act; and programs to develop instructional materials in languages for which such materials are commercially unavailable. (p. 10)

However, to provide the most effective service, the best procedure is to assess the situation and then select what seems to be the best course of action for responding to it. The purpose is not to weigh the relative merits of bilingual education or its manner of implementation, but rather to discuss what has been learned from this educational movement, and how this knowledge can help the educator to deal realistically with language minority students in whatever academic situation they may be found.

THE STUDENT

We noted that Eddie, our third-grade LEP student, was not a prototypical language minority student. To avoid the stereotyping that can result from a single example, we have decided to base our definition of the language minority student on Eddie and five other individuals who reflect the diversity of LMSs. These students differ in a number of significant ways. Their profiles were taken from actual case studies, and each provides background information important for teachers in facilitating two significant processes for the language minority student, the adjustment process and the learning process.

Ken

Ken is a 7-year-old first grader who attends a school on the Navajo reservation. He comes from a traditional Navajo family and speaks primarily Navajo. He rarely talks or writes in school. He has actually been observed to go through a whole day without uttering a sound. He was tested to determine if special education was appropriate or if he had a speech problem, but the results were negative. Nevertheless, he does have trouble remembering. His record indicates high absenteeism, and his performance reflects a short attention span. In comparison to other Navajo boys and girls in his class with similar language backgrounds, Ken has made relatively slow progress in English.

Angel

Angel is a high school student who has been in this country for 2½ years. He is originally from Ecuador. Angel is dominant in Spanish, yet after 1½ years in the bilingual class, he was elected president of the Honor Society. He plans to attend a local university to study chemical engineering.

Ana

Ana is a high school student who was born in the United States. However, her first language is Spanish. She is in a below-level class. Although Ana attempts to participate in class, she becomes confused and discouraged when the teacher asks her to use complete sentences.

Lin

Lin is an 11-year-old girl from Vietnam who has been in this country for less than three years. Her family is ethnically Chinese, and she speaks both Vietnamese and Chinese. On a scale of 1 to 4 (4 being equivalent to almost native ability in the language), Lin's current teacher rated her 3 in oral English proficiency. She ranks in the lowest reading group in English, the middle group in Chinese, and the top group in mathematics. The teacher describes Lin as extremely shy and quiet, frequently frowning and generally looking worried. The teacher also feels that Lin is reluctant to participate because of her limited English. Nevertheless, the teacher considers her to be intelligent and studious.

Gerardo

Gerardo is a 16-year-old, the eldest of five children living at home with his parents and grandmother. He came from a parochial school in the Dominican Republic and brought with him a very impressive school record. However, according to Gerardo's English teacher, he has shown little improvement in his acquisition of English since entering the school three years ago. As a result, while in eleventh grade he was referred to the special education department for evaluation. Gerardo is very competent in his native language. However, he has many negative opinions of life in this country. He also expresses negative feelings about himself and the school he attends. He feels that school here cannot be compared with the school he attended in Santo Domingo. "There we go to school to learn. It is not like that here. Here kids come to school to smoke and pass time, but not to learn" [translated from Spanish]. Gerardo feels that students do not respect teachers and, likewise, teachers show no respect for students. He speaks about learning English as "*esa baina,*" a condescending term implying that it is a waste of time.

Although people tend to think of language minority students as a rather homogeneous group, it is obvious from these profiles that they can be quite different, with unique needs and circumstances, diverse personalities, attitudes, and language abilities, and varying skills and interests.

In describing language minority groups, it is important to remember that groups and individuals differ not only in the languages they speak but in the cultural values that influence their actions and the experiences, skills, and interests they bring to the learning process.

The students we profiled differ in the following aspects, among others:

Birthplace and native language

Time in this country

Native language ability

Attitudes toward English, the target language, and the United States

Academic achievement

Personality

Manner of participation in school

Self-esteem

All of these factors can affect learning and adjustment and suggest the complexity of the problem for both learner and teacher.

STUDENT ADJUSTMENT

The process of adjusting to any new situation is rarely devoid of problems. When that process involves adjustment to a new environment, an unfamiliar language, a different set of values, and a school system that until recently was often oblivious to the complexity and intensity of these differences, the problem is greatly intensified. To understand the problem of adjustment faced by language minority students, the teacher must understand the experiences and background a student brings that are either congruent or in conflict with what the student encounters in the classroom and in the curriculum. This is especially important since the differences can lead to "culture shock," which is in turn associated with feelings of estrangement, anger, indecision, frustration, unhappiness, loneliness, or homesickness. The resultant feelings and behavior of the LMS in turn contribute to his or her eventual success or failure.

At a very personal level, there are two major areas in which cultural differences can create conflict and even shock for the language minority student. The first deals with the child-rearing practices that have socialized the child prior to his or her entry into the American school system. The second source of culture conflict is the language of the LEP student and the ways in which that language reflects a particular view of reality.

Culture and Socialization

Culture has been defined as a blueprint guiding the behavior of people in groups and nurtured by family life. Although some differences among families are idiosyncratic, others are clearly associated with differences in culture. The relationship between socialization and culture is evident during the child-rearing process. Very early in life, infants are taught the acceptable forms of interaction and participation: Unacceptable or intolerable behavior is chastised, and appropriate or well-mannered behavior is sanctioned. At a later age, children are given responsibilities and are expected to contribute to the family according to their culturally bound norms. In each of the aforementioned areas related to child rearing (forms of interaction and participation, sanctioning behavior, and responsibility taking), a potential conflict exists between the home and the school. This is especially true when the culture represented by the school or the teacher is different from the culture with which the child is most familiar.

The following is a classic example of this incongruity:

A teacher pats a child on the head as a gesture of affection. At home that same student has learned that this part of the body is sacred, and it is therefore disrespectful to touch it.

This case is particularly sad because it demonstrates that good intentions are not enough. A well-intentioned teacher created "cultural dissonance" (Philips, 1983; Mohatt & Erickson, 1981) for the student. The dissonance could have been minimized, if not totally avoided, if the teacher had had some understanding of the cultural background of the student. In teaching the LMS, this understanding is therefore not a frill but a necessity.

Behavioral differences across cultures are numerous. Saville-Troike (1978) and Hall (1959) discuss some of them. As we highlight these differences it is important to bear in mind that behaviors manifested by an individual or a family may not always be shaped by the culture but may simply represent differences idiosyncratic to that individual or family.

While some cultures encourage children to compete, others expect them to cooperate, discouraging and even punishing competition. Some cultures promote participation of children in adult events, while others discourage it. Silence among children is reinforced among some cultures; verbalization is encouraged among others. Cultures also differ in the degree to which they call attention to the individual. For example, some parents call on individual children to perform for visiting friends and relatives, while others avoid singling out children or anyone else in a gathering, regardless of how intimate the circumstances may be.

The rules for interaction also affect a child's use of language. What is appropriate or even polite behavior for greeting someone, initiating a conversation, or entering into an already established conversation differs from group to group. For example, asking someone how much he or she earns when first meeting is acceptable in some cultures, considered impolite in others.

Many children are taught at home what to expect and how to behave in school even before they enter kindergarten. The means by which behavior is encouraged or discouraged at home also affects the LMS's expectations and behavior in school. For example, sanctioning behavior on the part of the teacher may differ from that used at home. Some cultures encourage eye contact when reprimanding a child; others expect the child to lower the head out of respect. Some cultures emphasize astute listening; others encourage active questioning in school. Classroom behavior can also be affected if the home culture values cooperation but the school culture values competition. These examples of cultural differences comprise part of the structure of participation within a culture and are potential sources of cultural dissonance.

It is clear that the rules for participating and learning are not universal or culture-free; they are bound by the culture from which they emanate. These rules are not always obvious to the outsider. At times, even the insider or user has difficulty describing them. However, the differences in and of themselves are not a problem. For language minority children, the problem arises when the behaviors expected by the teacher and school are in conflict with those imposed at home. Researchers have recognized that learning can actually be facilitated when the values and demands of the school are congruent with home and community values, or at least not in dissonance with them.

Culture, Language, and Perception

The rules for socialization and interaction taught in the home are one way in which children learn the values of their culture. Another source of enculturation is in the forms of language available to the child. For example, a student who has always had to make a choice between formal and informal pronouns (for example, in Spanish, *tu*, informal "you," versus *Usted*, formal "you") faces both a language difficulty and an organizational or perceptual difficulty upon discovering that in English all individuals are addressed as "you," regardless of status or age. This same formal-informal dichotomy is present in many other languages, including French, Italian, Greek, and some dialects of Chinese. The choice of pronouns and verb endings in many of these languages is affected by the age and social status of the listener vis-à-vis the speaker. In effect, the formal-informal dichotomy causes the speaker of a language to view the world from a particular perspective and act accordingly. This supports the view that reality is affected by the categories and dichotomies that constitute a language and are available to its speakers. Brown (1980) described the relationship between language and culture as follows: "A language is a part of a culture and a culture is a part of a language; the two are intricately interwoven such that one cannot separate the two without losing the significance of either language or culture" (p. 124). He goes on to say:

> Language—the means for communication among members of a culture—is the most visible and available expression of that culture. And so a person's world view, self-identity, his systems of thinking, acting, feeling and communicating are disrupted by a change from one culture to another. (p. 129–130)

Clearly, differences of linguistic form affect more than language acquisition. They can also affect the process of cultural adjustment. Although adjustment to a different culture is indicated, the responsibility for change cannot be placed exclusively on the student. The responsibility of the teacher is just as great. Brown (1980) makes this point when he states:

> Both learners and teachers of a second language need to understand cultural differences, to recognize openly that everyone in the world is not "just like me," that people are not all the same beneath the skin. There are real differences between groups and cultures. We can learn to perceive those differences, appreciate them and above all to respect, value and prize the personhood of every human being. (p. 127)

Other Factors Affecting Adjustment

The adjustment process for LEP students is also influenced by the physical differences between their homeland and the United States as well as by the economic, political, and social experiences that caused their families to migrate. Consider the following situations, all potential sources of adjustment problems.

1. Educational adjustment when education in the native country is not mandatory or is limited to a small elite; a dress code is enforced; the approach used in instruction relies heavily on rote learning, extensive note taking, and/or limited movement or interaction among students in the classroom; and the teacher is highly revered.
2. Religious adjustment when there is no local house of worship that reflects the family's beliefs.
3. Political adjustment when a student comes from a country that is run by a dictatorship, under martial law, or threatened by military juntas.
4. Economic adjustment when a student is used to living well abroad and then finds himself or herself living poorly (the experience of some political refugees).
5. Geographic adjustment when a student comes from a rural region to live in a big urban center or when a family settles in an area inhabited by people of a different ethnic background rather than with people of their own national origin.
6. Climatic adjustment to weather that is markedly different from that experienced in the homeland.
7. Socioemotional adjustment when no one around the student speaks or understands the student's language.

This list represents only a handful of potential conflicts faced by newly arrived students as well as other LMSs, any one of which can lead to problems such as poor participation in classroom and other school activities as well as little motivation and interest in school. Unattended, these problems can lead to poor academic achievement and truancy and, more distressing, to dropping out of school altogether.

THE LEARNING PROCESS

The Role of Language in School Learning

Many researchers and theoreticians concur that formal schooling is directed at the acquisition of knowledge through the medium of language (Olson, 1977; Halliday, 1977; Cazden, 1979). If, however, the language being used to facilitate the acquisition of knowledge is foreign to the student, the acquisition of that knowledge must be affected. According to Wong-Fillmore (1982), the language used by teachers with non—English speakers serves a dual function at school: It conveys the subject matter to be learned, and it provides an important source of the input such students need in order to learn the school language (p. 283). Therefore, language, as the major vehicle of school instruction, presents a challenge to any student, but especially to the language minority student for whom the language of instruction may not be the language the child understands. Consider the many roles of language for these students:

1. Students must learn *about* language. They learn about its history, its grammar, and its system of meaning as well as about the literary heritage of people who speak it.
2. Students must learn to *use* language—to express themselves and to communicate ideas.
3. Students learn *through* language. The content of instruction is conveyed through language. Language is used to probe, stimulate, or clarify thinking.
4. Students demonstrate learning through language. Learning is gauged by language-dependent measures, such as oral and written examinations.
5. Students learn about group conduct and participation through formal and informal conversations and discussions. Language is used to regulate individual and group behavior and interactions.
6. Students express and acquire values, beliefs, and attitudes through communication with others.

According to Gage's (1972) conception of teaching, it is through the deliberate formulation and organization of utterances that teachers create the conditions that enable students to integrate and internalize concepts and ideas. Thus he describes a lesson as the exertion of a cognitive influence on a student, a process of transmission.

From another perspective, the Bullock report (1975) states:

> What the teacher has in mind may well be the destination of a thinking process; but the learner needs to trace the steps from the familiar to the new, from the fact or idea he possesses to what he is to acquire. In other words, he has to make a journey in thought for himself. (p. 141)

It is as if the student learns, in part, through a process of construction.

Whether one accepts the view that knowledge is transmitted or that knowledge is constructed, or whether one believes that the truth lies somewhere in between, there seems little disagreement that language is a powerful mediating force in school learning.

One of the earliest and clearest formulations of the view of language as a mediator is found in the work of the Russian psychologist Vygotsky (1978). He suggests that school learning is a profoundly social process that is mediated by language in two distinct ways: as "language turned outward" and "language turned inward."

By "language turned outward," Vygotsky was referring to the role of language in learning. That is, learning requires interaction, verbalization, and collaboration between two or more individuals: one who will guide, demonstrate, explain; the other who, by implication, will attend, question, and seek out information.

"Language turned inward" refers to the psychological process in which language is used to reflect on, organize, and rehearse newly acquired knowledge. This internal monologue or inner speech, which is said to have its origin in the social dialogue, is in fact a mental activity that makes it possible for individuals to direct, control, and regulate their own learning.

If we accept the notion that learning is mediated by the use of language turned outward and inward, we must allow for the active use of language in classes if learning is to occur. This requires that learning experiences be properly organized in order to promote cognitive development. The organization of these experiences should allow individuals to imitate or perform tasks with the support of others in their immediate environment. Thus language-mediated learning can positively affect or influence cognitive development.

Just as concepts are learned through the use of language, so too are they refined. According to Britton (1970), language is the principal means by which individuals form and organize mental representations of their experiences, which subsequently make it possible for them to classify, interpret, and understand future experiences and events. Moreover, it is through the verbalization of experiences, or through talk, that past or imagined experiences are reviewed and analyzed in ways that were not originally possible. Britton, however, emphasizes that more than the mere verbalization of experiences, it is social interaction through language that is important. Conversations are an important mode of learning since "in good conversation, participants profit from their own talking...from what others contribute and above all from the interaction—that is, from the enabling effect of each upon the other" (p. 238).

Like Vygotsky, Britton distinguishes between two types of talk that are essential modes of learning: spectator talk and participant talk. Spectator talk is talk to recount or re-create experiences, real or imagined. The prime purpose of spectator talk is to work on the world experience and to reorganize it in light of experiences not now engaged in but contemplated.

In contrast, participant talk is talk that accompanies action and is directed at getting things done. Specifically, participant talk is used to explore, theorize, gather information, and solve problems; it is talk that makes it possible to "turn confusion into order" and make sense of new, ongoing experiences.

In sum, both Vygotsky and Britton present powerful theories of how, through social interaction, the verbalization of ideas and information influences cognitive development and cognitive restructuring.

The problem for LEP students is that while the teacher and the text focus on content, often oblivious to the role of language in the process of acquiring knowledge, the students' limited knowledge of the language of instruction makes learning concepts a dual task. They must negotiate both the concepts and the language in which those concepts are presented. If the language already known and accessible to students is discouraged, or if they are penalized for using it, even privately, their potential for developing and exploring ideas through it is also repressed. Concepts, rather than being understood, explored, or clarified, are actually confused.

The Development of Language

Just as cognitive development is a complex process involving interaction between language and concepts, so too is the development of language. It involves more than the development of grammatical fluency or linguistic competence, as the process has been characterized in the past. More recently, researchers have agreed that before learning to use the forms of language and to manipulate its grammatical structures, children learn to put language to social use; that is, they develop sociolinguistic competence. Put simply, they learn how to use language to communicate and get things done (Bloom & Lahey, 1978).

The process of language development begins long before children utter their first words. Through crying, pointing, and other nonverbal forms, children begin communicating. Even at this early stage, their communication serves a variety of functions, including the expression of anger, satisfaction, agreement, and disagreement and the ability to make requests. Clearly, in the acquisition process, many functions of language are expressed prior to actual use of appropriate forms. Just as function takes precedence over form, comprehension of language takes precedence over its production.

By the age of 5, children are able to communicate in their native language. Over time this ability is fine-tuned; syntax gets more involved, and vocabulary expands. This ability involves knowledge of the discrete elements of the language. Most specifically, it includes a person's ability to manipulate these elements in the native language in new and creative ways. Children create with sounds (phonemes), word parts (morphemes), words (lexemes), and word order (syntax). For example, when children use words such as *goed* or *wented*, their creativity or "linguistic genius" (Chukovsky, 1968) is evident. By taking the stems *go* and *went* and overgeneralizing the inflectional ending –ed, they create a new past-tense form. Just as children who speak English natively create with English, so do those who speak other languages create with their native languages. Their ability to create is based on the fact that through the language acquisition process they develop a linguistic system of rules and the ability to use that system without necessarily being able to explain it. This ability is referred to as linguistic awareness.

Children who have learned a first language bring to the second language acquisition process a linguistic foundation. They have manipulated word parts—roots, stems, endings—as well as words themselves in the construction of utterances they have never heard before. It is this foundation that enables them to be as creative in the acquisition of a second language as they were in the acquisition of their native language. However, the creative construction process in second-language acquisition differs in some ways from that employed in native-language acquisition.

One of the biggest differences is the fact that second-language acquisition builds on knowledge and skills acquired during native-language acquisition. In learning a second language, one does not start from scratch. Many of these skills are similar across the languages and therefore transferrable. Most of the language-related skills that children possess prior to entering school are social in nature and have been labeled by Cummins (1981) as "basic interpersonal communication skills" (BICS). The degree to which children develop these communication skills in their native language (L_1) influences, in part, their development of the second language (L_2). Cummins describes this interrelationship as the "linguistic interdependence hypothesis." In essence, it states that the development of proficiency in L_2 is partially a function of L_1 proficiency at the time when intensive exposure to L_2 begins (Cummins, 1979).

Just as the knowledge and skills acquired in mastering one's native language can serve as a point of departure and enhance the acquisition of a second language, so too can they stand in its way. For example, when prior knowledge of the sounds, letters, or grammatical rules of one's native language are equal to those of the second language, there is a potential for positive transfer. However, when the forms and rules of the languages are different, the potential for negative transfer or interference exists. In effect, the native language serves as a filter through which the target language is both perceived and produced.

For example, at the level of syntax, the general rule for adjective placement in Spanish is "noun (N) + adjective (A)," while in English it is "adjective + noun." Students who use the Spanish N+A construction to produce an English utterance are incorrectly transferring a native-language rule to the second language. On the other hand, the rule for forming plurals in both English and Spanish requires the addition of *s* or *es*. The correct application of that rule to English is an example of positive transfer. (The circumstances under which that rule is applied are not exactly the same across the two languages, so there is also a potential for negative transfer under certain circumstances.)

While some errors made by ESL learners reflect negative transfer, many more reflect generalizations learners are making about the rules of the target language, independent of their knowledge of the native language. Both types of errors—those resulting from negative transfer and those from target-language overgeneralization—are an integral part of the second-language acquisition process, and both reflect the creative nature of that process. Too often, however, errors, regardless of their source, are seen by teachers as a sign of incompetence when in fact they are actually a reflection of competence—specifically, what a student knows about the language at a particular point in the acquisition process. As the student's system of rules becomes more refined and approximates more closely that of a native speaker, fewer interference errors are made, and more overgeneralizations occur. Hence the road to second-language acquisition is like a continuum, with errors serving as markers of what the student knows at any given point. This intermediate system, based on incomplete knowledge of the new language, is referred to in the literature as an "approximative system" (Richards, 1974) or as a student's "interlanguage" (Selinker, 1974). It is important to remember that errors are evidence of the rules language learners are deducing, and as such they can provide valuable information about what students know as well as what they need to learn about the new language.

Language Development and School Participation

Beyond grammatical or linguistic competence and subject-matter knowledge, participation in school requires that students have other kinds of knowledge and abilities.

Mehan (1979), for example, contends that students must know the context of academic subjects as well as the forms to convey their academic knowledge. They must know with whom, when, and where they can speak and act, and they must produce speech and behaviors that are appropriate for a given classroom activity. Students must be able to relate both academic and social behaviors to varying classroom situations by interpreting implicit rules (p. 133). For the LMS the task is complicated by the fact that the appropriate behavior patterns of the native country may be in conflict with what is expected in the American classroom, as discussed earlier.

Cummins (1981) supports the contention that classroom participation requires a particular type of language proficiency, "cognitive academic language proficiency" (CALP). He argues that CALP is often confused with proficiency in BICS. Cummins suggests that high levels of proficiency in CALP accompany high levels of school performance.

One of the basic distinctions between BICS and CALP is that the former is generally context-embedded, that is, found in a situation where there is contextual support for meaning. CALP is generally associated with a context-reduced situation, one with few contextual clues to meaning. Such is clearly the case with the language used in textbooks.

The problem for LEP students is twofold. While they may bring to the classroom a good command of the interpersonal forms of their native language, they are then introduced to, and expected to perform in, context-reduced academic forms of English without having developed either the academic forms of their native language or the interpersonal forms needed to interact in English. They are therefore doubly disadvantaged.

In sum, both Mehan and Cummins indicate that students must be able to decode and understand the informational content of instruction, as well as the procedures for classroom participation, in order to participate appropriately in classrooms and thereby gain access to instruction.

While these researchers agree that participation requires some degree of sociolinguistic competence on the part of students, they maintain that participation is not simply a matter of possessing fixed quantities of such competence. Nor does participation necessarily look the same for all children nor even for all members of the same culture. Student participation is said to be related to and affected by other factors.

In reviewing data collected on instruction in bilingual classes in the Significant Bilingual Instructional Features Study (SBIF), Romero (1982) found that the participation of the LMS was affected by at least four factors: language of instruction, oral English proficiency of the student, learning style of the student, and instructor's ground rules for participation. Apart from the extrinsic factors affecting participation, the form of that participation varied on at least six dimensions, as reflected in Figure 14.1. There was no one superior form of participation. Maximal participation was not always accurate, nor was minimal participation nonproductive or a reflection of incompetence. Just as individuals differ in their personalities and the experiences they bring to the learning process, so too do they differ in the ways in which they learn. Clearly, there is no one way to participate, and teachers need to make allowances for individual differences.

Factors Affecting Language Development

In the affective domain, Gardner and Lambert (1972) noted the importance of attitudes and motivation in learning a second language. Motivation was seen as taking two possible forms, an integrative orientation and an instrumental orientation. The integrative orientation motivates a student to learn a language because of a "sincere and personal interest in the people and culture represented in the other group" (p. 132). In some ways, it represents a desire to integrate into that culture. An instrumental orientation motivates a student to learn a language for its utilitarian function—to get a job or pass a test. While the integrative motivation was sometimes

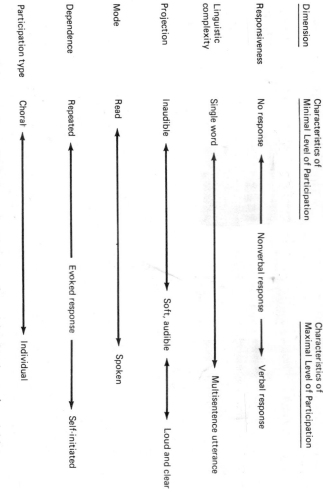

Dimension	Characteristics of Minimal Level of Participation		Characteristics of Maximal Level of Participation
Responsiveness	No response →	Nonverbal response →	Verbal response
Linguistic complexity	Single word ↔		Multisentence utterance
Projection	Inaudible ↔	Soft, audible ↔	Loud and clear
Mode	Read ↔		Spoken
Dependence	Repeated ↔	Evoked response ↔	Self-initiated
Participation type	Choral ↔		Individual

FIGURE 14.1   Some dimensions of students' oral participation in work activities.

found to be more productive, both instrumental and integrative orientations toward the language-learning task were helpful in assuring student success in learning a second language.

With respect to attitudes, Gardner and Lambert found that if a student's attitude was either ethnocentric or hostile toward the language under study, its effect on acquisition was negative. They saw the hostile or ethnocentric student as "perceptually insensitive to the language" and apparently "unwilling to modify or adjust his own response system to approximate the new pronunciational responses required in the other language" (p. 134). Language learners must be willing to identify with members of the target ethnolinguistic group if they are to accomplish the task of learning a new linguistic system. This does not mean that students must give up their own identity in order to take on that of another ethnolinguistic group. In another study reported in the same publication, Gardner and Lambert found that the status of the student's own minority language and ethnolinguistic group, within the larger community, must also be taken into account. The contention is that in bilingual communities, where differential prestige is accorded the languages and the ethnolinguistic groups involved, attention should be placed by *both* linguistic groups on the development of skills in the language more likely to be overlooked. This recommendation is based on the premise that there is an interrelationship between what we know and feel about our own language and how effectively we learn the new language.

According to Bloom (1980, cited in Brown, 1981), the process of learning a new language and becoming part of a second culture involves five different levels of affectivity. The first is *receiving*. A person must be aware of the surrounding environment and willing to accept and tolerate it, not avoid it. Recall our profile at the beginning of this chapter of Gerardo, who did just the opposite. He was aware of all

things and people in his environment, but he was unwilling to accept them as they were. In fact, he was determined to avoid them.

The second level of affectivity described by Bloom is *responding*—being willing to respond without coercion and then receiving satisfaction from that response. Gerardo's English teacher reported that he made little effort to participate in class activities, at times none at all. Gerardo himself stated that he found the class activities boring. The third level of affectivity, *valuing*, involves identifying, committing oneself to, and pursuing certain values. According to Gerardo, the things that he values, such as education, family, respect, and true friendship, are of little value here. *Organization*, the fourth level of affectivity, involves organizing values into a system of beliefs, determining interrelationships among them, and establishing a hierarchy within the system. If the first three levels have not been reached, attainment of level 4 is precluded. Finally, a personal value system serves as a guide for an individual's actions and attitudes about the world. Clearly, Gerardo has not yet learned to accept or even understand this new culture with its different values and attitudes. As a result, his acquisition of English and his willingness to become part of the American culture are negatively affected.

In the social domain, Wong-Fillmore (1976) found two basic interactional styles that motivated language use by LEP students, avoidance and risk taking. Avoiders refrain from using the target language and avoid putting themselves into situations in which they will be forced to use it. The result minimizes exposure to the language, a necessary requisite for language learning. In contrast, willingness and eagerness to immerse in language practice are characteristic of a risk taker. Making mistakes is a part of learning; language is explored through communication.

QUESTIONS TEACHERS ASK

Q. *What do effective bilingual teachers do?*

A. Effective bilingual teachers do what all effective teachers do—whatever works for them and for their students. Every individual is different, and so is every class. Changes may come quickly, slowly, or not at all. Finding the best approach for teaching a particular student or a given class requires experimentation, and this entails a certain degree of trial and error. However, experimentation need not be unguided. There is a growing body of research on effective teaching practices that can be very useful in expanding one's repertoire of instructional skills and techniques. With regard to bilingual instruction, much interesting and valuable research has been conducted in connection with the Part C [now Part B] Research Agenda. To understand more about truly effective bilingual instruction, refer to publications on the Significant Bilingual Instructional Features Study (SBIF; 1980–1982), which was funded by the National Institute of Education through a contract with the Far West Laboratory for Educational Research and Development. It is not possible to summarize here the full findings of this extensive study, but these were found to be the key features of effective bilingual instruction:

1. Effective bilingual teachers use two languages to mediate instruction. This involves conveying content in the native language as well as in the language of the school.
2. Effective bilingual teachers incorporate English language development in basic skills instruction. This promotes aquisition of the language as the student participates competently in instructional activities.

3. The effective bilingual teacher uses knowledge of the students' home culture while providing instruction. In doing so, the teacher (a) responds to and introduces culture-related referents, (b) makes instructional uses of the rules of discourse in the students' native language, and (c) observes the norms and values of the home culture.

Q. *How much time should be devoted to instruction in the native language and how much to instruction in English?*

A. It would be wonderful if we could state that, say, 49% of the instruction should be in L_1 and 51% in L_2. Unfortunately, it is not that simple. No matter what is found to be effective in one situation, there is no guarantee that it will be effective in another. Assuming that the bilingual program is a transitional one (as most are), at the end of a certain number of years, students are expected to have become proficient enough in English to receive monolingual instruction. As the teacher, you are to a large extent responsible for this happening, so your classroom behaviors must be guided by the knowledge of this very great responsibility. The percentage of time alloted to English will be dictated by the rate at which your students can progress comfortably in their acquisition of a second language. As in any group movement, it can be expected that some will be at the front and others at the back, but the important thing is that everyone keep advancing and that no one lag so far behind as to become lost. Knowing the time limit the school has imposed on the attainment of English proficiency, you may find it necessary to hurry your class along. Simply be aware of how hard you are pressing them.

Q. *How does one decide whether to provide bilingual or ESL instruction?*

A. Whether there is to be a bilingual program or an ESL program is usually determined by the combined regulations and policies of state and local educational agencies. In some states or municipalities, if there are a given number of LEP students in a district, speaking a common native language and at approximately the same grade level, the district is required to provide bilingual instruction. If the LEP student is isolated—that is, if there are few or no other students in the school that speak the same native language or if there is a wide difference in academic levels—it is customary to provide the student with instruction in English as a second language. Bear in mind that regulations and guidelines pertaining to the instruction of LEP students are not uniform throughout the nation, and in recent education-related legislation, the federal government has revealed a disinclination to impose anything that might be interpreted as national standards.

Q. *When children are placed in a bilingual program, isn't there a risk that they will never become proficient in English?*

A. This is an unreasonable fear. There are three types of bilingual education programs: (1) transitional programs, in which the object is to have the student attain proficiency in English as quickly as possible; the native language is used only as a means to this end; (2) maintenance programs, which provide ongoing instruction in the native language as well as English, so that the goal is true bilingualism; and (3) enrichment programs, which are usually modified maintenance programs in which English monolingual students participate to learn the language of the minority, who are in turn learning English. Regardless of its type, the major goal of every bilingual program is to teach LEP students to speak English; as important as maintenance and enrichment are, it is the English language development component that makes the program feasible. In addition, no ethnic enclave in this country can be completely isolated from the English language. The LEP student will hear it spoken in public, on television and radio, and see it written in books, magazines, newspapers, and various forms of advertising. Most likely, some of the students' peers will be proficient in English. Even if one were not to attend school at all, American society provides sufficient stimuli and motivation for the learning of English. Ironically, the irrational concern that bilingual education may not develop English language proficiency obscures the real danger, which is that monolingual education in English can lead to the loss of valuable native-language skills.

Q. *How can information be gathered on the LEP students' culture and experience and used in instruction?*

A.   Data on student backgrounds can be collected in a variety of ways as part of the instructional process. For example, students might be asked to fill in a time line with pictures or narratives of highlights of their lives. The teacher can provide visuals from which the LEP student can choose the most appropriate. As English proficiency increases, the student may also be asked to describe a typical day in the life of a student in the native country. Peers can be encouraged to ask the questions. If another student in the class is proficient in both the LEP student's native language and English, the bilingual student could serve as interpreter. By allowing LEP students to speak in their native language, its status is enhanced, and the monolingual children in the class are shown the value of being bilingual.

This information can be incorporated into units of study on the differences and similarities between the students' native language and culture and the language and culture represented by the school. It can then be used to make other students in the class aware of the differences that one encounters in a culturally diverse society.

Q. *What else should I know about my LEP students, and how can I obtain it?*

A.   To be able to avoid potential culture conflict, teachers need data on patterns of interaction with peers and with figures of authority, both in and out of school. By observing children interacting in a variety of contexts, with a variety of individuals, tentative hypotheses on modes of acceptable behavior, learning patterns, hierarchies of authority, and concomitant values can be identified.

In observing students interacting, teachers and administrators must be careful not to turn an observation of behavior into an evaluation of it. This can be the case when teachers approach other cultures with any degree of ethnocentrism or cultural snobbery. The function of the observation is simply to describe behavior without evaluating it. This is best accomplished by describing what a student does in different contexts, rather than by focusing on what the student does not do. Once observations have been made, the behaviors and generalizations deriving from them need to be confirmed either through outside readings or through adult informants.

Q. *How can I alleviate cultural conflict?*

A.   A primary requisite is that the teacher be informed about the cultures of the children in the class and to use that information in teaching. It is also important that LEP students develop knowledge of, and pride in, their language and culture. Conflicts resulting from cultures in contact can be handled through instruction. This might be done by having students read about other children who have gone through similar experiences or by discussing openly certain cultural differences that are potential sources of conflict.

Q.   *How can I provide effective instruction if I have only a few LEP students in my class?*
A.   There are many resources that can help you to meet the instructional needs of these students. Beyond the direct attention you provide, other students in the class can take turns serving as tutors. This type of interaction is said to be muturally beneficial in that it promotes cross-cultural understanding in natural ways. Situations that arise from these experiences may in turn be used for study and discussion by all students in the class. You might also consider the possibility of enlisting the aid of a school volunteer who speaks the language of the students. In some communities there are organizations that provide resource personnel. Such volunteers can provide essential cultural and background information that may give you a better understanding of your LEP students. More important, having someone who speaks the students' language is essential to establishing a channel of communication between the home and the school.

Beyond these human resources, there are instructional materials that can be used with or without a tutor to provide for meaningful activities related to the curriculum. For example, many teachers have found it effective to use "talking books," commercially recorded or recorded by other students or adults in the language that the students speak. LEPs may be given the opportunity to work independently with these during part of the school day.

As you avail yourself of the resources that are available, it is important that you schedule time each day for the LEP student to interact with you and the other students. Communication is at the heart of learning. By ensuring that the LEP students know they are as important to you as their English-speaking classmates, you will establish a climate in which they are comfortable. In this atmosphere, with patience and encouragement, the LEP students will eventually overcome their natural reticence and begin to attempt to speak English. This is only the first step in a long journey, but once it is taken, the going becomes progressively easier, for the teacher as well as the student.

Q.   *How can I obtain information on a learner's attitudes and motivation toward the language of instruction, given their importance in the language acquisition process?*
A.   Attitudes and motivation are manifested in behavior, not just in what one says about how he or she feels. Accordingly, they must be inferred from verbal and nonverbal behavior. Inferences can be drawn from observations of the following:

1. A student's behavior and body language when L_1 or L_2 is used for instruction.
2. The extent of participation of students during instruction in L_1 and L_2 and the manner in which they participate.
3. A student's verbal expressions of attitude toward the languages of instruction.
4. The student's use of language outside of school, for example, the language in which conversation is initiated, the dominant language of the children with whom

the LEP student interacts, the language in which the child responds when addressed in the native language or the second language, and the languages used at home with different individuals and for different purposes (with siblings, parents, grandparents, etc.; on TV and radio).

Q. *What should I know about my students' native language and related skills?*
A. First you must determine whether each student is literate in the native language. To determine the extent to which native-language literacy skills might be transferable to English, you should be aware of the type of writing system of the native language: Is it alphabetic or ideographic? If alphabetic, does it use the Roman, Cyrillic, Greek, or another alphabet? Do sound and symbols correspond across the two languages? If so, there is the potential for transfer; if not, there is potential for confusion. Areas of correspondence can be capitalized upon; areas of discrepancy can alert you to possible confusion.

Q. *When English is used as a medium of instruction with LEP students, what can the teacher do to promote its acquisition?*
A. An optimal second-language acquisition context has four basic characteristics:

1. The second language must be comprehensible to the student or rendered comprehensible through the use of concrete materials, visuals, and body-language clues.
2. The information conveyed through the second language must be interesting or relevant to the student.
3. Exposure to the second language must be sufficient to provide the opportunity for learning.
4. The learner must use the second language actively, to negotiate meaning. This can take the form of student-teacher or student-student interactions and dialogue.

Q. *What are some ways in which I can facilitate the English-language comprehension of the LEP students in my class?*
A. Here are four things you can do:

1. Paraphrase questions and statements to allow for different levels of proficiency on the part of students. Use synonyms to clarify the meaning of unknown words.
2. Make the language of the text (academic language) comprehensible by interpreting it in simple language using the everyday vocabulary of the children. When necessary, translate or switch codes to convey a word or concept that a student does not understand; then continue in English.
3. Enunciate clearly, but without exaggeration, and with your mouth in direct view of the students.
4. Encourage classroom discussion of new information to give students an opportunity to negotiate meaning.

Q. *How can I encourage LEP students to use English in class?*
A. Here are three suggestions:

1. Establish a classroom environment in which children are not afraid to take risks and to use English. Teach English monolingual students to understand language differences; let them know that there is nothing wrong with having an accent.

2. Ask questions that require different degrees of English proficiency in responding; that is, alternate directives that allow children an opportunity to demonstrate comprehension by responding nonverbally; questions requiring a yes or no answer; either-or questions in which the student chooses between two answers that have been included in the question, usually with a single word or a simple phrase; *wh–* questions (*who, what, when, where*) in which children must generate the vocabulary of the response, again usually single words or phrases; and why questions requiring greater knowledge of English.
3. When children respond to your questions and directives, focus on the content (the message) rather than on the form of the response.

CONCLUSIONS

The factors affecting the processes of adjustment and learning for language minority students and students with limited proficiency in English are complex. They include the background experiences of the child in the native country; the individual's modes of participation, interaction, and learning; native-language skills; and prior academic experience and achievement. Given the effect of these factors on learning, it is incumbent on teachers to collect information from LEP students and LMSs on their experiences in the native country, in the family, and, when appropriate and available, at previous schools. In so doing, the teacher of LEP students is placed in the role of learner. The information can be used by the teacher to identify possible sources of culture conflict and, simultaneously, to facilitate the social, cultural, and educational adjustment of the student to the classroom, the school, the community, and the country.

Our contention is that while ethnic and linguistic diversity within a classroom is viewed by many as a problem with which to contend, it can be turned into an asset from which both teachers and students can profit. For example, once collected, data can be used to inform and sensitize other students in the class to the differences that make for cultural diversity in this country. By necessity, the end goal must be productive and effective participation of language minority students in the American school system. However, we do not feel that this has to be accomplished at the expense of the native language or culture.

FURTHER READING

Barnes, D., Britton, J., & Rosen, H. (1969). *Language, the Learner and the School.* Upper Montclair, NJ: Boynton/Cook. Douglas Barnes's "Language in the Secondary Classroom," the heart of this book, aims at finding some answers to the use of language in the classroom. James Britton switches attention to the student: What function does talk—even ordinary, undemanding, talk for talk's sake—have in the development of thought? Finally, Rosen gives an account of wise language activities going on in some schools and suggestions for more.

Martin, N., Newton, B., D'Arcy, P., & Parker, R. (1976). *Writing and Learning across the Curriculum 11–16.* Upper Montclair, NJ: Boynton/Cook. This book is an outgrowth of the Schools Council Writing across the Curriculum Project, which emphasized the interrelationship of spoken and written language and sought to develop teaching techniques that would make writing more meaningful to students.

Tikunoff, W. (1983). *Applying Significant Bilingual Instructional Features in the Classroom.*

Rosslyn, VA: InterAmerica Research Associates, National Clearinghouse for Bilingual Education. Draws on extensive research in bilingual classrooms to identify techniques useful to teachers.

Wong-Fillmore, L. (1982). "Instructional Language as Linguistic Input." In L. C. Wilkinson (Ed.), *Communicating in the Classroom*. Orlando, FL: Academic Press. Explains the role of language in the classroom and the ways in which classroom language differs from everyday speech.

REFERENCES

Bloom, L., & Lahey, M. (1978). *Language development and language disorders*. New York: Wiley.

Britton, J. (1970). *Language and learning*. Middlesex, Eng.: Penguin.

Brown, H. D. (1981). *Principles of language learning and teaching*. Englewood Cliffs, NJ: Prentice-Hall.

Bullock, A. (1975). *A language for life*. Report of the Committees of Inquiry appointed by the Secretary of State for Education and Science. London: Her Majesty's Stationery Office.

Cazden, C. (1979). Language in education: Variations in the teacher-talk register. In J. E. Alatis and G. R. Tucker (Eds.), *Georgetown University Round Table on Languages and Linguistics: Language in public life*. Washington, DC: Georgetown University Press.

Chukovsky, K. (1968). *From 2 to 5*. Berkeley: University of California Press.

Cummins, J. (1979). Linguistic interdependence and the educational development of bilingual children. *Review of Educational Research, 49*, 222–251.

Cummins, J. (1981). The role of primary language development in promoting educational success for language minority students. In California State Department of Education, *Schooling and language minority students: A theoretical framework*. Los Angeles: Evaluation Dissemination and Assessment Center.

Gage, N. L. (1972). *Teacher effectiveness and teacher education*. Palo Alto, CA: Pacific Book Publishing.

Gardner, R. C., & Lambert, W. E. (1972). *Attitudes and motivation in second language learning*. Rowley, MA: Newbury House.

Hall, E. (1959). *The silent language*. New York: Doubleday.

Halliday, M.A.K. (1977). *Language as a social semiotic: The social interpretation of language and meaning*. Baltimore: University Park Press.

Larson, N., & Smalley, W. A. (1972). Becoming bilingual: A guide to language learning. *Practical Anthropology*.

Mehan, H. (1979). *Learning lessons: Social organization in the classroom*. Cambridge, MA: Harvard University Press.

Mohatt, R., & Erickson, F. (1981). Cultural differences in teaching styles in an Odawa school: A sociolinguistic approach. In H. T. Trueba, G. P. Guthrie, & K. H. Au (Eds.), *Culture and the bilingual classroom: Studies in classroom ethnography*. Rowley, MA: Newbury House.

Olson, R. (1977). From utterance to text: The bias of language in speech and writing. *Harvard Educational Review, 47*, 257–281.

Oxford-Carpenter, R. (1980). *Demographic projections of non–English-language-background and limited–English-proficient persons in the United States to the year 2000 by state, age, and language group*. Rosslyn, VA: Inter-American Research Associates, National Clearinghouse for Bilingual Education.

Philips, S. (1983). *The invisible culture: Communication in classroom and community on the Warm Springs Indian reservation*. White Plains, NY: Longman.

Richards, J. C. (1974). *Error analysis: Perspectives on second language acquisition*. London: Longman.

Romero, M. (1982, March). *Student response to classroom work activities based upon language of instruction.* Paper presented at the annual meeting of the American Educational Research Association, New York.

Saville-Troike, M. (1978). *A guide to culture in the classroom.* Rosslyn, VA: Inter-American Research Associates, National Clearinghouse for Bilingual Education.

Selinker, L. (1974). Interlanguage. In J. C. Richards (Ed.), *Error analysis: Perspectives on second language acquisition.* London: Longman.

U.S. Congress. House of Representatives. (1984). *Education Amendments of 1984.* 98th Cong., 2d sess. H.R. Report 98–1128.

Vygotsky, L. S. (1978). *Mind in society: The development of higher psychological processes* (M. Cole, V. John-Steiner, S. Scribner, & E. Souberman, Eds.). Cambridge, MA: Harvard University Press.

Wong-Fillmore, L. (1976). *The second time around: Cognitive and social strategies in second language acquisition.* Unpublished doctoral dissertation, Stanford University, Stanford, CA.

Wong-Fillmore, L. (1982). Instructional language as linguistic input. In L. C. Wilkinson (Ed.), *Communicating in the classroom.* Orlando, FL: Academic Press.

15 ETHNIC AND CULTURAL DIFFERENCES

Ursula Casanova

Recent interest in ethnic and cultural differences suggests that multiculturalism is a new phenomenon in this country. However, the United States has been a multicultural country from its beginnings. Many believe that it is precisely this variety that gives the country its strength and vitality. This view has helped to fuel current interest in multicultural education.

The recognition that many students find the school an alien environment has also contributed to the interest in multicultural education. Alienation may result when the student's acculturation prepares him or her for a social context that differs markedly from that of the school. In recent years, an emerging body of research has suggested that a discrepancy between home and school environments may be behind the lack of achievement of many such students.

A third reason for having an interest in ethnic and cultural differences is the pleasure and learning that may be derived from an understanding of the similarities that bind us and the differences that make us distinctive. Travel is a broadening experience because it puts us face to face with our common humanity as well as our cultural distinctiveness. The multicultural, multiethnic classroom also provides those opportunities if we only take them.

BACKGROUND

I intend to discuss ethnic and cultural differences, especially as they relate to teachers in their classrooms. Be forewarned, however, that ethnicity and culture are concepts difficult to define. Definitions vary with the definer's perspective—anthropological, psychological, social, or other. I will take the liberty of adopting definitions that are useful for our purposes and can be applied consistently throughout the chapter.

Ethnicity

The word *ethnic* comes from the Greek *ethnos*, meaning "folk" or "people." A dictionary of anthropology defines *ethnic* as "a group of people distinguished by common cultural characteristics, e.g. a linguistic group like the Bantu." But perhaps a more useful and appropriate definition for the purposes of this chapter is the one proposed by Iswajid (1974): "Ethnicity...refers to an involuntary group of people who share the same culture or to descendants of such people who identify themselves and/or are identified by others as belonging to the same involuntary groups" (p. 122). Ethnic groups are involuntary because we are born into the group; we do not choose it. And our identification with the group depends not only on self-identification but also on identification by others. Ethnic identity, then, is not easily shed, although outward manifestations designed to identify oneself or one's group may be more or less emphasized at different times. In the last decades, for example, many white ethnic groups, such as the Polish, Irish, and Ukrainians, have sought to emphasize their ethnicity, a phenomenon documented by Michael Novak (1971) in *The Rise of the Unmeltable Ethnics*.

Spicer and Thompson (1972) suggest three components implied by ethnic labels: cultural content, historical experience, and group image. In their view all three components must be present to form an ethnic group. The aspect of cultural content is easiest to understand. People who like similar music or food or who dress in characteristic ways express a shared cultural content. As we shall see, there are many other layers to this cultural content that are less easily observed but no less important.

The Jewish people offer a good example of a group that is most closely bound by historical experience. Although much cultural content is also shared, particularly the religious traditions, there are many Jewish subgroups that appear culturally dissimilar and whose main tie to other Jewish groups is a common historical experience.

A group image is sometimes ascribed by others to large groups that include a number of smaller groups that appear to share certain characteristics. The labels "Hispanic" and "American Indian" are examples of these. Each includes a number of groups who see themselves as distinct from others included under the same label. The general label tends to obliterate such differences and to assign to all subgroups characteristics that may be properly applied only to some members of the group. There are also times when members of these subgroups, such as Cubans, Mexican-Americans, and Puerto Ricans, may choose to group themselves under a general label since they do share a historical experience as well as a cultural content.

Sometimes concepts of ethnicity and race overlap; thus we have "blacks," "browns," and "whites." In that division, the blacks and browns are considered ethnics while the whites are not. This confuses ethnic identification, a social label, with race, a biological inheritance. The brown label, often used to refer to all people with a Spanish-American inheritance, for example, includes all three of the traditional major racial groups: Caucasoid, Mongoloid, and Negroid. It should be noted that the concept of race as a biological category is itself of dubious usefulness. Current opinion in anthropology rejects the idea of three distinct racial groups as scientifically inaccurate.

In other situations the ethnic label applied to the group is also applied indiscriminately to individuals within the group. This can be very risky. Take, for example, the case of a Vietnamese child raised by white, Anglo-Saxon, Protestant (WASP) parents in the United States. Such a child is not going to share the cultural content, historical experience, and group image of a Vietnamese child who also arrived in this country as a baby but was raised in a Vietnamese household. The former will remain a member of what is called the Mongoloid race and might be expected to share a Vietnamese ethnicity but will not behave in accordance with the customs and values of that ethnic group. The latter will likely be a full-fledged member of the Vietnamese group. The problem is that the ethnic label is more easily applied to groups than to individuals. We run a risk when we generalize the group labels to particular individuals. A Vietnamese child raised by WASP parents in the United States will be most comfortable with other WASPs, rather than with Vietnamese. In such a case the attachment to the ethnic group is only superficial, at least until adulthood. At that time such persons might decide to search for their origins and perhaps consciously choose to identify with their forebears. Unfortunately, sometimes social pressures are exerted on individuals, demanding that they behave in a manner congruent with the ethnic group to which they *appear* to belong rather than with the one with which they choose to identify.

The definition we have accepted indicates that we are all members of some ethnic group since we all identify ourselves and are identified as members of some groups and not of others. However, the term *ethnic* in the United States has traditionally been used to identify people who do not share the majority (WASP) culture. We will adhere to Iswajid's definition and consider WASP as an ethnic group. As we speak of differences, we will focus our attention on ethnic groups that differ from the majority because our public institutions, particularly the schools, have been shaped by the values of the majority ethnic group, the WASP. It is wise to remember, however, that institutions only reflect the values ascribed to them by the group that controls them. They do not have to be a certain way, and indeed there are many successful examples of schools in the United States and abroad that have chosen to reflect other ethnic and cultural traditions.

Culture

The word *culture* has undergone many changes. It derives from the Latin *cultura*, which originally referred to the cultivation of the soil. Like *ethnicity*, it has been defined in various ways according to the perspective assumed by the definer. The popular association of culture is with aesthetic interests, such as music and the arts. We refer to a person who is knowledgeable in those areas as "cultured." *Culture* is also used to refer to particular subgroups, such as the "drug culture."

Bullivant (1981) includes four dimensions within the concept of culture: (1) the physical environment; (2) the social environment; (3) the metaphysical environment, that is, otherworldly forces, both natural and supernatural, and issues such as life and death; and (4) a time continuum that includes knowledge of the past, traditions, and future orientation. He combines these four components in a comprehensive definition that includes knowledge and concepts embodied in symbolic and nonsymbolic ways of communication about the technology, skills, behaviors, values, beliefs, and attitudes that a society has evolved and modifies to give meaning to and cope with the problems of its existence. For our purposes we may simplify it to the sum total of ways in which a group of people think, feel, and react in order to solve problems of living in their environment. We need to keep in mind, however, that culture exists in a time continuum; therefore, it is not static. We must also remember that problems of living extend beyond the physical environment to the social and metaphysical aspects.

Differences

As we discuss ethnic and cultural differences, we will examine some of the ways in which people differ from one another as they attempt to solve problems in their environment. We will also discuss how these differences may affect learning in the school environment. For example, to a child reared in an urban environment, a request to "go get some fruit" is likely to mean something quite different than what the same request means to a child reared on a farm. The first may respond by asking for money to go to the store; the second, by going out to the orchard. These children will also react differently to lessons in school about fruit production. For the urban child such lessons are likely to be novel, while for the rural child they may only reiterate the obvious. Each of these children has grown up in a different setting, and each has learned different responses to the same problem. Neither response is better or worse than the other, but each would be considered inappropriate in the opposite environment. Similarly, each child will react to instruction differently according to the set of experiences he or she brings to the classroom. Some of these differences may be significant enough to interfere with instruction. Others may only be interesting or amusing. Part of the teacher's responsibility is to be sensitive to the existence of differences and to consider the potential for their interference with a student's academic progress.

In our discussion, culture and ethnicity will be considered as part of everyone's personal being rather than as special characteristics of people who differ from the dominant culture. At no time will the word *culture* be used to suggest artistic or intellectual achievement, nor will it be used to refer to surface differences such as style of dress or music. Culture includes all the ways in which people think, feel, and act as they try to solve their particular problems. Because these things are not static, we view culture as dynamic. Part of our humanity is the ability to learn and grow. Some changes, like learning that one buys fruit at the store, come easy; some, like acquiring different rules of politeness, are more difficult; and some behaviors, like looking away from or looking directly at a person to whom one is speaking, are almost impossible to change because they are unconscious.

Discussions about cultural differences are hazardous because they tend to solidify features and therefore may lead to stereotypes. Looking at cultures is somewhat like watching a changing landscape as we travel. All the time it seems the same, yet all the time it is also changing, until suddenly there is a definite, distinct difference that clearly demonstrates that we are in a different environment. Similarly, with culture it is difficult to identify subtle differences between people and much easier to see the obvious ones—language, for example. We must go beyond the obvious but always remain mindful that (1) such differences among cultural groups mask great individual variations within groups, (2) we know very little about these differences, and (3) the values attached to particular behaviors or characteristics are not inherent in these behaviors but rather are ascribed to them by the social context in which they exist. For example, being able to recognize the footprints of all the members of one's community is a highly valued skill in some Australian aboriginal societies. Recognizing all stock-exchange abbreviations is a highly valued skill in Western financial environments. Yet either skill would be totally useless, and therefore devoid of value, in the other social context.

The School Setting

Children entering school are also entering a new cultural setting. This is true even when the child has grown up in a white, Anglo-Saxon, Protestant home where the cultural overlap with the school is likely to be greatest. Recalling the earlier definition of *culture*, the school is itself a place where a group of people think, feel, and react in certain characteristic ways as they go about solving problems in their environment. Where else are children grouped in numbers of 25 to 30 in one room with one adult in charge? Where else are bells rung to signify changes in activities? Schools differ from one another in many ways, but in even more ways they are similar. There are certain rules of hierarchy, of turn taking, of valued behaviors that are generally accepted. A child's success in school depends to some extent on the ability to make a transition from the home or community culture to the school culture. The transition is easier where there is a high degree of congruence between the two settings.

Language differences (see Chapter 14) are likely to loom large in a child's transition, but we cannot assume that just because children speak English they have also learned all the social and linguistic rules that govern classroom interaction in the United States. In the school context, people relate to one another differently. Some of these relationships, such as when and how one gets access to the lavatory, are carefully planned and explicitly stated. Others are less conscious and only implicitly expressed, for example, that students are to speak to the teacher rather than among themselves. To succeed in the school setting, the child needs to be able to decode these social conventions, modify personal behavior, and adapt it to the school setting. Someone moving from the United States to Australia will first learn that vehicles are expected to travel on the left side of the road. This is clearly and explicitly stated. Less explicit are the host of habits that accompany this change: When crossing a street, one must look toward the right for oncoming cars. And since pedestrians follow the rules of vehicular traffic, they also walk on the left side of the sidewalk. To conduct oneself properly and survive in that environment, one must learn new rules and discard old habits.

Early Assumptions about Ethnic and Cultural Differences

We are not always aware of our tendencies to value certain behaviors and, conversely, to see other behaviors or characteristics as symptoms of deficiencies. The history of education is full of cases where cultural differences have been assumed to be indicators of moral or intellectual deficiencies. Modern U.S. history alone offers many examples. The Immigration Act of 1908 twisted what was already questionable data (the method for collecting and analyzing data would not withstand current standards for validity) to support legislation limiting the entry of nationals from southern and eastern European countries. The legislation stated that people from those countries were less able to learn and in general compared unfavorably with northern Europeans; it was therefore deemed justifiable to limit their entry in order to avoid hindering the country's development (Handlin, 1956).

More recently, large numbers of children have been labeled as culturally disadvantaged and in need of remediation. These children have been tested with tests originally designed to predict *school performance*, not innate ability. Sometimes these tests have been administered in a language to which the child has had only limited exposure. On the basis of such tests, many children have been diagnosed as lacking in intellectual development. This diagnosis has often proved to be a convenient cover for the school's inability to teach these students. The expression "culturally disadvantaged" has been applied to large numbers of people whose cultural behavior and characteristics differ from those represented by the schools. Remediation begins with an assumption that there is something missing, that something must be added; what the child brings and who the child is are matters of little consequence (Baratz & Baratz, 1985). It is very difficult for students to have high expectations for themselves when those around them assume that they are limited in their capacity to learn. It also becomes difficult for people to enter voluntarily a culture where they are considered inferior when by entering the culture they must accept their own inferiority.

As people, we are all subject to conscious and unconscious expectations and stereotypes. As educators, we must continually strive to dismiss preconceptions so as to provide our students with optimal opportunities for learning and developing their potential.

RESEARCH

Problems in This Research

The study of cultural differences is comparatively young as a scientific field. It is likely that interest in these differences began with accounts written by explorers and missionaries of the fifteenth through eighteenth centuries who were brought face to face with people who appeared very different from themselves. Many of these travelers wrote about their experiences, usually emphasizing differences and overlooking similarities that identified the groups as part of the human species. As a result, many of these people were classified as subhuman and treated accordingly.

The records left by these travelers became the basic source of data for the new sciences that arose around the middle of the nineteenth century. The emphasis on differences was also retained by the conquerors, who could favorably compare themselves as "civilized" and therefore superior to the "uncivilized" native inhabitants of the discovered territories. These early anecdotal accounts, sometimes exaggerated and quasi-fictional and only occasionally reliable and accurate, were the basis for many of the early theories about cultural differences. Many of these early theories became popularized and accepted as valid in spite of their dubious sources. The comparison of primitive societies with a childhood stage of development, the confusion of racial and cultural differences, biological explanations for differences, and the ascription of hierarchical positions to various groups were espoused by early social scientists and continue to haunt current interpretations of cultural differences (Cole & Scribner, 1974).

Recent research is much more rigorous and demanding. Scientists are expected to make detailed on-site observations and to use methods that have been shown to be reliable. However, the study of cultures and of cultural differences continues to be difficult. Culture combines many components: language, social relationships, kinship systems, technology, mythology. Each of these encompasses many subcategories. Language may be oral or written, formal or informal, and these aspects can be further subdivided, ad infinitum. It is difficult (sometimes impossible) to separate these components from one another. For example, is a particular vessel used in a religious ritual to be considered a part of pottery-making technology, aesthetic development, or religious practices?

In addition, researchers themselves are not culture-free. Their views, questions, analyses, and conclusions are influenced by their own cultural backgrounds. For example, a Japanese-American colleague related that people would often comment on her boyfriend's beautiful blue eyes. She had never noticed this attractive feature and in fact had to make a conscious effort to do so. She explained that when one grows up in a Japanese community, the shape and color of eyes and hair receive very little attention.

It is also difficult to separate out all the characteristics, such as gender, class, and place of residence, that are likely to influence a person's behavior. Are achievement differences, for example, more closely related to ethnic, class, or cultural differences?

Finally, cultures generally do not exist in isolation. Communication occurs continually across cultural bounds and influences behavior. The widespread availability of so-called ethnic foods across the United States is an example. Studies of isolated tribes in Africa have shown large differences in behavior within a given cultural group between individuals who live close to the roads and those who live distant from them (Cole & Scribner, 1974).

Culture and Intelligence

Intelligence is itself a cultural concept; that is, it may be differentially identified according to cultural setting. If we accept the definition of culture as the ways in which a group of people think, feel, and react in order to solve problems of living in their environment, it follows that intelligence will also be environmentally determined. People who are better able to solve problems in their environment will be considered more intelligent in that environment. In some environments, an Eastern religious community, for example, intelligence might mean the ability to be introspective. In our Western cultural tradition, it means the ability to deal with abstractions.

In Western industrialized countries, the concept of intelligence was solidified by the development of the intelligence test. The test was originally developed to identify students who would not do well in regular classrooms and would require special classes (Gould, 1981). Questions that did not predict school success were omitted from the intelligence test. It is therefore not surprising that a high IQ score is a good predictor of school success. However, the origins of the test have been forgotten in its application. A high IQ score is usually taken to mean that the owner is genetically endowed with a capacity called intelligence. This capacity is popularly believed to be unevenly distributed among the population according to class and race. This view is disputed by others who believe that environmental factors are the real determinants of intelligence as measured by IQ tests.

The strongest argument for genetic influence has been put forth by Jensen (1969). His position is based on his research with black and white populations in the United States. Jensen's position is that heredity is the most plausible explanation for individual differences as manifested in IQ scores. He believes that those differences cannot be adequately explained in terms of test bias and that the most commonly advanced environmental factors have proved wanting.

Jensen argues that IQ measures are analogous to measures of blood pressure, which show substantial heritability within racial groups, and that IQ differences are to be expected from an evolutionary standpoint. He cites research that has shown a white-black difference of 10 to 20 points in IQ in different regions of the country. His position is that IQ tests are free of bias, that they test an innate capacity called intelligence, and that the populations being tested (black and white) differ in terms of race but are otherwise essentially equal.

As stated earlier, the ascription to the IQ test of power to identify a particular capacity called intelligence extends its original purpose, which was to predict school success. There is no argument that performance on IQ tests does accurately predict the future school success of black and white populations. It is quite another thing to assume that those results indicate an inherited capacity that is unequally divided between the races. The definition of intelligence used by Jensen, and embodied in IQ tests, is itself a culturally biased label since it includes those skills that are valued in Western industrialized settings and excludes other types of skills. Unquestionably, the possession of these skills predicts success, but only in a similar setting. In this sense, intelligence tests are not very different from achievement tests, but results from the former are interpreted as unchangeable, whereas results from the latter may suggest the need for intervention.

Jensen used twin studies to argue for the immutability of genetic factors. Gage and Berliner (1984) use the same studies to show how a set of data may be interpreted in different ways to support either an environmental or a genetic cause. Identical twins reared in different homes were tested to determine whether their IQs were similar in spite of different environments. Comparisons of their IQs showed a correlation of .68, indicating a moderate to strong correlation between IQ and genetic factors. In another study, the differences in the same twins' scores were compared with differences in selected characteristics of their environment likely to contribute to educational advantage, including foster parent IQ and educational achievement. When compared in this way, the correlation between differences in the environment and differences in IQ was .79, indicating a strong relationship between environment and IQ. Thus it is possible to argue either that the IQs of twins reared apart are similar due to genetic factors or that they are different due to environmental factors.

Jensen's argument for the immutability of genetic factors has been called genetic determinism. According to this belief, intelligence is a genetic endowment independent of environmental conditions. Jensen applies this argument to differences in the performance of black and white individuals on IQ tests. He argues that the lower performance of blacks on IQ tests is indicative of genetic differences and is therefore permanent and immutable. Most researchers disagree with Jensen. Their disagreements may be grouped into three categories: those questioning the validity of race as the basis for genetic differences, those questioning the assumption that IQ and intelligence are synonymous concepts, and those questioning the assumption that white and black populations may be considered comparable for the purposes of research. Developing these arguments is beyond the purview of this chapter. Suffice it to say that the division of humanity into three distinct racial groups has been discarded by anthropologists, that the proper way to define *intelligence* is still being argued, and that the black population in this country has been subjected to what Gage calls "grievous experimental treatment" (Gage, 1972, p. 312). Beginning with slavery and continuing beyond emancipation to the present, this racial group has been the victim of isolation and discrimination. Jensen's basic assumption that blacks and whites can be considered comparable groups ignores or distorts that social reality.

A broader conception of intelligence has been more recently advanced by Gardner (1983). He argues that the IQ movement is only marginally based on a theory of how the mind works and adds that it fails to take into account the process of problem solving while relying heavily on skill in language and knowledge of facts. As a result, much of the information derived from IQ tests reflects knowledge gained from living in a specific social milieu.

Gardner proposes a theory of intellectual competence that entails a set of skills for problem solving. These skills should enable the individual to resolve genuine problems or difficulties that he or she encounters. In addition, intellectual competence must also entail the potential for finding or creating problems, thereby laying the groundwork for acquisition of new knowledge. These prerequisites, he argues, ensure that human intelligence is genuinely useful and important, at least in certain cultural settings.

Gardner finds persuasive evidence from research in cognitive psychology and neurobiology to support a theory of "multiple intelligences" (MI), or intellectual "frames." He admits to being unsure as yet of the exact nature or precise number of these intelligences, but he maintains that it is difficult to deny that "there exist at least some intelligences, that these are relatively independent of one another, and that they can be fashioned and combined in a multiplicity of adaptive ways by individuals and cultures" (p. 8).

Culture and Thought

Cognition as a field of study has been the object of a revival in the behavioral sciences and includes most of what was previously referred to as thought. It is a more encompassing concept than intelligence, the latter being more usually reserved for observable manifestations of thinking processes. Most psychologists would probably agree with Cole and Scribner (1974) that cognition includes the processes by which man acquires, transforms, and uses information about the world. This definition would include processes that in everyday speech might be referred to as thinking and perceiving. The study of cognition across cultural settings has intrigued researchers for many years but is plagued with difficulties.

Two leading researchers in comparative studies of how people think, Cole and Means (1981), have pointed out that the risk of error is incurred whenever the researcher (1) goes beyond the behavior observed under a particular set of circumstances to generalizations about how people think; (2) tries to interpret differences in performance by different groups that vary in many different, if unspecified, ways; and (3) tries to extrapolate from research on a narrow range of tasks in controlled settings to the world at large. Many widely publicized studies are vulnerable to this criticism, but too often their conclusions gain wide acceptance before they can be challenged. This is especially true when the conclusions reached fit popularly held beliefs.

Cognitive Skills

Work by Sigel and Anderson (1966) and others appeared to demonstrate that children from lower-socioeconomic backgrounds made less use of descriptive and categorical groupings and relied more on relationship groupings when classifying pictures in the Sigel Concept Styles Test (SCST). For example, they might classify a picture of a woman and a picture of a girl as mother and daughter rather than as women or female. Sigel suggested that such differences reflected social class differences in competence arising because fewer "distancing experiences" were available in lower-class homes. Simmons (1979) suggested that an alternative explanation might emerge if, for example, pictures having cultural relevance to the students were used. He constructed a test composed of such items and demonstrated that earlier results probably depended on the test items selected rather than on cultural differences in thinking. This example offers an illustration of the concerns expressed by Cole and Means (1981), who further cautioned that poor performance of a specific group on an experimental task cannot be taken as evidence that its members completely lack a specific ability or process. It only means that they do not show that particular ability or process when performing *that* task under *those* circumstances. However, such findings can affect our expectations and focus our attention on presumed deficits.

A. R. Luria (1979) emphasized that neither the components nor the functional systems into which mental functions are organized are already formed at birth. They are formed, instead, in the course of each individual's development and depend very closely on the social experiences of the child. Cole and Scribner (1974) illustrate what is meant by functional systems in a review of free-recall experiments. In those studies it was consistently found that educated and noneducated subjects performed differently. Although under some circumstances both groups showed efficient, organized recall, under standard experimental conditions the groups without schooling did not recall well, did not show much improvement after repeated exercise, and did not organize their recall categorically. Among those who had not attended school, organization by categories was used but did not play a controlling role in the recall itself. In the schooled groups, organization by categories was both the dominant mode of sorting and the control mechanism in recall. Thus each group demonstrates different functional systems, but both systems include the use of categorization. The fact that this difference in performance occurred under standard experimental conditions should be noted. Many studies of cross-cultural differences have relied solely on experimental situations and assumed that their findings constitute group characteristics. Cole and Scribner (1974) conclude that *we are unlikely to find cultural differences in the basic components of cognitive processes*, although there are differences in functional systems. After a thorough review of comparative studies of cognition, they add that "there is no evidence...that *any* cultural group wholly lacks basic processes such as abstraction, or inferential reasoning, or categorization" (p. 193). They suggest that cultural differences may be reflected in the way functional systems are organized. In their view, further research should attempt to uncover the culturally determined experiences that give rise to different dominant functional systems. For example, in the free-recall experiment, schooling appeared to be such an experiential factor. They also call for further research on the situational factors that call out certain functional systems.

Cognitive Styles

Other researchers have been concerned with differences in cognitive styles across population groups. This field of research arose out of concern that psychological research on perception had neglected the role of the perceiver, the person who does the perceiving. These researchers have argued that the act of perceiving needs to be examined in relation to the personality, needs, and values of the person doing it (Witkin & Goodenough, 1981). From there it is but a short leap to attempts to identify how groups differ in their perceptions.

John Ogbu (1982) writes about cognitive skills from the perspective of U.S. populations. He suggests a modification to the social sciences' definition of environment as parental, familial, and neighborhood factors. He agrees that cognitive skills and styles are acquired by children in the course of interacting with their environment but would extend the latter to include features of the wider society: economic systems, sociopolitical organization, and so on. He labels these "features of the macroenvironment" and suggests that these features determine cognitive roles and styles required for competence by role incumbents. Ogbu's view is compatible with Cole and Scribner's (1974) suggestion that cultural differences may reflect the way functional systems are organized. But while Cole and Scribner concentrate on comparisons of traditional and technoindustrial cultures, Ogbu attends to cultural experiences in the U.S. setting.

Ogbu cites research that distinguished between two opposite styles of thinking. These cognitive styles have been labeled differently by various researchers but always refer to sets of opposing characteristics. For example, an individual with an articulated or field-independent style, according to this research, shows ability to differentiate and organize features of the environment and approaches tasks objectively, functions well in formal organizational settings, and uses the analytical approach in abstracting information. The opposite style, variously called global, relational, or field-dependent, is characterized as more descriptive in approach, more likely to attend to global features, and more self-centered in its orientation to reality. Most researchers agree that these types originate in differences in socialization experience. Ogbu points out that in such studies, individuals reported to be global, field-dependent, relational, and concrete in their cognitive styles are found primarily in subordinate groups: women, Mexican-Americans, blacks, and Jewish boys from mother-dominated families. He argues that the competence associated with the different positions occupied by these groups in the society requires different types of cognitive styles that are adaptive to their positions as subordinates. He does not deny that these differences in cognitive styles exist but rather that the explanation of why they occur is inadequate (1982).

Ogbu's explanation for the existence of different cognitive styles across population groups contains an important caution for teachers. It is risky to accept group classifications that assign a particular way of behaving to all members of a group. Although gender and ethnicity may have an effect on a person's learning style (for example, some groups show a preference for learning cooperatively rather than competitively), individual members of any group are likely to vary in their preferences for certain learning styles. The teacher's task is to observe and note the differences and to offer a variety of alternatives for learning in the classroom. Variety in learning opportunities makes for a more interesting classroom, as it provides opportunities for different learning styles.

Culture and Communication

The apparent linguistic homogeneity of the United States masks many variations, both linguistic and nonlinguistic, that affect the success of cross-cultural communication.

Dialectical Differences.   The most obvious differences in language variety are those posed by dialectical differences. These are noticeable in the speech characteristic of different regions of the country. The dialectical difference most discussed in educational circles is probably Black English Vernacular (BEV), or Afro-American. For many years, BEV was assumed to be an error-laden version of standard American English. The work of Labov, Cohen, Robins, and Lewis (1968) showed that the street talk of blacks had distinct rules of its own and that this variety was capable of the same complexity of thought and expression as any other variety.

Acceptance of BEV as a rule-governed linguistic system does not diminish the fact that some of its pronunciation, word formation, and syntax characteristics are not understood by speakers of other English varieties. Most linguists now believe that BEV is probably related to Gullah, one of the three creole languages to have developed in the United States (the others are Louisiana Creole and Hawaiian Creole). Gullah developed as a hybrid of several African languages and English during the period of slavery. It is still spoken by some people along the North Carolina coast.

Black English Vernacular continues to exist for historical and social reasons. The isolation of blacks first due to slavery and later for reasons of discrimination has contributed to its maintenance. More recently, BEV has served, as do languages in many other settings, as a badge of ethnic group membership. Most blacks become bilingual in BEV and standard forms and use these selectively as appropriate.

According to Mitchell-Kernan (1972), black communities hold implicit rules of appropriateness that must be followed. For example, "proper talking," that is, using standard forms in informal situations, is likely to elicit censure. Occasions that call for switching from BEV to the standard form are those where an unfamiliar interlocutor or someone occupying an official position is present. These rules of appropriateness are similar to those followed in other bilingual communities.

Sociolinguistic Differences.   Sociolinguistics is the study of language in its social context. It is based on the assumption that the meaning of language cannot be separated from the context in which it occurs. These differences are particularly important to educators because conversation is a cooperative endeavor that depends on mutual assumptions and expectations about meaning.

Gumperz and Gumperz (1981) argue that individuals learn appropriate conversational behavior as a result of their participation in particular networks of relationship. When networks differ, as in ethnically mixed settings, conventions also differ, and communication can break down. Since these conventions operate below the level of consciousness, participants may be unaware that they are drawing incorrect inferences. For example, students may be incorrectly perceived as rude, uninterested, or "disadvantaged." In a classroom, the teacher is the one who decides what is or is not appropriate, but many of those decisions are based on conventions that are unique to the North American Anglo setting. According to these conventions, the teacher is the center of attention, and students are expected to look at the teacher and to respond to questions when called. Spontaneous speech on the part of students is frowned on, and every student is expected to complete his or her own work. When questions arise, students are to call on the teacher, not on their peers, for help, and activities occur in sequence according to a predetermined schedule. Question-and-answer sessions regularly follow what has been called the "switchboard" style, where the teacher calls on one child, who answers; the teacher responds, then calls on someone else, and so on. Most of these conventions are unspoken. They are classroom expectations that are usually unconsciously accepted by the students. If classroom rules are compatible with a child's home culture, problems are minimal, but if not, lack of understanding results.

School Culture versus Home Culture

The Gumperzes and other investigators believe that learning or failure to learn may be due to discontinuities between the norms and obligations that shape social relations in a child's home and community and those at school. That is, children's responses to school tasks are directly influenced by values and presuppositions learned in the home.

Several studies support this view. Susan Philips (1983), studying classrooms that combined American Indian and Anglo students, found a difference in the way members of these groups behaved as students. She found that the American Indian students were increasingly less likely to respond in class as they went up through the grades. She noticed their unwillingness to participate as speakers in the classroom and their tendency to gaze at each other, rather than at the teacher, when the latter was speaking. Philips compared this behavior to that of Anglo students, who she noticed were much more likely to look at the teacher, even when a fellow student was responding. In her conclusions, Philips suggests that such differences are due "primarily, although not entirely, to an incompatibility between Indian and Anglo systems for the regulation of turns at talk" (p. 115). Appropriate classroom behavior, by Anglo standards, requires the American Indian students to behave in ways that run counter to the expectations of socially approved behavior in their community. Philips explains that the Indian organization of interaction maximizes the control individuals have over their own turns at talk. This is achieved through three rules of turn taking: (1) address by a speaker is more often general than directed at a single individual; (2) immediate response to a speaker is not always necessary; and (3) speakers are not interrupted; they control the ends of their own turns. These features of turn taking contrasted with interaction in the Anglo classrooms, where the teacher determined who would speak and when, and when the student's turn to speak would end. The Warm Springs Indians studied by Philips were not accustomed to being addressed directly or to being told when and for how long they could speak. Thus, although the Warm Springs Indian students were English-dominant, their interactions were governed by the sociolinguistic rules of the Warm Springs community. The discrepancy between those rules and the rules operating in the Anglo classrooms contributed to their difficulties in those classrooms.

It also appears to be true that similarities in social identities and communication style have an influence on interactions. In his study of counseling interviews, Erickson (1975) found that such similarities positively influence the character and outcome of the interviews. He suggests that in face-to-face interaction, people use various combinations of ways of being alike, including but not limited to social class, nationality group, cultural sharing, and ethnicity. These similarities can contribute to the successful completion of the interaction, or, alternatively, differences can impede communication. This happens unconsciously even in situations where neutrality and fairness are intended. It appears that human communication is guided by learned and unconsciously produced verbal and nonverbal signals. Where speakers have synchrony, that is, when they share the set of signals guiding their communication, effectiveness is enhanced. In Erickson's study, the higher the synchrony between student and counselor, the higher also the amount of useful information gained by the student from the interview.

Scollon and Scollon (1981) support Erickson's findings. They argue that discrimination is mainly a problem of miscommunication. Fundamental differences in the value ascribed by different ethnic groups to communication contribute to miscommunication. The Scollons explain that these differences are based on values taught to members of the groups and constitute a significant aspect of their identity as individuals and as members of ethnic groups.

According to the Scollons, it is the discourse system—that is, the way ideas are joined into arguments, the way some of these ideas are selected for special emphasis, and the way emotional information about the ideas is presented—that causes the greatest problem in miscommunication. Since we tend to consider communication as a matter of grammar and vocabulary, the greatest potential for miscommunication occurs where the language being used by two speakers is the most similar, and understanding is therefore assumed. They urge caution in thinking that understanding is automatic just because speakers share a grammar and vocabulary.

The Scollons conclude that the solution to problems caused by interethnic differences in communication is not to eliminate individual and group differences in communicative style, but to cultivate a deep and genuine respect for these differences.

Nonverbal Communication

Nonverbal communication has become popular in the literature yet its importance in the classroom has received little attention. Perhaps the extension of sociolinguistics to include extralinguistic communication will signal the importance of these factors in instructional effectiveness.

The work of E. T. Hall (1976) and R. L. Birdwhistell (1970) gave early recognition to nonverbal communication. In their books and articles they have discussed the concepts of time, kinetics (the study of body movements), gazing, use of space, and other forms of nonverbal communication. They have also pointed out that these aspects of culture (what Hall calls the "hidden culture") differ across cultures. Since we are usually unconscious of its presence, nonverbal behavior can often underlie cross-cultural misunderstandings.

The presence of a synchronous teacher-student relationship was noted by Esmailka and Barnhardt (1981) in Athabaskan classrooms in Alaska. In an attempt to capture possible differences in teaching style, they observed teacher-student interaction in three classrooms taught by native teachers. Their first impression was that the students in these classrooms were not exhibiting the shy, passive behavior described as typical of American Indian students. Instead, they were eager to participate. Detailed analysis of videotapes revealed the ability of the teachers to "tune in" to the students through their rhythm and body movements so that the tempo of the teachers' speech responded to the students' tempo. The teachers also used less directive, more pupil-oriented instructional techniques.

Similar studies that focus on students and teachers of Hispanic background have been carried out. In many of these also, the teacher's cultural compatibility with the students appears to contribute to the effectiveness of instruction. Cazden, Carrasco, and Maldonado (1980) describe a Hispanic teacher's use of diminutives and endearments and an easy, relaxed rhythm that appeared to contribute to an extremely well functioning classroom.

These studies and similar ones enable us not only to understand that differences exist but also to know the what and the how of these differences. It is only through understanding the what and the how that we can hope to improve the cross-cultural climate of the classroom.

QUESTIONS TEACHERS ASK

Q.   *Why do students insist on associating only with others of the same cultural differences?*

A.   What gives rise to a particular behavior is not as important as the hasty labeling of students who do not conform to our expectations. We need to be as aware as those who do cross-cultural research that we are observing from our own cultural perspective and that our interpretation is always affected by unconscious beliefs and assumptions. We need to suspend judgment and become alert to patterns of behavior by the child, parents, or community that may be part of an underlying cultural system. Reflecting on our own reactions to the specific behavior can also help us to understand whether it is the behavior itself or our reaction to it that is the problem. For example, there may be various reasons why a student is consistently late to school. Some of these reasons may be cultural: Time is not an important issue in his or her culture, or the student is in charge of taking a younger sibling to the babysitter. Some reasons may be practical: There is no alarm clock in the house. On the other hand, it could be that the student is just lazy. We can determine the real reason only if we inquire with honest concern. If we decide in advance that the student is lazy, our approach to the student and parent will communicate censure and block possible communication. We also need to look at ourselves. Is the student's lateness a real problem to the student or to the class? Are we upset because the student is disrupting the class or missing instruction by coming in late, or is the lateness really insignificant and our reaction simply a cultural bias toward promptness? If the latter is the case, we can choose to ignore the lateness and accept our own discomfort, or we can honestly explain to the student and the parent that promptness is important to *us* and work at resolving whatever is causing the lateness.

Q.   *I have students of five different national origins in my class. How can I deal with cultural differences?*

A.   You cannot avoid dealing with such differences, since they are there every single day. The task is not to be responsive to one or five cultures but rather to have the kind of classroom where cultural differences are respected. It requires a high degree of sensitivity on the part of the teacher to be alert to manifestations of these differences and to smooth the way for children whose behavior may be quite different from that of others. In such a classroom time must be provided for discussion of differences so that respect for all may be enhanced. Discussions might start with, "This is how *we* do such-and-such. How do you do this in your culture?" They should not end there, however; there should also be times to explore why one person or group might find another person or group's behavior inappropriate. With older students, it might also mean covering both sides of a historical incident (e.g., how did Mexican history record the Battle of the Alamo?). It is not enough to discuss food or musical preferences, though these may be fun. Acceptance of cultural differences also means the acceptance of some conflict in the society. A multicultural society such as the United States can avoid conflict between groups by ignoring differences and acting as though everyone held the same beliefs and values and was equally respected socially. But such a social posture can result in resentment on the part of those who are reminded daily that they differ from that position and that all are not respected equally. Under careful teacher guidance, a multicultural classroom can provide a safe forum for airing those differences at a level appropriate to the students' maturity.

Q.   *Aren't notions of multiculturalism in conflict with the idea of the United States as a "melting pot"?*
A.   The notion of a melting pot is a pervasive myth with no grounding in reality. If "melting" had indeed occurred, U.S. society would display an intermingling of values and structures that would identify it socially, politically, linguistically, economically, and culturally as something quite different from the parent culture. When copper, tin, and other metals become a bronze alloy, none of these metals can be distinguished from the bronze that they become. By contrast, U.S. society can be separated into its cultural components and is clearly dominated by the English influence. Public institutions such as schools reflect that cultural bias.

Multiculturalism is the U.S. reality. There are many different cultural groups in this country. Politicians like to point to the richness of this variety and to celebrate its manifestations, usually by visiting "Little Italy" or similar sites at election time. But this is really a culturally rich country, at least potentially. Advancing multiculturalism can make that ideal we hold of the United States a reality. It also means changes. The preponderance of English threads in the U.S. social tapestry will eventually need to be balanced with threads of other styles and colors.

Q.   *Why do students insist on associating only with others of the same cultural group?*
A.   We all feel more comfortable with people who share our likes and dislikes, our history, and our language. In the Sun Belt states, it is common to find concentrations of immigrants from different geographic regions of the country. Certain types of stores attest to this—for example, New York–style delicatessens signal the presence of a concentration of New Yorkers, and a Mormon temple likewise marks the presence of midwesterners of that religious persuasion. However, these groups generally pass unnoticed because their members blend easily into a population that is almost entirely white, elderly, and English-speaking. Concentrations of people who are socially or ethnically different are more noticeable but not unusual, given human inclinations.

Other reasons why students might limit their associates are habit, fear of rejection, and fear for their safety. Schools are often the only places where students from different backgrounds have the opportunity to associate. It is not surprising that association does not come easily since they are exposed to few such models in the society.

Q. *How should I deal with the use of black dialect in the classroom?*
A.   The use of BEV in the classroom has been the subject of great controversy. Some people, among them respected black journalists like Carl Rowan and William Rasberry, take the position that tolerance of BEV in the classroom is incompatible with a good education and that black youngsters must achieve full control of standard English if they are to compete successfully in the real world. While accepting the importance of standard English for black students, many linguists believe that schools must recognize that these children speak a different dialect (BEV) when they enter school. They argue for instruction that will capitalize on their strengths and ease them into the standard version much as foreign language speakers might be. In 1980 a judge in Ann Arbor, Michigan, decided that schools in that city needed to be responsive to the needs of these students. His judgment requires educators in that city to become familiar enough with BEV to enable them to interact with their students in their instructional capacity.

Fishman and Lueders-Salmon (1972) point out that most of the world's school children are *not* taught to read and write the same language or language variety that they bring with them to school from their homes and neighborhoods. They suggest that the problem is not in the existence of multiple varieties of language but in the attitude held toward the variety.

They cite as an example the situation in Germany, where students arrive in school speaking a local dialect. This dialect is accepted matter-of-factly in the school, and no stigma is attached to its use since everyone uses it in informal situations. The instructional program assumes the need to transfer from the dialect to the standard version. This process is carried out effectively in a climate of acceptance.

Similarly, the acceptance of BEV as a legitimate informal language does not deny the need to transfer to standard English for purposes of formal expression. It does mean that the value of BEV as a vehicle of communication is accepted and that instructional procedures take into account areas of linguistic interference and provide for transitional stages in the process of transfer, much as we plan for speakers of other languages. It also means that BEV can retain its communicative use in informal situations and as a vehicle for creative expression. This finds ample precedent in the writings of William Faulkner, Tennessee Williams, Alice Walker, and many other noted American authors.

Q. *How can I change my school's instructional practice to make it more compatible with students' styles?*
A.   The recognition that this can be an important consideration is a significant first step. It is also useful to assume that lack of student academic progress or behavior that is not childlike—that is, extreme silence or extreme disorder—may indicate cultural incompatibility. One must also accept that teachers and schools operate within a cultural context themselves and that this context is capable of only moderate change. In addition, we all accept that students will be moving into that larger context and, therefore, that the school has a responsibility in preparing them to operate successfully in that larger context. It is understood that our aim is to improve cultural compatibility, not to duplicate the home environment in the school.

One place where this type of cultural modification has been accomplished with a high degree of success, as evidenced by high achievement and attendance, is the KEEP program at the Kamehameha School in Hawaii, a school that serves low-socio-economic-status, minority, dialect-speaking urban students. According to Jordan (1981), the program advocates "that in the selection of teaching practices, the children's culture be one of the factors to which attention is given" (p. 3). The goals for students in the Kamehameha School are similar to goals for students in other schools. The difference is that the leaders of KEEP assume that, given the children's culture, some teaching practices are more or less likely to elicit the behaviors and skills needed to reach the school's academic goals. Program organizers select those instructional practices that both correspond to the children's culture and allow the teacher to operate comfortably and effectively.

The KEEP program researchers found, for example, that the turn-taking rules used in most classrooms in the United States are culturally inappropriate for their students. They also found that an emphasis on decoding was inappropriate for this population. The program emphasizes comprehension and sight vocabulary, and decoding instruction takes place within that context. Decisions to operate in this manner were guided by recognition of the students' rich oral-heritage tradition. The participation structure has also capitalized on the importance Hawaiian culture places on the peer group in informal teaching and learning. KEEP students work at independent work centers, where they learn to help one another in completing their tasks.

The practices followed by KEEP may or may not work in a different setting. Their importance lies in their seeking to be responsive to their students' cultural needs and in achieving that goal without doing violence to the school's academic pursuits. It demonstrates what is possible given the assumptions mentioned, careful observation and study of student and community cultural preferences, and the willingness to expend time and energy in responding to these. The reward can be an improved classroom and school climate and increased participation by students.

Q. *Why is it that some culturally different students appear to fit very quickly in the classroom while others do not?*

A. Cultural compatibility can exist between groups that appear very different on the surface. Such compatibility facilitates a student's adaptation to the classroom environment. The Vietnamese offer a good example of this.

According to Dang Liem (1980), psychoreligious forces dictate the mode of living, way of thought, and manner of thought expression of the Vietnamese. Co-existing philosophies of Buddhism, Taoism, Confucianism, and Christianity constitute an amalgam that affects all Vietnamese regardless of their particular religious orientation. In responding to these cultural forces, the Vietnamese coincidentally behave in ways that are compatible with those of American educational institutions. "The virtuous man should strive constantly to improve himself by doing good deeds, and by renouncing sensual pleasures" (p. 11). This is taught by the Buddhist tradition, while Confucianism is a doctrine of social hierarchies that defines, through rigid rules, appropriate attitudes for each member of the society and prescribes a formula for social interactions between ruler and subject, father and son, and husband and wife. Dang Liem suggests that the Vietnamese tend to consider their employers as their mentors and as such expect them to give guidance, advice, and encouragement. The employee (and by analogy the student) is supposed to execute orders, perform the task quietly, and ask no questions and have no doubts about the orders. It is not difficult to see how children brought up in such a cultural tradition would adapt easily to the school situation. However, Dang Liem also points out that Vietnamese rules of politeness and tendency toward introspection are at odds with Western, particularly North American, straightforwardness, which they perceive as lack of intelligence or courtesy. A culturally different child may exhibit appropriate classroom behavior and yet feel very uncomfortable with the teacher or classmates. These differences need to be discussed in the multicultural classroom for what they are, differences in what we perceive and value as appropriate behavior.

Q. *How should I interpret lack of parental participation in school activities?*
A. As stated earlier, the first step is to suspend judgment. The second is to begin with the assumption that all parents are interested in their children and want the best for them. We can then build on this basic assumption. Since parents are interested, why are they not participating? A number of reasons can be identified very quickly: (1) A language difference impedes communication about or at school activities; (2) there is a cultural difference in perception about the appropriate role of the parents vis-à-vis the school; (3) parents' memories of their own school experiences may be unpleasant enough to discourage their participation as adults; (4) cultural differences between school personnel and parents get in the way of effective communication; (5) babies, work, or money may make demands that overpower any interest in participation. None of these suggests actual or perceived problems of discrimination, though these may also exist. The point is that we cannot judge parents without first examining all the possible reasons for their lack of participation and realizing that each implies a different solution.

Q. *How do these issues of ethnic and cultural differences affect school organization and management?*
A. Cultural issues in the organization and management of the schools are difficult to identify because they are so pervasive. We assume that there is only one way to run schools, and certainly there is much in school management that is prescribed by the bureaucratic structure in which they exist. However, institutions are run by people, and they can be made more responsive. Schools serving culturally different populations need personnel that are sensitive to the needs of those populations and that can be flexible in responding to those needs. The example of the Vietnamese points up the need for sensitivity in interpersonal communication to avoid offending parents and students. Other situations may require negotiating an understanding about school and parent roles. Puerto Rican parents, for example, tend to relinquish control over the education and discipline of their children to the school while retaining parental control over the children's activities; Anglo parents tend to behave exactly the opposite. Thus Puerto Rican parents do not easily get involved in what the school teaches: "You are the teachers," they will say, and they will tell their children, in reference to the principal or teacher, "While you're here, she's your mother. You do as she tells you." At the same time, they are likely to feel free to come into the school to get Maria so that she can stay home to babysit. Anglo parents, on the other hand, are more likely to get involved in curriculum decisions and less likely to surrender disciplinary measures to the school. They are also more likely to accept bureaucratic control over their children. Again, the issue is not which is "good" or

"right" but rather that these are differences that must be recognized if parents, students, and teachers are to work together effectively.

Q. *It seems that for some students, physical aggression is the only way to react. Am I supposed to accept this as just another cultural difference?*
A. For some students, the circumstances of their life are such that skill in physical aggression is as necessary to them today as literacy will be in their future. This does not mean that it needs to be accepted at school (indeed, many other behaviors specific to a cultural group would also be unacceptable—nudism, for example). Aggressive behavior may be appropriate for these students in their own neighborhoods because their safety may depend on it. It is not appropriate in a setting that is safe and secure. School personnel need to create such a setting and convince their students that they really are safe. It is then that aggressive behavior becomes inappropriate and unacceptable. Children who feel themselves in danger at school will continue to display aggressive behavior regardless of the sanctions imposed. In passing, we should note that aggression need not be physical. Many students avoid punishment by maintaining physical control while viciously attacking their classmates in word and deed. School personnel tend to pay more attention to physical displays and are often oblivious to or more tolerant of the less obvious acts of aggression.

Q. *How can I encourage students to work together while at the same time providing for their instructional needs?*
A. Cooperative learning techniques have been used successfully for this purpose. These techniques rely on the premise that people who work cooperatively toward a common goal encourage one another to do their best, help one another to do well, and end up respecting one another. These are the characteristics of many sport activities, which have now been successfully transferred to the classroom and to the pursuit of academic goals.

In a classroom where cooperative learning is being used, students work in heterogeneous groups to learn academic content. In most cases, students are rewarded for group performance. In order to do well, they must help one another learn. Educational research in these techniques has demonstrated that heterogeneous teams made up of high and low achievers, boys and girls, and members of different ethnic groups can succeed in achieving both affective and academic learning goals.

Three student-team learning techniques have now been extensively researched and found to increase student learning significantly: Student Teams Achievement Division, Team-Games-Tournament, and Jigsaw. A newer development is Team-Assisted Individualization (TAI), which is especially appropriate for use in heterogeneous math classes such as those containing mainstreamed, low-achieving, or gifted students (Slavin, 1983).

Students working together in classrooms that use these strategies are more likely to cross racial and ethnic lines in selecting their friends. They have also been found to make significant gains in achievement when compared to students in traditional classrooms. The possibility for accomplishing both of these important goals makes these strategies particularly appropriate for the multicultural classroom.

Q. *Are there any benefits to a multicultural classroom?*
A. Among the countless benefits are the following: Students can find out, in a

safe environment, how they look and sound to others who grew up in a different environment. They can learn to enjoy one another's celebrations, favorite foods, and games. They can learn about language—the many different ways in which we communicate, not only across different languages but also in the different varieties of English. They can learn about parts of their city or the world they might never visit. They can find out how different we are from each other and yet how, under all those differences, we are really very much alike. Most important is the satisfaction that you, as a teacher, can derive from a classroom where children communicate openly and respectfully about one another, where differences may be observed, learned from, enjoyed, and where one may even, when absolutely necessary, object to them.

Q.   *How can teachers and schools address the issues raised here?*
A.   For the last decade or so, there has been much talk about the need to develop multicultural curricula in our schools. There are many books on the subject, and space does not permit in-depth review of this literature. Several things need to be kept in mind, however:

1. The school is its own curriculum. That is, through its choices of content, organization, and methods of instruction, the school displays the values and attitudes of the people doing the choosing.
2. Multicultural education is not a subject matter, nor is it something only for social studies. Multiculturalism needs to be integrated into every course of study. How often are Indian or Chinese or Japanese selections heard in music class, for example? How often do we see American Indian art displayed outside of the Southwest (and sometimes not even there)?
3. Interethnic situations are likely to bring about conflict. This is to be neither feared nor ignored. Conflict is a reality of human interaction. Just as marriages may fail because conflicts go unresolved and disagreements are ignored, disagreements cannot be ignored in the classroom; they are bound to surface elsewhere. Schools can be safe environments where students can air their grievances, ask questions, and negotiate understandings.
4. Schools and teachers are not accustomed to dealing with these issues. Attempts to do so will require opportunities to discuss these ideas among district and school staff. Multiculturalism must begin with the adults.
5. Multicultural education is not a panacea. It will not resolve the real social inequities that remain in this country. We can only hope that students can begin to understand and respect one another and become concerned adults who can effectively grapple with those social conditions.

It is appropriate that a student have the last word in this chapter. This excerpt is by a Native American, Joseph H. Suina, who contrasts his memories of home and school. His recollection is a vivid example of the concerns expressed in this chapter.

The winter months are among my fondest recollection. A warm fire crackled and danced brightly in the fireplace and the aroma of delicious stew filled our one room house. To me the house was just right. The thick adobe walls wrapped around the two of us protectingly during the long, freezing nights. Grandmother's affection completed the warmth and security I will always remember.... Her shower of praises made me feel like the Indian Superman of

all times. At age five, I suppose I was as close to that concept of myself as anyone. . . .

    And then I went to school. . . . The classroom. . . had its odd characteristics.
It was terribly huge and smelled of medicine like the village clinic I feared so
much. The walls and ceiling. . . were too far from me and I felt naked. The
fluorescent light tubes were eerie and blinked suspiciously above me. . . .

    School was a painful experience during those early years. The English language
and the new set of values caused me much anxiety and embarrassment. . . . The
Dick and Jane reading series in the primary grades presented me pictures of a
home with a pitched roof, straight walls and sidewalks. . . . It was clear I didn't
have these things and what I did have did not measure up. At night, long after
grandmother went to sleep, I would lay awake staring at our crooked adobe
walls casting uneven shadows from the light of the fireplace. . . . My life was no
longer just right. I was ashamed of being who I was and I wanted to change right
then and there. Somehow, it became so important to have straight walls, clean
hair and teeth and a spotted dog to chase after. . .

FURTHER READING

On Multicultural Education

Appleton, N. (1983). *Cultural Pluralism in Education: Theoretical Foundation*. White Plains,
    NY: Longman. An exploration of current theories of multiculturalism and survey of
    related legal decisions. Includes excellent recommendations for teachers in multicultural
    classrooms.
Baker, G. C. (1983). *Planning and Organizing Multicultural Instruction*. Reading, MA:
    Addison-Wesley. An implementation plan for multicultural education at various levels
    within the educational system. Includes comprehensive discussion of what may be involved
    in the education and training of teachers for full implementation.
Bullivant, B. M. (1981). *Race, Ethnicity, and Curriculum*. Melbourne: Macmillan. A policy-
    oriented summary of a study of the effects of ideologies on educational provisions in six
    settings: Britain, Canada, Hawaii, Fiji, Australia, and the United States. Attempts to show
    how educational ideologies and models held of society affect what is being done to
    overcome the problems posed by pluralism.
Northwest Regional Laboratory—Washington Education Association. (1982). *Multicultural
    Education Training Program*. Seattle, WA: Washington Education Association. A compre-
    hensive program designed for staff development. Consists of 10 volumes, each devoted to a
    different aspect of this broad topic, e.g., linguistic dimensions, legislative issues, guided
    planning, and others. This program is a required course in teacher education at Portland
    State University.

On Linguistic Issues

Cazden, C. B., John, V. P., & Hymes, D. (1972). *Functions of Language in the Classroom*.
    New York: Teachers College Press. A collection of readings focusing on language as used
    in the communication between students and teachers in classrooms. Attempts to demon-
    strate how the meaning of language is embedded in the behavioral context in which it
    originates or in which it is used.
Scollon, R., & Scollon, S.B.K. (1981). *Narrative, Literacy, and Face in Interethnic Communi-
    cation*. Norwood, NJ: Ablex. Responds to the need for information about the dynamics of
    interpersonal communication among different ethnic groups. The authors rely on their

experience and research in Athabaskan communities in Alaska. However, their conclusions can be applied across interethnic settings.

On Cultural Differences in Cognition

Cole, M., & Scribner, S. (1974). *Culture and Thought: A Psychological Introduction*. New York: Wiley. An excellent introduction to the difficulties encountered in trying to determine whether there are cultural differences in cognitive processes. Through a review and critical analysis of experimental studies, the authors present useful information and relate it to contemporary social problems.

On Cooperative Learning

Slavin, R. E. (1983). *Cooperative Learning*, White Plains, NY: Longman. A review of the research on cooperative learning. Describes the distinguishing characteristics of different types of cooperative techniques and includes practical advice for interested teachers.

REFERENCES

Baratz, S. S., & Baratz, S. C. (1985). Early childhood intervention: The social base of institutional racism. In N. R. Yetman & Steele (Eds.), *Majority and minority: The dynamics of race and ethnicity in American life* (3rd ed., pp. 415–425). Boston: Allyn & Bacon.

Birdwhistell, R. L. (1970). *Kinesics and context*. Philadelphia: University of Pennsylvania Press.

Bullivant, B. M. (1981). *Race, ethnicity, and curriculum*. Melbourne: Macmillan.

Cazden, C. B., Carrasco, R. L., & Maldonado, A. (1980). The contribution of ethnographic research to bicultural-bilingual education. *Current issues in bilingual education*. Washington, DC: Georgetown University.

Cole, M., & Means, B. (1981). *Comparative studies of how people think*. Cambridge, MA: Harvard University Press.

Cole, M., & Scribner, S. (1974). *Culture and thought: A psychological introduction*. New York: Wiley.

Dang Liem, N. (1980, May). *Vietnamese-American intercultural communication*. Paper presented at the 30th International Conference on Communication: Human evolution and development, Acapulco, Mexico.

Erickson, F. (1975). Gatekeeping in the melting pot: Interaction in counseling encounters. *Harvard Educational Review, 45*, 44–70.

Esmailka, W., & Barnhardt, C. (1981). *The social organization of participation in three Athabaskan cross-cultural classrooms*. Final report to the National Institute of Education. (NIE-G-80-0064)

Fishman, J. A., & Lueders-Salmon, E. (1972). What has the sociology of language to say to the teacher? On teaching the standard variety to speakers of dialectal or sociolectal varieties. In C. B. Cazden, V. P. John, & D. Hymes (Eds.), *Functions of language in the classroom*. New York: Teachers College Press.

Gage, N. L. (1972). IQ heritability, race differences, and educational research. *Phi Delta Kappan, 53*, 308–312.

Gage, N. L., & Berliner, D. C. (1984). *Educational psychology*. Boston: Houghton-Mifflin.

Gardner, H. (1983). *Frames of mind: A theory of multiple intelligences*. New York: Basic Books.

Gould, S. J. (1981). *The mismeasure of man*. New York: W. W. Norton.

Gumperz, J. J., & Gumperz, J. C. (1981). Ethnic differences in communicative style. In C. A.

Ferguson & S. B. Heath (Eds.), *Language in the USA*. Cambridge, Eng.: Cambridge University Press.

Hall, E. T. (1976). *Beyond culture*. Garden City, NY: Doubleday Anchor Books.

Handlin, O. (1956). *Race and nationality in American life*. New York: Doubleday Anchor Books.

Iswajid, W. W. (1974). Definitions of ethnicity. *Ethnicity, 1,* 111–124.

Jensen, A. R. (1969). How much can we boost IQ and scholastic achievement? *Harvard Educational Review, 39,* 1–123.

Jordan, C. (1980). *The culturally sensitive selection of teaching practices*. Paper presented at the annual meeting of the American Educational Research Association.

Labov, W., Cohen, D., Robins, C., & Lewis, J. (1968). *A study of the non-standard English of Negro and Puerto Rican speakers in New York City*. Report on Cooperative Research Project 3288. New York: Columbia University.

Luria, A. R. (1979). Cultural differences in thinking. In M. Cole & S. Cole (Eds.), *The making of mind: A personal account of Soviet psychology*. Cambridge, MA: Harvard University Press.

Mitchell-Kernan, C. (1972). On the status of Black English for native speakers: An assessment of attitudes and values. In C. B. Cazden, V. P. John, & D. Hymes (Eds.), *Functions of language in the classroom*. New York: Teachers College Press.

Novak, M. (1971). *The rise of the unmeltable ethnics*. New York: Macmillan.

Ogbu, J. U. (1985). Minority education and caste. In N. R. Yetman & Steele (Eds.), *Majority and minority: The dynamics of race and ethnicity in American life* (3rd ed., pp. 426–439). Boston: Allyn & Bacon.

Philips, S. U. (1983). *The invisible culture: Communication in classroom and community on the Warm Springs Indian Reservation*. White Plains, NY: Longman.

Scollon, R., & Scollon, S.B.K. (1981). *Narrative, literacy, and face in interethnic communication*. Norwood, NJ: Ablex.

Sigel, I. E., Anderson, L. M., & Shapiro, H. (1966). Categorization behavior of lower- and middle-class Negro pre-school children: Differences in dealing with representation of familiar objects. *Journal of Negro Education, 35,* 218–229.

Simmons, W. (1979). The effects of the cultural salience of test materials on social class and ethnic differences in cognitive performance. *Quarterly Newsletter of the Laboratory of Comparative Human Cognition, 1,* 43–47.

Slavin, R. E. (1983). *Cooperative learning*. White Plains, NY: Longman.

Spicer, E., & Thompson, R. (1972). *Plural society in the Southwest*. New York: Interbook.

Suina, J. (n.d.). *And then I went to school*. Unpublished manuscript.

Witkin, H. A., & Goodenough, D. R. (1981). *Cognitive styles, essence and origins: Field dependence and field independence*. New York: International University Press.

16 IF MAINSTREAMING IS THE ANSWER, WHAT IS THE QUESTION?

Dianne L. Ferguson,
Philip M. Ferguson, and
Robert C. Bogdan

Special education did not begin in 1975 with the passage of Public Law 94-142, the Education of All Handicapped Children Act. But a new era in special education did begin then. Now, special educators define the terms of their debates about how best to educate children with disabilities according to the specifics of this landmark legislation. The enactment of P.L. 94-142 could be said to mark the passage of special education from childhood into adolescence, from which it may emerge into something like maturity. However, the infancy and youth of this educational stepchild need also to be remembered. Born of a spurious union of medicine and education and reared in an environment of social welfare and control, special education is today—as befits any self-respecting teenager—both reflective of and rebelling against its heritage.

HISTORY

The Early Days

The history of special education must not be presented as some Pollyannaish story of how dedicated professionals have worked together over the years to maintain steady progress in serving students with handicaps. The history is not one long litany of great achievements. Of course, there were dedicated people operating often with the best of intentions. And there has been notable progress in some areas. Nonetheless, many of the current problems of integration and classification are echoes of the loudly proclaimed fears and biases of special education's early leaders. Social historians over the past 20 years have revised our understanding of many of our basic social institutions (Lasch, 1977; Rothman, 1971). These historians remind us that if we want to learn the true history of medicine, it is better to look to the patients than the doctors. If you study the history of industry, you realize that there have been far more workers than owners. Similarly, what we need in the area of disabilities is not so much a history of special education as a history of disabled people and how they were involved with schools (as well as hospitals, asylums, and other institutions of public welfare). Such a social history of disabled people has not yet been written.

We will not fill the gap here. What we can do is comment on the social context of disabled people in America and how the rise of special education fits into that context.

The history of disabled people is, to a large degree, the history of poverty. In America, until the nineteenth century, disability was treated mainly from an economic standpoint (Rothman, 1971). People who were unable to survive independently, for whatever reason, were treated similarly. Circumstances varied since responsibility for such people did not go beyond the local community and often ended with the immediate family. What was common was the prominence given to the economic factor. Using the terms of the period, whether you were an idiot, a cripple, a drunkard, an orphan, an unwed mother, or a feeble widow with no children, it made little difference. Distinctions of pathology and etiology were not unknown, just irrelevant. If these "truly needy" could not be maintained by family or by assignment to the lowest bidders who tended such people for a fee, they usually ended up in the local almshouse. By the 1820s, nearly all the major cities and most towns or counties had such facilities as common repositories for any who could not maintain themselves.

Beginning in the 1820s and 1830s, the spirit of Jacksonian reform took hold in our new republic. Services for disabled people began to take a direction that was to last for most of the century and continue in many forms to this day. For the first time, the state began to assume responsibility for the care of disabled citizens. It went about meeting this responsibility by making distinctions where none had been made before. The distinctions were followed by separations. Large, segregated public institutions were established as the best solution for what were viewed as dangerous pathologies. A society newly concerned with burgeoning commerce felt the need to control the unproductive members of its cities (Rothman, 1971). Residential schools for deaf and blind children, asylums for those labeled insane or idiotic, large state prisons for the incorrigibles—all followed the same institutional pattern. After some brief initial overoptimism, the promised care came to be simple custody. Devoid of even superficial medical justification, the institutions, once established, continued in use as efficient custodians of society's deviant citizens.

Poverty remained central, although the specifics were now spoken of in the pseudoscientific jargon of institutional superintendents. The difference was that the upper classes now tended to see poverty as the cause of pathology rather than the result of it. The ever-increasing numbers of poor were seen as agents of social infection, passing on their defects and endangering the health of the republic itself. The solution was always the same: separate the affected individual from the poverty (i.e., from the family) and in so doing segregate the person from the larger society as well.

Even the beginnings of public education were founded on just such arguments. Henry Barnard, a noted advocate for public schooling, illustrated this new conception of the pathology of poor people in 1851:

No one at all familiar with the deficient household arrangements and deranged machinery of domestic life, of the extreme poor and ignorant, to say nothing of the intemperate—of the examples of rude manners, impure and profane language, and all the vicious habits of low-bred idleness, which abound in certain sections of all populous districts, can doubt that it is better for children to be removed as early and as long as possible from such scenes and such examples, and placed in an infant or primary school. (cited in Katz, Doucet, & Stern, 1982, pp. 348–349)

Of course, if a disability could be labeled, permanent removal was often possible. Another prominent reformer of this era, Samuel Gridley Howe, was one of the first to extend this notion of social pathology to insanity and retardation. For Howe, as for Barnard, Horace Mann, Dorothea Dix, and other reformers, the "social evils" such as idiocy could be properly blamed on the family in which the evil occurred, through the violation of "natural laws" (masturbation, drunkenness, intermarriage, ill health, etc.). All of this focused on a specific class of people to which, of course, Howe happened not to belong. Howe sounded the alarm for the state of Massachusetts in 1848:

The moral to be drawn from the prevalent existence of idiocy in society is that a very large class of persons ignore the conditions upon which alone health and reason are given to men, and consequently they sin in various ways. (Howe, 1848/1976, p. 34)

In the decades straddling the turn of the twentieth century, several developments coalesced that expanded public involvement with disabled children. They also dramatically expanded the number of children society chose to call disabled. Special-education classrooms began in the midst of a new wave of reform known as the Progressive Era. The first such classes probably began in the Cleveland school system in the 1870s (Mitchell, 1915). However, it was not until the 1890s that the practice was taken up by most of the major cities (Scheerenberger, 1983). By 1922, the Council for Exceptional Children had formed as a professional organization for the teachers of these now flourishing "ungraded classes."

At least three factors contributed to the rapid evolution of these special ungraded classes. First, universal compulsory schooling succeeded by the turn of the century—at least at the elementary level—in bringing together in one place large groups of children from widely separated strata of society, with differing intellectual abilities and ethnic backgrounds. By 1918, all of the states had some version of a compulsory school attendance law (Hoffman, 1975). Special education almost always began in our cities soon after the compulsory attendance laws were first enforced. The newly industrialized cities needed places for workers' children to be during the day. But once these children were in the schools, the system worked quickly to segregate large numbers of those who a few years earlier would never have entered the schoolhouse door. Most of the children who could not be handled in the regular classes were of southern European background (especially Italian). Almost always they were poor, and often they were judged recalcitrant or lazy. Special classes and entire schools were created as educational versions of the earlier almshouses. They were little more than catchall collections of students who for varieties of reasons were said not to fit in. The New Haven, Connecticut, system was described in 1902 as having three types of children lumped together in its special classes: "incorrigible boys, defective children, and children who speak no English" (Hoffman, 1975, p. 419).

A second factor greatly increased the efficiency with which school systems could sort children into the ungraded classes with a new patina of scientific objectivity. The Binet intelligence test was brought to America in 1908 by H. H. Goddard, a prominent institutional psychologist for retarded people. Whole new categories were popularized by Goddard and others. Terms such as *moral defective* and *moron* were used to refer to supposedly clinical entities newly identifiable by the powerful new IQ tests. In general, anyone scoring more than three years below his or her chronological age was automatically excluded from regular classes by most school systems. The linguistic and cultural biases of these tests, of course, were not insignificant factors when one realizes that in 1917, 70% of the students in New York City schools were immigrant children (Hoffman, 1975, p. 418). One of the other main advocates of intelligence tests, Lewis Terman, maintained throughout his career that people have significant intellectual differences from birth and that these differences are properly reflected in different social positions and occupational statuses. Terman also maintained the physical, emotional, and moral superiority of the gifted among us. The principles worked in reverse, too:

> Not all criminals are feeble-minded, but all feeble-minded persons are at least potential criminals. That every feeble-minded woman is a potential prostitute would hardly be disputed by anyone. Moral judgment, business judgment, social judgment, or any other kind of higher thought process, is a function of intelligence. Morality cannot flower and fruit if intelligence remains infantile. (cited in Gould, 1981, p. 181)

Even today, one hears echoes of Terman's pleas to keep intelligence tests out of politics and debates over social policy. But history tells us that the tests were never free of politics. Their value-laden nature says more about the similar prejudices of their creators and standardizers than about the different abilities supposedly diagnosed in the children tested.

A third development of a more conceptual nature provided the early intellectual justification for the segregation of special-education classes. As one general theory, this approach was called social Darwinism. One attraction of social Darwinism was that it could even justify the overwhelming numbers of poor urban immigrant children ending up in the special classes. Social Darwinism was most influential from 1870 to 1890. It nonetheless remained powerful, if not unchallenged, in the years before World War I, when Goddard and Terman were gaining influence. By this doctrine, social inequality was the inevitable by-product of evolution, just as certainly as biological variation. The poor and defective members of society were merely atavistic throwbacks to less advanced societies. (Thus "Mongolian idiocy" or "Mongolism" was a racist term based on the conviction that people with Down's syndrome were misplaced atavisms from the less advanced Oriental racial group. People with microcephaly—small heads—were similarly referred to as "Aztecs.") Terman and Goddard both carried the principles of social Darwinism to their logical extremes: lifelong segregation and eugenic sterilization. These earliest forms of tracking meant the special classes to be little more than feeder systems for the asylums, where segregation could be maintained to the grave. At least until the 1920s, most special educators publicly predicted institutional destinies for all their charges. The supervisor of special classes in Boston described the process in 1916:

> Most will agree that the ideal condition would be for many of the mentally defective to go from the school directly to the institution, and thus safeguard the public from inefficiency, unemployment, pauperism, vagrancy, degeneracy, and all the other social consequences of feeble-mindedness. (cited in Scheerenberger, 1983, p. 167)

That was said by a friend of disabled children; the enemies were not as hopeful.

As IQ scores became more and more entrenched in school administration, higher and higher scores came to be required for admission to special classes. Thus explicit exclusion of severely handicapped children became common. There remained plenty of candidates for special classes. The number of classes and students in those classes rose rapidly. Special education had lost its experimental status quickly and had become a recognized, if underfed, member of the educational family. By 1934, there were some 85,000 retarded students alone enrolled in special classes, in 427 cities (Scheerenberger, 1983, p. 201).

Recent History

From the 1930s through the 1960s, special education continued to expand. There was tremendous variation in types and numbers of programs from state to state, from city to city, and even from school to school. Most state laws were permissive about the education of disabled children. For those called "trainably retarded"—that is, with an IQ score from 25 to 50—educational programs were few and far between. For mildly handicapped students there was often a classroom in the basement, next to the boiler room or the janitor's closet.

An undercurrent of protest continued through these years. There were always a few educators arguing against segregation both as an effective educational strategy and as a violation of the children's rights. One educator of deaf children described the concept of mainstreaming, which he had promoted since the 1850s, as

> beneficial to both classes—to the deaf-mutes in enlarging their scope of thought by bringing their minds into contact with those of their more favored companions; beneficial yet more variously to those who hear and speak, quickening their perception, and improving mental development. (Gordon, 1885, p. 249)

One hundred years later, in 1953, an educator by the name of Tenny decried the "segregated nature of our special education programs." In very modern-sounding language, Tenny claimed that most special-education classes

> have prevented the non-handicapped majority from intimate social contact with the handicapped in school and probably also discouraged out-of-school contacts. Understanding and acceptance come about most readily through individual acquaintance; therefore, segregation should be eliminated wherever possible. (cited in Scheerenberger, 1983, p. 237)

Such statements always seemed to reflect quixotic battles against the windmills of special classes. Finally, in the 1970s, civil rights advocates joined forces with educational experts to apply the principle set forth in the 1954 school desegregation decision by the Supreme Court to special education as well as race: Separate education is inherently unequal education.

Perhaps the most important of the court cases in these pre–P.L. 94-142 years was the so-called PARC (Pennsylvania Association for Retarded Citizens) case. This case set forth five court-sanctioned principles, which in turn formed the foundation for the legislation to follow.

(1) Children with disabilities had systematically been denied a public education. (2) All children, regardless of handicap, could benefit from an education. (3) The Bill of Rights guaranteed all children a free appropriate public education if it was provided to any. (4) Parents had a right to due process protections regarding classification and placement decisions. (5) Children with disabilities were entitled to receive their education in the least restrictive environment possible. (Biklen, 1981)

Some four years after the PARC case, P.L. 94-142 was signed into law. For the first time, the federal government was setting minimal standards for the states to meet in their education of disabled children. Predictably, the law provoked as many questions as it answered. However, one basic fact was plain. For the first time, no school-age child could be excluded from the educational system by virtue of a handicapping condition.

Public Law 94-142

The process of interpreting and implementing P.L. 94-142 in America's schools has resulted in confusion, misconceptions, impediments, contradictions, and strong emotions on all sides. The concept of "least restrictive environment," a central element of the law, proves particularly slippery. With no mention of either mainstreaming or integration, the law reads:

Handicapped children in public or private institutions or other care facilities, are [to be] educated with children who are not handicapped.... Special classes, separate schooling, or other removal of handicapped children from the regular educational environment [may] occur only when the nature or severity of the handicap is such that education in regular classes with the use of supplementary aids and services cannot be achieved satisfactorily.

The presumption is that all kinds of students should learn together; integration is better than segregation. Further, the burden of proof is on those who would segregate. Segregation requires demonstration that the student cannot benefit from a more regular, integrated program. That is, all handicapped students have a legal right to have their educational needs met in the least exclusionary, least restrictive way possible.

The ensuing controversy was not entirely new. As we noted earlier, special educators began questioning the practice of segregated special classes during the 1960s (Reynolds, 1962; Dunn, 1968). A progression of court decisions, beginning with *Brown* v. *Board of Education* in 1954, gradually opened the way for more and more forms of desegregation. Finally, the development of the concept of "normalization" converged with "least restrictive environment," fueling and expanding the debate.

Normalization

While "least restrictive environment" evolved legalistically, using the reference points of exclusion and restriction, the evolution of "normalization" used the broadest possible reference point: all of society. The term was coined in 1959 by Neils E. Bank-Mikkelsen, then head of the Danish Mental Retardation Service. His influence led to the Danish Act of 1959, the stated purpose of which was "to create an existence for the mentally retarded as close to normal living conditions as possible." Focusing on outcome, Bank-Mikkelsen hoped to combat the "dogma of protectionism" and bring retarded people "the legal and human rights of all other citizens" (1969).

By 1969, the Swede Bengt Nirje had formulated a "principle" of normalization based on "making available to the mentally retarded patterns and conditions of everyday life which are as close as possible to the norms and patterns of the mainstream of society." Focusing on "normal means" of providing care and service, Nirje (1976) describes eight normal rhythms of life that should not be denied handicapped persons. These include normal rhythms of the day, week, year, and life cycle and normal opportunities to receive the respect of others, to live with the opposite sex, to live in typical housing, and to experience financial security.

By 1972, Wolf Wolfensberger had offered another formulation of the principle of normalization incorporating the Danish emphasis on normal outcomes with the Swedish one on normal means. In addition, he broadened the concept to refer to any handicapped or "devalued" person. In its briefest formulation, Wolfensberger's principle of normalization refers to "the use of culturally valued means in order to enable people to live culturally valued lives."

From its first publication in 1972, this definition and its implications have been the subject of much debate and misunderstanding, both in the literature and among service professions. Some people criticize normalization as ignoring real individual differences, as attempting to make people normal, or denying people relationships with their disabled peers. Still others find normalization "unrealistic," as "placing an undue burden" on people to change, as only really applicable to the most mildly disabled, or finally, as empirically unverified.

Wolfensberger (1980a, 1980b) has responded to such "misconceptions" of the principle of normalization. In so doing he reasserts normalization's implications for service. Agencies, including schools, that have a history of rejecting, segregating, or providing inadequate and inappropriate services to people with handicaps are challenged by the principle of normalization to do two things:

1. Provide services that will enhance both the skills and the social image of the handicapped.
2. Provide the services in a *manner* that effectively develops more skills while minimizing negative social images.

Mainstreaming

Much early controversy regarding mainstreaming resulted, in part, from the very use of the term. Legal emphasis on "regular educational environments" combined with normalization's reference to a person "functioning in the mainstream of society" resulted in two misconceptions: first, mainstreaming as physical placement in regular class, followed by mainstreaming as only for the appropriately eligible, that is, students with mild handicaps.

From 1969 to 1972, between 11,000 and 18,000 students previously labeled as "educable mentally retarded" were declassified and returned to regular classes (MacMillan, Jones, & Meyers, 1976). This occurred largely because of legislation altering the identification process—children had to be tested in their native language, and IQ cutoffs were lowered. Nevertheless, children previously judged as "failing" in regular classes were supposed ready to return to regular class with no further need of separate special assistance. Following such a pattern, early mainstreaming attempts apparently concluded that all children with handicaps, regardless of the severity of their handicaps or the intensity of their educational needs, must attend school in regular classes. One such oversimplified definition reads, "Mainstreaming is a form of educational programming that integrates special needs and non—special needs children in regular classrooms" (Meisels, 1978, p. 10).

This portrayal of mainstreaming has also provoked the most negative reactions from the teachers in those regular classrooms. Often the teachers had a legitimate complaint. Dumping children with continuing needs into an already crowded class-room with little or no support services did little but exchange one inadequate arrangement for another. Teachers who respond negatively to such dumping are too often attacked as betraying biases against disabled children. Although teacher bias has probably existed in some cases, the true target of these regular teachers' anger is not mainstreaming but the misuse of that term in a rigid, mechanical way.

Efforts to correct this narrow and erroneous view focused on the law's reference to "a continuum of services." Thus the Council for Exceptional Children described mainstreaming in 1975 as including a range of alternatives for students who need more specialized services than are available in regular classes. However, these alter-natives most frequently took the form of a continuum of discrete placement options. Not surprisingly, a national survey (Kenowitz, Zweibel, & Edgar, 1978) found that 70% of students labeled moderately handicapped and 69% of those labeled severely or profoundly handicapped were receiving educational programs in special-educa-tion centers (defined as "a separate facility designed exclusively for handicapped students"). Segregated, self-contained programs located in public school buildings (i.e., buildings that also contained classrooms for regular students) accounted for the remaining students in each category.

Clearly, few but the mildly handicapped had found their way to the mainstream by 1978. In fact, one early definition made this limitation explicit:

> Mainstreaming refers to the temporal, social, and instructional integration of *eligible* exceptional children with normal peers.... No categorical labels or classifications can be applied to any child to whom mainstreaming is applied.... Mainstreaming is *delimited* to the educational strategies which can be applied in *normalized educational service* for children with learning handicaps. (MacMillan et al., 1976, p. 3; emphasis added)

These and other authors (e.g., Birch, 1974) reacted to wholesale delabeling and dumping in the name of mainstreaming by restricting mainstreaming to those few handicapped students who were "most nearly normal." Apparently, the extent to which handicapped children could learn in the mainstream depended on the degree to which their "handicapped states" could be diminished.

Not only had mainstreaming been largely limited to meaning regular class placement for the most mildly handicapped students, but some argued that it had also become equated with regular class curriculum. Thirty years of specialized curriculum development for mildly handicapped students, emphasizing occupational, social, and other "basic life skills," seemed sacrificed.

PRESENT STATUS

Recent discussions counter earlier misapplications by returning to a broader formulation. The label "mainstreaming" is rejected in favor of "least restrictive educational opportunity" or just simply "integration." The concept is expanded beyond physical settings to include components of educational programming and meaningful interactions with nonhandicapped peers (Kenowitz et al., 1978). Attention has focused on integrated education for preschoolers with handicaps (Bricker, 1978) and issues unique to providing secondary students with the least restrictive educational opportunity (Wilcox & Bellamy, 1982). Most important is the increasing inclusion of *all* students with handicaps—even the most severely handicapped—into the debate and into public school (Brown, Wilcox, Sontag, Vincent, Dodd, & Gruenewald, 1977).

Integration for All Disabled Students?

Free from early misconceptions, the central conflict is now more clearly revealed—particularly in the case of integrating students with severe and profound handicaps. The conflict is between observing students' rights not to be discriminated against and meeting their educational needs; between supporting a valued choice and verifying an educational model. One key position statement says, "Not only do severely handicapped citizens have the *right* to be participating members of heterogeneous communities, but...such participation is *inherently good*" (Brown et al., 1977, p. 196; emphasis added). Furthermore, proponents argue, students with handicaps can (and do) learn things from their nonhandicapped peers that cannot be simulated in segregated settings. In fact, a review of research that compares special and regular class placements concludes that mainstreaming promotes social adjustment of students with handicaps (Carlberg & Kavale, 1980). Several qualitative studies have shown the academic value of modeling and natural reinforcers simply unavailable in segregated settings (Biklen, 1985; Bogdan, 1983a, 1983b). Studies supporting the positive effects of integration for handicapped students have focused on strategies for promoting positive attitudes and relationships (Gottlieb, 1980; Voeltz, 1982) and effects for different age groups (Appolloni & Cooke, 1978; Guralnick, 1981; Rynders, Johnson, Johnson, & Schmidt, 1980). Two reviews of research concerning severely handicapped students conclude that there is reason for optimism (Stainback & Stainback, 1981, 1982).

Conversely, another recent review of research (Gresham, 1982), focusing on social interaction and social learning through modeling, concludes that empirical research does not support the assumptions that mainstreaming results in improved attitudes of nonhandicapped students, increased social interaction between handicapped and nonhandicapped peers, and increased social learning of handicapped students from the example of the nonhandicapped. The review goes on to recommend social skills assessment and training *prior* to mainstreaming.

Does the Research Support Mainstreaming?

We concur with Blatt (1979) that research has nothing to do with *whether* we should continue the practice of integrating students with handicaps. Even if incontrovertible evidence were available to support integration, arguing on empirical grounds would still reflect a misdirected dependence on research to determine policies that are primarily value-based (Blatt, 1979; Center on Human Policy, 1979).

The argument for integrating black and white students is, of course, essentially the same as made here for disabled students. Integration of the races in educational settings has been national policy since 1954 on the grounds that "separate" can *never* be "equal." Racial disturbances, problems over busing, resistance from parents, or other developments never lead to denunciations of racial integration as a legitimate social goal. All that is questioned is how best to achieve that racial harmony. Yet when it comes to disabled children, bungled attempts at integration, dumping, lack of support services, and other problems lead frequently to calls to abandon the effort altogether. Integration *itself* is questioned in a way that would never be tolerated for racial issues. This is what is meant by saying that in its truest form, mainstreaming is a civil rights issue, not a matter for empirical research.

It is a matter of balance and priority. Not only is participation of handicapped children in integrated settings inherently good, "it is now feasible to arrange educational service delivery systems in ways that maximize the probability of such participation" (Brown et al., 1977, p. 196). These researchers proceed to suggest a variety of ways in which such service systems can accomplish such a goal. Among these dimensions are a natural ratio of handicapped to nonhandicapped students; functional, naturalized curricula; chronological age–appropriate educational environments; and physically accessible schools. Thus *whether* to integrate is not an appropriate research question. Increasingly, however, researchers investigate how integration of all handicapped students can be most effectively achieved (e.g., Biklen, 1985; Certo, Haring, & York, 1984; Stainback & Stainback, 1985).

Aspects of Integration

The tendency to equate mainstreaming with physical placement is a frequent misconception. The more recent preference for the concept of "integration" can fall prey to the similar error of failing to distinguish adequately between physical and social integration. A variety of authors point out that physical integration alone fails to meet goals of normalization or participation in heterogeneous communities. Yet little consensus has been reached on the meaning of social integration or, more important, how it can be achieved. One attempt to assess integration quantitatively (as part of Program Analysis of Service Systems [PASS]; Wolfensberger & Glenn, 1975) uses 14 separate "subscales."

It is more helpful to think of the concept of integration as multifaceted. Types or levels of integration (Dybwad, 1980; Nirje, 1980; Taylor & Ferguson, 1985) can be described from both the perspective of those being integrated and the perspective of those facilitating integration. The examples that follow describe types or levels of integration from both these perspectives. Although the school experience of students with handicaps will be emphasized, keep in mind that integration must apply to all areas of life.

Physical Integration.   Physical integration enables people with handicaps to share the same spaces as nonhandicapped people. Though not sufficient by itself, mere physical integration exposes handicapped and nonhandicapped students to one another and affords opportunities for social interaction and eventual integration. Some school districts disperse clusters of classes in a few buildings, as in the Albuquerque "side-by-side" approach (Thompson & Arkell, 1980). Other districts spread a few classes throughout a large number of schools, hoping to achieve the more or less natural proportion of students as found in society in general (Brown et al., 1977).

Functional Integration.   Once in schools, students should have access to all aspects of the school, such as the cafeteria, gym, swimming pool, library, transportation, and rest rooms. Often functional integration means that this access occurs at a different time—nonhandicapped students may not be present when a class of students with handicaps is scheduled to use the gym or library. Nevertheless, it represents an important extension of physical integration since students are not physically segregated in a single classroom or wing within the public school.

Social Integration.   Social integration comprises both impersonal and interpersonal social relationships. Physical and functional integration brings students into contact with a variety of persons with whom they can develop polite, impersonal social relationships. Hall monitors, crossing guards, cafeteria workers, librarians, and office workers are only a few of the people students casually greet, exchange information with, and get to know in the daily round of school life.

Social integration that is interpersonal refers more directly to interactions and relationships that develop between people, especially peers. Sometimes students develop close friendships, or perhaps just casual friendships as study partners, tutors, or lockermates. Attitudes of mutual respect, civility, and esteem are important elements of the relationships that develop as a result of social integration.

One other aspect of social integration is what some call personal integration (Nirje, 1980). This type of integration occurs through social relationships with especially significant people—parents, siblings, relatives, a spouse. Some services, for example, residential alternatives, should respect the needs and rights of people with handicaps to develop and sustain a satisfying private life.

Community Integration.   Community integration occurs when people with handicaps are able to participate as active members of a community. More and more frequently, community integration involves use of community sites for training and skill development. If students are learning to handle money in order to purchase food, clothing, or other desired things, they are more likely to learn in actual grocery, clothing, and department stores. This increasing functional emphasis in curricula for students with handicaps also advocates learning domestic and self-care skills in actual homes and vocational skills in actual job settings. Thus teachers address the skills their students need to use in the places where they actually need to use them. Even for very young students, community integration can mean learning to cross neighborhood streets, play in the local parks, and, eventually, to use public transportation.

Organizational Integration.   This general and expanding use of public generic services results from all the other forms of integration. Students with handicaps have no need of a separate, specialized educational organization, nor special transportation, health care, or other generic social, economic, or personal services.

THE CURRICULUM

Curriculum is sometimes thought of as synonymous with education. It is not. It is, however, more than just a published guide or teacher's manual. At its most basic, a curriculum answers the question "What do schools teach?" To a lesser extent, a curriculum also answers the question "How do schools teach?" It generally does not provide any direct information for the question "Why do schools teach what they do?" Further, deciding "what to teach" is rarely a straightforward process—such decisions are heavily value-laden. And in uncovering the how of teaching, another question is raised: "What happens to the curriculum as it filters through the particular beliefs and values of an individual teacher?"

In discussing curricular approaches for students with handicaps, we cannot do justice to this rich complexity. However, we will try to encompass the full range of students with handicaps. We suggest that if a curricular approach or instructional strategy can effectively serve students who are more difficult to teach—the most severely handicapped—it is also likely to work for students with mild or moderate educational needs. Thus we will often refer to examples from the experience of severely handicapped students.

What Are the Major Approaches to Curriculum Content?

Students with handicaps have long been associated with and identified by a series of failure motifs. In one way or another, they fail to learn enough, in the same way, or as quickly as schools and teachers are prepared to teach. Early efforts to accommodate the curriculum to some students' different learning resulted in a "watered down" version of regular class content. By the 1940s, the occupational education curriculum (Hungerford, 1943) was emphasizing vocational skills and getting jobs; the late 1950s brought a broader emphasis on basic life functions in the social learning curriculum (Goldstein & Seigle, 1958). Other curricula for handicapped students have variously emphasized such themes as areas of living (Love, 1968) or persisting life situations (Stevens, 1961).

Regardless of the exact content or its organization, these curricula reflect professionals' understanding of what education means and what students with handicaps ought to learn. We think there are three distinctively different approaches to the curriculum content and education that students with handicaps receive. We call these approaches (1) the developmental learner approach, (2) the clinical treatment approach, and (3) the functional skills approach (Ferguson & Searl, 1982). Some of these approaches encourage and facilitate integration of some students with handicaps; other approaches do not.

Developmental Learner Approach. This is the most widespread and general approach to education and curriculum content. Education for all students, regardless of their abilities or disabilities, seems to begin with this approach and with its key notion: that students learn skills and information in a predictable sequence and at a more or less predictable rate. Children learn to crawl before they walk, babble before they talk, talk before they read, and add before they multiply.

For students with disabilities, the developmental assumption states that the choices of what to teach should be drawn from the developmental learning sequences experienced by nonhandicapped children. This approach offers the advantage of the good example, as well as clear, well-defined, longitudinal sequences for teachers to follow. Several highly detailed developmental curricula have been developed specifically for handicapped—even severely handicapped—students (e.g., Fredericks et al., 1976; Cohen, Gross, & Haring, 1976). Particularly in the area of language, efforts have been made to employ other relevant approaches to "customize" developmental sequences for students with serious developmental delay. One well-known example combines psycholinguistic methods with a developmental approach (Miller & Yoder, 1972a, 1972b); another applies Piagetian developmental categories and stages to language learning (Bricker & Bricker, 1970, 1974).

While possessing some advantages, the developmental approach can create a variety of problems for students with disabilities. First, skills tend to be organized into domains—gross motor, language, self-help, social—and are often taught in an isolated manner without regard for the fact that activities generally require students to employ skills from several domains simultaneously.

Second, skills to be taught are frequently selected from developmental scales and measures. While useful for some aspects of assessment and evaluation, the psychometric criteria necessary for inclusion on a scale may have little relevance for a student's skills repertoire.

Third, deciding what skills to teach is based on the student's assessed developmental age rather than chronological age. The implied assumption behind such decisions is that students have an unlimited amount of time to acquire skills. Teenagers nearing adulthood who are still working on mastering skills most students of a much younger age have acquired may find themselves out of school with few of the skills needed to cope with adult living. The approach also does not include functional alternatives for skills that a student is clearly not going to acquire. Students with significant sensory or motor handicaps find no alternative functional sequence that will incorporate the necessary adaptations they need.

Finally, the developmental approach is heavily dependent on the notion of "readiness." Students are described as "delayed" or "behind" in development compared to the majority of their age-mates. The goal is to have the students become as able as their peers—to catch up to the developmental norm, or at least to narrow the distance between present performance and the norm.

One variation on the developmental approach to curriculum content is the basic skills approach. This approach assumes that in order to learn appropriate skills and behaviors that can be applied in a variety of environments and situations, one must master a core of basic academic skills. As in the developmental model, the teacher takes the skills of nonhandicapped students as models, but instead of using typical developmental sequences, new, highly detailed, individualized sequences are developed. Using the technique of task analysis, these new learning sequences can be tailored to the student's existing skills and unique learning patterns, thus assuring that each student will be able to apply skills successfully when needed (Barrett, 1979).

The basic skills emphasis on norm-referenced, terminal objectives but individual, student-referenced learning sequences is a strength. However, the focus on a core of academic and cognitive skills is a weakness for many students with handicaps. The basic core skills may never be acquired with enough facility to allow the student to apply and cross-reference such skills independently in general life situations.

Both the developmental and the related basic skills approaches can work for some students with handicaps. Use of a different sensory mode for instruction may help some students to catch up. Varying rates and proportions of new and review material in lessons can assist other students. Use of tape recorders, talking books, typewriters, and a variety of other easily made adaptations can permit many students with handicaps to learn efficiently in fully integrated situations.

But for some students, the developmental gap widens beyond the capacity of special "catch-up" sessions or strategies. Temporary removal from regular classes to resource rooms or part-time special classes too often ends up as certain students' terminal educational placement instead of a strategy to facilitate integration. These gaps may have less impact on younger students because the developmental-chrono-logical gap is proportionally smaller. However, older students who have failed to narrow the gap may find themselves permanently segregated.

Clinical Treatment Approach. The developmental learner approach—which dominates public education—is reinforced by another approach that has come to schools from settings more traditionally charged with serving and caring for the most severely handicapped.

Until very recently, the education, treatment, and programming for students labeled as severely handicapped have been characterized by frequent segregation, institutionalization, and weak to nonexistent programming, dominated by a commit-ment to a clinical treatment or "therapeutic" approach. Students are perceived as having deficits that need to be improved or overcome. A pathological reflex, high muscle tone, or any other interfering pattern of behavior must be eliminated, normalized, or otherwise gotten under control before positive, appropriate, more nearly normal patterns of behavior or learning can occur. Deficits are "treated" in fairly narrow, precise ways as a method of freeing a student for more traditional and familiar educational experiences.

Though most often experienced by students with severe handicaps, a version of this approach frequently applies to another group. Called the "eliminative" model by Wilcox and Bellamy (1982), the approach is less one of curriculum content than a perspective on how students learn. It is based on the assumption that students identified as having behavior problems cannot learn until their negative, maladaptive behaviors have been eliminated. Such maladaptive behaviors are thought to interfere so much that they crowd out any possibility of positive learning or development.

Both of these versions of the clinical treatment approach have very narrowly focused educational goals. There is less concern with helping students to participate within the typical mainstream or to catch up to the norm. Instead, the mission of teachers employing this approach is to overcome enough interfering behavior patterns to allow students to move on to other educational environments, where they will begin to develop the necessary positive skills to catch up and fit in. Thus this approach, too, relies on a strong notion of readiness. Students are not "ready" to learn until their negative, pathological, maladaptive behaviors have been eliminated or controlled.

This approach is applied at both the elementary and secondary levels, but the emphasis becomes more powerful and dramatic with older students. It is frequently used to justify moving or maintaining students in much more segregated and restrictive settings. Behaviors that can be tolerated or physically handled in younger, smaller children take on new dimensions of difficulty as students grow larger. Students can find themselves permanently segregated from mainstream public education on two counts: first, because they lack the readiness for successful integration, and second, because targeted behaviors or deficits can be controlled or eliminated only in a particular setting. The second has been described as becoming dependent on static structures (Crowner, 1979), and it works like this: Students whose behavior or handicap is manageable in one setting are assumed to be "ready" to move on to a less restrictive, more integrated setting. However, when moved, the maladaptive behavior recurs or the new staff cannot manage or care for the students easily enough. Therefore, the students clearly *need* the more restrictive setting because (1) they were not really ready or (2) it is the only setting in which they can maintain a positive learning attitude. While the approach might work for some students, this element of "catch-22" makes it problematic.

Functional Skills Approach.   One key difference in this approach is its direction. Decisions about what to teach, whether the student is a preschooler (Vincent, Salisbury, Walter, Brown, Gruenewald, & Powers, 1980) or a teenager (Wilcox & Bellamy, 1982), are made from outside the students. Unlike the developmental and clinical treatment approaches, which ask first what skills a student already possesses in order to build toward a long-range norm, the functional skills approach first asks what skills the student will need in the next environment entered. Through this approach, the discrepancy between that criterion and the student's present repertoire (Brown, Nietupski, & Hamre-Nietupski, 1976; Brown, Branston-McClean, Baumgart, Vincent, Falvey, & Schroeder, 1979) is assessed, and curricula are designed to bring the student's abilities into a closer correspondence with the concrete, practical expectations of the environments within which the student acts. The approach emphasizes that education should prepare students for the environment and demands they will encounter after public schooling is completed. Instruction is aimed at helping them make a successful transition to that environment, whether a college, a business, or a sheltered workshop.

Pursuing this goal requires that curriculum content be generated through a problem-solving process much less encumbered with the developmental readiness logic found in other approaches. Rather than following an established developmental sequence, no assumption is made about the order in which a child needs to learn skills. Instead, skills are taught in the order that, "when acquired most quickly, will accomplish some improvement in the [student's] ability to interact successfully with the environment" (Sailor & Guess, 1983).

This alternative method of determining curriculum content arose from efforts to design curricula for students with severe handicaps. These students frequently need to learn quite basic skills at a much older age than their nonhandicapped peers. Yet by virtue of their age they possess a very different learning history and repertoire than those possessed by nonhandicapped students when they learned the skills. They may also have specific physical, medical, or sensory limitations that prevent their acquisition of some skills. While use of this method may not be as critical for students with less severe handicaps, we think it can be quite useful.

Why should I use a functional approach? The approach to determining curriculum content overcomes several limitations of other approaches. First, it encourages the teaching of clusters of skills that span traditional domains. Thus generalization and functional use of newly learned skills is maximized, while acquisition of nonfunctional splinter or isolated skills is minimized. Second, skills that students need to perform frequently in their school, home, and community environments are selected. Thus skills with little relevance to a student's life, such as may be found on developmental scales or tests, are not selected for teaching. Third, since no order is assumed, students do not have to demonstrate some prescribed readiness. This is particularly helpful with older students who can learn clusters of skills appropriate to both their chronological age and their practical life needs.

Some authors (e.g., Sternberg & Adams, 1982) suggest that the apparent conflict between developmental and functional approaches is unnecessary. Instead they call for a "melding of the two models" into a "continuum of model emphasis." That is, decisions about what to teach should be made on the basis of chronological age expectations. It is perfectly appropriate to use a developmental approach for younger students, but then one must switch to a functional approach at a later age. The age to switch curriculum approaches should be made individually for each student on the basis of some "critical period" of change in expectations. However, these authors offer no guidance on how expectations would change or when they would change critically enough to warrant a shift in curriculum approach. While we agree that there is a great deal of overlap between the developmental and functional approaches, especially for younger students, we find three significant differences:

1. The functional skills approach can facilitate rather than impede integration of all students with handicaps (especially into their own nonschool communities).
2. The approach effectively teaches students skills they actually need to use.
3. The approach assists students to use their skills appropriately in a variety of school and nonschool environments.

Finally, we think the functional life-skills approach has the advantage of including *all* types of students, in terms of both age and intensity of need. Thus it can be quite flexibly applied to almost any student while encouraging maximum teacher creativity and autonomy in the design of individual curricula and instructional plans.

IMPLEMENTING INTEGRATION

In spite of controversy and apprehension, integration *has* occurred and *is* working in many schools across the country and for all kinds of students (Biklen, 1985; Taylor, 1982). As the policies and practices of integrated schooling become widespread, segregation of any student with handicaps becomes impossible to defend. Educators turn from arguing the merits of integrating to devising strategies for implementation in the face of very real obstacles. In large part, obstacles continue to exist because full, unconditional integration involves integration not just of students but also of teachers, programs and services, and administrative and bureaucratic systems.

Barriers to Integration

Organizational and Bureaucratic Barriers. In spite of P.L. 94-142, a variety of *legal barriers* remain in some states (Taylor, 1981). For example, relatively few states (e.g., Michigan and Wisconsin) mandate public education for all children from birth.

In many states, young children with handicaps continue to be legally excluded. There is also a need for model regulations and policies concerning graduation and competency requirements for students with handicaps to ensure their equal opportunity to earn diplomas.

Some groups of students who, for one reason or another, are involved with other social service agencies (e.g., adjudicated youth, institutionalized students, and students living in group homes, on military bases, and on reservations) are often denied their educational rights to a public education because of jurisdictional disputes between the agencies involved. Such *jurisdictional barriers* are often compounded by economic constraints due to a lack of effective funding mechanisms between such agencies. Similarly, some students living in financially overburdened or impoverished school districts may be denied a fully appropriate public education due to *economic barriers*. In many areas there remains a need for model legislation, regulations, and policies establishing funding and interagency mechanisms that protect students' educational rights both equitably and adequately.

Some geographic areas, particularly rural, sparsely populated ones, present *logistic barriers* to meeting students' educational needs. Students with handicaps that occur infrequently in the population or who are severely handicapped are particularly vulnerable since they are frequently the most difficult and costly students to serve. These same students are in greatest need of strong and effective advocates. However, parents, guardians, and other concerned advocates too often find their efforts thwarted by a variety of *political barriers*. Schools may only reluctantly share information with parents or may actively limit parent involvement in decision making through the use of overly technical language, formal meetings where parents are outnumbered and procedurally intimidated, or policies limiting regular access to teachers and classrooms.

One final organizational barrier to integration has turned out to be the *system of special-education categories*. Special education has been remarkably effective (especially since World War II) in establishing more and more narrow diagnostic labels. Each label then became redefined as a pathological entity residing somewhere inside children. As with any process of specialization, the main outcome has been a myth of expertise surrounding each disability. Learning-disabled children, therefore, can only be taught by "experts" in the arcane intricacies of learning disabilities. Teacher training programs at universities would not just certify graduates in special education but in particular etiologies and pathologies. Encouraged is a tendency toward "professional preciousness" (Sarason, 1972), whereby problems tend to be defined so as to require the services of traditionally trained professionals. This tendency has an inherently segregative impetus. As such, the very organization of special-education services works against the integration of children who are different. Regular teachers are denied access to information that would allow them the confidence and support to work with "labeled" students. Artificial shortages of support personnel are maintained by pushing this myth of expertise.

None of this denies that there are physical and behavioral differences between, say, a child with Down syndrome and a child with dyslexia. What it does claim is that the important differences have less to do with diagnostic labels drawn from a medical model and much more to do with prognostic educational objectives. Some students need more intensive educational programming focusing on basic skills. Others need much less intrusive remedial assistance. Some teachers need more intensive support services than others. These levels of programming needs cut across diagnostic categories. Indeed, many educators now believe that levels of need have as much to do with school expectations as with student characteristics (Apter, 1982; Sailor & Guess, 1983).

Students labeled as handicapped are more similar to typical children than different from them. They have varying educational strengths and weaknesses. Essentially, they are learners looking for an appropriate setting in which to learn. Our schools need to reflect this similarity by deemphasizing the traditional diagnostic labels of the past. Systems are beginning to reflect this change by organizing services in terms of program intensity and focus rather than arbitrary, child-blaming categories such as "trainable," "educable," "learning-disabled," and "autistic" (Wilcox & Bellamy, 1982).

This switch in orientation is also a type of integration in that it envisions a much more continuous shape to all programming options, regular or remedial. To be effective, of course, it has to be more than just a change in the names of classrooms. What goes on inside the classroom—both special and regular—is also changing in ways that assume integration instead of circumventing it.

Program Barriers.   Students with sensory, physical, and multiple impairments are effectively excluded from many educational opportunities and programs because of architectural barriers. They may have to travel far from their neighborhood peers, sometimes to attend segregated schools. They may be denied access to transportation because of inaccessible buses or denied independent mobility because of a school's lack of elevators, ramps, or braille signs. In some cases, classes or programs are inaccessible because of inadequate acoustics in rooms and buildings.

Even well-intentioned efforts can be thwarted by other kinds of technological barriers. These include many of the details of programming: creative, flexible curricula; effective assessment procedures; instructional techniques; adaptive devices. For example, many nonverbal students can learn to communicate effectively enough to participate in regular classes using alternative communication systems that range from manual-sign and symbolic-language boards to microcomputers with voice synthesizers. Although there has been dramatic growth in solutions to some of these technological programming problems, such new technology is not always widely disseminated and used.

Personnel Barriers.   By far the most formidable obstacles to implementing integrated educational programs for students with handicaps are attitudinal. Though all people with handicaps experience some social discrimination, certain groups are especially affected. These include students from racial or cultural minorities, those with severe handicaps, and those with particularly stigmatizing conditions (e.g., carriers of hepatitis B). Such attitudinal barriers occur among all types of school people: students, parents of both typical and handicapped children, teachers, administrators, school board members, and local citizen taxpayers. There is a continuing need systematically to foster positive attitudes toward people with significant differences in all realms of our society, including our schools.

Another kind of personnel barrier is the shortage of skilled professionals. Problems of turnover, fatigue, and frustration among special- and regular-education teachers only compound the need. Varieties of related and supportive personnel

—therapists, psychologists, teacher aides—are also in short supply. The most needy handicapped students suffer most from these kinds of personnel barriers.

Finally, a number of administrative practices and policies hinder the provision of appropriate public education to students with handicaps. Separate special-education administrative structures that parallel regular education structures can lead to problems of coordination, communication, and authority between regular- and special-education administrators.

These and other barriers pose great challenges for schools. Frequently, barriers overlap and interact, further complicating solutions. Some barriers impede only certain groups of students, while others can affect all students with handicaps. Nevertheless, "careful planning and preparation, creation of specialized support positions, development of facilitative policies, and other carefully planned strategies" (Taylor, 1982, p. 48) can succeed in implementing integrated education for all students with handicaps.

PROBLEMS IN INTEGRATION

Of course, what qualifies as a problem depends on one's perspective. Some teachers, both regular and special, feel their lack of experience with handicapped students (or some kinds of handicapped students) disqualifies them from participating in integration efforts. Others, like one kindergarten teacher we met, consider the integration of even severely multiple-handicapped students a challenge (see Bogdan, 1983a, for a description of this study):

> You know, I couldn't tell this to the other teachers because they wouldn't understand. But I've been teaching for seventeen years. It's always been easy for me, just natural. I never had to work at being a good teacher. Last year with Monica (a severely multiple handicapped student), and this, is the first time since I've been teaching that I really had to work. It was the first time I had really been challenged. And it's so exciting. I'm really earning my pay, but it's so interesting trying to find the answers. You keep telling yourself: "I know someone out there must have the answer to this particular question, I just have to find it." If I told that to the other teachers they would just laugh.[1]

Nevertheless, most people, quite understandably, are uncertain of how to act or what to do when they first encounter a new and different kind of student. Regular- and special-class teachers alike need various kinds of support.

The Students

"Are they dangerous?" "Can they talk?" "What's wrong with them?" "Why do they use that thing?" "Why do they flap their fingers?" Rather than steering a wide berth around new students and their teachers, questions like these should be asked. Principals can help by setting aside some time at a faculty meeting for the regular teachers to question the special-education staff about new students in the school. Support or resource staff can help the special-education teacher by, say, preparing a

[1]Teacher comments in this section are taken directly from researcher field notes or interview transcripts.

videotape illustrating the sorts of tasks the special program emphasizes. In one school, a staff person from a regional support team made just such a videotape, which included "before and after" video clips of students. One student who did not know how to hold a piece of chalk was later depicted using chalk to write letters. A nonverbal student later demonstrated her use of sign language to communicate. Slides or videotapes of students in their previous school setting shown to regular staff and students before their arrival can ease integration and acceptance.

Questions that are asked can be answered, but too often people fail to ask or report things that bother them. One example involved a new high school student labeled autistic. John had never been in a setting where the men wore ties and coats. He quickly became fascinated and would stop male teachers in the hall to "check out their labels," as his teacher referred to it. John would lift their ties and look under their coats, but to his teacher, the other male teachers seemed to be taking it in stride. It was only by accident, at a party, that this teacher discovered that John's behavior was causing quite a lot of comment among the faculty.

> Jeez, I didn't realize everyone was that concerned about it. I got right on it, and we ended it right way, by having John keep his hands in his pockets. But it upset me. I want people to tell me right away about those things so I can nip them in the bud.

What Should We Be Expected to Do with Them?

One common form of integration occurs through "teacher deals" (Biklen, 1985). A special-education teacher approaches a regular-education teacher suggesting that some particular students would "fit" or "work out" if integrated into the regular class. If the regular-class teacher agrees, integration occurs. The receiving teacher may obtain some informal support or even help from the special-education teacher if time permits and if the special-class teacher can arrange to release a volunteer, student intern, or aide. Usually, however, neither formal nor informal support or assistance is available. The teacher and the student are on their own. When successful, the teacher's efforts are often denigrated as resulting only from some sort of "super-teacher" activism rather than rewarded as creative, collaborative, and innovative. Lack of systematic support usually means that teacher deals risk frequent failure. At best, such deals are often fraught with difficulty and short-lived. Also, dependence on a teacher-deals strategy for implementing integration unfairly excludes most students with disabilities. With little or no assistance, teachers can only attempt to integrate students who require the fewest accommodations and the least support.

A related and equally stubborn problem is the general resentment felt by many regular-class teachers from having special-education students "dumped" into their classes. One shop teacher we met explained:

> Some of the students have just shown up in class and it might be a week or a month—whenever I finally ask—before I would find out that the kid was EMH [educable mentally handicapped] or something. The communication has often been totally at my initiative or just nonexistent.

While regular classroom teachers might logically turn to their special-education colleagues, and sometimes do, there remains an underlying resentment that the special-education teacher should have *offered* support. Yet, too often, special educators themselves need to be integrated first. They, too, have been segregated in separate schools, special units or wings. Their classrooms have been unfairly stigmatized by being located next to the custodian's office, in the basement, or in a remodeled closet. Their own professionalism either trivialized ("You've only got twelve kids? What a deal!") or unfairly characterized ("You must have so much patience!" "You are so giving. I couldn't handle it"), it is not surprising that many insulate their feelings by segregating themselves from other professional contact, choosing to protect themselves with the mantle of their conferred "special" status. Sometimes these teachers' own histories of stigmatization and segregation lead them to oppose integration efforts on the grounds that regular teachers cannot possibly understand, let alone teach, handicapped students. Their own segregation impedes everybody's integration.

This process of stigmatization through association with handicapped students can worry some regular teachers as well. Teachers of subjects often chosen for mainstreaming, such as music, art, gym, home economics, and shop, come to fear that the "brighter" students will not consider taking their subjects. One home economics teacher we encountered explained:

> I feel bad that more and more of the academically inclined kids are staying away from home economics. And sometimes I feel it's because they see the special-ed kids in my classes. I think maybe they say, "Well, I don't belong in that class. It has special-ed kids in it." It's frustrating.

All of these problems (and others) are real. None is simple to solve. Successful, enduring efforts to implement integration require broad, unconditional school district commitment and ongoing, systematic planning and problem solving. Involvement of a wide variety of school and community people is mandatory; teachers cannot integrate alone.

Here are a few specific strategies that administrators and teachers can use to facilitate integration of not only handicapped students but also their programs and their teachers.

- Establish a task force to develop a focused integration plan.
- Conduct in-service programs on the types of services and students involved in the proposed integration effort.
- Arrange visits for regular educators to the segregated programs, and vice versa.
- Locate programs in age-appropriate schools.
- Involve parents of both nonhandicapped and handicapped students in the planning and implementation of integrated programs.
- Arrange for visits, curriculum units, and special orientations for the nonhandicapped students.
- Make sure special-education teachers are on the same schedule and calendar as the regular teachers.
- Invite and encourage attendance of special-education faculty at all regular faculty meetings and social events.
- Locate special-education classrooms among regular classrooms to encourage mixing of both students and their teachers.
- Involve special-education teachers with nonhandicapped students through standard

duty assignments (bus or hall duty) as well as in leadership roles (as coaches, student council or yearbook adviser, chair of faculty committees).
• Anticipate teachers' needs for support, related services, or consultation, and develop a plan to provide them.

Once handicapped students are integrated into regular public schools and teachers have received appropriate preparation and are receiving continuing support, from both colleagues and administrators, the task of actually assisting the development of peer relationships between special and typical students can begin.

• Disperse students with disabilities into groups of nondisabled students within the classroom and school. In other words, avoid congregation of students with disabilities.
• Integrate support services such as speech therapy, remediation in reading or math, and other resource help into the classroom setting rather than sending students out for such services.
• Model appropriate language and social interaction with disabled students.
• Teach about differences as part of the regular curriculum.
• Structure social integration in the classroom through planned activities (e.g., role playing, biographical interviews, group projects, student reviews of one another's work).
• Teach nondisabled students about aids that are useful to disabled students (e.g., communication boards, wheelchairs, sign language, computers).
• Ensure, as much as possible, that students with disabilities follow the same or similar patterns of classroom and schoolwide activity scheduling as nondisabled students.
• Avoid references to, and language about, students with disabilities that might set them apart from the rest of the class (e.g., references to "our CP kids" or use of nicknames for disabled students but not for others).
• Where individualization is necessary for mainstreamed students, attempt to have it occur when other students are receiving individualized instruction.
• Comment positively on social interaction between disabled and nondisabled students.

CONCLUSION

Integrating disabled students into our nation's public schools is a long, frustrating, and difficult challenge. We have tried to establish that the challenge is an honorable one. The effort required is worthwhile. The educational result can be beneficial for all. Our children, disabled or not, require that we seek answers to the problems of integration at least as diligently as we have asked the questions.

FURTHER READING

Biklen, D. (1985). *The Complete School: Integrating Special and Regular Education*. New York: Teacher's College Press. An excellent guide for teachers and administrators. Includes fresh ideas about how to facilitate integration from the perspectives of administrators, parents, and teachers.
Brown, L., Nietupski, J., & Hamre-Nietupski, S. (1976). "Criterion of Ultimate Functioning."

In M. A. Thomas (Ed.), *Hey, Don't Forget about Me!* Reston, VA: Council for Exceptional Children. A key formulation of the instructional implications of normalization and integration. Brown and his colleagues first articulated the need for functional curricula in this article.

Certo, N., Haring, N. G., & York, R. (Eds.). (1984). *Public School Integration of Severely Handicapped Students.* Baltimore: Paul H. Brookes. Focusing on the newest group of students in public schools, this book includes chapters addressing systems change strategies, issues surrounding personnel preparation, curriculum innovations, and strategies for working with nonhandicapped students.

Flynn, R., & Nitsch, K. (Eds.). (1980). *Normalization, Social Integration, and Community Services.* Baltimore: University Park Press. An update on normalization and its implications for services, including chapters by Bank-Mikkelsen, Nirje, & Wolfensberger. In addition, it reports results and interpretations of deinstitutionalization, public school integration, community-based residential alternatives, and community-integrated adult service systems.

Guralnick, M. (Ed.). (1978). *Early Intervention and the Integration of Handicapped and Nonhandicapped Children.* Baltimore: University Park Press. A key formulation of integration for young children. Includes an important chapter by Bricker that provides a rationale for integration in addition to chapters on program design, instruction, and evaluation.

Horner, R. H., Meyer, L. H., & Fredericks, H. D. (Eds.). (1986). *Education of Learners with Severe Handicaps.* Baltimore: Paul H. Brookes. Describes a range of exemplary service strategies that support integration of severely handicapped students. Many of the successful service delivery models, curriculum innovations, and instructional procedures reported here have important implications for other less handicapped students.

REFERENCES

Appolloni, T., & Cooke, T. (1978). Integrated programming at the infant, toddler, and pre-school age levels. In M. Guralnick (Ed.), *Early intervention and the integration of handicapped and nonhandicapped children.* Baltimore: University Park Press.

Apter, S. J. (1982). *Troubled children, troubled systems.* Elmsford, NY: Pergamon Press.

Bank-Mikkelsen, N. (1969). A metropolitan area in Denmark: Copenhagen. In R. Kugel & W. Wolfensberger (Eds.), *Changing patterns in residential services for the mentally retarded.* Washington, DC: President's Commission on Mental Retardation.

Barrett, B. (1979). *Communitization and the measured message of normal behavior.* In R. York & E. Edgar (Eds.), *Teaching the severely handicapped* (Vol. 4). Columbus, OH: Special Press.

Biklen, D. (1981). *The least restrictive environment: Its application to education.* Syracuse, NY: Syracuse University, Special Education Resource Center.

Biklen, D. (1985). *The complete school: Integrating special and regular education.* New York: Teachers College Press.

Birch, J. (1974). *Mainstreaming: Educable mentally retarded children in regular classes.* Reston, VA: Council for Exceptional Children.

Blatt, B. (1979). A drastically different analysis. *Mental Retardation, 17,* 303–305.

Bogdan, R. (1983a). A closer look at mainstreaming. *Educational Forum, 47,* 425–434.

Bogdan, R. (1983b). Does mainstreaming work? is a silly question. *Phi Delta Kappan, 64,* 427–428.

Bricker, D. (1978). A rationale for the integration of handicapped and nonhandicapped preschool children. In M. Guralnick (Ed.), *Early intervention and the integration of handicapped and nonhandicapped children.* Baltimore: University Park Press.

Bricker, W., & Bricker, D. (1970). A program of language training for the severely handi-capped child. *Exceptional Children, 37*, 101–111.

Bricker, W., & Bricker, D. (1974). An early language training strategy. In R. Schiefelbusch & L. Lloyd (Eds.), *Language perspectives: Acquisition, retardation and intervention.* Baltimore: University Park Press.

Brown, L., Branston-McClean, M., Baumgart, D., Vincent, L., Falvey, M., & Schroeder, J. (1979). Using the characteristics of current and subsequent least restrictive environments in the development of content for severely handicapped students. *AAESPH Review, 4*, 407–424.

Brown, L., Nietupski, J. & Hamre-Nietupski, S. (1976). Criterion of ultimate functioning. In M. A. Thomas (Ed.), *Hey, don't forget about me!* Reston, VA: Council for Exceptional Children.

Brown, L., Wilcox, B., Sontag, E., Vincent, B., Dodd, N., & Gruenewald, L. (1977). Toward the realization of the least restrictive educational environments for severely handicapped students. *AAESPH Review, 2*, 195–201.

Carlberg, C., & Kavale, K. (1980). The efficacy of special versus regular class placement for exceptional children: A meta-analysis. *Journal of Special Education, 14*, 295–309.

Center on Human Policy. (1979). The community imperative: A refutation of all arguments in support of institutionalizing anybody because of mental retardation. Syracuse, NY: Author.

Certo, N., Haring, N. G., & York, R. (Eds.). (1984). *Public school integration of severely handicapped students.* Baltimore: Paul H. Brookes.

Cohen, M., Gross, P., & Haring, N. G. (1976). Developmental pinpoints. In N. G. Haring & L. Brown (Eds.), *Teaching the severely handicapped* (Vol. 1). Orlando, FL: Grune & Stratton.

Crowner, T. (1979). Developing and administrating programs for the severely and profoundly handicapped students in public school systems. In R. York & E. Edgar (Eds.), *Teaching the severely handicapped* (Vol. 4). Columbus, OH: Special Press.

Dunn, L. (1968). Special education for the mildly retarded: Is much of it justifiable? *Exceptional Children, 35*, 5–22.

Dybwad, G. (1980). Avoiding misconceptions of mainstreaming, the least restrictive environ-ment, and normalization. *Exceptional Children, 47*, 85–89.

Ferguson, D. L., & Searl, S. (1982). The challenge of integrating students with severe dis-abilities. Syracuse, NY: Syracuse University, Special Education Resource Center.

Fredericks, H., Riggs, C., Furey, T., Grove, D., Moore, W., McDonnell, J., Jordan, E., Hanson, W., Baldwin, V., & Wadlow, M. (1976). *The teaching research curriculum for the moderately and severely impaired.* Springfield, IL: Thomas.

Goldstein, H., & Seigle, D. (1958). *A curriculum guide for teachers of the educable mentally retarded.* Danville, IL: Interstate.

Gordon, J. C. (1885). Hints to parents of young deaf children concerning preliminary home training. *American Annals of the Deaf and Dumb, 30*, 241–250.

Gottlieb, J. (1980). Improving attitudes toward retarded children by using group discussion. *Exceptional Children, 47*, 106–113.

Gould, S. J. (1981). *The mismeasure of man.* New York: Norton.

Gresham, F. (1982). Misguided mainstreaming: The case for social skills training with handi-capped children. *Exceptional Children, 48*, 422–435.

Guralnick, M. (1981). The social behavior of preschool children at different developmental levels: Effects of group compositions. *Journal of Experimental Child Psychology, 31*, 115–130.

Hoffman, E. (1975). The American public school and the deviant child: The origins of their involvement. *Journal of Special Education, 9*, 415–423.

Howe, S. G. (1976). On the causes of idiocy. In M. Rosen, G. R. Clark, & M. S. Kivitz (Eds.),

The history of mental retardation: Collected papers (Vol. 1). Baltimore: University Park Press. (Originally published as *Report of commission to inquire into the conditions of idiots of the Commonwealth of Massachusetts.* Senate Document No. 51, 1848)

Hungerford, R. (1943). *Occupational education.* New York: Association for New York City Teachers of Special Education.

Katz, M. B., Doucet, M. J., & Stern, M. J. (1982). *The social organization of early industrial capitalism.* Cambridge, MA: Harvard University Press.

Kenowitz, L., Zweibel, S., & Edgar, E. (1978). Determining the least restrictive educational opportunity for the severely and profoundly handicapped. In N. G. Haring & D. Bricker (Eds.), *Teaching the severely handicapped* (Vol. 3). Seattle: American Association for the Education of the Severely and Profoundly Handicapped.

Lasch, C. (1977). *Haven in a heartless world: The family besieged.* New York: Basic Books.

Love, H. (1968). *Teaching the educable mentally retarded.* Berkeley, CA: McCutchan.

MacMillan, D., Jones, R., & Meyers, C. (1976). Mainstreaming the mildly retarded: Some questions, cautions, and guidelines. *Mental Retardation, 14*(1), 3–10.

Meisels, S. (1978). First steps in mainstreaming. *Early Childhood, 4,* 1–2.

Miller, J., & Yoder, D. (1972a). On developing the content for a language teaching program. *Mental Retardation, 10*(2), 9–11.

Miller, J., & Yoder, D. (1972b). A syntax teaching program. In J: McLean, D. Yoder, & R. Schiefelbusch (Eds.), *Language intervention with the retarded: Developing strategies.* Baltimore: University Park Press.

Mitchell, D. (1915). *Schools and classes for exceptional children.* Cleveland, OH: Survey Committee of the Cleveland Foundation.

Nirje, B. (1976). The normalization principle. In R. Kugel & A. Shearer (Eds.), *Changing patterns in residential services for the mentally retarded* (rev. ed.). Washington, DC: President's Committee on Mental Retardation.

Nirje, B. (1980). The normalization principle. Appendix: On integration. In R. Flynn & K. Nitsch (Eds.), *Normalization, social integration, and community services.* Baltimore: University Park Press.

Reynolds, M. (1962). A framework for considering some issues in special education. *Exceptional Children, 28,* 367–370.

Rothman, D. J. (1971). *The discovery of the asylum: Social order and disorder in the new republic.* Boston: Little, Brown.

Rynders, J., Johnson, R., Johnson, D., & Schmidt, B. (1980). Producing positive interaction among Down's syndrome and nonhandicapped teenagers through cooperative goal structuring. *American Journal of Mental Deficiency, 85,* 268–273.

Sailor, W., & Guess, D. (1983). *Severely handicapped students: An instructional design.* Boston: Houghton Mifflin.

Sarason, S. B. (1972). *The creation of settings and the future societies.* San Francisco: Jossey-Bass.

Scheerenberger, R. C. (1983). *A history of mental retardation.* Baltimore: Paul H. Brookes.

Stainback, W., & Stainback, S. (1981). A review of research on interactions between severely handicapped and nonhandicapped students. *Journal of the Association for the Severely Handicapped, 6*(3), 23–29.

Stainback, W., & Stainback, S. (1982). The need for research on training nonhandicapped students to interact with severely retarded students. *Education and Training of the Mentally Retarded, 17*(1), 12–16.

Stainback, W., & Stainback, S. (1985). *Integration of severely handicapped students with their nonhandicapped peers.* Reston, VA: Council for Exceptional Children.

Sternberg, L., & Adams, G. (1982). *Educating severely and profoundly handicapped students.* Rockville, MD: Aspen Systems Corp.

Stevens, G. (1961). An analysis of the objectives for the education of children with retarded mental development. In J. Rothstein (Ed.), *Mental Retardation*. New York: Holt, Rinehart and Winston.

Taylor, S. J. (1981). Traditional barriers to educational opportunity: Unserved/underserved children and young people in special education. Syracuse, NY: Syracuse University, Special Education Resource Center.

Taylor, S. J. (1982). From segregation to integration: Strategies for integrating severely handicapped students in normal school and community settings. *Journal of the Association for the Severely Handicapped, 7*(3), 42–49.

Taylor, S. J., & Ferguson, D. L. (1985). A summary of strategies utilized in model programs and resource materials. In W. Stainback & S. Stainback (Eds.), *Integration of severely handicapped students with their nonhandicapped peers*. Reston, VA: Council for Exceptional Children.

Thompson, J., & Arkell, C. (1980). Educating the severely/profoundly handicapped in the public schools: A side-by-side approach. *Exceptional Children, 47*, 114–122.

Vincent, L., Salisbury, C., Walter, G., Brown, P., Gruenewald, L., & Powers, M. (1980). Program evaluation and curriculum development in early childhood/special education: Criteria of the next environment. In W. Sailor, B. Wilcox, & L. Brown (Eds.), *Methods of instruction for severely handicapped students*. Baltimore: Paul H. Brookes.

Voeltz, L. (1982). Effects of structured interactions with severely handicapped peers on children's attitudes. *American Journal of Mental Deficiency, 86*, 380–390.

Wilcox, B., & Bellamy, G. (1982). *Design of high school programs for severely handicapped students*. Baltimore: Paul H. Brookes.

Wolfensberger, W. (1972). *The principles of normalization in human services*. Toronto, Canada: National Institute on Mental Retardation.

Wolfensberger, W. (1980a). The definition of normalization: Update, problems, disagreements, and misunderstandings. In R. Flynn & K. Nitsch (Eds.), *Normalization, social integration, and community services*. Baltimore: University Park Press.

Wolfensberger, W. (1980b). Research, empiricism, and the principle of normalization. In R. Flynn & K. Nitsch (Eds.), *Normalization, social integration, and community services*. Baltimore: University Park Press.

Wolfensberger, W., & Glenn, L. (1975). *Programs analysis of service systems: A method for the quantitative evaluation of human services* (3rd ed.) (Vols. 1 & 2). Toronto, Canada: National Institute on Mental Retardation.

17 GIFTED AND TALENTED

C. June Maker

THE GIFTED CHILD

Definitions

One of the most difficult questions we as educators, and indeed even as a society, must ask is, "What is giftedness?" The abilities or skills valued most highly or perceived as necessary for the survival or advancement of a culture are usually included in giftedness in that society. In a tribe whose survival depends on hunting wild game, for example, giftedness may be perceived as the ability to become an outstanding hunter, and in groups that are continually at war, an excellent warrior would be considered gifted. Individuals within these cultures or groups also perceive the phenomenon of giftedness differently. Thus the development of a universal definition of giftedness seems impossible or at best unlikely.

A related issue is that of describing talent. Some people use the words *gifted* and *talented* interchangeably. To others, they have different meanings. The most common way of distinguishing the two terms is to define *giftedness* as intellectual and academic ability and *talent* as abilities in the arts, leadership, athletics, mechanics, and other areas. Another is to consider giftedness as the highest level of ability in any area and talent as the next highest level. Both ways of distinguishing between the words seem to relegate talent to a less important position. Many individuals who use *gifted* to refer to intellectual or academic ability see it as more important than abilities in the other areas, and those who define *giftedness* as a higher level of ability often see services to the gifted as a greater priority than services to the talented except in athletics, where talent is highly rewarded by status and economic means.

Regardless of the common distinctions made between the terms *gifted* and *talented*, they will be used with the same meaning in this chapter. The concepts of giftedness and talent will be considered in their broadest sense, and many different kinds of abilities will be discussed.

From the early 1900s through the early 1960s, the concept of giftedness was limited to intellectual ability and academic achievement. The major criterion for

420

determining giftedness, by both researchers and practitioners, was either a score on an intelligence test (IQ) or a score on an achievement test. Sometimes these two scores were considered together.

As a result of changes in social climate in the 1960s and research on intelligence testing, perceptions of giftedness began to change. With the civil rights movement came an emphasis on the diversity of cultures and values and on the loss of potential in minority groups and people from poor families. Intelligence tests were attacked as being biased against these populations. Research on intelligence testing and the resulting predictions changed our view of IQ scores (Gallagher, 1966). At the same time, a variety of abilities other than intellectual and academic began to be recognized as valuable.

The most common definition of giftedness in current use is that adopted by the U.S. Office of Education (USOE; Marland, 1971), comprising people with demonstrated or potential ability in intellectual, creative, or specific academic areas, leadership, or the performing and visual arts. These are students who, because of their ability, require services or activities beyond those normally provided by the school. This definition includes many types of talent and defines giftedness in terms of educational need. A second definition that is gaining in popularity, and often incorporated into or used in conjunction with the USOE definition, is that proposed by Renzulli (1978). He suggests a three-ring conception of giftedness that includes above-average ability, creativity, and task commitment. He contends that these three clusters of characteristics interact as they are applied to any performance area and that evidence of them emerges early in life. Simply having these traits is not enough. One must apply them to some useful field of endeavor and is considered gifted only when actively engaged in high-level productive work.

Both these definitions recognize a wide range of abilities as valuable to our society. The major differences are that Renzulli's requires two clusters of abilities (above-average intellectual or academic ability, and creativity), in addition to task commitment or motivation, while the USOE definition suggests that individuals can possess any one type of ability or several abilities in various combinations.

General Characteristics

Students may be gifted in one or more areas. Some characteristics may be possessed by all types of gifted students, while other characteristics are unique to a certain type. Thus there is no such thing as a "typical" gifted child, but here are five examples to illustrate the many and varied traits they may have.

Alana.   Alana is a 5-year-old black child in kindergarten. She was reading at the fourth-grade level after being in school for only six months, so her teacher recommended that she be tested by the school psychologist. On the Stanford-Binet, she scored in the very superior range, with an IQ of 170. The psychologist and her teacher recommended that she be sent to a special school for the gifted or be accelerated to first or second grade. Her mother, who is a waitress at an expensive restaurant, and her father, who owns a very successful cleaning business, see no reason why she should be singled out as different and put into a higher grade. They will not even consider a special school. They "made it" on their own without any special help and believe Alana should do the same.

Alana is interested in many subjects but has become entranced with a neighbor's computer and word processor. She doesn't care about being friends with children of her own age but spends hours with the neighbors, who are in the fourth and fifth grades, and her older brother, who is in the fifth grade. She and her brother and their neighbors enjoy playing computer games and experimenting with the word processor.

In school, Alana gets bored very quickly with the activities of her classmates but enjoys working at her own pace in the individualized language arts program. She was very excited when her teacher suggested that she could go to the computer lab when she finished her work.

Claudia.   A seventh grader, Claudia is a beautiful brown-haired girl who is well liked by everyone. She has many friends with whom she spends a great deal of time listening to music, dancing, and talking. She considers her friends more important than school and is often late with her homework because she is busy with her friends. However, Claudia makes good grades in all her classes and achieves at an average or slightly above-average level in all subjects. She enjoys working on special projects with her friends. After she and several of her friends took a drama class together and enjoyed putting on two plays, they decided to join the drama club and continue with these activities. Claudia spends hours planning plays and drawing sketches of sets to share with her friends. In one of the plays for class, she designed all the costumes, sketched the scenery, and supervised the painting of the backdrops.

School has not always been easy for Claudia, however. From the time she was an infant, Claudia lived with her grandparents, who spoke only Spanish. Her parents were migrant workers and did not want her moved from place to place with them. Because she was a shy, quiet youngster, Claudia's teachers did not realize she was having problems with English, and she fell behind in achievement, especially reading. Claudia's artwork was beautiful, and she loved to please her teachers by drawing or painting for them. As a young child, Claudia had always been interested in drawing, painting, and crafts. She was not encouraged by her parents or grandparents, but her teachers saw this as a strength in such a quiet girl and encouraged her to continue.

In the third grade, things began to change for her. She had learned to speak English well and began to catch up in reading. Her grades improved throughout elementary school, as did her achievement. She continued to make beautiful illustrations for stories and to draw and paint for her friends. When she entered school, Claudia's IQ was 89; when tested again in third grade, her scores had risen to 115 on tests administered to the class as a group.

Freeland.   Freeland is a high school junior who loves athletic activities, clubs, and debate. He plays basketball, is captain of the debate team, and can be counted on to be at all meetings of the clubs. He is running for vice president of the student council this year but is also very interested in his studies. He is in advanced placement classes in math and science and in honors classes in English. Last year Freeland won top honors in the state science fair for his design of a solar energy collector. He is highly motivated and will work on projects alone or with a group.

Freeland has always been a good student and participated in special enrichment programs for gifted students when they were available at his school. Teachers loved to have him in class because he always knew the answers, was well behaved, and was always willing to complete extra assignments. Students respected him and asked him to help with their projects and assignments. They often chose him as group leader.

Freeland's parents, both from a white, middle-class background, are interested in his education and have provided him with many opportunities to pursue his interests. His father, a science professor at a university, would like to see him major in engineering at an Ivy League school in the East, but Freeland is more interested in going to school at the local university where many of his friends are already enrolled. He has participated in the precollege program there and knows his way around campus. Although his mother, a free-lance writer, would also like him to attend a well-known university, she believes that he should be allowed to choose his school and that he needs to spend more time narrowing his interests and deciding on a career before he decides where to go.

When tested by the school psychologist in fifth grade, Freeland scored in the superior range (IQ 132) on an intelligence test and showed achievement 1½ to 2 grade levels above his grade placement in most academic subjects. His achievement continues to be in approximately this range, and his interests are varied.

Jeannie.   Jeannie, a fourth grader, is a difficult child with whom to work. She seems to be bright but hates school. When the teacher asks a question, her answers are completely offbeat. She is always asking questions that annoy the teacher and take the discussion away from the central issue. Her work is sloppy and incomplete and always shows a different perspective. She completes assignments only when they are in an area in which she is interested. She hates arithmetic and refuses to learn her math facts. Her stories, which are interesting and imaginative, are seldom punctuated correctly, and her spelling is atrocious. Jeannie often distracts the other children with her funny anecdotes.

Jeannie's third-grade teacher, who was very concerned about her apparent ability and her poor performance, referred her for testing because she thought Jeannie might have a learning disability. There were no signs of learning problems, but the tests did show that she was capable of achieving at a much higher level than her performance showed (IQ 115). Her parents, however, did not evidence concern because her achievement was average or only slightly below in most areas.

Jeannie is the second child in a large family and spends a great deal of her time taking care of the younger children. Her mother, who takes in ironing, and her father, who paints houses and does other odd jobs, are struggling to make enough money to support the family and have little time to be concerned about her education. However, they want all their children to have the opportunities they did not have as youngsters. Since Jeannie seems to be a happy child at home, they see no cause for concern. Her stories and drawings are amusing to the family.

John.   John is a sixth grader who recently transferred to a boarding school near the Navajo reservation. His parents, who live in a rural area 50 miles from the nearest grocery store, had been concerned about the four hours a day he was spending riding a bus to and from school. They miss his help with the sheep but feel that he needs to make friends and continue his studies. John's father is a sheepherder, and his mother weaves rugs. His younger brothers and sisters still live in the family's one-room hogan and ride a bus to school.

In school, John is very quiet and has few friends. He prefers to work alone and would rather be given a structured task with clear guidelines than a more open-ended one. He seems to study all the time and completes all assignments conscientiously. His teachers are pleased with his dedication but wish he had more friends. Even though he works very hard, John's performance is not outstanding. His achievement is high in math and science, low in reading and language arts, and average in social studies. However, his teacher was surprised at his ability to operate equipment, since he had not seen most of it before, and at his willingness to attempt to repair anything that broke down in class. His teacher requests his help whenever she shows a film or uses any audiovisual equipment in class. She was amazed when John completely took apart the clock that was not working and put it back together. She was even more surprised when it worked!

When John was tested by the school psychologist, his scores on the Wechsler Intelligence Scale for Children—Revised were surprising. His verbal scores were average or slightly below, but his scores on the performance scale were superior, especially on the Block Design subtest.

As these brief vignettes illustrate, there are many differences among gifted students:

1. They come from a variety of cultural, economic, and geographic backgrounds.
2. They have differing degrees and types of motivation. Some wish to do well in school and work to please their teachers, while others do not seem to care about what happens in school or what their teachers think. Most, however, have a high degree of motivation to do things that interest them.
3. Some gifted students prefer to work alone, while others prefer to work with a small group.
4. They prefer varying degrees of structure in assignments or projects, but most seem to prefer less structure than students who are not gifted.
5. Patterns and levels of ability vary. Some gifted students have high abilities in all or most areas, while others have high abilities in only one area, with average to below-average abilities in others.
6. Not all have IQs in the very superior range. In fact, some children with superior talents in the visual or performing arts, mechanical, and leadership areas have average to slightly above-average IQs.
7. Some gifted students have excellent social skills with age-mates, while others prefer older children, and still others prefer to be alone.
8. Not all gifted students are successful in school or recognized as gifted by their teachers. Some are low achievers because their strengths are in areas other than those emphasized in school. Others are bored in school and are quickly "turned off" by it, while some seem to find alternative outlets for expressing and challenging their abilities. Still others lack prerequisite academic or linguistic skills, so their achievement is low until these skills are acquired.
9. Even though family background is an important factor in developing giftedness or in adjusting to it, families of gifted students exhibit very different profiles.

Some commonalities are also present:

1. Most gifted students have well-defined interests and demonstrate a high degree of motivation in their interest areas.

2. Most gifted students show early signs of talent or ability.
3. Gifted students are more advanced than their age-mates in the area of their talent but may be average or even below average in other talent areas or in skills.

ASSESSMENT: PRACTICES AND RESEARCH

Gifted and talented students can be identified through a variety of methods. In fact, the assessment process should include several methods so that children who need services will not be missed. Often the process consists of four stages: referral, screening, identification, and diagnosis of needs. Different methods and instruments are appropriate at each stage.

Referral

At the referral stage, various individuals are asked to nominate or refer students they believe are gifted and in need of special provisions or services. Sources for referral are parents, teachers, peers, members of the community (e.g., Boy and Girl Scout troop leaders, Sunday school teachers, music teachers), administrators, and themselves. Adult referral sources are more useful and more accurate if they are provided with (1) information about the characteristics of gifted students being sought out and (2) checklists or forms to use in describing the characteristics of each student being nominated. In self-referral, students should complete an application form and attach products that are examples of their talent. When asking other students to assist in the referral process, questions should be specific and include information that children can readily observe (e.g., "Who in your class always has unusual ideas?" "Who in your class is usually the first to think of new things to do or new games to play?").

Screening

Screening can be used as a supplement to referral as a means of getting names of more children who will be tested or observed closely to determine whether they need special services. If used in this way, scores from existing tests, such as standardized group tests of achievement, are examined to determine which children showing high potential have not yet been recognized. Additional tests or procedures can be administered or used in a search for other types of talent.

Screening can also be used to reduce the number of students who will be tested or observed more closely. Additional information is gathered on children who are referred, additional tests may be given to them as a group, and those who reach a certain level are then referred for further testing or observation. Those who do not reach the desired level are not considered in need of special services. If screening is used to reduce the number of students who will be tested or observed more closely, however, one must realize that some students will be missed because they are not recognized by their teachers, parents, or someone in the community and are not willing to nominate themselves. Jeannie and Claudia are examples of students who could easily be missed. Such unrecognized students are often the ones in greatest need of services.

Another problem is determining the cutoff point on a measure or test score above which students will be referred for further study and below which they will not be considered for a special program. Often these cutoff scores are too high, and students who do not achieve the criterion are not retested. Cutoff scores should be low enough to assure that very few children who are gifted would be missed. Even though there is no research indicating exactly what scores or criteria are most appropriate, it is clear that certain cutoff scores would be too high. For example, when using a group-administered IQ test as a screening measure, a cutoff score of 125 would be too high. Achieving a score this high on tests designed to be most accurate in measuring abilities near the average range (thus including very few items designed to measure abilities in the very superior range) is difficult. Missing one or two items can cause a 5- to 10-point IQ difference on some tests. To compound the problem, since the administration of an IQ test in a group setting does not allow interaction between examiner and examinees, many gifted students who think divergently or at a more sophisticated level than the thinking required by the test will miss seemingly simple items. Alana is an example of a highly gifted child who could be missed if a cutoff score is too high. Pegnato and Birch's (1959) classic study demonstrated that many students whose scores on individually administered intelligence tests are 160 or above would be missed if established cutoff scores on group-administered IQ tests were higher than 115. If children have not learned test-taking skills or if their language skills are low, they may perform poorly on these group-administered tests because the examiner has no way of knowing why an item was missed, whether the students understood the directions for completing an item or section. Claudia is another child who would probably not be considered for a gifted program because of her low English skills. Jeannie, a creative child, might view items in an unusual way, thus missing more than other children of similar ability. John's low language skills, coupled with the fact that very few group-administered tests of intelligence measure nonverbal skills, would probably prevent him from scoring at a high level.

Children who do not achieve a cutoff score or criterion on a certain measure should be retested at a later date and observed for possible indications of giftedness demonstrated in other ways. Some children, like Claudia, may acquire language skills that enable them to achieve at a higher level. Others, like Jeannie and John, may show giftedness or talent in areas other than intellectual ability.

Regardless of how they are used, screening procedures need to be inexpensive and applicable to large groups of children. They also need to be appropriate to the talent area of concern. One of the most common mistakes made in programs for the gifted is to use IQ or achievement scores as screening procedures regardless of the type of talent that is of interest. Since Claudia's strongest abilities, for instance, are in the visual and performing arts, she should not be expected to achieve a high score on an IQ test to be considered gifted in the visual arts and placed in a special program for students with similar talents. If, however, she is being considered for placement in a program for the intellectually gifted, she should be expected to score well on an IQ test. John (because of his mechanical ability) and Jeannie (because of her creativity) are other examples of students whose most outstanding abilities are in areas not appropriately measured by an intelligence test. Although Freeland is intellectually gifted, he also possesses outstanding leadership ability. His leadership ability is not indicated by his performance on an intelligence test but through his participation on the debate team and student council.

Here is a listing of possible screening procedures and instruments appropriate for the different types of giftedness in the USOE definition.

1. General Intellectual Ability
   a. Group-administered tests of intelligence such as the Developing Cognitive Abilities Test (DCAT) and the Otis-Lennon School Abilities Test (OLSAT)
   b. Group-administered nonverbal tests of intelligence such as Raven Progressive Matrices
   c. Group-administered tests of critical and higher-level thinking such as the Ross Test of Higher Cognitive Processes and the Watson-Glaser Test of Critical Thinking
2. Specific Academic Aptitude
   a. Group-administered tests of general achievement such as the Iowa Tests of Basic Skills and the Scholastic Aptitude Tests
   b. Group-administered tests of specific achievement
   c. Cumulative records of achievement and performance in various school subjects
   d. Teacher-designed inventories
   e. Criterion-referenced tests
3. Creative and Productive Thinking
   a. Group-administered tests of creative and productive thinking such as the Remote Associates Test (RAT) and the Group Inventory for Finding Creative Talent (GIFT)
   b. Group activities such as brainstorming
   c. Examination of students' creative products such as essays, stories, and poems
4. Leadership Ability
   a. Observation of students elected to leadership positions in school clubs or student government
   b. Structured simulation games or activities in which students must assume leadership roles
5. Visual and Performing Arts Ability
   a. Examination of students' original products such as drawings, paintings, and constructions
   b. Observation of students in dance classes, skits, role-playing situations, plays, band, orchestra, or choir

Identification

Identification is usually considered a second level of assessment. Students who are being considered for special services are administered additional tests, are observed further, or are interviewed to determine level or type of ability. Methods or instruments used at this stage can be more expensive or time-consuming because they will be used with a smaller number of students than the screening procedures. Here is a list of useful identification methods and instruments.

1. General Intellectual Ability
   a. Individually administered tests of intelligence such as the Stanford-Binet Test of Intelligence, the Wechsler scales, and the cognitive abilities portion of the Woodcock-Johnson Psychoeducational Battery
   b. Individually administered nonverbal tests of intelligence such as the Leiter International Performance Test
   c. Instruments listed as screening measures, if they have not already been administered (e.g., group tests of intelligence and critical thinking)

      d. Interviews with students and/or parents
2. Specific Academic Aptitude
      a. Individually administered tests of general achievement such as the Peabody Individual Achievement Test and the achievement portion of the Woodcock-Johnson Psychoeducational Battery
      b. Individually administered tests of achievement in a specific area such as Key Math
      c. Instruments and methods listed as screening measures, if they have not already been administered (e.g., group tests of achievement and cumulative records of achievement or performance in various school subjects)
      d. Interviews with students and/or parents
3. Creative and Productive Thinking
      a. Group and/or individually administered tests of creativity such as the Torrance Tests of Creative Thinking—Figural Form (TTCT–F) and Verbal Form (TTCT–V)
      b. Examination of several of each student's creative products such as stories, essays, and poems
      c. Interviews with students and/or parents
4. Leadership Ability
      a. Detailed observation of students in open-ended or structured situations such as student government activities, group projects, debate teams, playing on the playground at recess
      b. Interviews with other students regarding their perceptions of the leadership characteristics of each student being considered
      c. Interviews with the students and/or parents
5. Visual and Performing Arts Ability
      a. Auditions for musical and dramatic abilities, with professional musicians and actors as observers or judges
      b. Examination by professional artists of products such as drawings, paintings, and constructions
      c. Interviews with students, parents, and/or professionals outside the school who have worked with the student in the talent area

All assessment information compiled should be examined by a team of professionals familiar with the child to determine degree and area of giftedness, need for special services, and availability of appropriate services. The team must keep in mind the differences and commonalities in characteristics of gifted students and should carefully match each student's talent area with the most appropriate program. If the team finds that it needs additional information, it may defer until further diagnostic information can be collected. It may also decide that the student should be placed in a particular program on a trial basis while additional observations are being made or tests are being given.

Diagnosis

The purpose of diagnosis is to determine a child's specific strengths, weaknesses, interests, and preferences so that the most effective educational program can be provided or designed. The exact instruments or procedures to be used at this stage are determined by (1) the area of the child's giftedness, (2) areas of concern identified during the assessment process, (3) the goals of the program, and (4) any special requirements of the program.

The child's area of giftedness would suggest different diagnostic needs. For those with general intellectual ability, the teacher may need to know more about the patterns of ability or critical thinking skills. With regard to the visual and performing arts, further information may be needed on technique, ability to read music, or knowledge of various instruments.

Areas of concern may be indicated by results of testing and observation during the other stages of assessment. For example, a student's achievement on a standardized test may be very high, but an examination of grades shows either an inconsistent pattern (some high and some low) or a consistent pattern of low grades. Such a student may be bored in school, may have difficulties getting along with teachers, or may have a learning problem that is interfering with performance. Further testing, observation, or discussions with those who have worked with the student may be necessary to help develop a program.

Assessment in areas indicated by the special program's goals is necessary so that teachers can individualize. If the program is designed to develop critical thinking, for instance, the student's critical-thinking skills would need to be evaluated. If students are encouraged to pursue their own interests, an assessment of their interest areas would be helpful in the planning process.

The program itself may have certain requirements. For example, many programs for the gifted emphasize independent studies or self-direction. Even though in many of these programs such skills are developed as a part of the curriculum, in some programs many of these skills are prerequisites to successful performance. Students who enroll in independent studies with a teacher or are placed with a mentor are often expected to possess skills in working independently.

Research on Procedures and Instruments

Research on effective procedures and instruments for determining giftedness has been concentrated in six areas: the use of IQ scores for predicting success in school, the usefulness of IQ scores as indicators of overall intellectual ability, the use of achievement test scores to predict success in school or in occupations, the assessment of creativity, the relationship of intelligence to creativity, and the usefulness of other methods, including teacher judgment, in the identification of the gifted.

Generally, studies designed to validate the use of IQ scores to predict success in school or at work have shown that an intelligence test score is a good predictor of success in white, middle-class individuals (Gallagher, 1966; Wechsler, 1941; Cronbach, 1970; Horn, 1967; Terman & Oden, 1947). Terman and his colleagues, for instance, in their longitudinal studies of individuals who scored above 130 on the Stanford-Binet, found that these individuals received more honors in school, produced more scientific papers, were engaged in more high-level management positions, and produced more inventions, books, or other creative works than would be expected. Such research suggests that an IQ test would be a good tool for identification of giftedness in a white, middle-class group if giftedness is viewed as the potential to be productive in ways similar to those of Terman's group.

Earlier investigators seemed to assume that intelligence was stable and that it was largely a product of heredity. Later research indicated that these earlier conceptions were inaccurate. Scores on intelligence tests could be modified by a number of factors, especially by the provision of a stimulating environment (Gallagher, 1966). The fact that intelligence scores are modifiable suggests that when using them as an indicator of giftedness, one needs to reassess students who do not score high enough to be considered gifted since their scores may rise after enrichment experiences are provided or important skills are learned. Such reassessment is particularly important for students from disadvantaged homes or whose primary language before entering school is not English.

Though criticized by objectors to his methods, the research of J. P. Guilford (1959, 1967) has had a significant impact on the way educators of the gifted view intelligence. Guilford constructed a model of intelligence that predicted 120 separate abilities and conducted extensive research to identify these abilities. Through this research, Guilford called attention to the fact that most of the widely accepted measures of intelligence assessed no more than half of the identified or predicted abilities. This research emphasized the fact that a single IQ score could not be an accurate index of an individual's intelligence because there are, in fact, a number of "intelligences." Guilford defined *intellect* as a "system of thinking and memory factors, functions and processes" (1967, p. 290). The practical implication of this research is that IQ tests should not be the only measure of intellectual ability used in the identification process.

There are other problems beyond narrowness of focus and changes in scores associated with the use of IQ tests to identify intellectually and academically gifted students. Generally, IQ tests are criticized for focusing on "lower" mental processes such as knowledge, comprehension, and application and neglecting higher-level processes such as evaluation, analysis, and synthesis (Renzulli, Smith, White, Callahan, & Hartman, 1976). IQ scores usually have a low correlation, for example, with tests of critical thinking (Ross & Ross, 1976; Callahan & Corvo, 1980), yet critical-thinking skills are very similar to abilities described in theories of intelligence. Currently used tests of intelligence are also criticized because of their limitations for use with minorities and bilingual students (Martinson, 1975; Mercer & Lewis, 1978; Torrance, 1973, 1977b). IQ tests, especially those administered in a group, are also criticized because of the small number of items that discriminate at the highest levels of intelligence, thus creating a "ceiling effect" for identifying the gifted (Gallagher, 1985; Martinson, 1975; Silverman, in press). Sternberg (1982) criticizes their use (or overuse) as a single instrument for identification because their validity is questionable for some people, some purposes, and some instances.

Other researchers have examined achievement tests and found that there is little relationship between scores at the upper ranges and professional achievement at high levels (Hoyt, 1965; Mednick, 1963; Richards, 1967; Wallach, 1976; Wallach & Wing, 1969). The tests do have a high degree of success, however, in predicting academic performance and performance on similar tests.

A phenomenon of great interest to educators and researchers is creativity. Since achievement tests and IQ tests did not seem to predict originality or ability to develop novel solutions to problems and achievement tests did not predict productivity in careers, there was a need for a different kind of assessment. Torrance (1966, 1974, 1981) and others (Getzels & Jackson, 1962; Wallach & Kogan, 1965) developed tests designed to measure divergent thinking, originality, and other traits that could be clustered together and called "creativity." Although these tests have suffered from a great deal of criticism, they do seem to be better predictors of creative achievement in writing, science, medicine, and leadership than are IQ or achievement test scores (Torrance, 1969, 1972).

Another question of interest in this context is the relationship of creativity to intelligence. Even though Guilford, whose work stimulated much of the research on creativity, included the abilities usually so labeled as part of intelligence rather than separate from it, much research has focused on the differences between creativity and intelligence (Cattell, 1971; Getzels & Jackson, 1962; Harvey, 1981; Torrance, 1972; Wallach & Kogan, 1965). Researchers and practitioners both were quick to point out that currently used tests of intelligence measured very few of the abilities labeled "creativity" and that high performance on one type of test did not necessarily correlate with high performance on the other. Based on a synthesis of research, several writers have concluded that students who score high on tests of creativity usually score at least 120 on an IQ test (Gallagher, 1966; Torrance, 1977a), implying that a certain level of general intellectual ability is necessary for high creativity. Others see certain components of creativity as related to components of intelligence but other aspects as unrelated (Harvey, 1981; Horn, 1976). Writers have also concluded on the basis of reviews of research that there are personality and cognitive style differences between those who score higher on IQ tests and lower on creativity tests and those who have lower IQ scores but higher creativity scores (Cattell, 1971; Dellas & Gaier, 1970; Gallagher, 1966; Torrance, 1977a, 1981). A further interesting conclusion made by those who have reviewed the research is that the two groups just described (high IQ–low creativity, low IQ–high creativity) perform similarly on achievement tests and that those who are high on both creativity and IQ tend to be the most successful in school (Gallagher, 1966, 1985; Renzulli, 1978; Wallach & Kogan, 1965). This latter conclusion suggests that the abilities measured by tests of creativity or divergent thinking and the abilities measured by IQ tests should both be included in any model or theory of intelligence. A similar conclusion was reached by Guilford (1959, 1967), Sternberg (1982), Torrance (1966), and Cattell (1971) but was explained differently by each.

Methods for identifying giftedness other than IQ tests have also been studied. Varying degrees of success have been found using peer nomination (Torrance, 1972, 1977a; Friedman, Friedman, & Van Dyke, 1984; Maker, Morris, & James, 1981), parent nomination (Ciha, Harris, Hoffman, & Potter, 1974; Cornish, 1968; Jacobs, 1971), and teacher nomination (Borland, 1978; Gallagher, 1966; Gear, 1975a, 1975b; Renzulli et al., 1976). Most writers conclude, however, that identification of gifted students is greatly improved if the people doing the nominating are provided with structured rating scales or forms that require them to make judgments about specific traits rather than to make global decisions about whether or not a person is gifted and are given in-service training in the traits indicative of giftedness (Borland, 1978; Renzulli et al., 1976; Gear, 1975b; Maker et al., 1981). Maker and colleagues also suggest that nomination by teachers, peers, and parents is necessary because children who might otherwise be overlooked will be included. A major flaw in most of the studies assessing the usefulness of other methods is that a score on an individually administered IQ test is used as the final confirmation of giftedness. Low correlations between nomination by teachers or peers and IQ score could lead to several conclusions: that teachers and peers are not good identifiers of giftedness, that IQ tests are not good identifiers of giftedness, or that both are equally good identifiers but focus on different traits. The only way to decide which conclusion is most appropriate is to conduct longitudinal research on students identified by various methods and determine which method is the best predictor of giftedness in adults. Such research has not been attempted.

PROGRAM TYPES

Once students have been identified as gifted and in need of special services, a variety of programs can be designed to meet their needs. Models for delivery of services include special grouping arrangements such as ability grouping within the regular classroom in each subject area, consulting teachers who work with a small group of high-ability students in the regular classroom, resource teachers who work with gifted students from different classrooms (a "pull-out" program), special classes for gifted students, special seminars, and special schools for gifted students. Provisions for the gifted can also include various ways of allowing them to progress more rapidly through school, including continuous-progress curricula; grade skipping; compacting or telescoping (teaching the same content in a shorter time); early entrance into kindergarten, junior high, high school, or college; and advanced placement courses offering college credit. Other models provide needed services through counseling, work with a mentor in an area of talent or interest, internship programs, and provisions for independent study in an area of interest.

Research on Program Types

Educators often discuss program provisions and separate them into distinct groups—enrichment, acceleration, and special classes. Research has been designed to compare these major program types, and much debate has surrounded the question of which is best. Generally, studies showed enrichment programs to have positive effects (Clendening & Davies, 1980; Daurio, 1979; Gallagher, Greenman, Karnes, & King, 1960; Passow, Goldberg, & Link, 1961). However, in most cases, the success of the program varied depending on the interest and motivation of classroom teachers.

Evaluations of special classes or ability grouping have yielded mixed results, with some showing that the students in special classes had more positive attitudes and motivation for learning (Sumption, 1941; Hollingworth, 1931a; Drewes, 1963), others showing that students in special classes had a wider variety of interests (Sumption, 1941; Borg, 1964), and yet others showing that students in special groups were superior in achievement or skill development (Schwartz, 1942; Justman, 1954). Still others found no consistent differences favoring those in special classes or those in regular classroom settings (Borg, 1964; Goldberg, Passow, Justman, & Hage, 1965). What can be learned from this research is that changing the grouping of students without altering the curriculum or methods used to teach them cannot be expected to make a significant difference in the students' educational experience. As one researcher concluded, "Ability grouping is by no means a sufficient condition insuring greater academic achievement at any ability level. At best, it provides a framework within which enhanced learning may be more effectively planned and executed" (Goldberg, 1965, p. 41).

It should be noted, however, that the greatest fears of parents and others regarding the social and emotional development of their children in special classes are generally not well founded. In a review of such studies, Byers (1961) and Hollingworth (1931b) concluded that gifted students did not suffer as a result of ability grouping. Others (Passow & Goldberg, 1962; Bell, 1958; Grupe, 1961) also found that gifted students do not become "snobbish" or develop an "inflated ego" as a result of participating in a special program. Generally, their self-estimates tend to go down rather than up, probably because of the continued contact with others of similar or greater ability.

After a review of research prior to 1966, Gallagher (1966) concluded that research on acceleration is generally positive and that "the advantage of saving a year or two from a long investment in educational time does not seem to be diluted by social or emotional difficulties" (p. 100). Generally, if students are selected carefully and acceleration includes attention to gaps in knowledge or assistance in adjustment through counseling, students experience no adverse effects (Daurio, 1979; Stanley, 1976; Terman & Oden, 1947; Van Tassel-Baska, 1981; Whitlock, 1978).

As a result of several decades of research, we still do not have an answer to the question of which program type—acceleration, enrichment, or special classes—is best. In fact, the one conclusion that seems to emerge most clearly from this research is that what makes a difference is not the administrative arrangement or program type but the teacher, the curriculum, and the teaching methods used!

Gallagher, Weiss, Oglesby, and Thomas (1982) identified seven major administrative strategies currently in use in programs for the gifted: enrichment in the classroom, consultant teacher program, resource room/pull-out program, community mentor program, independent study programs, special class, and special school. The most popular among program directors at the state and local levels, parents, teachers, and others are the resource room model in the elementary grades and advanced classes in high school. Consulting teachers and enrichment are popular at the elementary level, and independent study and special schools are used frequently in high schools. Acceleration was not included in this list.

Research on the relative effectiveness of newer approaches such as the use of resource rooms and consulting teachers is notably lacking. In their review of studies of program effectiveness since 1966, Gallagher and his colleagues (1982) found no studies of the effects of many of these approaches. They reported that evaluation data regarding resource rooms were usually subjective and based on the perceived value of the skills learned and that there was no documentation of the effectiveness of the use of enrichment in the regular classroom either with or without the aid of a consulting teacher. Data regarding the use of independent study and the use of community mentors tended to be subjective and to consist of simply reporting that projects were completed. With regard to advanced classes, evaluation results consisted of objective achievement or aptitude test results showing that gifted students can learn advanced material in less time than is usually required. Special schools and classes seem to be able to demonstrate that one can select gifted students and provide a total curriculum for them.

In a review of research on enrichment and acceleration, Daurio (1979) concluded that while enrichment may be worthwhile for all students, no studies show enrichment to be superior to acceleration; there are minimal, short-lived social and emotional adjustment problems in children who have been accelerated; and accelerated students perform at least as well as controls on both academic and nonacademic measures.

The most important concept highlighted by this lack of research on program types is that such research is futile. It is time that educators and researchers in the field of education of the gifted abandon their attempt to determine which type is the most effective. Most likely, earlier results will be predictive of future results: Effectiveness depends on the characteristics and needs of the students, the teacher, the desired outcomes, and the methods and strategies used. Essentially, we need to design sophisticated research that examines a number of variables related to the question of success. Questions such as "What program types are most effective for what types of children under what conditions with what desired outcomes?" are more clear than "What is the most effective program type?" Two examples of such attempts are the little-known classic studies of different programs at the junior high school level. In the first study (Passow et al., 1961), four groups of talented students were matched on IQ, arithmetic performance, teacher ratings, and gender. One group received acceleration in content material, a second group took a curriculum designed to teach the "structure" of the subject, a third group took the regular curriculum with six enrichment units added, and a fourth group took the standard eighth-grade course. Achievement, mathematical competence, and attitudes were measured. Generally, the results showed the accelerated group to be superior to other treatment groups and all treatment groups to be superior to the controls. In a later, more extensive study with a larger population, Goldberg, Passow, Camm, and Neill (cited in Gallagher, 1985) studied two special curriculums and a regular curriculum in both accelerated and normally paced formats. They found that the programs ranked as follows: (1) School Mathematics Study Group (SMSG), accelerated; (2) University of Illinois Committee on School Mathematics (UICSM), normal; (3) UICSM, beginning earlier; (4) SMSG, normal; (5) traditional accelerated; and (6) traditional enriched. The most effective was a curriculum organized around key concepts in mathematics and taught in a more concentrated period of time. The least effective were traditional curriculums taught in an accelerated and enriched manner. This study suggests what the results of such research might reveal and indeed common sense might suggest: The most effective approaches are those combining different content, acceleration, and special grouping! If teaching methods and teacher skills had been examined, even more useful information could have been provided by the studies.

Curriculum and Teaching

Many researchers and practitioners (Gallagher, 1985; Kaplan, 1974; Maker, 1982a, 1982b; Renzulli, 1977; Seagoe, 1975) suggest that the curriculum for the gifted must be "qualitatively different" from the curriculum provided for all children. Educators should focus on providing different kinds of experiences rather than requiring more work. After his longitudinal studies, Terman (Seagoe, 1975) recommended systematic differentiated instruction emphasizing inductive rather than deductive reasoning, self-direction rather than teacher-led instruction, and logic. In addition, he suggested introducing a maximum of new ideas with a minimum of drill and repetition while employing concepts or principles rather than facts. Renzulli (1977) advocates that the gifted be provided with three types of enrichment: general exploratory activities to broaden and develop their interests, group training activities to develop thinking and feeling processes, and individual and small group investigations of real problems to allow in-depth study of topics of interest.

Maker (1982a), in reviewing the literature, suggests that there is general agreement in the field that the curriculum for the gifted needs to be based on the characteristics that make the children different and that it needs to take into account both the present traits and the probable future roles such children will assume. The present and future characteristics of the gifted suggest that the most appropriate curriculum includes different content (what is taught), different processes (how it is taught), an expectation that students will produce different products, and a different physical and psychological environment to facilitate the students' learning.

Based on her review, Maker (1982a) recommends certain general principles in the development of curriculum and teaching strategies for the gifted:

Content
1. Focus on the development of abstract ideas and general principles rather than on the teaching of facts. Facts should be presented as illustrations of a general principle or concept rather than as an end in themselves.
2. Teach complex ideas and concepts, including those that can be illustrated through content in several traditional disciplines.
3. Organize the teaching of information and the provision of experiences around key concepts and general principles.
4. Choose experiences and information carefully, using the criteria of usefulness and the contribution to an understanding of the underlying principles of a discipline as standards for deciding what experiences to provide and what information to teach.
5. Include information and concepts that are not a part of the regular curriculum, and sample systematically from major branches of knowledge.
6. Teach how to use research methods and investigation techniques that are important in the major fields of study.
7. Study the lives, characteristics, and major works of creative, productive, or eminent individuals in the major fields of study.

Process
1. Emphasize use rather than acquisition of information, focusing on the development of abstract reasoning skills.
2. Ask open-ended, provocative questions, and design activities that permit and encourage exploration.
3. Emphasize discovery learning and the development of inductive reasoning.
4. Require students to explain their reasons and support their conclusions.
5. Permit and encourage independent study and self-directed learning, but provide assistance in developing these skills.
6. Provide structured situations in which students can interact with other gifted students and can develop group participation and group leadership skills.
7. Pace the instruction and presentation of new materials rapidly so that students do not become bored.
8. Employ a variety of teaching methods, including discussions, lectures, learning centers, simulation games, field trips, committee work, and projects.

Products
1. Encourage students to develop products that address real problems.
2. Encourage students to direct their products toward real audiences of professionals whenever possible.

3. Require students to develop products that represent a synthesis or transformation of information rather than allowing them to summarize, paraphrase, or copy.
4. Provide for evaluation of products by audiences other than the teacher (especially the audience for whom the product was intended), and teach students skills in evaluating their own products.

Learning Environment
1. The learning environment should be student-centered rather than teacher-centered, focusing on student ideas and interests with an emphasis on discussions in which students interact with one another.
2. Teachers should encourage independence rather than dependence, with students assuming the responsibility for solving their own problems, even those related to classroom management.
3. The environment needs to be open rather than closed, permitting new people, materials, and things to enter and allowing new ideas, exploratory discussions, and the freedom to change directions when needed.
4. Teachers' reactions to student ideas and products must be accepting rather than judging. This does not imply that any standards should be lowered but that the teacher should make certain that ideas are understood before challenging them, should exercise caution in the timing of evaluative comments, and should evaluate ideas or products in a way that emphasizes both positive and negative aspects.
5. The physical and psychological environment must be complex rather than simple, including a variety of materials, references, and books, should include challenging tasks related to complex ideas, and should encourage use of sophisticated methods.
6. The learning environment should also permit high mobility, allowing movement in and out of the classroom, groupings within and outside the classroom, and access to different environments, materials, and equipment.

Even though writers and researchers emphasize the development of a curriculum that includes many modifications of the usual school curriculum, in reality the focus of most programs for the gifted is on processes. Certainly, the process is important and should continue to be emphasized. Positive change, or cognitive growth, occurs through children's *active* interactions with the environment (Blatt, 1969; Rest, 1974; Taba, 1964, 1966). They need opportunities to construct their own reality, organize the information they encounter, and draw their own conclusions. Gifted students need to use advanced levels of reasoning, receive feedback and critiques from the teacher, and then improve their reasoning. The teaching techniques that develop thinking skills and move children from one level or stage of cognitive development to the next are generally those labeled "process" or "how to think" activities. However, educators of the gifted have often placed so much emphasis on process that they have neglected the development of ideas and conclusions in the academic disciplines and the teaching of important concepts necessary as a foundation for further learning and creativity.

The teaching of processes must be combined with the teaching of important ideas and information. Even Parnes (1967; Parnes, Noller, & Biondi, 1966), who is known for his Creative Problem Solving Process, emphasizes the importance of an information base in the development of creative products. He explains that creative behavior is a function of knowledge, imagination, and evaluation and that sophisticated, creative products are seldom, if ever, developed by those who have not achieved a high level of understanding of the area in which they are working.

When dealing with the gifted or when attempting to develop higher levels of thinking, not just "any old content" will do. The content that forms the basis of the teaching process must be as rich and as significant as possible. Taba (1964, 1966) suggests that thinking skills can be taught through any subject matter but that it is impossible to separate content from process. The "richness" and significance of the content with which children work will affect the quality of their thinking, as will the processes used. Taba further suggests that there are certain "thought systems" in each discipline that contain both content and process. The examination of thought systems in the various disciplines would be an important activity both for teachers in the development of teaching strategies and for students as a part of the learning process.

RESEARCH ON CURRICULUM AND TEACHING STRATEGIES

Some of the guidelines presented earlier and advocated by leaders in the field receive their support through anecdotal evidence and experience rather than research. However, certain ideas have been studied in a systematic way.

There is support for the use of conceptually complex curricula (e.g., curricula that focus on complex, abstract concepts rather than factual information) for the gifted. Evaluations of the use of curricula developed in the 1960s after Bruner's (1960) book advocating emphasis on the "structure" of a discipline and key concepts rather than facts suggested that students at different levels of ability respond differently to such curricula. Generally, students with higher levels of ability profit more from the use of conceptually complex curricula than do children of lower ability (Lowman, 1961; Wallace, 1962; Grobman, 1962; Hanley, Whitla, Moo, & Walter, 1970).

Research on questioning strategies shows that teacher questions do make a difference and suggests that emphasis on questions requiring "higher levels of thinking" will develop abstract reasoning skills in students. In a landmark study, Gallagher, Aschner, and Jenne (1967) found that gifted students generally responded by using the level of thinking called for by the teacher. In other words, when teachers asked questions calling for higher levels of thinking, students responded with answers indicating a higher level of thought. Other research (Taba, 1964, 1966; Felker & Dapra, 1975; Watts & Anderson, 1971) has indicated that this phenomenon is true with groups of nongifted students also. Moreover, research on the use of certain creativity training programs has shown that changes in divergent thinking can be manifested as a result of such programs (Mansfield, Busse, & Krepelka, 1978; Feldhusen, Treffinger, & Bahlke, 1970; Callahan & Renzulli, 1974). Others have found that the use of certain teaching-learning models such as the Hilda Taba Strategies in programs for the gifted results in significant increases in critical-thinking skills (Maker, 1982a; Beckwith 1982).

There is support from research indicating that gifted students (1) prefer a less structured learning environment (Dunn & Price, 1980), (2) favor independent study more than their "average" peers (Stewart, 1979), and (3) prefer "achievement via independence" over "achievement via conformity" (Gallagher, 1966). In addition, gifted people prefer "complexity" over "simplicity" (MacKinnon, 1962; Dellas & Gaier, 1970; Terman & Oden, 1947).

Steele, House, Lapin, and Kerins (1970) conducted an extensive evaluation of programs for the gifted in Illinois, comparing average classes, classes for the gifted, and special demonstration classes for the gifted. Demonstration classes were considered the best examples of practices for the gifted and were selected to demonstrate effective teaching. These evaluators found that certain dimensions of classroom climate and emphasis differentiated the three types of classes. First, the teacher talked much less in the demonstration classes (only 10% to 25% of the time in 3% of average classes, 14% of regular gifted classes, and 21% of demonstration classes). Second, independence was permitted to a greater degree in demonstration classes, and students in the demonstration classes perceived that there were enthusiasm, excitement, and involvement in learning. By contrast, independence was encouraged in only a small percentage of average classrooms, and the students in 51% of average classrooms felt a lack of enthusiasm.

Student-centered classrooms have been shown to provide effective climates for achieving educational goals usually found in programs for the gifted (Chickering, 1969). For example, based on a review of research, Chickering concluded that children in student-centered classrooms were superior in motivation, in their ability to apply concepts, and in the use of group social skills. He summarized the research in this way: "The more highly one values outcomes going beyond acquisition of knowledge, the more likely that student-centered methods will be preferred" (p. 1140).

There has been very little research on the characteristics of successful teachers of the gifted except that of comparing the preferences of gifted students with the preferences of other students (Dorhout, 1983; Torrance, 1981) or surveying the opinions of experts (Dorhout, 1983; Frasier & Carland, 1980; Seeley, 1979). Generally, this research results in lists of desirable traits that include "all virtues of mankind" (Abraham, 1958). Maker (1975) summarizes the traits listed as important in teachers of the gifted:

- Intelligence
- Flexibility and creativity
- Self-confidence
- Wide variety of interests
- Sense of humor
- Fairness, firmness, patience
- Sympathy with the problems of gifted and talented children
- Clear understanding of self and role
- Willingness to devote extra time and effort to teaching
- Enthusiasm about teaching and the subject matter
- Willingness to be a facilitator rather than a "director of learning"
- Love of learning and desire to continue learning
- Enjoyment in working with gifted and talented children (adapted from p. 11)

She also summarizes the skills, knowledge, and attitudes believed to be important results of a teacher preparation program for teachers of the gifted:

- Extensive knowledge of the subject being taught and of related fields
- Understanding of human development
- Skill in developing a flexible, individualized curriculum
- Innovative approaches to teaching
- Utilization of teaching strategies that engage children in the higher orders of intellectual activity

- Student-centeredness
- Teaching ability in the regular classroom
- Ability to admit mistakes
- Willingness to be a guide rather than a dictator and to allow students to develop independence (adapted from p. 13)

More research is needed that analyzes teacher traits in an actual classroom interaction situation or attempts to isolate teacher behaviors or traits that have a positive impact on the learning of gifted students. Gallagher, Aschner, and Jenne (1967) found that the types of questions asked by teachers determined the kinds of thought processes used by gifted students. Schiever (1984) investigated the relationships among personality-type preferences and found that these preferences influenced certain observable behaviors: (1) Intuitives engage in more behaviors that stimulate higher-order thinking processes, (2) extroverts and intuitives show more enthusiasm, and (3) teachers who prefer a feeling mode are more sensitive and demonstrate a sense of humor. Length of teaching experience in classrooms for the gifted and in regular classrooms predicted the teachers' commitment to excellence and student-centeredness. The actual effects of such teacher behaviors on the development of gifted students needs to be investigated.

QUESTIONS TEACHERS ASK

Q. *Is it important to make a special attempt to identify gifted and talented students, or will they be easily found if they are "truly gifted"?*

A.   Students like Freeland and Alana will be easily spotted because they are very obviously gifted, and their abilities are in areas traditionally included in definitions of giftedness. They also make high scores on IQ and achievement tests, which are administered frequently in schools. Freeland would be more easily chosen than Alana because he is talented in many different areas and likes to please his teachers. He has high motivation, gets along well with his peers, and is interested in a variety of activities. In other words, his values and interests appear to match those of the school and his teachers. His parents, who are interested in his education, would probably nominate him for a gifted program if his teachers did not. Alana, on the other hand, may be easy to recognize as gifted now because she is still interested in school and has a teacher who is willing to make special provisions for her. However, if her teachers do not continue to provide the stimulation she needs, Alana may become bored in school, refuse to do what her teachers ask, and become an underachiever (Hollingworth, 1931b; Whitmore, 1980). Because she is highly gifted, she is less likely to get along well with her peers and more likely to need special provisions than are children who are not as highly gifted (Gallagher, 1966; Hollingworth, 1942; Terman & Oden, 1947).

Claudia would be identifiable now as an artistically talented student because of her illustrations of stories, her sketches of sets, and her supervision of the painting of sets. However, Claudia is also talented in intellectual areas and would be difficult to identify in these areas for the following reasons. When she first entered school, Claudia was quiet and shy, and since she spoke very little English, she did not participate actively in class. She also scored below average on an IQ test because it was administered in a language different from her own, and her language and conceptual differences were not taken into account in interpreting the scores (Gallagher, 1966; Maker et al., 1981; Torrance, 1977b). Claudia's achievement has not been outstanding at any time and is average or above-average now, even though she is capable of achieving at a much higher level.

Jeannie would also be difficult to identify because she hates school and does everything most teachers find annoying. Her answers are only remotely connected to the questions, she asks difficult questions that distract both the teacher and the other students, and she tells stories that make other children laugh. Jeannie does not pay attention to details and refuses to learn things that teachers perceive as important (math facts, punctuation, spelling). Generally, she does not conform to the expectations of adults and is not motivated to perform well in school, so she would be difficult to identify as a creatively gifted child (Torrance, 1977b; Whitmore, 1980).

John might not be considered gifted by some definitions. His talents lie in the nonverbal areas, especially in mechanics. Even the U.S. Office of Education's definition does not include mechanical ability as an area of giftedness. However, John's ability to operate equipment, to repair objects, and to take apart and put back together objects he has not seen before demonstrates a high degree of giftedness in this area. If his teachers are observant, they will notice this ability, but it would not show up on tests traditionally administered at school.

In deciding whether to make a "special effort" to identify gifted students, one must also consider the cultural, economic, and geographic background of the students. Children who come from advantaged homes have usually had more experiences that will help them be successful in school and help them perform well on tests (Gallagher, 1966; Kamin, 1974; Maker et al., 1981; Passow, 1972; Torrance, 1977b). Children from isolated rural areas may not perform as well in school because they have not had opportunities to learn information required on tests and have spent little time interacting with other children. Those with language differences also have problems with verbal tests.

Q.   *What is the best way to identify gifted students?*
A.   There is no "best way." Different instruments and methods are appropriate for the assessment of different talents, and different instruments work better with children from certain backgrounds. For instance, an IQ test would generally be appropriate for identifying intellectual ability. However, a group-administered test would be likely to miss a highly gifted child like Alana (Pegnato & Birch, 1959; Renzulli et al., 1976) because it contains so few items at the highest levels. For a student like Alana, especially one as young as she, the Stanford-Binet is the preferred instrument. Both group-administered and individually administered tests do not work well with students who lack experiences that are tested by information items or whose primary language is other than English (Bernal, 1974, 1978; Torrance, 1978). Students like Claudia and John would be difficult to identify with traditional IQ measures. Some experts recommend nonverbal tests of intelligence such as the Raven Progressive Matrices and the Leiter International Performance Scale (Maker et al., 1981; Maker, 1983), while others suggest culturally pluralistic assessments (Bernal, 1978; Mercer & Lewis, 1978), Piagetian measures (Bernal, 1974, 1978), and bilingual language proficiency scales (Bernal, 1978).

For identifying creative talent, one needs verbal and nonverbal tests of creativity or divergent thinking (Torrance, 1977a, 1977b, 1981). There is also some evidence that tests of creativity can be used in identifying children who will be high achievers, especially those from disadvantaged backgrounds or minority groups (Gallagher, 1966; Torrance, 1978; Wallach & Kogan, 1965).

Identification of leadership ability usually requires observation along with nomination by peers, and visual arts talent is best recognized by professional artists' examination of student products. Abilities in the performing arts usually are best recognized through auditions and performances judged by professionals in those areas.

There is evidence that teachers can become better identifiers of intellectual, academic, and creative giftedness if they are provided with structured observation tools and training in recognizing giftedness (Borland, 1978; Gear, 1975b; Renzulli et al., 1976). Results of research have also suggested that teachers may be helpful identifiers of children who are gifted but do not perform well on standardized tests (Barkan, 1982; High & Udall, 1983; Maker et al., 1981; Maker, 1983).

When using teacher nomination to select minority and disadvantaged students, however, one must exercise caution. Most of the checklists and rating scales used to guide teacher observation have been developed and validated only on an advantaged Anglo population. There is evidence to suggest that the most widely used rating scales, the Scales for Rating the Behavioral Characteristics of Superior Students (SRBCSS) (Renzulli et al., 1976), contain some subscales that are not appropriate for use with a Mexican-American population (Argulewicz, Elliott, & Hall, 1981; High & Udall, 1983). High and Udall (1983) also found that the ethnic and economic levels of schools influenced the numbers and types of students referred for gifted programs.

The most important conclusion that can be made from this research is that multiple instruments and procedures need to be employed in the identification process (High & Udall, 1983; Maker, 1983; Bernal, 1978; Gallagher, 1966) because no one method will be successful in identifying all students. Use of a case-study approach (Renzulli & Smith, 1977) is most appropriate because it allows flexibility and participation of a group of professionals in decision making and requires that a variety of information be included in the process.

Q. *Is it important to provide a special program to serve gifted students, or will they "make it on their own"?*

A.   One of the arguments heard most often from those who do not want to start programs for the gifted is that the gifted will be successful without any help from educators. Certainly, some students seem to need no intervention program. Children like Freeland seem to be interested in school and thrive on any assignment they are given. Others, like Alana, may become so bored in school that they are no longer challenged and feel that school is a nuisance. Children like Jeannie are often negative influences in a classroom and are not liked by their teachers. The usual school experiences do not meet these children's needs. A significant number of gifted students do not achieve at levels one would expect from their abilities (Whitmore, 1980; Terman & Oden, 1947; Fearn, 1982; Gallagher, 1966), and this underachievement is caused by a variety of factors, including the lack of appropriate programs or teaching strategies (Whitmore, 1980; Zilli, 1971). The most highly gifted students are those who most need special provisions (Hollingworth, 1942; Silverman, in press).

Many parents report that their children are remaining in school only because of the special program, and others report that the special program makes the rest of the day "bearable" for their children.

Support for the need to make special provisions also comes from the literature on giftedness among dropouts, delinquent populations, and suicides (Lajoie & Shore, 1981; Harvey & Seeley, 1984). These are individuals who definitely would not be considered "successful." One would expect to identify 3% to 5% of the normal population as gifted based on the normal curve. Lajoie and Shore (1981) concluded that there is at least the same percentage of gifted individuals among the disassociated groups just named as in the total population. In fact, Harvey and Seeley (1984) found that approximately 18% of the delinquent population they studied was gifted. These people are lost by and to the system because our educational system has apparently failed to provide appropriately for them.

One must also consider what gifted people are capable of achieving and the abilities they possess but are not using. Results of evaluations of programs for the gifted show that students grow significantly in critical-thinking ability (Beckwith, 1982; Maker, 1982a) and creative and productive thinking capabilities (Kolloff & Feldhusen, 1984) and that their social adjustment improves when they are in a special program (Gallagher, 1966). These results indicate that special programs can develop these potential abilities of gifted individuals.

Q. *How can we, as a society, justify making special provisions for a group of students who are already "advantaged"?*

A. Most educators subscribe to the philosophy that in a democracy, the purpose of education is to provide "equal opportunity" for all to achieve at the limits of their capabilities. If some have the ability to achieve at a higher level than others, it follows that they need different experiences—experiences that will provide opportunities needed for them to develop and express their abilities. Equal opportunity does *not* mean that the same educational program should be provided for all.

Many students who are included in and who benefit from programs for the gifted are not "advantaged." Some are handicapped, many are from poor families, and many are from minority groups. The numbers of such students are increasing in our programs as methods of assessment and identification improve and as educators' attitudes become more positive toward these students.

One should also consider the potential societal benefits of encouraging positive contributions from gifted individuals. A person who pursues his or her own interests (e.g., conducting research on a cure for cancer, composing a beautiful piece of music, developing new computer technology) and successfully reaches his or her goals can provide knowledge that could save or prolong lives, art that would enrich lives, and inventions that would make living easier or more comfortable for all. Special programs can provide a setting where gifted students can develop needed skills and gain or maintain their motivation to achieve at a high level. A special program can also decrease the possibility that gifted students will become bored or frustrated and turn their abilities and energies to antisocial acts. The large percentages of gifted students among delinquent populations and prisoners indicate that many gifted people do, in fact, express their talents negatively.

A final argument concerns the positive effects programs for the gifted have on the quality of education of the school as a whole. Many of the teaching methods that are considered essential for the gifted population are good for all children. An emphasis on problem solving, divergent thinking and creativity, interpersonal communication skills, and abstract reasoning skills would be valuable for students who are not gifted as well as those who are. House, Kerins, & Steele (1970), for example, found that many of the methods used in the gifted programs were being incorporated into the regular school curriculum in schools where a gifted program was operating.

Another positive effect of programs for the gifted is to focus attention on abilities rather than disabilities in all students. Focusing on strengths rather than weaknesses can have positive effects on classroom climate, students' self-concepts, and motivation to learn. This approach has the additional benefits of increasing levels of achievement in both strong and weak areas (Carlson, 1974; Torrance, 1977b).

Q. *How can I recognize a gifted or talented student in my classroom?*

A. Although there are many traits that indicate giftedness and many areas in which one can be gifted, in each area certain traits are usually found (e.g., intellectually gifted students usually demonstrate understanding of cause-and-effect relationships, recall information easily, and reason in more sophisticated ways than their age-mates). However, not all characteristics are observable in every student. Some traits are simply not present, and others may be hidden because of lack of experience, handicap, or lack of opportunities to express the ability (Renzulli, 1971). Maker (in press) presents indicators of giftedness that can be observed in the classroom, determined through examination of student products or observed when classroom modifications appropriate for the gifted are introduced (see Table 17.1).

Maker (in press) has identified six questions that teachers should ask in the process of screening and identifying the gifted. The best sources of information for answering each question are listed.

1. Is the student's performance on standardized tests significantly different from that of peers?

> Group-administered tests
>
> Individually administered tests

2. Does the student's performance in the classroom indicate superior abilities or talents?

> Classroom observations
>
> Product assessment
>
> Checklists for rating student

3. Does the child's behavior at home indicate superior abilities or talents?

> Interviews with parents
>
> Observation of child at home
>
> Checklists and rating scales
>
> Assessment of products developed at home

4. Does the student have a history of superior performance?

> Examination of school records

TABLE 17.1 INDICATORS OF GIFTEDNESS

Giftedness Observable in the Classroom

Intellectual (General)	Intellectual (Critical Thinking)	Academic	Creative
Demonstrates understanding of cause-and-effect relationships	Shows ability to judge the following:	Possesses a large store of information	Generates many ideas, solutions to problems, and answers to questions
Has rapid mastery and easy recall of information	whether a statement follows from the premises	Has advanced vocabulary and uses terms in a meaningful way within the subject area	Shows curiosity about many things and asks many questions
Has rapid insight into underlying principles and ability to make valid generalizations quickly in many areas	whether something is an assumption	Understands abstract concepts or key ideas important to the structure of the subject area	Demonstrates concern with changing, improving, and modifying objects, systems, and institutions
Reasons in more sophisticated ways than age-mates, including the use of logic and common sense	whether an observation is reliable	Makes valid generalizations about information and ideas in the subject area	Prefers complexity to simplicity
	whether a simple generalization is warranted	Understands and effectively uses the problem-solving methods or inquiry techniques characteristic of the field of study	Possesses cognitive flexibility, the ability to use perceptions and processes typical of several developmental levels in the development of products or ideas
	whether a theory is warranted	Recognizes and uses major sources of information in the subject area	Possesses a great degree of perceptual openness or an awareness of openness to both the outer world and the inner self
	whether an argument depends on an ambiguity	Possesses advanced skills in the use of reference tools related to the subject area	Is uninhibited in expressions of opinion and nonconforming; does not fear being different
	whether a statement is overvague or overspecific		Shows ambivalence toward traditional sex roles, interests, and characteristics
	whether an alleged authority is reliable		

Giftedness in Student Products

Intellectual and Academic

Demonstrates an application of basic information and methodology appropriate to the problem or question being investigated

Extends or transforms raw data, the student's existing knowledge, and/or the general principles in the applicable area of study

Demonstrates the use of critical and higher-level thinking skills

Designs for effective communication to an appropriate audience

Acknowledges information sources in a suitable way

Demonstrates consideration of varying points of view, conflicting data, and primary sources and reflects a reasonably thorough search of relevant sources

Demonstrates the use of details or explanations that enhance their meaning or appeal to the audience

Creative

Product shows evidence of the following:

viewing from a different perspective (visual, philosophical, historical, theoretical, logical, emotional)

reinterpreting (adapting objects to new ideas, shifts in meaning, redefining a problem, illustrating ideas, "highlighting")

elaborating (addition of details, adding to richness and color of a visual image, enhancing the product's appeal and uniqueness)

extending (going beyond) the known information (predicting, extrapolating, generalizing)

Observation of Effects Following Classroom Modifications

Intellectual and Academic

Include more teacher questions or activities that require critical thinking or higher levels of thinking. Observe the child's ability to answer, excitement, and interest.

Teach more abstract and sophisticated ideas or concepts. Observe the child's ability to comprehend the ideas, excitement, and interest.

Creative

Include more open-ended teacher questions or activities that require the production of unusual ideas or products. Observe the student's originality, flexibility, and elaboration in these ideas or products.

Include more open-ended teacher questions or activities that require the production of many different ideas or products. Observe the student's fluency (number of different ideas or different products) and flexibility (number of different categories of ideas and products).

Source: Renzulli et al., 1976; Ennis, 1964, pp. 600–610; Dellas & Gaier, 1970; Maker, 1982a.

445

Interviews with past teachers

Interviews with parents

5. Do modifications in the regular classroom provide enough challenges or opportunities for the child to develop his or her superior abilities?

Systematic modifications in the regular classroom program

Observation of the effects of modifications

Interviews with past and present teachers

Interviews with parents

Student interview

6. What are the differences between the child's performance on standardized tests
and his or her behavior in the classroom or at home?

Comparison of expected levels of performance with actual levels of performance

Gifted students often exhibit a high degree of motivation in their areas of
giftedness (Renzulli, 1978; Renzulli et al., 1976). However, since not all students who
are considered gifted by most definitions are highly motivated, some experts believe
that the fact that they do not exhibit these traits should not exclude them from a
special program (Whitmore, 1980). Many gifted students do not seem motivated in
school because the learning activities are not challenging or relevant, and these
children often become motivated when challenging activities are provided in an area
of interest (Whitmore, 1980). If one follows Renzulli's (1978) definition of giftedness,
however, students who do not seem motivated or who do not exhibit "task commitment" in an area of interest or talent would not be considered gifted.

Independence in learning, or the ability to be self-directed, is another characteristic usually found in gifted students (Treffinger, 1975; Renzulli et al., 1976).
However, this is another trait not found in all students who are gifted, and lack of
independence in learning should not exclude a child from a special program. The
development of skills related to self-direction is usually a goal of programs for the
gifted (Maker, in press) and often results from the development of motivation in an
area of interest (Treffinger, 1975).

Teachers who believe that some of their students are gifted but are not certain
can request assistance from a psychologist or specialist in the education of the gifted.
These individuals can give additional advice and can administer tests that will assist in
the identification process.

Q. *What can a teacher do in the regular classroom if there is no special.
program for the gifted?*

A. Several of the provisions and teaching methods described earlier in this
chapter can be implemented in the regular classroom. Individualizing instruction,
grouping students according to their abilities or interests, and providing supplemental
activities can be used to provide for the needs of gifted students. In addition, many
of the methods considered essential for the gifted can be of benefit to all children,
regardless of their ability. Since many of these methods are open-ended, allowing for
the expression of a variety of talents and many levels of ability, they are appropriate

for the encouragement of students who are gifted, above average, average, and possibly those who are slow learners. The teacher should also provide challenging experiences and opportunities in addition to using these open-ended methods.

Q.   *What can be done in the regular classroom to supplement the special program?*

A.   The most important fact to remember is that students are gifted the *entire day*. Even if there is a pull-out program or special classes in some subjects, the students' needs are not being fully met unless regular classroom teachers also modify their teaching techniques. Any of the methods presented in this chapter can be used to supplement the special program if one exists.

To achieve the objective of meeting the needs of gifted students for the entire day and week, one of the most significant things a teacher can do is cooperate with the teacher of the special program. Often the special program and the regular program are totally separate and unrelated. When a special program is established, teachers in the regular classroom often give up all responsibility for taking care of a child's giftedness because they assume that these needs are now being met. Sometimes they even resent the students' leaving the classroom and plan special events at times when gifted students are out of the room. This, of course, creates tension between teachers and competition for the children's attention. It is important to view the special program as an *extension* and *adjunct* to the regular curriculum and to plan coopera-tively for individual students.

The regular classroom teacher and the special classroom teacher should work in concert to enhance instruction for their students. They should visit and observe in each other's classrooms, share successful instructional strategies, communicate regularly about students' progress, and conduct joint parent-teacher conferences. The classroom teacher can support the work of the special teacher by avoiding the introduction of new material during the time gifted students are out of the class. If children always have to "make up" work they missed while in the special program, they will soon dislike the program. The special teacher can support the classroom teacher by planning activities that extend what is being taught in the classroom.

School administrators can facilitate cooperation between the classroom and special program teachers by providing time regularly for the teachers to plan together and discuss their respective programs and by including both teachers in the evaluation and reporting of pupil progress. Administrators can also promote a norm of colle-giality in their schools that encourages all teachers to share ideas, observe, and learn from one another.

Q.   *What is the best program model?*

A.   There is no best program model in the same way that there is no best way to identify gifted children. All types of programs can have positive effects. The administrative model used does not make as much difference as the teachers, the curriculum, and the teaching methods.

It does seem clear from practice, however, that a range of options would be necessary and desirable as a way to provide the best program for children who have a variety of needs. For instance, children like Alana might best be served by acceleration to a higher grade for either the whole day or part of a day. She is advanced in all subjects, prefers older children as friends, and is highly gifted. A special class for highly gifted students would benefit her also. Claudia, on the other hand, has friends her own age, does not achieve at a high level in all subjects, and enjoys nonacademic subjects. A special drama or art class as well as opportunities to work on productions as part of a club would benefit her. She could also be given opportunities to work with a special teacher or a mentor from the community on her artwork.

A student like Freeland needs a variety of programs and services. He needs advanced-level classes because of his high achievement and interest in several areas and needs opportunities for independent study either alone or with a group because of his strong interests, high motivation, and desire to study a topic in depth. He also needs opportunities to express and practice his leadership skills. Some of these needs can be met within the usual academic program, while others can be addressed through extracurricular activities. Jeannie, a creative, nonconforming student, may need an intensive program emphasizing the expression of her writing and artistic talents. She may also be served well in an enrichment program based in the regular classroom with a sensitive teacher.

A program in mechanics or opportunities to work with a mentor in a situation outside the school might meet John's needs. Since his achievement is high in math and science, John should be encouraged in these areas and given opportunities for independent study alone or with a group.

Since schools will have many gifted students with highly individualistic needs, a range of options must be available. There must also be a great deal of flexibility in the system to allow additional alternatives to be developed.

Q. *Many of the methods being advocated for use with the gifted seem to be good for all children. What is different about a gifted program?*

A. The teaching methods used with the gifted to develop abstract reasoning skills, critical-thinking skills, problem-solving abilities, and divergent thinking have been developed for use with all children and are not advocated for use solely with the gifted (Maker, 1982b; Renzulli, 1977). However, two points must be emphasized: (1) Although the skills and the methods used to develop them are good for all children, they are not in general use in classrooms, and such methods are *essential* for the gifted; and (2) the emphasis on such processes needs to be greater in programs for the gifted than in regular classrooms because gifted students tend to acquire basic skills more easily.

There is some evidence that modifications of what is taught, especially the emphasis on more conceptually based and conceptually complex content, may not be good for all students (Gallagher, 1975; Maker, 1982a). When evaluating curricula based on abstract concepts, some researchers have found that these materials were much more effective with intellectually gifted students. In units where fewer abstract concepts were presented, there were smaller gaps between the performance of students in different ability groups (Grobman, 1962; Hanley et al., 1970; Lowman, 1961; Wallace, 1962).

Q. *Should the program or methods be different for special populations of gifted students, such as minorities, the handicapped, or underachievers?*

A. All programs should be different to the extent that the needs of the children are different. Experts do not advocate separating groups of children from "special populations" (Maker, 1983; Torrance, 1977a) except those with common learning problems such as underachievers and the learning-disabled (Dowdall & Colangelo, 1982; Gallagher, 1966; Whitmore, 1980; Udall & Maker, 1983). Whitmore, for example, recommends a special intensive classroom for highly gifted underachievers because of their unique needs. If these "special populations" of children are included in the "regular" program, their possible unique needs must be addressed. For example, children from low-income homes may lack experience with paper-and-pencil tasks, may not have read widely, and may not have the wide variety of experiences (such as travel) that children from advantaged homes may have had. Thus these students would need field trips to broaden their experiences, more practice developing skills already possessed by other children, and more reading materials. Children from homes where English is not spoken or homes where English is a second language may need a bilingual program or extra instruction in English or basic skills so that they can participate effectively in the gifted program. Where there are large groups of students with language differences, students lacking basic skills, or students with learning difficulties, an intensive program can be provided just for these students for one to three years with the goal of accelerating the acquisition of language, basic skills, and skills for overcoming or coping with learning problems. When ready, these students can enter the regular gifted program (Maker et al., 1981; Whitmore, 1980).

CONCLUSION

There are a variety of perspectives on the education of the gifted, and research results are inconclusive on a number of issues but decisive on a few.

There are a number of definitions and conceptions of giftedness. Although there is no consensus on the most acceptable definition, professionals agree that many types of giftedness exist and that these types can be found in a variety of combinations.

Very few characteristics can be found in all gifted students, but commonalities do exist, especially within categories (types) of giftedness. Because of these varied traits, no one method of identification is best for any type of giftedness or any subgroup of the population. However, research and practice clearly indicate that multiple measures should be employed and that identification and assessment procedures should be consistent with the definition of giftedness and with the type of programs or provisions from which alternatives are selected for each student. Decisions regarding placement should be made by consensus of professionals rather than by relying simply on scores or compilations of scores.

There is little consensus regarding which program type is best or the relative benefits of each. However, professionals agree that a variety of provisions is needed to serve the needs of a varied population. The service delivery model used (self-contained class, resource room) does not by itself cause a program to succeed or fail. The teaching methods, content of the classes, and characteristics and skills of the teacher must be appropriately matched to the needs of the learners.

FURTHER READING
General References

Passow, A. H. (Ed.). (1979). *The Gifted and the Talented*. 78th Yearbook of the National Society for the Study of Education. Chicago: University of Chicago Press. Contains many articles written by prominent individuals in the field of education of the gifted. Some provide reviews of research, while others review theory and practice. Topics range from identification and assessment to services for special subgroups of the gifted and methods of program evaluation.

Seagoe, M. V. (1975). *Terman and the Gifted*. Los Altos, CA: William Kaufmann. A review and synthesis of Lewis M. Terman's longitudinal study of 1,000 gifted students through adulthood, written by a woman who worked closely with Terman on later follow-up studies. Summarizes the research in a readable way.

Definitions and Types of Giftedness

Bloom, B. S. (1982). "The Role of Gifts and Markers in the Development of Talent." *Exceptional Children, 48,* 510–522.

Bloom, B. S., & Sosniak, L. A. (1981). "Talent Development vs. Schooling." *Educational Leadership, 39,* 86–94. Research on the factors involved in development of high-level talent. Implications for policies and practices are also presented.

Guilford, J. P. (1975). "Varieties of Creative Giftedness: Their Measurement and Development." *Gifted Child Quarterly, 19,* 107–121. An important article because of the impact of Guilford's model of intelligence on policies and practices. Reviews Guilford's work and its implications for defining giftedness.

Identification

Richert, E. S. (1982). *National Report on Identification: Assessment and Recommendations for Comprehensive Identification of Gifted and Talented Youth*. Sewell, NJ: Educational Improvement Center—South. A panel of experts reviewed and assessed various tests and other methods used to identify giftedness. Lists of tests, address lists, and references are very comprehensive. A useful handbook for anyone developing a program for the gifted.

Treffinger, D. J. (Ed.). (1984). *Gifted Child Quarterly, 28*(4). The entire issue of this journal is devoted to discussions of the identification of gifted students. Different approaches are described.

Curriculum and Teaching

Gallagher, J. J. (1985). *Teaching the Gifted Child* (3rd ed.). Boston: Allyn & Bacon. Although most of this book is devoted to teaching methods, it also covers issues and practices related to program design, identification, and program evaluation. Many teaching ideas and reviews of literature are presented.

Maker, C. J. (1982). *Curriculum Development for the Gifted*. Rockville, MD: Aspen Systems Corp. One of the few books devoted entirely to the design and development of curricula appropriate in programs for gifted students. General principles for differentiating the curriculum are provided, along with a review of practices and research and examples of model programs at various grade levels.

Maker, C. J. (1982). *Teaching-Learning Models in Education of the Gifted*. Rockville, MD: Aspen Systems Corp. Currently, this is the only reference in which teaching-learning models commonly used in programs for the gifted are reviewed and explained. A chapter about each model contains a description, examples of teaching activities to use with the gifted, a review of research on effectiveness, lists of curriculum materials, and lists of references.

Special Populations

Seeley, K. R. (1983). *Journal for the Education of the Gifted, 6*(3). The entire issue of this journal is devoted to discussions and research related to the education of minorities, the handicapped, and females—subgroups often underrepresented or inappropriately served in programs for the gifted.

Whitmore, J. R. (1980). *Giftedness, Conflict, and Underachievement.* Boston: Allyn & Bacon. A very readable book, this reference provides case studies of highly gifted students who were underachievers in school. The special program designed for them is described, and the results obtained with each student (now adolescents or adults) are explained. Research and literature on underachieving children are also reviewed.

REFERENCES

Abraham, W. A. (1958). *Common sense about gifted children.* New York: Harper & Row.

Argulewicz, E. N., Elliot, S., & Hall, R. (1981). *A comparison of ratings for Anglo and Mexican-American gifted children on the Renzulli-Hartman Scales for Rating the Behavioral Characteristics of Superior Students.* Unpublished manuscript, Arizona State University, Tempe.

Barkan, G. H. (1982). *A comparison of ratings on the Scales for Rating Behavioral Characteristics of Superior Students between Mexican-American and Anglo children nominated by their peers.* Unpublished manuscript, University of Arizona, Tucson.

Beckwith, A. H. (1982). Use of the Ross test as an assessment measure in programs for the gifted and a comparison study of the Ross test to individually administered intelligence tests. *Journal for the Education of the Gifted, 5*(2), 127–140.

Bell, M. E. (1958). *A comparative study of mentally gifted children heterogeneously and homogeneously grouped.* Unpublished doctoral dissertation, Indiana University, Bloomington.

Bernal, E. M., Jr. (1974). Gifted Mexican-American children: An ethnoscientific perspective. *California Journal of Educational Research, 25,* 261–273.

Bernal, E. M., Jr. (1978). The identification of gifted Chicano children. In A. Y. Baldwin, G. H. Gear, & L. J. Lucito (Eds.), *Educational planning for the gifted: Overcoming cultural, geographic, and socioeconomic barriers.* Reston, VA: Council for Exceptional Children.

Blatt, M. (1969). *Studies of the effects of classroom discussion upon children's moral development.* Unpublished doctoral dissertation, University of Chicago.

Borg, W. R. (1964). *An evaluation of ability grouping.* U.S. Office of Education Cooperative Research Project No. 577. Logan: Utah State University.

Borland, J. (1978). Teacher identification of the gifted: A new look. *Journal for the Education of the Gifted, 2*(1), 22–32.

Bruner, J. S. (1960). *The process of education.* Cambridge, MA: Harvard University Press.

Byers, L. (1961). Ability grouping: Help or hindrance to social and emotional growth? *School Review, 69,* 449–456.

Callahan, C. M., & Corvo, M. L. (1980). Validating the Ross test for identification and evaluation of critical thinking skills in programs for the gifted. *Journal for the Education of the Gifted, 4*(1), 17–26.

Callahan, C. M., & Renzulli, J. S. (1974). The effectiveness of a creativity training program in the language arts. *Gifted Child Quarterly, 11,* 538–545.

Carlson, N. A. (1974). *Using the creative strengths of a learning-disabled child to increase evaluative effort and academic achievement.* Unpublished doctoral dissertation, Michigan State University, East Lansing.

Cattell, R. B. (1971). *Abilities: Their structure, growth, and action.* Boston: Houghton Mifflin.

Chickering, A. W. (1969). *Education and identity.* San Francisco: Jossey-Bass.

Ciha, T. E., Harris, R., Hoffman, C., & Potter, M. W. (1974). Parents as identifiers of giftedness: Ignored but accurate. *Gifted Child Quarterly, 18,* 191–195.

Clendening, C. P., & Davies, R. A. (1980). *Creating programs for the gifted.* New York: Bowker.

Cornish, R. (1968). Parents', teachers', and pupils' perception of the gifted child's ability. *Gifted Child Quarterly, 10*(2), 34, 14.

Cronbach, L. J. (1970). *Essentials of psychological testing* (3rd ed.). New York: Harper & Row.

Daurio, S. P. (1979). Educational enrichment versus acceleration: A review of the literature. In W. C. George, S. J. Cohn, & J. C. Stanley (Eds.), *Educating the gifted: Acceleration and enrichment*. Baltimore: Johns Hopkins University Press.

Dellas, M., & Gaier, E. L. (1970). Identification of creativity: The individual. *Psychological Bulletin, 73*, 55–73.

Dorhout, A. (1983). Student and teacher perceptions of preferred teacher behaviors among the academically gifted. *Gifted Child Quarterly, 27*, 122–125.

Dowdall, C. B., & Colangelo, N. (1982). Underachieving gifted students. *Gifted Child Quarterly, 26*(4), 179–184.

Drewes, E. (1963). *Student abilities, grouping patterns, and classroom interaction*. U.S. Office of Education Cooperative Research Project No. 608. East Lansing: Michigan State University.

Dunn, R., & Price, G. E. (1980). Identifying the learning style characteristics of gifted children. *Gifted Child Quarterly, 24*, 33–36.

Ennis, R. H. (1964). A definition of critical thinking. *Reading Teacher, 18*, 599–612.

Fearn, L. (1982). Underachievement and rate of acceleration. *Gifted Child Quarterly, 26*, 121–125.

Feldhusen, J. F., Treffinger, D. J., & Bahlke, S. J. (1970). Developing creative thinking. *Journal of Creative Behavior, 4*, 85–90.

Felker, D. P., & Dapra, R. A. (1975). Effects of question type and question placement on problem-solving ability from prose material. *Journal of Educational Psychology, 67*, 380–384.

Frasier, M. M., & Carland, J. (1980). A study to identify key factors that affect the establishment of a positive relationship between teachers of the gifted and regular classroom teachers. *Journal for the Education of the Gifted, 3*(4), 225–227.

Friedman, P. C., Friedman, R., & Van Dyke, M. (1984). Identifying the leadership-gifted: Self, peer, or teacher nominations? *Roeper Review, 7*(2), 91–94.

Gallagher, J. J. (1966). *Research summary on gifted child education*. Springfield, IL: Office of the Superintendent of Public Instruction.

Gallagher, J. J. (1975). *Teaching the gifted child* (3rd ed.). Boston: Allyn & Bacon.

Gallagher, J. J., Aschner, M. J., & Jenne, W. (1967). *Productive thinking in classroom interaction*. Reston, VA: Council for Exceptional Children.

Gallagher, J. J., Greenman, M., Karnes, M., & King, A. (1960). Individual classroom adjustments for gifted children in elementary schools. *Exceptional Children, 26*, 409–422, 432.

Gallagher, J. J., Weiss, P., Oglesby, K., & Thomas, T. (1982). *Report on education of the gifted* (Vol. 1). Unpublished manuscript, University of North Carolina, Chapel Hill.

Gear, G. H. (1975a). *Effects of the training program "Identification of the potentially gifted" on teachers' accuracy in the identification of intellectually gifted children*. Unpublished doctoral dissertation, University of Connecticut, Storrs.

Gear, G. H. (1975b). Teacher judgment in identification of gifted children. *Gifted Child Quarterly, 20*, 478–489.

Getzels, J. W., & Jackson, P. W. (1962). *Creativity and intelligence*. New York: Wiley.

Goldberg, M. (1965). *Research on the talented*. New York: Teachers College Press.

Goldberg, M., Passow, A. H., Justman, J., & Hage, G. (1965). *The effects of ability grouping*. New York: Columbia University Press.

Grobman, H. (1962). Some comments on the evaluation program findings and their implications. *Biological Sciences Curriculum Study Newsletter, 19*, 5–29.

Grupe, A. J. (1961). *Adjustment and acceptance of mentally superior children in regular and special fifth-grade classes in a public school system.* Unpublished doctoral dissertation, University of Illinois, Urbana.

Guilford, J. P. (1959). Three faces of intellect. *American Psychologist, 14,* 469–479.

Guilford, J. P. (1967). *The nature of human intelligence.* New York: McGraw-Hill.

Hanley, J. P., Whitla, D. K., Moo, E. W., & Walter, A. S. (1970). *Man: A course of study: An evaluation.* Cambridge, MA: Education Development Center.

Harvey, S. (1981). A new view of the relationship between creativity and intelligence. *Journal for the Education of the Gifted, 5*(4), 295–307.

Harvey, S., & Seeley, K. R. (1984). An investigation of the relationships among intellectual and creative abilities, extracurricular activities, achievement, and giftedness in a delinquent population. *Gifted Child Quarterly, 28,* 73–79.

High, M. H., & Udall, A. J. (1983). Teacher ratings of students in relation to ethnicity of students and school ethnic balance. *Journal for the Education of the Gifted, 6*(3), 154–166.

Hollingworth, L. S. (1931a). How should gifted children be educated? *Baltimore Bulletin of Education, 2,* 195–197.

Hollingworth, L. S. (1931b). Personality development of special class children. *University of Pennsylvania Bulletin* (18th Annual *Schoolmen's Week Proceedings*), *31,* 442–446.

Hollingworth, L. S. (1942). *Children above 180 IQ.* Yonkers, NY: World Book.

Horn, J. L. (1967). Intelligence: Why it grows, why it declines. *Trans-Action, 5*(1), 23–31.

Horn, J. L. (1976). Human abilities: A review of research and theory in the early 1970's. *Annual Review of Psychology, 27,* 437–485.

House, E. R., Karins, C. T., & Steele, J. M. (1971). *The gifted classroom.* Urbana-Champaign, IL: Center for Instructional Research and Curriculum Evaluation.

Hoyt, D. P. (1965). *The relationship between college grades and adult achievement: A review of the literature* (Research Rep. No. 7). Iowa City, IA: American College Testing Program.

Jacobs, J. (1971). Effectiveness of teacher and parent identification of gifted children as a function of school level. *Psychology in the Schools, 8,* 140–142.

Justman, J. (1954). Academic achievement of intellectually gifted accelerants and non-accelerants in junior high school. *School Review, 62,* 142–150.

Kamin, L. J. (1974). *The science and politics of IQ.* New York: Wiley.

Kaplan, S. N. (1974). *Providing programs for the gifted and talented: A handbook.* Ventura, CA: Office of the Ventura County Superintendent of Schools.

Kolloff, P. B., & Feldhusen, J. F. (1984). The effects of enrichment on self-concept and creative thinking. *Gifted Child Quarterly, 28,* 53–57.

Lajoie, S. P., & Shore, B. M. (1981). Three myths? The overrepresentation of the gifted among dropouts, delinquents, and suicides. *Gifted Child Quarterly, 25,* 138–143.

Lowman, L. M. (1961). An experimental evaluation of two curriculum designs for teaching first-year algebra in a ninth-grade class. *Dissertation Abstracts, 22,* 502. (University Microfilms No. 61-2864)

MacKinnon, D. W. (1962). The nature and nurture of creative talent. *American Psychologist, 17,* 484–495.

Maker, C. J. (1975). *Training teachers for the gifted and talented: A comparison of models.* Reston, VA: Council for Exceptional Children.

Maker, C. J. (1982a). *Curriculum development for the gifted.* Rockville, MD: Aspen Systems Corp.

Maker, C. J. (1982b). *Teaching-learning models in education of the gifted.* Rockville, MD: Aspen Systems Corp.

Maker, C. J. (1983). Quality education for gifted minority students. *Journal for the Education of the Gifted, 6*(3), 140–153.

Maker, C. J. (in press). Assessment of gifted students. In B. Berdine (Ed.), *Educational assessment in special education.* Boston: Little, Brown.

Maker, C. J., Morris, E., & James, J. (1981). The Eugene Field project: A program for potentially gifted young children. In National/State Leadership Training Institute on the Gifted and Talented (Ed.), *Balancing the scale for the disadvantaged gifted*. Los Angeles: National/State Leadership Training Institute on the Gifted and Talented.

Mansfield, R. S., Busse, F. V., & Krepelka, E. J. (1978). The effectiveness of creativity training. *Review of Educational Research, 48,* 517–536.

Marland, S., Jr. (1971). *Education of the gifted and talented*. (Report to the Congress of the United States by the U.S. Commissioner of Education.) Washington, DC: Government Printing Office.

Martinson, R. A. (1975). *The identification of the gifted and talented*. Reston, VA: Council for Exceptional Children.

Mednick, M. T. (1963). Research creativity in psychology graduate students. *Journal of Consulting Psychology, 27,* 265–266.

Mercer, J. R., & Lewis, J. F. (1978). Using the System of Multicultural Pluralistic Assessment (SOMPA) to identify the gifted minority child. In A. Y. Baldwin, G. H. Gear, & L. J. Lucito (Eds.), *Educational planning for the gifted: Overcoming cultural, geographic, and socioeconomic barriers*. Reston, VA: Council for Exceptional Children.

Parnes, S. J. (1967). *Creative potential and the education experience* (Occasional Paper No. 2). Buffalo, NY: Creative Education Foundation.

Parnes, S. J., Noller, R., & Biondi, A. (1966). *Guide to creative action*. New York: Scribner.

Passow, A. H. (1972). The gifted and the disadvantaged. *National Elementary Principal, 51*(5), 24–31.

Passow, A. H., & Goldberg, M. L. (1962). The talented youth project: A progress report, 1962. *Exceptional Children, 28,* 223–231.

Passow, A. H., Goldberg, M. L., & Link, F. (1961). Enriched mathematics for gifted junior high school students. *Education Leadership, 18,* 442–448.

Pegnato, C. C., & Birch, J. W. (1959). Locating gifted children in junior high schools: A comparison of methods. *Exceptional Children, 25,* 300–314.

Renzulli, J. S. (1971). Talent potential in minority group students. *Exceptional Children, 38,* 437–444.

Renzulli, J. S. (1977). *The enrichment triad model: A guide for developing defensible programs for the gifted and talented*. Wethersfield, CT: Creative Learning Press.

Renzulli, J. S. (1978). What makes giftedness? Reexamining a definition. *Phi Delta Kappan, 60,* 180–184.

Renzulli, J. S., & Smith, L. H. (1977). Two approaches to identification of gifted students. *Exceptional Children, 43,* 512–518.

Renzulli, J. S., Smith, L. H., White, A. J., Callahan, C. M., & Hartman, R. K. (1976). *Scales for Rating the Behavioral Characteristics of Superior Students* (SRBCSS). Wethersfield, CT: Creative Learning Press.

Rest, J. (1974). Developmental psychology as a guide to value education: A review of "Kohlbergian" programs. *Review of Educational Research, 44,* 241–257.

Richards, J. M., Jr. (1967). Prediction of student accomplishment in college. *Journal of Educational Psychology, 58,* 343–355.

Ross, J. D., & Ross, C. M. (1976). *Ross test of higher cognitive processes: Administration manual*. San Rafael, CA: Academic Therapy Publications.

Schiever, S. W. (1984). *An investigation of teacher characteristics*. Unpublished manuscript, University of Arizona, Tucson.

Schwartz, W. P. (1942). *The effect of homogeneous classification on the scholastic achievement and personality development of gifted pupils in elementary and junior high schools*. Unpublished doctoral dissertation, New York University.

Seagoe, M. V. (1975). *Terman and the gifted*. Los Altos, CA: William Kaufmann.

Seeley, K. R. (1979). Competencies for teachers of gifted and talented children. *Journal for the Education of the Gifted, 3*(1), 7–13.

Silverman, L. (in press). *Gifted education: Providing for gifted and talented learners*. St. Louis: Mosby.

Stanley, J. C. (1976). The case for extreme educational acceleration of intellectually brilliant youths. *Gifted Child Quarterly, 20*, 66–75.

Steele, J. M., House, E. R., Lapan, S., & Kerins, T. (1970). *Instructional climate in Illinois gifted classes*. Urbana: University of Illinois, Center for Instructional Research and Curriculum Evaluation.

Sternberg, R. J. (1982). Lies we live by: Misapplication of tests in identifying the gifted. *Gifted Child Quarterly, 26*(4), 157–161.

Stewart, E. D. (1979). Learning styles among gifted/talented students: Preferences for instructional techniques. *Dissertation Abstracts International, 40*, 4503A-4504A. (University Microfilms No. 8003762)

Sumption, M. R. (1941). *Three hundred gifted children*. Yonkers, NY: World Book.

Taba, H. (1962). *Thinking in elementary school children* (USOE Cooperative Research Project No. 1574). San Francisco: San Francisco State College. (ERIC Document Reproduction Service No. ED 003 285)

Taba, H. (1966). *Teaching strategies and cognitive functioning in elementary school children* (USOE Cooperative Research Project No. 2404). San Francisco: San Francisco State College.

Terman, L. M., & Oden, M. H. (1947). The gifted child grows up. In *Genetic studies of genius* (Vol. 4). Stanford, CA: Stanford University Press.

Torrance, E. P. (1966). *Torrance tests of creative thinking: Norms. Technical manual*. Princeton, NJ: Personnel Press.

Torrance, E. P. (1969). Prediction of adult creative achievement among high school seniors. *Gifted Child Quarterly, 13*(2), 71–81.

Torrance, E. P. (1972). Career patterns and peak creative achievements of creative high school students twelve years later. *Gifted Child Quarterly, 16*(2), 75–88.

Torrance, E. P. (1973). Assessment of disadvantaged minority group children. *School Psychology Digest, 2*, 3–10.

Torrance, E. P. (1974). *Torrance tests of creative thinking: Norms. Technical manual*. Lexington, MA: Ginn.

Torrance, E. P. (1977a). *Discovery and nurturance of giftedness in the culturally different*. Reston, VA: Council for Exceptional Children.

Torrance, E. P. (1977b, June). *Perspectives on the status of the gifted: Current perspectives*. Paper presented at the 1977 Summer Institute on the Education of the Gifted/Talented, Columbia University, Teachers College, New York.

Torrance, E. P. (1978). Ways of discovering gifted black children. In A. Y. Baldwin, G. H. Gear, & L. J. Lucito (Eds.), *Educational planning for the gifted: Overcoming cultural, geographic, and socioeconomic barriers*. Reston, VA: Council for Exceptional Children.

Torrance, E. P. (1981). Predicting the creativity of elementary school children (1958–80)—and the teacher who "made a difference." *Gifted Child Quarterly, 25*, 55–62.

Treffinger, D. J. (1975). Teaching for self-directed learning: A priority for the gifted and talented. *Gifted Child Quarterly, 19*, 46–59.

Udall, A. J., & Maker, C. J. (1983). A pilot program for elementary age, learning-disabled gifted students. In L. H. Fox, L. Brody, & D. Tobin (Eds.), *Learning-disabled/gifted children: Identification and programming*. Baltimore: University Park Press.

Van Tassel-Baska, J. (1981, December). *The case for acceleration*. Paper presented at the CEC-TAG Topical Conference on the Gifted and Talented, Orlando, FL.

Wallace, W. L. (1962). The BSCS 1961–62 evaluation program: A statistical report. *Biological Sciences Curriculum Study Newsletter, 19*, 22–24.

Wallach, M. A. (1976). Tests tell us little about talent. *American Scientist, 64*, 57–63.

Wallach, M. A., & Kogan, N. (1965). *Modes of thinking in young children: A study of the creativity-intelligence distinction*. New York: Holt, Rinehart and Winston.

Wallach, M. A., & Wing, C. W., Jr. (1969). *The talented students: A validation of the creativity-intelligence distinction.* New York: Holt, Rinehart and Winston.

Watts, G. H., & Anderson, R. C. (1971). Effects of three types of inserted questions on learning from prose. *Journal of Educational Psychology, 62,* 387–394.

Wechsler, D. (1941). *The measurement of adult intelligence* (2nd ed.). Baltimore: Williams & Wilkins.

Whitlock, B. W. (1978). *Don't hold them back.* New York: College Entrance Examination Board.

Whitmore, J. R. (1980). *Giftedness, conflict, and underachievement.* Boston: Allyn & Bacon.

Zilli, M. G. (1971). Reasons why the gifted adolescent underachieves and some of the implications of guidance and counseling to this problem. *Gifted Child Quarterly, 15,* 279–292.

PART FOUR

The School

Richard H. Hersh, Editor

Elementary and secondary school teaching is an isolating occupation. Teachers have few opportunities for conversations with other adults about what is going on in their classrooms. They seldom work together on joint tasks, and the main activities in teachers' work lives take place behind closed doors and away from the possibility of close supervision or assessment by other adults.

Given the nature of the teaching occupation, one would think that classroom effects are the most powerful of school determinants of student learning. In fact, we have recently determined that school-level factors are also extremely important in affecting student learning—both directly (for example, school attendance policies) and indirectly by affecting teachers' attitudes and behaviors. Boyer (1983) noted that teachers who work in a school with an effective principal have definite advantages over teachers whose competence and commitments may be the same but who are in schools with less effective principals. Results of a survey of teachers in Los Angeles indicated that teachers consider school administrators to be the most important help in their being more effective teachers, as well as the greatest hindrance (Ward & Tickunoff, 1984). Further, teachers in schools with the principals considered less effective stated that they wanted to move to the schools with the most effective principals. The stability of the teaching force, however, was very high in schools with more effective principals. Further, the very organization of the school can affect teachers' attitudes and behavior. Ashton, Webb, and Doda (1982) found that teachers' sense of efficacy was higher in an open, team-approach junior high than in a traditional junior high school.

Three of the chapters in this section examine school-level factors in relation to classroom teachers. In Chapter 18, Ken Duckworth and Doug Carnine examine the literature on principal leadership and how effective principals interact with teachers in their schools. Some important lessons can be learned from this literature. In Chapter 19, Michael Cohen looks at the school effectiveness literature in terms of what it would mean for a school to use that literature for improvement. In Chapter 20, Judith Warren Little uses the framework of the school as a workplace to describe the very small number of schools across the country whose organization allows teachers to interact with one another as colleagues. They talk to each other about schooling, experiment with new ideas, and observe each other in the classroom. As she points out, schools with norms of collegiality and experimentation have been shown to be effective. However, engendering these norms is an extremely difficult task, and one that takes an extensive period of time.

The final chapter in this section deals with an aspect of the teacher's role that is often ignored in the literature, in evaluations of teachers, and in training: teachers' relations with parents and the community. The community exerts a strong effect on the school and classrooms through norms that students bring to the classroom and that influence policy decisions at the school district and school board level. The very same school program can be implemented in very different ways, depending on the type of community the school serves (Popkewitz, Tabachnick, & Wehlage, 1982). Parents are also in a position to support the education of their children through structuring homework time, becoming involved in the school, and lobbying for changes in the system. Chapter 21 explores the literature on the ways in which parents can support their children at home, the effects of parental involvement in the schools on student learning, and ways in which schools can increase parental involvement.

This part, then, moves out of the classroom and into the school and the community. The chapters remind us that not all the action in education takes place in the classroom.

Virginia Richardson-Koehler
Senior Editor

REFERENCES

Ashton, P. T., Webb, R. B., & Doda, N. (1982). *A study of teachers' sense of efficacy* (Final Report to the National Institute of Education No. 400-79-0075). Gainesville: University of Florida, College of Education.

Boyer, E. (1983). *High school.* New York: Harper & Row.

Popkewitz, T., Tabachnick, B., & Wehlage, G. (1982). *The myth of educational reform.* Madison: University of Wisconsin Press.

Ward, B., & Tikunoff, W. (1984). *Conditions of schooling in the Los Angeles Unified School District: A survey of the experiences and perceptions of the teachers in the Los Angeles School District.* Report prepared for the United Teachers of Los Angeles. San Francisco: Center for Interactive Research and Development.

18 THE QUALITY OF TEACHER-PRINCIPAL RELATIONSHIPS

Kenneth Duckworth and Douglas Carnine

Willard Waller once described the relationship of teacher and student as one of "institutionalized conflict" (1932). One might describe the relationship of teacher and principal as one of "institutionalized ambivalence." The formal organization of the school suggests a hierarchical relationship in which the principal directs and supervises instruction. This sort of relationship does occur in some countries where the principal is "head teacher." In the United States, however, the reality is that teachers prefer and enjoy considerable autonomy within the classroom and that principals exercise little direct supervision over instruction. Nonetheless, the two actors are interdependent in many ways.

Dan Lortie has published an influential study of elementary school teachers as an occupational group and has recently finished a parallel study of elementary school principals.[1] In *Schoolteacher*, Lortie wrote that teachers'

> acceptance of the principal's authority is coupled with definite ideas on how that authority should be deployed. They agree that it should be mobilized to serve teacher interests; parents should be buffered, troublesome students dealt with, and chore-avoiding colleagues brought to heel. Most respondents seem to favor a light rein on themselves; some, however, prefer the principal who checks them closely and carefully. [Teachers] stand ready, it seems, to award deference and loyalty to principals who make their authority available to teachers; that authority can help them achieve working conditions which favor classroom achievement and its rewards. (1975, p. 200)

---

[1]Because the preponderance of research deals with elementary schools, we will focus on that setting.

However, it should be noted that the portrait Lortie drew of teachers' notions of "working conditions which favor classroom achievement" was a hazy, impressionistic portrait. Lortie's teachers "discuss achievement test performance...as if they are uncertain of the tangibility of measured gains or the rightfulness of their claiming credit of them" (1975, p. 128). The implication is important: Where the "craft" of teaching is hard to define, the exchange of deference and loyalty to the principal in return for facilitation of teaching is problematic.

In his recent study of principals, Lortie (1982) argues that these exchanges are the primary activities of principals, whose "core relationship" is with the teachers in their schools. Rather than enjoying a role that is complementary to classroom instruction, however, the principal occupies a role that is merely "residual" to teaching: The principal does what no one else is assigned to do in the school. This residual role does not overlap neatly with the subordinate, accountable role the principal holds in the school district. Hence principals may experience conflict with teachers over the appropriate extension of the principals' authority and also between the demands placed by the central office and claims of the teachers. This role ambiguity is poignantly expressed in principals' replies to Lortie's question, "What's your most difficult task?" The majority mentioned the evaluation and supervision of teachers.

In arguing the importance of teacher-principal relationships, we are guided by research on effective teaching practices such as the evaluation of Follow Through models conducted by Jane Stallings (1975) and the Beginning Teacher Evaluation Study conducted by Charles Fisher and colleagues (Fisher, Berliner, Filby, Marliave, Cahen, & Dishaw, 1980). Such practices can be subsumed under the general concept of direct instruction as defined by Barak Rosenshine: "academically focused, teacher-directed classrooms using sequenced and structured materials" (1979, p. 38). Of importance here is the fact that teaching behaviors are defined in relationship tc student achievement gains in a way that places both teachers and principals in a situation of accountability. The haze (in Lortie's picture of teachers' notions about conditions for student achievement) is lifted, and the question arises, if the teacher is not teaching in this way, why not? Once teachers and principals begin to ask this question—and know that the *other* is asking the question—the stage is set for the improvements to be discussed in this chapter.

A second set of studies deals with "effective schools." Michael Cohen summarizes this research in Chapter 19, and Judith Warren Little's Chapter 20 elaborates on the special importance of teacher collegiality in effective schools. Our point is that teachers and principals are *interdependent* in making schools effective. If, as the effective schools research suggests, a school is to exhibit a coherent curriculum, high priority for academic goals, positive beliefs about student potential, and an orderly climate to sustain and protect instructional lessons, principals and teachers must cooperate in sustaining them. It is the principal who represents the interests of the school as a whole and who can play an important role in initiating and encouraging this cooperation; the principal can also be an important partner in cooperative enterprises. On the other hand, the prevailing loose linkage between teaching and administrative activities allows teachers to sabotage such a collective orientation simply by asserting their autonomy. Hence the principal cannot do it alone; teachers are architects of the school community as well.

A third set of studies to be drawn on in this chapter deals with principal leadership. To some extent these studies developed in response to findings that principal leadership is a characteristic of "effective schools." A good summary of the findings on principal leadership was provided by Caroline Persell (1982, pp. 6–25), from which we concluded that principals of effective schools

display commitment to academic goals,

create a climate of expectations and respect,

develop their own organizational potency,

are forceful and energetic,

exercise interpersonal skills,

provide instructional leadership,

facilitate instruction, especially through discipline,

devote time to instructional matters, and

observe, monitor, and evaluate classroom teaching.

Research on the leadership of the principal has a longer pedigree than that suggested by the recent studies of effective schools, however. Research on the principal's leadership style achieved considerable prominence in the 1960s with studies by Andrew Halpin (1966) and others on the principal's reputation with teachers of emphasizing teacher task performance (called "initiating structure") and the personal well-being of teachers (called "consideration"). These concepts of task-oriented and person-oriented leadership continue to exercise influence on the imagination of current researchers, generating a search for personal traits and specific managerial behaviors that help principals to gain greater control over the direction and quality of classroom teaching and to motivate and sustain teachers' efforts in the classroom. Both elements are included in Persell's summary.

The personal style of the principal was given central emphasis in a recent study of effective principals by Arthur Blumberg and William Greenfield (1980). They concluded that the principal's personal management style, rather than particular management behavior, determines the impact on teachers. The effective principal was described as holding "a rather individualistic and idiosyncratic ideology toward his/her job" (p. 197). The principals in the study exhibited a personal vision, a propensity to take the initiative in changing states of affairs, an efficient handling of routine tasks to allow focusing of available resources on personal goals (a sense of control), a commitment to quality, and personal persuasiveness.

An elaborate development of the personal-style approach is to be found in the recent study of Florida school principals by Sheila Huff and her colleagues (Huff, Lake, & Schaalman, 1982). Comparing a mixed sample of elementary, middle, and high school principals selected to include both effective and average principals, the study used the "critical incident" method to identify general capacities, dispositions, and propensities of such principals. These researchers found that six "basic" competencies seemed to be common to all principals in the sample (and presumably might be used as a means of screening for the occupation) and that an additional eight "optimal" competencies distinguished effective from average principals (and might serve as selection criteria for particular positions). The total list of 14 competencies was grouped in four clusters (p. 29).

Clusters	Basic Competencies	Optimal Competencies
Purpose and direction	1. Commitment to school mission	2. Sense of control
Cognitive skills		3. Monitoring
		4. Ability to recognize patterns
		5. Perceptual objectivity
		6. Analytical ability
Consensus management	7. Concern for image	10. Persuasiveness
	8. Participatory style	
	9. Tactical adaptability	
Quality enhancement	13. Coaching skills	11. Commitment to quality
	14. Firmness in enforcing quality standards	12. Focused involvement in change

The researchers emphasized the findings that effective principals do not dictate but persuade. In general, the study plays down the importance of elaborate knowledge about instruction and highlights what we might call general practical intelligence. The study's findings are consonant with Blumberg and Greenfield's findings. With its longer and more specific list of competencies, however, there is a danger in the Florida study of constructing a procrustean bed and trying to fit all principals to the same mold, regardless of differences in personal characteristics or situations.

Other researchers have sought to describe the effective principal in terms of management behavior rather than personality. For example, the program of research at the Far West Laboratory conducted by Steven Bossert, David Dwyer, Brian Rowan, and Ginny Lee emphasized the *variety* of management strategies employed by effective principals (Bossert et al., 1982; Dwyer, Lee, Rowan, & Bossert, 1983). Although personal characteristics were described in this research, primary attention was given to management behavior. These researchers emphasized that management strategies should be evaluated in terms of organizational *functions* that have to be fulfilled for schools to be effective. This takes us a step further, because it suggests a common *target* for principals with different personal characteristics or situations. The question becomes what impact a management strategy has on the work of teachers. In an initial set of case studies of effective principals, Dwyer and his colleagues found that some principals use a human relations approach while others use a rationalistic approach, possibly depending on the overall experience level of their teachers. These researchers emphasized the importance of good relations with local parents and community members and the principal's ability to negotiate the political system of the local district. Paperwork and committee work necessary to maintain the school as a public institution were delegated and carefully supervised.

Such research helps us to deflate exaggerated and unrealistic images of instructional leadership by the principal. It suggests that the message of instructional leadership is transmitted by selecting teachers who are compatible with the instructional philosophy of the principal, keeping school a pleasant place to be, communicating to students that their education is a serious matter of high priority to the school, and troubleshooting problems in instruction and student behavior. It reminds us that many *routine* administrative functions are in fact critical for the classroom's integrity as an instructional setting. Dwyer and colleagues classify the routine functions as "monitoring, information control and exchange, planning, direct interaction with students, staff development and hiring, and overseeing building maintenance" (1983, p. 53). Institutional cycles of public education drive some of these administrative functions, such as the management of events surrounding the opening and closing of school, vacations, and required testing days.

The Far West Laboratory research does not provide information about the substance of staff development and curriculum development activities, which may be episodic and periodic and less visible to a research strategy of direct observation of a slice of school life. However, it is likely that such infrequent events provide a substantive base for the routine administrative processes these researchers describe. Daily contact with the principal may serve teachers as a reminder of things previously discussed at greater length.

This, then, is a representative sampling of three burgeoning areas of research—effective teaching, effective schools, and effective principals—that can help us to construct an image of the desired quality of working relationships between principals and teachers.

TEACHER-PRINCIPAL RELATIONSHIPS IN EFFECTIVE SCHOOLS

Our task now is to project an image of the quality of working relationships between teachers and principals in effective schools. Although this image may seem to be idealized, it can help us identify elements in the current state of affairs that need change and orient our efforts to make change. We approach this task by taking in turn the perspectives of a teacher and a principal trying to think through the implications of the research just discussed.

What Does the Teacher Need from the Principal?

The teacher using the classroom instructional practices recommended by the research on effective teaching needs a set of teaching goals, objectives, and strategies that are clarified and confirmed by the principal. The principal should be knowledgeable about good teaching, monitor and provide feedback on the progress of students, and arrange for demonstrations of new strategies as necessary to cope with new problems. Conversely, the principal should not indicate to the teacher that other values generally take precedence over those teaching goals and objectives. Teachers need the backbone of organizational policy to sustain their efforts during initially fumbling attempts with new strategies, to maintain a sense of equity among teachers in terms of effort, and to persuade students and parents who expect to be treated as exceptions that cooperation with a more demanding regime is for the good of all. Although teachers need discretion to adapt the school program to different classes of students, they need consistent standards and expectations from administrators.

In addition, the teacher needs encouragement and reward for persevering in the difficult tasks—in preparing lessons for different students' states of readiness and in teaching actively rather than falling back on the various seatwork strategems that reduce the amount of time the teacher must be onstage. The principal can establish an expectation for good teaching by the way he or she conducts faculty meetings and staff development activities, and these occasions can provide inspiration for the teacher who otherwise might wonder whether anyone cared. The principal's monitoring and feedback are also occasions for giving teachers the recognition they deserve. Such events can also communicate the principal's determination to remedy slack teaching.

Most of all, the teacher needs the principal to protect the activities of teaching and to provide resources without which neither teaching nor learning can proceed effectively. Jane Stallings has suggested several areas in which the principal can make a real contribution: by preventing lesson interruptions, by reducing absenteeism and lateness, and by obtaining the various materials teachers need to work with students at different levels of readiness (1981). The principal can also provide resources in the form of skills development opportunities for teachers and special learning problem services for students—including the general problems of home and peer relationships. Resources include support in dealings with parents who want special treatment and students who disrupt lessons. These considerations are consistent with the clusters of purpose and direction, cognitive skills, and quality enhancement identified in the study of Florida principals.

Whereas the purposes and rewards of good teaching may need direct action by the principal (and hence may depend on personality differences), the resources correspond to the general functioning requirements of the classroom discussed by Bossert and his colleagues. Hence the principal may satisfy these needs indirectly, through subordinates.

Even in the area of leadership, however, the principal can help the teacher indirectly as well as directly. The principal can bring together the teaching faculty in a community that develops norms about instruction. Such norms, like positive expectations for student performance, sustain a teacher through difficult times. How the principal accomplishes this community maintenance task is likely to vary from school to school, depending on the mix of teachers, the mix of problems, and the personal style of the principal. The cluster called consensus management in the Florida study seems useful here. Once established, however, the teacher community can "substitute" for principal leadership in fulfilling many of the teachers' needs.

The principal is in a position to build and sustain that community through the organizing of teacher collaboration and through symbolic gestures that represent the community and its values. Teachers collectively need the principal to project the image of the effective school in public settings.

What Does the Principal Need from the Teacher?

The principal needs to have the goals of student learning continually brought to his or her attention by teachers; moreover, the principal needs teachers to provide the elaboration of such goals that can give a sharp picture of classroom events rather than abstractions. The principal, however, does *not* need mechanical implementation of instructional programs; instead, the principal needs teachers who will take the time to make thoughtful adaptations of programs to varying circumstances and who will keep the purposes rather than the procedures in mind. The principal, even with a highly structured program, needs teachers who will enliven classroom instruction. The principal also needs teachers who do not tie him or her down continually with numerous small problems for which they expect immediate attention.

The principal needs appreciation for attempts to exert leadership in instruction; it is too easy for teachers to discourage a principal by raising problems as barriers to his or her involvement rather than as occasions for adjustments. Principals are rewarded by evidence that they have helped students; teachers are in a position to provide this evidence and in general to give principals opportunities to interact with students on nondisciplinary matters. When a principal must confront a slack teacher, the principal needs other teachers who will judge the case on its merits rather than automatically close ranks. Conversely, when a principal seeks to honor an effective teacher, the principal needs company in the celebration rather than jealousy over imagined slights.

The principal needs information from teachers in order to improve school management. The principal also needs assistance in carrying on development work, such as new curricula or teaching strategies. Finally, the principal needs to be able to delegate some of the routine administrative tasks to teachers in order to free up time and energy for developing thoughtful approaches to instructional problems.

In short, the principal needs a partnership with teachers. This is so because the principal needs cooperation in extending the role from a residual one to a complementary one. Even more important, however, is the life that can be brought to school-level deliberations about instructional problems by teachers who are committed to the school as well as to their particular classroom groups. Without this life, the principal can get bogged down in abstractions and details rather than bringing personal skills to bear on the real concerns of teachers.

WHAT ARE THE BARRIERS TO GOOD TEACHER-PRINCIPAL WORKING RELATIONSHIPS?

The teacher or principal who reads the foregoing may be forgiven for skepticism about the possibility of achieving the quality of working relationships depicted. The real cause for concern is the reader who says, "Why, we're already doing all of that." The reality is that the ideal image of teaching and administration presented is rare, according to descriptive research reviewed by Keith Leithwood and Deborah Montgomery (1982). Such research on the broad range of schools—as opposed to research on exemplary situations—indicates that the status quo presents institutional barriers to the sort of working relationships advocated.

What Are the Institutional Constraints?

Schools as institutions are oriented to a plurality of goals that are stated in generalities and often conflict with one another. The plurality and vagueness of goals have been characterized by James March (1978) as leading to a decoupling of teaching and administration and a sacrifice of excellence in any one endeavor to a satisfactory level of functioning across the variety of endeavors undertaken.

John Meyer (1980) goes further in characterizing the agenda of the institution as incompatible with the working relationships advocated. Meyer points out that schools are supported by society to provide graduated status increments for children as they move from infancy to adulthood. In this view, the orderly progress of grade levels and traditional subjects resembles a yearly parade, and the expectation is not for achievement but for participation and ultimate receipt of the credential of the high school diploma. Given this charge by society, teachers are concerned with observation of the daily, weekly, and grading-period rituals, and administrators are loath to be confronted with evidence that suggests discrepancies between the educational credits awarded to students and the real levels of student achievement and rates of learning. This highly critical view of education should not be dismissed hastily. There is evidence that school reforms attempting to tighten the coupling of administration with teaching and both with learning have run into political opposition as well as internal managerial problems. The prolonged legal challenge to competency-based graduation requirements in Florida is an example. Whether current experiments with merit pay for teachers will fare better is a matter of doubt to many thoughtful observers.

Whether schools are loosely coupled organizations because divergent and vague goals tend to cancel one another out or because schooling is a social ritual in which the maintenance of face is paramount, the result in any event is a distancing of teachers and principals from one another on issues of task performance. Where personalities permit, there may be a general cordiality about working together in the same building with the same children, and this cordiality often passes for what we call collegiality. In collegial as opposed to merely cordial relationships, however, conversation dwells on work as often as on social topics, and the tone is of mutual interest rather than mutual complaint. There are schools, though, where personalities do not mesh so well and where neither cordial nor collegial relationships exist. Teachers and principals work in their separate worlds, and their main link may be the school office secretary.

In addition to the organizational research already mentioned, there has grown up a literature of descriptive studies on the principal's daily work behavior that is in accordance with the view just presented. Among these are studies by Harry Wolcott (1973), Donald Willower and his students (Martin & Willower, 1981; Kmetz & Willower, 1982), and Van Cleve Morris and his colleagues (Morris, Crowson, Hurwitz, & Porter-Gehrie, 1981). Principals seem to devote their time to a myriad of brief and often unscheduled meetings with people who have problems. It is hard for principals to focus efforts continuously or systematically on the instructional program in these conditions. This impression of intuitive and reactive behavior is paralleled in descriptive studies of teacher work. Christopher Clark and Robert Yinger (1979) have described teachers as oriented to activities and materials rather than objectives and strategies and have found them unable to articulate the major decisions they make about instruction. (Clark and Yinger report that teachers exhibit an underlying rationale in practice but apparently have little occasion to verbalize it.)

In addition to traditions of administrative disregard for instruction and teacher orientation to coverage of the material, school personnel work under a common set of imperatives and constraints that derive from legal and institutional regulations that limit their ability to enjoy the kind of working relationships advocated.

Principals, for example, are required to evaluate teachers on a periodic basis. Whereas in a fully articulated system this activity would be predictable and presumably legitimate, given the vagueness of goals and lack of monitoring of instruction described, evaluation becomes a chronic source of tension. As a result, teachers are guarded in what they allow a principal to see and are circumspect in public declarations about goals. Feedback from the principal may be interpreted as a personal attack and may make the teacher defensive. Ironically, merit pay, a policy proposed to improve school effectiveness, could aggravate the tension between principals and teachers around evaluation.

Another major constraint on the agenda of teacher-principal relationships is the increasing inclusion of policy issues in teacher employment agreements negotiated under collective bargaining, which has been documented by the research of Steven Goldschmidt and his colleagues (Goldschmidt, Bowers, Riley, & Stuart, 1983). Where teachers' classroom practices are protected by contract language, principals may come to regard attempts to improve teaching as a mine field and withdraw even further from involvement in instructional matters. In some schools, every question of improving instruction and curriculum may be screened through the language of the contract. Goldschmidt and colleagues found that negotiated policy *is* implemented.

Overcoming Institutional Constraints

The incentives for principals and teachers to transcend the situation just described may be very limited. The rumor mill among school administrators at conventions is often rife with accounts of people who have gone out on a limb and been fired. In contrast, there is a bleak comfort in the belief that there are excellent reasons—stemming from the malice or incompetence of district personnel and school board members, the potential jealousy and hostility of other principals and teachers who may fear the establishment of new benchmarks of practice, and the innate limitations of the students—for adhering to the conventional standoff.

Another disincentive to implementation of the recommendations of the research on effective teaching and effective schools is the teacher's commitment to professional autonomy. Teachers continue to prize freedom to do as they wish "once the classroom door is closed." Normative incentives to join together in creating a school culture that incorporates effective techniques are lacking where even the union can count on teacher loyalty only in showdowns with administration.

A major limitation on the development of teacher-principal working relationships is the scarcity of resources. Researchers like Philip Jackson (1968) point to the incredible volume of classroom interactions in which a teacher engages daily. To some extent, the interactive press is a key finding in research on administrative behavior as well (Morris et al., 1981). The work of simply coping with this volume of interaction drains energy and time that might be used in planning how to master the situation and reduce the burden. The problem is especially keen where students exhibit a wide range of levels of readiness for learning. In general, time is a scarce resource.

The level of teacher and principal skills for engaging in and monitoring direct instruction may likewise be low. There is a widespread suspicion that preservice training has not succeeded in imparting such skills and that further in-service training is needed. Recent research by Meredith Gall and his colleagues, however, indicated that such in-service training appears to be fragmented and poorly integrated with school policy on the instructional program (Gall, Haisley, Baker, & Perez, 1983). Hence programs to build teacher skills systematically and with principal participation are rare and vulnerable. They are often the first casualties in budget cuts and are generally undercut by the attitudes of those teachers and administrators who prefer things as they are. Bruce Joyce and his colleagues (Joyce, Hersh, & McKibbin, 1983) found many teachers to be passive or withdrawn about new developments in teaching practice, and Gene Hall and William Rutherford (1983) found many principals to avoid involvement in movements to improve teaching.

Each of these authors identifies teachers and principals who are more active in seeking out change, however, and the role of such people in bringing about system-wide change will be considered next.

IMPROVING WORKING RELATIONSHIPS

Teachers and principals are interdependent and need to develop cooperative working relationships. Under increasing public pressure and more complex legal constraints, however, the relationship of teachers and administrators may enter a vicious cycle of distrust and opposition unless countervailing steps are taken to initiate a positive cycle of trust and cooperation.

The literature on leadership suggests that a central figure is essential in introducing and sustaining the symbols of progress. The principal has the major responsibility for moving his or her relationship with teachers to a more positive tone. However, the principal depends on allies for the critical mass required for change, and so the principal must develop a supportive teaching staff, either through persuasion or replacement, transferring adversaries to other schools when necessary and bringing in teachers who are supportive of the vision to be shared.

What Can the Principal Do?

The principal's contribution to moving a school beyond the status quo might well begin with an examination of how he or she uses time and how discretionary time might be expanded in the interest of sustained communication with teachers about classroom instruction. Teachers need to be aware that the principal is making this effort, because an immediate effect of the principal's experiment in time management is likely to be a delay in principal response to momentary problems. Teachers will either have to assist one another more—for instance, by developing cooperative time-out arrangements for unruly students or sharing materials in short supply—or they will have to anticipate problems.

For the principal to increase communication with teachers requires collective and one-on-one arrangements. The principal may join in discussions of teacher groups dealing with instructional improvement and act as a colleague rather than as a boss. The principal may supplement the daily tour of the physical plant with more prolonged visits to classes to appreciate what teachers and students are doing. The principal may gain further ground from participating in lessons either as a co-teacher or as an occasional substitute teacher. If, as David Dwyer and his colleagues suggest, the real influence of the principal on teachers occurs day by day in the course of routine interaction, that interaction should be focused on the instructional program as well as on logistical problems.

The side effects of such communication and participation are manifold. First, the teacher begins to see the principal as the "knowledgeable colleague" described by Richard Williams (1980). Second, the principal develops a reputation for concern with teaching problems and interest in teaching successes. Third, the principal builds a repertoire of ideas to share with other teachers as the occasion warrants.

A next step is cooperative problem solving. The principal can engage the teachers individually and collectively in the search for better practice. The principal can bring curriculum development and staff development efforts into a more organic relationship. The principal must be willing, however, to deliver on promises of assistance for teachers and to bend district requirements to enable teachers to explore new options. Susan Johnson (1982) has described the team spirit in schools where the principal's willingness to step around the contract in the interest of the common good is reciprocated by teachers. In this way, school organizational processes—including routine administrative functions—generate the "effective school" climate described by Stewart Purkey and Marshall Smith (1982). Feelings of community and collaborative problem solving grow out of a pattern of committee work and principal-teacher discussions.

In developing this problem-solving activity, principals need to remember that teachers may approach the research on effective teaching from different levels and angles. Since the research is based on natural variation, it is to be expected that some teachers may already be using effective practice. Identifying these and building a special role for them in the schoolwide effort is a task requiring administrative tact. Other teachers may not be teaching well and may need to be protected in schoolwide improvement efforts; if they feel vulnerable, they are likely to become defensive. In addition, the administrator is likely to find teachers for whom the profile of effective teaching is either too structured or too interactive and who operate effectively with a modification of the profile. Here the principal has to be able to articulate the underlying function of the teaching behavior so that the teacher can see whether personal variations accomplish the function. For example, a teacher may feel that diagnosis of student learning problems is better done in the midst of daily classwork than in a separate planning session. The critical question is whether the teacher is able to take a fresh look at all children performing below expectations in the midst of the daily routine or whether some children become invisible under a cloak of familiarity. Similarly, some teachers may be what Bruce Joyce calls "omnivores" with respect to staff development and may benefit from a more teacher-driven program than those who respond more passively to a program structured by others. Again, the point is that teachers be stimulated to review their teaching and incorporate new strategies; how this is accomplished in any particular school may vary with the people involved.

What Can the Teacher Do?

The implications of research on effective schools are seldom drawn for what the *teacher* can do to improve the leadership and support given by the principal. Yet Lortie's (1982) depiction of the principal's role suggests that principals are highly susceptible to incentives of teacher support and morale. Moreover, to the degree that teachers are taking a hand in policy formation via the collective bargaining route, teachers will have a say in the definition of the principal's work role and conditions through the contract. Hence it is important to start thinking about how teachers can effect changes in their own performance and in principals' performance.

The teacher attitude that the invisible administrator is the best administrator ("run the school and leave me alone in my classroom") is counterproductive.

Principals can advance the interests of teachers and respond to their needs only if principals have current and in-depth knowledge of those interests and needs. Hence it is important for the teacher to make frequent personal contact with the principal. This means seeking out the principal for reasons other than fixing lights and fans. The teacher may invite the principal to observe a particular classroom activity or attend teacher planning meetings. To follow up, the teacher needs to reinforce the principal's efforts to keep abreast of classroom progress and provide resources for teacher projects. This means using faculty meetings for teacher praise of principal activities as well as vice versa.

Of course, one can never eliminate the hierarchical forces generating tension between the teacher and principal roles (e.g., over contract items and formal evaluations). We would suggest, however, that teachers as well as principals can exert some control in defining the context of their interaction and incentives for the principals' performance.

The teacher *group* is more potent than the individual teacher in improving the tenor of principal-teacher relations. Chapter 20 indicates how teachers as colleagues can provide a proactive group in a faculty to catalyze principal support efforts. A corollary to this is that teacher colleagues can provide the critical mass necessary to get principal-initiated projects off the ground and can demand influence over such projects as an exchange. Teachers also can socialize the principal about instructional improvements by involving the principal in staff development efforts. Beverly Showers (1983) has provided such a role for principals in her peer-coaching projects, although she prefers to use teacher colleagues in the actual coaching activities. Experience in training for coaching relationships can give the principal intimate knowledge of the processes and dynamics of such a relationship and enable the principal to support teachers acting as colleagues.

With respect to the formal and hierarchical aspects of principal performance, teachers can assist the principal in devoting more energy to instruction by reducing the tendency of their colleagues to place the principal perpetually "on call" for minor problems. Teachers can develop collective resource stockpiles and cooperative time-out arrangements to reduce the frequency of requests for principal help and the frequency of disciplinary referrals. The research on the fragmentary and reactive nature of principals' work indicates that basic ground rules about principals' duties need to be changed if principals are to devote blocks of time to instructional improvement processes.

Finally, teachers, as increasingly potent influences on the organization, can accept responsibility for the school as a whole rather than just their classroom. If teachers are perceived as being uninterested in the principal's responsibilities, the principal may brush off criticism offered constructively by teachers with the thought, "They don't understand the reason for this; they're just complaining." Where teachers articulate and fulfill the legitimate obligations they have to the school, they are in a much stronger position in daily feedback to the principal about particular organizational factors that are damaging to the work of teaching. If this sounds like a major role change, it is. The residual role of the principal will shift to overall stimulation and facilitation of good teaching when some of the other duties at present exercised by the principal are taken on by teachers singly and in groups. Delegation of administrative tasks must be accepted in exchange for instructional leadership.

In looking to the school principal for assistance in improving their work, teachers need to be aware that principals differ in their style (just like teachers). Gene Hall and William Rutherford (1983) found that principals can be "initiators," "managers," or "responders" with respect to change. With an "initiator" principal, the teacher may need to cultivate the principal's sense that the change was the principal's idea in order to avoid threatening the need for proactiveness Blumberg and Greenfield found among their effective principals. Teachers with a "responder" principal may need to "get their act together" thoroughly and with public support before the principal comes around. Teachers with a "manager" principal probably need to reassure the principal that school equilibria will not be upset in the change process, and that may mean forming a united front in dealing with the district.

Teachers need likewise to be aware that principals deal with many teachers and have to balance the demands of all. Supporting the principals' message that teacher uniqueness is limited and that there are commonalities and universal dimensions to good teaching is one way to contribute to the principal's ability to weld a facultywide approach together rather than scatter energies among individual teachers.

CONCLUSION

The research on the effective teacher, the effective school, and the effective principal indicates that teachers and principals are interdependent with respect to their impact on the quality of education students receive. Interdependence requires cooperation, and cooperation depends on collegial working relationships. Schools as they are, however, inhibit the development of such collegiality. Only by building trust through frequent interaction and problem solving can principals generate a cycle of increasing cooperation, but they need teachers to support and reward their efforts to overcome institutional constraints on good working relationships.

FURTHER READING

Bossert, S., Dwyer, D., Rowan, B. & Lee, G. (1982, Summer). "The Instructional Management Role of the Principal." *Educational Administration Quarterly, 18,* 34–64. Provides a comprehensive account of research on the principal's opportunities to exert educational leadership. The target for such leadership may be either school climate or the organization of the instructional program and school day.

Carnine, D., Gersten, R., & Green, S. (1982). "The Principal as Instructional Leader: A Second Look." *Educational Leadership, 40*(12), 47–50. Describes how supervision and support of teachers' work can come from sources other than the principal. The principal's role may be indirect rather than direct in improving the quality of teaching.

Darling-Hammond, L., Wise, A., & Pease, S. (1983). "Teacher Evaluation in the Organizational Context: A Review of the Literature." *Review of Educational Research, 53,* 285–328. Describes the pitfalls in teacher evaluation that prevent most efforts from having any effect on the quality of teaching. The steps necessary to make evaluation more constructive are carefully developed.

Duckworth, K. (1983, Spring-Summer). "The Agenda, Incentives, and Resources of School Improvement." *R & D Perspectives.* Available free from the Center for Educational Policy and Management, University of Oregon, Eugene, OR 97403. This short article criticizes the "quick fix" mentality regarding school improvement and describes how a consortium of small school districts mounted an effective program of collaboration between teachers and administrators in improving the quality of instruction.

Hall, G., Rutherford, W., Hord, S., & Huling, L. (1984). "Effects of Three Principal Styles on

School Improvement." *Educational Leadership, 41*(2), 22–31. Describes three types of school principals—initiators, managers, and responders—and argues, on the basis of research, that initiators are more effective in bringing about school improvement.

Joyce, B., Hersh, R., & McKibbin, M. (1983). *The Structure of School Improvement.* White Plains, NY: Longman. Describes the processes of refining, renovating, and redesigning schools for improved teaching and learning. A paradigm for organizing effective staff development is presented.

Leithwood, K., & Montgomery, D. (1982). "The Role of the Elementary School Principal in School Improvement." *Review of Educational Research, 52,* 309–339. Argues, on the basis of research, that effective elementary principals share with teachers the goal of promoting student learning as a first priority. Such principals work toward collaboration with teachers but never sacrifice the student achievement goal to staff congeniality.

Murphy, J., Hallinger, P., & Mitman, A. (1983). "Problems with Research on Educational Leadership: Issues to Be Addressed." *Educational Evaluation and Policy Analysis, 5,* 297–305. Cautions against a superficial image of the principal as educational leader and alerts the reader to the steps by which principals build authority. The authors argue that principals build authority through successful transactions with the *external* environment as much as through collaborative transactions with teachers within the school.

Purkey, S., & Smith, M. (1983). "Effective Schools: A Review." *Elementary School Journal, 83,* 427–452. Provides another comprehensive account of the characteristics of schools that produce student achievement beyond expectation. Like Bossert et al., Purkey and Smith distinguish between change in climate factors, which may take longer to accomplish, and change in organizational factors, which may proceed rapidly.

REFERENCES

Blumberg, A., & Greenfield, W. (1980). *The effective principal: Perspectives on school leadership.* Boston: Allyn & Bacon.

Bossert, S. T., Dwyer, D., Rowan, B., & Lee, G. (1982, Summer). The instructional management role of the principal. *Educational Administration Quarterly, 18,* 34–64.

Clark, C., & Yinger, R. (1979). Teachers' thinking. In P. L. Peterson & H. J. Walberg (Eds.), *Research on teaching: Concepts, findings, and implications.* Berkeley, CA: McCutchan.

Dwyer, D., Lee, G., Rowan, B., & Bossert, S. T. (1983). *Five principals in action: Perspectives on instructional management.* San Francisco: Far West Laboratory.

Fisher, C., Berliner, D., Filby, N., Marliave, R., Cahen, L., & Dishaw, M. (1980). Teaching behaviors, academic learning time, and student achievement: An overview. In C. Denham & A. Lieberman (Eds.), *Time to learn.* Sacramento: California Commission for Teacher Preparation and Licensing.

Gall, M., Haisley, F., Baker, R., & Perez, M. (1983). *The relationship between inservice education practices and effectiveness of basic skills instruction.* Eugene: University of Oregon, Center for Educational Policy and Management.

Goldschmidt, S., Bowers, B., Riley, M., & Stuart, L. (1983). *The extent of educational policy bargaining.* Eugene: University of Oregon, Center for Educational Policy and Management.

Hall, G., & Rutherford, W. (1983, April). *Three change facilitator styles: How principals affect improvement efforts.* Paper presented at the annual meeting of the American Educational Research Association, Montreal, Canada.

Halpin, A. (1966). *Theory and research in administration.* New York: Macmillan.

Huff, S., Lake, D., & Schaalman, M. L. (1982, November). *Principal difference: Excellence in school leadership and management.* Report submitted to the Council of Educational Management, Department of Education, State of Florida by McBer & Co., Boston.

Jackson, P. (1968). *Life in classrooms.* New York: Holt, Rinehart and Winston.

Johnson, S. M. (1982). *Teacher unions and the schools*. Cambridge, MA: Harvard University, Institute for Educational Policy Studies.

Joyce, B., Hersh, R., & McKibbin, M. (1983). *The structure of school improvement*. White Plains, NY: Longman.

Kmetz, J., & Willower, D. (1982, Fall). Elementary school principals' work behavior. *Educational Administration Quarterly, 18*, 62–78.

Leithwood, K., & Montgomery, D. (1982). The role of the elementary school principal in program improvement. *Review of Educational Research, 52*, 309–339.

Lortie, D. C. (1975). *Schoolteacher: A sociological study*. Chicago: University of Chicago Press.

Lortie, D. C. (1982). The complex work relationships of elementary school principals. In K. Duckworth & W. DeBevoise (Eds.), *The effects of collective bargaining on school administrative leadership: Proceedings of a conference*. Eugene: University of Oregon, Center for Educational Policy and Management.

March, J. (1978). American public school administration: A short analysis. *School Review, 86*, 217–250.

Martin, W., & Willower, D. (1981, Winter). The managerial behavior of high school principals. *Educational Administration Quarterly, 17*, 69–90.

Meyer, J. (1980). Levels of the educational system and schooling effects. In C. Bidwell & D. Windham (Eds.), *The analysis of educational productivity: Vol. 2. Issues in macroanalysis*. Cambridge, MA: Ballinger.

Morris, V., Crowson, R., Hurwitz, E., Jr., & Porter-Gehrie, C. (1981). *The urban principal: Discretionary decision-making in a large educational organization*. Chicago: University of Illinois at Chicago Circle.

Persell, C. (1982). *Effective principals: What do we know from various educational literatures?* Paper presented at the NIE Conference on Principals for Educational Excellence in the 1980s, Washington, DC.

Purkey, S. C., & Smith, M. S. (1982). *Effective schools: A review*. Paper presented at the NIE Conference on Research on Teaching: Implications for Practice, Washington, DC.

Rosenshine, B. (1979). Content, time, and direct instruction. In P. L. Peterson & H. J. Walberg (Eds.), *Research on teaching: Concepts, findings, and implications*. Berkeley, CA: McCutchan.

Showers, B. (1983). *Transfer of training: The contribution of coaching*. Eugene: University of Oregon, Center for Educational Policy and Management.

Stallings, J. A. (1975). Implementation and child effects of teaching practices in Follow Through classrooms. *Monographs of the Society for Research in Child Development, 40* (Serial No. 163), 1–119.

Stallings, J. A. (1981). What research has to say to administrators of secondary schools about effective teaching and staff development. In K. Duckworth et al. (Eds.), *Creating conditions for effective teaching: Proceedings of a conference*. Eugene: University of Oregon, Center for Educational Policy and Management.

Waller, W. (1932). *The sociology of teaching*. New York: Wiley.

Williams, R. (1980). Implementing practices in elementary schools based on BTES: Implications for the principal. In C. Denham & A. Lieberman (Eds.), *Time to learn*. Sacramento: California Commission for Teacher Preparation and Licensing.

Wolcott, H. (1973). *The man in the principal's office*. New York: Holt, Rinehart and Winston.

19 IMPROVING SCHOOL EFFECTIVENESS: LESSONS FROM RESEARCH

Michael Cohen

The 1980s have witnessed the birth and rapid growth of an "effective schools" movement, in which educators at all levels, from the classroom to the state education department, have turned to an accumulating body of research on schooling practices that influence student learning. For example, a recent study (Miles & Kaufman, 1985) indicates that there are nearly 40 effective schools programs operating in some 1,750 school districts and almost 7,500 schools in virtually every state in the country. This is double the number found in a 1983 study (Miles, Farrar, & Neufeld, 1983), and every sign suggests that such programs will continue to spread rapidly in the coming years.

In contrast, as recently as 1980 there were probably no more than a handful of schools involved in effective schools programs, and perhaps not many more educators familiar with research on effective schooling practices. Further, in the 1970s the prevailing wisdom, at least in the education research community if not among educators at large, was that the key to having an effective school was to find one serving predominantly white and upper-middle-class students. For schools serving a poor and minority clientele, there were no schooling practices that consistently enhanced student achievement. In large part, this was the legacy of early studies of school effectiveness, such as those conducted by Coleman and colleagues (1966) and by Jencks and coworkers (1972), whose major findings were that students' achievement was more heavily dependent on their family background than on the characteristics of the schools they attended.

One of the major reasons that these and other early studies of school effectiveness failed to find effective schooling practices lies in their nearly exclusive focus on

474

the availability of particular educational resources (i.e., experienced and credentialed teachers, library books, lab equipment, and the like) rather than on the ways in which such resources were actually used on a day-to-day basis in schools (Cohen, 1982). During the 1970s, researchers shifted their emphasis away from educational resources toward educational practices, focusing on such issues as classroom organization and management, instructional practices, and school leadership. In addition, considerable attention was devoted to identifying, describing, and analyzing the practices used by teachers and administrators in classrooms and schools serving predominantly poor and minority populations in which student achievement levels were considerably higher than would be expected on the basis of student background.

The findings from these studies of unusually effective teachers and schools form the core of the "effective schools" research. When considered together with other studies of teaching and schooling, the effective schools research provides us with a conceptual framework for thinking about schools. Such a framework can provide educators with a powerful set of lenses, enabling them to develop a deeper understanding of the forces that shape and influence behavior and interactions in their own schools and classrooms. Further, it can assist them in identifying, selecting, or modifying practices that will be most effective in their own settings.

SCHOOL IMPROVEMENT

The effective schools studies since the mid-1970s have been important in part because of the way in which they have shaped the thinking of state and local policymakers and administrators about the nature and possibilities of school improvement. Among the more important lessons from the research are the following:

1. Schools Can Make a Difference

As noted, early research on school effectiveness, conducted by Coleman et al. (1966), Jencks et al. (1972), and others, found that family background contributed much more heavily to school performance than did school characteristics. These findings were widely misinterpreted at the time as saying that "schools don't make a difference," that there is nothing that schools can do to overcome the educational disadvantages produced by minority-group status and poverty (Cohen, 1982). More recent studies (e.g., Brookover, Beady, Flood, Schweitzer, & Wisenbaker, 1979) have challenged this view by identifying schools serving predominantly poor and minority populations in which student achievement levels are higher than expected for those students. The argument here, as developed by Edmonds (1979), is that if *some* schools can teach poor and minority students effectively, *all* can, if they employ the knowledge base regarding effective practices. While subsequent research has highlighted some technical difficulties in identifying effective schools based on student test scores (Dwyer, Lee, Rowan, & Bossert, 1983), the point still remains. While no one seriously debates the importance of family background, we no longer believe that schools are unable to teach students from all backgrounds effectively. This shift in beliefs has important symbolic value, both for raising the performance expectations teachers and administrators have of their students and for mobilizing public and political support for school improvement.

2. The School Is the Fundamental Unit of Reform

The effective schools findings are generally understood to imply that educational reform efforts have to be targeted primarily to the school building as an institution, rather than to individual teachers or entire school districts. This is in part accidental and tautological: When you look for effective *schools*, you are likely to conclude that schools (rather than teachers or districts) are where the action is. More important, however, it reflects appropriate recognition of the effect that the school context, especially the behaviors of the principal and the teaching staff, has on the teaching strategies and practices of individual teachers (Bossert, Dwyer, Rowan, & Lee, 1982). The school culture—the norms, values, and belief systems that characterize the school—seem inherently to be properties of schools, rather than entire districts, because of the relative physical and bureaucratic isolation of schools from the other schools and the central office of the local district. Consequently, not only is the school seen as the primary unit of reform, but analysts such as Cohen (1983) and Finn (1984) argue that schools require considerable autonomy and discretion in determining their own policies and standards. It should be noted that while in principle it is widely agreed that the school is the key unit of reform, in practice much of the recent wave of educational reform policies appears further to centralize authority at the state or local district level and correspondingly to reduce latitude for educators in individual school buildings (Cohen, 1985).

3. School Improvement Should Reduce the Professional Isolation of Teachers

Related closely to point 2, the research strongly suggests the importance of increasing the opportunities for teachers to work together with their peers. Historically, teaching has been a profession in which work is typically performed in isolation from one's colleagues (Lortie, 1975). This has had several undesirable consequences, including the limited codification of successful practices and the virtual absence of systems to provide ongoing technical support to teachers when needed. In effective schools, however, teachers frequently work and interact with one another. They are involved in staff development programs together, offer and receive assistance from one another, and share ideas and experiences about teaching. Consequently, their morale is often higher and their enthusiasm greater. Under such circumstances, teachers are often more willing to experiment with new approaches and are more effective in meeting their students' needs (Rosenholtz, 1984). Significantly, some proposed reforms of the teaching profession, such as the introduction of career ladders in Charlotte-Mecklenburg, NC, or the state of Tennessee, seem implicitly to recognize the need to create structures that increase the likelihood that teachers will interact collegially with one another.

4. School Staff Cannot Engage in School Improvement Efforts on Their Own

Meaningful and sustained changes in schooling practices require support and assistance from outside the school, in the form of technical assistance and training, leadership and guidance, and resources (Crandall et al., 1982; Louis, Rosenblum, & Molito, 1981). While the individual school buildings should be the unit of reform, the role of the local superintendent in providing leadership, in the form of both pressure to improve and assistance and resources to support improvement, is critical. Further, particularly with respect to the implementation of complex improvements based on the effective schools research, it needs to be clearly understood that implementation and improvement are long-term processes that unfold over a period of years.

These four lessons provide an important part of the *context* of our thinking about improving school effectiveness. We now turn our attention to the *content* of school improvement, by providing a framework for thinking about the ways in which teachers and building administrators can organize their own efforts and orient the behavior of their students, in order to promote student learning most effectively.

THE CONTENT OF SCHOOL IMPROVEMENT

I organize the research findings on school effectiveness into four broad domains of schooling: classroom teaching practices, school-level instructional management and coordination, school culture, and instructional leadership. Other reviewers (e.g., Bossert, Dwyer, Rowan, & Lee, 1982; Cohen, 1983; Edmonds, 1979; and Purkey & Smith, 1983) have used different frameworks for synthesizing essentially similar findings. I make no claim here that this framework is necessarily better than any others; in fact, I urge readers to consult these other works as well in order to obtain somewhat different perspectives on issues of school effectiveness.

The particular framework employed here permits several important distinctions that I find helpful for thinking about school improvement. One useful distinction is between organizational levels within the school. Certain practices or variables, such as instructional practices and the classroom conditions that permit their successful application, operate primarily at the classroom level, where the work of teaching and learning occurs. Other practices operate primarily at the school level. They shape classroom practices, integrate the work of teachers across classrooms, and provide some orderly progression to the learning experiences students accumulate as they move from one grade to the next (Cohen, 1983). Distinguishing between classroom and school-level practices is useful for school improvement because it enables educators to be clear about where primary responsibility for changes rests and where to look for evidence that desired changes are actually occurring.

A second useful distinction is between curricular and instructional practices, which are primarily instrumental and technical in nature, versus the decidedly more social aspects of schools—the expectations, values, and beliefs that govern the behaviors of individuals and groups within the school. Of interest here are practices that integrate diverse participants into a common, more or less committed whole and that direct time and energies to support the instructional mission of the school. This distinction is not hard and fast, for in reality both the social and technical aspects of schooling are interwoven. For example, the way in which the instructional program is organized influences teachers' interaction patterns and work norms; conversely, teachers' beliefs and expectations influence their classroom management and instructional practices.

Analytically distinguishing between technical and social aspects of schooling is important for several reasons. First, it enables us to think clearly about different aspects of school life. Second, it reminds us that promoting instructional effectiveness in schools requires improving teaching practices and school management, the technical core of the school, as well as school culture, the social side of the school, simultaneously, because they are inextricably intertwined. Teaching practices, leadership styles and management practices, school goals, belief systems, and the like cannot be readily separated from one another and worked at in a piecemeal fashion. Put somewhat differently, changing instructional practices or other teacher behaviors involves altering not only what teachers do but how they think about their behavior and the meaning they and others give to it as well.

The first two domains to be considered, classroom teaching and school-level curricular coordination, pertain largely to the technical side of schooling, at both the classroom and building levels. The third domain we will consider, the culture of the school, clearly refers to the social side. In our discussion, we will focus on both classroom and school-level concerns, addressing the school level in more detail. The final area we will address, school leadership, focuses on both the technical and social side of schools. It does so intentionally, underscoring the need for leaders to pay careful attention to the entire operation of the school, ensuring that specific curricular decisions and teaching practices are carried out in a climate that supports the instructional goals of the school.

Classroom Teaching Practices

Since much of the rest of this volume focuses in considerable detail on classroom practices that promote student learning, it is unnecessary to review that literature here. It is important, however, that we clearly illustrate the ways in which teaching practices already identified as effective are embedded in the larger context of the school and thus can be influenced by school improvement programs. Our attention here will therefore be selective rather than exhaustive, focusing on major practices reviewed elsewhere in this volume and examining the linkages between the classroom level and the school level.

One of the major classroom variables determining student achievement is academic learning time (ALT). Berliner (1979) has already shown how teachers' planning, management, and instructional decisions influence ALT. Time on task is also subject to schoolwide influences. As an obvious example, the lengths of the school year and day place upper limits on the total amount of instructional time available. Further, scheduling decisions, such as the timing of assemblies, pep rallies, athletic practice, and the like, also determine the quantity and availability of instructional time. Instructional programming decisions, such as the existence of special or remedial pull-out programs, as well as day-to-day decisions regarding which students receive special services and when they are to be delivered, can influence individual students' opportunity to learn particular subject matter in their regular classroom setting.

Schoolwide policies and practices can also have powerful influences on engaged time as well. For example, school discipline policies that are clearly announced and effectively and fairly enforced can limit intrusions into or disruptions of instructional time. Similarly, clear rules about when the loudspeaker can and cannot be used during the school day can eliminate potential intrusions, which are often particularly disruptive of instruction time (Benhke et al., 1981).

Teachers' classroom management practices have been shown to be related to engaged time and student achievement levels. Effective classroom managers establish classroom rules, procedures, and routines at the very beginning of the school year, teach them to students, and constantly monitor and reinforce them throughout the year. In addition, effective managers are able to plan, organize, and implement instructional activities in ways that maximize student engagement and minimize time lost due to disruptions, transitions from one activity to the next, and the like. (See Brophy, 1983, for a review of this research.) Important for our purposes is not the details of effective management practices but rather the fact that the management practices and skills of individual teachers are subject to influence from the school. For example, schoolwide staff development and in-service training focused on classroom management can be a particularly powerful strategy to address classroom level management issues. Further, when in-service training is accompanied by opportunities for teachers to observe, assist, and consult with one another, the likelihood of strengthening the management practices of individual teachers increases considerably.

Another illustration of how aspects of effective classroom teaching can be influenced by the larger school environment is the case of teacher expectations and role definitions. Effective teachers have a high sense of efficacy; they believe that they are effective and can affect the learning of students (Armor et al., 1976; Berman, McLaughlin, Bass, Pauly, & Zellman, 1977; Ashton, Webb, & Doda, 1982). Such teachers believe that instructing students in curriculum content is important; they accept responsibility for teaching, and reteaching if necessary, until students master content. They create a businesslike, task-oriented environment. Through clear instructions to students, monitoring behavior, and their choice of materials and activities, they create classrooms in which students are held accountable for their work (Brookover et al., 1979; Brophy & Evertson, 1976; Rosenshine, 1979; Stallings & Kaskowitz, 1974).

This sense of efficacy and concomitant positive expectations are especially important in classrooms with large concentrations of low-achieving students, for it is apparently easy for teachers to let the previous low academic performance of students translate into low expectations about subsequent performance. A voluminous literature documents that teachers treat low- and high-achieving students differently within the same classroom. (For excellent reviews, see Cooper, 1979, Brophy, 1982b, and Cooper & Good, 1984.) For example, teachers often give low-achieving students less opportunity and less time to respond to questions, criticize them more frequently, praise them less frequently or inappropriately, and generally pay less attention to and demand less from them. There is some tentative evidence that teachers with a high sense of efficacy are those who are the least likely to engage in classroom behaviors that transmit lower expectations to low achievers (Ashton, Webb, & Doda, 1982).

Again, what is important for our consideration here is the growing realization that teachers' sense of efficacy and their performance expectations for their students are in part a function of the larger school context. Schools in which teachers are provided the encouragement and opportunity to share ideas and experiences about teaching practices, instructional problems, and the like are schools that also promote the development of positive expectations on the part of teachers (Ashton et al., 1982; Rosenholtz, 1984). The opportunity to learn from one another and solve problems together typically generates both enthusiasm and strategies that promote positive expectations in teachers.

School-Level Instructional Management and Coordination

In general, research on school-level practices is less well developed than research on classroom practices. Studies are fewer, findings across studies are less frequently replicated, and descriptions of specific practices are fewer. Nonetheless, with respect to the management and coordination of instruction, several themes emerge.

There is general agreement that the curriculum and the instructional program in effective schools, especially in elementary schools, are tightly coupled. Essentially, this means that school goals, grade level, and classroom instructional objectives, instructional content and activities, and measures of pupil performance are all carefully aligned (Edmonds, 1979; Brookover et al., 1979; Wellisch, MacQueen, Carriere, & Duck, 1978; Levine & Stark, 1982; Weber, 1971). Students are exposed to a well-ordered and focused curriculum, and the instructional efforts of teachers and other instructional staff are consistent and cumulative.

This close relation among elements of the instructional program has several implications. First, schools should have instructional goals that are clear, public, and agreed upon, that form the basis of the selection of objectives, content, and materials, and that are developed through some type of planning process implemented at the building level. Second, differences among classrooms in time allocated to the same content should not be extreme. Extreme differences probably reflect the substitution of teacher preferences for formal school goals and expose children in different classes to functionally different curricula that are not adequately matched to school goals or performance measures (Berliner, 1979). Consequently, tight coupling implies that norms granting autonomy to teachers behind the closed door of the classroom carry less weight than the shared goals of the professional staff. Third, expectations and instructional activities of nonclassroom specialists (e.g., resource teachers, reading specialists) should support the efforts of classroom teachers. Fourth, a well-coordinated instructional program seems to require the use of achievement tests or other student performance measures, to focus instructional efforts and to detect programmatic weaknesses. Fifth, tight coupling implies an overlap between the content of instruction and the content of material used to measure pupil performance.

The findings about tight coupling, like those about effective teaching, may seem obvious. Nonetheless, tight coupling in schools is far from routine. For example, a recent study (Freeman et al., 1983; Porter, 1983) that examined in detail five commonly used fourth-grade mathematics textbooks found relatively little overlap between test content and textbook content. More specifically, according to Porter, "the percent of textbook topics covered by a test ranged from 21 to 50 percent" (p. 10). In short, if the selection of textbooks and the selection of tests are not carefully coordinated by schools or school districts, there is a good chance that students will not be tested on what they have been taught nor learn the content on which they are tested. In either case, the result is the same: diminished school effectiveness as measured by gains on the standardized tests.

Shared Values and Culture

A number of studies and analyses (Brookover et al., 1979; Wynne, 1980; Grant, 1982; Rutter, Maughan, Mortimore, Ouston, & Smith, 1979; Purkey & Smith, 1982; Cohen, 1981a, 1981b) suggest that effective schools generate a strong sense of community, with commonly shared goals and high expectations for student and staff performance and mechanisms for sustaining motivation, commitment, and identification with school goals.

The norms and values that unite individual members of a school into a cohesive community are academic as well as practical and social (Rutter et al., 1979). Positive expectations for student performance communicate the primacy of the instructional mission of the school and the obligation of both teachers and students to participate in it (see Brookover et al., 1979; Rutter et al., 1979). However, as Grant (1982) persuasively argues, community in schools also requires the creation of a moral order, which entails respect for authority, genuine and pervasive caring about individuals, respect for their feelings and attitudes, mutual trust, and the consistent enforcement of norms that define acceptable behavior. Such a strong social order creates an identity for the school, provides meaning to membership in it, and reduces alienation. And, as the work of Rutter et al. (1979) demonstrates, school "ethos" not only increases achievement but also improves student behavior and attendance and reduces the incidence of delinquency.

The importance of a shared moral order should not be underestimated. Schools are fragile social institutions, easily disrupted by conflict in or around them. Formal controls over the selection and activities of staff are weak (Bidwell, 1965; Lortie, 1969; Weick, 1976), and especially in public schools, control over the selection of students is limited or nonexistent. Students, in turn, are the involuntary clientele of the schools (Bidwell, 1971; Spady, 1974); their willing engagement in the formally prescribed activities of the school must be treated as problematic rather than taken for granted. The situation is further complicated because teaching and learning require not only compliance but also commitment and engagement. Under such circumstances, schools cannot rely simply on coercive power to bring about order. Rather, schools are normative organizations (Etzioni, 1975) that must rely on the internalization of goals, the legitimate use of authority, and the manipulation of symbols to control and direct the behavior of participants. Therefore, the kind of climate described by Grant and Rutter becomes an important precondition for effective instruction.

There is useful research regarding more specific aspects of school cultures that influence achievement. In particular, work norms among faculty appear to be especially important determinants of school effectiveness. Little (1981) highlights two norms that contribute to successful schools. One norm is collegiality, the notion that the work of teachers is shared work, not work to be done exclusively in the isolation of the classroom. Successful schools, then, are characterized by a large number of interactions, involving a large proportion of the staff, about numerous aspects of teaching. Extensive interactions and the expectation that they will and should occur are powerful mechanisms for integrating the work of the school and generating commitment and shared values among teachers.

A second norm, that of continuous improvement, reflects the expectation that all teachers continue to improve instructional practice, not just beginning teachers. Such a norm is enacted in schools through continuous analysis, evaluation, and experimentation with instructional practices. When both of these norms are present and salient in a school, there will be frequent talk among teachers about the practice of teaching (as distinct from talk about the backgrounds of students, the influence of external environments on schools, etc.); frequent observation of teaching by teachers; and teachers working together to plan, design, research, and prepare materials for teaching (Little, 1981). These practices, in turn, are likely to result in the development of shared values and a commitment to improve instructional effectiveness.

Other recent research also highlights the importance of teacher collegiality. Ashton, Webb, and Doda (1982) compared teachers in a traditionally organized junior high school with teachers in a multigraded, team-organized middle school, each school of comparable size and serving comparable student bodies. Among other things, they found that the team organization, which required collective decision making about instructional matters, and the multigraded organization, which ensured that teachers on the same team instructed the same students, enhanced teacher efficacy. Teaching became shared work, and sustained interaction focused on solving the problems of students and improving the practices of teachers. Professional isolation among teachers was reduced. Also reduced were the ambiguity over effectiveness inherent in the work of teaching (Lortie, 1975) and the debilitating self-doubts that typically accompany this ambiguity. Furthermore, enhanced efficacy was frequently reflected in more positive classroom teaching.

There is also considerable evidence to suggest that student norms and interactions are powerful determinants of school effectiveness. Peer groups provide important role models and informal rewards for students. They often powerfully shape students' perceptions of the importance of schoolwork and influence the extent to which a student commits time and energy to academic work (see Coleman, 1961; McDill & Rigsby, 1973; Cusik, 1973; Spady, 1970). Peers are also potentially important instructional resources since under certain circumstances they can provide tutoring and other forms of help to their classmates (see Cohen & Anthony, 1982; Peterson & Wilkinson, 1982; Webb, 1982).

Evidence is growing that peer group norms and peer interaction in schools are not determined solely by the characteristics of students or their family backgrounds. Rather, to a considerable degree, they are responses to the structure and climate of the school and classroom, as these are shaped by teachers and administrators (see Grant, 1982). For example, research findings indicate that the placement of students in curricular tracks, classrooms, and instructional groups influences students' choice of friends, patterns of interaction, and academically relevant group norms (see Alexander, Cook, & McDill, 1978; Alexander & McDill, 1976; Bossert, 1979). Further evidence suggests that classroom reward structures can influence academic norms and the frequency with which students help one another on academic tasks. For example, Slavin (1980, 1983) created cooperative reward structures in classrooms by assigning students to mixed-ability teams that competed on academic games. The competition was arranged so that individual students representing their teams competed against other students of similar ability so that all students had roughly equal chances of success. This cooperative reward structure has been demonstrated in numerous experiments conducted over a range of content areas and grade levels to increase the frequency of peer tutoring and cooperation. Since team members have an incentive to coach one another, peer group norms are shifted toward greater encouragement of academic achievement and involvement, significantly increasing academic achievement.

In short, the evidence suggests that schools are more effective when informal norms governing faculty and student behavior are consistent with formal academic goals. It further suggests that organizational aspects of the instructional program, as well as the leadership by the principal, can create an environment that supports instructional improvement and furthers student learning.

Instructional Leadership

There is near universal agreement among researchers and educators alike regarding the importance of instructional leadership for school effectiveness. Further, there is also nearly universal consensus that the principal needs to play a major (though not always exclusive) role in providing instructional leadership. There is considerably less agreement, however, on the particular strategies, tactics, and behaviors that constitute effective leadership on a day-to-day basis. This is partly a function of the relative infancy of research on the work of principals; there has been far less study of the role, behaviors, and effectiveness of principals than there has been of teachers. It is also partly a function of the nature of leadership itself, because leadership is often symbolic, indirect, and highly varied from situation to situation. Nonetheless, certain aspects of the instructional leadership role of the principal are increasingly coming into focus as research in the area progresses.

First, *leadership is situational in nature.* To be effective, a principal's leadership style has to be matched to the particular conditions in the school. For example, Bossert (1985) suggests that principals working with experienced and highly professionalized staffs might employ rather indirect leadership styles, simply suggesting ideas or raising questions with individual staff members and otherwise providing the necessary resources and latitude for good teachers to carry out good ideas. In contrast, in schools with inexperienced staff, the principals may need to employ much more direct supervisory strategies.

Second, *leadership is visible.* Regardless of their particular leadership styles, effective principals have a visible presence in their schools (Dwyer et al., 1983). They accomplish this by spending a good deal of each day in the halls, classrooms, lunchroom, library, and all other locations in the building. Because of their visibility, effective principals are aware of developments within the building and have a constant flow of information available to them.

Third, *leadership requires a vision of instructional improvement* (Blumberg & Greenfield, 1980; Manasse, 1985). Effective principals articulate this vision to the staff and others in the school and use this vision to guide their many daily interactions (Blumberg & Greenfield, 1980; Little, 1981, 1982). In instructionally effective schools, this vision takes the form of an emphasis on achievement. Effective principals tend to emphasize achievement (Gross & Herriot, 1965; Wellisch et al., 1978) by setting instructional goals, developing performance standards for students, and expressing optimism about the ability of students to meet instructional goals.

Put somewhat differently, effective principals are keenly aware of the classroom factors that promote achievement and have a conception of the variety of strategies and tactics they can use to strengthen those practices:

Each of the principals clearly articulates direct and remote links between their actions and their schools' instructional systems. It appears that successful principals always ask themselves how a particular decision will affect the learning environment within their own schools and classrooms. Although each principal expresses his or her own instructional philosophy, the guiding elements of that philosophy are strikingly similar to the factors that derive from effective teaching research. . . . They analyze and work with their teachers to guarantee that school activities reinforce, rather than detract from, their classroom's instructional programs. (Bossert, 1985, p. 46)

What is being suggested here is that the specific leadership behaviors and strategies of principals will of necessity vary from school to school depending on both the context of the school and the personality of the principal. Having said that, however, a constant characteristic of effective instructional leaders is that they have a clear sense of the particular "levers" in their school that can be used to influence instruction, and they deliberately go about working those levers to create and sustain conditions that promote effective instruction.

Fourth, *leadership focuses on school culture as well as on technical instructional practices*. As argued earlier, the social aspects of schooling, the ethos of the school, are critical preconditions for the enactment of technically sound instructional practices. Effective principals recognize this and employ strategies to strengthen the school culture. These often involve the use of rituals, such as pep rallies, assemblies, reward programs, and the like, which provide meaning to school membership, identify and celebrate achievement and success in school life, and define valued behaviors. These tools can be used to highlight and reward academic success for students.

Principals can shape the work norms among faculty. According to Little (1981, 1982), principals contribute to the development of collegiality and continuous improvement in several ways. First, they announce that they expect staff to be knowledgeable about effective practices and to participate in efforts to improve instruction. Second, they model desired behaviors by participating in instructional improvement activities themselves. Third, they reward teachers who are effective and who are trying to improve. Finally, they protect teachers who are implementing new practices from a variety of competing demands on their time and energies, in order to improve the likelihood of success for those teachers.

USING RESEARCH FOR SCHOOL IMPROVEMENT

The predominant mode of using the effective schools research has been to incorporate the findings into effective schools programs or school improvement programs designed for implementation at the school-building level. These programs have been developed by a broad range of agencies, including local, intermediate, and state education agencies, regional laboratories, and universities (Miles & Kaufman, 1985). Although programs vary in their particulars, they typically incorporate the following key features.

First, *school leadership or planning teams*, consisting of the principal, representatives of teachers and other professional staff, and sometimes parent, community, or student representatives, provide overall guidance to the school's efforts. The team is generally reponsible for conducting a needs assessment, identifying targets for improvement, developing improvement plans and overseeing their implementation, and assessing the results and effects of improvement activities.

Second, the programs use *assessment instruments based on the effective schools research*. The instruments are typically questionnaires or interview guides, often supplemented by school records and data on student achievement and background. The general strategy here involves engaging the school staff in comparing current schooling practices with those identified as optimal in the research. On the basis of these comparisons, as well as the input of the school staff and the informed judgments of the school improvement team, priorities for school improvement are identified.

Third, program developers provide some sort of technical assistance. Rarely is the staff in the school expected to implement a school improvement entirely on its own. At a minimum, most program developers provide training or assistance in the steps of the improvement process (e.g., formation of a school improvement team, interpretation of data) and in the substance of the effective schools research. In some cases, the developer will also provide training in specific areas (classroom management, instructional leadership) or will identify specialists who can provide and resources for obtaining needed training and assistance.

To date, there has been little systematic research into the experience of schools participating in such programs or into the impact of these programs on student achievement. Early evidence from a few programs in New York City (Clark & McCarthy, 1983) and Milwaukee (McCormack-Larkin & Kritek, 1982) does suggest that these programs can indeed be successful, even though they are not invariably so.

Implementing an Improvement Program

Since there has been so little study of school improvement programs, it is impossible to provide a comprehensive guide to implementing them (for an excellent research-based, practical guide, however, see Loucks-Horsley and Hergert, 1985). But we can review some practical suggestions to keep in mind when initiating such a project.

First, use the research findings to supplement your professional experience and wisdom, not to supplant it. The point here is to recognize that the implications of the research need to be tailored to the particular dimensions of your own school, not mechanistically adopted. More than anything else, the research provides you with a set of lenses through which you can view your school, focusing your attention on a range of critical practices and the ways in which they are tied together. Among other things, this means that you ought to approach any data you collect on current practices with a degree of skepticism, recognizing that even data from well-developed effective schools instruments represent only the starting point for discussions of a school planning team regarding aspects of the school program needing improvements. The perceptions, beliefs, and past experiences of school staff also need to be brought to bear on the interpretation of any more formal data and in the identification of priority problems to work on.

Second, it is important not to spend too much time in the early stages of the project on needs assessment and problem definition activities (Loucks-Horsley & Hergert, 1985), for several reasons. First, school staff have limited time and energy to devote to school improvement efforts. It is therefore more important to engage those limited resources on actions directed toward improving something than to squander them on deciding what needs to be improved. Further, as a review of the research suggests, many different aspects of schooling are inherently interrelated, so working on one problem in the school is likely to have spillover effects in other areas. For example, a program to reduce the chaos in the school lunchroom is likely to improve the conditions for instruction during the period after lunch and can begin to engender a more positive school spirit as well. Having the entire staff participate in an in-service training program on classroom management will not only improve instruction but could also alter staff interaction patterns and work norms.

Finally, few aspects of schooling remain static. Most "needs" are moving targets anyway, and the nature of the problems a school improvement team begins to address will change over the course of time. Consequently, getting a precise "fix" on a problem is less critical than deciding on a direction and beginning to move, recognizing that your understanding of a particular problem will change as you begin to work on it.

Third, design early improvement efforts for success, stacking the deck, if necessary. This means several things. First, when selecting a problem to tackle, don't hesitate to start with relatively small and simple objectives. For example, if there is a choice between a massive curriculum change on one hand and developing and implementing a policy to reduce student tardiness on the other, it may make sense to work on the tardiness first. This is especially so if you anticipate encountering significant pockets of skepticism or resistance among the staff or if your school has a weak history with prior improvement efforts. The aphorism that "nothing succeeds like success" is particularly apt here, and the general strategy ought to be to tackle small but meaningful problems first, building a track record of success, demonstrating seriousness of intent, and persuading, by example, that the school staff can, in fact, successfully tackle problems by working together.

Concomitantly, it often makes sense to involve the strongest and most committed staff in the initial implementation activities. For example, the school planning team may decide that peer coaching would be a sensible way to work on instructional improvement and build collegiality. If so, they should try this out with a small number of volunteer staff who are comfortable with the idea and secure enough to be observed frequently. This is not the time to pick either the weakest or the most recalcitrant teachers and recruit them into the project. The opportunities for failure would be too great, remaining activities too readily threatened. A more successful strategy in this case would involve starting with a small group of committed staff, providing the support and encouragement to facilitate success, and gradually expanding participation over time to include other staff. This would allow plenty of time and opportunity to persuade or, if necessary, pressure less willing staff to participate in the project activity.

Another related point is to be tolerant of a wide variety of needs and activities in the early stages of the process. While some schools may immediately be ready to tackle thorny and sensitive issues of improving intruction through frequent peer observations, clinical supervision, and the like, many other schools will be a long way from those strategies at the outset. Schools may need to start their improvement efforts by focusing on such diverse targets as keeping the public areas of the school clean and litter-free, ensuring that both students and faculty arrive to class on time, or developing symbolic evidence of the schools' commitment to academics, through the use of special assemblies, reward programs, slogans, and the like. Although these activities may not seem to be squarely focused on improving intructional effectiveness, they are in fact related to that goal. Further, they may be necessary first steps in a longer-term project, enabling the staff to build the experience and skill of working together on common problems.

Finally, the preceding point out withstanding, it is important to ensure that over time the project activities begin to focus directly on the heart of the schooling process. Ultimately, this should involve fairly comprehensive activities to improve curriculum and instruction and to promote the norms of collegiality and continuous improvement.

FURTHER READING

Kyle, R.M.J. (Ed.). (1985). *Reaching for Excellence: An· Effective Schools Sourcebook.* Washington DC: Government Printing Office. This book contains a number of excellent, well-written summaries of the most important research on effective teaching and schooling practices at the elementary and secondary levels. In addition, it analyzes the implications of current research for local district and state education policies. Finally, it contains a specific, detailed guide to existing effective schools programs.

Loucks-Horsley, S., & Hergert, L. F. (1985). *An Action Guide to School Improvement.* Alexandria, VA: Association for Supervision and Curriculum Development. An excellent guide to conducting a school improvement program. Written for teachers and principals, it reviews the major steps in a school improvement program, suggests strategies for conducting them, and identifies potential problems and recommends ways of coping with them.

Purkey, S. C., & Smith, M. S. (1983). "Effective Schools: A Review." *Elementary School Journal, 83,* 427–452. An excellent overview and critique of research on effective schooling practices. Provides a useful framework for understanding the research and its most important implications for practice.

REFERENCES

Alexander, K. L., Cook, M. A., & McDill, E. L. (1978). Curriculum tracking and educational stratification. *American Sociological Review, 43,* 47–67.

Alexander, K. L., & McDill, E. L. (1976). Selection and allocation within schools: Some causes and consequences of curriculum placement. *American Sociological Review, 41,* 963–980.

Armor, D., Conry-Oseguera, P., Cox, M., King, N., McDonnell, L., Pascal, A., Pauly, E., & Zellman, G. (1976). *Analysis of the school-preferred reading program in selected Los Angeles schools.* Santa Monica, CA: Rand Corp.

Ashton, P. T., Webb, R. B., & Doda, N. (1982). *A study of teachers' sense of efficacy* (Final Report to the National Institute of Education No. 400–79–0075). Gainesville: University of Florida, Department of Education.

Benhke, G., Labovitz, E. M., Bennett, J., Chase, C., Day, J., Lazar, C., & Mittleholtz, D. (1981). Coping with classroom distractions. *Elementary School Journal, 81,* 135–155.

Berliner, D. (1979). Tempus educare. In P. L. Peterson & H. J. Walberg (Eds.), *Research on teaching: Concepts, findings, and implications.* Berkeley, CA: McCutchan.

Berman, P., McLaughlin, M. W., Bass, G., Pauly, E., & Zellman, G. (1977). *Federal programs supporting educational change: Vol. VII. Factors affecting implementation and continuation.* Santa Monica, CA: Rand Corp.

Bidwell, C. E. (1965). The school as a formal organization. In J. G. March (Ed.), *Handbook of organizations.* Chicago: Rand McNally.

Bidwell, C. E. (1971). Students and schools: Some observations on client trust in client-serving organizations. In W. R. Rosengren & M. Lefton (Eds.), *Organizations and clients.* Columbus, OH: Merrill.

Blumberg, A., & Greenfield, W. (1980). *The effective principal: Perspectives on school leadership.* Boston: Allyn & Bacon.

Bossert, S. T. (1979). *Tasks and social relationships in classrooms: A study of classroom organization and its consequences.* New York: Cambridge University Press.

Bossert, S. T. (1985). Effective elementary schools. In National Institute of Education, *Reaching for excellence: An effective schools sourcebook*. Washington, DC: Government Printing Office.

Bossert, S. T., Dwyer, D., Rowan, B., & Lee, G. (1982, Summer). The instructional management role of the principal. *Educational Administration Quarterly, 18*, 34–64.

Brookover, W. B., Beady, C., Flood, P., Schweitzer, J., & Wisenbaker, J. (1979). *School social systems and student achievement: Schools can make a difference*. New York: Praeger.

Brookover, W. B., & Lezotte, L. (1979). *Changes in school characteristics coincident with changes in student achievement*. East Lansing: Michigan State University, Institute for Research on Teaching.

Brophy, J. E. (1983). Classroom organization and management. *Elementary School Journal, 83*(4), 265–286.

Brophy, J., & Evertson, C. (1976). *Learning from teaching: A developmental perspective*. Boston: Allyn & Bacon.

Clark, T., & McCarthy, D. P. (1983). School improvement in New York City: The evolution of a project. *Educational Researcher, 12*(4), 17–24.

Cohen, E. G., & Anthony, B. (1982, March). *Expectation-state theory and classroom learning*. Paper presented at the annual meeting of the American Educational Research Association, New York.

Cohen, M. (1981a, August). *Effective schools: Toward useful interpretations*. Paper presented at the Summer Instructional Leadership Conference of the American Association of School Administrators, Washington, DC.

Cohen, M. (1981b). Effective schools: What the research says. *Today's Education, 70*(2), 46–49.

Cohen, M. (1982). Effective schools: Accumulating research findings. *American Education, 18*, 13–16.

Cohen, M. (1983). Instructional, management, and social conditions in effective schools. In A. Olden & L. D. Webb (Eds.), *School finance and school improvement: Linkages for the 1980s*. Cambridge, MA: Ballinger.

Cohen, M. (1985). Introduction to special issue on policy implications of effective schools research. *Elementary School Journal, 85*, 277–279.

Coleman, J. S. (1961). *The adolescent society*. New York: Free Press.

Coleman, J. S., Campbell, E. Q., Hobson, C. J., McPartland, J. M., Mood, A. M., Weinfield, F. D., & York, R. L. (1966). *Equality of educational opportunity*. Washington, DC: Government Printing Office.

Cooper, H. M. (1979). Pygmalion grows up: A model for teacher expectation, communication, and performance influence. *Review of Educational Research, 49*, 389–410.

Cooper, H. M., & Good, T. L. (1984). *Pygmalion grows up: Studies in the expectation communication process*. White Plains, NY: Longman.

Crandall, D. P., et al. (1982). *Helping schools get better: Strategies for school development in the 1980s—Final report*. Andover, MA: The Network.

Cusik, P. A. (1973). *Inside high school: The students' world*. New York: Holt, Rinehart and Winston.

Dwyer, D., Lee, G., Rowan, B., & Bossert, S. T. (1983). *Five principals in action: Perspectives on instructional leadership*. San Francisco: Far West Laboratory.

Edmonds, R. (1979). Some schools work and more can. *Social Policy, 9*, 28–32.

Etzioni, A. (1975). *A comparative analysis of complex organizations* (2nd ed.). New York: Free Press.

Finn, C. E. (1984). Towards strategic independence: Nine commandments for enhancing school effectiveness. *Phi Delta Kappan, 65*, 8.

Freeman, D., Kuhs, T., Porter, A., Floden, R., Schmidt, W., & Schwille, J. (1983). Do textbooks and tests define a national curriculum in elementary school mathematics? *Elementary School Journal, 83*, 501–513.

Grant, G. (1982). *Education, character, and American schools: Are effective schools good enough?* Syracuse, NY: Syracuse University.

Gross, N., & Herriot, R. E. (1965). *Staff leadership in public schools: A sociological inquiry.* New York: Wiley.

Jencks, C. S., Smith, M., Ackland, H., Bane, M. J., Cohen, D., Gintis, H., Heyns, B., & Michelson, S. (1972). *Inequality: A reassessment of the effect of family and schooling in America.* New York: Basic Books.

Levine, D. U., & Stark, J. (1982). *Instructional and organizational arrangements and processes for improving academic achievement in inner city elementary schools* (Final Report to the National Institute of Education No. NIE-G-81-0700). Kansas City: University of Missouri, Center for the Study of Metropolitan Problems in Education.

Little, J. W. (1981). *School success and staff development: The role of staff development in urban desegregated schools* (Final Report to the National Institute of Education No. 400-79-0049). Boulder, CO: Center for Action Research.

Little, J. W. (1982). The effective principal. *American Education, 18*(7), 38–43.

Lortie, D. C. (1969). The balance of control and automony in elementary school teaching. In A. Etzioni (Ed.), *The semiprofessions and their organization.* New York: Free Press.

Lortie, D. C. (1975). *Schoolteacher: A sociological study.* Chicago: University of Chicago Press.

Loucks-Horsley, S., & Hergert, L. F. (1985). *An action guide to school improvement.* Alexandria, VA: Association for Supervision and Curriculum Development.

Louis, K. S., Rosenblum, R., & Molito, J. (1981). *Strategies for knowledge use and school improvement: A summary.* Cambridge, MA: Abt.

McCormack-Larkin, M., & Kritek, W. (1982). Milwaukee's Project RISE. *Educational Leadership, 40*:16–21.

McDill, E. L., & Rigsby, L. C. (1973). *Structure and process in secondary schools: The academic impact of educational climates.* Baltimore: Johns Hopkins University Press.

Manasse, A. L. (1985). Improving conditions for principal effectiveness: Policy implications of research. *Elementary School Journal, 85*(3), 439–463.

Miles, M. B., Farrar, E., & Neufeld, B. (1983). *The extent of adoption of effective schools programs. Vol. 2, Review of Effective Schools Programs Prepared for the National Commission on Excellence in Education.* Cambridge, MA: Huron Institute.

Miles, M. B., & Kaufman, T. (1985). A directory of programs. In R.M.J. Kyle (Ed.), *Reaching for excellence: An effective schools sourcebook.* Washington, DC: Government Printing Office.

Peterson, P. L., & Wilkinson, L. C. (1982, March). *Merging the process-product and sociolinguistic paradigms: Research on small group processes.* Paper presented at the annual meeting of the American Educational Research Association, New York.

Porter, A. (1983). The role of teaching in effective schools. *American Education, 19*(1), 9–12.

Purkey, S. C., & Smith, M. S. (1982). *Effective schools: A review.* Paper presented at the NIE Conference on Research on Teaching: Implications for Practice, Washington, DC.

Rosenholtz, S. (1984). *Myths* (No. TQ84–4). Denver, CO: Education Commission of the States.

Rosenshine, B. (1979). Content, time, and direct instruction. In P. L. Peterson & H. J. Walberg (Eds.), *Research on teaching: Concepts, findings, and implications.* Berkeley, CA: McCutchan.

Rutter, M., Maughan, B., Mortimore, P., Ouston, J., & Smith, A. (1979). *Fifteen thousand hours: Secondary schools and their effects on children.* Cambridge, MA: Harvard University Press.

Slavin, R. E. (1980). Cooperative learning. *Review of Educational Research, 50*, 315–342.

Slavin, R. E. (1983). *Cooperative learning.* White Plains, NY: Longman.

Spady, W. G. (1970). Lament for the letterman: Effects of peer status and extra-curricular activities on goals and achievement. *American Journal of Sociology, 75*, 680–702.

Spady, W. G. (1974). The authority system of the school and student unrest: A theoretical exploration. In C. W. Gordon (Ed.), *Uses of sociology of education.* 73rd Yearbook of the National Society for the Study of Education. Chicago: University of Chicago Press.

Stallings, J. A., & Kaskowitz, D. (1974). *Follow Through classroom observation evaluation, 1972–73.* Menlo Park, CA: Stanford Research Institute.

Webb, N. (1982, March). *Predicting learning from student interactions: Defining the variables.* Paper presented at the annual meeting of the American Educational Research Association, New York.

Weber, G. (1971). *Inner city children can be taught to read: Four successful schools* (Occasional Paper No. 18). Washington DC: Council for Basic Education.

Weick, K. E. (1976). Education organizations as loosely coupled systems. *Administrative Science Quarterly, 21,* 1–19.

Wellisch, J. B., MacQueen, A. H., Carriere, R. A., & Duck, C. (1978). School management and organization in successful schools. *Sociology of Education, 51,* 211–226.

Wynne, E. A. (1980). *Looking at schools: Good, bad and indifferent.* Lexington, MA: Lexington Books.

20 TEACHERS AS COLLEAGUES

Judith Warren Little

Research has yielded rich, detailed descriptions of the work of teachers. These descriptions present two quite different portraits of teachers' professional lives. In large numbers of schools, and for long periods of time, teachers are colleagues in name only. They work out of sight and hearing of one another, plan and prepare their lessons and materials alone, and struggle on their own to solve most of their instructional, curricular, and management problems.

Against this almost uniform backdrop of isolated work, some schools stand out for the professional relations they foster among teachers. These schools, more than others, are organized to permit the sort of "reflection in action" that Sykes (1983a, p. 90) argues has been largely absent from professional preparation and professional work in schools. For teachers in such schools, work involves colleagueship of a more substantial sort. Recognition and satisfaction stem not only from being a masterful teacher but also from being a member of a masterful group.

This chapter examines the possibilities and limits of collegiality among teachers. In framing a view of collegiality, I have relied primarily on three groups of studies. Studies of the professional "workplace" character of successful schools have drawn attention to collegial relations among teachers and to the ability of administrators or teacher leaders to foster those relations. Studies of organized teacher teaming have underscored some of the benefits of teacher collaboration but have also raised questions about the stability and continuity of work groups in schools. The teaming studies help to place face-to-face cooperative work amid a wider spectrum of joint action by teachers. Finally, studies of school improvement, teacher preparation, professional development, and the implementation of innovations have all identified certain inescapable and consequential relations among teachers and between teachers and administrators that spell the difference between success and disappointment.

I am indebted to Tom Bird for his part in formulating many of the ideas reflected in this chapter and to Patrick Shields for his assistance in reviewing the literature.

The accumulated research has made obvious the contrast between the conditions of professional work that prevail in most schools and the conditions that have been achieved in a much smaller number of schools or districts. Side by side with a devastating picture of professional isolation among experienced teachers and trial-and-error survival of beginning teachers are descriptions of institutions that have organized to promote professional collaboration and to give assistance to those just learning to teach.

These latter schools, in which collegial relations prevail, are urban and rural, large and small. They are more often elementary and middle-level schools than they are high schools (Cusick, 1980), but not exclusively so (Bird & Little, 1985). In them ordinary people, relying on ordinary budgets and confronted with the ordinary ebb and flow of energy, goodwill, and creativity, accomplish extraordinary things. As a basis for action, the differences in sheer numbers between the many isolating schools and the rare collegial schools are of less moment than the differences in their organizational character.

This is a literature of school life. Granted that there are larger phenomena at stake, requiring a broader sweep, it remains true that the educational goals we hold for our children and our communities are achieved, or are compromised, one school at a time. Taken together, recent studies have generated an increasingly sophisticated grasp of the professional structure of teaching in schools. The discoveries of the 1970s and 1980s make our understanding of collegiality less crude, our enthusiasms more carefully tempered.

Finally, this literature is theoretically, methodologically, and practically rich. It promises a conceptualization of conditions in schools that plausibly support learning to teach and the steady improvement of teaching over time. It draws on the perspectives and methods of several academic disciplines. And its questions, methods, and findings engage the intellectual curiosities, day-to-day experiences, and professional aspirations of teachers and others with whom they work.

WHAT DIFFERENCE DO COLLEAGUES MAKE?

The reason to pursue the study and practice of collegiality is that, presumably, something is gained when teachers work together and something is lost when they do not. The teachers who put aside other activities in order to work with colleagues, the principals who promote and organize such work, the superintendents who endorse it, and the school boards that pay for it must all be convinced that the benefits are substantial; in effect, the perceived benefits must be great enough that the time teachers spend together can compete with time spent in other ways, on other priorities that are equally compelling or more immediate.

Teachers' professional encounters with one another assume greater importance when placed against future demands on schools and on the teaching profession. At stake is a profession that attracts able and talented candidates by affording them work that is intellectually stimulating, personally meaningful, economically rewarding, and well regarded in the larger community (Lyons & McCleary, 1980; Sykes, 1983a). Equally at stake is an image of schools organized to improve steadily (or to adapt rapidly) by tapping the collective talents, experience, and energy of their professional staffs (Bird & Little, 1986; Little, 1985; Glickman, 1985; Lieberman & Miller, 1984).

Emerging visions of the teaching profession and of the school as a professional environment are in tension with inherited traditions. On the whole, tenacious habits of mind and deed make the achievement of strong collegial relations a remarkable accomplishment: not the rule, but the rare, often fragile exception.

Do Students Benefit When Teachers Work Together?

The teacher-student relationship is both the major *obligation* to which teachers are held and the primary source of *rewards* in teaching (Ashton, Webb, & Doda, 1982; Mitchell, Ortiz, & Mitchell, 1983; Lortie, 1975). The relations that teachers establish with fellow teachers or with other adults will—and must—be judged by their ability to make teachers' relations with students more productive and more satisfying.

Some studies offer vivid accounts of the classroom payoffs that follow teachers' joint efforts. Teachers who have worked together closely over a period of years celebrate their accomplishments by pointing to gains in the achievement, behavior, and attitude of students. In one study of six urban schools, teachers in an elementary school attributed schoolwide academic gains and improvements in classroom performance to the fact that they had worked in grade-level teams once a week for two years to tie their curriculum and instruction to principles of mastery learning (Little, 1981). Teachers in a junior high school traced both their remarkable gains in math achievement and the virtual elimination of classroom behavior problems to the revisions in curriculum, testing, and student placement procedures they had achieved working as a group (Bird & Little, 1985).

In the eyes of these teachers, the benefits of working together have outweighed the advantages of working alone. The quality of program in which students participate, the sense of program coherence and faculty cohesiveness that students detect, and the consistency in expectations that students encounter all figure prominently in teachers' descriptions (see also Rutter, Maughan, Mortimore, Ouston, & Smith, 1979).

By other accounts, however, the classroom benefits of shared work are not so readily apparent. Fledgling team efforts founder when participants find them too thin a resource for meeting the daily pressures of the classroom. Observing the apparent instability of teaming efforts in 16 elementary schools, Bredo (1977) speculates that the "immediacy" of classroom tasks places a premium on rapid decision making, close coordination of activities, and basic agreements about standards and procedures. Unaccustomed to planning curriculum together or to arriving at collective agreements about instruction or management, teachers often find their first efforts clumsy and unrewarding. The time spent in meetings appears to be time lost in meeting the requirements of lesson planning and instruction. Predictably, "unproductive" meetings are abandoned in favor of more familiar and satisfying routines. In one elementary school, only teachers' commitment to try a pilot program for a full two-year term saw them through the first six months of learning to work productively together (Little, 1981).

Skeptics doubt the benefits of teacher collaboration. Some protest that extensive out-of-classroom time is suspect. Others maintain that the press for cooperation may lead individual teachers to succumb to peer pressure, leading to compliant implementation of ideas with little merit or to robotlike activity that stifles variety.

The influences that shape students' learning, attitudes, and actions are interwoven and cumulative. Productive peer relations among teachers, where they exist, are difficult to disentangle from the many other contributors to the classroom environment and student success. The composition and character of a class, the quality of a teacher's moment-by-moment decision making in the classroom, the latitude for teachers to make curricular and instructional choices, the school's allocation of time and other resources for joint work, and the stability of the general environment all enter into the equation.

We know relatively little about the specific mechanisms by which collegial relations among teachers operate to the benefit of students. Is it that lesson planning improves as people press each other to say not only what they do with students, but why? Is it that the toughest, most persistent problems of curriculum, instruction, and classroom management get the benefit of the group's experience? Is it the combined sense of confidence and obligation that teachers carry into the classroom? Is it the peer pressure to live up to agreements made and ideas offered? Is it that in making teaching principles and practices more public, the best practices are promoted more widely and the weakest ones are abandoned? Is it simply that close work with colleagues affords a kind of stimulation and solidarity that reflects itself in energetic classroom performance and holds talented teachers longer in the profession? Are the rate and quality of classroom innovation higher? Or does the sheer visibility of teachers at work with one another, or closely in touch with one another throughout the day or week, deliver its own message to students?

In the eyes of enthusiasts, the answer lies in some complex and elusive combination of all these possibilities. Each of these and several more possible interpretations are threaded throughout the available literature. They read as plausible explanations for the way collegial influences might operate, but they have not yet been subject to systematic inquiry.

What Do Veteran Teachers Gain from Close Colleagues?

The advantages of collegial work, as experienced teachers describe them, center around one theme: breaking the isolation of the classroom. Over time, teachers who work closely together on matters of curriculum and instruction find themselves better equipped for classroom work. They are frequently and credibly recognized for their professional capabilities and interests. And they take pride in professional relationships that withstand differences in viewpoint and occasional conflict.

Instructional Range, Depth, and Flexibility.   The relationship between teacher collaboration and instructional quality has been examined in a series of studies by Elizabeth Cohen (1981) and her associates at Stanford. In early stages of the work, they found significant correlations between teaming arrangements and teachers' capacity to accommodate new curriculum. Cooperation served teachers well as they worked to understand and apply new ideas, methods, and materials.

In subsequent phases of work, the Stanford group posed this question: Do teaming arrangements in turn expand schools' and teachers' ability to achieve even greater complexity? Questionnaire data from teachers in 16 elementary schools produced mixed results. Members of teams begun in 1973 did not report appreciably greater variation in classroom materials by 1975, leading the research group to doubt whether team structures operate to enrich an instructional or curricular repertoire.

Yet there was some evidence that teaming did enhance reflective decision making in the classroom. In one substudy, Intili (1977) found strong relationships between all her measures of reflective decision making by teachers and their participation in a cooperative group that met often and worked together intensively (see also Cohen, Deal, Meyer, & Scott, 1979; Bredo, 1975).

This is fundamentally a question of what teachers can and do achieve by working together. Is collaborative work productive mainly for responding to shifts in external circumstances? For organizing to understand and apply ideas developed by others, or to regroup when the community population or preferences shift? Or is a team-based organization a resource for development? Preliminary assessments of what a team can accomplish were based on a readily measurable but narrow definition of "greater complexity," that is, variation in instructional materials. The Stanford studies examined how teams accommodated the demands of new curriculum, requiring new methods and materials in the classroom; the very circumstances may thus have acted to limit the volume of instructional variation among the team members, making it appear that the team structure served only to manage existing requirements but did little to foster new alternatives.

Recent studies have enlarged our view of the complex tasks that draw teachers into work together and of the range of benefits that their work may yield. The complexities introduced by a new curriculum create one compelling reason for teachers to work together; an even more complex challenge, it appears, is to examine and refine the existing curriculum and instruction of a group and to select and implement improvements on a continual basis.

In schools where teams have seen it as their obligation to propose new ideas and methods or to continue the development of a curriculum over time, there is persuasive evidence that complex variations in materials, instruction, and classroom-based social organization have developed as a consequence of joint effort (Bird & Little, 1985). In one junior high school, two of the four "core" academic departments worked together closely over five years with the explicit aims of improving students' academic achievement and enriching the learning environment of classrooms. Originally convened by the principal as a study group, the teachers' task was to examine their present practices in light of available classroom research and to develop alternatives consistent with the principles they discovered. Over time they revised their own approach to curriculum development, lesson planning, testing, and student placement. They expanded their instructional repertoire by relying less on whole-group direct instruction and by introducing selective use of cooperative or student team learning.

In the two "active" departments, teachers argued that their collaboration produced an expanded pool of ideas, materials, and methods and a collective ability to generate higher-quality solutions to problems. The evolving coherence and vitality in the curriculum, the rate of instructional innovation, the frequency and depth of discussion about instructional and classroom management issues, and the demonstrated academic, social, and affective gains among the students all far outstripped the two other academic departments in the same school whose members lacked the same shared purposes and engaged in far less collective action. The habits and structures of group work have enabled teachers to attempt innovations in curriculum and instruction that they could not have implemented as individuals, for example, a full-scale field experiment to test curriculum alternatives in social studies.

In sum, the early Stanford studies credited team work with easing the burden of new external demands but left it uncertain that teachers who work together will achieve a level of instructional sophistication that they would not ordinarily reach by working alone. Subsequent in-depth case studies have confirmed the finding that team structure alone is insufficient to advance instructional practice; crucially, however, they have also expanded our view of the potential consequences that may flow from joint action and have underscored the importance of a group's perceived purposes and obligations in shaping its tasks and probable outcomes (Little & Bird, 1984a). The conclusions that one draws from the experiences of closely orchestrated, task-oriented groups in schools are consistent with conclusions drawn from other studies of organization: The accomplishments of a proficient and well-organized group are widely considered to be greater than the accomplishments of isolated individuals (Blau & Scott, 1962).

Influence and Respect.   The more "public" an enterprise teaching becomes, the more it both requires and supports collective scrutiny. Among the most public environments for teaching has been the open-space school, and it is from studies of open-space schools that many of the insights about teacher-to-teacher interaction and influence have been drawn. Meyer and his colleagues at Stanford found that teachers in open-space schools exerted more influence on others and accorded their colleagues more influence on their own teaching than did teachers in conventional settings (Meyer, Cohen, Brunetti, Molnar, & Lueders-Salmon, 1971; Bredo, 1977). Teachers in open-space schools were more likely to believe that their peers' evaluations of them were important and were well founded (Marram, Dornbush, & Scott, 1972).

In open-space schools, teaching is made public by circumstance. Sheer visibility creates a degree of mutual dependence and influence not required by more conventional single-classroom arrangements. But visibility has its limits. Even (or especially) in open environments, teachers inevitably concentrate their attention and energy close at hand, on their own students. Even in open-space environments, something more is needed to convert mere attentiveness to a systematic, reciprocal influence on the conceptions and practices of teaching.

The highest levels of reciprocal influence reported by teachers were reserved for schools in which teachers were both routinely visible to one another (i.e., open-space) and were routinely and intensively involved in teams; in these settings, teachers' knowledge about and reliance upon one another were most essential (Meyer et al., 1971). The greater the opportunities for involvement, (e.g., the more "balanced" the participation in group meetings), the greater the influence felt by the participating individuals and the higher their satisfaction with the team (Molnar, 1971). Summing up these findings, Cohen (1981) observes: "Two very different kinds of team inter-action are taking place in these...schools; one produces many influential teachers and the other produces few" (p. 182).

A combination of visibility (teaching planned for and done in the presence of others), shared responsibility, and widespread interaction heightens the influence of teachers on one another and on the school as a whole. In the 1970s, the open-space movement promoted precisely that combination. In the 1980s, when open-space schools have diminished in popularity, it is a combination harder to find. The developing enthusiasm for peer observation and peer "coaching" provides one surrogate for day-by-day visibility; what peer observation cannot achieve in daily contact it gains in concentration (Showers, 1985).

This is a scenario in which both teachers and principals stand to gain. Joint work offers a form of professional autonomy that is not protection from scrutiny or freedom from external demand but is instead heightened control over work that resides in the group. Based on an investigation of teachers' and principals' influence over decisions relating to pupil management, curriculum, teaching methods, and other aspects of school and classroom life, Johnson (1976) developed a typology of extensive and intensive collaboration. In the schools with the highest levels of extensive collaboration (many people) and intensive collaboration (frequent interaction on key decisions), both principals and teachers felt more influential than either group felt in less interactive settings (see also Barnett, 1982).

Career Rewards and Daily Satisfactions.   Through work with others, teachers shape their perspectives on their daily work and revise or confirm their assessments of their career choices.

Teachers in schools known for high rates of innovation and team work distinguish carefully between end-of-year weariness and career burnout. Some teachers say they require periods of "on-the-job sabbatical" to slow the pace of constant innovation, to consolidate gains, and to ensure that multiple innovations form an integrated whole in the classroom. Their enthusiasm for teaching, however, has been sustained in large part by collective efforts to learn and apply new ideas (Little, 1981; Bird & Little, 1985).

Working together to understand and improve life in the classroom, teachers reduce the "endemic uncertainties" (Lortie, 1975, p. 134) that ordinarily make a teacher's hold on success so tenuous. Instead of grasping for the single dramatic event or the special achievements of a few children as the main source of pride, teachers are more able to detect and celebrate a pattern of accomplishments within and across classrooms.

Virtually no research has been conducted on the long-term effects of teacher collaboration on career commitment or orientation. In an occupational and organizational culture that makes intensive collaboration hard to find, teachers who value shared work may find themselves less rather than more satisfied in teaching, ready to leave rather than stay. In the short run, professional recognition, professional involvement, and professional influence prove to be powerful substitutes for less accessible rewards (see Ashton et al., 1982).

Do Beginning Teachers Benefit from Close Colleagues?

Virtually all teachers in American schools assume full responsibility for student learning and for the independent management of a classroom from their first day on the job. Unlike the more gradual, incremental introduction that newcomers receive to other occupations, entry into teaching has been labeled "abrupt," "unmediated," and "unstaged" (Lortie, 1975; Nemser, 1983). Asked how they have learned to teach, teachers over and over report that they have learned "on my own," "by trial and error," or "it was sink or swim" (Ryan, 1970; Little, 1981; Fuchs, 1969). A prevailing belief that teaching is learned by independent trial and error is reflected in (and sustained by) norms that constrain the interaction between experienced and novice teachers and by the relative scarcity of organizational arrangements for assistance and support by universities, districts, or schools (Doyle & Nespor, 1984).

Critics of this short, survival-oriented induction period argue that it serves neither teachers nor students well. Mutual assistance, they propose, would make new recruits less isolated, more self-confident, more proficient in the classroom—and more inclined to continue in teaching past the first one or two years (Copeland & Jamgochian, 1985). By this view, a first-year teacher might properly be described as a "well-started novice" (Clark, 1984) for whom the subtleties and complexities of masterful teaching are introduced gradually.

A distinction is in order between the social support that puts newcomers at ease and the professional support that advances one's knowledge and practice of teaching. Many beginning teachers are indeed made welcome in their first assignments. Experienced teachers take newcomers "under their wing" and show them around the building, introduce them to faculty members and other staff, show them where to locate books and supplies, and offer to be available for help: "If you need anything, just ask." Other first-year teachers are not so fortunate, of course, and remain as socially isolated as they are professionally unsupported. In neither case, typically, is a beginning teacher's relationship with other teachers systematically directed toward learning to teach (or learning to teach in this school, in this community, and with these students).

Without diminishing the import of moral support and emotional solidarity, the central issue here is one of professional relations that go well beyond the usual "buddy" arrangement. The classroom successes and failures of novice teachers are little affected by the general friendliness of the staff or by broad school philosophy (Veenman, 1984). Less common—and arguably more critical—are professional encounters that bring experienced teachers and beginning teachers close to the class-room together and that plausibly influence the competence and confidence of the beginning teachers.

Organized assistance may permit beginning teachers to achieve a balance between practical fluency and conceptual understanding, between the press to accumulate the "tricks of the trade" (Lortie, 1975, p. 77) and the opportunity for slowly evolving understanding of underlying conceptual principles (Nemser, 1983, p. 161). Recent research provides insight into two possibilities. First, research into the character of the mentor-protégé relationship (Gehrke & Kay, 1984) examines the part that senior colleagues play in offering direct assistance to beginning teachers. Second, research on school-level norms of collegiality (Little, 1982) provides a basis for examining the ways in which schools are organized—or not—as environments for learning to teach.

Traditions of Apprenticeship or Mentoring.   Meaningful mentoring relations between experienced and beginning teachers are the exception· rather than the rule. Such relations are applauded by the few teachers who have experienced them and are widely considered to be a superior but uncommon arrangement for learning to teach.

The admiration that teachers express for the basic concept of mentoring stands in sharp contrast to a fundamental reality in the culture of teaching: Teachers learn to teach not only through experience but through solitary experience. In addition, the available evidence on the dynamics and consequences of mentoring and other organized support is meager and uneven. Reviewing the records of supervised intern-ships, McDonald (1980) was unable to detect any differences in the evaluations received by first-year interns and those received by beginning teachers in more conventional arrangements. McDonald's findings serve to curb unwarranted enthusiasm. Nonetheless, they deserve some closer scrutiny. In reading the program reviews, one is reminded that we have little data on potentially consequential variations in the scale and intensity of assistance. We still know little about the ability of supervisors to assist first-year teachers or to construct evaluations that well represent their development (but see Wilburn & Drummond, 1984). We apply few methods, either in research or practice, that help us to detect evolving approaches to teacher planning and reflectivity. These developments in the way teachers think about and plan for their work with students may not be highly visible in a beginning teacher's behavior, particularly in the first few months of teaching, when the translation of intent into practice is often unpolished. Recent studies centering on the "prideful occasion" in learning to teach (Feiman-Nemser & Buchmann, 1985) or on student teachers' reflective examinations of their unsuccessful lessons (Borko, Lalik, Barksdale, & Yon, 1985) hold promise.

Lortie's analysis of socialization and induction into teaching, published in 1975, still rings true. However, in the dozen or so years since Lortie's landmark work, researchers have chronicled three developments that have prospects for altering professional relationships between the beginning teacher and experienced colleagues.

First, preservice teacher education programs have been examined for the pattern of beliefs, habits, and skills they convey with regard to learning to teach and for their contributions to the socialization of teachers into the beliefs and customs of an occupation (Lacey, 1977; Feiman-Nemser & Floden, 1985). Some institutions have revised entire curricula to tackle the commonly held perception of teacher education students that they have nothing to learn from their formal preparation programs (Book, Byers, & Freeman, 1983). Others have launched programs designed to introduce the perspectives and habits of collegiality by organizing support teams that make prospective teachers mutually responsible for one another's learning (Copeland & Jamgochian, 1985). Still others have acknowledged that encounters between beginning teachers and their assigned supervisors are typically infrequent, unfocused, and uncoordinated (Griffin et al., 1983) and have concentrated on strengthening the quality and frequency of assistance from university and school-based supervisors of student teachers (California State University, 1984) or first-year teachers (Wilburn & Drummond, 1984; Tisher, 1980). Schools that are deliberately and thoughtfully organized to accommodate the interests and requirements of student teachers have been described (Lanier, 1983; Weyand, 1983; Bird & Little, 1985).

Second, improvements in teacher evaluation policies and procedures have increasingly been targeted to the first-year teacher (Darling-Hammond, 1984). Based in part on a progressive apprenticeship model, these district evaluation policies have combined frequent observation with consultation and assistance.

Finally, the expanded professional opportunities and rewards that accrue to exemplary teachers under the terms of various state and local initiatives have routinely been accompanied by new professional obligations. Such initiatives explicitly alter the expected professional relations between experienced teachers and beginning teachers. In a variety of career ladder plans, in the California Mentor Teacher Program, and in other master teacher or teacher adviser programs, experienced and highly regarded senior teachers are asked to assume the obligation for assisting new teachers (Schlechty, 1984; Career Ladder Research Group, 1984; Wagner, 1985; Southern Regional Education Board, 1984).

The expanded professional roles introduced by these initiatives and by other incentives programs constitute a radical departure from historical precedent in the teaching occupation. While master or mentor teacher designations give credit to superior knowledge, skill, and energy, they also fly in the face of longstanding precedents of "noninterference" (Pellegrin, 1976). Experienced teachers ordinarily refrain from intervening in the struggles of novice teachers, while those same novices request assistance with specific problems only when certain that their basic competence is not in question (Newberry, 1977).

In the absence of formal supervisory authority, even the most accomplished teachers are reluctant to assert their own knowledge and experience with fellow teachers. Among the 180 teachers who responded to Gehrke and Kay's (1984) survey on career issues, almost 60% claimed to have had some kind of "mentoring" relationship in learning to teach, but only three teachers named a fellow teacher as a mentor (p. 22).

The precedents of noninterference are powerful, and claims to individual autonomy are closely guarded. Even teachers designated as master teachers, mentors, or advisers are humble about their expertise and uncertain about how to enter into relations that will be both rigorous and respectful (Little, Galagaran, & O'Neal, 1984; Bird, Shulman, St. Clair, & Little, 1984). Teachers who were designated as "assisters" precisely because of their knowledge and skill still "struggled with the 'collegial/expert' dichotomy" in their relations with teachers (Goodman & Lieberman, 1985, p. 8). Yet teachers accustomed to well-supported collaborative work more readily accorded to one another the right to take the lead on issues of curriculum and instruction (Schmuck, Runkel, & Langmeyer, 1971). And in teacher surveys aimed at uncovering teachers' rights of initiative on matters close to the classroom, teachers routinely approved of greater professional assertion by teachers and administrators than they were accustomed to seeing in practice (Bird & Little, 1985).

The conditions, forms, and consequences of mentor-protégé relations in learning to teach deserve closer attention, not only because of the inevitable costs associated with altered induction arrangements but also because the relevant outcomes go well beyond ensuring adequate technical performance in the classroom. The wider set of outcomes includes beginning teachers' sense of personal and institutional efficacy, their capacity to grapple intellectually with crucial substantive problems in education, their inclination to work and learn with colleagues, and their professional commitment to teaching as a career.

Learning to Teach in a "Collegial School."   As environments for learning to teach, highly "collegial" schools offer an alternative to the "sink or swim" image of learning to teach. Nonetheless, "collegial" schools do not necessarily make hospitable settings for novice teachers. Schools that are well organized to foster (and benefit from) the continued development of experienced, pedagogically sophisticated teachers are not necessarily well organized to assist beginning teachers. While the two environments are not mutually exclusive, neither are they identical.

A faculty accustomed to team work may nonetheless prove ill equipped to receive novice teachers. Established collegial teams have a standard of productivity, a fast pace, a shared language, and an accumulated knowledge base that may prove hard for beginning teachers to assimilate. A student teacher placed in one highly teamed school was impressed by the "constant exchange of ideas and careful planning for the team's mix of students" but was "ambivalent about the pressure she feels when the whole team is working together on a unit" (Lipsitz, 1983, pp. 150–151). Teachers working together to improve their work provide a good model of professional relations but create a demanding situation for first- and second-year teachers.

Newcomers to a highly coordinated faculty may unwittingly jeopardize the agreements and achievements of a group. In one recent study, experienced middle-school teachers acted in concert on hard-won agreements about curriculum instruction and classroom management but found their agreements difficult to maintain when the rights of eight student teachers to "experiment" outweighed the rights of the experienced group to state expectations and preferences (Little & Bird, 1984b).

Still, schools with habits of collaboration appear well equipped to adapt quickly and systematically to assist beginning teachers. In the study just described, the experienced teachers, accustomed to group problem solving, met to share their impressions of the student teaching program. The meeting uncovered the frustrations of individuals but also revealed commonalities of circumstance and purpose among the master teachers; it ended with an agreement to "get organized" with respect to student teaching. Within the first eight weeks of school in the fall, seven master teachers met twice on their own and twice with a university supervisor to arrive at a policy to govern student teaching in the building.

I have concentrated on the significance of collegial support for novice teachers. But veteran teachers also periodically find themselves in unfamiliar and challenging situations that test the limits of their knowledge and experience. The special advantages (and special difficulties) of the mentor-protégé relation and the well-established collegial group are no less significant to experienced teachers who, after several years in the classroom, must now tackle new subjects, new grade levels, or new instructional methods. Finally, overt guidance (mentoring) and involvement in a support group have been described as crucially important features of programs that prepare skilled teachers to adopt leadership roles in teaching (Kent, 1985; Goodman & Lieberman, 1985).

Benefits to the School

Increasingly, schools must bolster public faith and enlist public support by showing that they are capable of meeting complex demands with an ever more diverse student population. Yet the twin requirements that schools show steady improvement and that teachers "be professional" cannot plausibly be satisfied by the individual efforts of even the most capable, energetic, and dedicated teachers.

One feature of steadily improving schools is that they are organized to influence teaching (Bird & Little, 1986). Teaching in such schools is a public enterprise. The broad values that guide daily decisions, expectations for student learning, ideas about how children learn and what we as a society wish them to learn, the planning and conduct of instruction, recurrent dilemmas in fostering student motivation and judging student progress, the principles for organizing life in classrooms—all receive the collective attention, scrutiny, insight, and refinement of peers acting as colleagues.

Schools stand to benefit in three ways from promoting closer collegial ties among teachers. Schools benefit first by simply orchestrating the daily work of teaching across classrooms. Teachers, students, and parents all gain confidence in their knowledge of what is taught throughout the program and why. Teachers are better prepared to support one another's strengths and to accommodate weaknesses.

Second, schools that promote teacher-to-teacher work tend to be organized to examine and test new ideas, methods, and materials. They are adaptable and self-reliant in the face of new demands; they have the necessary organization to attempt school or classroom innovations that would exhaust the energy, skill, or resources of an individual teacher.

Finally, schools that foster collegiality are plausibly organized to ease the strain of staff turnover, both by providing systematic assistance to beginning teachers and by explicitly socializing all newcomers to staff values, traditions, and resources (Little, 1985).

Colleagues and the Teaching Profession

Members of a profession are colleagues not merely in name but also with regard to the core ideas, principles, and practices of their work (Etzioni, 1969; Marram et al., 1972). Judged by this standard of strong peer relations, teaching is at a disadvantage. Teachers have prided themselves on their individual accomplishments; the "culture of teaching" is grounded in values of independence (Feiman-Nemser & Floden, 1985).

Strong peer relations are not a treasured part of an occupational culture. Nor does a set of core ideas and practices form a body of disciplined knowledge upon which daily action and judgment rest (Schlechty, 1985). Unlike medicine, in which daily uncertainties and ambiguities are eased by an accepted body of practice (Fox, 1957), teaching celebrates no body of accepted pedagogical practice.

Even now, the terrain that is usefully mapped by research on teaching is small. Teachers' practical knowledge has been disparaged as idiosyncratic and atheoretical ("a matter of style"), treated as having little value as a basis for collective scrutiny or action (Buchmann, 1983; Feiman-Nemser & Floden, 1985). Relations among teachers, either in or out of school, have not been organized "to promote inquiry or to add to the intellectual capital of the profession" (Lortie, 1975, p. 56).

Responsibility for accumulating, evaluating, and disseminating knowledge about teaching and learning has not been vested in teachers. Teachers have few mechanisms for adding to the knowledge base in teaching and leave no legacy of insights, methods, and materials at the close of a long career (Little, 1985). The knowledge base in teaching, such as it is, receives neither the close attention nor the loyalty of those who teach or those who are preparing to teach (Lanier & Little, 1986; Book et al., 1983; Feiman-Nemser & Floden, 1986).

Recent analyses suggest that the traditional attractions to teaching have diminished, confronting prospective teachers with "uncertain rewards in a careerless profession" (Sykes, 1983b, p. 110; see also Sykes & Devaney, 1984; Lortie, 1975). Neither the opportunity for more shared work with fellow teachers nor expanded career advancement possibilities will substitute for public esteem, adequate salaries, and satisfactions in the classroom. Yet we would make too little of the drawing power and holding power of strong collegial ties if we failed to take account of the way teachers themselves speak of their most productive work relations.

In the past, neither obligations held in common nor achievements rewarded in common have bound teachers as a group. The alliances forged by the union movement have concentrated on protecting teachers against abuses in personnel practice.

The obligation that teachers owe to one another has yet to encompass matters of professional practice on any large scale. What is absent from current research findings is perhaps as telling as what is present: No one is evaluated, either positively or negatively, on the basis of contributions they have made to the knowledge base of the profession or to the teaching proficiency of others.

Recent state initiatives to expand professional opportunities and rewards in teaching (e.g., Wagner, 1985) suggest that a tightened set of collegial ties and a heightened set of collegial controls may be in the offing. These developments, both political and professional, have prospects for altering relations among colleagues in major ways.

Career ladder and other incentive plans have highlighted teachers' demonstrated expertise as a basis for introducing status differences into a traditionally egalitarian profession (Bird, 1985). Under the terms of such plans, experienced senior colleagues acquire both the obligation and the opportunity to assert leadership in the improvement of teaching. Whatever efforts may be made to soften the implications (e.g., by labeling master and mentor teacher positions as "more work for more pay"), the basic assumptions seem inescapable (Bird et al., 1984).

In addition, the rapid developments in classroom-based research since the mid-1970s, combined with an economic and political climate that presses schools to demonstrate "excellence," have drawn the attention of policymakers to the essential competence of teachers. Debates over the "knowledge base in teaching" are no longer academic.

WHAT TEACHERS DO AS COLLEAGUES

Like most broad images, collegiality shows its peculiar architecture only close up. In some schools, collegiality among teachers is an inescapable fact of life and work (Little, 1982). In those schools, certain critical practices are clearly in evidence.

Talk about Teaching

Colleagues talk to one another about teaching often, at a level of detail that makes their exchange both theoretically rich and practically meaningful. While teaching is not the only topic of their conversation, it is a prominent one. No visiting stranger—or new teacher—would have to search long to uncover it. Discussions are heard in the faculty lounge, in hallways, standing in the office, in workrooms, in unused classrooms. The teachers' lounge is not reserved for "letting off steam" or for "jousting and griping" (Lieberman & Miller, 1979, p. 61; see also Woods, 1984; Hammersley, 1984).

Colleagues' efforts to speak clearly, fully, and concretely about their work help to take the mystery out of teaching without diminishing its essential artistry. This helps to make clear the understandings that teachers hold about connections between their actions and student learning (Bussis, Chittenden, & Amarel, 1976). It illuminates underlying principles and ideas in a way that allows teachers to understand and accommodate one another, to assist one another, and sometimes to challenge one another.

Productive talk about teaching is not mere shop talk. The standard of productive talk is not satisfied by casual "war stories" or "experience swapping" (Rosenholtz &

Kyle, 1984). It requires familiarity with and high regard for principles and conclusions derived not only from immediate classroom experience (Hargreaves, 1984)
but also from the thinking, experience, and observations of others (Weyand, 1983).

Shared Planning and Preparation

Together, colleagues plan, prepare, and evaluate the topics, methods, and materials of
teaching. Working in concert, they reduce their individual planning time while
increasing their pool of ideas and materials. In grade-level or subject-area groups, or
in interdisciplinary teams, they arrive at agreements about curriculum emphasis, pace,
and sequence. They work together to design and prepare the content of teaching:
course outlines, unit objectives, tests, and other materials. They meet to evaluate the
progress of students and to decide or recommend student placements. They take joint
responsibility for a group of students, though instances of actual joint teaching are
less common (Cohen, 1981). In all these ways, they build program coherence, expand
individual resources, and reduce individual burdens for planning and preparation (see
also Barnes & Dow, 1982).

Examples of shared planning and preparation are frequent and varied at the
elementary and junior high or middle-school levels (Little, 1982; Little & Bird,
1984a; Lipsitz, 1983) but are less evident in high school. In a fruitless search for staff
networks in two large midwestern high schools, Cusick (1980) encountered a well-
established pattern of individual entrepreneurship among teachers. Competition over
student enrollments and a premium on securing students' attendance and cooperation
led to a proliferation of electives that gave teachers little to discuss (or plan) with one
another. (Indeed, the rewards attached to individual entrepreneurialism made more
for competition than cooperation among teachers.) Teachers' involvement in student
sports or other activities cut into time for shared work with other teachers, and a host
of out-of-school commitments further eroded teachers' opportunities and interests in
collegial pursuits. While examples of shared work are not unknown at the high school
level (Bird & Little, 1985), and individual departments or small groups may prove
highly cohesive (Ball & Lacey, 1984), schoolwide patterns of collegiality are far more
prevalent at the elementary and middle levels.

Classroom Observation

The presence of observers in classrooms is a common event in schools that promote
collegial work. Administrators in these schools devote the time and study necessary to
make their own observations fruitful (Little & Bird, 1984a) and free up observation
time for teachers working together on improvement projects of their own (Weyand,
1983). Increasingly, classroom observation has developed as a professional development resource for teachers at work with teachers; descriptions of peer observation,
peer coaching, and targeted videotaping now appear in both the research and practitioner literature (Showers, 1985).

We can distinguish between sheer "visibility," as a fact of life in some schools,
and systematic observation, as an organized practice of administration or professional
development. By teaching within sight and sound of one another, as in open-space
plans, teachers are made attentive to the judgments and preferences of their peers
(Meyer et al., 1971). By engaging in systematic observation, teachers explore central

issues in student learning and consider teaching practices and their improvement (Bird & Little, 1985).

For both administrators and teachers, the requisite incentives, skills, habits, and opportunities associated with good observation appear hard to come by. One recent study prompted this description:

> In one of five schools, classroom observation is so frequent, so intellectually lively and intense, so thoroughly integrated into the daily work and so associated with accomplishments for all who participate, that it is difficult to see how the practices could fail to improve teaching. In still another school, the observation practices approach this standard. In three of the five schools, however, the observation of classroom life is so cursory, so infrequent, so shapeless and tentative that if it were found to affect instruction favorably we would be hard-pressed to construct a plausible explanation. (Little & Bird, 1984a, p. 12)

Training Together and Training One Another

Colleagues teach one another about new ideas and new classroom practices, abandoning a perspective that teaching is "just a matter of style" in favor of a perspective that favors continuous scrutiny of practices and their consequences. Without turning creative individuals into robots who all teach precisely the same way, teachers view the practices of teaching as professional practices, open to scrutiny, discussion, and refinement. Formal occasions of in-service training are organized so that teachers can train together and train one another, with opportunity for follow-up in classrooms. Informal study groups provide an opportunity for teachers and administrators to "get smarter together" and to develop small-scale experiments in curriculum, instruction, and classroom management (Weyand, 1983).

A record of classroom success earns teachers in collegial schools the right (or even the obligation) to teach others, either informally through a peer-coaching arrangement or formally in in-service workshops (Bird & Little, 1985). (Talented teachers in less collegial settings are made acutely uncomfortable at the prospect of teaching their peers; described by admirers as "prophets without honor in their own land," such teachers confine their energies to their own classrooms or conduct in-service workshops in far-flung schools or districts.)

Each of these practices and perspectives brings teachers close to one another's work with students. Together, such views and habits have been summed up as norms of collegiality and continuous improvement (Little, 1982). They make up a pattern of joint action that relies in part on face-to-face teamwork and in part on other forms of coordination and mutual accommodation.

A lot of what passes for collegiality does not add up to much. When teachers meet only occasionally on questions of logistics, broad curriculum outlines, or school-level matters, they are unlikely to engage in close mutual examination of how they think about teaching, plan for teaching, or handle teaching demands in the classroom. Closer to the classroom is also closer to the bone—closer to the day-by-day performances on which personal esteem and professional standing rest. The prospects for conflict are high (Martin, 1975; Metz, 1984).

The closer one gets to the classroom and to central questions of curriculum and instruction, the fewer are the recorded instances of meaningful, rigorous collaboration. In case narratives of exemplary middle schools, for which interdisciplinary teaming is a central philosophical tenet, Lipsitz (1983) describes closely integrated team work in only one of four schools. In that school, teachers hammer out agreements about curriculum emphasis and instructional approach and develop materials jointly. So crucial is teaming to the daily work that team members rarely miss a day's work and have been known to give "calamity day" awards to individuals who were not devoting a full measure of time, thought, and energy to the group effort. In the remaining three schools, however, teams met infrequently, and team decisions had less immediate bearing on teachers' classroom decisions.

SUPPORTING TEACHERS AS COLLEAGUES

The key practices of colleagues are most likely to make a difference where they are a patterned, integral, inescapable part of day-to-day work.

How Common Is Collegial Work?

Overall, collegiality is rare. Most teachers can point to a treasured colleague, but few work in schools where cooperative work is a condition of employment. Many teachers are satisfied with their peer relationships, but few claim that those relationships make their way into the classroom. Many schools offer congenial work environments, but few offer a professional environment that makes the school "as educative for teachers as for students" (Shulman, 1983).

Pellegrin (1976) describes an effort to uncover the extent of perceived interdependence among teachers. Teachers were asked to create two lists. On the first, they were to name persons other than students on whom they depended most heavily to perform their job effectively. On the second, they were to name any person whose job was so closely related to their own that the two jobs must be performed collaboratively in order for each to be effective. The first set was termed "dependence relationships," and it was small (a mean of 4); the second set was labeled "essential relationships," and it was smaller still (a range from 0 to 2.5, with a mean of 1.). Pellegrin elaborates:

> These data show that the types of relationships specified by teachers consist primarily of those that deal with the provision of resources (facilities and materials), psychological and social support, advice, and exchange of ideas. It is quite rare for *task* interdependencies to be mentioned. (p. 368, emphasis in original)

Characterizing schools as places with "a division of labor low in interdependence" (p. 353), Pellegrin emphasizes that teachers rarely interact with one another to complete the main obligations of their work. Similarly, only one-quarter of the teachers surveyed by Lortie (1975, p. 193) reported having frequent contact with other teachers for purposes of jointly planning classes, reviewing student work, or sharing responsibility for classes. Lortie concludes that task-oriented cooperation among teachers is likely to be "permissive rather than mandatory" (p. 194; see also Cohen, 1981). Special programs (such as federally funded categorical programs) have been credited with promoting or requiring close cooperation among teachers (e.g.,

McLaughlin & Marsh, 1979), but most alliances among teachers appear to be informal, voluntary, and distant from the real work in and of the classroom.

How Stable Is Collegiality in Schools?

Collegial relations and structures have proved relatively fragile (Cohen, 1976; Cohen et al., 1979). A shift in building leadership can alter the governing values and priorities, the opportunities created in a master schedule, and the incentives and rewards associated with collaborative work. Relationships, habits, and structures that have taken years to build may unravel in a matter of weeks (Little & Bird, 1984b; Little & Long, 1985).

A fairly constant refrain in the literature and in the field is that cooperative work among teachers is scarce, fruitless, or hard to maintain. Organized work groups come and go, or their membership changes drastically over time. When one team of researchers returned after two years to schools in which more than half the faculty had been actively involved in school-level curriculum implementation teams, they found less than 15% still participating (Cohen, 1976, p. 59).

Although the term *collegiality* may at first bring to mind face-to-face interaction among teachers, concentration on formally organized teams may have led researchers to overestimate (or wrongly conceive) the problem of instability. An example serves to illustrate. Eight middle-school teachers were intent on making the annual influx of student teachers a more productive experience. They formed a group, confirmed a group leader, and met four times early in the school year to arrive at a policy to govern the involvement of university supervisors, student teachers, and school-based master teachers. When they had completed their work, they ceased meeting, having agreed that each would use the policy to govern his or her own work in the student teaching program. Judged strictly by a set of measures limited to visible face-to-face teaming, the group might have appeared "unstable" when it ceased to gather regularly after four meetings. In fact, the group was better organized at the end than at the beginning to achieve its teacher training goals and to preserve the integrity of valued approaches to curriculum and instruction (Little & Bird, 1984b, p. 13).

The problem of stability can be pursued as a problem of sustaining a pattern of cooperative work among a "reciprocally interdependent staff" (Cohen, 1981, p. 188). The central question about collegiality thus becomes, "Under what conditions would we expect to find relations among teachers that were rigorous enough and durable enough to have any demonstrable effect on conceptions and practices of teaching?" (Little & Bird, 1984b, p. 8). Two fundamental conditions appear crucial to joint action among teachers: interdependence and opportunity. Shifts in either condition may produce a fluctuation in visible group effort ("instability").

Interdependence.   Teachers are interdependent when they must depend on one another, regardless of personal preference. Interdependence is not chosen but is imposed by circumstance. It is one thing for teachers to depend on each other to observe the bell schedule. It is quite another for them to depend on each other for information about good teaching practices or for lesson plans designed according to shared pedagogical principles. To be relevant to their joint action, interdependence must be perceived or felt in some way by teachers. The perspective taken here is consistent with Pellegrin's (1976) orientation to essential relationships but differs from the stance taken in some of the early teaming studies, in which the term *interdependence* is used interchangeably with *interaction, cooperation,* or *co-presence* (Bredo, 1977; Cohen, 1981).

Opportunity.   Joint action cannot occur where it is impossible or prohibitively costly in organizational, political, or personal terms. Bureaucratic conditions such as schedules, staff assignments, and access to resources may or may not be conducive to shared work among teachers. Cultural conditions, including beliefs and norms of interaction among teachers, may permit, support, or discourage close collaboration.

Interdependence and opportunity have no necessary relation. Persons can understand fully that they are dependent on one another in some crucial ways that affect their respective reputations and fortunes but still have no opportunity to work together for mutual benefit. Persons may have substantial opportunity for work together but be at a loss to understand why it is important that they should or what would be sacrificed if they did not.

How Are Collegial Relations Supported in Schools?

Unlike many of the skills described elsewhere in this book, the habits and skills of colleagueship cannot be mastered alone. Further, they are not readily introduced by the initiative of a single teacher, however skillful and well intentioned. This may seem a painfully obvious point, but it is meant to underscore the organizational as well as professional character of collegiality.

Six dimensions of support are prominent in the literature: (1) symbolic endorsements and rewards that place value on cooperative work and make the sources of interdependence clear; (2) school-level organization of staff assignments and leadership; (3) latitude for influence on crucial matters of curriculum and instruction; (4) time; (5) training and assistance; and (6) material support.

Public Endorsements and Institutional Policy.   Principals and others in positions of influence promote collegiality by declaring that they value team efforts and by describing in some detail what they think that means. A teacher leader in one school emphasizes, "It's important to *say the words,*" while a teacher in another school laments, "They may believe it's important, and I agree, but that's never been communicated" (Little & Long, 1985). Among Lipsitz's (1983) successful middle schools, the most heavily teamed school was one in which the principal and team leaders conveyed their own faith in the power of interdisciplinary teams to make the school better for students. In schools where teaming came lower on a principal's list of priorities, cooperative efforts were less frequent, less focused on fundamental questions of curriculum and classroom instruction, and less binding on the decisions of individual teachers in classrooms.

High levels of joint action are more likely to persist where there is a "policy" in favor of teaming, in which the reasons for interdependence are articulated by both district-level and school-level leaders, and opportunity is afforded by the routine organization of staff assignments, time, and other resources (Cohen, 1981). In a study of administrators' influence on teachers' collegiality and innovation, Bird and Little (1985) confirmed earlier speculation that school-level support for teaming required a combination of public endorsements, material and technical support, opportunity, and reward. Districts promote teaming (or not) in part through the policies and procedures they employ for selecting, placing, and evaluating principals (Little & Long, 1985). Together, districts and schools where shared work prevails have a policy of teamed work explicitly tied to improvement goals. Working together is "the way we do things here."

School Organization and Teacher Leadership. Cooperative work among teachers, as a matter of organizational principle or institutional priority, is the exception rather than the rule in American schools. One might be led to ask, "What have the environment and norms of schools to do with teachers' performance as...colleagues and leaders in the advancement of teaching?" (Bird & Little, 1985b, p. 13).

School-level reorganization into teams has been found to increase interaction, collegial influence, and reciprocal influence (Cohen, 1981). In one of four middle schools portayed by Lipsitz (1983), each of eight academic teams is responsible (as a team) for the learning experiences of approximately 150 students. Each team has relative autonomy with respect to scheduling, grouping assignments, staff assignments, and the development of curriculum units or instructional approaches. With the encouragement of the principal, and led by assigned team leaders, these academic teams take full advantage of organizational resources. They use their common planning times to arrive at agreements about curriculum, instruction, and the organization of students. In this case, the *opportunity* to work together afforded by the schedule and by the staff organization is matched by teachers' felt *obligation* to work together on behalf of students.

Team-based staff organization goes a long way toward permitting cooperative work but does not guarantee it. In yet other middle schools studied by Lipsitz, for example, teachers assigned to the same teams or "houses" met only in a perfunctory manner to resolve routine matters of scheduling or student placement and had little to do with each other on issues that strike close to the heart of daily classroom experience. Even in the one highly teamed school, commitment to the team ethos is uneven. In contrast to the eight academic teams, the unified arts team in the same building has neither a small community of students to call its own (student loyalties are to academic teams), nor a compelling interest in producing a coordinated curriculum, nor daily common planning periods in which to develop any version of a combined program. The experience of teaming has been far less rewarding (and rewarded) for the unified arts teachers than for teachers on the academic teams.

One aspect of a team work policy appears to be a form of organization in which leadership is broadly distributed among both administrators and teachers, who in turn provide groups with direction, continuity, and support. In schools where teaming has been well established, a common pattern has been to invest team leaders, department heads, grade-level chairs, or resource teachers with special authority for organizing and leading work on curriculum and instruction (Lipsitz, 1983, Little & Bird, 1984b). The main contribution of the principals in team-oriented middle schools has been "to make the school larger than one person" (Lipsitz, 1983, p. 284).

Although the assignment of teachers to formal leadership positions is a departure from established precedent in the teaching profession, it is an accepted tradition in some schools. Lipsitz describes a group of team leaders who, with reduced teaching loads, are responsible for leading curriculum development and other improvement-related work in an exemplary middle school; they receive no more pay than their colleagues, but receive reduced teaching loads and other perks of status, such as dinner with out-of-town visitors at a good restaurant (Lipsitz, 1983). A study of leadership in junior and senior high schools provides still other examples (Bird & Little, 1985). Informal teacher leaders in a junior high school receive no more money than their colleagues but "settle for fame." Increasingly, they are called on to conduct in-service training in their own and other schools and to consult with administrators, policymakers, and researchers. In a senior high school, the role of department head has been moved steadily away from book ordering and other paperwork toward responsibilities for curriculum development, program evaluation, and consultation with teachers.

Establishing effective team leadership and cultivating reciprocity and respect among team members turn out to be complex tasks in their own right. Most school-based teams, unlike work groups in industry, tend to be equal-status groups in which leadership roles are rarely assigned and in which professional deference is simply assumed ("you just have to be a decent person"). The equal-status assumption is compelling. Even when principals speak of team leaders, teachers may deny their existence (Cohen, 1981) or their effectiveness (Arikado, 1976). Other studies have demonstrated that there are almost no mechanisms by which teachers can emerge as leaders for purposes of leading work on teaching, even when they have been acknowledged as exemplary classroom teachers (Bird, 1985).

Latitude for Influence. Teachers' investment in team planning appears to rest heavily on the latitude they have to make decisions in crucial areas of curriculum, materials selection, student assignments, instructional grouping, classroom activity, and the assessment of student progress. One junior high school principal supported curriculum projects and study groups on instructional research as the vehicles for building teachers' involvement with one another and their collective attention to program improvement (Weyand, 1983). In another school fiercely committed to a team structure, the principal negotiated with district curriculum supervisors to win his teachers the right to design and use their own curriculum units (Lipsitz, 1983).

Work together requires some topic of compelling importance to work on. (Teaming for the sake of teaming is predictably short-lived.) Teams are more likely to form when the work at hand is complex enough to make two (or six) heads better than one and to make it probable that the reflected glory of the team will outshine success that each member could expect from working alone. According to Cohen (1981), complex tasks generate uncertainty, for which lateral relations between teachers serve as a source of problem solving, information processing, and coordination.

Forces outside the school curtail teachers' latitude and incentive to act. Some are the legacy of a "feminized" occupational culture in which teachers (mostly women) nurture the young and administrators (mostly men) tend to issues of policy, program, and management (Feiman-Nemser & Floden, 1985; Boston Women's Teachers' Group, 1983).

Other forces reflect the battle currently being waged over the control of teaching and teachers. As states specify curriculum standards and as districts move toward uniform curriculum content, teachers have less apparent room to explore curriculum alternatives. The proliferation of classroom-based research has spawned efforts to create ever more prescriptive, technically precise requirements for effective teaching, eroding still further teachers' latitude or obligation to exercise professional judgment or to articulate professional values. As a decade of research on effective teaching and effective schools makes its way to state legislatures and local school boards, research discoveries are converted to evaluation criteria and competency standards. In the view of Sara Freedman and her colleagues, this increasingly prescriptive stance echoes the nineteenth century, when, ironically, "the highly prescriptive nature of teaching—in which neither teacher nor student could deviate from a set norm—exonerated both of them from responsibility for upgrading the education of pupils" (Boston Women's Teachers' Group, 1983, p. 277). In some states, simultaneous efforts to expand teacher incentive plans and to control the quality of instruction and curriculum are in considerable tension.

Such forces operate in many respects from a distance. They are necessarily mediated by the day-to-day forces that operate closer to the school and the classroom, but they cannot be ignored.

Time and the Master Schedule.   Common planning periods, regularly scheduled team or subject-area meetings, and the judicious use of release time all support cooperative work among teachers (Weyand, 1983; Little & Bird, 1984b).

The opportunities for collaborative work among teachers are enhanced or eroded by the school's master schedule. The master schedule determines whether any two teachers who have students, subjects, or other interests in common will have time together during the school day. The master schedule makes room, or not, for all teachers to be available for a block of time each day or each week. The master schedule gives reason, or not, for teachers to work together on a program for a group of students taught in common.

Differences in scale are crucial. "Morning meetings," made possible by an all-school early-morning planning period, allow teachers to work on problems of curriculum and instruction with the persistence and regularity needed to achieve continuity and depth or to resolve disagreements. Monthly or quarterly meetings, say teachers, cannot have the same effect.

Training and Assistance.   To forge a group that lasts through time (and through tough times) and that creates achievements worth celebrating is no small challenge. Most teachers can imagine an "ideal" team; many have been part of at least one group that has taken pride in its accomplishments. Most can also tell tales of teams gone awry, situations in which they have given more than they have received or have been bored, frustrated, confused, overburdened, insulted, or insulting.

Cooperative work places unfamiliar and pressing demands on teachers. In an environment where teachers work mostly with students, mostly out of sight and sound of others, cooperative work among adults is often less polished and practiced. In a profession in which the norm of not interfering with another teacher's views or practices is powerful, serious and sustained collaboration with regard to curriculum and instruction represents a radical departure.

Teacher work groups succeed in part by mastering specific skills and by developing explicit agreements to govern their work together. One observer of team work comments, "Team meetings have been observed where no one has helped team members with such simple techniques for saving time as using an agenda" (Cohen, 1976, p. 61). Task-related training and assistance bolster the confidence that teachers have in one another for work outside the classroom, as in long-term planning, curriculum development, or peer observation. Assistance in effective group process and group leadership has helped teachers master the routines of scheduling regular meetings, using an agenda, prioritizing issues, facilitating discussion, and reaching closure on decisions and tasks. The ability to distinguish issues that deserve group attention from those that can be handled by a team leader or can be left to individual prerogative can keep a group from becoming bogged down in an "overreliance on consensus" (Cohen, 1981, p. 186). Participants in groups with clear internal policies regarding participation have consistently been more satisfied with their work together (Bredo, 1977).

Even in less formal collaborations, specific skills and perspectives of working with a colleague are critical. In effect, teachers count on their collective ability to do good work on the problems of teaching without doing damage to one another as teachers. They sum up their accomplishments as "trust."

Recent portraits of collegial relations among teachers have shed some light on the mysteries of trust (Little et al., 1984). Lacking the intimacy that confirms trust among family members or long-time friends, team members must rely on other evidence that they do not intend harm to one another. They create trust as the consequence, not the precondition, of close interaction by displaying professional reciprocity clearly and concretely in each small exchange.

Among the guarantors of reciprocity are (1) *shared language* for describing and analyzing the problems of curriculum and instruction; (2) *predictability* in group dealings, including rules for group process and especially for airing and resolving disagreements; (3) talk that concentrates on *practices and their consequences* rather than people and their competence; and (4) *sharing equally in the obligations* to work hard, to credit one another's contributions, and to risk looking ignorant, clumsy, or foolish.

Material Support. The quality and availability of reference texts and other materials, adequate copying equipment, consultants on selected problems, and other forms of material and human support appear to be crucial—but often under-estimated—contributors to teachers' ability and willingness to work successfully together. In one recent study (Bird & Little, 1985), teachers in one junior high school and one high school regarded themselves as well supported (as entire faculties) in part because they had large, multicapability copying machines staffed by aides. In these schools, teachers had both time and inclination to plan together. In two other high schools, where 100 teachers competed for time at two small and fragile copiers, entire planning periods were spent standing in line; time and inclination for group work were in short supply.

At its strongest—most durable, most rigorously connected to problems of student learning, most commanding of teachers' energies, talents, and loyalties—cooperative work is a matter of school policy. Team efforts receive public endorsements and accolades; are supported by time, space, materials, and staff assignments; and are demonstrably tied to the school's ability to educate the young. Teachers tackle tasks of adequate complexity to require and reward individuals' participation. Team leadership is adequate to ensure continuity, direction, and full participation.

Together, these aspects of policy and support may lend stability and continuity to joint action among teachers, equipping them to orchestrate the daily work of teaching, to get better at their work over time, and to provide adequate support to inexperienced teachers.

CONCLUSION

Serious collaboration, by which teachers engage in the rigorous mutual examination of teaching and learning, turns out to be rare. Teachers create realistic, insightful chronicles of the difficulties they encounter. Collaborative efforts run counter to historical precedent, tending to be unstable, short-lived, and secondary to other priorities. Compromises in substance are made to preserve camaraderie (or camaraderie alone is mistaken for sturdier stuff). As teachers probe issues close to the classroom, they generate heat as well as light. An emphasis on cooperation may place a premium on coherence and uniformity at the expense of individual inventiveness and independent initiative. Cooperation on any meaningful scale will almost certainly require rethinking the present organization of human and material resources.

Yet the enthusiasms expressed by teachers about their collaborations are persuasive. When schools are organized to promote joint action, the advantages of collegial work groups are varied and substantial. Teachers' work as colleagues promises greater coherence and integration to the daily work of teaching. It equips individuals, groups, and institutions for steady improvement. And it helps to organize the schools as an environment for learning to teach.

The professional relations that we might legitimately describe as collegial are neither mysterious nor subtle. Colleagues stand out. They can be seen and heard. The value placed on joint action is heard in the talk among teachers who pursue questions or joint projects even in odd moments during a crowded day. It is evident when teachers invite observation, seek opportunities to watch others at work, or coach one another to master specific new classroom approaches. It is evident when teachers organize to "get smarter together." Colleagues can be found before and after school, with materials spread out on a table and discussion in full swing; individuals argue some preferences fiercely and put aside others, with the intent of arriving at agreements they can live with. Finally, colleagues make themselves felt by organizing to make the study of teaching and the work of teaching public, to learn from and with one another.

The institutional supports for collegiality, where they exist, are, like the practices themselves, neither subtle nor mysterious. Humans are remarkably sturdy and stubborn characters. No one can make anyone do much of anything, whether it's to teach well or to work well with others. Both, at bottom, are labors of love and skill. Neither can be coerced, but both can be supported. Faculties who work together are by nature no more generous in spirit, quick in mind, lively in humor, or inventive in action than faculties in other schools, but by habit and interaction, they come to appear so.

For teachers to work often and fruitfully as colleagues requires action on all fronts. The *value* that is placed on shared work must be both said and shown. The *opportunity* for shared work and shared study must be prominent in the schedule for the day, the week, and the year. The *purpose* for work together must be compelling and the task sufficiently challenging. The *material resources and human assistance* must be adequate. And the *accomplishments* of individuals and groups must be recognized and celebrated.

The press toward steady improvement of schools, teaching, and teacher education lends urgency to the continuing study of professional relations among teachers as colleagues. Research since the mid-1970s has come close to the internal lives of classrooms and schools, with substantial gain. Foremost in the gains we can expect in the 1980s and 1990s will be new understandings of how, and with what effect, schools promote leadership in teaching by teachers.

FURTHER READING

Bird, T., and Little, J. W. (1986). "How Schools Organize the Teaching Occupation." *Elementary School Journal, 86*(4), 495–511. Argues that the issue of teacher collegiality is more properly (and broadly) an issue of the way schools are organized for steady improvement. This piece, first prepared for the California Commission on the Teaching Profession, ends with proposals for policy and program initiatives.

Cohen, E. (1981). "Sociology Looks at Team Teaching." *Research in Sociology of Education and Socialization, 2*, 163–193. Presents a cogent overview of the main discoveries about organized teacher teamwork that were generated by Stanford University researchers during the 1970s. Prospects for and limitations of organized teacher work groups are discussed.

Lortie, D. (1975). *Schoolteacher: A Sociological Study*. Chicago: University of Chicago Press. This classic analysis of the teaching occupation remains fundamentally accurate more than a decade after its publication. Chapters on teacher preparation and induction, daily work, and career rewards convey some of the costs of isolation in teaching and some of the conditions that perpetuate teacher isolation generation to generation.

Pellegrin, R. J. (1976). "Schools as Work Settings." In R. Dubin (Ed.), *Handbook of Work, Organizations, and Society*. Skokie, IL: Rand McNally. Based on studies of teaming conducted at the University of Oregon, this article contributes an important and useful formulation of interdependence among colleagues.

REFERENCES

Arikado, M. S. (1976). Status congruence as it relates to team teacher satisfaction. *Journal of Educational Administration, 14*, 70–78.

Ashton, P., Webb, R., & Doda, N. (1982). *A study of teachers' sense of efficacy* (Final Report to the National Institute of Education No. 400-79-0075). Gainesville: University of Florida, College of Education.

Ball, S. J., & Lacey, C. (1984). Subject disciplines as the opportunity for group action: A measured critique of subject sub-cultures. In A. Hargreaves & P. Woods (Eds.), *Classrooms and staffrooms: The sociology of teachers and teaching*. Milton Keynes, England: Open University Press.

Barnes, R., & Dow, G. (1982). Looking at topic-centred teaching. In G. Dow (Ed.), *Teacher learning*. London: Routledge & Kegan Paul.

Barnett, B. (1982, March). *Subordinate teacher power and influence in schools*. Paper presented at the annual meeting of the American Educational Research Association, New York.

Bird, T. D. (1985, April). *The formation of instrumental status differences among teachers*. Paper presented at the annual meeting of the American Educational Research Association, Chicago.

Bird, T. D., & Little, J. W. (1985). *Instructional leadership in eight secondary schools* (Final report to the National Institute of Education). Boulder, CO: Center for Action Research.

Bird, T. D., & Little, J. W. (1986). *School organization of the teaching occupation*. Prepared for the California Commission on the Teaching Profession. San Francisco: Far West Laboratory.

.Bird, T. D., Shulman, J., St. Clair, G., & Little, J. W. (1984). *Expanded teacher roles: Mentors and masters, interim report.* San Francisco: Far West Laboratory.

Blau, P., & Scott, W. R. (1962). *Formal organizations.* San Francisco: Chandler.

Book, C., Byers, J., & Freeman, D. (1983). Student expectations and teacher education traditions with which we can and cannot live. *Journal of Teacher Education, 34*(1), 9–13.

Borko, H., Lalik, R., Barksdale, M., & Yon, M. (1985, April). *What is successful teaching? An examination of student teachers' developing understandings of teaching.* Paper presented at the annual meeting of the American Educational Research Association, Chicago.

Boston Women's Teachers' Group (S. Freedman, J. Jackson, & K. Boles) (1983). Teaching: An imperiled "profession." In L. Shulman & G. Sykes (Eds.), *Handbook of teaching and policy.* White Plains, NY: Longman.

Bredo, E. (1975). *Collaborative relationships on teaching problems: Implications for collegial influence, team morale, and instructional practices* (Tech. Rep. No. 45). Stanford, CA: Stanford University, Center for Research and Development in Teaching.

Bredo, E. (1977). Collaborative relations among elementary school teachers. *Sociology of Education, 50,* 300–309.

Buchmann, M. (1983). *The use of research knowledge in teacher education and teaching* (Occasional Paper No. 71). East Lansing: Michigan State University, Institute for Research on Teaching.

Bussis, A. M., Chittenden, E. A., & Amarel, M. (1976). *Beyond surface curriculum: An interview study of teachers' understandings.* Boulder, CO: Westview Press.

California State University (1984). *A comprehensive plan for improvement of pre-service teacher education through clinical supervision of student teachers.* Long Beach: Office of the Chancellor.

Career Ladder Research Group (1984). *Career ladders in Utah: A preliminary study.* Salt Lake City: University of Utah and Utah State Office of Education.

Clark, C. (1984, April). *Research on teaching and the content of teacher education.* Symposium presentation at the annual meeting of the American Educational Research Association, New Orleans.

Cohen, E. (1976). Problems and prospects of teaming. *Educational Research Quarterly, 1,* 49–63.

Cohen, E. (1981). Sociology looks at team teaching. *Research in Sociology of Education and Socialization, 2,* 163–193.

Cohen, E., Deal, T. E., Meyer, J. E., & Scott, W. R. (1979). Technology and teaming in the elementary school. *Sociology of Education, 52,* 20–33.

Copeland, W. D., & Jamgochian, R. (1985). Colleague training and peer review. *Journal of Teacher Education, 36*(2), 18–21.

Cusick, P. A. (1980). *A study of networks among professional staffs of two secondary schools.* East Lansing: Michigan State University.

Darling-Hammond, L. (1984). The Toledo (Ohio) Public School intern and intervention programs. In A. Wise, L. Darling-Hammond, M. W. McLaughlin, & H. T. Bernstein (Eds.), *Case studies for teacher evaluation: A study of effective practices.* Santa Monica, CA: Rand Corp.

Doyle, W., & Nespor, J. (1984). *Learning to teach.* Austin: University of Texas, Research and Development Center in Teacher Education.

Etzioni, A. (1969). *The semi-professions and their organization.* New York: Free Press.

Feiman-Nemser, S., & Buchmann, M. (1985, April). *On what is learned in student teaching: Appraising the experience.* Paper presented at the annual meeting of the American Educational Research Association, Chicago.

Feiman-Nemser, S., & Floden, R. (1986). The cultures of teaching. In M. Wittrock (Ed.),

Handbook of research on teaching (3rd ed.). Washington, DC: American Educational Research Association, pp. 505–526.

Fox, R. (1957). Training for uncertainty. In R. Merton, G. Reader, & P. Kendall (Eds.), *The student physician*. Cambridge, MA: Harvard University Press.

Fuchs, E. (1969). *Teachers talk: Views from inside city schools*. Garden City, NY: Doubleday.

Gehrke, N. J., & Kay, R. S. (1984). The socialization of beginning teachers through mentor-protégé relationships. *Journal of Teacher Education, 35*(3), 21–24.

Glickman, C. D. (1985). The supervisor's challenge: Changing the teacher's work environment. *Educational Leadership, 42*(4), 38–40.

Goodman, L., & Lieberman, A. (1985, April). *Effective assister behavior: What they brought and what they learned*. Paper presented at the annual meeting of the American Educational Research Association, Chicago.

Griffin, G., Barnes, S., Hughes, R., Jr., O'Neal, S., Defino, M., Edwards, S., & Hukill, H. (1983). *Clinical preservice teacher education: Final report of a descriptive study*. Austin: University of Texas, Research and Development Center for Teacher Education.

Hammersley, M. (1984). Staffroom news. In A. Hargreaves & P. Woods (Eds.), *Classrooms and staffrooms: The sociology of teachers and teaching*. Milton Keynes, England: Open University Press.

Hargreaves, A. (1984). Experience counts, theory doesn't: How teachers talk about their work. *Sociology of Education, 57*, 244–254.

Intili, J. K. (1977). *Structural conditions in the school that facilitate reflective decision making*. Unpublished doctoral dissertation, Stanford University.

Johnson, R. (1976). *Teacher collaboration, principal influence and decision-making in elementary schools* (Tech. Rep. No. 48). Stanford, CA: Stanford University, Center for Research and Development in Teaching.

Johnson, S. M. (1982). *Teacher unions and the schools*. Cambridge, MA: Harvard University, Institute for Educational Policy Studies.

Kent, K. (1985). *A successful program of teachers assisting teachers*. San Rafael, CA: Marin County Office of Education.

Lacey, C. (1977). *The socialization of teachers*. London: Methuen.

Lanier, J. (1983). Tensions in teaching the skills of pedagogy. In G. Griffin (Ed.), *Staff development*. 82nd Yearbook of the National Society for the Study of Education. Chicago: University of Chicago Press.

Lanier, J. E., with Little, J. W. (1986). Research on teacher education. In M. Wittrock (Ed.), *Handbook of research in teaching* (3rd ed.). Washington, DC: American Educational Research Association, pp. 527–569.

Lieberman, A., & Miller, L. (1979). The social realities of teaching. In A. Lieberman & L. Miller (Eds.), *Staff development: New demands, new realities, new perspectives*. New York: Teachers College Press.

Lieberman, A., & Miller, L. (1984). *Teachers: Their world and their work*. Alexandria, VA: Association for Supervision and Curriculum Development.

Lipsitz, J. (1983). *Successful schools for young adolescents*. New Brunswick, NJ: Transaction Press.

Little, J. W. (1981). *School success and staff development: The role of staff development in urban desegregated schools*. Boulder, CO: Center for Action Research.

Little, J. W. (1982). Norms of collegiality and experimentation: Workplace conditions of school success. *American Educational Research Journal, 19*, 325–340.

Little, J. W. (1985, April). *Schools' contributions to teaching as a profession*. Paper presented at the annual meeting of the American Educational Research Association, Chicago.

Little, J. W., & Bird, T. D. (1984a, April). *Is there instructional leadership in high schools? First findings from a study of secondary school administrators and their influence on teachers' professional norms*. Paper presented at the annual meeting of the American Educational Research Association, New Orleans.

Little, J. W., & Bird, T. D. (1984b). *Report on a pilot study of school-level collegial teaming*. San Francisco: Far West Laboratory.

Little, J. W., Galagaran, P., & O'Neal, R. (1984). *Professional development roles and relationships: Principles and skills of advising*. San Francisco: Far West Laboratory.

Little, J. W., & Long, C. (1985). *Portraits of school-based collegial teams*. San Francisco: Far West Laboratory.

Lortie, D. (1975). *Schoolteacher: A sociological study*. Chicago: University of Chicago Press.

Lyons, G., & McCleary, L. (1980). Careers in teaching. In E. Hoyle & J. Megarry (Eds.), *World yearbook of education 1980: Professional development of teachers*. London: Kogan Page.

Marram, G. D., Dornbush, S., & Scott, W. R. (1972). *The impact of teaming and visibility of teaching in the professionalism of elementary school teachers* (Tech. Rep. No. 33). Stanford, CA: Stanford University, Center for Research and Development in Teaching.

Martin, W.B.W. (1975). The negotiated order of teachers in team teaching situations. *Sociology of Education, 48*, 202–222.

McDonald, F. J. (1980). *Study of induction programs for beginning teachers*. Princeton, NJ: Educational Testing Service.

McLaughlin, M. W., & Marsh, D. D. (1979). Staff development and school change. In A. Lieberman & L. Miller (Eds.), *Staff development: New demands, new realities, new perspectives*. New York: Teachers College Press.

Metz, M. H. (1984, August). *Faculty culture: A case study*. Paper presented at the annual meeting of the American Sociological Association, San Antonio, TX.

Meyer, J., Cohen, E., Brunetti, F., Molnar, S., & Lueders-Salmon, E. (1971). *The impact of the open-space school upon teacher influence and autonomy: The effects of an organizational innovation* (Tech. Rep. No. 21). Stanford, CA: Stanford University, Center for Research and Development in Teaching.

Mitchell, D., Ortiz, F., & Mitchell, T. (1983). *Work orientation and job performance: The cultural basis of teaching rewards and incentives* (Report prepared for the National Institute of Education, Grant No. NIE-G-80-0154). Riverside: University of California.

Molnar, S. (1971). *Teachers in teams: Interaction, influence and autonomy* (Tech. Rep. No. 22). Stanford, CA: Stanford University, Center for Research and Development in Teaching.

Nemser, S. F. (1983). Learning to teach. In L. S. Shulman & G. Sykes (Eds.), *Handbook of teaching and policy*. White Plains, NY: Longman.

Newberry, J. M. (1977, April). *The first year of experience: Influences on beginning teachers*. Paper presented at the annual meeting of the American Educational Research Association, New York.

Pellegrin, R. J. (1976). Schools as work settings. In R. Dubin (Ed.), *Handbook of work, organizations, and society.* Skokie, IL: Rand McNally.

Rosenholtz, S. J., & Kyle, S. J. (1984, Winter). Teacher isolation: Barrier to professionalism. *American Educator, 10–15*.

Rutter, M., Maughan, B., Mortimore, P., Ouston, J., & Smith, A. (1979). *Fifteen thousand hours: Secondary schools and their effects on children*. Cambridge, MA: Harvard University Press.

Ryan, K. (1970). *Don't smile until Christmas: Accounts of the first year of teaching*. Chicago: University of Chicago Press.

Schlechty, P. (1984, April). *A school district revises the functions and rewards of teaching*. Paper presented at the annual meeting of the American Educational Research Association, New Orleans.

Schlechty, P. (1985, April). *Teaching as a profession: What we know and what we need to know about teachers*. Paper presented at the annual meeting of the American Educational Research Association, Chicago.

Schmuck, R., Runkel, P., & Langmeyer, D. (1971). Using group problem-solving procedures. In R. A. Schmuck & M. B. Miles (Eds.), *Organizational development in schools.* Washington, DC: National Press Books.

Showers, B. (1985) Teachers coaching teachers. *Educational Leadership, 42*(7), 43–48.

Shulman, L. S. (1983). A perspective on effective schools. In *Making our schools more effective: Proceedings of three state conferences.* San Francisco: Far West Laboratory.

Southern Regional Education Board (1984). *State actions: Career ladders and other incentive plans for school teachers and administrators.* Atlanta: Southern Regional Education Board.

Sykes, G. (1983a). Contradictions, ironies and promises unfulfilled: A contemporary account of the status of teaching. *Phi Delta Kappan, 65,* 87–93.

Sykes, G. (1983b). Public policy and the problem of teacher quality: The need for screens and magnets. In L. Shulman & G. Sykes (Eds.), *Handbook of teaching and policy.* White Plains, NY: Longman.

Sykes, G., & Devaney, K. (1984). *A status report on the teaching profession.* Prepared for the California Commission on the Teaching Profession.

Tisher, R. (1980). The induction of beginning teachers. In E. Hoyle & J. Megarry (Eds.), *World yearbook of education 1980: Professional development of teachers.* London: Kogan Page.

Veenman, S. (1984). Perceived problems of beginning teachers. *Review of Educational Research, 54,* 143–178.

Wagner, L. (1985, April). *The Mentor Teacher Program: California's foray into differentiated staffing.* Paper presented at the annual meeting of the American Educational Research Association, Chicago.

Weyand, J. (1983). *Reflections on getting good.* Prepared for the Far West Laboratory for Educational Research and Development, San Francisco. Loveland, CO: Thompson Valley School District.

Wilburn, K. T., & Drummond, R. C. (1984, April). *Peer supervision: A study of peer teachers in Florida's Beginning Teacher Program.* Paper presented at the annual meeting of the American Educational Research Association, New Orleans.

Woods, P. (1984). The meaning of staffroom humour. In A. Hargreaves & P. Woods (Eds.), *Classrooms and staffrooms: The sociology of teachers and teaching.* Milton Keynes, England: Open University Press.

21 PARENTS AND THE COMMUNITY

Sandra Tangri and Oliver Moles

The little red schoolhouse and its three-story glass-and-concrete version exist in social environments that are financially responsible for their survival and that depend on the quality of their performance to sustain economic productivity and political stability. It is therefore odd that the exchanges between schools and their communities are so often not reflective of this interdependence.

When the public school system and the country were much younger, the social and physical distances between teachers and the community they served were generally less than they are now. Teachers lived in the immediate community, and because they were unmarried (by law or custom), they often lived with a family whose children they taught. Parent-teacher "conferences" might take place at the dinner table. In any case, parents, teachers, and students saw one another in contexts other than the school, and "reversals" of authority occurred naturally.

Some of these features survive in smaller, often rural districts, but in the large urban public school, easy, frequent, and diverse contact between parents and schools has become the exception rather than the rule. The result is the widespread perception that "many schools seem content to 'run the public's business' without bothering to involve the public" (Gonder, 1981). This isolation from the community has contributed to several problems now being faced by the schools, the most important of which are a lack of confidence expressed at various times by the minimum competency movement and the failure of bond issues. Many school personnel, on the other hand, feel increasingly and unreasonably burdened with the fallout from social changes beyond their control (desegregation and busing, undersocialized or undersupervised children) and less and less appreciated or respected.

The withering of community has been accompanied by the "erosion of the educative function of the school" (Goodlad, 1981, p. 333). Reversal of this process will require new efforts to restore the integration of the school with its social environment, the community. This community includes, but is not limited to, the parents of the students attending the school. Thus there are two foci for this chapter:

involving parents in the educative process and involving other adults, institutions, enterprises, and agencies.

The constraints that limit involvement with the schools are perhaps better known than the degree and diversity of motivation for such involvement. Among the frequently cited constraints to parental involvement are (1) social conditions, including the rise of single-parent and dual-earner families, cuts in funding of programs for parental involvement, transient neighborhoods, and fears about personal safety; (2) perceptions by parents that school staff are apathetic and indifferent or hostile to their participation; and (3) reciprocal beliefs by school staff that parents are apathetic or that they do not want to get involved or don't have the skills to make meaningful contributions. In the secondary schools, additional issues are experienced as barriers to parental participation in the educational process, including (1) parents' beliefs that they have limited influence on their teenage children; (2) lack of knowledge and skills on the part of both parents and teachers about how to create suitable roles for parents at the secondary level and how to make use of other community resources; (3) logistic difficulties arising from multiple teachers for each child and teachers often having over 100 students in a semester; and (4) changes in the children's own feelings about their parents' coming to school (Murray n.d.; Stough, 1982; Tangri & Leitch, 1982; Moles, 1982; Davies, 1981). Finally, there is Lightfoot's (1978) argument that schools and parents have inherently conflicting perspectives on the educative process because of their different roles vis-à-vis the child. One additional attitudinal barrier that has constrained the greater participation of businesses in vocational and other educative programs is the wariness of school personnel about the potential value biases that business involvement might bring (Gonder, 1981).

On the other hand, there is also evidence that there is a strong desire on the part of both parents and school staff for more community participation (Tangri & Leitch, 1982; Stallworth & Williams, 1983; Gallup, 1978; Thornberg, 1981). The challenge, therefore is to find ways to capitalize on this motivation and the potential resources it could bring to the education of children.

CITIZEN SERVICE IN THE SCHOOLS

Parent Participation in School Governance

The concept of parent participation in educational decision making is closely linked to democratic ideals of citizen participation in the affairs of government. It has been defended on both ideological and practical grounds. The ideological rationale is that people affected by decisions of public institutions should be involved in making those decisions. The practical one is that enduring and positive change is most likely when those affected are involved in the planning and decision making (Davies, 1976). Governance participation includes representation on district or school-level policy and advisory committees, planning councils, other governing bodies and even the use of parents as regular advisers to teachers in classroom affairs.

Public participation was given a major boost in the 1960s and early 1970s with federal requirements for parent advisory councils (PACs) under Title I of the Elementary and Secondary Education Act, Head Start, Follow Through, and the Education for All Handicapped Children Act. During the 1970s a few states—California, Florida, and South Carolina—also mandated advisory councils at the school-site level.

The requirement for PACs under Title I has now been dropped by the federal government and replaced with a general requirement to consult with parents in the development of new programs under the Education Consolidation and Improvement Act. Nevertheless, some states and localities continue to require or encourage PACs, and the Education Commission of the States (1980) has recommended that states emphasize during the 1980s a policy of building citizen participation in the educational process.

These mixed signals suggest that parent participation in school governance bears close examination and lead to the following questions.

How Interested and Involved Are Parents in School Governance?   Recent surveys of large numbers of elementary school parents, teachers, and principals in six southwestern states inquired about parents' interest and participation in school decision making (Stallworth & Williams, 1983). Of most interest to parents were involvement in decisions on classroom discipline, amount of homework assigned, setting school behavior rules, and evaluating how well children are learning. However, in each of these areas, principals and teachers thought that parent involvement would be much less useful than the parent ratings would indicate.

Of least interest to parents was participation in decisions on hiring and firing principals and teachers and on having more multicultural or bilingual education in the schools (Stallworth & Williams, 1982). Thus parents seem mainly interested in governance matters close to the classroom and issues that bear directly on their children's performance.

On an overall assessment of various parent involvement roles, principals and teachers rated parents least important as decision makers. Stallworth and Williams (1982) conclude that parents would become more involved in school decisions if they had more opportunity and that action or inaction by school personnel, rather than parental apathy, is the key.

Information on the use of parent advisory groups before the federal requirements were dropped comes from a comprehensive analysis of parent involvement in four federal education programs: ESEA Title I, ESEA Title VII (bilingual education), the Emergency School Assistance Act (for desegregating schools), and Follow Through (Melaragno, Keesling, Lyons, Robbins, & Smith, 1981). Regulations for each program require an advisory board with parent members. Among many projects observed at some length, only 30% had parent advisory groups with *major* involvement, where they made decisions or recommendations that resulted in changes. Follow Through had more active parent participation than the other three programs, apparently because of its very explicit regulations promoting active advisory groups. The advisory groups did display a wide range of nongovernance activities like serving as a means of communication with parents, providing training to them at meetings, and helping with project activities at the schools.

How Can Parent Advisory Groups Be Made More Active?   Factors contributing to active advisory groups point to actions by school or project personnel like training parents in group processes, having effective parent leaders, and staff attitudes that parents should be involved in project decisions and are capable of doing so (Melaragno et al., 1981).

The effects of parent participation in school governance are less well documented

and present a mixed picture. On the one hand, there is evidence that parent participation increases parents' satisfaction with schools (Comer, 1980). The study of parent
involvement in four federal education programs showed that advisory groups also
influenced the availability and quality of additional resources, allowed for information exchange, and developed better working relationships with staff. Where parent
contributions were considered valuable, parents developed pride in the project and
the school and satisfaction from knowing they could influence project decision
making. Parent involvement did not shift the project away from its main goals
(Melaragno et al., 1981).

On the other hand, the evidence for effects on student achievement is mixed.
Several researchers find a link between the existence and activities of parent advisory
groups and student achievement as well as fewer absences and behavior problems
(Armor et al., 1976; Comer, 1980; Guttentag, 1972). Others have found no effects on
students achievement (Wagenaar, 1977).

Thus the benefits for children's academic performance of having parents in
governance roles are uncertain. When parents serve in governance roles, there is no
obvious and direct link to children's learning, although connections can be made in
terms of the parents' sense of efficacy, information about school operations, and other
factors that could enhance motivation and educational skills for parents and children.

The common experience is that parent involvement does not detract from
program goals and instead makes for greater parental satisfaction with schools and
better working relationships with school staff. Where these are valued in their own
right, parent participation in school governance seems well worth the effort.

Paid Aides in the Classroom

Some schools hire aides who help teachers work with individual students, groups of
students, or whole-class instructional activities. The aides may be parents or other
local citizens; they most often work in elementary schools.

Few school studies have examined the use of paid aides, perhaps in part because
they are usually employed along with other innovations, making it difficult to determine the effects of each separately. An exception is the study of four large federally
funded educational programs where two-thirds of the observed school projects had
paid instructional aides (Melaragno et al., 1981). A major consequence of their
involvement was that the aides became resources to other parents by explaining the
instructional program to them, answering their questions, and recruiting other
parents to participate in project activities. The aides reported greater self-confidence
and personal satisfaction as they realized they were performing important functions.
Some sites reported that students had more positive attitudes toward schoolwork and
better conduct and attendance because their parents or neighbor parents, working as
aides, could observe them. Some sites also reported that the innovative tutoring skills
of aides and their understanding of student needs gave project teachers new respect
for the paid parent aides.

In some of the projects, parents of other students began asking questions more
freely, apparently because they felt that the aides "spoke their own language" and
could therefore explain the program and their children's progress better. On the other
hand, a few teachers said that involving parents as aides was too time-consuming and
mostly a hindrance. On balance, however, what evidence there is suggests that parent

aides can enhance not only their own personal development but also student motivation and performance and communication with other parents.

Volunteers

In an era of declining school resources, the use of community volunteers is particularly appealing to supplement the work of school staff in the classroom and other school settings. But beyond the economic incentive, the use of volunteers can also produce other benefits. Their work can enhance communication between the school and the community and can build support for the schools. It can create among parents and citizens a better understanding of what schools do and can help school staff appreciate more the problems faced by parents and other citizens. For example, over half the senior citizen volunteers and teachers in one program felt that their attitudes toward each other had improved (National School Volunteer Program, 1983). It is even claimed that when parents volunteer, students develop greater motivation for learning.

Who Volunteers, and How Are They Used?   A recent national survey estimated that volunteers were used in some capacity in 79% of the public school districts in the country, more so in elementary schools (88%), but also in secondary schools (60%). Parents were the most common volunteers, followed by older citizens, students, and business employees. This study calculated that for every dollar spent, school districts received $50 in volunteer services based on the number of hours volunteers contributed and assuming that pay for such work would be at $5.00 per hour (Thomas, n.d.).

A less optimistic picture comes from the study of parent involvement in four federal educational programs where very few projects tried to obtain parent instructional volunteers. But those who did volunteer were usually found to play an important instructional role—working with individual students or small groups of students to reinforce skills being taught and contributing to decisions on lesson plans and activities for students with whom they worked. Training of parent volunteers and allowing time for them and teachers to plan activities and discuss past activities seemed especially important to successful programs (Melaragno et al., 1981).

Information from two diverse states, Florida and Minnesota, throws further light on the use of volunteers. In Minnesota, 18,275 volunteers contributed an average of 10.5 hours per person. Slightly over half had been recruited by school staff, about 20% came on their own initiative, and 14% were recruited through the PTA or other school-parent-community organizations. A little over half the volunteers were parents or other immediate family members of students. Volunteers worked on advisory committees, special projects, and short-term resource presentations and less often provided individualized assistance to students and help with extracurricular activities (Minnesota Department of Education, 1982).

In Florida, 54 of the state's 67 school districts had districtwide volunteer programs in the 1981–1982 school year (Florida Department of Education, 1983). A statewide coordination and communication network and state-funded matching grants aided their efforts. Florida also has a statewide program to involve the private sector and gives annual awards to schools, superintendents, and volunteers.

What Makes Volunteer Programs Successful? The Florida state volunteer coordinator believes that the support of the district superintendent and the principal are essential to the success of volunteer programs. From the Minnesota survey come other ideas for making volunteer programs more effective: (1) appropriate techniques for recruiting and training volunteers, (2) workshops on orientation of volunteers and in-service training for principals and teachers on the use of volunteers, (3) training of staff in the supervision of volunteers, and (4) consideration of legal and financial aspects of volunteer programs. Also mentioned was the evaluation of individual volunteer performance and evaluation of the overall volunteer program. Very little is known in this area. Although programs can turn out large numbers of volunteers performing a variety of needed services for schools, the benefits to students remain to be documented.

HOME-SCHOOL RELATIONSHIPS

Home-School Communication

There are a number of ways of contacting parents aside from encounters with those who regularly work at school or sit on advisory boards. The parent-teacher conference is one, and workshops and training sessions for parents are also fairly common. But other opportunities arise when parents visit the school or can be created by phone calls, notes, home visits, and even having parents pick up report cards at the school (Murray, n.d.).

Home-school communications may be constricted by a number of conditions such as legal regulations, local school policies and practices, personal experiences of each participant, and differing expectations. In workshop materials on productive parent-school-teacher relationships, the National Education Association (1982) points out that parents have no obligation to communicate with schools and may even hesitate to become involved. The NEA concludes that it is therefore the responsibility of the schools to contact parents as needed and to minimize barriers that tend to overwhelm parents, such as inflexible time schedules, use of status symbols, and the presence of more school staff than parents in conferences.

What, then, can be learned from studies to help educators improve the practices of home-school communication? First we must know the extent of home-school communications.

National surveys have recorded high levels of school contact by parents: up to 87% of parents with some contact and about 70% meeting with or writing to a teacher in the previous two years. Almost half had attended a PTA meeting or volunteered at school. Those with more contacts were more highly educated, had higher incomes, lived in rural areas, and had greater confidence in public school teachers (Cantril, 1979). But a study of four federal education programs found that the most frequently used home-school communication mechanisms were written messages (newsletters, bulletins, and flyers), which provided little opportunity for parents to respond. Personal interaction between parents and staff were quite uncommon, aside from parent meetings and open houses where time for personal discussion is limited. Parent coordinators did make some home visits, and their work was seen as a way to facilitate home-school interaction (Melaragno et al., 1981). This detailed study suggests that without a special emphasis, parent contacts are likely to be brief and infrequent.

Parent involvement does not always have the same effects. In one large study of elementary schools, parent involvement as measured by parent contacts with teachers and interest in pupil progress affected student achievement only in majority-black schools. The authors suggest that in middle-class white schools, parents are mainly involved when student achievement is unsatisfactory, whereas in black schools the parents may actually influence the way the school helps children achieve (Brookover, Beady, Flood, Schweitzer, & Wisenbaker, 1979).

There is some additional evidence that under specific conditions, communication between school personnel and parents by phone calls, personal contacts, and other means improves attendance and school performance and may also increase parent-initiated contacts with the school. Since excessive absenteeism is linked to poor school performance and negative attitudes toward school, there are important reasons for trying to improve attendance as well as school performance.

Phone Contacts

One time-consuming but potentially rewarding means of contact is the telephone. When the principal called parents of first- and second-grade children with many absences, their attendance improved, and parents also reported absences due to illness more regularly (Parker & McCoy, 1977). In another study, calls from the school secretary were as effective as those from the principal; in each case, absenteeism was reduced by about one-third (Sheats & Dunkleberger, 1979).

Telephone calls can be effective at the secondary level too. School systems are experimenting with computerized calls to parents when high school students are absent; they report substantial increases in attendance (LaFraniere, 1983).

Recorded messages have also been used to tell parents what children were learning in class and how parents might help them. When weekly messages were provided during most of the school year, parents were highly satisfied with the service. In the third-grade classes studied, student test scores were higher when parents reported doing more of the suggested home activities, but in the fourth grade no consistent relationship was found. Teachers tended to run out of new ideas for parental assistance, and the tests probably measured somewhat different competencies than those embodied in the parent activities (Marshall & Herbert, 1981).

In another study, recorded messages giving academic and nonacademic information were left for parents of first graders (Bittle, 1975). When spelling words were included, this improved spelling performance more than sending the words home with a note to parents. When the message asked for the return of permission slips and money for picnic drinks, all the parents and children obliged, thus saving teachers time in bookkeeping and reminders.

On the negative side, the NEA (1982) notes that use of the telephone has certain limitations, such as the limited free time of teachers at school and in evenings, the interruption of family life, the tendency to demand an immediate response without giving parents a chance to think over situations that call for remedial action, and the frequent lack of records of calls made. These conditions suggest that phone contacts must be planned carefully, conducted discreetly, and used selectively for the maximum benefit, especially when the intent is to solicit the cooperation of parents in remedying student deficiencies.

Home Visits

The home visit, an intensive form of home-school communication, does seem to produce striking effects in the context of the Follow Through Parent Educator Program. These parent educators regularly visit parents of first to third graders to discuss current classroom instruction and to present supplementary activities parents can undertake with their children. Compared to their older siblings who had no Follow Through experience, those entering the Parent Educator Program is Richmond, VA, in 1969 through 1972 dropped out of school subsequently less often, and girls were less often held back in grade. Although there were no differences on special education placement, the average placement was over twice as long for the siblings as for the program participants (Olmsted, 1983). Thus the benefits of such intensive contacts seem to run far into the future.

In another study, teachers were trained to improve communication skills with parents and then made home visits. Both attendance and grades improved in comparison to classes without such activities (Shelton & Dobson, 1973). It is not clear how much of the gains should be attributed to the training per se or whether teachers favored children whose families they visited. Nevertheless, taken together, these studies do suggest that attendance and achievement can be increased by personal contacts with parents at home.

Parent-Teacher Conferences

The parent-teacher conference has rich potential. The exchange of information can give parents and teachers valuable insights on creating more effective learning experiences in the school and at home. Both parties consider the conference necessary for students' educational growth. Despite this potential, teachers usually have little formal training for parent-teacher conferences and must rely on experience gained on the job. Because conferences often occur when students are in trouble, parents and teachers are often fearful and defensive during them.

Useful procedures for teachers to use in the conference include interpersonal communication skills such as warmth, attentiveness, and responsiveness (Rotter & Robinson, 1982) and conference skills such as how to handle parents' resistance to negative information about their children and how to build a view of parents as equals who want the best for their children (Losen & Diament, 1978). Losen and Diament also discuss preparing for the parent-teacher conference, including guidelines for protecting parents' due process rights, interpreting test scores, and knowing when a conference is needed.

Some large school systems have developed parent-teacher conferences to a high level. For example, Houston holds conferences for all grade levels twice a year. School is recessed early; 15-minute interviews are scheduled through two afternoons and evenings, and businesses are urged to give employees leave time. Teachers have computer printouts of student test scores for parents. The printouts also suggest ways parents can help children in areas where they have scored low. For high school students, the printouts show career interests and steps needed to enter related occupations. Booklets of tips for parents to help children learn are also available. Large numbers of parents turn out for these conferences. Most of the parents and teachers are highly satisfied with this process. Indianapolis has a similar program (Collins, Moles, & Cross, 1982).

Surprisingly little attention has been given to effects on students. In a study of second graders, some randomly selected parents had a conference with the teacher every other week for 12 weeks while others did not. There was no difference between the groups in children's acquisition of math concepts. Low-achieving students did have more positive attitudes toward math after the parent conferences, but among average and high-achieving pupils, attitudes became more negative (Buchanan, Hansen, & Quilling, 1969).

In secondary schools, parents are more likely to talk to a counselor than a teacher about their children's performance. An intensive study of two inner-city junior high schools disclosed some major obstacles to full use of the conference. Counselors often did not communicate parental concerns to the teachers, and conferences usually ended without a plan of action or agreement on meeting again to assess progress. Staff development work and a better structure for staff coordination might improve such situations (Tangri & Leitch, 1982).

These studies suggest that the amount of parent-teacher conference contact is not as important as how conferences are conducted. Extensive contact may even be counterproductive for some students. Instead, the available research suggests a need for staff training on ways of relating to parents in a nonthreatening manner and building a sense of partnership with them. Having information on student skills progress to give to parents also seems to attract them. Finally, a structure for following up parent and teacher concerns in the school and home and for continued consultation as needed would appear useful at all grade levels.

Parent Education and Training

Besides parent-teacher conferences and other school visits, parents are displaying a willingness to become involved with schools on a more intensive, continuing basis. In a 1978 Gallup poll, eight in ten parents of school children thought that parents should attend evening classes once a month to learn how they can improve children's behavior and increase their interest in school work. Parent training in preschool intervention programs has been shown to produce immediate and long-term achievement gains (Goodson & Hess, 1975).

As children begin school, a common objective of parent training activities is to change the academic or social behavior of children by working directly with their parents. This objective is approached by teaching parents various skills including behavior modification techniques or specific tasks like how to implement a home reading program. Parents may be instructed in weekly sessions for up to several months, in one-time meetings, or even by mail. By working with parents, investigators have been able to decrease inappropriate student behavior and increase academic performance. Working with parents seems even more effective in these areas than counseling individual students (Filipczak, Lordeman, & Friedman, 1977). However, in a study of four federal education programs, systematic efforts to train parents for home tutoring were rare. On the other hand, one-time workshops on how to help children with school skills or on making instructional games were very common (Melaragno, 1981).

Where well-designed programs and evaluations have been conducted, results are promising. Graue, Weinstein, and Walberg (1983) identified 29 controlled studies of parent training programs over a 10-year period (1970–1980) and subjected them to a metanalysis. Ninety-one percent of all comparisons favored the program groups over their controls, and the typical program raised students' performance well above the mean of the control group. Specially trained teachers or paraprofessionals were more effective than professional parent trainers, and semester-length programs were less successful than those lasting only five to six weeks.

These findings suggest that parent training can indeed be beneficial for student achievement in basic subjects but that lengthy and professionalized training may be counterproductive. Although not all results have been positive, other kinds of effects have also been recorded, including parent and teacher self-reports of change, parent satisfaction, and changes in parent and student self-concepts. Issues of cost effectiveness, self-selection of possibly more motivated parents, and how to elicit parent participation are not discussed much in the literature on parent training (Filipczak et al., 1977).

Limitations

The studies just cited provide encouraging evidence of home-school communication effects on student performance. Other studies, however, show effects only with particular groups in particular subjects, or at certain grade levels. For example, Armor and his colleagues (1976) showed that parent-teacher contact via classroom and home visits was an important factor in the achievement of sixth-grade black children but that such contacts were weak predictors for Mexican-American children. The authors note that this may have been because they failed to include some key variables, such as English-language fluency.

Effects may also vary by grade level and subject matter. In a supplementary reading program that emphasized parent-teacher contacts of various kinds, more contacts produced greater reading gains among first graders. By the fourth to eighth grades, a few contacts produced gains, but large numbers of contacts were detrimental (Iverson, Brownlee, & Walberg, 1981). All the children in this study were reading one to two years below grade level, and the authors suggest that under-achieving older children may resent being singled out because of their lack of success.

A project with first and second graders in New York City encouraged parents to visit the classroom and talk with teachers, to attend school programs on child development, and to help with school activities. Newsletters with information on educational activities were sent home, teas were arranged, and later, personal contacts by other parents were made. The researchers concluded that only after several years of concerted effort were the effects of parent participation discernible (Heisler & Crowley, 1969). A similar cautionary note comes from reading of Comer's (1980) experience in inner-city schools of New Haven. A great variety of parent-school contacts were developed, but student achievement increased only years after the initiation of the project.

HOME LEARNING ACTIVITIES

Children engage in learning activities with their parents and other family members from infancy onward. The range of such activities is vast and changes with the child's age, family circumstances, and many other factors. Three kinds of home learning activities are singled out for discussion here because of their relevance to schooling and the opportunities parents have to use them: homework assistance, home tutoring, and enrichment activities.

Homework Assistance

A recent metanalysis of 15 studies found a moderately large effect of assigned homework and very large effects when homework was either commented on or graded by the teacher (Paschal, Weinstein, & Walberg, 1983). The weight of the evidence indicates that homework is important when taken seriously by students and teachers. But what of parent roles?

Here the systematic information is meager. Parents are often advised to set aside a place, a time, materials, and resources for doing homework. The National Assessment of Educational Progress found no higher math achievement scores among 17-year-olds who had a specific place to study, but more did well who had dictionaries and other reference books at home (Education Commission of the States, 1977).

Other common recommendations are that parents should encourage children to do their homework and do it well, to evaluate their completed homework on a regular basis, to discuss ideas related to homework topics, and to set an example of concentrating on learning tasks. These are all plausible suggestions that have considerable intuitive appeal, but the studies to support them have not been done. Instead, some other actions by parents of older children seem to hold promise. A national study of male sophomores that analyzed a number of factors determined that five were independently related to hours of homework performed: the amount of homework assigned, academic program, father's education, parent knowing the student's whereabouts outside of school, and parents' monitoring of school performance (DiPrete, 1981). The last two factors pertain much less to the immediate homework task than to broad levels of awareness and supervision of adolescent children's activities.

School systems have tried to facilitate homework performance with a variety of advice and guidance and some interesting innovations such as the "homework hotline." One of the first districts to try it, Philadelphia, found that about 10% of the hotline calls were from parents (Collins et al., 1982). Teachers who staff hotlines help callers locate resources and understand the logic of assigned tasks without actually solving problems for them.

A project with second graders from a low-income area tried to improve their mathematics performance by increased home-school contact (Buchanan et al., 1969). Pupils in three classes were randomly assigned to several interventions, including individual parent-teacher conferences every other week for 12 weeks that involved homework assignments for the students. Parents were asked to check completed work with the child and return it at the next conference. The assignments were largely drill and practice. On average, parents attended about half the conferences. This intervention produced no better acquisition of math skills and concepts than conferences without reference to homework or homework assignments without attempting to involve parents.

Thus evidence of benefits for student achievement comes mostly from large-scale studies of older children. It suggests several things: Home educational resources such as dictionaries and encyclopedias are important, and so is the monitoring of school performance and after-school activities. Structuring learning opportunities in these broad ways has more empirical support regarding older students than specific actions like checking homework, signing it, or having a special place to study. But whether these popular forms of advice to parents are helpful to younger students doing homework remains to be seen. Younger students may be less self-disciplined and need more structure in homework situations, so specific guidance could very well be beneficial to them.

Home Tutoring

The idea of training parents to extend the instructional process into the home is an intriguing one. Done well, it could mobilize parent interest in the child's education, add to teaching time at low cost, and increase student performance. There is strong support for the idea of parents as home tutors among parents, school staff, and school system officials (Stallworth & Williams, 1983). What, then, do we know about the effectiveness of such a strategy?

In a recent review, Leler (1983) has identified 18 well-designed studies of home instruction and children's academic achievement. Each is described in some detail, and many show the ways schools work to involve parents as well as the ways parents work with their children. Of these 18 studies, 13 produced positive results on one or more achievement variables, and 5 showed no difference between involved and uninvolved families on any measure. Since none of the studies produced negative results and over two-thirds showed some positive findings, the overall picture for training parents as home tutors is encouraging.

It should be noted that all these studies concerned parents of elementary school children, most often those in the lower grades. However, a number of the projects worked with low-income minority or poorly educated parents, so the benefits of home tutoring are not restricted to mainstream parents and children.

There are several processes by which greater achievement may be produced. Three chains of events have been identified, all of which begin with a parent learning how to teach his or her own child and then teaching the child new skills (Stanford Research Institute, 1973). This increases the child's academic skills, increases the child's academic motivation by seeing that the parent believes education is important, and improves the parent's self-image. Perceiving new personal competence, the parent may communicate confidence to the child. Greater confidence, new skills, and enhanced motivation should all help the child to perform better on tests.

The Stanford Research Institute (1973) presented some evidence for the activation of each chain in home instruction. They concluded that the child's sense of confidence and control may be the strongest of the three factors but that it is difficult to tell which chain is occurring or is the most powerful.

To sustain parent participation, schools can, for example, send home weekly teacher comments on pupil test scores and ask parents to return records of completed home instruction daily. In one study of kindergartners, these did not produce any higher student achievement than when parents only attended a 90-minute initial training session on conducting home practice (Niedermeyer, 1969). In another program, parents were given a two-week comprehensive exposure to reading methods, diagnostic methods, and learning theories. They also watched the child being taught with the recommended techniques. Parent instruction was then under the supervision of professionals. Children made greater gains in oral reading than a comparison group but did not make greater gains on an achievement measure (Murray, 1972). Other studies of complex training reviewed by Leler (1983) are similarly disappointing. As noted earlier, Graue and colleagues (1983) also found that professional trainers, formalized training, and long programs were not particularly beneficial.

The lack of success of such elaborate arrangements suggests that simpler, less intrusive approaches may work equally well if not better. It appears that parents can use initial instruction and less intensive contacts and materials well enough to produce noticeable improvement. Close supervision could even undermine confidence by keeping parents constantly on display and concerned with the quality of their tutoring.

The Parent Education Follow Through Program is a well-established and well-documented approach to home tutoring in the lower grades. It emphasizes home learning activities demonstrated by the parent educator that are related to work in the classroom but take advantage of family activities and materials found in the home.

This parent education program has identified certain desirable teaching behaviors for parents and teachers. These include preparing the learner, asking questions with more than one correct answer, getting learners to ask questions, praising them for learning, and correcting mistakes without criticism. Results show that after training, parents used more such behaviors than other comparable parents. In several studies, the use of home learning activities by parents correlated with the child's reading achievement and sometimes also with math test scores (Olmsted & Rubin, n.d.)

This shows that regular contact with parent educators can give parents the teaching skills and information to supplement coursework that in turn helps their children achieve well in the basic subjects. The resources required to pay parents as paraprofessional educators are considerable, but the results are very encouraging. More generally, home tutoring under sustained guidance does show clear student learning benefits both in this Follow Through model and in a number of other related approaches. Complex training does not seem necessary.

Home Educational Enrichment

What Can Parents Do to Enrich Their Children's Learning at Home? Research demonstrates that it is what parents do in the home more than their educational or occupational status that influences children's performance.

The encouragement of simple home activities with strong educational aspects is exemplified in the Home Learning Lab (Rich, 1976). Every other week for 16 weeks, first-grade parents were sent suggestions for activities with their children to reinforce and supplement math and reading. These children gained more in reading than a control group, and black children in the program gained more in both reading and math than their counterparts in the control group. This enrichment technique has been used in a number of other school systems and with a variety of elementary school students.

Many kinds of home enrichment activities can be promoted by educators; taken together, all seem to have a positive impact on parents and children. A recent comprehensive study of first-, third- and fifth-grade teachers in Maryland (Epstein, 1983) illustrates this point very nicely. Epstein identified five broad kinds of parental practices to stimulate home learning encouraged by some of these teachers. The five practices included reading to children and having them read to parents, encouraging home discussions, informal learning activities such as playing family games or using common items to teach skills as in the Home Learning Lab, contracts for parents to supervise assignments, and teaching parents how to tutor or make learning materials for use with children at home. When adopted by parents, these activities could increase "achievement press," academic guidance, and student exploration of the larger environment, three of the home experiences Bloom (1981) sees as influencing school achievement.

Teachers who often used the practices found ways to involve all parents regardless of their educational level, whereas other teachers of children in low-education families felt that these parents would not be willing or able to help their child at home (Epstein, 1983). Thus strong users of these practices found ways of working with poorly educated parents, despite the common belief that such parents are unable to assist their children's education. District-level policies may also encourage teachers to stress certain kinds of parent involvement (Epstein, 1983).

The parents of students who had these teacher leaders in parent involvement were more likely to feel they should help their child at home, understood more of what their child was being taught at school, and rated these teachers more highly in overall teaching ability than parents of students in nonleader classrooms. It appears that extensive efforts to involve parents also helped parents feel more positive about home learning activities and about the teachers who encouraged them (Epstein, 1983).

Some teachers also pointed out problems in home enrichment efforts, such as the time demands on teachers, parents, and students; the stress on children and parents when home learning activities are ineffective; and the competing need for parents to develop children's social and emotional skills as well as their intellect. But others noted children's improved basic skills, better parent-teacher cooperation, and more useful parent-student interaction (Epstein & Becker, 1982). Students of the teacher leaders did report more positive attitudes toward school, more regular homework habits, and more similarity and more familiarity between the home and school than students in nonleader classrooms (Epstein, 1982). And students gained more in reading achievement over the year in classes with teacher leaders in parent involvement even when other factors contributing to achievement were taken into account (Epstein, 1984).

Since the teacher practices were aimed at stimulating home reading, family discussions, and other activities of a largely nonmathematical nature, the gains in reading take on greater significance, and the lack of effects on math are understandable. All this suggests that while successful programs to stimulate home educational enrichment involve considerable planning as well as effort and dealing with competing demands, they can be effective even for busy and poorly educated parents and their elementary school children. However, we know little about the kinds of parental assistance most useful for students in secondary schools.

Motivating Children

Much could be written on the family interactions that encourage children's academic motivation, but the key question for our purposes is how schools might help parents to motivate children. This kind of assistance is nicely illustrated in a study by Smith (1968) that involves a more thorough restructuring of the home environment than is evident in the previously cited studies.

Parents of children in second and fifth grades attended group meetings where they were instructed in ways to model a regard for learning and to help with homework completion. They were asked to read to their child, read in their presence, ask questions about their child's work and praise their efforts, and arrange a quiet place and regular time for homework. Their children made greater gains in reading vocabulary over a five-month period than children in a matched comparison group.

In this approach, one sees an emphasis on the content of intellectual skills, the value of praise and parental interest in children's work, and also modeling of interest in reading. No doubt there is consideration of the motivational aspects in many parent involvement programs, but this study highlights the combination of forces that asisst children's home learning and suggests that attention to this variety of parental actions can be more significant than a focus on only the instructional aspects.

EMPLOYED MOTHERS AND SINGLE PARENTS

The idealized two-child family with a father as breadwinner and mother as home-maker is less and less common today. A variety of family forms now coexist, in sometimes uneasy relationship to each other and the schools. Two that deserve special attention because of their numbers are families with employed mothers and single parents. Current estimates are that almost half of all children can expect to live in a single-parent home at some time (Seligson, Genser, Gannett, & Gray, 1983).

Considerable information is now emerging on home-school relations and the school performance of children in these kinds of families. In addition, the after-school care of children of employed mothers is receiving attention in research and policy.

Children of Employed Mothers

Several recent reviews of research have come to the same conclusion: that the employment of mothers has no universally positive or negative influence on children (Heyns, 1982; Hoffman, 1980). The only common experience is that families are better off materially and have less time together when mothers are employed (Kamerman & Hayes, 1982).

How Much Are Employed Mothers Involved with Their Children's Education?   School staff should not assume a lack of interest in education simply because mothers work outside the home. Most available evidence suggests that working parents spend no less time than non-working parents in educational activities with their children, such as monitoring or helping with homework (Tangri & Leitch, 1982; Medrich & Roizen, 1981) and strive to keep in touch with their children's school performance (Espinosa, Naron, & Lewis, 1983). They do naturally spend less time working in schools, but in two predominantly black inner-city junior high schools, more employed mothers said they went to school to keep in touch with their child's progress, and about the same proportion as nonemployed mothers kept in touch by phone. Though fewer of the employed went to PTA meetings, in several other ways the employed mothers were more positive about doing things for the school (Tangri & Leitch, 1982).

Another intensive study of families with two working parents also showed that most made significant efforts to maintain close contacts with teachers and schools. But for this and other family needs to be met, the study found that workplaces need to allow flexible short-term leave, especially for parents with young children. And schools need to give early warning of school problems, adjust their schedules, and plan well in advance in order to involve two-earner families (Mason & Espinosa, 1983). For example, employed parents have a much stronger preference for seeing school staff in the mornings or for talking on the phone in the evenings (Tangri & Leitch, 1982).

Children of Single Parents

A recent review of numerous studies does not find uniformly negative effects of living in a single-parent household (Hetherington, Camara, & Featherman, 1981). While most children and parents find the period surrounding divorce a stressful time, long-term problems may be lessened by support from friends, relatives, neighbors, and teachers. Children from one-parent homes do tend to receive lower grades, display more disruptive behavior in school, and have poorer attendance.

Several factors may contribute to this. Circumstances in the one-parent home sometimes result in children's inability to concentrate and to employ effective study habits. For example, multiple demands and stresses on divorced mothers may prevent their family life from having the regularity that helps children to come to school well prepared and on time. The lower evaluations these children receive may also reflect the tendency of teachers to rate more favorably children who conform to school routines and who are generally well behaved (Hetherington et al., 1981).

The difficulties of children from one-parent families may also be in the eye of the beholder. Two groups of teachers viewed a videotape showing social interaction of an 8-year-old boy. One group was told the boy's parents were divorced, the other group that he lived with both natural parents. Teachers rated the divorced child more negatively on happiness, emotional adjustment, and coping with stress (Santrock & Tracy, 1978). In another study, teachers were observed to direct more negative behavior toward children of divorce in the first year following the divorce, but by the second year there were no differences (Hetherington, Cox, & Cox, 1979).

How Can Teachers Help Children of Single Parents?   The stress of divorce itself seems most critical in the first year. During this period, children respond best to a relatively structured and predictable school environment (Hetherington et al., 1979). Positive adjustment also depends on qualities of the teacher, such as attentiveness, warmth, supportiveness, and assignment of reasonable responsibilities. Such an environment may be more important to young children who cannot structure their own relationships as older children can and to children experiencing more stress at home. Parents' encounters with schools may also contribute to lower performance. From information on 1,200 single parents across the country, over one-third had heard school personnel make specific negative comments about one-parent families, and almost half had heard them mention "broken homes" or other stereotypes. Over half said they had to take time off from work for conferences with teachers, and few schools provided care for younger children during school activities. Less than 10% reported that noncustodial parents received report cards or notices of school activities, although one-third noted that noncustodial parents may attend parent-teacher conferences (Clay, 1981).

Such experiences reduce the flow of information about student performance and family-related factors that could be influencing student progress. Negative comments about one-parent families also breed hostility, weaken the resolve of single parents to cooperate with the schools, and add to feelings of demoralization. Stereotypes can affect children's self-concepts too and help to create the expected negative behavior as a kind of self-fulfilling prophecy. Both staff attitudes and school practices will have to change before single parents will be able to participate effectively and comfortably in planning the education of their children with school personnel.

After-School Child Care

If present trends continue, the number of young children with two employed parents will increase in the 1980s and 1990s and with this the need for care arrangements for the hours when children are not in school. Children of single parents may be in special need of care before and after school. Already three-fourths of the single mothers of elementary school-age children work outside the home.

With such numbers likely to increase, it is important for educators to understand the child-care arrangements parents make, their concerns regarding these arrangements, and the reactions of the child to this significant part of the children's day. What happens then may affect children's preparation for school, their leisure-time interests, and even their emotional state.

Working parents use a great variety of arrangements, including self-care, care by friends, relatives, or neighbors, care centers, and organized recreation or lessons. No definitive national data exist on the number of children in different kinds of after-school care.

School-based after-school programs are relatively uncommon. In a recent survey among older children, 5% in Virginia and 10% in Minnesota were involved in such programs (Applied Management Sciences, 1983). Important elements of a good after-school care program include: the quality of the staff, ratio of staff to children, meaningful parent involvement, affordable fees, exclusive use of space, and a variety of activities for children at varying levels of development (Seligson et al., 1983).

Using the school building for before- and after-school care has several advantages: no transportation problems, a familiar and usually available facility, possibly lower costs from donated space, and encouraging parent support for public schools. School-based programs also have their problems, such as staff resistance to increased responsibilities and use of their space and the need for operating guidelines and clear policy on the relationship between the program and the school (Seligson et al., 1983). In the Virginia and Minnesota study, parents who used school-based programs were more satisfied than with any other kind of arrangement. They liked the parent involvement and educational activities for children and not having to transport children to another site after school (Applied Management Sciences, 1983).

Some localities have developed after-school care on a large scale. Miami has a countywide program in a majority of its elementary schools. Teachers act as program managers, and volunteers and paid staff provide direct care, education, and recreational activities. Fees are uniform, but programs vary. More affluent schools offer a range of educationally stimulating activities, including computer courses, while the less affluent provide tutoring, help with homework, and fewer added services (Perrault, 1983). Without a sliding-fee scale, programs do not attract as many low-income families and tend to offer different services.

There is growing interest in school-based programs, including a bill in Congress and action by at least a few state legislatures, educational associations, and local school systems. With the clear advantages of such programs, we may expect to see further consideration of this solution to the problem of after-school care.

CONCERNS WITH OLDER STUDENTS

Student Conduct

How Can Schools Help Parents Improve Student Conduct?   Students and teachers often mention the need for greater parent involvement to reduce disruptive acts in schools (National Institute of Education, 1978). A powerful incentive is the law that in all states makes parents personally responsible for school vandalism by their child if it results from lack of supervision or misdirected parenting (Wilson, 1983).

A variety of actions involving parents can be taken by schools to minimize disruptive behavior. One favored by parents themselves is notifying them at the earliest opportunity when conduct problems occur (Gotts, n.d.). Another study has found that counseling parents was more successful in reducing classroom behavior problems than direct counseling with the student (Taylor & Hoedt, 1974).

A very active relationship with parents of disruptive young people is exemplified in the Accountability in Citizenship Training program in the Jacksonville public schools. Students in grades 5 through 7 identify problem behaviors and write contracts agreeing to change one behavior at a time. Some parents are trained to visit the homes of student participants and help parents develop the desired behaviors in their children. The helped parents have been shown to provide more encouragement and reinforcement of positive behaviors (Collins et al., 1982)

A number of other examples of home-based reinforcement also appear effective in motivating children's acceptable school behavior. Various kinds of reinforcers, such as consumables, earned privileges, and verbal praise, can be administered by parents when informed of children's performance by frequent notes from school. Individual or group instruction and even letters have been used to instruct parents, and the time required of parents and teachers seems small (Barth, 1979).

On the level of group strategies, special staff and student teams have been trained to try to reduce school crime. High school teams were most effective when they tried to increase communication within the school and between the school and the community. One vehicle for this was the creation of joint parent, teacher, and student task forces. Effective middle-school teams worked to improve teacher-parent relationships (Grant & Capell, 1983).

Other strategies are incorporated in programs that help parents develop more effective child-rearing skills. Parent training has been recommended to enhance skills such as parent-child communication, to improve the fairness and moderation of family discipline, to reinforce and model desired behavior, and to provide opportunities for children to participate successfully in family life. Family crisis intervention services via family skills development also appears effective in reducing delinquent behavior and, presumably, school misbehavior as well (Hawkins & Weis, 1980).

Altogether, a great variety of home-school linkages to improve student conduct are possible, ranging from early discussion of problem behavior through reinforcement of specific acceptable behaviors to the development of communication and human relations skills in parents.

Absentees and Dropouts

How Can Schools Help Parents Improve Their Children's Attendance? Student absenteeism is a concern to both parents and school officials. Increasing daily attendance was seen as the most important of a number of possible school activities to improve academic achievement by school district officials in a national survey (Wright, 1983). Secondary school parents have also emphasized their desire to be informed quickly when children's performance or attendance drops (Gotts, n.d.).

This suggests that perhaps the most essential thing a school can do with parents is tell them promptly when students are absent. This has been done by a number of schools and school systems. Some use regular staff to search class records for absentees and then call parents. But when numbers of absentees are large, other schools supplement the regular staff with work-study students, paid aides, or volunteers (Collins et al., 1982; Tangri & Leitch, 1982). A few are also experimenting with computerized telephone dialing machines that play a recorded message, for example, "Your child was absent from school today. Please contact the school." Some considerable success is reported for these methods, especially in schools with high absence rates (LaFraniere, 1983). Although these monitoring approaches may not work with "hard-core" truants, prompt notification allows parents to use their influence to increase children's school attendance before truancy becomes a habit.

Because truancy and low grades are the strongest predictors of dropping out of school (Brantner & Enderlan, 1972), successful efforts to reduce absences also improve retention. Most effective programs combine involvement of nonschool agencies or parents and more individualized—sometimes more career- or vocationally oriented—instruction. Among the community resources involved have been law enforcement personnel and probation officers (Sweetwater Union High School District, 1982), businesses (Phillips & Rosenberger, 1983), and an autonomous social agency with varied public agency contacts and diverse facilities and programs (Berkowitz, 1971). Lotto (1982) summarizes her review of effective dropout prevention programs by listing four shared characteristics: (1) the use of multiple strategies integrated within a single program, (2) concentrating resources on a small target population, (3) placing potential or actual dropouts in environments dissimilar to traditional schools, and (4) emphasizing vocational education and work experience. (The last two items are discussed further in the final section of this chapter.)

Sex Education

Pressure on schools to provide some form of sex education grew with the awareness of the incidence of and problems associated with teenage pregnancy and childbearing. Information about the distribution, content, or effectiveness of sex education in the schools is not very good. According to Moore and Burt (1982), estimates of the number of school systems offering sex education is between 10% and 55%. Of particular interest here is the finding by several studies that a majority of states leave the decision as to whether to provide sex education to local school officials. Given the uncertainty of our knowledge even about how many schools offer such programs, it is clearly not possible to present a systematic evaluation of the effects of programs. However, a descriptive overview of exemplary programs has been provided by Kirby, Alter, and Scales (1979). What we do know is that (1) most existing sex education programs last for a total of less than 10 hours; (2) few go beyond providing information on reproductive anatomy, menstruation, venereal disease, and ethical standards, and fewer than 40% cover contraception; (3) few include parental involvement or programs for parents; (4) the majority of the well-planned courses are offered in high schools and colleges; and (5) few junior high schools focus on sexual and emotional feelings toward the opposite sex (Moore & Burt, 1982). Most critically, it appears that nonschool programs seem more likely than school-based ones to cover the more controversial topics of most interest to teens, such as contraception, sexual decision making, values, feelings, and premarital sex:

> The success of non-school programs in handling these topics is important to note, especially since non-school programs typically have more community involvement in shaping their programs than schools have. This suggests that, properly handled, programs including controversial topics can receive significant community support. (Moore & Burt, 1982, p. 64)

How Can "Significant Community Support" for Sex Education Programs Be Achieved?   In a survey of 23 communities, Scales (1982) found that observing the following "rules" tended to "offset outrage" and garner community support: (1) Use small community committees rather than large ones, (2) conduct community surveys, (3) make sure the programs discuss sexual abstinence, (4) provide staff training, (5) adopt written policies, and (6) involve parents in the program. In fact, 8 of the 31 states with policies on sex education mandate parental involvement in the program. Kirby, Alter, and Scales (1979) report that some of the most successful programs emphasize parental involvement at both the planning and operational stages of programs. In addition, several programs include education or training for parents that complements what the students receive. These are designed to give parents more accurate information about sexuality today, provide them with information about what topics are being covered in the students' classes, and hopefully improve communication between teenagers and their parents. There is reason to believe that such programs increase parent-child communication (Institute for Family Research and Education, 1977) and possibly contribute to delayed intercourse and better use of contraception (cited in Moore & Burt, 1982, p. 68).

An example of such a program is the Seminars for Parents on Family Living/Sex Education being conducted in seven New York City school districts (Collins, et al., 1982). There are five elements in the program. First is the parent orientation in which staff work with parent organizations in each district to conduct orientation sessions. Next, workshops are held to train a cadre of parents and other community adults who can in turn organize and train other parents. Third, workshops are held for teachers, supervisors, and counselors that are based on a needs assessment conducted earlier for them. Then a community resource referral network is organized, to assist students and parents. Finally, a District School Health Advisory Council is developed. This includes representatives of local public and private agencies and organizations concerned with school health and family living or sex education in the larger context of school health. The council provides broad community perspectives and support.

Specific and detailed techniques for creating successful parent discussion groups are described by Hereford (1963) in the context of a community education program on parent-child relations in Austin, Texas. Although this program was primarily aimed at changing parental attitudes, similar techniques can be employed in the context of a more bidirectional exchange among parents, educators, and students.

What Methods Are Most Effective and What Topics Need to Be Covered?   Although school programs rely more heavily on lectures than nonschool programs, the use of discussion methods, role playing, audiovisual materials as stimuli to discussion, values clarification exercises, and similar approaches are the techniques that were best received by students (Kirby et al., 1979). Approaches that teach specific problem-solving skills (Maracek, 1981) or training in decision-making and interpersonal skills (Blythe, Gilchrist, & Schenke, 1981) have the advantages of not encountering community opposition because they stress skill acquisition rather than sex-specific information and of being transferable to other areas of life.

What Can Schools Do Once Teenagers Get Pregnant?   Today's conventional wisdom is that the worst thing that can be done to a pregnant teenager is to force her out of school. Expulsion leads to significantly worsened outcomes in education, employability, and dependency (Moore & Waite, 1977). Zellman (1981) found in her field studies on 11 school districts around the country three kinds of programs that are designed to meet the educational needs of pregnant teenagers: inclusive curriculum programs, which offer general education and a range of special coursework and services; relevant coursework for credit in a supplementary curriculum to the regular classes the students attend; and noncurricular programs that do not grant credit but do provide relevant instruction and other services. Zellman does not provide a comparative evaluation of these three approaches to the needs of pregnant teenagers. In all of them, nonschool resources play an important part.

An example of the first type of program is the Educational Services for School-age Parents (ESSP; 1983). This program provides educational, nutritional, social, and health services to expectant school-age students in the public school system. The program is carried out at the Family Learning Center (FLC) in New Brunswick, NJ, which provides small classes with highly motivated teachers and emphasizes satisfactory academic achievement, maternal and child health, and nutrition. The student is also helped to reach appropriate social agencies and encouraged to attend informal rap sessions with the head teacher and guidance counselor. The program's nurse contacts the student's obstetrician and makes sure the records are complete, follows her progress, and sees to it that regular appointments are kept. After delivery and a two-week maternity leave, a student may continue her classes at the FLC for six weeks. This period of adjustment facilitates her entry into the double role of mother and student and encourages her to complete her education. The program was initiated in 1969, validated in 1973 by ESEA Title III, and has greatly decreased dropout rates of pregnant students and improved the birth weight of their babies.

OFF-CAMPUS EDUCATION AND USE OF COMMUNITY RESOURCES

Although most of the issues dealt with in this chapter and in the literature on the relationship between schools and the public concern how schools relate to parents whose children are in the school, a significant amount of educational activity for students is provided through the auspices of community organizations in cooperation with the schools. Such organizations represent a potentially large resource to the school.

Vocational and Career Education Programs

The 1978 Vocational Education Act (PH 90-576) provided for national and state advisory councils and required that these councils solicit parent participation. The councils were to conduct evaluations of vocational education programs, disseminate the findings, and make recommendations to the secretary of education for transmittal to Congress regarding such programs. Many vocational education programs have been launched, many are still operating, and some have been evaluated. However, there has been no national evaluation of such programs. Published reports of such programs generally focus on those that appear to be working well, and a few have investigated what portions of the student body are being served best by the program. There is little or no discussion of such programs at the elementary school level; we assume that if there is any attention to vocational issues, it takes the form of sporadic or annual visits by parents or other community persons who speak to individual classes about their own occupations.

At the secondary level, however, some very ambitious and well-thought-out programs are being carried out.

By What Criteria Are These Programs Judged Successful?   At least three kinds of criteria have been used to evaluate such programs. One set of criteria concerns the impact of the program on students' performance in traditional academic subject matter and school attendance; another set of criteria consist of what the student learns about vocations, the "real world," and how to cope with that world; a third set is the degree of satisfaction expressed by various constituencies, including educators, parents, the students, and the general community. The criteria applied vary with the nature and goals of the program. We will focus on programs that require students to engage in some form of off-campus activity. Thus we will not cover vocationally related courses offered within the school (such are typing, shop, accounting, and journalism), nor programs limited to school visits by outside professionals and other workers. The programs reviewed here have been considered successful by one or more of these criteria.

What Do These Programs Look Like?   A huge variety of programs take students off campus for some part of their education, ranging from an occasional field trip to a steady, paid job. What they all have in common is adult supervision of the activity, integration of the activity with the students' academic requirements, and participation by members of the larger community who are not the participants' parents. The nature and amount of this participation varies a lot.

Adopt-a-School

This program matches a particular school with a particular business on the basis of a needs survey by teachers. The coordinating agency tries to find a business that meets students' needs. For instance, in Denver, a school where attendance was identified as a major problem was paired with a corporation that owns two sports teams so that good attendance could be rewarded by having lunch with a sports hero (a very effective reinforcement). A school with a largely Hispanic student body was paired with a Hispanic-owned firm. The businesses may take students on tours of the business, let them try out equipment, give demonstrations of new technology, and develop minicourses (some of which are based on their own personnel training procedures). Some Adopt-a-School programs may involve primarily campus-based activities.

In another project, a bank, two teachers, and the Colorado Council on Economic Education developed a course that combined simulation games on various aspects of the economy with interviews in the community of persons representing different points of view and perspectives on the issues. Both the bank and the council provided resources for the course, including salary for a college economics professor who evaluated the course materials and acted as liaison for the various groups (Gonder, 1981).

Adopt-a-School partnerships may have as many as three coordinators: one at the business, one at the school, and one for parents (whose role varies with each project). This program seems to fare best when the coordinator has no direct ties with either the school system or the business establishment and can therefore act as a neutral broker. Concerns about the potential pro-business bias can be met by examination of the proposed materials. If they are basically good but have some bias, teachers can teach about the bias in the classroom (Gonder, 1981).

The Adopt-a-School program works well in large cities with an organized business community and a well-developed Chamber of Commerce but may not be as successful where these conditions do not obtain. It also tends not to involve other potentially interested constituencies like labor unions, nonprofit organizations, and community colleges. The consortium approach addresses these issues.

The Consortium Approach.   This approach is being used by about 30 local communities and states and usually consists of a central coordinating council composed of representatives from the schools, business community, labor, and government agencies. Their function is to provide a forum for traditional adversaries, to provide information, and to serve as a clearinghouse to connect the education and business communities. The councils are part of the national network Work Education Consortium, and each council receives funds from the U.S. Department of Labor (through one of three nonprofit agencies, the National Manpower Institute, the American Association of Community and Junior Colleges, or the National Alliance of Businessmen). Their common goal is to smooth the transition from education to work. For example, the Council of Southeastern Michigan got two federally funded agencies on the council to pay for computerizing a data bank on jobs. Terminals are placed throughout the county in school counselors' offices, public libraries, and state employment offices. The Livonia (MI) Council sponsored career-planning workshops for laid-off teachers. The Oakland (CA) Council did a survey and discovered that counselors, teachers, and community groups did not know how to contact employers. It set up a clearinghouse that linked nearly 1,200 young people with employers (mostly for informational interviews) in its first six months of operation.

Experience-based Career Education (EBCE). There are over 100 EBCE programs across the nation. The programs promote career exploration and academic and life-skills learning through individual projects that require multiple placements in workplaces in the local community. The programs emphasize general rather than specific career skills, are targeted to all students, combine learning about career interests with academic and personal learning objectives, and allow students to play a major role in shaping their own program. Neither the students nor the community participants are paid (National Institute of Education [NIE], 1976). The key to the success of the program is the matching of student interests with different adults in the community performing their usual daily activities (NIE, 1976). The programs are linked through the National EBCE Association.

Metanalyses of the effects of EBCE (Bucknam & Brand, 1983; Bucknam, 1976) show that EBCE students gained more than students in the typical high school curriculum on several scales pertaining to career development, life attitudes, and academic skills and that these gains are significantly larger than those of students in the regular high school curriculum. The analyses also show that the program is more successful with rural and urban students than with suburban students and more successful for poor than for middle-income students. These findings counter the argument that experiential programs serve only a narrow band of the student spectrum and serve least well those who need it most.

Programs Not Related to Work Education

There are other school-based programs that provide students with important learning experiences outside the classroom but are not particularly considered vocational, career, or work education programs. Yet like these, they use community resources and contribute to the community as well as to student learning.

The Community as a Classroom. The Parkway program in Philadelphia consists in part of simply using donated space in the community (church basements, YWCA buildings, etc.) to hold regular classes, thus saving the district the cost of constructing new classrooms and schools. Other classes are held at least some of the time in locations pertinent to the subject matter: for example, an electricity course in the utility company building, history classes at Independent Historical Park, biology classes at a nature center. Students earn academic credit for volunteer work in hospitals, museums, and local businesses. And some students actually take college courses in the community. Although some students cannot handle the autonomy and responsibility, and sometimes there are logistical mishaps, most assessments of the program have been very positive. On one index of success, time to completion of high school, the program tends to be more successful than the traditional high school, graduating many students in three years rather than four (Gonder, 1981).

The Community as Textbook.   An experiment in Rabun County, GA, to teach students "oral cultural journalism" has blossomed into a quarterly magazine (*Foxfire*) which is self-supporting even with 10 paid staff members, a constellation of school courses, and a series of books published by Anchor/Doubleday. Royalties from the books pay the salaries for seven teachers who teach courses in photography, folklore and Appalachian music, record production, and video journalism, to cite a few. Other fruits from this project include a newsletter (*Hands On!*) that exchanges information on publishing with similar projects nationwide and a textbook on cultural journalism (*You and Aunt Arie*). Aunt Arie is a local folk heroine whose life story provided the impetus for this project (Gonder, 1981).

Learning from Volunteering and Other Roles.   This is a course written by the National Information Center on Volunteerism (NICOV) and taught through the schools in cooperation with community groups. Students spend part of the week in class and the rest of the class time volunteering in the community. They learn the economic role of volunteers, careers and job-seeking skills, and facts about their community. A teacher, a staff person from a volunteer bureau, and a member of a community service organization run the program as a team. The volunteers meet about every 10 days to discuss their experiences.

The National Commission on Resources for Youth is a clearinghouse for diverse projects involving youth in meaningful innovative roles. Examples are curriculum development, tutoring of other students, peer counseling, citizenship training on issues like tenants' rights and ecology, and operating businesses. One example of this last type of project was three companies—an architecture company, an accounting company, and a construction company—formed by Manual High School in Denver to build and rehabilitate homes. In Cobb County, GA, another type of project gave students training in archaeology when a high school student discovered a valuable archaeological site.

What Do Schools, Parents, and the Community Get Out of Such Programs?

In addition to the good public relations that businesses create when they contribute to such programs, they also derive several more tangible benefits. The most important of these is the improvement of skills in the labor pool from which businesses draw their work force. The combination of an EBCE program, internships, and magnet schools proved so successful in Dallas that Texas Instruments amended their employment policy of hiring only people with AA degrees to permit hiring of Career Center graduates. In addition, employees get a morale boost from their involvement with the students and the sense of value the program gives to their own work.

Schools derive both direct and indirect benefits from the program. There are, first of all, the tangible contributions of time, expertise, and equipment that businesses and the larger community donate to such programs for instructional purposes.

The school system can also receive direct assistance for itself from businesses. Again in Dallas, businesses were asked to help the school district become more efficient in personnel procedures, food services, purchasing, distribution, and management. The increased efficiency and demonstration of concern for cost effectiveness created a climate of greater public confidence in the schools, which also helped get the bond issue passed.

Schools can also receive many forms of assistance from the community in designing and implementing the school desegregation program. A Dallas advertising agency donated time to raise $100,000 for making two professional-quality films to promote the desegregation plan in that city, and a community committee set up a speakers' bureau and information network for the same purpose.

Finally, schools involved with successful programs like these tend to report lower absenteeism, truancy, and dropout rates (Bucknam, 1976). Indeed, these are often among the measures of success of the program.

Teachers benefit from career exploration, Adopt-a-School, and vocational programs by expanding their professional contacts in the nonacademic community. More formally, some teachers receive internships in business to update their skills. In the Parkway program, teachers are excited about teaching strategies that work.

In a comparative evaluation of three different educational programs in a single racially and economically mixed high school, Coleman and Beckman (1980) found that all three programs (EBCE, Distributive Education, and Vocational Office Training) appeared to meet the needs of both the schools and the students.

Although no formal evaluation exists for most of these programs (except for EBCE), the experiences of these communities are worth learning from, as they suggest a tremendous variety of ways for schools to enrich their curricula, improve their cost-effectiveness, and build community support by drawing on the diverse resources of their own communities.

FURTHER READING

Becker, H. J., & Epstein, J. L. (1982). "Parent Involvement: A Survey of Teacher Practices." *Elementary School Journal, 83*(2), 85–102. Describes findings from a statewide survey of elementary school teachers. Fourteen techniques to involve parents were investigated. Differences in teacher use of the techniques by grade level, educational level of parents, and other conditions are discussed.

Collins, C. H., Moles, O., & Cross, M. (1982). *The Home-School Connection: Selected Partnership Programs in Large Cities.* Boston: Institute for Responsive Education. Contains profiles of 28 home-school collaboration programs in operation during the 1980–1981 school year, site visit reports on seven of these programs, a discussion and synthesis of findings across the programs, and notes toward designing a comprehensive home-school program. The programs focused on grades 4 through 12 in schools of the largest cities in the country.

Comer, J. P. (1980). *School Power: Implications of an Intervention Project.* New York: Free Press. A report on the massive and successful Baldwin-King Project in New Haven, conducted by the Yale Child Study Center. A detailed and graphic description useful for learning the mechanisms that create commitment.

Davies, D. (Ed.). (1981). *Communities and Their Schools.* New York: McGraw-Hill. Twelve chapters by different authors on the most central topics of school-community relations: governance, use of community resources, concepts of school-community relations, and so on. Both theoretical and extremely practical. Many descriptions of actual programs across the country and how they work are presented.

Henderson, A. (1981). *Parent Participation—Student Achievement: The Evidence Grows*. Columbia, MD: National Committee for Citizens in Education. This is an annotated bibliography of over 30 studies, mostly from the 1970s, that examines parent involvement and student achievement. In a foreword the author concludes that the form of parent involvement is not critical if the program is well planned, comprehensive, and enduring.

Leler, H. (1983). "Parent Education and Involvement in Relation to the Schools and to Parents of School-aged Children." In R. Haskins and D. Adams (Eds.), *Parent Education and Public Policy*. Norwood, NJ: Ablex. Reviews the best-designed studies of school programs to assist parents and indicates the most promising approaches to parent education. Findings from individual studies are discussed in detail in relation to family, school, and community impact models of parent involvement.

Lightfoot, S. L. (1978). *Worlds Apart: Relationships between Families and Schools*. New York: Basic Books. This report of an intensive, long-term study of the parent-school relationship provides excellent descriptions and insights into the social and psychological dynamics that thwart as well as enrich that relationship. Attention is paid to both race and class issues, and the perspective is well balanced.

Melaragno, R. J., Keesling, R. J., Lyons, M. F., Robbins, A. E., & Smith, A. G. (1981). *Parents and Federal Education Programs: Vol. I. The Nature, Causes, and Consequences of Parent Involvement*. Santa Monica, CA: Systems Development Corp. This is the summary volume of an extensive study of ESEA Title I, ESEA Title VII (bilingual education), the Emergency School Aid Act, and Follow Through before the first three were put into block grants. Five kinds of parent involvement were examined in 1979 at 57 locations, and detailed findings and conclusions on each kind of involvement are presented.

Moles, O. C. (1982). "Synthesis of Recent Research on Parent Participation in Children's Education." *Educational Leadership*, 40(2), 44–47. This short overview describes some effects of parent participation on children's achievement, ways in which parents participate, some barriers to home-school collaboration, and promising school programs to involve parents. The article shows that there is considerable interest among parents and educators in fostering more parent involvement in education.

Moore, K. A., & Burt, M. R. (1982). *Private Crisis, Public Cost: Policy Perspectives on Teenage Childbearing*. Washington, DC: Urban Institute Press. A thorough review of research and policy options on every aspect of the teenage pregnancy issue. Concludes with a chapter on policy recommendations, some of which are aimed at schools and their communities.

National Institute of Education. (1976). *Experienced-based Career Education: A New Approach to Secondary Education*. Washington, DC: U.S. Department of Education. Provides a general description of the elements of EBCE, its functions and goals, and distinctive features of the program that account for its effectiveness.

REFERENCES

Applied Management Sciences. (1983). School-age day care study: Executive summary. Silver Springs, MD: Author. (Mimeographed)

Armor, D., Conry-Oseguera, P., Cox, M., King, N., McDonnell, L., Pascal, A., Pauly, E., & Zellman, G. (1976). *Analysis of the school-preferred reading program in selected Los Angeles minority schools*. Santa Monica, CA.: Rand Corp.

Barth, R. (1979). Home-based reinforcement of school behavior: A review and analysis. *Review of Educational Research, 49*, 436–458.

Berkowitz, L. (Ed.). (1971). *Staying in school: An evaluation of a program to prevent school dropouts* (Final Report). New York: Educational Alliance.

Bittle, R. G. (1975). Improving parent-teacher communication through recorded telephone messages. *Journal of Educational Research, 69*(3), 87–95.

Bloom, B. S. (1981). *All our children learning.* New York: McGraw-Hill.

Blythe, B., Gilchrist, L. D., & Schenke, S. (1981). Pregnancy prevention groups for adolescents. *Social Work, 26,* 503–504.

Brantner, S. T., & Enderlan, T. E. (1972). *A comparison of vocational and nonvocational high school dropouts and retainers.* Harrisburg: Pennsylvania State University, Research Co-ordinating Unit for Vocational Education.

Brookover, W. B., Beady, C., Flood, P., Schweitzer, J., & Wisenbaker, J. (1979). *School social systems and student achievement: Schools can make a difference.* New York: Praeger.

Buchanan, A. E., Hansen, P. J., & Quilling, M. R. (1969). Effects of increased home-school contact on performance and attitudes in mathematics. Madison: University of Wisconsin, Research and Development Center for Cognitive Learning. (ERIC Document Reproduction Service No. ED 036 446)

Bucknam, R. B. (1976). The impact of EBCE: An evaluator's viewpoint. *Illinois Career Education Journal, 33*(3), 32–36.

Bucknam, R. B., & Brand, S. E. (1983). EBCE really works. *Educational Leadership, 4*(6), 66–71.

Cantril, A. H. (1979). The school-home community relationship: An interpretive summary of the public view. Report prepared for the U.S. Office of Education.

Clay, P. L. (1981). *Single parents and the public schools: How does the partnership work?* Columbia, MD: National Committee for Citizens in Education.

Coleman, D., & Beckman, C. A. (1980). *The ecology of youth participation in work settings: Implications for linking home, school, and work for facilitating communication between youth and adults.* (Tech. Rep.). Columbus: Ohio State University, National Center for Research on Vocational Education.

Collins, C. H., Moles, O., & Cross, M. (1982). *The home-school connection: Selected partnership programs in large cities.* Boston: Institute for Responsive Education.

Comer, J. P. (1980). *School power: Implications of an intervention project.* New York: Free Press.

Davies, D. (1976). *Schools where parents make a difference.* Boston: Institute for Responsive Education.

Davies, D. (Ed.). (1981). *Communities and their schools.* New York: McGraw-Hill.

DiPrete, T. A. (1981). *Discipline, order, and student behavior in American high schools.* Chicago: National Opinion Research Center.

Education Commission of the States. (1977). *Analysis of supplemental background questions on homework and TV.* Denver: Author.

Education Commission of the States. (1980). *Report of the ECS Priorities Committee.* Denver: Author.

Educational Services for School-age Parents (ESSP). (1983). *Educational programs that work.* San Francisco: Far West Laboratory.

Epstein, J. L. (1982, March). Student reactions to teachers' practices of parent involvement. Paper presented at the annual meeting of the American Educational Research Association, New York.

Epstein, J. L. (1983). *Effects on parents of teacher practices of parent involvement* (Rep. No. 346). Baltimore: Johns Hopkins University, Center for Social Organization of Schools.

Epstein, J. L. (1984, April). *Effects of parent involvement on change in student achievement in reading and math.* Paper presented at the annual meeting of the American Educational Research Association, New Orleans.

Epstein, J. L., & Becker, H. J. (1982). Teachers' reported practices of parent involvement: Problems and possibilities. *Elementary School Journal, 83,* 103–113.

Espinosa, R., Naron, N., & Lewis, S. (1983). *Work and family life among Anglo, black, and Mexican-American single-parent families: Executive summary.* Austin, TX: Southwest Educational Development Laboratory. (Mimeographed)

Filipczak, J., Lordeman, A., & Friedman, R. M. (1977, April). *Parental involvement in the schools: Toward what end?* Paper presented at the annual meeting of the American Educational Research Association, New York.

Florida Department of Education. (1983). *Interlock: Florida school volunteer program directory.* Tallahassee: Author.

Gallup, G. H. (1978). The 10th annual Gallup poll of the public's attitudes toward the public schools. *Phi Delta Kappan, 60,* 33–45.

Gonder, P. O. (1981). Exchange school and community resources. In D. Davies (Ed.), *Communities and their schools.* New York: McGraw-Hill.

Goodlad, J. I. (1981). Education, schools, and a sense of community. In D. Davies (Ed.), *Communities and their schools.* New York: McGraw-Hill.

Goodson, B. D., & Hess, R. D. (1975). *Parents as teachers of young children: An evaluative review of some contemporary concepts and programs.* Washington, DC: U.S. Department of Health, Education and Welfare, Office of Education.

Gotts, E. E. (n.d.). *Ways that effective home-school communications change across grade levels.* Charleston, WV: Appalachian Educational Laboratory. (Mimeographed)

Grant, J., & Capell, F. J. (1983). *Reducing school crime: A report on the school team approach.* San Rafael, CA: Social Action Research Center. (Mimeographed)

Graue, M. E., Weinstein, T., & Walberg, H. J. (1983, April). School-based home instruction and learning: A quantitative synthesis. Paper presented at the annual meeting of the American Educational Research Association, Montreal, Canada.

Guttentag, M. (1972). Children in Harlem's community-controlled schools. *Journal of Social Issues, 28*(4), 1–20.

Hawkins, J. D., & Weis, J. E. (1980). *The social development model: An integrated approach to delinquency prevention.* Seattle: University of Washington, Center for Law and Justice. (Mimeographed)

Heisler, F., & Crowley, F. (1969). *Parental participation: Its effect on the first grade achievement of children in a depressed area.* Wyandanch, NY: Union Free School District 9. (Mimeographed)

Hereford, C. F. (1963). *Changing parental attitudes through group discussion.* Austin: University of Texas Press.

Hetherington, E. M., Camara, K. A., & Featherman, D. L. (1981). *Cognitive performance, school behavior, and achievement of children from one-parent households.* Paper prepared for the National Institute of Education.

Hetherington, E. M., Cox, M., & Cox, R. (1979). Family interaction and the social, emotional, and cognitive development of children following divorce. In V. Vaughn & T. B. Brazelton (Eds.), *The family: Setting priorities.* New York: Science and Medicine Publishing Co.

Heyns, B. (1982). The influence of parents' work on children's school achievement. In S. B. Kamerman & C. D. Hayes (Eds.), *Families that work: Children in a changing world.* Washington, DC: National Academy Press.

Hoffman, L. W. (1980). *The effects of maternal employment on the academic attitudes and performance of school-aged children.* Paper prepared for the National Institute of Education.

Institute for Family Research and Education. (1977). *Community life programs for parents: A training manual for organizers.* Syracuse, NY: Author.

Iverson, B. K., Brownlee, G. D., & Walberg, H. K. (1981). Parent-teacher contacts and student learning. *Journal of Educational Research, 74,* 394–396.

Kamerman, S. B., & Hayes, C. D. (Eds.). (1982). *Families that work: Children in a changing world.* Washington, DC: National Academy Press.

Kirby, D., Alter, J., & Scales, P. (1979). *An analysis of U.S. sex education programs and evaluation methods*. Washington, DC: U.S. Department of Health, Education and Welfare.

LaFraniere, S. (1983, Dec. 14). The computerized truant officer. *Washington Post*, B-1.

Leler, H. (1983). Parent education and involvement in relation to the schools and to parents of school-aged children. In R. Haskins & D. Adams (Eds.), *Parent education and public policy*. Norwood, NJ: Ablex.

Lightfoot, S. L. (1978). *Worlds apart: Relationships between families and schools*. New York: Basic Books.

Losen, S. M., & Diament, B. (1978). *Parent conferences in the schools*. Boston: Allyn & Bacon.

Lotto, L. S. (1982). The holding power of vocational curricula: Characteristics of effective dropout prevention programs. *Journal of Vocational Education Research, 7*(4), 39–48.

Maracek, J. (1981). Psycho-Social Workshop presentation at the annual meeting of the Population Association of America, Washington, DC.

Marshall, G., & Herbert, M. (1981). *Evaluation report: Recorded telephone messages—a way to link teacher and parents*. St. Louis: Central Midwest Regional Educational Laboratory.

Mason, T., & Espinosa, R. (1983). *Executive summary of the final report: Working parents project*. Austin, TX: Southwest Educational Development Laboratory. (Mimeographed)

Medrich, E. A., & Roizen, J. A. (1981). *The serious business of growing up*. Berkeley: University of California Press.

Melaragno, R. J., Keesling, J. W., Lyons, M. F., Robbins, A. E., & Smith, A. G. (1981). *Parents and federal education programs: Vol. 1. The nature, causes, and consequences of parental involvement*. Santa Monica, CA.: Systems Development Corp.

Minnesota Department of Education. (1982). *A report on a study of volunteerism in Minnesota school districts*. St. Paul: Author.

Moles, O. C. (1982). Synthesis of recent research on parent participation in children's education. *Educational Leadership, 40*(2), 44–47.

Moore, K. A., & Burt, M. R. (1982). *Private crisis, public cost: Policy perspectives on teenage childbearing*. Washington, DC: Urban Institute Press.

Moore, K. A., & Waite, L. J. (1977). Early childbearing and educational attainment. *Family Planning Perspectives, 9*(5), 220–225.

Murray, B. B. (1972). *Individualized amelioration of learning disability through parent helper—pupil involvement*. Clarksville, TN: Austin Peay State University.

Murray, S. R. (n.d.). *Stimulating parental involvement in secondary schools: Things that get in the way*. Washington, DC: Public Schools.

National Education Association. (1982). *Productive relationships: Parent-school-teacher*. Washington, DC: Author.

National Institute of Education. (1976). *Experience-based career education: A new approach to secondary education*. Washington, DC: U.S. Department of Education.

National Institute of Education. (1978). *Violent schools—safe schools: The safe school study report to the Congress* (Vol. 1). Washington, DC: U.S. Department of Health, Education, and Welfare.

National School Volunteer Program. (1983). *The idea bulletin*. Alexandria, VA.: Author.

Niedermeyer, F. C. (1969). *Effects of school-to-home feedback and parent accountability on kindergarten reading performance, parent participation, and pupil attitude*. Doctoral dissertation, University of California, Los Angeles.

Olmsted, P. P. (1983). *Long-term effects of Parent Education Follow Through program participation*. Chapel Hill: University of North Carolina, School of Education.

Olmsted, P. P., & Rubin, R. I. (n.d.). *Linking parent behaviors to child achievement: Four evaluation studies from the Parent Education Follow Through program*. Chapel Hill: University of North Carolina, School of Education. (Mimeographed)

Parker, F. C., & McCoy, J. F. (1977). School-based intervention for the modification of excessive absenteeism. *Psychology in the Schools, 14*, 84–88.

Paschal, R. A., Weinstein, T., & Walberg, H. J. (1983, April). *The effects of homework on learning: A quantitative synthesis.* Paper presented at the annual meeting of the American Educational Research Association, Montreal, Canada.

Perrault, G. (1983). After-school day care. *Networker, 4*(3), 1, 6.

Phillips, G., & Rosenberger, T. (1983). Breaking the failure cycle in an inner-city high school. *NASSP Bulletin, 67,* 30–35.

Rich, D. K. (1976). The relationship of the home learning lab technique to first grade student achievement in the archdiocese of Washington, D.C., schools. *Dissertation Abstracts, 37,* 5509–A.

Rotter, J. C., & Robinson, E. H., III. (1982). *Parent-teacher conferencing.* Washington, DC: National Education Association.

Santrock, J. W., & Tracy, R. L. (1978). Effects of children's family structure status on the development of stereotypes by teachers. *Journal of Educational Psychology, 70,* 754–757.

Scales, P. (1981). Sex education and the prevention of teenage pregnancy: An overview of policies and programs in the United States. In T. Ooms (Ed.), *Teenage pregnancy in a family context.* Philadelphia: Temple University Press.

Scales, P. (1982). Offset outrage: Let parents help land your sex education program. *American School Board Journal, 169*(7), 32–33.

Seligson, M., Genser, A., Gannett, E., & Gray, W. (1983). *School-age child care: A policy report.* Wellesley, MA: Wellesley College, Center for Research on Women.

Sheats, D., & Dunkleberger, G. E. (1979). A determination of the principal's effect in school-initiated home contacts concerning attendance of elementary school students. *Journal of Educational Research, 72*(6), 310–312.

Shelton, J., & Dobson, R. L. (1973). An analysis of a family involvement-communication system in a Title I elementary school (Final report.) (ERIC Document Reproduction Service No. ED 082 091)

Smith, M. B. (1968). School and home: Focus on achievement. In A. H. Passow (Ed.), *Developing programs for the educationally disadvantaged.* New York: Teachers College Press.

Stallworth, N. T., & Williams, D. L., Jr. (1982). *Executive summary of the final report: A survey of parents regarding parent involvement in the schools.* Austin, TX: Southwest Educational Development Laboratory.

Stallworth, J. T., & Williams, D. L., Jr. (1983). *Executive summary of the final report: A survey of school administrators and policy makers.* Austin, TX: Southwest Educational Development Laboratory.

Stanford Research Institute. (1973). *Parent involvement in compensatory education programs.* Menlo Park, CA: Stanford Research Institute.

Stough, M. F. (1982). *Lowering barriers to home-school communication: In search of a redefinition of parent involvement. The perceptions of 482 parents as expressed in personal interviews.* Washington, DC: U.S. Department of Education.

Sweetwater Union High School District. (1982). Operation stay in school. *Superintendent's Communicator, 3*(2).

Tangri, S. S., & Leitch, L. M. (1982). *Barriers to home-school collaboration: Two case studies in junior high schools* (Final Report to the National Institute of Education).

Taylor, W. F., & Hoedt, K. C. (1974). Classroom-related behavior problems: Counsel parents, teacher, or children? *Journal of Counseling Psychology, 21,* 3–8.

Thomas, M. D. (n.d.). *Volunteerism in public education.* Salt Lake City, UT: Salt Lake School District.

Thornberg, K. R. (1981). Attitudes of secondary principals, teachers, parents, and students toward parent involvement in the schools. *High School Journal, 64,* 150–153.

Wagenaar, T. C. (1977). *School achievement level vis-à-vis community involvement and support: An empirical assessment.* Columbus: Ohio State University, Mershon Center.

Wilson, J. L. (1983). Parental responsibility for student vandalism. In *School Law Update, 1982*. Topeka, KS: National Organization on Legal Problems in Education.

Wright, D. (1983). *School district survey of academic requirements and achievement: Early release*. Washington, DC: U.S. Department of Education, National Center for Education Statistics. (Mimeographed)

Zellman, G. L. (1981). *A Title IX perspective on the schools' response to teenage pregnancy and parenthood* (Rep. No. R–2759/1 NIE). Santa Monica, CA: Rand Corp.

PART FIVE

Professional Issues

Lee S. Shulman, Editor

Many recent reforms, such as career ladders and mentor teacher programs, are designed to enhance the teaching occupation in order to attract more academically able individuals into teaching and in order to keep effective teachers in the classroom. These reforms are moving on two fronts: the conditions of schooling, and the rewards and career opportunities for teachers. The conditions of schooling are well described in Chapter 23, by Henrietta Schwartz and George Olson. School violence, poor facilities and equipment, large class sizes, and disrespectful attitudes on the part of students can make schools unpleasant places for teachers and students alike. Further, teachers do not have the amenities offered in other professions. For example, teachers do not have access to telephones except in the school office or the public booths. Rewards are few and far between. Beginning salaries of teachers, adjusted for 12 months, are lower than for any other field requiring a bachelor's degree, and they peak sooner and at a lower level than other college-degree-level occupations (National Education Association, 1984).

Will these recent reforms attract to the occupation the high-caliber individuals that many feel avoid teaching? Will they change the public image of teaching that caused a writer for *Newsweek* (1984, September) to describe teaching as "the most scorned quasi-profession in America"? And will we at last be able to say that teaching is a profession?

An occupation that is a profession has a formal knowledge base that can be passed on to people entering the occupation. As indicated in many chapters in this book, the formal knowledge base for teaching is growing. Another condition for an occupation to be a profession is that its members be attentive to the occupation's professional aspects. Professionals attend informational conferences, read professional journals, develop codes and norms for behavior, govern their own behavior, and pay close attention to the state of their profession. Teachers have done this, to a certain degree, through their various organizations. But teachers as a group still do not govern their own lives or pay attention to the state of teaching.

The chapters in this section cover some critical aspects of the teaching occupation that do not necessarily directly affect what happens in the classroom but can affect who gets into the classroom, how much they are paid, the level of stress felt on a daily basis by teachers, and, to a certain degree, how teachers feel about themselves as professionals. These factors have a lasting effect on the education system as a whole and are as important to the future of our children as the specific techniques used by teachers in the classroom.

In Chapter 22, Susan Moore Johnson provides a history of collective bargaining and summarizes the literature on the effects of bargaining on salaries, on the ways teachers spend their time, and on student learning. Stress and burnout is the topic of Chapter 23, by Schwartz and Olson. Clearly, the conditions of schooling today cause much stress, but the authors point out that some of this can be alleviated by the individual teacher or the school organization. In Chapter 24, David Schimmel presents several controversial legal issues of the day—discipline, due process, and religion in the schools—and the responsibilities of teachers in relation to these issues. Finally, Lovely Billups and Marilyn Rauth of the American Federation of Teachers present a model for teachers to become actively engaged in the translation of research into practice, in itself a type of research. Billups and Rauth feel that such active involvement will help to break down the barriers between teaching and research and will help to professionalize the occupation.

These chapters are a modest attempt to begin to outline the issues that need to be addressed as teachers move toward governing their own professional lives and improving those conditions that stand in the way of effective practice.

Virginia Richardson-Koehler
Senior Editor

REFERENCES

National Education Association. (1984). *Prices, Budgets, Salaries, and Income: 1983.* Washington, DC: National Education Association.
Why teachers fail. (1984, September 24). *Newsweek*, pp. 64–70.

22 COLLECTIVE BARGAINING

Susan Moore Johnson

Teachers have always been uneasy about teacher unionism. Having acquired a modicum of professional status, they have shunned unions' blue-collar image. Believing that teaching advances the social good, they have suspected that collective bargaining might compromise the public interest. Prizing autonomy, teachers have been concerned that written contracts might constrain their practice. Preferring collegial, reciprocal relationships with administrators, they have anticipated that collective bargaining would pit labor against management. Being a circumspect lot, teachers have objected to labor's seeming endorsement of strident confrontation.

Despite these tensions, over the course of this century teachers have exchanged the image of public servants for that of hard-bargaining teacher advocates, a shift many people regard as an unfortunate compromise of professional standards. Low pay, low status, and administrative abuse promoted union growth. By 1982, 91% of all teachers belonged to either the National Education Association or the American Federation of Teachers, and approximately 89% of all school districts with more than 1,000 students bargained collectively with their professional staff (Mitchell & Kerchner, 1983, p. 214).

During the early days of teacher bargaining, there were conflicting expectations about what teacher unionism would mean for teachers and schools. Some educators and commentators anticipated that collective bargaining would legitimate teacher influence on educational policy, while others feared that it would promote union control of schools. Some anticipated that it would advance constructive reform of schooling, while others thought that it would stultify improvement efforts and rigidly standardize practice. Many hoped that collective bargaining would augment the teachers' professional standing; some predicted that it would debase both them and their work.

After two decades of collective bargaining, it is possible to review what teacher unionism has meant for teachers and their schools. Since the mid-1960s, educational researchers have sought to identify and interpret the effects of collective bargaining.

Their findings provide tentative answers to questions often posed in the debate about teacher unionism: What issues do contracts address? How uniform and consistent are the effects of collective bargaining? How has negotiation affected principals' authority and principal-teacher relationships? Have teachers' rights and protections been increased? Has collective bargaining changed their work load or enhanced their roles as policymakers? Has it affected student achievement? What difference has collective negotiation made in teachers' wages? Has it affected their professionalism?

In exploring each of these questions, the following discussion focuses primarily on the organizational effects of teacher unionism, with some attention to its effects on wages. Although a number of empirical studies have addressed these issues, educational labor relations remains a relatively unexamined topic. A final assessment of collective bargaining must await more extensive investigation of all outcomes of the process, including little-explored topics such as strikes, changes in governance, effects of negotiated staffing policies, and changes in district resource allocation.

A brief review of the development of teacher unionism and collective bargaining practices will provide a background for the discussion about effects that follows.

BACKGROUND

When the National Teachers Association, forerunner of the National Education Association (NEA), was formed in Philadelphia in 1857, its membership included both teachers and school officials who sought to "elevate the character and advance the interest of the profession of teaching, and...promote the cause of popular education in the United States" (Wesley, 1957, pp. 23–24). The American Federation of Teachers (AFT), founded in Chicago in 1916, also sought to "elevate the character of the profession of teacher," but its membership was restricted to classroom teachers, and its attention centered more on wages and conditions of work, "the rights to which [teachers] are entitled" (Commission on Educational Reconstruction, 1955, pp. 27–28).

Throughout the first half of this century, the AFT and the NEA pursued separate courses. Stressing their professional orientation, NEA leaders resisted teachers' efforts to commit the organization to higher teacher salaries. AFT members, who resented the NEA's avoidance of the salary issue, nonetheless disapproved of strikes and resisted close affiliation between their union and organized labor. Wayne Urban (1982) observes that "even at its most militant, the AFT pursued improved working conditions, as well as higher standards for entry-level teachers, in language which appealed to teachers' desire for occupational respectability" (p. 139).

Between 1919 and the early 1970s, the relative strength and influence of the AFT and NEA shifted repeatedly in response to a variety of influences—the two World Wars, the Great Depression, McCarthyism. Neither enjoyed sustained strength or influence, and the wages and status of teachers remained low.

There is no single explanation for the dramatic change in the size and power of teachers' unions during the 1960s. National concern about public education, galvanized by the Russians' launching of *Sputnik*, promoted speculation about a teacher shortage and generated proposals for pay increases, which bolstered the unions' efforts. Also, the ranks of teachers were increasingly male after World War II, and this new interest group with families to support began to press for higher wages and to endorse more aggressive action by their organizations.

The growth of teacher unionism was partly attributable to an increasing bureaucracy in education. Bruce S. Cooper (1982) explains:

> Public school educators, then, were reacting to the centralization and consolidation of American public schools; the regimentation that resulted from local, state, and federal regulation of schools; and the impact of uniformity brought about by the single salary schedule, tenure regulations, and certification and recertification requirements. (p. 6)

In addition, the 1960s were a time of attention to personal rights and social causes. Groups that had once been acquiescent actively pursued their aims; teachers advocated their self-interests as well. Some argue that the most important of the many factors promoting growth in union membership and bargaining activity was the intense rivalry between the NEA and the AFT. In 1960, the AFT represented 50,000 teachers and the NEA 14 times that number. The NEA advertised "professionalism," and the AFT promised attention to wages and working conditions. Many teachers wanted both, and the goals and strategies of the two organizations all but merged. Membership in both organizations surged, and by 1978 the AFT reportedly had 500,000 members while the NEA claimed 1.7 million.

The enactment of state collective bargaining laws was both a cause and a consequence of that growth. During the 1960s and 1970s, one state after another passed laws requiring local schools boards to recognize and negotiate with local teachers' unions. These laws defined the scope of issues that might or must be bargained and set forth administrative boards to oversee the process. By the mid-1980s, 33 states and the District of Columbia required local school boards to negotiate with teachers. Ten states authorized teachers to strike when efforts to reach a contract settlement fail.

Assessing the effects of such dramatic change is important but difficult. Although much has been written about educational labor relations, little of that writing is based on empirical research. Most journal articles recount the experiences of one local district, present the advice of a single administrator or teacher, or advocate the position of labor or management. Much of the empirical research that has been done centers on salary scales rather than school practices, and attempts to measure the effects of collective bargaining on teacher salaries by comparing wage increases in unionized and nonunionized districts. Research studies that examine the nonwage effects of collective bargaining typically use one of two methods, contract analysis or field study. With the first, researchers usually use quantitative methods to compare contract contents and to determine how negotiation has affected local educational policies. With the second, typically qualitative studies, researchers visit the local districts and seek to understand the negotiation process, contract administration, and the effects of negotiated policies on school practice. Our discussion will draw mainly from the conclusions of the qualitative studies because they are currently most directly applicable to local decision making. However, it must be emphasized that this research is exploratory and not conclusive. There is much yet to be investigated before we can generalize about these findings.

It is important to mention one additional caveat. The effects of collective bargaining are, for the most part, inextricable from the effects of many other forces that have reshaped public education since the 1960s—declining enrollments, inflation, federal aid to education, desegregation, and reduced school revenues. Because collective bargaining has interacted with these and other factors, we can't know what schooling might have been like if it had not been for collective bargaining. We can only describe current labor practices and their apparent effects on today's schools.

WHAT ISSUES DO TEACHER CONTRACTS ADDRESS?

Teacher contracts typically cover a wide range of subjects including wages, hours, working conditions, and, increasingly, matters of educational policy. Some contracts are short (15 pages) and cover only a few basic issues—pay, length of the workday and workyear, grievance procedures, teacher assignment, and meeting requirements. Others are long (100 pages) and set forth detailed policies regulating many additional issues—class size, reduction in force, transfers, nonteaching duties, teacher aides, union representatives, promotions, supervision and evaluation, preparation time, duty-free lunch, in-service meetings, policy committees, building maintenance, and student discipline.

In seeking to identify trends in the nonsalary items of collective bargaining agreements, Lorraine McDonnell and Anthony Pascal (1979) compared the 1970 and 1975 contracts of 155 local districts. They found a "convergence of collective bargaining outcomes" over time, that is, less variation in contract contents in 1975 than in 1970 (p. 31). However, they also found that of the 11 key provisions they had identified, only four—grievance arbitration, class hours, pupil exclusion, and teacher evaluation—were included in the majority of 1975 contracts, leading them to conclude that although "organized teachers have successfully negotiated a number of provisions that have constrained the traditional prerogatives of school management," the gains "have been neither universal nor total" (1978, p. 35). These researchers concluded that teachers had "significantly improved their working conditions and increased their influence over school and classroom operations." They "now play a major role in decisions about the length and composition of the school day, how teachers are evaluated, and how supplementary personnel are used in schools" (1979, p. vii).

It is important to distinguish between the presence of a contract provision and the relative strength of that provision. Contracts can be comprehensive yet do little to advance teachers' interests. For example, an agreement calling for an eight-hour workday defines the limits of teachers' in-school responsibilities but does not reduce them. Similarly, a provision stating that the school board will work to reduce class size provides little assurance of smaller classes. In general, the formal literature reports frequencies of contract items rather than comparisons of contract provisions addressing the same issue.

While informative, contracts can only tell what has been formally negotiated. We can read words, but we don't know the understanding behind the words. Contracts don't tell how provisions are interpreted by local teachers and administrators or whether they are complied with and enforced. Because contracts often address similar issues with similar language, many people conclude that the effects of collective bargaining are quite consistent across unionized districts. However, field studies that investigate the negotiation and implementation of these contracts have complicated that view.

How Consistent Are Educational Labor Practices?

The very word *union* implies uniformity. It is generally assumed that one of the primary goals of unionism is the standardization of personnel practices and work rules. In the belief that strength comes in unified numbers, employees submit their individual interests to the group's interests. Many opponents of collective bargaining believe that the standardizing forces of unionism are strong and that eventually all unionized teachers will comply with the same list of minimal job requirements while all school officials will be constrained by the same set of procedural requirements and limts of their managerial prerogatives.

Similarly, some who study educational labor relations focus on the uniformity of collective bargaining outcomes. For example, having examined data from approximately 5,000 teachers in more than 250 school districts, Randall Eberts (1982) generalizes about time allocation of unionized teachers and about "what collective bargaining has done to education in general in this country." He reports that through negotiation, teachers "reduced the amount of time they spent in instruction by about ten minutes a day" and spent more time on preparation, administrative, and clerical tasks and in meetings with parents (pp. 93–96).

By contrast, other researchers explore the diversity of effects within general trends. For example, Charles Kerchner and Douglas Mitchell (1981) describe "generational" patterns in the negotiation practices of eight local districts in Illinois and California while also documenting in some detail the variation within those patterns.

In my own study of six local districts selected for their diversity on a number of variables (Johnson, 1984), I identified a number of general consequences of bargaining for schools: Principals have less formal authority, and teachers can exercise more power; school personnel practices are increasingly standardized, and grievance procedures reinforce the hierarchical structure of schools; teachers, whose work obligations have been defined and often reduced, can rely on their contracts and unions to protect their jobs (pp. 14–15).

But within these general trends, I also found considerable variation both among and within districts. Teachers in the six districts had neither pursued nor won the same rights and protections, and differences in contract language produced differences in teacher work patterns and school practices from district to district. Labor practices were variously collaborative, cooperative, or contentious. Some local unions aggressively represented teacher interests, while some others were cautious and unassertive. Some district office administrators preferred centralized management of labor relations, while others maintained more decentralized organizations (pp. 164–165).

In addition to the variation in labor practices from district to district, there was variation from school to school within those districts. In some sample schools, the contract was quite prominent and rigorously enforced, while in others within the same district it was barely mentioned or teachers knowingly bent it "for the good of the school." There were schools with hostile labor relationships and many grievances and schools with cordial labor relationships and no grievances. There were schools where a number of teachers did little more than the contract required and schools where most teachers went well beyond its minimal demands.

Unquestionably, teacher unionism has exerted similar influences on schools and school districts. By its very nature, collective bargaining augments the rights of teachers, constrains the powers of management, centralizes contract negotiation, and standardizes contract administration. Yet labor practices and collective bargaining outcomes in both the public and private sectors are considerably more diverse than many believe.

From the perspective of local teachers and administrators, it is important in any analysis of collective bargaining outcomes to identify both general trends and variations within them. To emphasize only what is uniform, predictable, and certain is to suggest that local actors, from the negotiating table to the offices and classrooms of the district, are puppets in a predetermined play. In fact, local teachers and administrators intentionally and substantially regulate the impact of teacher unionism on their schools. Conversely, to attend to diversity and ignore identifiable trends or patterns would mask the fact that collective bargaining has changed and continues to change public schools.

Why Do Local Labor Practices Vary?

There are at least three factors that promote diversity in educational labor relations: the decentralized character of teacher unionism, strong norms of professional autonomy among teachers, and unresolved debates about educational policy and practice.

First, unlike the auto- or steelworkers, teachers have no single national union negotiating on their behalf. Each of the approximately 10,000 local teachers' organizations that bargain does so independently. Priorities and strategies are influenced, but certainly not controlled, by the national organizations. NEA and AFT field representatives furnish their local affiliates with research, advice, training, and bargaining expertise, but final decisions about priorities, tactics, and settlements rest with local teachers. NEA and AFT officials advocate strong contracts that protect teacher rights and advance teacher interests, but they acknowledge the independence of the locals. In fact, the national unions probably exert more direct influence in the state legislatures than at the many local negotiating tables.

The autonomy of each teachers' union results largely from the decentralized governance of American education. Local school districts are funded primarily by local governments and are controlled by local school boards comprised of lay citizens. Only in Hawaii are the school boards unified into a single district and governed at the state level. Therefore, local contract settlements reflect local values and practices, are influenced by local personalities, and are constrained by local budgets and the failures of local tax levies.

Second, teachers as an employee group value their independence and would likely oppose relinquishing control of local bargaining even if governance structures permitted it. Strong professional norms support teacher autonomy and resist standardization of teaching practice. The failures of "teacher-proof" curricula stand as testimony to that independence. Teachers affiliate with unions cautiously and endorse union positions selectively, accepting the rhetoric and tactics that are consistent with their values and priorities while rejecting those that are not.

Third, although teachers generally agree that they deserve higher pay and better working conditions, they differ about what issues should be negotiated, what particular contract provisions are best, and what negotiation trade-offs are wisest. For example, should the workday be defined to protect teachers from unreasonable administrative demands or remain undefined to preserve teachers' professional discretion? Is it better to relieve teachers from supervisory duties and thus provide them with more preparation time, or does the civilizing presence of teachers in the cafeteria outweigh the benefits of additional time for planning and conferences? Do performance-based layoffs, designed to retain better teachers during periods of reduction in force, benefit schools more than seniority-based layoffs, which minimize uncertainty and divisiveness? Because the process of schooling is complex, its intended outcomes are many, and its instructional theories are varied, teachers often differ among themselves about the anticipated effects of alternative contract provisions and compromises.

RIGHTS AND ROLES

Before collective bargaining, virtually the only protections most teachers had against unfair treatment were patronage and tenure laws shielding teachers who had successfully completed probationary teaching from sudden, unwarranted dismissal. While tenure provided job security for experienced teachers, it did not protect nontenured staff, nor did it provide any teachers with a course of redress for administrative actions short of dismissal. Union contracts provide teachers with new rights and protections by defining procedures for evaluation, transfer, and reduction in force, as well as by empowering teachers to challenge administrative decisions through the grievance process.

Grievance Procedures

Grievance procedures are often called the "heart" or "guts" of the contract because without them, the rest of the contract is unenforceable. They specify a series of steps and deadlines by which an employee can initiate a complaint, receive a response, and pursue it, if necessary, to a higher level. Typically, the meeting at the first step is held with the building principal, the second with a central office administrator, the third with the school board, and the final before a neutral arbitrator who renders a binding decision. McDonnell and Pascal (1979) found in their analysis of contracts that grievance procedures culminating in arbitration were included more frequently than any other key provision. By 1975, 83% of the contracts they had studied had them (p. 12).

The range of issues that may be formally protested varies by contract. In some cases, grievances must allege specific contract violations, while in others they may challenge a wide range of administrative actions. Although in most districts relatively few grievances are formally filed—it would be unusual to have more than five in a school per year—many more are informally raised. Principals report that the threat of grievance and arbitration hearings, which can be time-consuming and emotionally taxing, promote administrative compliance with the contract. Kerchner and Mitchell (1981) conclude, "Grievance threats force management to give attention to situations that they might have preferred to ignore. Since managerial time and attention are scarce, the ability to file a grievance is a powerful attention-getting device"

(p. 6:25). Grievance procedures have greatly augmented the power of teachers. Principals, who used to be accountable only to district officials or their school board, have become accountable to the teachers they supervise.

Teacher Evaluation

Union contracts also regulate the process of teacher evaluation. They specify who will conduct the evaluations—typically principals or department heads—and how frequently they will be completed—usually annually or once every three years. Most contracts also specify the number of classroom observations on which evaluations are to be based and provide teachers with the right to include written responses in their personnel files. Although teachers' substantive challenges of their evaluations are rarely upheld, violations of procedure—deadlines, postobservation conferences, the provision of written prescriptions for improvement—often are. It is the union's vigilant attention to such procedural violations and their skillful defense of teachers whose procedural rights have been abridged that complicate and sometimes reverse disciplinary actions that reach arbitration.

Layoff and Transfer Procedures

Negotiated layoff and transfer procedures provide further protection for teachers against administrative caprice and abuse. In some districts with declining enrollments, these contract provisions have recently become more important to teachers than wage settlements, for they determine job security. When layoff provisions include non-seniority criteria such as merit, needs of the school district, or professional development, the layoff decisions necessarily become subjective. Consequently, unions typically pursue seniority-based layoff and transfer language, and junior teachers often support these efforts because they see no other fair way to make difficult decisions.

Though not subjective, seniority is not necessarily an evenhanded criterion. It penalizes those most recently hired, often minorities. Moreover, if seniority is blindly applied without attention to other factors such as teachers' qualifications for specific courses or the continuity of a class, its problems can outweigh its benefits (Johnson, 1984, p. 260). Strict seniority transfer procedures that provide school site administrators with no opportunity to screen or assign teachers concern principals greatly. As one principal in a district with such contract language said:

> If I could have one wish, it would be to be able to conduct a thorough interview and to observe potential teachers in my school. I believe that the selection of the staff should be the number one most important responsibility of the principal. (Johnson, 1984, pp. 80–81)

Principals complain about seniority-based provisions that cause them to lose outstanding teachers, to inherit less effective or unqualified teachers, or to endure domino sequences of seniority-based transfers. However, most do not advocate performance-based layoffs as an alternative. Rather, they support modified seniority provisions that would allow some administrative discretion in assigning staff and would ensure some stability within a school over time (Johnson, 1984, pp. 74–80). For example, principals might be entitled to select from the three most senior teachers seeking transfer, or they might be guaranteed that no teacher would be involuntarily transferred more often than once in three years.

How Has Collective Bargaining Affected Principals' Authority?

Before collective bargaining, principals' authority over their teachers was virtually unchallenged. Howard S. Becker reported a teacher's view in 1953:

> The principal is accepted as the supreme authority in the school: "After all, he's the principal, he is the boss, what he says should go, you know what I mean...He's the principal and he's the authority, and you have to follow his orders. That's all there is to it." This is true no matter how poorly he fills the position. The position contains the authority.... (p. 183)

Teacher contracts have reallocated formal authority in schools, limiting the power of principals to manage and discipline their staffs and empowering teachers to challenge principals' actions through grievance procedures. R. Theodore Clark, Jr. (1981), commenting on the "very real loss of authority by building principals," concludes:

> Rather than having the final say, the principal is now frequently caught in the middle of the adversarial battle between the teachers on the one hand and central-office administrators and the board on the other. To suggest that this has made the job of being a principal less attractive merely states the obvious. (p. 87)

It would be inaccurate, however, to view labor relations at the school site as simply a struggle for power between labor and management. The sides are not always clear, and in at least four important ways, principals are not strictly managers.

First, virtually all principals were themselves teachers and therefore have considerable understanding of and sympathy with teachers' work. As Dan Lortie (1982) reminds us, principals were initially socialized as teachers, and "resocialization from teacher to principal is not complete" (p. 55).

Second, principals see their work centered in their schools rather than in the central office. The work relationships that matter to them are those with teachers and students rather than with other administrators. When Lortie asked a sample of principals how they would spend an additional 10 hours,

> 39 percent said that they would like more time with students. The central office was given the lowest percentage, the thrust then is *into* the school, not upward; they place the most value on relationships with teachers and students. (p. 61)

Third, principals in many states are themselves union members who negotiate written agreements with their school boards. When the *American School Board Journal* surveyed principals in January 1976, 86% said they were "in favor of state laws that will guarantee their right to bargain directly with school boards and will force school boards to negotiate directly with principals" (Betchkal, 1976, p. 25). Bruce Cooper (1982), who has studied the unionization of principals extensively, concludes that "the roots of principals' discontent appear to be somewhat similar to those of teachers: job security, low pay, and poor working conditions." He notes also that principals have special concerns as middle managers:

Although these administrators carry the titles, expectations, and responsibilities of leaders, they lack the resources, authority, and access to the top policy-making councils.... Caught in the middle, they see themselves as neither truly management nor part of the rank-and-file employee groups like teachers. (pp. 16–17)

Principals are, therefore, seldom anti-union and often sympathetic with union objectives. In many districts their wage settlements are tied directly or indirectly to those achieved by teachers in bargaining, further reinforcing the teacher-principal alliance.

The fourth reason that principals do not see themselves strictly as managers under collective bargaining is that although they bear the greatest responsibility for administering the teachers' contract, they seldom participate actively in negotiating it. They may inform central office administrators of their priorities, and in some cases they may be asked to review tentative agreements, but they rarely sit at the table and negotiate.

For these reasons, then, principals do not usually view collective bargaining as a standoff between them and their teachers, nor do they routinely regard teacher unionism as undermining their position. When 65 principals were asked whether their authority had been undermined by collective bargaining (Johnson, 1984), some were adamant that it had, but most contended that it had not. Many respondents distinguished between formal and informal authority. One said:

Certainly the collective agreement doesn't add to the authority of a principal. However, power in a job is based on job performance, not on the authority of the position. This provides more potent power than you can use. When I think back to 1961 and compare that with now, in many ways I can get more from my teachers than my principal could have gotten from me and that was before collective bargaining. If you rely on the authority of the position, not on the power that is based on confidence, then there's a problem. (pp. 153–154)

Has Collective Bargaining Changed Working Relationships between Teachers and Principals?

Although collective bargaining creates the potential for highly formalized relations between teachers and principals—close enforcement of the contract, rigid adherence to defined work rules, and regular resort to grievance procedures—teachers and principals generally resist and discourage this formalism (Johnson, 1984). Many contract provisions, such as those that regulate supervisory duties or the use of preparation periods, are informally renegotiated to fit the priorities and practices of a particular school. Teachers report that they file grievances only when they cannot resolve problems personally with their principals. Administrators report that most teachers go well beyond the minimal contract requirements. Both teachers and principals recognize that rigid contract enforcement is not in either's best interests, since it typically provokes similarly inflexible responses from the other side. As one principal explained, if there were a teacher "who made me walk the chalk line, then I'd make that teacher walk the chalk line" (Johnson, 1984, p. 158).

Moreover, collective bargaining regulates only part of what is important to teachers. Because they continue to rely on their principals for much that makes effective teaching possible—an orderly and secure building, a balanced teaching assignment, sufficient supplies and books—principals continue to exert considerable power despite teacher unionism. However, collective bargaining has changed their work. School site management is more difficult and requires them to participate in ongoing negotiation and compromise with their teachers. As one principal explained, "I can't say 'be there' or 'do this' anymore" (Johnson, 1984, p. 85).

McDonnell and Pascal (1979) concur that "collective bargaining has made the principal's job more difficult" and further contend that "the principal plays a central role in determining whether collective bargaining works in the school building." They explain:

> Truly effective principals usually accept collective bargaining and use the contract both to manage their building more systematically and to increase teacher participation in school decisionmaking. Less effective principals may view the contract as an obstacle to a well-run school and then use it as an excuse for poor management. (p. 81)

In my own work (Johnson, 1984), I also found that differences in principals' administrative styles were central in determining the levels of teacher service, the extent of contract enforcement, and the quality of labor relations at the school site. Principals who combined high expectations with fairness and respect for teachers appeared to manage labor relations most effectively (pp. 154–157).

Although principals even in strong union districts can manage their schools well, there is no question that very restrictive contracts or very aggressive unions can make principals' work unpleasant and trying and can divert attention from other responsibilities or opportunities to improve the schools. Contract provisions defining work responsibilities of teachers introduce additional managerial demands for principals.

EFFECTS ON TEACHERS AND STUDENTS

How Has Collective Bargaining Changed Teachers' Work Load and Responsibilities?

Before teachers could negotiate the terms and conditions of their employment with school boards, administrators might require them to teach extra courses or large classes, to monitor student behavior throughout the day and throughout the building, to attend evening PTA meetings, and to chaperon student dances. The job was regarded as a whole—professional commitment to serve the school in whatever ways the administration deemed necessary.

Some administrators abused these powers, and some teachers resented spending large portions of their time on noninstructional responsibilities. Over time, contract negotiators defined such matters as the length of the teacher's workday and workyear, class size, preparation time, and supervisory duties. Each of these issues will be considered briefly.

Length of the Workyear.   State legislatures have had a larger role than teacher negotiators in defining the length of the school year. Most school districts require teachers to be at work four or five days beyond the 180 typically required by the states. Unionized districts that once required substantially more time beyond the legislated year have in some cases reduced that time in negotiations. In his study of nine local districts, Charles Perry (1979) found that all but one of those studied discussed the school calendar at the bargaining table. However, only five specified the length of the school year and school day in their contracts. Perry concluded, "All five of these systems experienced a trend toward the minimum school year required by state law" (pp. 12–13).

Negotiations over the teachers' workyear usually depend on money rather than teachers' willingness to work. Union negotiators will consider more workdays if teachers are offered additional compensation, but financially constrained school boards often must trade the days they once had for smaller salary increases.

Length of the Workday.   Perry (1979) also found that three districts of his sample had negotiated reductions in school days from 30 to 55 minutes (p. 13). By contrast, in the six districts in my study (Johnson, 1984), the instructional days, which ranged from five hours and 40 minutes to seven hours, had remained constant since the 1950s, when many schools had been on double session. However, teachers' workdays, which ranged from six hours and 15 minutes to eight hours, had been reduced through bargaining. One district required teachers to be present in school one hour beyond the school day, while another permitted teachers to arrive and leave with the students; the remaining four districts fell between these extremes (pp. 86–87).

There is no clear evidence about the ideal length of the teachers' workday. Although contracts determine the work hours of some teachers, staff often stay longer than their contracts require. Many teachers contend that long in-school workdays are not necessarily productive, especially since teachers frequently prefer to do additional preparation at home. But it is clear that contractual workdays that begin and end with the students' school days provide no guaranteed time for parental conferences, grade-level meetings, collegial planning, or after-school help and therefore potentially compromise the educational program.

Class Size.   A topic of intense negotiations in many districts, class size is a central concern for teachers and their unions. Some support class size limits in the name of better instruction; others do so in the name of job security. Some contracts include class size limits that must be adhered to; others include class size goals to be honored if finances and staffing permit. From the perspective of management, class size limits are fundamentally a financial matter; smaller classes are desirable but cost more. Many administrators recall teaching classes of 40 or 45 students and agree that smaller classes permit better instruction.

However, the experiences of several districts suggest that class size limits can be instructionally problematic if they are rigidly applied (Johnson, 1984). For example, the contract of one urban district includes limits of 33 students for all classes without regard to subject or level. By contrast, another local district sets both a schoolwide average of 23 and a classroom maximum of 28, thus allowing a school's staff and administration to have classes of varying sizes for different subjects or groups of students. Therefore, in negotiation, the application of class size limits may deserve as much attention as the limits themselves.

Preparation Time.   Many union contracts also guarantee in-school preparation time for teachers, typically 45 minutes per day. Although many high school teachers have long had free periods, elementary school teachers have recently won the right to preparation time through collective bargaining. Perry (1979) found that elementary school teachers in most of the nine school systems he studied did not win preparation time until the early 1970s and, "in at least three systems, still do not enjoy as much preparation time as their counterparts at the secondary level" (p. 13).

The major dispute about preparation time is not about its need but about its use. Unions contend that teachers should have discretion over the time; management often argues that administrators should specify its use. In most districts, principals report with satisfaction that teachers use the time appropriately—for student conferences, staff meetings, or lesson preparation. However, in districts that permit teachers both to arrive and leave with students and to use preparation time as they see fit, administrators report some dissatisfaction with their lack of authority over its use (Johnson, 1984, pp. 100–101).

Nonteaching Duties. Nonteaching duties, including building supervision and extracurricular activities, are addressed by most contracts, although the particular provisions vary widely. Kerchner and Mitchell (1981) argue that as a result of collective bargaining, "there has been a clear cleavage between the 'regular' and the 'extra' duties for teachers and...the presence of this cleavage is changing the curriculum of schools to emphasize organized activity in the classrooms and deemphasize the extra-curriculum" (p. 1:12). Teachers' interests do, in fact, center on their classrooms, and they support efforts to reduce required noninstructional activities. They typically regard instruction as professional work and supervision as custodial work.

In practice, teachers in all districts assume some supervisory duties, although collective bargaining has certainly reduced the number and restricted the kind. Cafeteria supervision, a duty generally loathed by teachers and worried over by principals, is probably the most hotly negotiated nonteaching duty. Teachers in most districts have now negotiated duty-free lunch and in some cases have been freed of cafeteria duty as well. In other districts with multiple lunch periods, teachers have both a duty-free lunch and responsibility for cafeteria supervision. Many districts hire aides to keep order in the teachers' absence, but they often do not command the respect of students. Consequently, principals, who, as Dan Lortie (1982) observes, are the "possessors of residual obligations" (p. 54), spend considerable time supervising both the aides and the students. Teachers and administrators agree that inadequate cafeteria supervision can lead to classroom problems, but neither group willingly assumes responsibility for the matter (Johnson, 1984, p. 107).

By reducing their supervisory roles, teachers stress that they are not to be regarded as caretakers but as professionals with instructional expertise. Teacher contracts reflect these preferences. However, while these negotiated changes permit more efficient use of professional time, they also reduce the supervisory capacity of schools.

Teacher attitudes toward participation in extracurricular activities are somewhat different. Many teachers express interest in sponsoring clubs or special activities but believe that such participation should be voluntary rather than required. Most school districts have long compensated teachers with stipends or released time for selected extracurricular work such as coaching football, directing the marching band, or advising the newspaper staff. But negotiation has increased the number of activities that carry stipends.

Some districts that bargain collectively still require teachers each to sponsor at least one after-school activity: others state that such participation will be voluntary;

yet others make participation voluntary and pay virtually all participants. A varied range of extracurricular activities is available under all three arrangements, and administrators report that student apathy or after-school work presents more problems for the extracurricular program than teacher contracts do (Johnson, 1984, p. 93), a perception evident in the work of Larkin (1979) and Lewin-Epstein (1981). However, where participation is voluntary, a small number of teachers carry much of the responsibility, and principals must rely on persuasion or informal pressure to ensure that all activites are covered (Johnson, 1984, p. 83).

Contract provisions defining teachers' work obligations were introduced to limit administrative abuse of their time, energy, and commitment, and by most reports they have done so. But in some cases such provisions have been written so restrictively that they penalize students and compromise the school program or make school adminis-tration unnecessarily onerous. Collective bargaining has reduced the scope of teacher duties. If, ultimately, teachers' responsibilities are to be limited to classroom teaching, school officials may have to redefine public education's traditional structure and pro-gram to accommodate those negotiated changes.

Has Collective Bargaining Enhanced Teachers' Roles as Policymakers?

Over time, one goal of unionism has been to ensure teachers a greater role in educational policymaking. This has been achieved at the state level by lobbying about such issues as school finance, tenure, and teacher certification. Locally, it has been achieved through negotiating educational policies, including class size, length of the school day, and teacher assignment. In addition, local teachers have won greater roles as ongoing participants in the policymaking process.

Many teacher contracts include provisions establishing faculty advisory com-mittees that meet regularly with principals on matters of school policy. In addition, some contracts further strengthen the teachers' policymaking roles by establishing liaison committees with superintendents and other district administrators. Such com-mittees promise a greater policymaking role for teachers, but they function unevenly. On the basis of their fieldwork, McDonnell and Pascal (1979) conclude:

> School-site committees also vary greatly in schools even within the same district. In one district with contractually mandated committees, a central office adminis-trator noted that they are "all over the map" in terms of effectiveness, ranging from adversarial to cooperative working relationships. Some actually co-administer the building while others have no influence. (p. 77)

Teachers often do not seek to participate in such groups. As Lortie observed in 1975, teachers' attention

> is centered on instructional outcomes and relationships with students. Scant attention is paid to other aspects of the teacher's role; pride is not evoked by participation in schoolwide affairs. The classroom is the cathected forum—not the principal's office or the professional association. (p. 131)

In 1979, Daniel Duke, Beverly Showers, and Michael Imber studied teachers' involve-ment in decision making and found that although teachers in the sample believed "in the principle of shared decision-making," they thought that the time and organization costs outweighed the potential benefits.

One explanation for teachers' reluctance to participate in local policymaking committees is that, given their advisory status, the success of these committees is largely a function of the administrators' attitudes toward teacher participation. If principals believe that shared decision making is good for them and their schools, such committees are usually active and address a wide range of issues such as textbooks, supervision, and budget. However, if principals discourage or oppose teacher participation in school policymaking, such committees become forums for ritualized discussions. A teacher in one district described the principal's response in her school:

> He would come into the faculty advisory committee meetings like a used car salesman—smiling and pretending to hear everything, pretending to listen. But he didn't do anything in response. By the second semester, the committee was not even active. (Johnson, 1984, p. 45)

Teachers quickly withdraw from such purposeless endeavors and seek other avenues of influence.

Although teachers' policymaking powers are generally limited to advisory roles, there are instances where districts have negotiated contracts empowering teachers to stall or veto administrative decisions. Such contract provisions can lead to teacher control of policy that may be no better than the administrative control it replaced.

Some union critics have expressed concern that collective bargaining agreements will eventually regulate all educational policy, dictating curriculum and teaching methods. There is little evidence to support such a concern. Teachers seek contracts that protect their professional autonomy, and they would likely oppose union efforts to prescribe programs just as they resist administrative efforts to do so.

Has Collective Bargaining Affected Student Achievement?

Underlying both critics' apprehension and advocates' optimism about teacher unionism was the expectation that it might ultimately affect student achievement. It might, some said, improve teacher morale, permit more efficient use of teachers' time, promote professional involvement in policymaking, and thereby lead to better instruction and student achievement. Conversely, others said that collective bargaining would reduce instructional time, focus teachers' attention on compensation rather than the quality of their work, and undermine administrative authority within the school, thus reducing the quality of instruction and diminishing student achievement.

As anyone who works in schools well knows, and as researchers have repeatedly confirmed, it is virtually impossible to determine what effect any single factor has on student achievement, whether it be the curriculum, per pupil expenditures, teacher preparation, class size, or collective bargaining. Schooling is a complex process, and much that affects its outcomes—student abilities, parental attitudes, funding—is well beyond the control of teachers and the scrutiny of research.

In discussing the problem of identifying collective bargaining's effects on student achievement, Robert E. Doherty (1981) observes, "We sometimes attribute to bargaining certain changes in educational performance on the sole ground that one preceded the other. As Samuel Johnson once observed of physicians, they tended to mistake subsequence for consequence" (p. 64). Doherty himself concludes that "bargaining has not brought about a substantial improvement in student achievement. But neither can it be shown that bargaining has in any significant way been responsible for the decline in achievement" (p. 75). Similarly, Randall Eberts and Joe Stone (1983) studied the effects of collective bargaining in union and nonunion schools and concluded that the net difference in student achievement was "negligible" (p. 166).

Such studies of unionized and nonunionized districts, which seek to determine the effects of collective bargaining on student achievement, tend to obscure a more important question for local policymakers. The issue for most unionized districts is not whether to bargain collectively but rather, given collective bargaining, which contract provisions support good instruction and which undermine it. Although researchers have yet to answer complicated questions about the effects of particular factors on student learning, common sense suggests that different contract provisions will affect student achievement differently.

Reduced class size might promote better instruction, but inflexible class size limits might compromise it. A defined workday for teachers might protect their professional time, but a workday that includes no time for staff planning might lead to a disorderly curriculum. In the absence of conclusive research evidence, local negotiators should carefully weigh the anticipated effects of any proposed contract provision on classroom instruction and seek to negotiate agreements that enhance the educational program.

What Difference Have Collective Negotiations Made in Teacher Wages?

Better pay has always been the biggest rallying cause of teacher unionism. Teachers who were reluctant about labor affiliation often were persuaded to join by the promise of higher wages. Far more research has been conducted on the question of collective bargaining's effect on teachers' wages than on any other issue of educational labor relations. The studies have provoked intense methodological debates and led to further studies. As with student achievement, it is difficult to isolate the effects of collective bargaining. Because contract settlements in unionized districts influence those of nonunionized districts, it is not possible simply to compare salaries in the two and identify the difference that bargaining makes.

Most people who have studied the question have concluded that collective bargaining has made only a modest difference in teachers' wages (Cooper, 1982, p. 84). David Lipsky and John Drotning (1973) studied the salary settlements of unionized and nonunionized districts in New York State one year after enactment of collective bargaining legislation. They concluded that when the salary differences between these two groups of districts were adjusted for other factors, such as salary levels before collective bargaining and the ability of the district to meet salary demands, "collective bargaining...had no effect on teacher salary levels" (p. 35).

More recently, Charles Perry, in his 1979 study of nine local districts, reached similar conclusions:

> Collective bargaining in these systems has continued to add varying amounts to the total cost of salary settlements, but the cumulative effect of these increases on average teacher salary, overall budget size, and percent of budget devoted to teacher salaries has not been substantial in aggregate terms. (p. 12)

Some researchers have concluded that the effect of collective bargaining on wages is higher than the 5% to 9% others have estimated. Jay Chambers (1980) estimates that the effect is between 8% and 14% (p. 11). Eberts and Stone (1983) conclude that although teachers' wage gains during the early 1970s were small, "union gains increased substantially by the late 1970s, reaching a level comparable to the average union wage-premium in the private sector" (p. 166).

Undoubtedly, the methodological debate about collective bargaining's effects on wages will continue. Additional bargaining gains in fringe benefits have generally not been included in such studies, but increasingly, unions pursue such untaxed income as part of their compensation packages. We do not yet know how the total packages or the proportions of wages and fringe benefits compare in unionized and nonunionized districts.

One very important question that has received little research attention is how collective bargaining affects resource allocation within a district. One might expect that whatever the local funds available, organized teachers would garner a higher share of it for salaries than nonunionized teachers. It is generally agreed that teachers are underpaid and that competitive salaries are important in attracting new teachers. But school budgets are limited, and only a portion of them can be allocated to salary increases. Building maintenance, supplies, and support staff make their own demands. Better understanding of the effects of collective bargaining on local allocation practices would inform local negotiators as they cope with diminishing resources.

Has Collective Bargaining Affected the Professionalism of Teachers?

The prospect of enhanced professional status has led many teachers to support unions despite their reservations about organized labor. During the early days of collective bargaining for teachers, educational commentators differed about the anticipated effects the process might have on teachers' professionalism. In *Education as a Profession*, Myron Lieberman (1965) optimistically advocated collective bargaining as a means of professionalization. By contrast, George W. Brown, writing in the *American School Board Journal* in 1966, warned that unionism would make teaching unprofessional:

> There was a voice that spoke for children. Sometimes it was pleading; often it cajoled; on rare occasions it rang with authority...speaking the cause of children. The voice was that of the teaching profession.... That voice still speaks, but its tones have become strident and shrill. The words are demanding and the posture threatening. Where it had spoken of children, it speaks of bargaining. Where it had pleaded for educational opportunity, it now demands negotiations. Where it had appealed to the human conscience, it now appeals to sanctions. (p. 11)

Because definitions vary about what professionalism for teachers means, assessments of the effects of collective bargaining on that professionalism will vary as well. However, after two decades of negotiations, it appears that collective bargaining has enhanced certain elements of teachers' professional standing and diminished others.

First, by successfully negotiating and lobbying for pay scales, pension plans, health benefits, and job security, unions have, over the course of the century, transformed teaching from itinerant work—between 1900 and 1920, the median number of years of teaching was five (Urban, 1982, p. 16)—to a career. Although the opportunities for advancement in teaching are limited, the career is stable and predictable. Tenure, seniority rules, and due process protect experienced teachers from sudden, arbitrary dismissal.

Second, in both state legislatures and local districts, teachers' roles in policymaking have been augmented. Teachers and their unions cannot control all educational policy, but their influence through lobbying and bargaining is substantial. Major policymaking committees at all levels of government include teacher representation, and the union position is typically given serious attention. Locally, by negotiating such issues as class size, evaluation practices, and work hours, teachers have direct influence over professional decisions. By gaining access to grievance and arbitration procedures, teachers have won the power to exert their policymaking influence and to enforce their rights.

Although unionism has secured long-term employment for teachers and augmented their power to regulate their practice, it has not substantially increased public regard for them or their work. Teachers still are ranked far below doctors and lawyers on the list of desirable professions, and recent research about the failure of teaching to attract highly qualified candidates suggests that its relative standing may fall rather than rise. Collective bargaining has not achieved the high wages for teachers that might command greater public regard. Certainly, the public recognizes the power that teacher unions wield when they strike and close down a major school system. But intimidating the public does not win its esteem. Instead the public sees union members pursuing pay with demands, threats, and job actions. The media convey images of ruffians aggressively pursuing their self-interests rather than professionals acting in the best interests of children. Margaret Haley, one of the early leaders of the AFT, contended in 1920 that "there is no possible conflict between the interest of the child and the interest of the teacher" (Donley, 1976, p. 20). The public appears to remain unconvinced.

A fundamental obstacle to teachers' achieving the professional status of doctors and lawyers is that teachers are employed rather than self-employed. Given the structure of public education, teachers cannot be independent contractors, setting their own hours, fees, and conditions of work. Collective negotiations underscore their dependent, subordinate status. The school board has what teachers need, and in order to get it, they must adopt uniform demands and unite in a show of strength. Professionalism implies independence and autonomy; unionism suggests uniformity and solidarity.

In 1969, Lortie noted the strong norms of equality among teachers and observed that "they seem to share a kind of 'uniformity pact' whereby agreement is secured among teachers that all should, insofar as extrinsic rewards are concerned, be treated largely alike.... Equality, it seems, is the foundation of their autonomy" (p. 363). However, as publicly employed teachers, that autonomy is ultimately limited, and thus their professionalism is limited as well.

Mitchell and Kerchner (1983) argue further that because collective bargaining rationalizes teaching and formalizes the supervisory role of administrators, teaching is more like labor, where supervisors directly assess employees' performance, and less like a profession, with peer review.

Recently, in the case of *NLRB* v. *Yeshiva University* (1980), the Supreme Court blocked faculty members' efforts to unionize, saying that they were "managerial" employees who were "in effect, substantially, and pervasively operating the enterprise." In essence, the faculty members' roles as professionals prohibited their organizing as employees. This case suggests the irony of teachers' pursuit of professional status. They have unionized in order to achieve professional autonomy, but they might be prohibited from bargaining collectively if they achieve it.

In 1967, Robert Doherty and Walter Oberer speculated about the prospects for teachers' achieving professional status through collective bargaining:

> Teachers have always sought professional status. Ironically, they may achieve this status by first learning how to act like militant trade unionists, thus securing the economic base that will allow them to concentrate on professional problems. Whether they succeed in making this transition or merely continue to pursue the trade union route is a matter almost beyond conjecture. (p. 125)

Teachers have not secured that economic base, and their unions have not focused attention on those professional problems. Amid the current debate about schooling and teaching, however, there is talk of change. Some argue that discussion of professional problems cannot await the time when teachers have secured high salaries. In fact, as Albert Shanker, president of the AFT, has suggested, perhaps teachers must begin to review their own work critically and to consider alternative professional structures in order to win higher wages. It is the first instance in the more than two decades since collective bargaining began that union leaders have advocated a critical review of teaching. It may promise more for the professional status of teachers than all of the combative rhetoric that preceded it.

CONCLUSION

Teacher unionism takes many forms, and collective bargaining has many effects. Some of those effects have improved teaching and schooling; some have not. In many instances, collective bargaining has improved the lot of teachers, democratized school policymaking, and improved both working and learning conditions. In a few cases, negotiated agreements have diminished teaching services, excessively constrained administrators, and reduced professional accountability. The particular set of outcomes in any district is a function of local priorities, politics, finances, and personalities.

Although little can be said about the general effect of collective bargaining on student achievement, it seems clear that the character of labor relations at any particular school site has consequence for the teaching and learning that take place there. Schools are interdependent organizations that do not function effectively if teachers and administrators define their roles rigidly or enforce contract provisions inflexibly. Fortunately, in most cases, teachers do far more than the contract requires, and principals and teachers recognize the importance of cooperation and compromise. Their roles as educators take precedence over their roles as employees or managers.

Despite the fact that people, rather than contracts, usually run schools, there are exceptions. Labor relations can become formal and hostile; contract language can be rigorously enforced. Therefore, the details of written contracts are critical and deserve at least as much attention at the bargaining table as wages. Narrow contractual definitions of the principal's powers or the teacher's responsibilities can establish standards and practices that fall short of the complex needs of the school. Negotiators must anticipate the consequences of any new contract provision on the school as an organization and the work that goes on there. They must strike an appropriate balance between student interests and teacher interests and between teacher rights and administrative discretion.

Teachers who had hoped to achieve high pay and public status through unionism are probably disappointed, for neither has been achieved. Perhaps it is too soon to judge, but perhaps these expectations were unrealistic, given that public teaching is public work, subject to the limitations of the public purse. Teachers' working conditions have unquestionably improved; they have gained considerable control over their practice. They have also achieved public recognition—of their plight. It is possible that teachers might have retained a bit more public regard if they had rejected unionism and patiently pursued their work, but there is little to suggest that they would have been better off. Public servants, like public services, are not well tended.

Collective bargaining is established practice in most school districts, and the major issues of teachers' working conditions have been negotiated. Major changes in contracts over the next decade seem unlikely. However, collective bargaining as a policymaking process may be at a turning point. Its adversarial format, which has always been somewhat at odds with teachers' values, is increasingly dysfunctional in an era of decline. More and more, negotiators face problems that cannot be resolved by bullying or splitting the difference between extreme positions. A new process of constructive negotiations is called for in which problems are solved cooperatively while all interests are taken into account (Fisher & Ury, 1981). Though difficult to develop, such a process is more consistent with teacher norms than traditional adversarial bargaining. Teachers can be problem solvers as well as teacher advocates. To the extent that their professional values shape the bargaining process, educational labor relations will serve both teachers and schools better.

FURTHER READING

Cooper, B. S. (1982). *Collective Bargaining, Strikes, and Financial Costs in Public Education: A Comparative Review.* Eugene, OR: ERIC Clearinghouse on Educational Management. This comprehensive review of the literature addresses three central questions about educational labor relations: What are the causes of bargaining and union activity in schools? What are the nature and causes of strikes? How has collective bargaining affected the costs and provision of education?

Cresswell, A. M., & Murphy, M. J. (1980). *Teachers, Unions, and Collective Bargaining.* Berkeley, CA: McCutchan. A broad discussion of the literature on educational labor relations, addressing a wide range of issues, from the history of unionism to its impact on school governance and politics.

Eaton, E. E. (1975). *The American Federation of Teachers, 1916–1961.* Carbondale: Southern Illinois University Press. Examines the beginnings of the union movement, the central figures, similarities among local organizations, the place of the AFT in the pattern of American educational history.

Fisher, R., & Ury, W. (1981). *Getting to Yes: Negotiating Agreement without Giving In.* Boston: Houghton Mifflin. An informative guide to the process of principled negotiations in which participants pursue their own interests while acknowledging the interests of others. The discussion includes examples from a wide variety of domestic, local, national, and international arenas.

Johnson, S. M. (1984). *Teacher Unions in Schools.* Philadelphia: Temple University Press. This field study examines the day-to-day impact of teacher unions on the public schools. It concludes that the outcomes of teacher bargaining have been varied and that the principal is central in determining the impact of unionism at the school site.

Lipsky, D. B. (1982). "The Effect of Collective Bargaining on Teacher Pay: A Review of the Evidence." *Educational Administration Quarterly, 18*(1), 14–42. Examines the effects of collective bargaining on teacher salaries. After comparing and contrasting the methods and findings of 16 studies designed to examine the issue, the author concludes that teacher salaries are only slightly higher than they would have been in the absence of collective bargaining.

McDonnell, L. M., & Pascal, A. H. (1979) *Organized Teachers in American Schools.* Santa Monica, CA: Rand Corp. This study, comprised of both a quantitative analysis of contract data and fieldwork in 15 districts, concludes that teachers have significantly improved their working conditions and increased their influence over school and classroom operations. However, the researchers conclude that bargaining has not significantly affected classroom operations or the quality of educational services.

Mitchell, D. E., & Kerchner, C. T. (1983). "Labor Relations and Teacher Policy." In L. S. Shulman & G. Sykes (Eds.), *Handbook of Teaching and Policy.* White Plains, NY: Longman. Discusses the implications of current labor policies for teaching practices. The authors argue that collective bargaining has made teaching more like labor and less like professional work.

Urban, W. J. (1982). *Why Teachers Organized.* Detroit: Wayne State University Press. This historical study of teacher unionism between 1890 and 1930 examines rivalries between the NEA and the AFT as well as the policies and practices of local unions in New York City, Atlanta, and Chicago.

REFERENCES

Becker, H. S. (1953). The teacher in the authority system of the public school. *Journal of Educational Sociology, 27,* 128–141.

Betchkal, J. (Ed.). (1976). The brewing—and perhaps still preventable—revolt of school principals. *American School Board Journal, 163*(1), 25–27.

Brown, G. W. (1966). Teacher power techniques. *American School Board Journal, 152*(2), 11–13.

Chambers, J. G. (1980). *The impact of bargaining statutes on the earnings of public school teachers: A comparison in California and Missouri.* Stanford, CA: Stanford University, Institute for Research on Education Finance and Governance.

Clark, R. T., Jr. (1981). Commentary. In G. W. Angell (Ed.), *Faculty and teacher bargaining: The impact of unions on education.* Lexington, MA: Lexington Books.

Commission on Educational Reconstruction. (1955). *Organizing the teaching profession.* Glencoe, IL: Free Press.

Cooper, B. S. (1982). *Collective bargaining, strikes, and financial costs in public education: A comparative review.* Eugene, OR: ERIC Clearinghouse on Educational Management.

Doherty, R. E. (1981). Does teacher bargaining affect student achievement? In G. W. Angell (Ed.), *Faculty and teacher bargaining: The impact of unions on education.* Lexington, MA: Lexington Books.

Doherty, R. E., & Oberer, W. E. (1967). *Teachers, school boards, and collective bargaining: A changing of the guard.* Ithaca: New York State School of Industrial and Labor Relations.

Donley, M. O., Jr. (1976). *Power to the teacher.* Bloomington: Indiana University Press.

Duke, D., Showers, B. K., & Imber, M. (1979). *Costs to teachers of involvement in school decision-making.* Stanford, CA: Stanford University, Institute for Research on Education Finance and Governance.

Eberts, R. (1982). Research presentation. In K. Duckworth & W. DeBevoise (Eds.), *The effects of collective bargaining on school administrative leadership: Proceedings of a conference.* Eugene, OR: Center for Educational Policy and Management.

Eberts, R., & Stone, J. (1983). *Unions and public schools: The effects of collective bargaining on American education.* Lexington, MA: Lexington Books.

Fisher, R., & Ury, W. (1981). *Getting to yes: Negotiating agreement without giving in.* Boston: Houghton Mifflin.

Johnson, S. M. (1984). *Teacher unions in schools.* Philadelphia: Temple University Press.

Kerchner, C. T., & Mitchell, D. (1981). *The dynamics of public school collective bargaining and its impact on governance, administration, and teaching.* Washington, DC: National Institute of Education.

Larkin, R. W. (1979). *Suburban youth in cultural crisis.* New York: Oxford University Press.

Lewin-Epstein, N. (1981). *Employment during high school: An analysis of high school and beyond.* Chicago: National Center for Educational Statistics.

Lieberman, M. (1965). *Education as a profession.* Englewood Cliffs, NJ: Prentice-Hall.

Lipsky, D. B., & Drotning, J. E. (1973). The influence of collective bargaining on teachers' salaries in New York State. *Industrial and Labor Relations Review, 27,* 18–35.

Lortie, D. C. (1969). The balance of control and autonomy in elementary school training. In A. Etzioni (Ed.), *The semiprofessions and their organizations.* New York: Free Press.

Lortie, D. C. (1975). *Schoolteacher: A sociological study.* Chicago: University of Chicago Press.

Lortie, D. C. (1982). The complex work relationships of elementary school principals. In K. Duckworth & W. DeBevoise (Eds.), *The effects of collective bargaining on school administrative leadership.* Eugene, OR: Center for Educational Policy and Management.

McDonnell, L. M., & Pascal, A. H. (1978). Organized teachers and local schools. In M. F. Williams (Ed.), *Government in the classroom.* New York: Academy of Political Science.

McDonnell, L. M., & Pascal, A. H. (1979). *Organized teachers in American schools.* Santa Monica, CA: Rand Corp.

Mitchell, D. E., & Kerchner, C. T. (1983). Labor relations and teacher policy. In L. S. Shulman & G. Sykes (Eds.), *Handbook of teaching and policy.* White Plains, NY: Longman.

NLRB v. *Yeshiva University,* 100 S.Ct. 856 (1980).

Perry, C. R. (1979). Teacher bargaining: The experience in nine systems. *Industrial and Labor Relations Review, 33,* 3–17.

Urban, W. J. (1982). *Why teachers organized.* Detroit: Wayne State University Press.

Wesley, E. B. (1957). *The NEA: The first hundred years.* New York: Harper & Row.

23 STRESS AND BURNOUT
Henrietta Schwartz and George Olson

STRESS IN TEACHING

History suggests that vivid descriptions of reality can sometimes help to transform society. At the turn of the century, Upton Sinclair's vivid descriptions in *The Jungle* of conditions in the slaughter yards of Chicago provoked reforms in the food-processing industry. Movie and television records, through the portrayal of the suffering and human toll caused by war, have influenced public opinion and action. If the descriptive record is powerful enough to arouse the readers' or viewers' emotions and engage their intellect, a popular demand to change the situation can result.

Profoundly moving descriptions of severe problems in the nation's public schools already exist, and they reflect a real concern and a need to address issues that affect the growth and development of our children. Teacher stress—its effects on school personnel and on children—confronts everyone with a critical problem that has far-reaching effects. Descriptions of stress in the lives of urban teachers especially may be sufficient to move the reader both emotionally and rationally. For example, it is difficult for anyone who cares about public schooling to remain indifferent in the face of accounts such as these:

Plaster falling from the ceiling was creating a safety hazard.

"Street people," juveniles not in school, irate parents, and other outsiders could enter and roam the halls.

School and community representatives were unable to prevent the operation of a methadone clinic on the same block as the school.

There were no textbooks in some classes, and a new teacher was told to use old copies of *Reader's Digest* as texts.

The potential for positive parental involvement was virtually nonexistent because school personnel and parents frequently criticized and were hostile toward each other.

The teachers' restrooms lacked adequate facilities.

Midterms were canceled because the school ran out of paper.

Racial tensions among school personnel provided role models encouraging racial separation rather than integration among students.

Teachers were faced with the threat of transfer and layoff throughout the school year.

The descriptive records and interviews with teachers provide jarring examples of the stressful conditions of urban teaching in the 1980s. Fortunately, the same records contain information needed to propose solutions to these problems. A number of recent, systematic studies add to the descriptive record and offer recommendations to the educators for the reduction of occupationally related stress experienced by urban teachers. One such study found that all the variables affecting members of the school environment could be categorized in three groups: concerns for status, concerns for security, and concerns for sociability (Schwartz, Olson, Ginsberg, & Bennett, 1983). Public school teachers suffer from low self-esteem and from a sense that their efforts are not valued highly (status); they feel physically and/or financially threatened (security); and adult contact during the day is severely limited (sociability). Much of the discussion in the ensuing pages will revolve around these three concepts and their relationship to teacher stress.

These findings disturb those of us who still believe teaching to be a noble profession and public schooling to be one of the great institutions of democratic America. The results of extensive research show that the profession as a whole is under great stress and that schools consequently are not educating youth as they should. The research does, however, provide some ideas that could benefit all teachers and their students by improving the conditions of teaching and learning. We will survey some of these possibilities.

RESEARCH FINDINGS

Defining Teacher Stress: Symptoms and Consequences

Stress is part of daily existence at home and at work; its symptoms and consequences have been documented for many years. It operates among all ages, occupations, races, sexes, socioeconomic classes, and religions. Physiologically, stress is a response by the mind and body to an environmental change or a stimulation called a *stressor* (Selye, 1956). Stress can serve to promote physical and psychological well-being, or it can debilitate, sometimes severely, both mentally and physically. Individuals suffering from excessive stress lose job motivation, feel emotionally exhausted, develop low emotional affect expressed in depersonalized attitudes toward students, and have reduced self-esteem. Other psychopathological problems and psychosomatic symptoms result in increased teacher absence on sick leave.

Individuals vary, however, in reacting to stress. What is debilitating stress for one person may be a positive stimulant for another. Some individuals cope well in stressful situations, while others fall apart or "burn out." Burnout has been defined as "physical, emotional, and attitudinal exhaustion" (Hendrickson, 1979). Stress may be manifested on the job in low staff morale, absenteeism, or high job turnover. Some of the institutional variables that have been related to dysfunctional stress are feelings of ineffectiveness on the job, anonymity, powerlessness, and confinement for long periods of time. Physical and psychological disorders that may result from negative reactions to stress include coronary heart disease, asthma, kidney and gastrointestinal disease, hostility, depression, and nervous disorders (National School Resource Network, 1981). In Newell's view (1978–1979), dysfunctional stress has reached epidemic proportions in schools: "Stress is one of the worst health problems all teachers have to contend with." The descriptive and analytical research studies reviewed examined stressors hypothesized to be related to the development of un-productive stress in schools. The nature of the studies and the methodologies employed do not suggest clear causality, but they do point to correlations between certain conditions and practices with various levels of stress. The descriptions and analyses allow us to offer some ideas about how schools can minimize conditions related to stress among the adult populations of schools.

Kyriacou and Sutcliffe (1978), regarded as pioneers in the field, reviewed the research on teacher stress, looking at teacher dissatisfaction primarily in British schools. British and American teachers were found to be dissatisfied with clerical tasks and supervisory duties at school (McLaughlin & Shea, 1960; Lortie, 1975), to be dissatisfied with poor working conditions (Payne, 1974; Dunham, 1977), and to suffer from poor human relations (Lortie, 1975; Dunham, 1977; Rudd & Wiseman, 1962). Assorted other aspects of teaching, such as student behavior problems, contri-bute to the pattern (Caspari, 1976; Hargreaves, 1976; Lowenstein, 1975). In follow-up studies of teachers in 1978 and 1979, Kyriacou and Sutcliffe found that approxi-mately 20% of respondents in the United Kingdom (19.9% in 1978; 23.4% in 1979) rated being a teacher as either very stressful or extremely stressful. In a replication of that study, Feitler and Tokar (1981) surveyed almost 4,000 teachers in the United States and concluded that although the perceived *levels* of stress were higher in England, a higher *proportion* of American teachers experienced some stress in teaching.

Anderson and Iwaniki (1981) examined the relationship between burnout and teacher motivation and listed three stages of burnout as identified by Maslach and Jackson (1978):

1. Increased feelings of emotional exhaustion and fatigue
2. Negative, cynical attitudes toward clients
3. A tendency to evaluate oneself negatively

Bloch (1978) studied 250 teachers with symptoms of physical trauma and/or prolonged psychic stress, a stress level he likened to "combat neurosis." Bloch suggests that teachers can survive in stressful schools if proper procedures are initiated. These procedures include preparedness, opportunity for sharing, morale, and crisis intervention, as well as introducing the three R's of rotation, rest, and recuperation into the school setting.

Data from a study of *environmental* stress on over 4,000 Chicago teachers (Cichon & Koff, 1978) indicate that Maslow's (1970) theory of need hierarchies can explain the link between the work situation and the way it is perceived. The study found that teachers were most stressed by teaching events associated with fear for safety and concerns about job security. In a replication of the Chicago study, conducted in Portland, OR, Catterton (1979) found, consistent with the Chicago study, that safety and security, management tensions, job performance, and peda-gogical functions were the four factors related to teacher stress.

Other studies reported sources of "dissatisfaction" among teachers (Rudd & Wiseman, 1962) or of "bothersomeness" (Cruickshank, Kennedy, & Meyers, 1974) and identified heavy teaching loads, large classes, shortage of time, and feelings of inadequacy as among the chief dissatisfactions. Other studies identify motivation and control of students as two of the main problems. In a 1980 poll conducted by Gallup for the National Education Association, 60% of 1,000 teachers sampled identified paperwork as their number one problem. In a sample of 164 teachers in a large urban district, Bruner and Felder (1983) identified several themes in teachers' dissatisfaction with their work. This dissatisfaction centered around lack of job security and mobility, inadequate teaching resources, excessive or inconvenient work hours, and unpleasant classroom environment.

In a survey of its readership, *Instructor* magazine (Landsmann, 1978) found that 75% of respondents said their sick days were related to stress or tension. Sources of reported stress were many, including physical safety, the physical environment, lack of teaching material, discipline problems, public pressure on teachers, too many students in a class, schedules that do not allow for breaks, and lack of preparation or in-service training for new programs.

These findings and numerous subsequent studies clearly indicate the presence of dysfunctional stress among teachers; the phenomenon is serious enough to warrant in-depth investigations to determine whether and to what extent instruction suffers as a result.

Stressors: Causes for Stress in Schools

Interpersonal Relations and Stress: The Psychological Workplace.   The role of teachers' relationships with other professionals has been shown to be a crucial variable in determining levels of (and reactions to) stress. School environment, for example, affects the general stress level of the professional staff. Koff, Laffey, Olson, and Cichan (1981) found that suburban schools feature less stress due to student discipline problems than do urban schools. According to Koff et al., the feeling of a psychological community of professionals working together toward a common goal is an important antistress factor.

We know that schools with high student populations (over 1,000 pupils) feature high-stress environments (Farber & Miller, 1981). In this context, the physical environment can influence the individual's overall perception of working conditions and cause sufficient strain to create pathological reactions in some individuals. For example, an unsightly or decaying physical plant is a stressor for all administrative and teaching personnel and the students.

Nina Gupta (1981) has indicated the importance of a healthy work environment to the welfare of employees in connection with role stress, which she defined as individuals' perception that they cannot meet the demands of their role to the satisfaction of others. The importance of role stress in causing stress and burnout symptoms is becoming more prominent in the literature and will be discussed later.

Principals and teachers alike risk burnout due to job-related stress. It is certain that each group influences the other in causing or alleviating burnout, and it is possible for principals and teachers to alleviate the stress each imposes on the other (Bruner & Felder, 1983; Frey & Young, 1983). Few investigators have examined the stress problems of both teachers and principals simultaneously, although the literature on stress shows that teacher-principal relationships are a major focus of study.

In "Stress and the School Administrator" (Koff, Laffey, Olson, & Cichon, 1981), both statistical analyses of numerical data and written responses to questionnaires supported the presence of certain themes of stress: conflicts among administrators and teachers (such as unsatisfactory teacher performance reports), student conflicts, and problems and threats to security and status (a perceived lack of control). In Olson's 1983 review of research in administrator stress covering studies conducted between 1977 and 1983, one of the most commonly reported categories of stress for administrators was interpersonal relations, including staff evaluations, resolution of conflicts among school personnel and community members, and maintaining rapport with school personnel.

Stress is passed down the school hierarchical ladder from the district office to the principal, from the principal to the teacher, and from the teacher to the student. Stress is also transmitted back up the ladder. The networks of interpersonal relationships (the sociability factor) within the school cultural system—in addition to the factors of security and status—influence the nature of the school organizational climate, which in turn is a factor in stress etiology (Bolding, 1982; Bedian, 1981). Clearly, an atmosphere of tension from numerous interpersonal conflicts is conducive to system-wide dysfunctional stress. The question is, what combination of people, procedures, beliefs, and behaviors in what combination of physical facilities can best promote teaching and learning in a state of creative tension?

A considerable body of research since the mid-1970s focuses on the principal's role in causing and alleviating stress (Burscemi, 1981; Frey & Young, 1983; Holifield, 1982; Bruner & Felder, 1983). Some earlier work was done on the relationship of the principal's leadership style and teacher satisfaction. Muth (1973) found that teachers in the Chicago area perceived successful principals as using ascribed authority rather than coercion or influence. Gmelch (1978) argues that in order for principals to be effective at reducing stress, they must first be reeducated. He calls upon principals to accept the responsibility for maintaining a positive climate in the schools and for training staff to cope with the demands of the job. Much of the effective schools literature in the 1980s, as well as popular press reinterpretations of the literature, highlights the crucial role of the building principal in setting the climate and morale in the school. Some of the specific research findings have identified this and other role relationships as a crucial variable.[1]

Role Definitions and Role Insufficiency. The psychological workplace of schools has been examined from another perspective in addition to that of principal-teacher and teacher-teacher relationships: the concept of teachers' expectations of support from their professional environmental structure. This concept differs slightly from the simple interpersonal power relationship between principal and teacher; that is, an important source of teacher stress has to do with teachers' expectations of the responsibilities of administrators in making the school system run well. Stressors best understood as "role insufficiency" reflect teachers' perceptions that administrators are not helping them as they should—a quite different matter from a concern with the direct power principals have over teachers in evaluations and other security-related questions.

Thus, for example, the chief stress-producing context variable identified in

---

[1]There is always an interaction among the individual, the role, the organization, and the environment. One of the most comprehensive discussions of the behavioral outcomes of this interaction is found in Getzels, Lipham, and Campbell (1968).

Bruner and Felder's (1983) study was a "lack of support from building administration concerning student discipline." Farber (1982) notes that many teachers see the
principal's office as opposing the faculty, unresponsive to teacher needs, or self-
serving. Schwartz et al. (1983) report that many teachers view the principal as
making numerous demands (both in the classroom and outside it) without providing
adequate resources—an example of role insufficiency. Other examples are provided
by Coates and Thoreson (1976), who reviewed the literature on teacher anxiety
especially for sources of teacher concern and found a link between work overload and
teacher anxiety. Added to this was the anxiety involved in performing the teacher role
under conditions that made high performance difficult—meeting individual needs,
balancing "no failure" policies with ensuring minimum standards, planning lessons,
grading papers, and finding time for remedial work. Lortie (1975) also found these to
be sources of discontent for teachers.

McCarrey (1965) found that teachers who were high in need of independence or
low in tolerance of authoritarianism were more satisfied (and less stressed) in a school
that used participatory decision making. Miller (1979) concludes that "administrative
behavior is a highly important factor in facilitating good staff morale" (p. 15). One
practice that Miller suggests administrators follow is to "praise and give credit to
teachers when it is warranted" (p. 25). And in attempting to determine how supervisors can reduce stress, Goens and Kuciejczkyk (1981) suggest that administrators
should provide support, leadership, and quality feedback for teacher concerns.

Institutional Variables Contributing to Teacher Stress.   There has been a
parallel attempt to identify and examine institutional variables that raise the levels of
teacher stress. These conditions can be summarized as follows:

1. Lack of mobility, low turnover, few new teachers, public attacks and budget
   reversals, bad press (Reed, 1979)
2. Lack of direct teacher involvement in decision making, no control over the job
   environment, involuntary transfers, little chance to interact with other adults
   (Cichon & Olson, 1978; Newell, 1978–1979; Reed, 1979)
3. Long hours, lack of supplies, too much paperwork, large classes, no planning time
   (Sullivan, 1979; Coates & Thoreson, 1976; Feshbach & Campbell, 1978)
4. Discipline and management of disruptive children; threats of violence; assaults on
   colleagues, verbal abuse (Cichon & Koff, 1978; Coates & Thoreson, 1976;
   Feshbach & Campbell, 1978)
5. Muzzling teachers after a violent incident; teacher discouraged from talking about
   or reporting stressful incident, principal harrassment, transfer denied (Bloch,
   1978)
6. Stress related to doing a good job; maintaining self-control when angry, teaching
   below-average students (Cichon & Koff, 1978)

Crime in the schools has long been a major source of teacher stress, although its
impact on teachers has not yet received much attention. The National Institute of
Education's *Violent Schools, Safe Schools* study (1978) found that 5,200 of the
nation's teachers are physically attacked at school in a month's time; nearly one-fifth
of the attacks required medical treatment. The NIE study found a relationship
between class size and teacher victimization: The higher the average number of
students in classes, the higher was the teacher's risk of being abused, attacked, and

robbed. The study also reported that teachers with high proportions of low-ability students, underachievers, behavior problems, and low-income minority students were more likely to be victims. Teachers who had been victimized were more likely to assess their schools and students negatively, and the NIE study speculated that these negative assessments both reflected and affected the reality of the classroom.

The pattern and the affective value of both principal-teacher and teacher-teacher relationships is captured in the concept of "school climate." Schools with "open" climates typically have positive role relationships, exhibit a sense of purpose and participation, and are productive in task accomplishment. Schools with "closed" climates are characterized by formal relationships, tension between superiors and subordinates, and varied perceptions of the goals of the organization. Stress-producing conflict often occurs between members of the same power echelon, and some findings suggest that the institutional variable of climate may be directly related to such conflicts. Ponder and Mayshark (1974) studied schools with open and closed climates as defined by the Halpin and Crofts (1963) Organizational Climate Description Questionnaire. Teachers in the closed-climate school took significantly more days of sick leave, suggesting that teachers in closed-climate schools experienced more stress-induced illness. In more recent studies, Young (1978) concludes that administrative support would help reduce the frustrations that give rise to high anxiety levels, that periods of stress could be prevented by perceptive principals assisted by concerned members of the school setting.

Teachers' Coping Strategies

An integrative review of the literature of the causes and probable consequences of teacher stress, including often ignored personal variables, was presented by Hoover-Dempsey and Kendall in their NIE-sponsored study (1982). Hoover-Dempsey and Kendall identified three general themes from the occupational stress literature: support from peers, role-related factors in the workplace, and person-environment compatibility.

Coping with job-related stress is assisted chiefly by two related sets of variables: personal resources (problem-solving skills and communication skills in particular) and social support, particularly from coworkers. Personal response—"personal action designed to change the individual's perception or experience of stressors" (Hoover-Dempsey & Kendall, p. 95)—was by far the most frequently cited category of coping response. Some job-related strategies were cited: teacher preparation, collegial interaction, and administrative intervention. It was pointed out, however, that while these strategies were most frequently cited in the research on coping with stress, the strategies themselves "have not been subjected to systematic design or evaluation of effectiveness" (p. 96).

Kepler-Zumwalt (1982) identified personality factors that enable teachers to feel and act positively about their job situations. Initiative and strong internal locus of control were two factors found to characterize teachers who were effective and had positive feelings about teaching. Not surprisingly, a sense of autonomy, mutual respect, and feedback from colleagues were factors found to enable teachers to feel positive even under adverse conditions. A mutual appreciation for autonomy and respect for personal judgment, as norms of the teaching subculture, were thought to be at the heart of such positive feelings. Citing other research to support these findings, Kepler-Zumwalt summarized teachers' suggestions for changes that would improve or maintain job satisfaction (in order of priority): smaller classes, additional support services for students, greater supervisor support, and improvement in the physical environment.

A recent study by Spencer-Hall (1982) examined the relationship between teachers' home and school lives. Data from four areas of teacher experience were collected: personal history, intraschool experience, extraschool relationships, and activities and staff development. Results indicated that overlap of home and school environments often had deleterious effects on both situations, with chronic depression and upsets in emotional equilibrium the frequently reported result. The level of stress experienced was often tied to individual home-situation variables such as marital status, presence of children, and economic level. Further research on stress will need to consider these factors, which undermine support necessary for coping successfully with stress.

In school, teachers' coping strategies were seen by Spencer-Hall as a range of extreme responses to the stressful aspects of school life. Stressed teachers reacted to their students by becoming either nurturing mother figures or harsh disciplinarians and by either doing the absolute minimum of classwork or deliberately overworking themselves and their students. In dealing with administrators, some adopted a passive conflict-avoidance stance, while others rebelled openly. Although these extreme reactions to dysfunctional stress were seen by researchers as nonconstructive, they were the norm in this particular population of teachers. The most successful coping technique was also reported as the most difficult to achieve: A very few teachers compartmentalized their lives, employing elaborate scheduling and structuring strategies to the point that no conflicting overlap was allowed. This highly structured and disciplined approach was practiced most commonly by persons with unusually favorable domestic situations.

Teacher attitudes toward staff development as a personal coping mechanism indicated needs that are not being met by the established programs. Miller (1979) posits that one of the most effective methods of countering stress is to develop a support system for sharing the burden, which can be comforting during high stress periods. Bloch (1978) insists that "the opportunity to report directly to the school board about unfair administration, overcrowded classrooms, violence," and other stressors would assure teachers that someone is listening and that needed remedial measures may be taken.

A Holistic Study of Stress

Some of the studies cited so far have dealt with more than one of the three areas, but by 1980 it was apparent that a research methodology was needed that could integrate the environmental, institutional, interpersonal, and personal aspects of stress on the job. The data-collection strategies would have to include the classical survey techniques but would depend heavily on the more inclusive ethnographic methodologies of the anthropologist, including key informant interviews, participant and nonparticipant observations, and content analysis of documents over at least a two-year period.

In 1980, the National Institute of Education supported such a holistic three-year study to look at six schools in two metropolitan areas. The study was designed to provide the "thick descriptions" that would illuminate working conditions in schools as a factor in teacher stress and burnout. This study (Schwartz et al., 1983) and its findings form the basis of the remainder of this chapter.

The investigators viewed each of the six sites as a microculture—each unique, but sharing certain universal characteristics with the others. Data were collected to describe how each school addressed the following "cultural universals":

1. A *value system* that indicates the preferred ways of doing things or specifying what is good and what is bad
2. A *world view* or cosmology that specifies the beliefs concerning the position of humankind in the cosmos and the limits individuals must adhere to in the school, the community, the church, or the classroom
3. A *social organization* that governs individual and group relationships even to the point of determining forms of verbal address
4. A *technology*, a body of knowledge and skills used to perform the tasks necessary for the system to function and survive (for a school, this would include knowing how to read and how to count)
5. An *economic system* that regulates the allocation of goods and services in the school and the classroom
6. A *political system* regulating individual and institutional behavior that specifies how decisions are made; how power, authority, and influence are acquired and used; and who participates in what decision
7. A *language* uniquely suited to the educational process or the subject matter of the classroom
8. An *aesthetic system* that defines what is beautiful, creative, and artistic
9. A *socialization process* or educational process that regularizes the transmission of knowledge to the neophytes, the unlearned ones in the group

This cultural-universals model provided a conceptual framework that allowed the investigators to develop detailed comparable descriptions of each of the six schools. It permitted the examination of stressors in the schools from the individual, institutional, and environmental perspectives. The model also specified that each culture must provide the members of the culture with *status* (feelings of being a worthwhile individual doing a worthwhile job), *security* (fiscal rewards, physical safety, and job security), and *sociability* (the time and opportunity to interact with other adults and discuss personal and professional issues in an atmosphere of trust and respect). When systems or cultures did not provide the individual with feelings of status, security, and sociability, the individual displayed the classic systems of dysfunctional stress described earlier.

From a cross-site analysis of data from the six schools, seven major categories of stressors were identified: security, governance/leadership, budget cuts, student issues, staff relations, lack of respect, and barriers to teaching.[2] Two categories of stressors pervaded all six schools and cut across security, status, and sociability: the *lack-of-respect syndrome* and *barriers to teaching*. Both led to the dysfunctional stress symptoms that precede burnout.

Lack-of-Respect Syndrome.   Teachers' frequent perceptions that they are held in low esteem by administrators, students, parents, and the general public contribute to

[2]For a complete discussion of these variables, see Schwartz et al., 1983.

a major stress-producing factor, referred to here as the lack-of-respect syndrome. Teachers feel they receive too few rewards and too little support or appreciation. A typical comment reflecting this perception is "You see and hear only the bad, seldom the good. No one cares."

Teachers perceive that directives that affect their job performance are forced on them from above. At the same time, they perceive that they have little input into the decision-making process, that little opportunity is given to them to express ideas to policymakers, and that administrators manipulate them and can be either too authoritarian or too nondirective.

Adding to these tensions, teachers describe students as increasingly disrespectful, uninterested, disruptive, and verbally abusive. Parents often disapprove of teachers' work. Even colleagues on the staff form cliques and are unable or unwilling to work cooperatively.

Security concerns heighten feelings of powerlessness, as teachers believe they are forced to work in unsafe conditions in jobs that may or may not have long-term protection. Budget cuts affect funds for materials, maintenance, and repairs, and teachers see their work environment and their control over that environment deteriorating around them. Teachers not only see fewer opportunities for advancement but also must worry about preserving the status quo. They feel trapped in what now may seem to be a dead-end job, with no assurances that working conditions and job security are not likely to erode further. Teachers, then, seem not to get the respect they feel they deserve. They feel powerless, deflated, and generally unappreciated, for they see themselves held responsible for negative situations over which they have little or no control.

Barriers to Teaching.   Obstacles to carrying out the expected duties of a professional educator are uniformly stressful. Principals expect teachers to do a variety of nonteaching functions, from patrolling halls to lunchroom duty to taking attendance in a homeroom. Boards of education demand copious and often repetitive paperwork, whether it be new forms, daily lesson plans, or mastery learning cards completed for all students at each level of achievement. New mandates requiring students to leave class for special instruction often are perceived as disruptive to lessons. Teachers also express strong resentment at having to function as security personnel to bolster safety inside schools. Intrusions and the threat of intrusions into classrooms by outsiders are very unsettling; many teachers seem preoccupied with the potential for such occurrences. In their view, teachers seek extensive training to teach, not to become quasi-police.

Similarly, all teachers in the Schwartz et al. study felt burdened by shortages of supplies and equipment and by depressing conditions, all of which made even their routine tasks difficult. Lack of paper, textbooks, and testing materials was a common reality. Cracked walls, falling plaster, and poorly maintained bathrooms all have a negative psychological effect on teachers. In addition, teachers felt that an inordinate amount of time was required to discipline an increasing number of disruptive students.

Despite these hindrances and distractions, extra time was needed to bring low-ability or low-achieving students up to levels where they could begin to learn appropriate material. Colleagues seemed unable or unwilling to pool resources and collectively resolve common problems. In short, teachers feel that the system is replete with mandates and shortages that consume valuable time needed for "settling in" and just teaching. In effect, it is not the act of teaching itself but *obstacles to it* that cause the teachers stress.

The stress-causing factor is, therefore, a deteriorating condition that teachers feel powerless to change, at least within the near future. The challenge for the future appears to concern how to remediate, and cope with, this situation in the interim. Since school personnel agree about conditions in these schools, the challenge is systemwide and not a problem for teachers alone, but without positive feelings of status, security, and sociability, teachers burn out, drop out, or are carried out. The survivors certainly are not interested in new statewide or systemwide initiatives or curriculum change projects ordered from above. The social organization and political system in highly stressed schools rob teachers of their opportunities for collegiality, innovation, and the creativity of peer interaction. Significant here is that these systems also rob teachers of a voice in the curriculum decisions that are at the core of their professional identity.

DECREASING STRESS IN SCHOOLS: STARTING POINTS

What can practitioners do? As Chapter 18 argues, collaboration between the principal and the teachers is essential for schools to be effective. We believe that collaboration of both parties involved in the policy decision-making process enhances the overall goal of increased status, security, and sociability for teachers and also clarifies predetermined administrative roles in the cultural matrix.

The literature clearly indicates the need for a formal resolution of teacher-administrator conflict with a coherent approach to solving problems as they arise. Organized statgies that deal with the causes of stress are demonstrably superior to strategies that merely address stress symptoms in progress. This means that a comprehensive approach is required, one that takes into account the nature of the entire school, the personalities of the staff, and all of the numerous variables involved.

The relevant factors in stress prevention are summarized by the concepts of status, security, and sociability. These encompass the sociocultural needs of any member of any cultural system, including teachers. When any of these needs are threatened, stress results.

It should be noted that our study (Schwartz et al., 1983) and others summarize only the aspects of the work environment that appeared to inhibit the needs of teachers. Neither our study nor most of the others concentrated on identifying aspects of the school environment that might have supported teachers' efforts. It is possible to argue that the conclusions drawn from this and other studies imply a world more dreary than real; after all, the positive side of teachers' lives was not examined. But it is difficult to argue that these stressors are acceptable, no matter what else is occurring in any of the schools. It is difficult to suppose that the existence of such stressors would not have some negative effect on the potential for effective teaching and maximum student learning.

What can the teacher, the administrator, the parent, the school board member do to minimize these stressors and to provide the skills for coping with the normal levels of stress found in any workplace? Let us examine questions and answers that suggest some ways to overcome barriers to teaching, increase respect for teachers, allow teachers to regain some control over their environment, and help teachers to enjoy and feel secure in their work. The answers to the questions describe the conditions conducive to a healthy teaching and learning environment, to excellence in teaching, and to positive and productive human beings.

Status

Q. *To what extent is schooling valued by parents and society, and does this value level affect the practice of teaching?*

A. The public perception is that conditions in the schools are deteriorating, that teachers and administrators are not as competent as they used to be. Declining general aptitude scores are cited by some as evidence. Low public confidence is reflected in a lack of financial support through bonds or increased school taxes. The popular press has expressed serious criticisms of schools and of teachers in particular. Expressions of low-valuation perceptions by the general public damages teachers' psychological well-being and eventually their ability or willingness to pursue excellence in teaching.

In the six schools in the Schwartz et al. (1983) study, stressors include isolation, lack of recognition, disrespect from the community and the general public, obstacles to teaching in the form of nonteaching duties, and responsibilities laid at the door of teachers by the same community parties who were disapproving.

Until the general public, the media, and local communities acknowledge the difficult role of the teacher in the public schools through increased funding, career ladder opportunities, and appreciation, teachers will continue to experience dysfunctional stress. Occupational-role research provides ample evidence that excessively stressed workers do not perform their duties well. Perhaps criticism of teachers would be more instructive if classroom stress were better understood. The ability of the teaching profession to attract the best and the brightest students is directly related to the public view of the profession, to its incentive system, and to its practitioners' perceptions of their future in the profession. At least in the schools studied, there seems to be a genuine image crisis. Until teachers themselves and the public come to value teaching more, we can expect stress to remain high and the negative consequences of that stress to remain.

Q. *How can the general public be informed about the physical and psychological stressors in teaching?*

A. A general public informed about the physical and psychological stressors in teaching can work toward solving stress problems more effectively in the schools. A pervasive but unspoken problem like stress cannot be addressed before it is acknowledged as legitimate and in need of attention. But the informing process must start with the schools themselves.

The individual school sites can take the lead in structuring interaction between teachers and the community. The school can begin the creation of supportive teacher networks that can be organs for expressing teacher concerns to the community, as well as social networks for helping teachers handle stress effects. There remains the direct method of informing the legislative bodies of the situation and applying pressure for needed changes. Teachers' unions can lobby for proschool legislation.

Concentrated efforts must be made to inform educators and the public about the importance of considering and addressing two major aspects of stressors in schools: (1) stressors related to the physical, financial, organizational, managerial, and status conditions of schools (e.g., poor security, discipline problems, decaying facilities, mismanagement, lack of supplies) and (2) stressors more generic to teaching itself. Teacher preparatory institutions, school administrators, board members, and the public must acknowledge the negative impact of stressful working conditions on teachers and the educational process and take action to remedy the working conditions related to dysfunctional stress.

Some specific suggestions have already been mentioned. Here is a brief list of some current practices in schools throughout the country that seem to be helpful in informing the public and the policymakers about the nature of teaching in the public schools:

1. The *Take-a-Class* program is based on the Native American principle that one should walk in another's moccasins for a mile before criticizing. In this program, businessmen, reporters, school board members, and parents take on the curriculum and instruction of a typical classroom for a week, a day, a morning, or an afternoon and try to cope. The regular curriculum must be the focus of the activity, not games or free-play period. Where the plan has been tried, most visitors come away with an increased appreciation and respect for the work of the teacher.

2. The *Adopt-a-School* program allows a business, civic group, or university to become the sponsor and patron for a given school. The patron has the responsibility of attempting to help the school obtain the resources it needs and cannot get from public funds, install new programs such as computer literacy, create learning bridges between high school and college by student and teacher exchanges, and generally work with the school staff to enhance the instructional and extracurricular programs.

3. *Publicizing special features of the instructional program* can be done through the use of news releases to local papers, inviting reporters to observe special programs, inviting parents to visit the school regularly, scheduling breakfasts with the principal and selected teachers, and arranging public performances by the school teams, fine arts and performing arts groups, spellers, readers, and so on.

4. *Released time for teachers* can free them to visit with parents, community groups, and local policymakers to talk about the school, students, and themselves.

Q. *How can resources best be allocated within schools to satisfy minimal classroom needs for equipment and supplies in a way that is equitable?*

A. Lack of adequate supplies has been a complaint of teachers probably throughout history. People charged with allocation of supplies have historically had to judge the seriousness of the complaints and deal with the problem as fairly as possible. In the six urban schools studied, the lack of materials was severe enough to hinder the normal teaching functions. In one school, written midterm exams were impossible because no paper suitable for duplication was available, and there had been little paper available for the entire semester. In another school, the total supply budget averaged about $25 per teacher for the entire year. Two of the six schools had whole classrooms with no textbooks available to them. A more common observation was aging audiovisual equipment lying dormant due to lack of funds for repairs (bulbs, overhead transparencies, etc.).

At the "gut" level, lack of instructional materials is a status-threatening issue. It is demeaning to be denied the basic tools for carrying out the known tasks of one's job. An important initial action would be to give the supplies problem the importance it commands. Decisions about procedure and implementation would follow more easily. Stress should decrease when the people involved are assured of the fairness of the effort. Such relief could indeed help marshal the collaborative efforts of concerned school personnel to obtain more of what is indeed most needed.

Questions concerning the equitable allocation of available supplies deserve serious consideration. A systematic acquisition and distribution scheme agreeable to the interested parties needs to be developed and implemented. Methods and procedures for such a task already exist; they need only be adapted. Teachers will cope much more willingly if they recognize the process as equitable. This demands, at the very least, teacher input into the decision process of allocation, a decision area over which teachers typically have only powers of request.

There is no single ideal approach to resource allocation for all schools; school situations differ in the amount of resources available and methods employed to allocate them. One must expect, therefore, that the solution to the allocation problem must be local and will take the time and effort of a number of school personnel.

Three principles to be observed at the local level are these:

1. The resource problem is an important one that must be addressed by all involved; therefore, a representative resources planning group should include members of the administration, the teachers, and others involved to make allocations and get additional resources.
2. Distribution must be fair, and all must suffer or gain equally unless the majority of the faculty endorses or requests a deviation.
3. The parents must be informed of their responsibility to provide children with the tools of instruction not provided by the state, and children must be taught to use resources wisely.

Q. *How can the teaching career be modified to improve the professional image of teachers and provide professional options reflecting the variety of contributions teachers can make?*

A. Principals, teachers, and other educational staff should have regularly scheduled time for collegial interactions that enhance professional skills, promote the sharing of ideas, minimize the isolation of the classroom, and improve communication. Many teachers lament somewhat bitterly the tedium and continual pressure associated with closed-campus policies and desire more opportunity to mix either professionally or socially with their colleagues. The real stressor under such conditions is isolation and a resultant feeling of alienation. The opportunity to share concerns is praised in schools where regular preparation time is provided. The collegial interaction is identified as a positive factor in dealing with day-to-day problems. Participation and support by the school principal are important ingredients in such problem solving.

New staffing patterns and career ladders for teachers need to be explored. Such alternatives allow teachers to remain part-time in the classroom, while having the opportunity to be rewarded professionally and economically for specialized training, study, and ability in other educational roles. At a 1984 conference sponsored by the

California Roundtable on Education on the topic of how to enhance the professional image of teachers, 100 teachers, administrators, business executives, and university and state department staff developed a list that included the following priority concerns:

- Establishment of career ladders and differentiated staffing
- Extension of the formal training period with additional supervised clinical experiences
- Provision for time and support for group and individual professional development (Smith, 1985)

Improving the teacher's professional image will necessarily involve change at all stages of professional life: preparation, practice, and what can be referred to as "passing the torch." Such a model would begin with an extended period of specialized training in undergraduate school with many opportunities to observe and work in schools under the supervision of teachers and other staff. Clearer and more rigorous standards for entry into the professional phase of the program need to be developed. An internship or apprenticeship under the supervision of a mentor, a master teacher, or, better yet, a university professor or a combination of these would be required for receipt of certification. In the second stage, practice, the assistant teacher would start on the beginning step of the differentiated career ladder. Teachers would proceed through the ranks of associate teacher and professor teacher only after demonstrating increased skills, knowledge, and expertise at each level. Peer evaluation with administrative input would be the vehicle for advancement. Each movement up the teachers' career ladder carries with it increased responsibilities and increased monetary and status rewards.

In the third stage, passing the torch, the professor teacher would serve in a mentor role, work on curriculum development in a master-teacher role, and work with university faculty in an action-researcher role, but always devoting a part of each workyear to teaching students.

The structural changes required by this system would need the cooperation of school boards, universities, teachers' organizations, and the public. But the professionalization of the teaching staff depends on the willingness of teachers to become professionals before any other consideration.

Security

Q. *What can be done about unsafe conditions in schools so that teaching is unimpaired by threats to physical security?*

A. Boards of education should establish mechanisms for assessing school needs for protecting school personnel and students from physical harm and from the psychological strain created by unsafe conditions. School authorities, city governments, and community members should cooperatively take action to increase safety in and around the schools.

Personal safety is a major concern of a large majority of school personnel in urban schools. Fears for personal safety and personal property stem from limited control over volatile students, unsafe neighborhoods, school intruders, and, in some cases, hostile parents. Because problems differ greatly from site to site, blanket procedures are clearly not the answer. Under present economic conditions, massive additional funding for security is unlikely. Innovative methods must be employed, making better use of existing monetary and human resources. District and individual school needs must first be assessed and action planned to address specific causes and problems.

Teachers frequently perceive boards of education as acting independently and unilaterally in making demands on teachers. In this case, a cooperative effort would have far more chance of success. The personal safety issue provides an opportunity for higher-level administrators to respond positively and specifically to a general problem. Individual schools will likely need little encouragement to seek solutions to security problems, but they will require information and support in considering which solutions are most cost-effective. It may be that a simple "buddy system" in walking to the parking lot after school would solve most of the security problems at one school, while a procedure for escorting visitors to and from classrooms would work well at another school. Community and city government involvement in resolving security problems is essential. Perhaps a citizens' watch group for "latch-key" children and other neighborhood problems could be organized by the school.

School systems' maintainance of the school and grounds should be regularly reviewed and corrected when found to be inadequate. The importance of the school to the community and the status of the teachers are reflected in the attention given to the maintenance of facilities. Above all, teachers must be consulted about, and involved in, any plan to remedy the situation at the local site.

Q. *How can preservice and in-service teacher education programs increase teacher awareness of potential stressors, provide coping skills, and develop preventive strategies?*

A. As part of the final stage of data collection in the Schwartz et al. study, teachers were asked to identify the coping strategies they employed to deal with stress. Two things stood out. First, there was no clear pattern to the responses, and many of the strategies suggested were clearly dysfunctional: for example, "working through lunch," "drugs," and "sleeping a great deal." Second, teachers found it hard to express or describe their own responses to stressors and appeared unprepared to take planned, positive action to deal with them. These experienced teachers had little knowledge of coping strategies for stress. Further investigation revealed that pre-service teacher education programs generally do not give high priority to the issue of coping with stress on the job.

In a very real sense, teachers' expectations for their teaching role have been violated. They did not expect, when they began teaching, a hostile and uncaring work environment, where respect and rewards for good teaching are difficult to earn. They did not expect to encounter a deteriorating physical and academic environment, nor did they expect to fear for their personal safety. Finally, they did not expect the dramatic change brought on by fluctuations in the national economy. Even if many of these problems could have been anticipated, the extent and complexity of the problems collectively could not. Threats to personal safety serve to heighten anxiety felt from other areas. All such negative perceptions heighten the impressions and fears that teachers' control of the work situation is declining.

Teachers must regain some of the control they feel they have lost. Prospective teachers must be prepared for the environment they will face. Thus in both preservice and in-service training, teachers must be involved in a way that encourages realistic perceptions and expectations of their work environment. Such infusions of reality, however, must be bolstered with feasible strategies for coping with or changing undesirable conditions. No one should have to work in an environment where he or she is made to feel unworthy, unsafe, and unappreciated.

For preservice programs of teacher education, prospective teachers must become better acquainted with the prevailing environmental forces, especially those that prevent and hinder the teaching and learning process and possibly demean the teaching process. Teachers should be able to recognize these forces and the fact that they must deal with these factors constructively if they are to survive. Equally important, therefore, is the provision for going beyond recognition and identification to positive treatment of the problems. Methods and strategies are needed to treat these negative forces, and it must be expected that such treatment is part of the job of teaching.

Prospective teachers will require early and varied experiences (clinical and simulated) in dealing with debilitating conditions, conditions actually experienced by the teachers studied. Prospective teachers should know on a firsthand basis about hostile parents, unmotivated and unprepared students, and lean or nonexistent budgets for support of teaching and learning. In addition to the joys of working with children and learning, prospective teachers will need to know about assertive discipline, fund raising, and literally winning friends and influencing people in bureaucracies. Perhaps courses in communication in complex organizations should be required for teachers. Novice teachers will need to practice coping successfully, as individuals and as group members, with such problems during their preservice programs. Beginning teachers especially will have to be willing and able to seek help and support from available sources. The teacher training institutions must examine their programs in concert with their colleagues in the field to blend theory and practice appropriately.

Here are some successful joint stress reduction programs that have been implemented at local sites:

- Cross-role cadres composed of teachers, administrators, parents, and interns who work together over a three- to five-year period on problem solving, project development and evaluation, policy generation, and so on
- Regular stress reduction groups led by professional consultants from the university
- Personal and professional counseling-clinic services using advanced interns under the supervision of a university professor
- Exercise and fitness programs at the school, offered by student teachers or interns from the university
- Coaching and buddy systems for feedback and for practicing new instructional strategies
- Training programs for principals in creating positive climates in their schools

Prospective and experienced teachers have to be prepared first and foremost to provide effective instruction. To survive in depressed and deteriorating workplaces, however, they will also need the ability to structure and build an environment for learning. This may require developing assertiveness and a refusal to accept poor conditions coupled with a determination to improve them. How do teachers deal with a "zero" supply situation, lack of heat and light, threats to personal safety? How do they react in a constructive fashion to the continual threat of losing their jobs? Stress is heightened when teachers realize that there is little chance of any outside intervention to change these conditions and that they themselves lack the training in how to treat them individually.

Many teachers observed by Schwartz et al. were innovative and successful in providing effective instruction in spite of poor working conditions. But the psychological, physical, and financial costs to teachers were considerable. Treating symptoms has its rewards, and the ability to cope should not be underestimated, but coping ability should be viewed as an avenue toward treating a cause—a process, not an outcome. If teachers can indeed cope with poor conditions, maintaining a reasonable amount of control over the environments they face, they may be able to move to the next stage, formulating and implementing ways of improving the environment.

This kind of "crisis intervention" may be a new role for teachers, one that may be met with resistance and reluctance from a number of quarters. However, it may be the most feasible and palatable approach for lasting impact and change. Major change is needed, and major change never comes unchallenged. Although this places responsibility squarely and perhaps unfairly on the teachers, it has the positive feature of direct benefit to teachers for acceptance of the extra work involved. If such approaches indeed give teachers greater control over their work environment, the benefits of control could be far-reaching for teachers as individuals and as professionals.

Q. *How can teachers better manage the multitude of teaching and managerial tasks that are required of today's teacher?*

A. Preparation of lesson plans, grades, attendance records, and records of student competencies are tasks directly related to teaching, and teachers do not generally report these tasks as stressful. The administrative paperwork and other noninstructional duties *are*. In one area, for example, frustration levels rose when the board of education reversed in the middle of processing its demands for multiple copies of forms and called for new sets of forms instead. Obviously, there is a genuine need for reporting. However, if documentation interferes with teaching and other educational activities, no purpose is served.

Teachers feel and believe there is not enough time to carry out adequately the tasks requested of them. Consequently, they must juggle and prioritize their activities, leaving some unaccomplished. Tasks that are not specifically teaching-related and take time away from preparation or teaching are perceived very negatively. Teachers believe strongly that the time spent in doing non-teaching-related tasks robs students of learning time.

Teachers are under pressure to produce more than in the past, to increase student achievement as well as respond to all administrative requests satisfactorily. From many quarters (parents, media, superiors, government figures), teachers are blamed for declining achievement and poor discipline; little attention is paid to other causal factors in this negative cycle. These factors combine to produce feelings of futility in teachers. Teachers would prefer to treat these as low-priority items, but with the uncertainty surrounding the security of their jobs, they cannot. They perceive themselves in a no-win situation.

What can be done to alleviate this situation? First, principals could seek a clearer understanding of the dilemma their teachers face and take an active hand in helping them deal with it. Principals could translate and communicate the rationale behind their own and board of education demands for carrying out nonteaching tasks. Teachers find most frustrating tasks they are required to perform that have no apparent benefit or rationale; if teachers could see more reason and benefit in what they are being asked to do, they would be more accepting.

Second, teachers could be provided with some feedback concerning the results of their non-teaching-related efforts. If different reporting schemes were implemented, for example, at the very least teachers should know the reason for the change. They should then be informed of the positive benefits of the revised system, even if those benefits are not directly related to them personally.

Third, the requests for nonteaching tasks should be reviewed periodically by the people requiring them. Are they needed and necessary? Are the data gathered used for good purposes? Is it indeed valuable for teachers to perform this nonteaching function (e.g., supervision of the lunchroom)? If the answers to these questions are not yes, the requirement should be considered for elimination. Teachers should be made aware of and involved in this monitoring process. Where teachers can be involved in the decision-making process, they should be. If teachers were a part of the process of determining nonteaching functions, they would be less apt to become frustrated by them.

What initiative can teachers take to ensure their own participation? Teachers have at least two avenues open to them. The first is to obtain support for their analysis of their situation. Can they assess in an objective manner the extent to which they are adequately managing their situation? Is some agency or individual willing to give a third-party assessment of the extent to which the work situation is unreasonable in its demands? Teachers need some verification of their dilemma, some unbiased opinion that validates their claims. Assistance in this regard might be available from sources with an interest in the problem, such as research institutions, teacher training programs, and parents.

The second approach is to work with the principal to reach some agreement on the importance of the problem. Many principals function successfully in a buffer role between teachers and forces outside the school. In some schools that Schwartz et al. studied, teachers and principals alike saw this as a valuable function where it was operating well. In other schools, many teachers resented being "sheltered" and expressed the feeling that their principal was unresponsive to problems and was not keeping them informed. It was clear that some meeting of the minds was needed in these cases if any relief was to be obtained. Clarity of expectations by both parties is essential to any stress reduction effort.

Sociability

Q. *How can principals best learn to handle stress-related problems of school personnel?*

A. Opportunities should be provided for school principals, through both pre-service and in-service programs, to improve their leadership ability, including skills in management, communication, assessment of the school climate, and structure of learning environments. They should know how to use and support action research strategies as tools for improvement.

The principal has tremendous influence on the degree of stress perceived by teachers in each school. Whether stress levels are relatively high or low, the principal is seen as a major determining factor and is therefore perceived as having the potential both to solve and to cause school problems. Indeed, the principal can directly influence conditions by controlling material and human resource allocations, security procedures, performance evaluations, and discipline measures. For these reasons, principals need a highly developed set of leadership and management skills and need also to expand such expertise to cope with the persistent and changing demands of the job.

More specifically, principals should be encouraged to focus on fostering two-way communication between faculty and administration. Clear and consistent articulation of expectations is essential. Principals should involve teachers in the decision-making process, minimize intrusion of managerial requirements on the teaching and learning process, secure the school from outside threats and disruption, allow for fair and equal treatment of all teachers, and promote the positive image of the school and its personnel in the community.

Q.   *How can teachers combat feelings of frustration and deal with stressors in the workplace?*

A.   The tedium, isolation, and frustration that teachers experience in various teaching environments has already been discussed, particularly with respect to school policies that inhibit adult interaction during the school day. Whether feelings of isolation result from lack of adult contact or from a sense of noninvolvment in decisions that affect working conditions, the overall result is a feeling of futility, one that harms teaching effectiveness. A complicating factor is that each school environment differs sufficiently from the others so that no single treatment applies to all situations. Thus the causes of such feelings, their roots, and their intensity can vary from school to school. Needed, therefore, are strategies, as generic starting points, that individual school faculties can employ flexibly to counteract these feelings of isolation and frustration.

In the school systems studied by Schwartz et al., and not necessarily in the schools themselves, two successful strategies were identified. The first was to try to adapt stress reduction strategies that have been successfully used in business, industry, and social service agencies, such as quality circles and problem-solving groups. It is crucial, however, that such strategies ensure two-way communication and joint decision making. Without this, the strategy becomes manipulative and insincere in the eyes of teachers.

The second strategy was the development of a support group among teachers themselves. Under austere budget conditions, teachers experienced job insecurity due to the threat of involuntary transfers, changes in teaching assignments, or layoffs. Many teachers feel their span of control over their work is diminishing. Support is needed to help teachers face such threats with positive action and regain control over their lives. If support groups are successful, efforts can be refocused on the task of teaching. Teacher organizations are a logical delivery mechanism for such services because they can provide them in a less threatening environment. It must be recognized that such action will require resources, an appropriate method of establishing such groups, and service centers for individual schools.

For teachers to take greater charge of their work situation, they must have a professional forum for discussion and planning. Such structures have always been needed in the past and have been successful to some extent. The need for such structures has grown by virtue of recent changes in conditions and increases in demands on teachers. It may therefore necessitate a reformulation of the way administrators and teachers view the job of teacher. Stress is understandably high and needs to be alleviated with realistic measures that will have lasting impact on the causes of stress and provide more than a Band-Aid to the wounds already inflicted.

Q. *How can the relationship between teachers and boards of education ensure that goals, expectations, and reasons for decisions are better understood?*

A. Boards of education should assess the impact of their decisions on daily life in classrooms and schools and on the teaching and learning process. Teachers often perceive boards of education as distant and insensitive to actual classroom and school needs. According to teachers, boards of education need closer contact with schools. This could be achieved through systematic structures, such as forums, town meetings, and regular visits by board members, which allow significant input from principals and school facilities. It is also likely that many board directives might be better received if staff fully understood the rationale behind them. Mandates to do things without explanations create frustrations that might be easily avoided. Staff awareness of the reason for a directive would allow for valuable input as to whether or not a particular course of action is actually meeting its goal.

CONCLUSIONS

Conditions in Urban Schools

The descriptions presented in this study are admittedly dreary and, as one critic put it, "devastating." This is partly attributable to the subject at hand: Looking for working conditions related to the dysfunctional stress is bound to be a bit dismal. It must be noted that there are instances of success in urban education, and in many urban areas, longstanding trends of declining test scores are being reversed. That such positive reversals are taking place is especially worthy of respect and recognition, given the odds against such successes. The point is not to condemn urban education but to understand its plight and offer constructive ways to improve the situation.

The descriptions included in case-study material in the research seem to be qualitatively different from descriptions of other workplaces and of nonurban schools. Do the constant bombardments to status, security, sociability, and teaching reflect systems in disarray? Do these urban schools simply reflect the anomie and social malaise attendant to urban decay? If so, then in addition to looking at conditions related to dysfunctional stress among teachers and administrators, the gap between teachers' ideal expectations about teaching and the reality of maintaining law and order in the building should be the focus of reform, as should the prevailing governing structures.

Clearly, more work must be done to detail the training and coping strategies of the remarkable educators who do work effectively in these difficult situations. Short-range solutions should include coping and change strategies taught to teachers and administrators at the preservice and in-service stages. Long-range plans call for systematic restructuring and sweeping reforms for cities and their schools to combat the decay reflected in the case studies.

Finally, if one were to assume, for the sake of argument, that the conditions described in these case studies are representative of large numbers of urban schools, dysfunctional stressors will only increase and make the school workplace more unbearable. The problems then become more political and more social, and research to deal with solutions might better be couched in comparative terms: Is the dysfunctional stress level in urban schools comparable to or worse than levels in other urban institutions such as hospitals, welfare agencies, and juvenile detention homes? At what point will we as a society refuse to tolerate these conditions or to subject our children to them?

On the other hand, if it is assumed that schools as workplaces can be divorced from the disease of urban decay—as some institutions, such as great symphony orchestras, urban universities, banks, and even some schools have been—the questions could be focused on remediation of the stressors identified in the Schwartz et al. and other studies.

The School as a Workplace

To study working conditions in schools is to view schools necessarily as workplaces—unique workplaces by comparison to many other institutions. Schools have multiple and sometimes contradictory functions, produce few tangible and easily accessible products, exercise limited control over the selection and removal of their clientele, and are commonly organized in ways that limit adult interaction. In addition, schools include populations that cross an unusually wide range of generations. Many teachers seem inadequately prepared, and sometimes indisposed, to deal with these unique aspects, and adjusting to them proves to be stressful. As long as the unique aspects remain unanticipated and strategies for positively responding to them are neither found nor employed, they will remain stressful.

Urban schools as workplaces, because of their deteriorating conditions, may present a higher potential for stress than nonurban schools do. The Schwartz et al. study concluded that stress for teachers was generally attributable to a lack of respect and to barriers to carrying out the tasks that teachers had been trained to perform. It seems that teachers find themselves in a kind of catch-22 situation. If they adjust to existing conditions, they may be accepting norms of behavior and success that are contrary to their basic beliefs and expectations. However, if they attempt to maintain standards different from the mainstream, standards more congruent with their own expectations for teaching performance and responsibilities, they literally may not survive. Stress may be attributable to being forced to choose among two very undesirable alternative courses of action, neither of which gains them self-respect or respect from others or enables them to carry out their expected duties and tasks.

Further, the study of schools as workplaces suggests strongly that stress is not the sole property of teachers but is experienced by all school personnel—teachers, administrators, clerical and maintenance personnel—and by the students. There is a danger in attributing stress to one or another role group in a school, lest the individual nature of the role or person be targeted for the cause. Therefore, treatments for stress need to be system-based efforts, not designed solely for one or another role group.

The questions and answers posed earlier identify actions needed, such as collaboration, increased communication within and to the public, more data of the case-study type (particularly of success stories), and documented experimentation with new roles. The field needs to experiment with career ladders for teachers, differentiated staffing structures, and innovative recruitment and training efforts. Detailed descriptions of successful school-by-school efforts to improve working conditions would be an important contribution. The available lists of characteristics of effective schools are not useful unless they are accompanied by details of the structure, function, content, and processes used to achieve an identifiable level of effectiveness. Then questions like the following could be addressed: How much and what kind of discipline is enough for effectiveness? What should be the "clear expectations" set by the principal for teachers and students? How does an administrator restore a sense of efficacy in a teaching staff, a belief in the worthiness of what schools and teachers do? What steps should be taken to build a culture of mutually reinforcing expectations and activities, and how long will it take? The success stories tell us it can be done; effective schools and teachers are not the result of magic. Teachers want to and can be effective, given time, support, and resources; principals can and do make a difference, and the central office and boards of education can help with the tasks. But whatever improvements take place will do so at the school-building and classroom levels, and that is where the resources, planning, follow-through, and attention must be concentrated. Proposed changes must be perceived by school personnel as improvements, or the objectives fail. Good teachers, like good schools, are committed, self-confident, active, able, focused, well organized, flexible, and tolerant—another list that is not particularly meaningful without improvements in the processes by which we select, train, and employ such people. Any additional inquiry or program implementation concerning how to reduce dysfunctional stress in schools should address these three areas of selection, training, and working conditions in schools.

FURTHER READING

National Association of Secondary Schools Principals Bulletin, December 1981. A number of articles in this issue are devoted to the theme of coping with stress. Three are of particular interest.

In "Supervisors: Do They Induce or Reduce Stress?" Goens and Kuciejczyk provide supervising strategies for managing stress. While they acknowledge the potential of supervisors as stress inducers, they support the idea of clarifying expectations, using listening and reward techniques as positive conflict resolution mechanisms, and eliminating role incongruities as successful strategies for stress reduction.

In "Teacher Stress: A Descriptive Study of the Concerns," C. V. Dedrick, R. H. Hawkes, and J. K. Smith found rather striking differences in male and female teachers in their ranking of sources of stress. Males and females agreed on only 3 of 11 identified sources of stress. Disruptive students and student apathy were two that were ranked as highly stressful and agreed upon by most of the 400 teachers sampled. Fully 57% of the sample had seriously considered a career change in the recent past.

In a study by Koff, Laffey, Olson, and Cichon, "Executive Stress and the School Administrator," a Teaching Events Stress Inventory was adapted for distribution to a national sample of NASSP and NAESP principals. Most interesting was the analysis of principals' comments that identified causes of stress (staff reduction, teacher evaluation and dismissal), described low-stress schools (smaller schools, nonpublic schools), and methods of conquering stress (acceptance of stressors, physical fitness, adequacy of planning and organization).

Farber, B. (1982). *Stress and Burnout: Implications for Teacher Motivation.* Available through ERIC.

Gupta, N. (1981). *Organizational Antecedents and Consequences of Role Stress among Teachers.* Available through ERIC.

Kepler-Zumwalt, K. (1982). *What Are the Factors Which Enable Some Teachers to Maintain Positive Attitudes about Their Jobs?* All three papers are available through ERIC. Each probes beyond teacher input and analyzes stress in a manner comparable to that of Schwartz et al. (1983).

REFERENCES

Anderson, M., & Iwaniki, E. (1981, April). *The burnout syndrome and its relationship to teacher motivation.* Paper presented at the annual meeting of the American Educational Research Association, Los Angeles.

Bedian, A. G., Armnekis, A. A., & Curran, S. M. (1981, April). The relationship between role stress and job related, interpersonal, and organizational climate factors. *Journal of Social Psychology, 113*(2), 247–260.

Bloch, A. (1978, October). Combat neurosis in inner-city schools. *American Journal of Psychiatry,* 1189–1192.

Bolding, J. T., & Van Patten, J. J. (1982). Creating a healthy organizational climate. *Administrators' Update, 3*(3). (Washington, DC: American Association of University Administrators)

Bruner, A., & Felder, B. (1983, March). Problems teachers encounter: How difficult is teaching? What is the principal's role? *National Association of Secondary Schools Principals Bulletin, 67.*

Burscemi, J. (1981). Practical Solutions for administrators to reduce stress in the classroom. *Illinois School Research and Development, 18*(5), 34–38.

Caspari, I. E. (1976). *Troublesome children in class.* London: Routledge & Kegan Paul.

Catterton, B. (1979). *Teaching Stress Events Inventory: Portland study of teachers.* Washington, DC: American Federation of Teachers.

Cichon, T. J., & Koff, R. H. (1978, March). *The Teaching Events Stress Inventory.* Paper presented at the annual meeting of the American Educational Research Association, Toronto, Canada. Analysis by J. Laffey.

Cichon, T. J., & Olson, G. E. (1978). Psychometrics and observations: Issues in a dual approach to the study of classroom learning environments. *Curric Inquiry, 8,* 133–153.

Coates, T. J., & Thoreson, C. E. (1976, Spring). Teacher anxiety: A review with recommendations. *Educational Research, 46,* 159–184.

Cruickshank, D. R., Kennedy, J. J., & Meyers, B. (1974). Perceived problems of secondary school teachers. *Journal of Educational Research, 68,* 154–159.

Dunham, J. (1977). The effects of disruptive behavior on teachers. *Educational Review, 29,* 1981–1987.

Farber, B. (1982, March). *Stress and burnout: Implications for teacher motivation.* Paper presented at the annual meeting of the American Educational Research Association, New York.

Farber, B., & Miller, J. (1981). Teacher burnout: A psychoeducational perspective. *Teaching College Record, 83*(2).

Feitler, F., & Tokar, E. (1981, April). *Teacher stress: Source, symptoms, and job satisfaction.* Paper presented at the annual meeting of the American Educational Research Association, Los Angeles.

Feshbach, N., & Campbell, M. (1978). *Teacher stress and disciplinary practices in schools.* Paper presented at the annual meeting of the American Orthopsychiatric Association, San Francisco.

Frey, D., & Young, J. (1983). Methods school administrators can use to help teachers manage stress. *National Association of Secondary Schools Principals Bulletin, 67,* 73–78.

Getzels, J., Lipham, J., & Campbell, R. (1968). *Educational administration as a social process: Theory, research, and practice.* New York: Harper & Row.

Gmelch, W. (1978). Principals' next challenge: The 20th century art of managing stress. *National Association of Secondary Schools Principals Bulletin, 62*(415), 5–13.

Goens, A., & Kuciejczyk, J. (1981). Supervisors: Do they induce or reduce teacher stress? *National Association of Secondary Schools Principals Bulletin, 65,* 24–28.

Gupta, N. (1981). *Organizational antecedents and consequences of role stress among teachers* (Final report). Austin, TX: Southwest Educational Development Laboratory.

Halpin, A., & Crofts, D. B. (1963). *The organizational climate of schools.* Chicago: University of Chicago, Midwest Administrative Center.

Hargreaves, D. H . (1976). The real battle of the classroom. *New Society, 35,* 207–209.

Hendrickson, B. (1979). Teacher burnout: How to recognize it, what to do about it. *Learning, 7*(5), 37–39.

Holifeld, J. (1982). An analysis of junior high/middle school teachers' perceptions of factors affecting teacher job stress and principals' perceptions of ways to alleviate or manage teacher job stress. *Dissertation Abstracts International, 42*(4A), 1401.

Hoover-Dempsey, K., & Kendall, E. (1982). *Stress and coping among teachers: Experience in search of theory and science* (Final report). Nashville, TN: George Peabody College and Vanderbilt University.

Kepler-Zumwalt, K. (1982). *What are the factors which enable some teachers to maintain positive attitudes about their jobs?* (Final report). New York: Columbia University, Teachers Center.

Koff, R. H., Laffey, J. M., Olson, G. E., & Cichon, D. J. (1981). Stress and the school administrator. *National Association of Secondary Schools Principals Bulletin, 65*(449).

Kyriacou, C., & Sutcliffe, J. (1978). Teacher stress: Prevalence, sources and symptoms. *British Journal of Educational Psychology, 48,* 159–167.

Kyriacou, C., & Sutcliffe, J. (1979). Teacher stress and satisfaction. *Educational Research, 21*(2), 89–96.

Landsmann, L. (1978). Principals may be hazardous to their teachers' health. *National Elementary Principal, 57,* 69–72.

Lortie, D. C. (1975). *Schoolteacher: A sociological study.* Chicago: University of Chicago Press.

Lowenstein, L. F. (1975). *Violent and disruptive behavior in schools.* Hemel Henstead, Great Britain: National Association of School Masters.

Maslach, C., & Jackson, S. (1978). Job burnout: How teachers cope. *Public Welfare, 36*(2), 56–58.

Maslow, A. (1970). *Motivation and personality.* New York: Harper & Row.

McCarrey, L. R. (1965). *Job satisfaction as related to participation under varying administrative behaviors.* Eugene, OR: Oregon School Study Council.

McLaughlin, J. W., & Shea, J. T. (1960). California teachers' job satisfaction. *California Journal of Educational Research, 11,* 216–224.

Miller, W. (1979). O. K. *Dealing with stress: A challenge for education.* (Phi Delta Kappa Educational Foundation No. 130, pp. 5–30)

Muth, R. (1973). Teacher perceptions of power, conflict, and consensus. *Administrator's Notebook, 21.*

National Institute of Education. (1978). *Violent schools-safe schools: Safe School Study Report to the Congress.* Washington, DC: U.S. Department of Health, Education and Welfare.

National School Resource Network. (1981). *Stress and burn-out in the schools.* Washington, DC: Author.

Newell, R. (1978–1979). Teacher stress warning: Teaching may be hazardous to your health. *American Teacher,* 16–17.

Olson, G. (1983, April). *The stressors of school administrators: A synthesis of recent research.*

Paper presented at the annual meeting of the American Educational Research Association, Montreal, Canada.

Payne, J. (1974). *Educational priority: Vol. 2. EPA surveys and statistics.* London: Her Majesty's Stationery Office.

Ponder, L. D., & Mayshark, C. (1974). The relationship between school organizational climate and selected teacher health status indicators. *Journal of School Health, 44,* 123–125.

Reed, S. (1979, March). What you can do to prevent teacher burnout. *Principal, 58,* 67–70.

Rudd, W.G.A., & Wiseman, S. (1962). Sources of dissatisfaction among a group of teachers. *British Journal of Educational Psychology, 32,* 275–291.

Schwartz, H., Olson, G., Ginsberg, R., & Bennett, A. (1983). *Schools as a workplace: The realities of stress* (National Institute of Education Rep. No. G-80-0011). Chicago: Roosevelt University.

Selye, H. (1956). *The stress of life.* New York: McGraw-Hill.

Smith, B. O. (1985, June). Research bases for teacher education. *Phi Delta Kappan, 66,* 685–690.

Spencer-Hall, D. A. (1982). *Teachers as persons: Case studies of the lives of women teachers* (Final report). Warrensburg: Central Missouri State University.

Sullivan, C. (1979). *Sources of anxiety within the school setting as reported by Emory University pre-service and in-service teachers: A descriptive study.* Atlanta: Emory University.

Young, B. B. (1978). Anxiety and stress: How they affect teachers, teaching. *National Association of Secondary Schools Principals Bulletin, 62,* 78–83.

24 CONTROVERSIAL LEGAL ISSUES OF THE 1980S

David Schimmel

During the 1980s the issue of student rights and administrative control reached unprecedented levels of political debate and public confusion. From local school boards to the White House, there were cries of alarm and demands for change. Two issues have been at the center of this debate: discipline in the schools and prayer in the classrooms. On the first day of 1984, for example, a White House report on school violence attacked Supreme Court decisions that guaranteed due process to students, claiming that due process interfered with effective discipline. A few weeks later, the president of the United States in his State of the Union address called for a constitutional amendment to permit prayer in the schools and for tuition tax credits for parents of students in private and religious schools.

Issues of student rights are not new. In 1969, the Supreme Court ruled that the Constitution does not stop at the schoolhouse gate but protects the rights of students in America's classrooms. During the 1970s, these rights were expanded and clarified in an explosion of court decisions. Although many parents, teachers, and administrators initially criticized these decisions, they were generally followed by school authorities and ignored by politicians. But by the 1980s, the president and other political leaders led a backlash of dissatisfaction with education and focused on discipline, due process, school prayer, and tuition tax credits as issues of major concern.

This debate left many educators feeling frustrated and angry about our political and legal system. They viewed judges as improperly interfering with educational decisions and imposing unnecessary legalistic procedures on the schools. They saw the law as a source of anxiety and uncertainty, as an adversary rather than an ally. As a result, educators are often intimidated by the threat of a lawsuit, often fail to exercise legitimate authority, and then blame judges for problems that have little to do with the law. That is why educators need to become legally literate—especially about issues of discipline, due process, and religion in the schools. By becoming legally literate, teachers and administrators can understand better how the legal system works and how it can work to improve education.

DISCIPLINE AND DUE PROCESS

In 1975, a sharply divided Supreme Court ruled that students facing short sus-pensions are entitled to the due process protections of the Fourteenth Amendment. This decision that split the High Court continues to divide the country. A federal task force appointed by President Reagan stated that due process requirements "deprive school administrators of the tools they need to control school violence." Others, however, believe that due process in schools leads to more positive student attitudes toward school rules, discipline, law, and education. Whatever position educators take on the issue, it is important that the debate be based on an accurate understanding of the legal principles involved. Otherwise, the issues are confused by error, and laws are mistakenly attacked as the cause of a problem while the real causes remain hidden. To avoid these mistakes, let us examine what courts have and have not said about a series of controversial issues that have confused the discipline debate.

Due Process

Due process simply refers to fair procedures. It is based on the Fourteenth Amend-ment, which provides that no state shall "deprive any person of life, liberty or property without due process of law." When school officials punish students, this is considered "state action" since schools obtain their authority from the state. Thus when administrators deprive students of a "liberty" or "property" right, the Four-teenth Amendment applies. This generally means that before severe punishments are imposed on students, the students are entitled to due process of law.

Due process is not a rigid concept consisting of a series of fixed steps and technical rules. Rather it is an elastic, flexible process that varies according to the severity of the punishment. In cases of minor punishment such as detention, courts will probably feel that no legal procedures are due. However, in cases such as expulsion, more extensive requirements are due because of the greater seriousness of the penalty.

Due Process and Suspension

Students are entitled to due process before they are suspended, ruled the U.S. Supreme Court in the landmark case of *Goss* v. *Lopez* (1975). The case began after students from the Columbus, OH, schools were suspended without a hearing. Some were punished for documented acts of violence. Others, like Dwight Lopez, were suspended although they claimed to be innocent bystanders. No evidence was presented against them, and they were never told what they were accused of doing. Lopez and a group of other students who were suspended for up to 10 days without a hearing claimed that this violated their right to due process of law. The Supreme Court agreed.

According to the Court, the U.S. Constitution does not require states to establish public schools. But once they do, students have a "property" right, which may not be withdrawn on grounds of misconduct without "fundamentally fair procedures." A suspension of up to 10 days is not so minor a punishment that it may be imposed "in complete disregard of the Due Process Clause," wrote the Court. "The total exclusion from the educational process for more than a trivial period is a serious event in the life of the suspended child." If the charges against them are recorded in their records, they could damage the students' standing with their teachers and "interfere with later opportunities for higher education and employment."

In cases of suspension, what procedures are due? Less than most educators imagine. In *Goss*, the Supreme Court explained that due process is a flexible and practical concept and does not require a rigid set of procedures to be applied in all situations. However, it does require at least that students facing suspension "must be given *some* kind of notice and afforded *some* kind of hearing."

The Court explained the kind of informal notice and hearing that are required before a short suspension. There are two steps. First, "the student is given oral or written notice of the charges against him." If the student admits the accusation, no other procedures are required before determining punishment. However, "if he denies them," the student is entitled to "an explanation of the evidence the authorities have and an opportunity to present his side of the story."

There are exceptions to the notice and hearing requirement. If a student poses a continuing danger to himself or others or poses "an ongoing threat of disrupting the academic process," he may be "immediately removed from school." In such cases an informal hearing should be held "as soon as practicable."

On the other hand, in cases where facts are in dispute, additional procedures might be appropriate. Suppose, for example, that a student who is accused of taking part in a disruptive demonstration in the cafeteria denies the charge and claims he was in Ms. Smith's class. A reasonable administrator would check the student's story with Ms. Smith before suspending him. In cases such as this, the Supreme Court suggested that the disciplinarian might decide "to summon the accuser, permit cross examination, and allow the student to present his own witnesses." As a result, the administrator's "discretion will be more informed" and "the risk of error substantially reduced." The Court, however, declined to require these additional procedures but left them to the disciplinarian's discretion.

Informality of Procedures

Will the due process required by the Court before suspension take extensive time or turn the school into a courtroom? No. The process required in cases of short suspension need not be formal or time-consuming. According to *Goss*:

> There need be no delay between the time "notice" is given and the time of the hearing. In the great majority of cases, the disciplinarian may informally discuss the alleged misconduct with the student minutes after it has occurred.

What is required by the Court is what most good administrators have been doing for decades—informing students of the rules they are accused of breaking and discussing the alleged misbehavior with them before imposing punishment. As Justice White observed:

> It would be a strange disciplinary system in an educational institution if no communication was sought by the disciplinarian with the student...to let him tell his side of the story in order to make sure that an injustice is not done. (*Goss*, 1975)

Additional Procedures

The informal notice and hearing outlined by the Court in the *Goss* case is the minimum procedure required under the Constitution before suspension. Many disciplinary codes have gone beyond this minimum. Some require that students have a right to invite parents and/or teachers to a hearing preceding suspension. Others require verbal and written communications between principals and parents and have added an appeal procedure. Some administrators believe that these added steps make their disciplinary process more effective. Others feel that they are an unnecessary burden. Many educators erroneously believe that these procedures are legal requirements of due process and have been imposed by courts. Such added procedures are matters of administrative discretion, not requirements of constitutional law.

Due Process and Expulsion

Although there has been no Supreme Court decision on the question, other courts have indicated that due process requires relatively formal procedures prior to expulsion. Unlike a short suspension, expulsion has quite serious consequences on a student's educational and occupational life; therefore, more extensive procedures are due. In cases of expulsion, courts generally require that students be notified in writing of the charges against them, the time and place of the hearing, a description of the hearing procedures, and the evidence that will be presented by the administration. At the hearing, students may be advised by their parents or a lawyer, may present evidence and witnesses on their own behalf, may cross-examine witnesses against them, and may record the proceedings. The decision of the hearing officers or board should be in writing, should be based only on the evidence presented at the hearing, and should be accompanied by a right of appeal.

In *Dixon* v. *Alabama* (1961), involving the expulsion of a college student, a federal appeals court wrote:

> By its nature, a charge of misconduct depends upon a collection of the facts...easily colored by the point of view of the witnesses. In such circumstances, a hearing which gives the Board or the administrative authorities...an opportunity to hear both sides in considerable detail is best suited to protect the rights of all involved.

Thus the process due before a student is expelled is more extensive than in the case of a short suspension. However, judges do not require a "full-dress judicial hearing" or that courtroom rules of evidence be followed. What is required, according to *Dixon*, are the "rudiments of an adversary proceeding" that gives students a reasonable opportunity to defend against changes that might lead to their expulsion.

Minor Punishments

Is due process always required before a student is punished? No. Courts do not require due process in disciplinary matters that do not seriously affect students. For example, if students complained to a judge that they were given detention, extra homework, or written warnings without a hearing, the judge would probably refuse to consider the cases because they do not "implicate constitutional values." Or the judge would apply the legal maxim *de minimus non curat lex* ("the law does not deal with trifles") to these situations and rule that student complaints about minor punishments should be taken to the school board, not to the courts. This does not mean that the courts approve of any arbitrary punishment, only that minor disciplinary conflicts are considered to be educational, not legal, matters.

These principles are illustrated by a 1983 federal decision (*Bernstein* v. *Menard*). The case involved a Virginia student who was dismissed from a high school band for refusing to go on a band trip because of a dispute with his bandmaster. The court found that "the punishment prescribed for the boy as a result of his unpleasant encounter with the bandmaster was *de minimis*." According to the judge, if the boy

> accepted the punishment meted out by the bandmaster, be it considered fair or unfair, ...he would have accepted a transitory embarrassment and humiliation which he might remember with distaste for the rest of his life or, more likely, which might have taught him to be more respectful of those placed in authority over him. Whatever the event, it is clear that the Constitution of the United States of America was not offended.... If bandmasters must be concerned that their every disciplinary decision is subject to a constitutional standard to be judged in a federal court, harmony and rhythm will disappear from the musical scene.... Suits such as this trivialize our Constitution.

This case does not mean that a decision to remove a student from a school organization is unimportant. Nor does it suggest that there should not be school procedures for resolving such disputes. In fact, this case was considered "at every level of the school hierarchy." Under these circumstances, the judge simply ruled that the established procedures available to the student were more than adequate and that the dispute was not a constitutional matter to be decided by the federal courts.[1]

Subjective Judgments in Academic and Extracurricular Activities

Is due process required in all important school decisions affecting students? No. Due process generally does not apply to academic matters (such as grading) or to student selection for participation in extracurricular activities that are not based on objective criteria. In academic and educational matters (as contrasted with disciplinary procedures), courts are reluctant to substitute their judgment for the judgment of educators.

A recent Wisconsin decision (*Karnstein* v. *Pawaukee School Board*, 1983) dealing with election to the National Honor Society (NHS) illustrates the court's view on these matters. Walter Karnstein was academically eligible for membership in the NHS but was not selected by the school's faculty committee. Because there was no opportunity for Karnstein to be heard by the committee or to appeal the committee's decision, he went to court claiming a violation of his right to due process.

The court recognized that election to the NHS was an important honor for students and might be valuable when applying for college. However, the judge had

> no trouble concluding that an applicant for membership in the NHS has no constitutionally protected liberty or property interest in election to the society.

---

[1]Virginia law even provides review of such disputes in local courts.

The procedures governing the selection process, therefore, need not afford to an applicant the requirements of due process of law.

In a comment relevant to similar school decisions, Judge Evans noted:

> Selection is a mere "honor" no different, except in degree, from such things as being picked to star in the school play or being named to serve as captain of the basketball team.... Most honors are alike in that some individual or committee must review what someone has accomplished and make a subjective judgment of whether that conduct is deserving of reward or recognition. Inherent in such a system is the possibility of error.... Courts would indeed be entering into a prickly briarpatch were they to get involved in reviewing these kinds of subjective judgments. (*Karnstein*, 1983)

Thus courts will not review decisions of this sort to determine if they were wise or correct. As long as the decisions are not clearly discriminatory, the court held that Karnstein's constitutional rights were not violated even if the decision not to elect him to the NHS was wrong.

However, if a student is removed or prohibited from participating in an extra-curricular activity based on facts in dispute, the situation might be different. For example, in a New Hampshire case (*Duffley* v. *New Hampshire Interscholastic Athletic Association*, 1983), John Duffley withdrew from school during his sophomore year due to illness, but he was ruled ineligible for basketball as a senior because the state athletic association doubted the legitimacy of his sophomore withdrawal. Duffley wanted a hearing to prove that his illness was serious, but the association refused, explaining that no hearing was required since there was no constitutional right to play basketball.

The Supreme Court of New Hampshire ruled that Duffley was entitled to a hearing. The court explained that interscholastic athletics are more of a "property interest" than a "mere privilege" since such activities "are considered an integral and important element of the educational process" and may determine a student's ability to attend college. The court concluded that "the right of a student to participate in interscholastic athletics is one that is entitled to the protection of procedural due process." Therefore, in New Hampshire, students cannot be denied eligibility from interscholastic competition without some type of "notice and an opportunity to be heard"—especially when decisions are based on objective facts in dispute, not on subjective judgments of a student's ability.

Procedural Omissions

If some aspect of due process is not followed, is the punishment automatically invalid? Not necessarily. It depends on the severity of the punishment and whether the omission might have impaired the fairness of the process or prejudiced the result.

Some courts hold that there are certain essential elements of due process and that schools must adhere to this minimum—especially in cases of serious punishment. Thus in a Wisconsin expulsion case, a federal court ruled that a student must receive an adequate written notice of the charges and sufficient opportunity to prepare for the hearing—even when the student admitted the conduct. On the other hand, a recent decision by the Supreme Court of Vermont reflected a more flexible position.[2]

The Vermont case involved Eric Rutz, a student who was expelled after he admitted selling a small quantity of marijuana in his high school. Rutz went to court to enjoin his expulsion because the school failed to follow its own procedures, which required that students receive a "written notice" of the expulsion hearing containing the charges. Justice Peck acknowledged that some courts hold that written notice is "an inflexible sine qua non of due process" and that if schools adopt disciplinary regulations, "they must be strictly and literally complied with *necessarily* under pain of reversal." But the Vermont Supreme Court wrote that this view was "too rigid" and "inflexible" and limited the court's capacity "to accomplish true justice." According to Justice Peck, the critical question is "whether the student's interests have been properly protected so that he was not prejudiced by the failure to give written notice." "If that question can be answered in the affirmative," wrote the court, "we would hold, generally, that there has been no necessary violation of the due process clause." Since Rutz admitted receiving "actual notice of the charges," the failure to provide written notice did not result in "any prejudice" against him. Based on the facts of this case, the court held that there was no violation of Rutz's due process rights because there has been "substantial compliance" with the school's regulations, and the student "has not been prejudiced by any failure of strict compliance." However, Justice Peck warned that schools are still expected to comply with their own rules and that when there is noncompliance, "the potential for a due process violation is ever present, threatening reversal."

A similar result was reached by a federal appeals court in the case of Michael McClain, who was suspended for more than seven months for bringing a switchblade to his high school (*McClain* v. *Lafayette County School Board*, 1982). Michael argued that his due process rights were violated because he was not informed of the names of his accusers, the right to be represented by counsel, or the right to confront witnesses. Furthermore, since the administration played tape recordings of witnesses, there was no opportunity for cross examination. Despite the omission of these procedural requirements, the court ruled against the student. The judge acknowledged that under some circumstances what was done "might be a denial of due process," but not in this case. The reason, wrote the judge, is that "Michael had conceded his guilt and has never afterward denied it." Since the student had an opportunity to present his side of the case and did not deny the wrongdoing, the court concluded that "there was nothing fundamentally unfair or legally prejudicial in the proceedings."

Legal Representation

Generally, courts have held that students facing expulsion are entitled to have a lawyer present for consultation and advice. But it is not clear whether students have a right to have their attorney cross-examine witnesses. A recent federal case ruled that there was no such right in a college disciplinary hearing (*Hart* v. *Ferris State College*, 1983). The court feared that giving lawyers the right to cross-examine witnesses in

[2]*Keller* v. *Fochs* (1974); *Rutz* v. *Essex Junction Prudential Committee* (1983).

expulsion cases might result in colleges' having their own attorneys participate in the hearing to ensure that their witnesses "not be harassed" and that the students' witnesses "be subject to equally searching cross-examinations," thus escalating a school's administrative procedure into a "full-dress judicial hearing." It is probable that the same reasoning would apply to public schools, where due process might require that students or parents (but not lawyers) have the right to cross-examine on the theory that the burdens of giving lawyers this right far outweighs its benefit.

Suspension of Transportation

Can schools suspend a student's right to bus transportation without due process? According to a federal appeals court, they can. The case arose in New Hampshire after the Nashua School Board implemented a policy suspending bus service for five days for all students on buses where serious disruptions occurred if the guilty students could not be identified (*Rose* v. *Nashua Board of Education*, 1982). Objecting parents went to court, claiming that their children's due process rights were violated since they did not cause the trouble and that their transportation was unfairly suspended without a hearing because of the misbehavior of others. But the court ruled against the parents.

The court explained that since the suspension of bus transportation for five days "caused only inconvenience, not loss of educational opportunity or other significant injury, we believe it is a 'de minimus' deprivation that does not call for constitutional due process protection."

Even if there were a constitutionally protected property interest involved in suspending the bus transportation, Judge Breyer asserted that the students "received the 'process' they are due." He acknowledged that a prior hearing might prevent the innocent from being punished along with the guilty. But such a process would require the schools to abandon their current suspension policy, which was instituted because they were unable to identify the specific troublemakers. Under the circumstances of this specific case, the court refused to require greater procedural protections—particularly when such procedures "would merely prevent the implementation of a reasonable disciplinary policy aimed at securing the safety of the children riding school buses."

Miranda Warnings

Must students be advised of a right to remain silent before being questioned by school officials about alleged offenses? No. In 1980, Daniel Boynton was expelled from a Maine school for using marijuana. Boynton claimed that his punishment was based on an admission that was obtained after an unconstitutional hearing. The student argued that his due process rights were violated because the principal and vice principal questioned him for over an hour, during which time they denied him permission to leave and failed to advise him of his right to remain silent.

Since Boynton was notified of the alleged infraction and given an opportunity to be heard before his initial suspension, the court ruled that he had received the process that was due, and that the extensive questioning by the principals was not unconstitutional. The judge held that Boynton need not be advised of a right to remain silent.

The court concluded that the warnings that police must give suspects in criminal cases are not applicable "to interrogations conducted by school officials in furtherance of their disciplinary duties" (*Boynton* v. *Casey*, 1982).

Cross Examination

A student's right to confront and cross-examine hostile witnesses depends on the circumstances. Confrontation and cross examination are generally not required before short suspensions. However, in cases of long-term suspension or expulsion, the opportunity to cross-examine witnesses is usually required—especially when there is a conflict about the facts of the case. A 1982 California decision (*John A.* v. *San Bernardino City Unified School District*) illustrates how courts react to this issue.

The case arose when a fight erupted on the San Bernardino High School campus after a football game. Following an investigation by the vice principal, a 14-year-old student, John A., was expelled for 6½ months based on signed statements from several other students that he "took part in an unprovoked attack." Neither of the injured boys nor any of the witnesses testified at the hearing. And John strongly denied the charges.

John's lawyer contended that his client had a right to confront and cross-examine the witnesses against him. The administrators argued that they must be able to discipline students without subjecting their accusers to cross examination "because otherwise fear of retaliation would make students reluctant to give information on disciplinary matters." And there was evidence that there had been threats of retaliation in the past. But the court ruled that there was no evidence in this case that witnesses were unwilling to testify "or that by testifying they would subject themselves to a substantial risk of harm." Therefore, under such circumstances, where evidence is in sharp dispute and witnesses are readily available, schools may not rely solely on written reports to expel a student.

On the other hand, the California Supreme Court acknowledged that confrontation and cross examination are not always required. In fact, the court wrote that a school board may rely "upon statements and reports when it finds that disclosure of identity and producing the witnesses would subject the informant to significant and specific risk of harm." Although the U.S. Supreme Court has never considered this question, the California court's conclusion appears to provide sound advice: When evidence indicates that there is a significant risk of harm to a witness, a school board may use written or tape-recorded testimony in a hearing without disclosing the identity of the witness. But where there is no specific risk to a witness and the facts are in dispute, a student should not be expelled without a chance to cross-examine his accuser.

RELIGION AND EDUCATION

In March 1984, the United States Senate and House of Representatives debated a constitutional amendment to overturn earlier Supreme Court decisions prohibiting prayer in the public schools. President Reagan joined the debate and said "I believe that the loving God who has blessed our land...should never have been expelled from American's classrooms" (Church, 1984). The president also lobbied in favor of the amendment, which began: "Nothing in this Constitution shall be construed to prohibit individual or group, vocal or silent prayer, in public schools or other public institutions."[3] Although a majority of the senators voted in favor of this proposal, it failed to receive the two-thirds needed to pass. But the religious and political leaders who supported the proposal (which is favored by about 80% of the people) promised to try again. And the 1985 Supreme Court decision on silent prayer further fueled this dispute.

Prayers in School

Is school prayer permitted if students who do not wish to participate are excused? No. The U.S. Supreme Court has clearly ruled that school prayer laws are unconstitutional and that an excusal provision does not save such laws.

A major Supreme Court case on this issue, *Abington School District* v. *Schempp* (1963), involved a Pennsylvania law that included the Lord's Prayer and Bible reading as part of opening exercises. The law allowed students to be excused upon the written request of their parents. Despite this provision, two students and their parents felt that these "religions activities" violated their constitutional rights. The parents feared that if they had their children excused, they would be considered "oddballs" and perhaps "un-American atheists." The Court ruled in favor of the students.

In this 1963 decision, Justice Clark noted that the First Amendment prohibits Congress and the states from making laws "respecting an establishment of religion or prohibiting the free exercise thereof." To guarantee that the government is neutral in religious matters, it should not pass any laws unless they have a "secular purpose" and their "primary effect neither advances nor inhibits religion." Applying these principles to this case, the Court found that the required recitation of the Lord's Prayer and Bible reading were an unconstitutional "religious ceremony."

Why doesn't the parents' right to excuse their children from the religious exercises save the law? In an earlier case, the Court explained that when the power, prestige, and support of the government are placed behind a particular religious belief or practice, "the indirect coercive pressure upon religious minorities to conform" to the prevailing "officially approved" religious practice is plain. The Court emphasized that prohibiting school prayers does not interfere with the religious freedom of the majority. While the free exercise clause prohibits government from denying anyone the right to freedom of religion, "it has never meant that a majority could use the machinery of the State to practice its belief."

In a related decision (*Engel* v. *Vitale*, 1962), the Supreme Court struck down a school board requirement that students should begin each day by reciting a non-denominational prayer. Doesn't prohibiting school prayer indicate a hostility toward religion? "Nothing," wrote Justice Black, "could be more wrong." The Bill of Rights, explained the justice, tried to put an end to government control of religion and prayer, but it "was not written to destroy either." The Court concluded that "it is neither sacriligious nor anti-religious to say that each separate government in this country should stay out of the business of writing or sanctioning official prayers and leave that purely religious function to the people themselves."

[3]The amendment proposed by Senate majority leader Howard Baker also stated: "No person shall be required by the United States or by any state to participate in prayer. Neither the United States nor any state shall compose or mandate the words of any prayer to be said in public schools."

Intent of the Framers

Aren't the Court's antiprayer decisions inconsistent with the intention of the framers of the Constitution? This is a matter of considerable debate among scholars. In fact, the state of Alabama defended its school prayer laws on the basis of arguments by conservative historians that the Constitution "was intended only to prohibit the federal government from establishing a national religion" and was not intended to apply to the states. But as a federal appeals court has pointed out, this argument has been considered and rejected by the Supreme Court, "which is the ultimate authority on the interpretation of our Constitution." Thus the court voided Alabama's voluntary prayer statute with these words: "The fact that the prayer law is voluntary and non-denominational does not neutralize the state's involvement. The state must remain neutral not only between competing religious sects, but also between believers and non-believers" (*Jaffree* v. *Wallace*, 1983).

Silent Prayer or Meditation

Since the late 1970s, many states have passed "moment of silence" statutes, and courts have been divided over their constitutionality. In Massachusetts, for example, a federal court upheld a state law requiring public schools to observe a minute of silence for "meditation or prayer" (*Gaines* v. *Anderson*, 1976). According to the court, the law does not require prayer: "All the statute requires students to do is be silent." The court explained that a moment of silence may serve several secular purposes: It might "still the tumult of the playground," help start the day on a calm note, and help students learn self-discipline. While *requiring* silent prayer would be unconstitutional, the Massachusetts law is "framed in the disjunctive" and simply *permits* meditation or prayer. Thus the court concluded that the law takes "a neutral position that neither encourages nor discourages prayer"—it accommodates those who wish to pray silently as well as those who wish to reflect on nonreligious matters.

On the other hand, a federal court in New Mexico held unconstitutional a state statute that authorized a minute of silence "for contemplation, meditation or prayer" (*Duffy* v. *Las Cruces Public Schools*, 1983). The court found that the goal of the law's sponsor was to draft a bill "which would authorize some form of prayer in our public schools." The court also found that the insertion of the words *contemplation* and *meditation* was "solely for the purpose of attempting to disguise the religious nature of the bill." By providing a time for prayer, the legislature "placed the imprimatur of the State on that religious activity" and thus has "impermissibly advanced religion."

In 1983, a federal court went even further and invalidated a New Jersey law that provided a minute of silence "for quiet and private contemplation or introspection" and said nothing about prayer (*May* v. *Cooperman*). The judge ruled that the law violated the establishment clause because it had "no overwhelming secular purpose" and because the history and circumstances of this legislation "point inescapably to an essentially religious purpose."

In the wake of these conflicting decisions, the U.S. Supreme Court ruled on an Alabama law that authorized a minute of silence in all public schools "for meditation or voluntary prayer." In a controversial 1985 decision in *Wallace* v. *Jaffree*, the High

Court held the law unconstitutional. In the process, the justices not only explained their reasons for rejecting the statute but also suggested how legislatures could pass moment-of-silence statutes that would be constitutional.

The challenged law was enacted in 1981, when Alabama already had a statute authorizing a moment of silence "for meditation." The legislative purpose of the new law was "to return voluntary prayer" to the public schools. And that was the problem. When a statute is challenged under the establishment clause, the Court emphasized, the state must show that it has a secular purpose.

In this case the record was clear. "The statute," wrote Justice Stevens, "had no secular purpose." It was enacted "to convey a message of state endorsement and promotion of prayer." According to the Court, the addition of "or voluntary prayer" to the existing moment-of-silence statute "indicates that the state intended to characterize prayer as a favored practice." Justice Stevens concluded that such an endorsement is not consistent with the established principle of complete government neutrality toward religion.

In an unusual concurring opinion, Justice O'Connor explained why this decision would not necessarily make the 25 moment-of-silence laws in other states unconstitutional. According to Justice O'Connor, state-sponsored silence is different from state-sponsored vocal prayer or Bible reading in two ways. A moment of silence "is not inherently religious," and students who are silent "need not compromise" their beliefs. "The crucial question," wrote the justice, "is whether the state has conveyed...the message that children should use the moment of silence for prayer" (*Wallace* v. *Jaffree*, 1985).

This decision did not resolve all of the questions surrounding moment-of-silence laws, but it resolved most of them. First, statutes or school district policies that require moments of silence "for prayer" are clearly unconstitutional. Second, those that simply provide for moments of silence and say nothing about prayer will not violate the establishment clause unless they are based on a clear legislative purpose to encourage prayer. Third, statutes that provide for silent "meditation or prayer" but have no secular purpose are unconstitutional. Fourth, meditation or prayer laws that have plausible educational purposes will probably be upheld. Justice Powell indicated in his concurring opinion that he would have voted to uphold the challenged Alabama law "if it also had a clear secular purpose." And Justice Powell's view is probably shared by a majority of the Court.

Student Prayers

May schools permit student-initiated prayers at assemblies? In a 1981 Arizona case, a federal appeals court said no (*Collins* v. *Chandler Unified School District*). The case involved a high school student council that requested permission to allow student volunteers to open assemblies with prayers. After the administration approved the plan, a parent challenged the practice as unconstitutional.

The appeals court indicated that there was "no meaningful distinction between school authorities actually organizing the religious activity" and officials "merely 'permitting' students to direct the exercises." Since opening the assemblies with prayers has no secular purpose, since their primary effect is to advance religion, and since they occur in the "coercive setting" of the public school, they were held to violate the establishment clause.

Extracurricular Prayers

May schools encourage the reciting or singing of prayers at extracurricular activities? Not according to a recent federal court decision (*Doe* v. *Aldine Independent School District*, 1982). The case concerned a Texas high school that posted the words of a prayer over the entrance of its gymnasium and sang or recited the prayer at athletic contests, pep rallies, and graduation ceremonies, often led by the principal. Although these events are part of the school's regular extracurricular activities, they are voluntary and take place before or after school hours. The prayer said: "Dear God, please bless our school and all it stands for. Help keep us free from sin, honest, and true, courage and faith [*sic*] to make our school the victor. In Jesus' name we pray, Amen."

The school argued that the prayer had a secular purpose of instilling "school spirit or pride" and "contributes to an increase in morale" and "lessens disciplinary problems." However, the court rejected this rationale because a school "cannot seek to advance nonreligious goals and values, no matter how laudatory, through religious means." As the judge noted, if a school could use religious means to further nonreligious goals, "any religious activity of whatever nature could be justified by public officials on the basis that it has a beneficial secular purpose." The court concluded that the practice of "initiating, leading or encouraging" the recitation or singing of a school prayer at school-sponsored events and the posting of the prayer on school property was in violation of the First Amendment to the Constitution.

Prayer Clubs

May administrators permit a student-initiated prayer club to meet at school? The answer depends on the precise facts of the case. As noted, school officials may not encourage students to pray. But according to one federal court, when students voluntarily request permission to form a prayer club to meet on the same basis as any other student organization, they may have the constitutional right to do so.

The case arose in Pennsylvania's Williamsport Area High School when the administration refused to recognize Petros, a nondenominational student "prayer fellowship" that wanted to meet during the school's regular activity period two mornings each week. School officials argued that recognition of Petros would violate the establishment clause. But the court disagreed (*Bender* v. *Williamsport Area School District*, 1983).

First, the purpose of the school in creating the activity period was not to promote prayer or religion. Rather it was to promote a wide range of intellectual and social interests. The fact that a religious group wishes to use this activity period on the same basis as the other groups does not convert the policy's purpose to a religious one.

Second, the policy does not have the "primary effect" of advancing religion. More than 25 student groups—with interests ranging from government and sports to music and social service—use the activity period. According to Judge Nealon:

> The fact that a small portion of public funds would be expended for the lighting and heating of the facility to be used by Petros does not, standing alone, indicate that the primary effect of an equal access policy would be to advance religion.

The court concluded that the number and spectrum of student groups at the high school indicates that "recognition of Petros would benefit religion only incidentally."

Unlike the school prayer cases in which teachers encourage the religious activity and students who do not wish to participate must conspicuously absent themselves, the situation in Williamsport is far different. There is no "en masse" recitation of religious doctrine at the start of the school day. Students may choose a variety of activities or none. And Petros has agreed to fewer benefits than other organizations, doing without space in the school paper or access to the school's public address system. Thus students are "not likely to view the Petros meetings as an endorsement of religion by the school." Moreover, the faculty adviser would attend meetings to keep order (as a policeman at a religious rally in a public park), not to encourage religious activity. Finally, Judge Nealon emphasized that his decision does not hold that voluntary school prayer should always be permitted, only that under the facts of this case, these students should not have been discriminated against and prohibited from organizing Petros because of its religious content.

In a similar New York situation, however, the Second Circuit Court of Appeals ruled that it was not unconstitutional for school administrators to deny Students for Voluntary Prayer permission to conduct communal prayer meetings in a classroom before school (*Brandon* v. *Board of Education of Guilderland Central School District*, 1980). The school board argued that "authorizing student-initiated voluntary prayer would have violated the Establishment Clause by creating an un-constitutional link between church and state." The court agreed.

Judge Kaufman conceded that granting all student groups, including religious organizations, access to school facilities reflects a legitimate secular purpose—the encouragement of extracurricular activities. But the court felt that there were two problems with the students' proposal. The voluntary student prayer meetings would occur during school hours and "would create an improper appearance of official support, and the prohibition against impermissibly advancing religion would be violated." Second, "excessive involvement" of the state in religious matters would result if the students' request were granted since "official supervision" is required of all school activities to maintain order, and in this case "to guarantee that partici-pation in the prayer meetings would always remain voluntary."

Thus prayer clubs is another religion and education issue on which lower courts are divided. Although the Supreme Court has permitted prayer clubs on college campuses (*Widmar* v. *Vincent*, 1981), it has not ruled on the issue in public schools. However, in comparing the Pennsylvania and New York cases just examined, the former seems to be reasoned more carefully and appears to be more in line with the Supreme Court's trend of decision.

Religious Holiday Activities

Are Christmas observances unconstitutional in public schools? Not necessarily. It depends on the type of observance. A federal case that arose in South Dakota (*Florey* v. *Sioux Falls School District 49-5*, 1979–1980) provided some clarification on this complex and sensitive issue.

The controversy arose when two kindergarten classes rehearsed, memorized, and then performed for parents a Christmas assembly replete with religious content. Part of the assembly consisted of a "beginner's Christmas quiz" that included exchanges between the teacher and the students such as the following:

TEACHER: Where had they [the angels] made a bed for Christ, the blessed Savior's head?

CLASS: In a manager in a cattle stall.

TEACHER: What is the day we celebrate as birthday of this One so great?

CLASS: Christmas.

As a result of complaints about this Christmas assembly, the school board developed a policy on the observance of religious holidays that included the following rules:

1. Schools may observe holidays "which have a religious and a secular basis."
2. "Music, art, literature and drama having religious themes are permitted as part of the curriculum" if presented in a "prudent and objective" manner.
3. The use of religious symbols as teaching aids is permitted provided they are displayed as "an example of the cultural and religious heritage of the holiday and are temporary."

Several parents argued that the rules that allowed religious songs and symbols were unconstitutional, but a federal court disagreed. In evaluating the constitutionality of the rules, the court applied the three-part test developed by the Supreme Court. First, do the rules have a secular purpose? Since the rules limit holiday observances to those that have "both a religious and a secular basis," they prohibit holiday observances that are solely religious. Furthermore, Judge Heaney explained, since religious themes must be presented in an objective manner and religious symbols can only be used as temporary teaching aids, the motivation behind the rules "was simply to ensure that no religious exercise" was part of official school activities. Unlike rules encouraging religious activities such as school prayer, the Sioux Falls rules are simply "an attempt to delineate the scope of permissible activity...not to mandate a program of religious inculcation."

Second, do the rules have the primary effect of advancing religion? Again the court said no. The judge observed that much of art, literature, and music associated with holidays such as Christmas have acquired a significance that is no longer strictly religious but has "become integrated into our national culture and heritage." Since permitted programs must be presented objectively and must deal with the secular or cultural basis of the holidays, the court concluded that the advancement of a "secular program of education" and not religion "is the primary effect of the rules." The court used the "beginner's Christmas quiz" to illustrate the difference between an activity that primarily advances religion and programs permitted by the rules. The quiz, wrote the judge, was a "predominantly religious activity which exceeded constitutional bounds" and would be prohibited by the new rules.

Third, do the rules unconstitutionally entangle the Sioux Falls schools in religion? No, ruled the court. Rather than entangling the schools with religion, "the rules provide the means to ensure that the district steers clear of religious exercises."

Teaching the Bible

Is it unconstitutional to teach about the Bible in public schools? Not necessarily. In the *Schempp* case (*Abington* v. *Schempp*, 1963), the U.S. Supreme Court prohibited "devotional Bible reading" to open the school day as an impermissible religious activity. However, the Court emphasized that the use of the Bible in public school was not necessarily unconstitutional. In the words of the Court, "the Bible is worthy of study for its literary and historic qualities" and "when presented objectively as part of a secular program of education" would not violate the First Amendment. Thus Bible courses must be examined individually to determine whether they are impermissible religious instruction or whether they are objectively presented as part of the regular curriculum.

Such a question arose in Bristol, VA, when parents challenged the local Bible course that was taught in the fourth and fifth grades (*Crockett* v. *Sorenson*, 1983). The course was prepared by the Ministerial Association and was sponsored by a council of ministers and lay church representatives that hired, supervised, and paid the teachers. Although Judge Kiser found that the curriculum and methods were appropriate for the grade levels, he ruled that the Bible course was unconstitutional because the evidence showed that the course "was initiated as a religious exercise" to "inculcate religious beliefs in the students." As the judge noted, it would be difficult to find any Bible program sponsored and supervised by the Protestant churches and not subject to control by secular authority that can be considered an "objective academic course of study."

Judge Kiser suggested the following guidelines for all public school systems that wished to teach about the Bible without violating the Constitution:

1. The school board should supervise and control the course, prescribe the curriculum and teaching materials, and hire and fire the teachers as it does for all other courses.
2. Teachers should be certified and chosen without regard to their religious beliefs.
3. The course should be offered as an elective, and there should be no indoctrination concerning the truth or falsity of the biblical materials.

Equal Time for Creationism

May states require that schools that teach about evolution must also teach about creation? Not according to a federal court in Arkansas, which ruled that the state's Balanced Treatment for Creation-Science and Evolution-Science Act was unconstitutional (*McLean* v. *Arkansas Board of Education*, 1982). Act 590, which was passed in 1981, was challenged as "an establishment of religion prohibited by the First Amendment." In a carefully reasoned 23-page opinion, Judge Overton examined the history, purpose, and effect of both the Arkansas act and the establishment clause.

In the first section of his opinion, the judge observed that the preservation of our communities from divisive pressures by religious groups or of coercion of religious groups by government requires strict confinement of the state to instruction other than religious, leaving indoctrination in a chosen faith to the individual's church and home. Examining the purpose of the act, the court found that the bill's sponsor was motivated "solely by his religious beliefs and desire to see the Biblical version of creation taught in the public schools." One supporter of Act 590 wrote, "I view this whole battle [to pass the Act] as one between God and anti-God forces." The act was passed without legislative investigation or debate, and the state produced no evidence to indicate that anyone considered the act to have any "legitimate educational value." The court concluded that "it was simply and purely an effort to introduce the Biblical version of creation into the public school curriculum" and therefore had no secular legislative purpose.

Second, the court found the evidence "overwhelming" that the effect of the act "is the advancement of religion in the public schools." This conclusion was based on an analysis of the act itself. The court, for example, found that the act's definition of "creation-science" as including "sudden creation of the universe, energy and life from nothing" is "not merely similar to the literal interpretation of Genesis" but is "identical and parallel to no other story of creation." Furthermore, the court found that "creation-science" as defined in the act "is simply not science" because its concepts depend on "a supernatural intervention which is not guided by natural law [and] is not testable." The creationist's methods do not take data, weigh them against opposing scientific data, and then reach conclusions. Instead, wrote the court, "they start with a conclusion and refuse to change it regardless of the evidence." Since creation science "has no scientific merit or educational value as science," Judge Overton concluded, "the *only* real effect of Act 590 is the advancement of religion."

Since the act mandates "balanced treatment" for creation science and evolution *and* prohibits instruction in any religious doctrine or references to religious writings, "administrators and teachers face an impossible task." How, asks the court, "is the teacher to respond to questions about a creation suddenly and out of nothing?" Or how will a teacher explain "the occurrence of a world-wide flood" as required by creationist theory? Since the only source of answers to these questions is found in Genesis, the state will inevitably be entangled with religion under Act 590. Thus involvement of state officials in screening texts for impermissible religious references and in upholding the act's prohibition against religious instruction "create an excessive and prohibited entanglement with religion."

Judge Overton acknowledged that a majority of the American public thinks that creation science should be taught if evolution is taught. However, the application of First Amendment principles is not determined by majority vote. Under our Constitution, wrote the court, "no group, no matter how large or small, may use the organs of government, of which the public schools are the most conspicious and influential, to foist its religious beliefs on others."

Religious Schools that Discriminate

Can the government deny tax exemption to religious schools that engage in racial discrimination because of their religious beliefs? Yes. In a case decided in 1983 (*Bob Jones University* v. *United States*), the U.S. Supreme Court ruled that the Internal Revenue Service properly denied tax-exempt status to Goldsboro Christian Schools because of a racially discriminatory admissions policy.[4] The school maintained that its policy was motivated by a religious belief based on their interpretation of the Bible and holds that any "mixing of the races is...a violation of God's command." Therefore, the school argued, denial by the government of tax-exempt status "violates their free exercise rights under the religion clauses of the First Amendment."

The Supreme Court acknowledged that the school's discriminatory policies were based on sincere religious beliefs and that a denial of tax benefits would have a negative impact on the operation of their religious schools. However, the Court noted

---

[4]The Goldsboro Christian Schools case was combined with the Bob Jones University case because they both raised the same constitutional issue.

that "not all burdens on religion are unconstitutional" and that the government may justify a limitation on religious freedom if it can show that it is "essential" to accomplish an "overriding" or "compelling" governmental interest. According to the Court, "The government has a fundamental, overriding interest in eradicating racial discrimination in education." Since such discrimination violates a "most fundamental public policy," the Court concluded that the abolition of racial discrimination in schools is a "compelling government interest that substantially outweighs whatever burden denial of tax benefits places on [the school's] exercise of their religious beliefs."

State Aid for Religious Education

May states provide tax deductions to parents who send their children to religious schools? Probably. Although it is unconstitutional for states to provide direct support for religious education, the Supreme Court ruled in 1983 that it is constitutional for states to allow tax deductions to parents for tuition of dependents attending any elementary and secondary school.

The case (*Mueller* v. *Allen*) arose when Minnesota taxpayers challenged a state statute providing for deductions of up to $700 per dependent for "tuition, textbooks, and transportation." The plaintiffs claimed that the law violated the establishment clause by providing financial assistance to religious schools because about 95% of the Minnesota students that attend private schools are enrolled in sectarian institutions. But a divided Supreme Court upheld the statute in a decision that will be used as a guide by other states looking for constitutional ways to aid religious schools.

On behalf of the majority, Justice Rehnquist rejected the notion that "any program which in some manner aids an institution with religious affiliation" violates the establishment clause. He then applied the Court's three-part test to determine whether the Minnesota law was constitutional. First, he wrote that the state's decision "to defray the cost of educational expenses incurred by parents—regardless of the type of schools their children attend—evidences a purpose that is both secular and understandable." Among the legitimate secular purposes of this law are "ensuring that the state's citizenry is well-educated," "assuring the continued financial health of private schools," and providing an "educational alternative for" and "wholesome competition with our public schools."

The more difficult question is whether the Minnesota law has "the primary effect of advancing the sectarian aims of the nonpublic schools." The majority concluded that it does not. The most important reason is that the tax deduction "is available for educational expenses incurred by *all* parents," including those whose children attend public as well as private schools. Justice Rehnquist distinguished this case from unlawful schemes to provide public aid "only to parents of children in *nonpublic* schools." Unlike direct payments to religious institutions, which would be prohibited by the establishment clause, this case concerns only an "attenuated financial benefit, ultimately controlled by the private choices of individual parents, that eventually flows to parochial schools from the neutrally available tax benefit" granted under this Minnesota law. Finally, the Court ruled that the statute does not "excessively entangle" the state in religion.

EDUCATIONAL IMPLICATIONS

What are the educational implications of the cases outlined in this chapter and of the political controversies that surround issues of discipline, due process, and religion in the public schools? Four implications are of special significance: the need for more educators to become legally literate, the need to avoid legal liability, the need for more research concerning the educational impact of legal decisions, and the need to understand legal principles rather than to know the results of specific cases.

Legal Literacy for Educators

In February 1984, a group of teachers met at UCLA to discuss the White House report *Disorder in Our Public Schools* (Working Group, 1984). At that meeting, more than three-fourths of the teachers agreed with the report's assertion that court-required due process before suspension was too cumbersome and time-consuming and interfered with effective discipline. This is because the educators erroneously believed that the process required by courts before suspension gave students the right to have parents present, to cross-examine their accusers, to present witnesses on their behalf, and to appeal the principal's decision.

When the teachers were asked if they would favor a policy allowing students to have their parents and the complaining teacher participate in a conference with the principal before suspension, all of the teachers said yes. Yet such a policy would go far beyond the informal due process required by the Supreme Court before short suspensions.

The UCLA meeting illustrates the dangers of legal illiteracy among educators: the failure to understand the flexible nature of due process, the mistaken belief that the law requires schools to apply courtroom procedures in all suspension cases, and the tendency for educators to blame the courts for excessive procedures that are voluntarily adapted by local administrators or school boards. As a result of legal misunderstandings, educators are intimidated by fear or threat of suit, fail to use proper authority, and criticize courts for problems they have not caused. There is a need for more educators to become legally literate: to understand education law as it applies to the schools, to see law as a source of knowledge and power (not as a source of fear and anxiety), and to understand how law can be used to improve education.

Avoiding Legal Liability

In 1975, the U.S. Supreme Court ruled that school officials could be held personally liable for money damages for violating a student's clearly established constitutional rights (*Wood* v. *Strickland*). This decision heightened the anxiety of many educators concerning the dangers of being sued by disgruntled students and parents. If students can prove that their rights are violated knowingly or maliciously, judges can award punitive damages for such deliberate unconstitutional behavior.

In most cases, however, where constitutional violations are the result of oversight rather than intent, the fear of being held personally liable often exceeds the actual risk. This is because courts will award only nominal or token damages unless students can prove actual monetary losses or can prove that their rights were intentionally violated (*Carey* v. *Piphus*, 1978). And this is usually difficult to do. Furthermore, even if educators are found liable, they often are (or should be) protected by personal, associational, or school district liability insurance. But no one wants to suffer through a lawsuit as a defendant. Therefore, the best protection against liability is to practice preventive law—to build the protection of constitutional rights into the school's policies and procedures with the advice of competent legal counsel.

Research Needed

Even if educators were clearly informed about what the law does and does not require, there still might be fundamental differences about the impact of the law on education and inadequate research to inform the debate. The White House report again provides a timely example. The report uses anecdotal evidence to argue that due process interferes with effective discipline. On the other hand, some contrary evidence suggests that due process facilitates discipline. This includes a 1979 study by Cynthia Kelly indicating that in schools that observe due process, students are more likely to have positive attitudes toward school rules, the legal system, and schooling. Reports from a 1983 Bush conference indicate that in Los Angeles schools, the second-largest system in the nation, administrators intentionally use more due process than required by law because they believe such procedures help them develop better educational alternatives for disruptive students (Schimmel & Williams, 1984–1985). And some psychological theories indicate that due process makes discipline and punishment more effective (Schimmel & Eiseman, 1982). Despite the arguments on both sides of this issue, there have been no major, systematic studies to answer the question, Does due process interfere with discipline? Nor has there been much research on other educational legal issues examined in this chapter. For example, would informal due process in academic matters interfere with education? Does fear of retaliation prevent students from testifying against one another? Is it possible to allow students to be advised by an attorney without transforming a school hearing into a legalistic, adversarial procedure? Can courses on religion or the Bible be taught in an "objective" and "impartial" manner? Can schools provide time for silent meditation without promoting religion? What has been the result of curriculum designed to provide a balanced treatment of creation science and evolution? Research results on questions such as these are needed to enlighten the debate among educators, lawyers, and judges on issues of due process and religion in the schools.

Principles More Important than Decisions

Many educators are more interested in learning how the courts have decided a specific controversy than in understanding the principles underlying that decision. But for teachers and administrators who shape and interpret educational policy, it is much more important to understand the legal principles than to know who won the legal battle. This is because the outcome of a particular case may have little bearing on another case involving the same subject if the facts of the two cases are different. On the other hand, the same basic constitutional principles apply to similar types of controversies even if the specific facts differ.

The judicial decisions concerning silent meditation, Bible teaching, and creationism illustrate this point. In each of these cases, the courts ruled that the practices in question violated the Constitution. Knowing these results, it might be reasonable to believe that it is unconstitutional for a public school to sponsor meditation or to teach the Bible or the Genesis story of creation. But such a generalization would be wrong under many circumstances. Thus it would generally not be unconstitutional to teach about the Bible (including the Genesis story of creation) as part of a course in the history of literature or world religions. Nor would a school-mandated moment of silence for meditation necessarily violate the First Amendment. Whether these practices are in conflict with the establishment clause depends on whether they have a "legitimate secular, educational purpose" and whether their "primary effect" is to promote religion. Thus it is far more important to understand these basic constitutional principles, which courts apply to all establishment clause cases, than to know who won a particular judicial controversy.

The cases in this chapter have illustrated how educators are frequently caught in the crossfire of legal and political conflict. Without adequate legal knowledge, teachers and principals are often trapped between constitutional values and community pressures. But as legal understanding increases among educators, they can become more effective practitioners of preventive law and better able to manage the legal and political controversies surrounding issues of due process and religion in the public schools. Thus legal literacy can become a constructive tool for educators to use to protect both constitutional values and the quality of schooling.

FURTHER READING

Crockenberg, V. A. (1984). "An Argument for the Constitutionality of Direct Aid to Religious Schools." *Journal of Law and Education, 13*, 1. Argues that the establishment clause of the First Amendment was not intended to prohibit the government from providing direct financial assistance to religious schools and that providing such aid would not have a politically divisive impact in the United States.

Epley, B. G. (1985). "Crime and Punishment: The Judicial Role in School Discipline and Substantive Due Process." *Education Law Reporter, 19*, 65. Reviews a series of recent student punishment cases and concludes that the judiciary wants "to protect the right of school officials to discipline students in the manner they deem appropriate."

Fischer, L., & Schimmel, D. (1982). *The Rights of Students and Teachers.* New York: Harper & Row. Summarizes key controversial cases on discipline, due process, religion, and other constitutional issues confronted in the public schools.

Mawdsley, R. D. (1984). "*Lynch* v. *Donnelly*: A New Constitutional Standard in Establishment Cases?" *Education Law Reporter, 18*, 805. Examines the traditional judicial analysis of cases, including the establishment clause and education, and suggests that future Supreme Court decisions might be more accommodating to "our nation's rich heritage." Submitted by the Administrative Council at Liberty Baptist College.

Pfeffer, L. (1984). *Religion, State, and the Burger Court.* New York: Prometheus Books. A detailed study of Supreme Court decisions on religion between 1969 and 1984 by a leading advocate of church-state separation.

Rossow, L. F. (1984). "Administrative Discretion and Student Suspension: A Lion in Waiting." *Journal of Law and Education, 13*, 417. Explains why administrators must do more than follow procedural due process in student suspension cases; schools must also be concerned with the principles of substantive due process—fair warnings, proportionality, equal application, and nondiscrimination.

Schimmel, D., & Eiseman, J. (1982). "School discipline." *Update on Law-related Education, 6*(2),

23–25, 51–53. Argues that the due process of law requirements of the Constitution and the courts are in harmony with good education and effective discipline.

Schimmel, D., & Fischer, L. (1977). "Discipline and due process in the schools." *Update on Law-related Education, 1*(2). A summary and analysis of two landmark Supreme Court decisions—on corporal punishment and due process—that have been widely publicized and frequently misunderstood.

Sorenson, G. P. (1985). "Equal access for voluntary student prayer groups: A legal dilemma." *Education Law Reporter, 19*, 461. A discussion of the Equal Access Act of 1984 and judicial decisions concerning student-initiated religious activities in the public schools.

Zirkel, P. A. (1984). "A practical analysis of prayer-related cases." *Education Law Reporter, 18*, 521. Reviews and analyzes judicial decisions concerning school prayer, silent meditation, and student prayer groups.

REFERENCES

Abington School District v. *Schempp*, 374 U.S. 203 (1963).

Bender v. *Williamsport Area School District*, 563 F. Supp. 697 (1983).

Bernstein v. *Menard*, 557 F. Supp. 90 (E.D. Va. 1983).

Bob Jones University v. *United States*, 103 S.Ct. 2017 (1983).

Boynton v. *Casey*, 543 F. Supp. 995 (D. Me. 1982).

Brandon v. *Board of Education of Guilderland Central School District*, 635 F.2d 971 (1980).

Carey v. *Piphus*, 435 U.S. 247 (1978).

Church, George J. (1984, March 19). Mixing politics with prayer. *Time*, pp. 12–15.

Collins v. *Chandler Unified School District*, 644 F.2d 759 (1981).

Crockett v. *Sorenson*, 568 F. Supp. 1422 (1983).

Dixon v. *Alabama State Board of Education*, 294 F.2d 150 (1961).

Doe v. *Aldine Independent School District*, 563 F. Supp. 883 (1982).

Duffley v. *New Hampshire Interscholastic Athletic Association*, 446 A.2d 462 (1983).

Duffy v. *Las Cruces Public Schools*, 557 F. Supp. 1013 (1983).

Engel v. *Vitale*, 370 U.S. 421 (1962).

Florey v. *Sioux Falls School District 49-5*, 464 F. Supp. 911 (1979); 619 F.2d 1311 (1980); Cert. Den. 101 Sup.Ct. 409 (1980).

Gaines v. *Anderson*, 421 F. Supp. 337 (1976).

Goss v. *Lopez*, 419 U.S. 565 (1975).

Hart v. *Ferris State College*, 557 F. Supp. 1379 (1983).

Jaffree v. *Wallace*, 705 F.2d 1526 (1983).

John A. v. *San Bernardino City Unified School District*, 654 P.2d 242 (1982).

Karnstein v. *Pawaukee School Board*, 557 F. Supp. 565 (E.D. Wisc. 1983).

Keller v. *Fochs*, 385 F. Supp. 262 (1974).

Kelly, C. A. (1979). *Due process in the schools: The view from inside*. Unpublished doctoral dissertation, Northwestern University, Evanston, IL.

May v. *Cooperman*, 572 F. Supp. 1561 (1983).

McClain v. *Lafayette County School Board*, 673 F.2d 106 (1982).

McLean v. *Arkansas Board of Education*, 592 F. Supp. 1255 (1982).

Mueller v. *Allen*, 103 S.Ct. 3062 (1983).

Rose v. *Nashua Board of Education*, 679 F.2d 279 (1st Cir. 1982).

Rutz v. *Essex Junction Prudential Committee*, 487 A.2d 1368 (1983).

Schimmel, D., & Eiseman, J. (1982). School discipline. *Update on Law-related Education, 6*(2), 23–25, 51–53.

Schimmel, D., & Williams, R. (1984–1985). Does due process interfere with school discipline? *High School Journal, 18*(2), 47–51.

Wallace v. *Jaffree*, 53 L.W. 4665 (1985).

Widmar v. *Vincent*, 102 S.Ct. 269 (1981).

Wood v. *Strickland*, 420 U.S. 308 (1975).

Working Group on School Violence/Discipline. (1984, January 3). *Disorder in our public schools*. Memorandum for the Cabinet Council on Human Resources, presented to Ronald Reagan.

25 TEACHERS AND RESEARCH

Lovely H. Billups and Marilyn Rauth

Is teaching a profession? Consider some of the criteria of true professions. Do teachers share a common technical language that reflects specialized knowledge unknown to the lay person? Would the public consider it a criminal act to practice teaching without a license? Are teachers' special skills acknowledged by the public in the prestige, working conditions, or economic rewards they enjoy? Because an unequivocal yes cannot be given to any of these questions, teaching has always been relegated to semiprofessional status.

One of the results of the recent education reform movement has been public focus on the art of teaching. Concerns are being expressed about how teachers are trained, selected, nurtured, and evaluated. Too often, the philosophy of teaching condoned through current practices appears to be "do as well as you can and hope things turn out all right." But there is a rising tide against mediocrity that demands a more substantive philosophical base for those who will be instructing the nation's youth and providing them with skills to survive and prosper in an increasingly complex world.

It is our contention that good teaching is science as well as art. For too long it has been difficult to delineate between these two sets of behaviors. Effective teachers seem to exude natural talent, which prompts the public to cling to the adage, "Good teachers are born, not made." The same belief applied to doctors in the mid-1800s. However, the medical profession launched its own "reform movement" and established standards and procedures that resulted in medical practice becoming a highly prestigious and financially rewarding profession. There are lessons to be learned from this. Certainly, individuals bring varying levels of talent to the art of teaching, but this does not negate the existence of specific skills and knowledge that can be acquired or measured. In fact, quite a bit of evidence supports efficient, productive teaching practices.

EFFECTIVE TEACHING

Effective teachers demonstrate that they are clearly in charge of classroom activities by knowing their subject matter, setting academic goals for students, presenting

624

instructional materials and concepts, monitoring student progress, and providing feedback to students and parents. Coker, Medley, and Soar (1980) estimate that approximately 50% of effective teaching strategies involve basic logic, but the remaining 50% are counterintuitive, meaning that success depends on doing exactly the opposite of what seems obvious. The process of calling on students for recitation is a case in point. The natural inclination of the teacher could easily be to ask the question and then call on students who raise their hands to answer. Effective teachers know, however, that this approach can lead to a select group of students constantly providing answers. These students "pull" the teacher's attention, and what may appear to the teacher as random turn taking can easily result in reactions to the attention pullers. Effective teachers devise a series of turn-taking "patterns" that are rotated in order to provide more students with the opportunity to respond and participate actively in the learning process.

Stressing the complexity of teaching, David Berliner notes that a teacher makes at least 10 nontrivial decisions an hour (1984, p. 6). Is this an appropriate question to ask Johnny? Is Mary ready to move from single-digit to double-digit multiplication? Which instructional aids should be used to support a lesson on the concept of infinity? How can Sarah's poor composition be corrected or graded without discouraging her from doing written assignments? Such decisions are made daily in the course of at least 1,500 interactions with individual students while supervising 30 or more students in a class.

Classroom Management

Managing students' individual and group behavior while providing instruction can be monumental tasks. Regardless of age, students are concerned about where to put their personal belongings, when and how they may retrieve them, what are the processes for entering and leaving the room, what is deemed "acceptable" behavior in class. These and other functions are carefully woven into the classroom process of effective teachers to the end that a minimum of time is diverted from instruction. Effective classroom management helps to create an environment in which learning can take place.

A great deal of recent research on effective teaching is based on classroom observations that describe actual techniques of more effective teachers. Although it is researchers who report findings, the source of this information is real teachers, real students, and real classrooms. As a result, we are learning a great deal about time on task, group management, feedback and praise, interactive teaching, learning styles, cooperative team grouping, and strategies for teaching reading and other content areas. (For an excellent review of this literature, see Brophy and Good, 1986.) A large portion of this research was conducted at the elementary school level, but more and more studies in secondary education are being produced. What is quite clear is that effective teachers demonstrate specific pedagogical skills. They have been derived from a combination of training and experiences and are cardinal to success as a classroom teacher. Teaching is not something that anyone who knows the subject matter can do.

Educational research, whether conducted by teachers, researchers, or both in collaboration, generates a good deal of technical knowledge about classrooms and the science of teaching. If teachers are made aware of useful research knowledge and its implications, they can more effectively control daily classroom outcomes. Understanding of this technical knowledge is important to teachers since research unequivocally portrays the complexity of the teaching process, negating all contentions that the person without professional training can teach as well as anyone else. Unfortunately, the research base for teaching has yet to be incorporated in any meaningful way in the training of prospective teachers.

There are many effective style variations among teachers, characterized as the "intangible art of teaching." But art alone does not make a teacher. Complementing this must be a specialized set of skills grounded in a professional knowledge base. Together they comprise the science of teaching. It is the combination of art and science that makes a professional teacher.

PROBLEMS

Beyond public perceptions, which tend to disavow teaching as a scientific profession, problems hinder the direct use of educational research by teachers.

Perceptions

Teachers find research reports of great length to be cumbersome and complicated by statistical data and research terminology they do not understand. From their point of view, the findings offer no "recipes" for direct application in the classroom. They perceive researchers as too far removed from the classroom, thus having little understanding of day-to-day classroom activities. Research credibility is weakened through teachers' perception that findings of various studies usually contradict one another. Finally, they are skeptical of research because they feel it uses teachers and students as "guinea pigs" for experiments.

Researchers, on the other hand, admit that they may not have the "language" with which to communicate with teachers. Further, they are dismayed by teachers' desire for instant remedies. They are also mindful that teachers have not developed as users of research because the teachers' training process traditionally neglects substantive research orientation. Finally, researchers rarely receive feedback from teachers concerning the results of research concepts applied in the classroom.

Although there is evidence of truths in the allegations made by teachers and researchers that contribute to a mutual lack of communication, there are also many misconceptions that can be corrected. Later we will describe a process devised to neutralize negative attitudes to the end that teachers perceive educational research as useful knowledge about what they do. Once research is mainstreamed into everyday practice in the classroom, lines of communication are opened, and researchers can receive feedback necessary to refine and continue their work.

Mandates

Educational program mandates, often viewed as guarantors of accountability, can in many instances be counterproductive. Teachers spend up to 1,000 hours a year in isolation with students. Even the most ambitious teacher evaluation programs net only 15 to 20 hours of observation. Teachers must believe in what they teach and the process by which they teach it. Only individual commitment has sustained value in changing teaching practice.

Teaching children is an isolating experience for adults. Most teachers see very little of their peers during the average workday. They are closed behind classroom doors and interact with their students for hours at a time. There is little opportunity to exchange ideas with colleagues. Classroom observations are limited, and sufficient time to discuss the implications of classroom observations is almost obsolete. So teachers are left pretty much to their own devices, often for months between classroom visits. They will do what they deem best to do, and when they need help they will either seek out a colleague or suffer in silence. Mandated programs have only fleeting impact on teacher performance, except to produce as "show and tell" exhibits when supervisors come to visit.

Almost as self-defeating as the practice of pretending to use mandated programs is the lethargy that overcomes teachers in the top-down decision-making process. Researchers and teacher trainers are well aware of teachers' reluctance to change practice, often justifiably so, because of their experiences with "hand-me-down" programs.

A workable approach, then, for getting teachers to apply research-based strategies to classroom teaching would be to give teachers a chance to investigate and understand the research concepts and then make decisions about how the techniques can or cannot be implemented in their classrooms. The professional teacher, trained in inquiry and problem solving, can be trusted with this responsibility.

This process is of a high-risk nature to administrators and policymakers who are convinced that teachers, like students, must be told *what* to do, *how*, and *when* (rarely why), or it will not be done. A fallacy of this thinking lies in the reality that teachers' conditions of isolation provide very effective methods of resisting mandates. Teaching is a very private act. Yet mandates continue, even though little change is effected in teaching or learning.

Misapplication of Research Information

Improper use of research in classrooms is more prevalent than is comfortable to imagine. A closer look at the methods of research implementation at the school level provides clues as to why programs fail.

Research-based programs fail when teachers lose confidence in them. This may be due to inadequate preparation of teachers or insufficient funding. It is also the result of teachers perceiving, often correctly, that the program represents no improvement over existing methodology. Problems are exacerbated by mandates that force teachers to meet unrealistic time lines and produce irrelevant reports.

A case in point involves the current use of the Synthesis of Instructional Functions (Rosenshine, 1983). Several teaching effectiveness programs draw on these functions to guide teacher behaviors in developing an instructional lesson. The process advises teachers to begin the instructional period with a review of the previous lesson, then present new information, direct a practice session, provide feedback, assign independent study, reteach, and so on. Much of the process is familiar to almost all teachers, but the formula serves to emphasize the importance of teacher-directed instruction and reminds teachers of the value of sequential instructional patterns. Instead, teachers are required to *write* the six or seven steps (depending on the program) for each lesson, resulting in a waste of time and resources.

Redundant experiences for teachers violate the intent of the research and are no more productive than classroom exercises that require students to write already learned multiplication tables 100 times. Likewise, unrealistic demands that impose time limitations for program implementation in classrooms regardless of individual need or group dynamics diminish teachers' confidence in the validity of the research. A 16-week lockstep program may not allow sufficient time for teachers to reteach lessons not learned the first time around. The resulting chicanery on the part of teachers who must find their way around the process is counterproductive to the research design and does not inspire teachers to look to research for answers.

Other instances of misapplication of research abound. Madeline Hunter, who created a research-based training program to improve teaching effectiveness, found it necessary to publish an article called "What's Wrong with Madeline Hunter?" (1985), in which she confronted numerous myths about the program and misunderstandings that led to abuse. No, the model should not be viewed as an evaluation system. No, administrators should not expect teachers to use every element of effective instruction in every lesson. No, training cannot be completed in a day or even a year. No, principles of learning are not absolutes. No, excellence in teaching cannot be mandated. This partial list of Hunter's caveats underscores common practice in the schools, which subverts promising programs by undermining teacher expertise and ignoring known principles of effective staff development. One Florida school system, implementing a new research-based teacher evaluation process, sent guidelines to evaluators that included numerous references to a criterion called "teacher witness." What these evaluators should have been looking for was "teacher withitness," a term coined by researcher Jacob Kounin (1970) to describe the teacher's ability to monitor many different things going on in the classroom simultaneously. Are there administrators out there today looking for that unknown quantity, "teacher witness," and teachers whose careers are being affected by it?

BENEFITS OF RESEARCH: THE AFT PROJECT

Historically, there has been a gap between educational research and classroom practice. Teaching, consequently, has been denied a general text for its basic skills. At best, results of educational research have been shared in a rather haphazard and careless fashion. Some teachers are exposed to Bloom's *Taxonomy* during teacher training; some hear about it in special workshops; most do not use it in the practice of teaching. Many teachers read about Piagetian theory; few understand it. All teachers of mathematics were herded into the "new math syndrome" (for which researchers rather than mathematicians were erroneously blamed). Students failed, and teachers rebelled. From the teacher's perspective and often the public's, researchers concocted theoretical formulas in their ivory towers with little understanding of the real world of the classroom.

The distance between research and practice is perpetuated by conditions that allow researchers to exchange most of their information only with one another. On occasions when research is made accessible to teachers, neither its length, its form, nor its language is meaningful to practitioners. Dissatisfaction with these conditions and encouragement from results of more practical research generated since the 1960s prompted the American Federation of Teachers to pilot a dissemination program that would help close the gap between research and practice.

Supported by a two-year grant from the National Institute of Education, the AFT developed the Educational Research and Dissemination Program (ER&D), a process that resulted in the sharing, examination, and evaluation of research results directly by teachers. The process necessitated interactions among educational factions for whom communication had been difficult. But it proved to be an excellent rallying point. Teacher union members and school principals had to agree to mutual support of the program at the school level. Researchers and teachers collaborated in discussions about the implications of research findings. Teacher center directors served as the first ER&D local site coordinators and were in frequent contact with school-district central administration. AFT staff, ourselves included, consulted with state education agencies, NIE staff members, university professors, and researchers. The complexity of this undertaking emphasized how thin these lines of communication normally were.

Development of the Educational Research and Dissemination Program from its inception in 1981 evolved from a longstanding belief on the part of AFT's leadership that optimal teaching is a complex process requiring the use of experientially and scientifically based judgmental skills as well as extensive subject-matter knowledge.

Without a grounding in science, the art of teaching could never be considered a profession. No one with experience in the classroom would argue there is one "right" way to teach. But it made sense that some instructional strategies would be more effective than others in given situations. Among the many problems that hindered the development of the science of teaching was the primitive methodology employed in educational research for many years, which produced little information to guide teacher education or classroom practice. Eventually, more sophisticated methodological techniques developed, and researchers began studying what more effective teachers actually did in the classroom. This produced the foundations of a validated research base on effective teaching and classroom management strategies. Does this mean that research offers absolute answers in defining effective practice? To date, no one can make this claim. Research is, however, a powerful tool in the hands of teachers to enable them to analyze and reflect on teaching strategies, goals, and values.

There is a dire need for a systematic process through which teachers can gain personal access to information about what they do. Both the process and the information disseminated through the process have to be precise yet eclectic, accurate yet flexible. Teachers are inundated by "canned" prescriptions for teaching that promise full-course servings of classroom strategies with little effort on the part of the teacher (except for an abundance of recordkeeping) to impart the curriculum to students effectively. Often these programs tout "teacher-proof" aspects of the process as most desirable. "Students working independently most of the class period" is a popular program characteristic. Yet findings from research on teacher-directed instruction caution against long periods of independent study for students without teacher intervention. Teachers need access to this kind of information to consider in lesson planning. Teachers need access to research results to add to the stockpile of resources that influence their instructional decision making.

Process

Convinced that the results of educational research generated in the preceding two decades could be of practical value to teachers and dismayed by the episodic use of research-based information in classrooms, the American Federation of Teachers developed a dissemination mechanism to link research to practice. The AFT felt that as a teacher union, it was trusted by the membership and could therefore encourage teachers to review research information and experiment with new ideas without imposing the threat of evaluation. Development and implementation of the process was multifaceted and largely influenced by the challenges and dilemmas described earlier in this chapter. The pilot program, funded by NIE, was orchestrated by national staff members of AFT's Educational Issues Department with guidance from a three-panel advisory board of nationally renowned educational researchers.

Early on, a code of ethics was established to govern the spirit of the program. The union as a peer-level disseminator would guarantee a *voluntary*, nonthreatening, nonjudgmental environment for program participants. The teacher center staff development concept served as a model. Further, the nature of research used in the program would be applicable in the classroom, meaning that studies would be sought (especially in initial program stages) that were based on actual classroom situations and whose findings could be implemented by teachers, either individually or collectively.

Key Players

In addition to funding, NIE provided project monitors and members of the research and dissemination staff who were available as advisers and consultants throughout pilot stages of the program. This input, combined with consistent guidance from the advisory board of researchers and educators from the Institute for Research on Teaching, Far West Laboratory, and Teachers College–Columbia University helped set the project on the right track.

The union's support of the program was another crucial element. AFT's Educational Issues Department, committed to continuing professional growth of the membership, directed program development using a national staff of three and the director of the department. This team worked out guidelines and parameters for program participants and developed the research implementation process.

Program participants included the local union structure, which in the beginning included AFT locals in San Francisco, New York, and Washington, DC. Since then the number of participating locals has grown to almost 90. Within each local, the ER&D is directed by a local site coordinator (LSC). The role of the LSC has evolved from a purely administrative function as liaison among the local union leadership, the school district, AFT staff, and teacher participants to include the work of training teachers in the research and its application.

Those who disseminate research to teachers are called teacher research linkers (TRLs). These are the program players who operate at the core of the program, linking research with teachers at the building level. Past research indicates that the human element in innovation and change is crucial. The ER&D program did not depend solely on the distribution of printed research information to teachers, but instead was heavily reliant on a cadre of carefully selected human disseminators who could interact with their colleagues as they reviewed the research. TRLs, as well as LSCs, were screened for some general characteristics, including these:

Good leadership qualities

Good rapport with fellow teachers and administrators

Perception by peers as an effective practitioner

Initiative as a risk taker and innovator

Good interpersonal and communication skills

Willingness and ability to commit time to the program

There is no doubt that the selection of participants who possess many more positive and professional characteristics than negatives was of tremendous benefit to program process.

Identifying Usable Research

In the initial stages of the program, project staff with assistance from the advisory board discovered several factors to be critical in identifying potential research that would be viewed as useful for classroom use by a wide range of teachers in various settings.

Perceived Need.   It was clear through national and local union contacts with members that managing behavior and improving student achievement were priority concerns among teachers. As the program developed, teacher participants opened up to the idea that research findings could be helpful to their practice and began to request studies in other areas of concern, such as class size, multicultural classroom settings, and grouping.

Practical Application.   The research selected would have to provide a framework that suggested relevant strategies for daily classroom application. Further, the research should enhance experiential knowledge and established practice and allow teachers to "walk away" with a plan that could be put into effect as soon as possible. This aspect of immediacy began to diminish as the program progressed. Teachers tended to engage in more in-depth discussions of the meaning of research concepts and were increasingly discriminating about how and when they would apply concepts in the classroom.

Generic Scope.   Since the project staff would be working with teachers across all grade levels and disciplines, the research had to have implications for all teachers. We were concerned that most of the research had been done at the elementary level and concentrated on student achievement in reading and mathematics. As we developed "translations" of research and conducted training sessions, we relied on our own experience as teachers and that of the TRLs for validating the general applicability of research findings. In spite of initial reluctance on the part of secondary school teachers to accept findings from research done at the elementary level, the research information *sold itself.* Eventually, high school teachers agreed that relevant information about effective classroom management or effective teaching could, with minor adaptations, be applied in classrooms at all grade levels.

Consistent Findings.   Teachers often view research as contradictory in nature; findings from one study may refute another. To help neutralize this perception and lend to the credibility of research and the project, we consciously sought a validated body of knowledge that consistently signaled a clear message about effective teaching practices. Once attitudes were changed and a greater appreciation for research developed, we were able to offer "contradictory" findings to challenge TRLs' thinking. Most often they concluded that findings were not contradictory but rather represented the pursuit of different research questions.

Observation-based Data.   The first research presented to TRLs was based on actual classroom observation, or "real" classrooms. TRLs were more receptive to this kind of research because it gave them the chance to look vicariously into other teachers' classrooms and see what constituted more and less effective practice. Studies used during the pilot period covered these topics:

> Beginning of the Year Classroom management (Emmer & Evertson, 1980)
>
> Teacher Praise (Brophy, 1981)
>
> Direct Instruction (Brophy & Good, 1986)
>
> Group Management (Kounin, 1970)
>
> Time on Task (Denham & Lieberman, 1980)

After the first two years, these topics were included:

> Cooperative Teams Learning (Slavin, 1983)
>
> Communication in the Multicultural Classroom (Erikson, in press; Boggs, 1972)
>
> Student Motivation (Brophy, 1983; Weiner, 1979; Bandura, 1982; Deci, Schwartz, Scheinman, & Ryan, 1981)

Translation and Transformation

An initial assumption regarding teacher use of research information was that seldom are findings reported in terms understandable to the practitioner. Statistics and research jargon are appropriate tools of the research community but present difficulty for the teacher. Further, most researchers are not willing to set forth the implications for practice. Attempts to provide translations for practice have often resulted in educational policy mandates framed in prescriptive "research says" absolutes. The underlying philosophy for this project was to present research information as a resource framework, nonthreatening in nature, that would encourage teacher investigation, problem solving, and self-evaluation. We therefore attempted to identify basic research concepts, illustrated by *suggestions* for practice within each narrative and reinforced through accompanying training activities.

In sum, project staff became convinced that research statistics needed to be interpreted clearly and significant relationships delineated with clarifying comments for teacher use. Reporting of research findings would have to allow for reflection and introspection by teachers, rather than providing only prescriptive how-tos, to promote inquiry and understanding. While teachers may need specific information on a single study, conclusions and findings from a wide body of studies, such as those provided in syntheses and reviews, would have to be cited to aid in translation for teacher use.

One of the most important insights gained in this program was that translation of research into language meaningful to teachers is only one step in facilitating implementation of research strategies in the classroom. What really bridged the gap between research and practice was a process now referred to as "transformation" of the research concepts shared with teachers.

In this transformation process, the "meaning" of the research as useful information was constructed as AFT staff and local TRLs engaged in an interaction with the research content. The process encompassed several steps, established through the training process:

1. Neutralization of negative attitudes toward research and development of trust and peer-to-peer interaction
2. Training in and discussion of research concepts for classroom use
3. Strategy development for implementation in practice and validation of research
4. Development of the TRL as a researcher disseminator

These steps and the transformation process could not have come about simply by reading the research translations. It was only after working with the research concepts in depth over an extended period of time that they became an integral part of the teacher's repertoire of skills.

Most TRLs were as doubtful of the potential of educational research to influence practice as any other teachers. Although TRLs had been selected on the basis of their being outstanding teachers, it was evident that most of them were not research "users." The task was to capitalize on the assets TRLs brought with them—union membership, peer respect and trust, teaching effectiveness, willingness to investigate innovations—to develop their receptivity to research information.

TRLs associate membership in the union with trust and the provision of positive benefits. This allows them to pursue investigations of the research within a nonthreatening, nonevaluative framework. It is also necessary to assure TRLs that they are valued as individuals who have developed valid teaching styles and whose opinions are important.

Training Sessions

Sessions are held approximately once every three weeks for a minimum of two hours. A typical session involves investigations of the research concepts and discussion. As TRLs share their perceptions, they learn from one another and become a cohesive group. Often the research concept is reinforced through the use of project-developed, group participation activities that simulate classroom situations universally experienced by teachers.

A portion of each session is also devoted to TRLs' making personal selections of research strategies they would implement in the classroom. Documentation forms are supplied so that TRLs can plan what they will try, in addition to how and when. The strategies are applied in classrooms during the period between sessions. TRLs report on their experiences at the following meeting and analyze the reasons for success or failure.

Developing Interest in Specific Findings.   Combining our own experiences as classroom teachers with interactions through the teacher union structure, we had a good sense of teachers' major concerns. As we reviewed the research on classroom management and teaching effectiveness, we extracted research concepts that related easily to classroom-specific situations teachers could recognize. Training activities were built around these to enhance understanding of the research by developing a "tangibility" between concept and practice.

Validating Research.   The process of transforming research into consumable form for classroom use made it possible for TRLs to validate the usefulness of the research. TRLs felt comfortable commenting on the appropriateness of applying research-based strategies at specific age or grade levels or in certain school environments. Moreover, they began to pose questions to researchers based on classroom experiences and developed individual strategies using research findings. Significantly, successful teachers confirmed the research findings and validated the strategies as good practice.

A profile of the teachers who became research linkers revealed that the research studies were "put to the test" in a wide variety of teaching situations. Our initial concern was that the research we had selected had been conducted primarily at the elementary school level, and we certainly did not anticipate the variety of teaching situations to which the research would be exposed.

Mainstreaming Research.   Important in keeping the transformation process moving was the task of getting teachers to incorporate research into the mainstream of their thinking as professionals. This suggested that teachers perceive research as more than a supplement to their lives as teachers but instead as an essential element in developing good practice. There is evidence that this was a viable goal. Experienced TRLs stated that the research validated their practice but that it had taken years of struggle as isolated individuals for them to develop successful programs and strategies.

Strong recommendations for incorporating classroom-applicable research findings in teacher training programs were made not only by TRLs but also by teacher participants at systemwide ER&D staff development training sessions conducted by TRLs. Experienced teachers said it would have been helpful to have been exposed to the research-based information earlier in their careers. While it can be argued that educational research is indeed included in preservice training, the message to researchers and higher education people may be that more attention should be paid to *what* research is used and the *form* in which it is presented. It would appear that this is an area of specific interest to NIE and research institutions as they consider more effective methods of disseminating research and to teacher training institutions as a possible design for program improvement.

Disseminators

The role of the cadre of teachers identified as teacher research linkers (TRLs) involved a complicated network of behaviors. Essentially, TRLs were required to become familiar with research concepts, implement research strategies, disseminate research findings, develop other teachers as users of research, and solicit feedback from teachers to keep the lines of communication open between teachers and researchers. Moreover, they were pledged to maintain the integrity of the program by guaranteeing voluntary, nonevaluative involvement of participants.

Training trainers was a very important aspect of the program. TRLs who had previously functioned as trainers were apprehensive about their role as presenters. Even with the level of trust that evolved in the TRL group process, they admitted to feeling nervous during practice sessions. Training, therefore, included information and activities on adult learning theory, teacher change, and skills necessary for facilitating group discussion.

As part of the development of this role, TRLs were asked to think beyond their own classrooms to the classrooms of others. Those who became the most successful disseminators began reviewing concepts with an "other" orientation, asking, what information will be most helpful to other teachers?

Institutions of Higher Education

Program collaboration with colleges and universities was designed to accomplish the following: (1) provide an ongoing supply of relevant research in areas identified by local teachers, (2) "translate" the research for teacher consumption, (3) keep teachers abreast of current research, and (4) perpetuate lines of communication between teachers and researchers. These, in addition to the continuous training of new TRLs to disseminate the research, would serve to institutionalize the ER&D program process at each site.

THE VISITING PRACTITIONER PROGRAM

Without new research translations, the ER&D program would die after TRLs had studied and experimented with the original findings summarized by the national office staff or after TRLs had shared the information with other teachers in the school system. The ongoing nature of this process and teachers' desire to know more about the craft aspect of teaching required a steady influx of new information.

Because teachers were not trained as researchers, we looked to the research institutions. Stanford University faculty, who were impressed with TRL training sessions they observed, paved the way for establishing the visiting practitioner program.

During the 1983–1984 school year, a San Francisco teacher, trained as a TRL, spent a sabbatical year as the first "visiting practitioner" at Stanford. The university waived tuition and fees, enabling the teacher to attend classes and interact with faculty and students in a variety of ways. One class helped the teacher read and interpret research. Others provided knowledge related to the research translations being done. AFT project staff had decided that credit would not be offered for the visiting practitioner experience to maintain a peer relationship between teacher and university faculty. Although visiting practitioners initially questioned this, they later felt it had been a good idea.

There were many outcomes of the first visiting practitioner experience. First, two new research translations, accompanied by training activities, were produced, on cooperative teams learning and communication in the multicultural classroom. Second, a new dialogue developed between teachers in San Francisco and faculty at Stanford. A number of university faculty participated in teacher-sponsored staff development programs. The visiting practitioner was able to act as broker in promoting a bilingual program, developed at Stanford, in San Francisco schools. In fact, a teacher-in-charge at an alternative elementary school was willing to experiment with the program and serve as a model for other schools in the district. University faculty and students gained new insights from the teacher on the real world of the classroom and schools. Both researchers and teachers emerged with new respect for one another. Third, the visiting practitioner maintained ties to the school system by continuing to train TRLs throughout the year.

In 1984–1985, the second visiting practitioner at Stanford developed a new research translation on student motivation, trained new TRLs, and worked with the Far West Laboratory to document the perceptions of TRLs, teachers with whom TRLs shared research information, and administrators of the effects of the ER&D process on teaching in 14 initial sites.

The visiting practitioner program owes a great deal to the Hewlett Foundation and Stanford University, which provide major funding. Hewlett monies also make it possible for the visiting practitioner to attend the annual meeting of the American Educational Research Association. Here the teacher has the opportunity to discuss the results of implementation of research concepts face to face with researchers, as well as to obtain new knowledge.

Because of the success of this program, nine teachers participated in visiting practitioner programs at six research universities in the 1985–1986 school year. Universities have been most cooperative in waiving tuition and fees, providing a part-time graduate research assistant to work with the visiting practitioner, and assigning a knowledgeable professor as mentor. Many school systems have willingly provided sabbatical leaves; some are less cooperative.

There are several additional outcomes of interest of the visiting practitioner program. Teachers are finding that theoretical research, if done well, can also contribute to practice. They are also developing research skills of their own. The visiting practitioner from Rush-Henrietta, NY, for example, will work with Syracuse University to summarize research on adult education theory and effective dissemination techniques, experiment with the findings in the local ER&D program, and draw implications that will strengthen the dissemination component in sites throughout the country. Without fanfare, the truly professional teacher is emerging.

PROFESSIONALISM IN TEACHING

Teaching in its present state can in no way be characterized as a profession, not because the nature of its mission is unprofessional but because treatment of those who perform the service is unprofessional. Dictionary definitions of *profession* refer to "occupation or calling, especially one requiring learning, engaged in for money." AFT president Albert Shanker states, "For most of us, *professional* describes someone who is *expert* in his or her field and who thus requires little or no supervision and has a high degree of decision-making power" (1985, p. 313).

Frequent analogies are made between the professional status of doctors and lawyers and the status of teachers. One common comparison centers around the use of research information to guide practice. Surgeons are constantly citing the latest research-based techniques applied in the operating room. They have a technical language that gives them unique ownership of the surgical process. Surgeons are held in high esteem by the public.

Not so the case for teachers. Even as relevant information about effective ways of teaching emerge from research, methods of disseminating and applying the concepts at the classroom level remain antiquated. Teacher disinterest in research is in vogue, reflected in the reaction, "What do researchers know about what goes on in classrooms?" Derisiveness toward research usually reflects researchers' frustration at their lack of understanding functions. Many supervisors and administrators are comfortable repeating the same ineffectual process imposed on them in the past, which did very little to improve their teaching or supervisory skills. Shanker tells of expert teachers, some with years of experience and doctorates, who do not receive satisfactory ratings on evaluations because they do not conform to the *detailed lesson plan mandate* (1985, p. 314). In other cases, marginal or unsatisfactory teachers, having submitted to the ritual, receive good evaluations.

These practices do not make a profession. Robert Glaser, speaking of higher standards and education reform, states, "We are urged toward excellence but observe that, despite inspiring instances of professional excellence, *the educational profession is seriously undernourished by modern knowledge*" (Glaser, 1984, p. 4). Applauding reform reports that influenced policymakers' increasing awareness of good practice, Glaser reminds us that education is one of the least research-supported professions.

To the credit of the National Academy of Education, recently convened to discuss the relationships between research and practice, emphasis was shared equally between theoretical research and the "experiences and problems of practical application," which "inform research" and consequently "suggest investigations for the development of new theory" (Glaser, 1984, p. 5). It is this new focus on research, which recognizes the importance of its practical use, that will ultimately influence research acceptance at the school level.

Since 1981, a successful research dissemination process has been expanding and flourishing. The more than 600 teacher research linkers involved in AFT's Educational Research and Dissemination Program are aware of the importance of the research role in guiding effective practice. The program motto is "Knowledge is power." Program participants realize the important connections between scientific understanding and practical application. They are also aware that the influence of research in designing educational programs is weakened by lack of in-depth exploration of the underlying concepts by those in the classroom. Teacher investigations of research support the process of inquiry and decision making and provide essential feedback to researchers. Those who have been specially trained and who are expert at what they do, who participate in the decision-making process and are adequately paid, can rightfully lay claim to the title "professional."

Overall implications for the development of teachers as users of educational research refer to general perceptions of teachers as professionals. More specifically, the research information can be used toward the upward mobility of classroom teachers who wish to assume more broad-based responsibility in the teaching role. Staff-differentiated roles initiated in recent education reform proposals provide opportunities for "expert" teachers to climb career ladders by supervising the professional development of new teachers, assisting in the growth of experienced teachers, reviewing texts, and developing programs and curricula. Although these are non-traditional duties for teachers, such actions will support higher professional standards of practice. Inherent in this process is the need for a validated knowledge base to guide practice.

This can be the best of times for teachers and researchers. The "ivory tower" reputation cannot have been comfortable for most researchers. They need vehicles to interact with teachers and substantiate their findings. On the other hand, teachers could not continue to defend their practice on the basis of emotional or intuitive arguments. It is one thing to say that an overload of paperwork is personally burdensome to teachers. It is quite another to argue that excessive paperwork detracts from instructional class time during which teachers should be interacting with students. Educational research can alert teachers to the best available evidence regarding daily classroom operations. Less effective teachers can find remedies for self-improvement. Effective teachers find that educational research reinforces expert teaching practices and inspires professionalism by promoting the *science* of teaching.

REFERENCES

Anderson, L. (1985). What are students doing when they do all that seatwork. In C. Fisher & D. Berliner (Eds.), *Perspectives on instructional time* (pp. 189–200). White Plains, NY: Longman.

Bandura, A. (1982). Self-efficacy mechanism in human agency. *American Psychologist, 37*(2), 122–147.

Berliner, D. (1984, February 16). Testimony before the Governor's Task Force on Teacher Education, University of Arizona.

Berliner, D. (1985). Laboratory settings and the study of teacher education. *Journal of Teacher Education, 36*(6), 2–8.

Boggs, S. T. (1972). The meaning of questions and narratives to Hawaiian children. In C. Cazden, V. P. John, & D. Hymes (Eds.), *Functions of language in the classroom* (pp. 299–327). New York: Teachers College Press.

Brophy, J. (1981). On praising effectively. *Elementary School Journal, 81,* 269–278.

Brophy, J. (1983). Conceptualizing student motivation. *Educational Psychologist, 18,* 200–215.

Brophy, J., & Good, T. (1986). Teacher behavior and student achievement. In M. Whittrock (Ed.), *Handbook of research on teaching* (pp. 328–375). New York: Macmillan.

Coker, H., Medley, D., & Soar, R. (1980). How valid are expert opinions about effective teaching? *Phi Delta Kappan, 62,* 131–134.

Deci, E., Schwartz, A., Scheinman, L., & Ryan, R. (1981). An instrument to assess adults' orientations toward control versus autonomy with children: Reflections on intrinsic motivation and perceived competence. *Journal of Educational Psychology, 73,* 642–650.

Denham, C., & Lieberman, A. (Eds.). (1980). *Time to learn.* Washington, DC: National Institute of Education.

Emmer, E., & Evertson, C. (1980). *Classroom management at the beginning of the school year* (R&D Report No. 6005). Austin, TX: University of Texas, Research and Development Center for Teacher Education.

Erikson, F. (in press). Anecdote, rhapsody, and rhetoric: Devices and strategies for cohesion in a discussion among black American adolescents. In D. Tannen (Ed.), *Coherence in spoken and written discourse.* Norwood, NJ: Ablex.

Glaser, R. (1984). Improving education: Perspectives on educational research. In National Academy of Education (Ed.), *The necessity for research in education: An Introduction* (pp. 4–8). Washington, DC: National Academy of Education.

Hunter, M. (1985). What's wrong with Madeline Hunter? *Educational Leadership, 42*(5), 57–60.

Kounin, J. (1970). *Discipline and group management in classrooms.* New York: Holt, Rinehart and Winston.

Rosenshine, B. (1983). Teaching functions in instructional settings. *Elementary School Journal, 83,* 335–352.

Shanker, A. (1985). The revolution that's overdue. *Phi Delta Kappan, 66,* 311–315.

Slavin, R. (1983). *Cooperative learning.* White Plains, NY: Longman.

Stallings, J. (1981). *What research has to say to administrators of secondary schools about effective teaching and staff development.* Paper presented at Conference on Research and Administration, Center for Educational Policy and Management, Eugene, OR.

Weiner, B. (1979). A theory of motivation for some classroom experiences. *Journal of Educational Psychology, 71,* 3–25.

AUTHOR INDEX

SUBJECT INDEX